ELEVENTH EDITION

Death, Society, and Human Experience

Robert J. Kastenbaum
Arizona State University

PEARSON

Boston Columbus Indianapolis New York San Francisco Upper Saddle River
Amsterdam Cape Town Dubai London Madrid Milan Munich Paris Montreal Toronto
Delhi Mexico City São Paulo Sydney Hong Kong Seoul Singapore Taipei Tokyo

Editorial Director: Craig Campanella
Editor in Chief: Dickson Musslewhite
Publisher: Karen Hanson
VP, Director of Marketing: Brandy Dawson
Executive Marketing Manager: Kelly May
Managing Editor: Maureen Richardson
Project Manager, Production: Shelly
    Kupperman
Operations Supervisor: Mary Fischer
Senior Operations Specialist: Sherry Lewis
Design Director: John Christiana

Cover Designer: Pat Smythe
Cover Image: © Jügen Fälchle/Fotolia
Supplements Editor: Mayda Bosco
Digital Media Editor: Thomas Scalzo
Full-Service Project Management and
    Composition: Revathi Viswanathan,
    PreMediaGlobal
Printer/Binder: R.R.Donnelley's
Cover Printer: Lehigh Phoenix
Text Font: PalatinoLTstd

Credits and acknowledgments borrowed from other sources and reproduced, with permission, in this textbook appear on page 502.

Library of Congress Cataloging-in-Publication Data
Kastenbaum, Robert.
Death, society, and human experience/Robert J. Kastenbaum.—11th ed.
        p.   cm.
    Includes bibliographical references and index.
    ISBN-13: 978-0-205-00108-8 (alk. paper)
    ISBN-10: 0-205-00108-4 (alk. paper)
    1. Death—Psychological aspects. 2. Death—Social aspects.
    I. Title.
    BF789.D4K36 2012
    306.9—dc23

                                                    2011030228

10 9 8 7 6 5 4 3

PEARSON

                              ISBN-13: 978-0-205-00108-8
                              ISBN-10:   0-205-00108-4

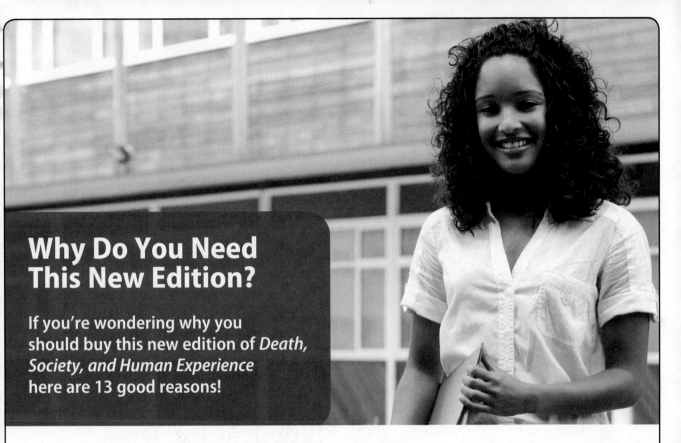

Why Do You Need This New Edition?

If you're wondering why you should buy this new edition of *Death, Society, and Human Experience* here are 13 good reasons!

1. Terror management theory is re-examined in the light of recent studies.

2. The discussion of death legalization is updated, as it is approved in another state, and controversy rages in several others.

3. Death attitudes and practices through the centuries are discussed, including Aries' stimulating perspective.

4. A discussion of how the human mind projects death thoughts into the universe—and yet often denies it in everyday life.

5. Exploration of selective attention and fatal errors in people who are in decision-making situations.

6. St. John Bosco's version of stages of dying, radically different from those described by Elizabeth Kubler-Ross, is brought forward for consideration.

7. A discussion on troubling data indicates that pain and other symptom relief is still not provided for many terminally ill hospital patients.

8. New discussion of ethical and legal issues regarding the harvesting and merchandising of transplant organs from impoverished or imprisoned people to the more affluent.

9. A new look at the neuropsychological perspective of suicide. Is suicide related to disorders in the brain?

10. Discussion of the effectiveness of the response to high suicide rates among active military personnel and veterans.

11. Discussion of child murders committed by desperate parents.

12. A review of the "stages of grief." Are they a story made up to make sense of disturbing and chaotic events?

13. Discussion of the extent to which various nations and cultures agree on what is "the good death".

*For Cynthia
and for those
you have loved . . .*

CONTENTS

PREFACE

We are not alone. We have more than 300 million compatriots if we live in the United States of America. There is no point in making this number more specific, because at least one infant will have made its debut before you finish reading this paragraph, and the total continues to rise day after month after year. On planet Earth, we are companioned by nearly 7 billion of our carbon-based species. There are more humans alive today than at any previous time in history, and, as you may have noticed, far more competition for parking spaces. On numbers alone, the human project seems to be doing well but all these lives end.

The first business of life is to stay alive. Ask the blades of grass that struggle up to the sunlight through the hard surfaces of a city street. Ask our resourceful adversaries, the virus and the microorganism, who continue to reinvent themselves whenever we launch a new pharmacological assault. Ask the child of a devastated homeland who has already experienced massive loss, stress, and deprivation but is determined to survive, and does. Ask nurses, paramedics, and physicians who have seen people make remarkable recoveries, seemingly because they had such a strong will to live. Ask firefighters why they risk their own lives to save people they've never met.

Even at its most resourceful and fortunate, life does not succeed indefinitely. All those millions and billions of us have been given a limited time offer by life, and most will also experience the death of people who are precious to us. That is a pretty good reason for having a book such at this and courses focused on dying, death, and grief. For many years, society ignored death, the dying, and the grieving person. The rule of silence created more problems than it solved. There was little comfort for the dying or grieving person, and little counseling for the troubled mind of the suicidal person. Inadequate communication interfered with potentially supportive relationships. Health care professionals had their own share of misery: responsible for care of the "incurable" (as dying people often were known) yet not prepared to deal with mortality in their own thoughts and feelings.

Many people participated in the systematic avoidance of death. They paid the price in anxiety and burdensome defenses. Other people brooded alone, haunted by death-related anxieties. Still others challenged death by risky actions; these episodes turned passive anxiety into active thrills but, too often, resulted in serious injury or death. Few had the opportunity to reflect on mortality with the help of a sensitive instructor and knowledge-based writings. There was little peer support for the nurse who dared to "get involved" with dying patients by actually being with them, the teacher who allowed students to discuss their death fears and bereavement experiences, or the researcher who deviated from the mainstream to explore our response to mortality. Funny thing, though: let death come a little too close to one's own life, and the same people who had looked askance at the local "death lady" now approached her for counsel and comfort.

The field of research and practice sometimes known as *thanatology* started to take shape in the 1960s, mostly in Western Europe and North America (Chapter 14). Like the other early "deathniks" back then, I had to learn almost everything on the go. Our professional training had not prepared us for encounters with mortality. The first time I stepped into a death and dying classroom was as the instructor, and the same held true for many other death educators who followed. It still seemed odd to be studying death. Eventually I figured out that thanatology was actually the study of life—but with death left in. As the 1970s began, we had the emerging hospice movement, a scattering of classes and workshops, media attention, and *Omega,* the first peer-reviewed journal devoted to death and dying.

We didn't have a textbook, though, so I wrote one. I thought that we should call on experiences, knowledge, and insights from many perspectives. No field had all the answers, and most had been reluctant even to raise the questions. Easy generalizations had already appeared in public and professional discourse. Whoa! Let's not become attached to hasty conclusions, especially those that satisfy our wish-fulfillment needs. This meant that the knots of uncertainty, inadequate evidence, and conflicting perspectives had to be identified and acknowledged, even if this posed a burden for reader and author.

I thought a lot about the people who would read this book. Some would be working toward or engaged in a human services career. Others would be following their curiosity. There would also be people—many—who had experienced traumatic death-related situations that continued to trouble them. For still other people, death-related issues would be ongoing: a roommate is suicidal; a family member is dying; they might themselves have a life-threatening condition. There is a give-and-take in the classroom that no book can accomplish on its own. Nevertheless, authors should respect the diverse life experiences and circumstances that people bring with them. It also seemed to me that authors should continue to be contributors to research, theory, and practice, and so the first and all succeeding editions include some sharings from my own work.

ABOUT THE ELEVENTH EDITION

This book is intended to contribute to your understanding of your relationship with death, both as an individual and as a member of society. For example, you will learn:

- How your personal attitudes and experiences compare with those of other people, as well as with the available research findings. This will be accomplished through self-inventory quizzes in several chapters.
- How our thoughts and feelings about death develop from early childhood and how we struggle with anxiety and denial as we move toward a mature and effective view of death.
- How mass media and computer-mediated programs can influence our attitudes, risk factors, and relationships.
- What very different ideas and meanings have been associated with death throughout the centuries.
- How and why the "Undead" have survived into our own times.
- How the ideas of "death" and "dead" have become and remained unsettled in our own time.
- How social forces and events affect the length of our lives, how we grieve, and how we die—in nations ravaged by disease, poverty, and violence, as well as in our own.
- How dying people are perceived and treated in our society, and what can be done to provide the best possible care.
- Why the "Good Death" is a difficult but valuable ideal.

- How hospice (palliative care) continues to change and develop.
- What choices and decisions we have about the way we are treated at the end of our lives.
- What stresses and risks caregivers to terminally ill people and their families experience.
- How people respond to the sorrow and anxiety of grief and the challenge of moving on with their lives.
- Why the funeral and memorialization process is still with us today after so many centuries, and how it is changing.
- Who is most at risk for suicide, and who is most likely to become either a killer or a victim of homicide.
- What is happening in the continuing controversy over euthanasia and physician-assisted death.
- What is becoming of faith and doubt about an afterlife.
- How we can help others cope with their death encounters.

NEW TO THIS EDITION

- Terror management theory is re-examined in the light of recent studies
- Assisted death legalization is approved in another state, and controversy rages in several others.
- Death attitudes and practices through the centuries: Aries' stimulating perspective.
- How the human mind projects death thoughts into the universe—and yet often denies it in everyday life.
- Explores selective attention and fatal errors in people who are in decision-making situations.
- St. John Bosco's version of stages of dying, radically different from those described by Elizabeth Kubler-Ross, is brought forward for consideration.
- Troubling data indicates that pain and other symptom relief is still not provided for many terminally ill hospital patients.
- Ethical and legal issues regarding the harvesting and merchandising of transplant organs from impoverished or imprisoned people to the more affluent.
- Is suicide related to disorders in the brain? A new look at the neurophysiological perspective.

- How effective has been the response to high suicide rates among active military personnel and veterans?
- Child murders committed by desperate parents.
- Are "stages of grief" a kind of story made up to make sense of disturbing and chaotic events?
- To what extent do various nations and cultures agree on what is "the good death?"

These and other topics recognize interactions between individual and society. It is true that we live and die as individuals. However, it is also true that we live and die within a particular society during a particular time in world history. Preoccupation with our thoughts and feelings as individuals could lead us to lose sight of the larger picture in which social dynamics so often influence the timing, mode, and experience of dying as well as our basic interpretations of life and death.

We draw upon the best available scholarship and research as well as upon the words of people who have found themselves in the middle of death-related situations. We note the limitations of present knowledge and offer alternative interpretations. It is our intention to present information clearly but without undue simplification.

I welcome you personally to this book and to the course to which this book may contribute. Take advantage of your instructor's expertise: Do not hesitate to ask questions and share your experiences. Explore the ever-growing literature on the human encounter with mortality. Discover what observers from many different perspectives can offer us. Now join us in one of humankind's oldest—and newest—voyages of discovery.

ACKNOWLEDGMENTS

I appreciate the comments offered by the following reviewers: Patrick Ashwood, Hawkeye Community College; J. Meredith Martin, University of New Mexico; and Allen Richardson, Cedar Crest College. It was also good to hear from other instructors and readers who had useful suggestions to make.

I hope you will find this book helpful in your explorations of death, society, and human experience.

A NOTE FROM THE PUBLISHER ON SUPPLEMENTS

Instructor's Manual and Test Bank (ISBN 0-205-00110-6): The Instructor's Manual and Test Bank has been designed to assist teachers in their efforts to prepare lectures and evaluate student learning. For each chapter of the text, the Instructor's Manual offers different types of resources, including detailed chapter summaries and outlines, learning objectives, discussion questions, classroom activities, and much more.

Also included in this manual is a Test Bank offering multiple-choice, true/false, fill-in-the-blank, and/or essay questions for each chapter. The Instructor's Manual and Test Bank is available to adopters at www.pearsonhighered.com.

MyTest (ISBN 0-205-00111-4): The Test Bank is also available online through Pearson's computerized testing system, MyTest. MyTest allows instructors to create their own personalized exams, to edit any of the existing test questions, and to add new questions. Other special features of this program include random generation of test questions, creation of alternative versions of the same test, scrambling question sequence, and test preview before printing. Search and sort features allow you to locate questions quickly and to arrange them in whatever order you prefer. The Test Bank can be accessed from anywhere with a free MyTest user account. There is no need to download a program or file to your computer.

PowerPoint Presentations (ISBN 0-205-00112-2): Lecture PowerPoints are available for this text. The Lecture PowerPoint slides outline each chapter to help you convey sociological principles in a visual and exciting way. They are available to adopters at www.pearsonhighered.com.

MySearchLab: MySearchLab provides a host of tools for students to master a writing or research project, It provides online access to reliable content for Internet research projects, including thousands of full articles from the EBSCO ContentSelect database a complete online handbook for grammar and usage support. A tutorial on understanding and avoiding plagiarism, and AutoCite, which helps students correctly cite sources

Is death our greatest fear, as many observers have
concluded? Perhaps they should have added, "That's
why it can be such a thrill to dance at the edge of
existence."

As We Think About Death

Union General John Sedgwick was killed during the battle of Spotsylvania on May 8, 1864, while watching Confederate troops. His last words were, "They couldn't hit an elephant at this dist. . . ."
—quoted by John Richard Stephens (2006, p. 161)

Chilling whistles preceded horrible booms, and Antonia found herself listening for each whistle to end, fearing the worst, then letting her breath out when she heard someone else's life exploding.
—Diane Ackerman (2007, p. 58)

. . . we are taught not to contemplate the possibility that all being is ephemeral—including our own. But san men remind us of it every day: as our trash goes, so one day, go we. No wonder we need to hate them.
—Robin Nagel (2008)

I felt like we were going to get thrown out of the car numerous times, and I had zero control in anticipating which direction we were thrown next. I'm glad we hit it again before I could think about it or I might not have done her again.
—Anonymous rollercoaster enthusiast (2008)

One man was stretchered away after he was hit in the back by a bull with its horn and another man who had tripped had a lucky escape when the animal simply tripped over him. . . . "You're not even thinking. You're just sprinting. The elation at the end of it. You're just ecstatic," said a 23-year-old accountant from Adelaide, Australia, Jim Atkinson
—CNN (2004)

"His brow was perfectly calm. No scowl disfigured his happy face, which signifies he died an easy death, no sins of this world to harrow his soul as it gently passed away to distant and far happier realms."
—U.S. Civil War Confederate soldier,
quoted by Drew Gilpin Faust (2008, p. 21).

Every year women arrive at the Herart Public Hospital in Afghanistan with burns so severe that they die. These are women who were killed for bringing "dishonor" to their families by violating a rule, or who failed to bring a suitable dowry when married.

—Leela Jacinto (2002)

In the land of the Uttarakurus grows the magic Jambu tree, whose fruit has the property of conferring immunity from illness and old age, and, by means of this fruit, they lengthen their lives to a thousand years or even, in some accounts, to eleven thousand years . . . among other things, their realm includes landscapes of precious stones and trees from whose branches grow beautiful maidens.

—Gerald J. Gruman (2003, p. 33)

Life is supposed to go on. Yes, there is death, but not here, not now, and surely not for us. We wake to a familiar world each day. We splash water on the same face we rinsed yesterday. We talk with people whose faces are familiar. We see so much of what we have seen many times before. It is so comforting . . . this ongoingness of daily life. Why disturb this pattern? Why think of death? Why make each other anxious? And why do anything that would increase our risk? Here are a few quick, if perhaps not entirely satisfying answers:

- General Sedgwick led an eventful life, but is remembered now for his inadvertently famous last words. Did he deny his immediate danger to set a bold example for his troops, to cover up his own fear, or perhaps just because he would not think of taking advice from a junior officer? Denial of vulnerability can be a fatal gesture.
- Death anxiety sometimes arises in a moment and passes almost as quickly when the threat evaporates. Not so for Antonia and her family in Warsaw, as the great city was first bombed extensively and then occupied by the Nazis, who used every method within their means to discover, torture, and kill anybody who might oppose their rule. Normal life had been replaced by 24/7 emergency alert. Death was no longer an abstraction or a remote and mysterious event: it was life that now seemed elusive, perhaps unattainable.

- We can't help but think of death. It's their fault, the sanitation workers who haul our garbage away. That is the considered opinion of New York City sanitation worker Robin Nagel, who is also a professor of anthropology. She notes that we live in a high-consuming, rapid-disposing culture that tries to keeps death and the dead at the farthest margins of our physical and emotional space. We are uneasy in the knowledge that there is no permanence in our lives. Today's bargain purchase is tomorrow's garbage. We, who have purchased, used, and discarded so much, will ourselves be hauled off some day, and then what? What will it all have meant? "Why Do We Love to Hate San Men?" (op. cit.). Well, Professor Nagel has just told us.
- Who can resist the opportunity to be scared out of our wits on a diabolical rollercoaster or gored and trampled by a bull? Each year so many people crowd into the northern Spanish town of Pamplona that they become almost as much a menace to each other as the six bulls who rush down cobblestone streets. (Fifteen have died and hundreds have been injured since the first bull run in 1911.) The "ecstasy" of outrunning death is hard to understand for those who organize themselves around the avoidance of mortal anxiety. Our friend "Anonymous" tries out the biggest and baddest rollercoasters, and does it over and over again. It's the thrill of terror and the joy of survival. Not only do accidents

Sanitation workers in New York City are just doing their job, but anthropologist (and fellow employee) Robin Nagel observes many people anxiously associate the disposal of trash with their own mortality in a throw-away society that has difficulty in facing the realities of impermanence and death.

occur, usually attributed to inadequate attention to safety issues (Johnson & Williams, 2007), but the cardiovascular risk is serious enough to elicit medical warnings (Peck, 2005). Healthy volunteers experienced sharp rises in blood pressure during a brief ride, and several had potentially life-threatening cardiac responses. People with cardiovascular conditions are placing themselves at risk on the more daunting amusement park rides—as are those with silent (previously undetected) medical problems. Apparently, then, we like to avoid unnecessary risk and mortal terror—except when we don't. Why? Because there's fun in it, the intensified feeling of being alive when we dance at the edge of survival (see *edge theory*, this chapter).

- In the mid-nineteenth-century United States, people thought often and intensely about death. No family was secure from the threat of virulent epidemics and lethal infections, especially during or after childbirth. Fortunately, they knew how they were supposed to think about death. Guidebooks for Christian living and dying were relied on by many families. The Civil War brought death on an unprecedented scale and in horrifying forms. The loss of young lives was devastating to families on both sides of the conflict. What made these losses all the more unbearable was the fact that sons, brothers, husbands, and fathers

had died far from home, bereft of comfort and spiritual ministry, and possibly in a despairing state of mind. The Confederate soldier quoted by Faust (p. 21) was providing a welcome service when he described his cousin's death in such positive terms in a condolence letter. It was best if his relatives could be made to believe that their young man had ended his life at peace with himself and God. How people died reflected on how they had lived and hinted at what would be their estate in the afterlife (see also the *good death* in Chapter 15).

- Young women, even girls as young as 11, have set themselves on fire, choosing extremely painful deaths over lives enslaved to men they did not want to marry. Such events are still occurring in Afghanistan, and other places where females are regarded as disposable property. Some of these deaths are finally coming to general attention, as when Shakiba, a 19-year-old Afghan woman, was interviewed by television from the hospital bed in which she would soon die. Shakiba's family sold her to become a man's second wife. "My family was selling me and I didn't know what else to do." Women between 14 and 20 years of age who were desperately trying to escape marriages to older men have carried out most of the self-immolations. The daughters were being married off for a "bride price" intended to help the rest of the family survive. But families themselves have also been accused of killing daughters for being uncooperative or for having violated their society's rigid sexist code of conduct. Not only death, then, but death in youth, and not only death in youth, but death preceded by intense suffering—these were chosen over lives that seemed even worse.

- Through the centuries, most people died before what we now would consider to be midlife. Many did not even survive childhood. Perhaps this is one reason why the folklore of ancient times is filled with stories about fortunate people who lived so long that they hardly needed to think about death. The Uttarakurus were supposed to live in the far north of India, but similar tales flourished in Greek, Persian, Teutonic, Hindu, and Japanese lore, among others. One of the oldest Hebrew legends speaks of the River of Immortality, which some scholars believe provided the background for Christ being identified with the Fountain of Life. The idea that in a faraway place there were refreshing waters that could extend life and perhaps also renew youth was still credible enough to gain funding for Ponce de Leon's expedition to Florida (although skeptics suggest it was gold lust all the way). Fear of dying could be attributed to the prevailing short life expectancy. If only we could *do* something about death, we wouldn't have to be thinking about it so often!

Some families today cherish fading photographs of relatives who died years ago of pneumonia, tuberculosis, cholera, typhoid, scarlet fever, infantile paralysis, and other widespread diseases. One hoped to survive the diseases that threatened children and young adults. One hoped for the chance to realize personal dreams for a good life. Perspectives have changed about what to do when life isn't good. There are now increasing demands for release from life when the quality of that life has been reduced by painful or incapacitating illness. Death, once the problem, is being regarded as the answer by a growing number of people.

In this chapter we begin our exploration of thoughts, knowledge, attitudes, and feelings about death. We will consider many world societies, although our focus is on the United States. It is not enough, though, to attend only to the way other people think about death; therefore, this chapter also provides the opportunity to take stock of our own dealings with mortality. First, we gather around the campfire and spare a few thoughts for our ancestors.

A HISTORY OF DEATH?

We have already touched a little on the history of death. In fact, one might grumble that all of history is just death warmed over. The people who did those things, or had those things done to them—their lives, no matter how lively, have been absorbed into yesteryear. Grumbles aside, the history of death is so interwoven with life that scholars have hesitated to take it on. Try to encompass

life and death in the big picture, leaving nothing out and placing everything in balanced perspective? Good luck with that! Therefore, in this book we offer historical perspectives in many specific areas, e.g., hospice care, euthanasia, terrorism, and afterlife beliefs. One scholar stands out, however, for his effort to identify basic themes in attitudes toward death over an extended period. Phillipe Aries had already made substantial contributions to the history of family life (1987) and the social construction of childhood (1962). Aries's influential work (1981) energized the study of death from a historical perspective. He attempted to reconstruct the history of European death attitudes, focusing on approximately a thousand years after the introduction of Christianity up to the present time. He drew most of his observations from burial practices and rituals surrounding the end of life. Aries's book is a treasure of information regarding how our ancestors lived with death.

What does Aries extract from this daunting mass of observations? Four psychological themes and their variations: *awareness of the individual; the defense of society against untamed nature; the belief in an afterlife;* and *belief in the existence of evil.* These themes have unfolded through the centuries.

Death was primarily a community event in the earliest human societies. The community or tribe could be seriously weakened by the loss of its members, and the survivors feared even more for their lives. Nature was dangerous, so the death of the individual was relatively "tame." How the community would keep itself strong and viable was the challenge.

Ritualization was a way of protecting fragile human society from the uncontrollable perils of nature and malevolent gods. Death and the dead had to be dealt with constantly. Much of the danger resided in potential harm from the dead, who might return with a vengeance. The dead as well as death were tamed by requiring them to return only under specified occasions and conditions. Mostly, the early Christian dead were assigned the role of peaceful sleepers. Speak not ill of them.

About a thousand years into the Christian era, a darker shadow fell over prevailing attitudes: the death of the self became the most intense concern.

People became more aware of themselves as individuals. This was associated with a heightened sense of vulnerability. It was their very own life, their very own soul that was at stake. And there was a lot more to life. The quality of life was improving, so people were reluctant to surrender the pleasures of earthly life unless postmortem bliss was assured. *The hour of death became the most important hour of life.* The Ave Maria became a fervent prayer for a good death. Death was no longer simply a natural part of life: it was make-or-break with individual destiny. This transformation became evidence in burial practices: the body and face were now covered and concealed, taken out of nature.

Next came what might be called twisted death. Rationalism and science were contributing to an increasingly progressive and sophisticated worldview; however, at the same time, death became more entwined with both violence and sexuality. In other words, death had become strange, alien, and sometimes perverted.

Furthermore, a specific dark fear becomes "viral" throughout the world: being buried alive. Horror is on the loose as people recoil but are fascinated at the image of life and death so closely mingled, perhaps with forbidden sexuality as a terrifying temptation. Sex and death would remain strange bedfellows as a cross-cultural theme still having its say.

Attitude change did not stop at this point. Next into prominence came the death of the other. This took place within the context of widespread technological advances and the growing importance of family life and privacy. People lived more as members of a tight-knit family than as cogs in the larger society. Death had become more personal—individual grief breaking through communal ritual. "What the survivors mourned was no longer the fact of dying but the physical separation from the deceased" (p. 610). Death now was neither tame nor wild. It could be viewed as a beautiful adventure. This social reconstruction of death was made possible by the dismissal of purgatory, Hell, and an eternity of suffering. Death was revisioned as a guilt-free trip. One could therefore contemplate the mysteries and wondrous transformations rather than tremble at the threshold of damnation. Best of all,

death meant reunion with loved ones. Heaven had been improved with an extreme makeover that promised reunion with loved ones, a projection of the earthly good life into a forever space.

Next? *The invisible death* made its impact in the nineteenth century and continues its dominance today. It does not revoke the death of the other, but takes us to a different place in the mind. "Death became dirty, and then it became medicalized" (p .612). Why? Because "success" had become everything. The opposite of absolute success was absolute failure, and that was the new role assigned to death. This meant that it was a kindness to protect people from knowledge of their imminent death: enter denial! Avoidance, misrepresentation, and denial had an effect that could hardly have been more unthinkable in earlier eras. It was spiritual deprivation—deprived of the opportunity for that transformative deathbed moment. Distracted from their own final passage and shorn of interpersonal support and communal ritual, people now died neither in grace nor in peril of damnation. If death were no longer an evil, it was no longer a sacred passage either. It was just, well, failure of the machine.

Aries offers many examples in support of his conclusions. His book is little short of a revelation for those who have never attended to the connection between our social constructions and how we live and die. Nevertheless, Aries's conclusions have not escaped challenge. It is possible to read history in more than one way. Perhaps he emphasized one source of data too much while ignoring others. In any event, he does not delve into the history of death attitudes and practices in Africa, Asia, and the Pacific Islands. A fair assessment is that Aries has made a remarkable contribution for one scholar as he pioneered a vast and neglected realm of human experience.

For a brief, intensive immersion in the history of death, a top recommendation is Barbara W. Tuchman's (1978) authoritative and richly illustrated *A Distant Mirror. The Calamitous 14th Century.* Here we find death raw, up close and personal, and in command of town and country, crown and church. Another informative read is John R. Hall's (2009) *Apocalypse.* He traces the history of doom-saying from antiquity to the present. If you have ever wondered about the end of the world, here is the opportunity to catch up with what others have been imagining through the centuries. Many entries on specific historical developments are offered in the encyclopedias listed at the end of this chapter. And I wouldn't mind it if you felt like reading my book, *On Our Way: The Final Passage Through Life and Death.*

Philosophers were most active in pondering death when abstract thought burst through with unprecedented enthusiasm during the Golden Age of Greek antiquity. What is the world made of? What is really real, and what is illusion? How do we know anything, and how do we know that we know it? What is the good? And what are we to make of this limited run on earth? In later centuries, philosophers mostly whistled past death, and it is only in recent years that a few have tried to pick up where the ancients left off. Jacque Choron (1973) offered a concise and reliable survey of *Death in Western Thought*, but good luck in snagging a copy! As a challenging sample of early philosophical thought, here is what one maverick passed along:

> So death, the most terrifying of ills, is nothing
> to us, since so long as we exist, death is not with
> us, but when death comes, then we do not exist.
> It does not then concern either the living or the
> dead, since for the former it is not and the latter
> are no more. (Epicurus, Third century B.C.)

Neither the living nor the dead should be concerned about death. Instead, we should cultivate a pleasurable life of learning and friendship. Epicurus illustrated this approach by creating a garden community that welcomed people of all backgrounds who wanted to live here and now in a peaceful and friendly manner. It is said that, remarkably, this community endured for 500 years. Is that a philosophy we should live by—or we entitled and condemned to worry about our mortal endings?

NOT THINKING ABOUT DEATH: A FAILED EXPERIMENT

As a society, we have tried not thinking about death. Most of us completed our school days without being exposed to substantial readings and discussions about dying, death, grief, and suicide. Who would have taught us, anyway? Our teachers were products of the same never-say-die society. Death did surface sporadically as an event remote from our own experiences. For example, X many gunmen murdered each other in a famous shoot-out. Some king or other died and somebody else grabbed the throne on a date we might need to remember for the exam. Occasionally, interesting people died or people died in interesting ways; otherwise, death had little to do with us.

Students who persevered to a graduate degree received only further lessons in death avoidance. Nurses, physicians, psychologists, social workers, and others who would be relied on to provide human services were not helped to understand their own death-related feelings, let alone anybody else's. During these long years, even clergy often felt unprepared to cope with the death-related situations they would face. Few of their instructors had themselves mastered the art of ministering to the dying.

The media also cooperated. Nobody died. Nobody had cancer. Lucky "Nobody"! Instead, people would "pass away" after a "long illness." Deaths associated with crime and violence received lavish attention, then as now, but silence had settled over the deaths of everyday people. When a movie script called for a deathbed scene, Hollywood would offer a sentimental and sanitized version. A typical example occurs in *Till the Clouds Go By* (1946), a film that purported to be the biography of songwriter Jerome Kern. A dying man tries to communicate to a friend his realization that this will be the last time they see each other, but the visitor obeys the Hollywood dictum of avoidance and pretense. As a result, the friends never actually connect, never offer significant words of parting to each other. A physician then enters the room and nods gravely to the friend, who immediately departs. Another mortal lesson from Hollywood: The moment of death belongs to the doctor, not to the dying person and the bereaved. Audiences today see this scene as shallow and deceptive. One student spoke for many others in complaining, "It was as phony as can be—what a terrible way to end a relationship!" A new question has arisen, though: Does the fascination with grisly corpses and mangled body parts on television programs such as *CSI* literally depersonalize death? Is immersion in gory details just another maneuver to avoid emotional confrontation with the death of a person?

Not thinking about death was a failure. People continued to die, and how they died became an increasing source of concern. Survivors continued to grieve, often feeling a lack of understanding and support from others. Suicide rates doubled, then tripled, among the young, and remained exceptionally high among older adults. Scattered voices warned us that in attempting to evade the reality of death, we were falsifying the totality of our lives. Who were we kidding? Neither an individual nor a society could face its challenges wisely without coming to terms with mortality.

It is still difficult to think about death, especially when our own lives and relationships are involved. Nevertheless, enforced silence and frantic evasion seem to be less pervasive. There is an increasing readiness to listen and communicate.

Listening and Communicating

More physicians are now listening and communicating. Patients and family members feel more empowered to express their concerns, needs, and wishes. Physicians feel more compelled to take these concerns, needs, and wishes into account.

Some people have a ready-made answer that dismisses open discussion of death: "There's nothing to think about. When your number's up, it's up." This idea goes back a long way. It is part of that general view of life known as *fatalism*. Outcomes are determined in advance. There's nothing we can do to affect the outcomes so why bother? There is something to be said for respecting the limits of human knowledge and efficacy. But there is also something to be said for doing what we can to reduce suffering and risk within our limits. The person who is quick to introduce a fatalistic statement often is attempting to end the discussion before it really begins. It is what communication experts call a *silencer*.

Fatalistic attitudes in today's world are perhaps more dangerous than ever. As we will see, many deaths in the United States can be attributed to lifestyle. Our attitudes, choices, and actions contribute to many other deaths across the entire life span. Ironically, it is the belief that there is no use in thinking about death and taking life-protective measures that increase the probability of an avoidable death.

YOUR SELF-INVENTORY OF ATTITUDES, BELIEFS, AND FEELINGS

We have touched briefly on a few of the death-related questions and beliefs that are current in our society. Perhaps some of your own thoughts and feelings have come to mind. One of the most beneficial things you can do for yourself at this point is to take stock of your present experiences, attitudes, beliefs, and feelings. This will give you not only a personal data baseline but will also contribute further to your appreciation of the ways in which other people view death.

Before reading further, please begin sampling your personal experiences with death by completing Self-Inventories 1–4. Try to notice what thoughts and feelings come to mind as you answer these questions. Which questions make you angry? Which questions would you prefer not to answer? Which questions seem foolish, or make you want to laugh? Observing your own responses is part of the self-monitoring process that has been found invaluable by many of the people who work systematically with death-related issues.

Each of the inventories takes a distinctive perspective. We begin with your knowledge base, sampling the information you have acquired regarding various facets of death. This is followed by exploring your attitudes and beliefs. We then move on to your personal experiences with death. Finally, we look at the feelings that are stirred in you by dying, death, and grief. Our total view of death comprises knowledge, attitudes, experiences, and feelings—and it is useful to identify each of these components accurately. For example, if I fail to distinguish between my personal feelings and my actual knowledge of a death-related topic, I thereby reduce my ability to make wise decisions and take effective actions.

Please complete the self-inventories now.

Inventory 1

Your Knowledge Base

Fill in the blanks or select alternative answers as accurately as you can. If you are not sure of the answer, offer your best guess.

1. Your friend wants to live as long and possible—and would change species to do it. Which of the following species has the longest verified life-span?

    a. Bat _____   c. Lobster _____

    b. Cat _____   d. Queen termite _____

2. Most baby boomers:

    a. Do not believe in Heaven _____

    b. Believe in Heaven, but not in ghosts _____

    c. Believe in Heaven, but do not expect to go there _____

    d. Believe in Heaven, and expect to go there _____

3. How many deaths are there in the United States each year? _____

4. The leading cause of death for the population in general is _____

5. A person born in the United States a century ago had an average life expectancy (ALE) of about _____ years.

6. A person born in the United States today has an ALE of about _____ years.

7. In the nation of _____, ALE has dropped from 63 to only 34 years over the past quarter of a century. Why?

8. There is a new entry among the 10 leading causes of death in the United States. This is _____

9. What is the leading cause of fatal injuries in the United States? _____

10. A seriously ill person is in the hospital and not expected to recover. How much time is this person likely to spend alone each 24-hour day?

11. Homicide rates in the United States have been consistently highest in:

    New England _____

    Mountain states _____

    Southern states _____

    West north central states _____

12. Does your state recognize an advance directive for end-of-life medical care as a legal and enforceable document?

    Yes_____ No_____

13. A suicide attempt is most likely to result in death when made by a/an

    a. Young woman

    b. Young man

    c. Elderly woman

    d. Elderly man

14. Cryonic suspension is a technique that is intended to preserve a body in a hypothermic (low-temperature) state until a cure is discovered for the fatal condition. How many people have actually been placed in cryonic suspension, and how many revived?

15. The earliest childhood memory reported by most adults is an experience of _____.

16. The two states that have legalized physician-assisted death are _____ and _____

17. Palliative care most often has relief from _____ as its top priority.

18. What was placed inside the chest of a royal Egyptian mummy, and why?

19. In the United States, cremation is now chosen by about one person in _____.

20. Near-death experience reports have several key elements in common with G-LOC. What is G-LOC? _____

21. Jack Kevorkian, M.D., "assisted" in the death of more than 100 people. How many of these people were terminally ill? _____

22. "Periodic mass extinctions" have totally eliminated many species and taken a tremendous toll of life. The three most recent mass die-offs are thought to have been caused by _____.

23. The Harvard Criteria offered an influential guide to the diagnosis of _____.

24. _____ is the philosopher who turned down the opportunity to escape his unjust execution, and instead used the occasion to explain to his friends why death should not be feared.

25. PTSD has been receiving increased media attention lately. What is it? _____

Answers to self-inventory questions are found later in this chapter. Not going to peek, are you?

Inventory 2

My Attitudes and Beliefs

Select the answer that most accurately represents your belief.

1. I believe in some form of life after death:

   Yes, definitely _____

   Yes, but not quite sure _____

   No, but not quite sure _____

   No, definitely _____

2. I believe that you die when your number comes up. It's in the hands of fate.

   Yes, definitely _____

   Yes, but not quite sure _____

   No, but not quite sure _____

   No, definitely _____

3. I believe that taking one's own life is:

   Never justified _____

   Justified when terminally ill _____

   Justified whenever life no longer seems worth living _____

4. I believe that taking another person's life is:

   Never justified _____

   Justified in defense of your own life _____

   Justified when that person has committed a terrible crime _____

5. I believe that dying people should be:

   Told the truth about their condition _____

   Kept hopeful by sparing them the facts _____

   Depends upon the person and the circumstances _____

6. In thinking about my own old age, I would prefer:

   To die before I grow old _____

   To live as long as I can _____

   To discover what challenges and opportunities old age will bring _____

7. To me, the possibility of nuclear weapon warfare or accidents that might destroy much of life on earth has been of:

   No concern _____

   Little concern _____

   Some concern _____

   Major concern _____

8. To me, the possibility of environmental catastrophes that might destroy much of life on earth has been of:

   No concern _____

   Little concern _____

   Some concern _____

9. Drivers and passengers should be required to wear seat belts.

   Yes, agree _____

   Tend to agree _____

   Tend to disagree _____

   No, disagree _____

10. The availability of handguns should be more tightly controlled to reduce accidental and impulsive shootings.

    Yes, agree _____

    Tend to agree _____

    Tend to disagree _____

    No, disagree _____

11. A person has been taken to the emergency room with internal bleeding that is likely to prove fatal. This person is 82 years of age and has an Alzheimer's disease–type dementia. What type of response would you recommend from the ER staff?

    Comfort only _____

    Limited attempt at rescue _____

    All-out attempt at rescue _____

12. You have been taken to the emergency room with internal bleeding that is likely to prove fatal. You are now 82 years of age and have an Alzheimer's disease–type dementia. What type of response would you hope you receive from the ER staff?

    Comfort only _____

    Limited attempt at rescue _____

    All-out attempt at rescue _____

13. Another round of chemotherapy has failed for a woman with advanced breast cancer. The doctor suggests a new round of experimental therapy. She replies, "I wish I were dead." What do you think should be done—and why?

    _____

    _____

    _____

Inventory 3

My Experiences with Death

Fill in the blanks or select the most accurate alternative answers.

1. A. I have had an animal companion who died.
        Yes   No
    B. How I felt when my pet died can be described by words such as _____ and
        _____.

2. The following people in my life have died:

    Person   How Long Ago?

    A. _____
    B. _____
    C. _____
    D. _____
    E. _____

3. The death that affected me the most at the time was _____.

4. How I felt when this person died can be described by words such as _____ and _____.

5. This death was especially significant to me because
    _____
    _____.

6. In all the circumstances surrounding this person's death, including what happened afterward, my most positive memory is of
    _____.

7. My most disturbing memory is of
    _____
    _____

8. I have conversed with dying people:
    Never _____   One person _____
    Several people _____ Many people _____

9. I have provided care for a dying person.
    Never _____   One person _____
    Several people _____ Many people _____

10. I have known a person who attempted suicide.
    Not to my knowledge _____
    One person _____
    Several people _____

11. I have known a person who committed suicide.
    Not to my knowledge _____
    One person _____
    Several people _____

12. I have known a person who died in an accident.
    Not to my knowledge _____
    One person _____
    Several people _____

13. I have known a person who was murdered.
    Never _____
    One person _____
    Several people _____

14. I have known a person who died of AIDS-related disease.
    Not to my knowledge _____
    One person _____
    Several people _____

15. I know a person who has tested positive for the AIDS virus.
    Not to my knowledge _____
    One person _____
    Several people _____

    _____
    _____

Inventory 4

My Feelings

Select the answer that most closely represents your feelings.

1. I would feel comfortable in developing an intimate conversation with a dying person.

    Yes, agree _____   Tend to agree _____

    Tend to disagree _____   No, disagree _____

2. I would hesitate to touch someone who was dying.

    Yes, agree _____   Tend to agree _____

    Tend to disagree _____   No, disagree _____

3. My hands would tremble if I were talking to a dying person.

    Yes, agree _____   Tend to agree _____

    Tend to disagree _____   No, disagree _____

4. I would have more difficulty in talking if the dying person was about my age.

    Yes, agree _____   Tend to agree _____

    Tend to disagree _____   No, disagree _____

5. I would avoid talking about death and dying with a person who was terminally ill.

    Yes, agree _____   Tend to agree _____

    Tend to disagree _____   No, disagree _____

6. I would avoid talking with a dying person if possible.

    Yes, agree _____   Tend to agree _____

    Tend to disagree _____   No, disagree _____

7. I have had moments of anxiety in which I think of my own death.

    Never _____   Once _____

    Several times _____   Often _____

8. I fear that I will die too soon.

    Yes, agree _____   Tend to agree _____

    Tend to disagree _____   No, disagree _____

9. I have no fear of death as such.

    Yes, agree _____   Tend to agree _____

    Tend to disagree _____   No, disagree _____

10. I have no fears associated with dying.

    Yes, agree _____   Tend to agree _____

    Tend to disagree _____   No, disagree _____

11. I feel good when I think about life after death.

    Yes, agree _____   Tend to agree _____

    Tend to disagree _____   No, disagree _____

12. I am anxious about the possible death of somebody I love.

    Yes, agree _____   Tend to agree _____

    Tend to disagree _____   No, disagree _____

13. I am grieving over somebody who has already died.

    Yes, agree _____   Tend to agree _____

    Tend to disagree _____   No, disagree _____

14. I have a hard time taking death seriously: It feels remote to me, and not really connected to my own life.

    Yes, agree _____   Tend to agree _____

    Tend to disagree _____   No, disagree _____

15. I have some strong, even urgent, feelings regarding death these days.

    Yes, agree _____   Tend to agree _____

    Tend to disagree _____   No, disagree _____

Note: Questions 1–6 are part of a scale introduced by Hayslip (1986–1987).

SOME ANSWERS—AND THE QUESTIONS THEY RAISE

Here are the answers to Self-Inventory #1:

1. Lobster it is, at age 170. Bat, 30; cat 36; queen termite, 50 (Kirkwood, 2010). If lobstering does not satisfy your friend, suggest morphing into a bristlecone pine tree, some of which have survived for thousands of years. Perhaps you can outdo your friend as a hydra, which is (theoretically) immortal.

2. Most members of the baby boomer generation believe in ghosts and in their own acceptance into Heaven, though they judge that many other people will not make it (Chapter 13).

3. More than 2 million people die in the United States each year. The most recent data report lists 2,443,387 deaths (Chapter 3).

4. Heart disease continues to be the leading cause of death in the United States (Chapter 3).

5. A person born in the United States *in 1900* had an ALE of 47 years (Chapter 3).

6. A person born in the United States *today* has an ALE of nearly 78 years (Chapter 3).

7. Zimbabwe, beset by AIDS, poverty, and societal disorder, has suffered a severe reduction in ALE (Chapter 3), after having previously achieved one of the highest levels ever in Africa.

8. Alzheimer's disease has become the eighth leading cause of death in the United States, an unfortunate consequence of the aging of the population and the limited success so far in preventing or treating this condition (Chapter 3).

9. Motor vehicle accidents have long been the most common cause of fatal accidents in the United States. Among elderly people, falls are the second most common type of injury fatality (Chapter 3).

10. Seriously and terminally ill people were alone almost 19 hours a day, according to a hospital study (Chapter 4).

11. Homicide rates have been consistently the highest in Southern states (Chapter 9).

12. Yes—all states do! (Chapter 6).

13. A suicide attempt is most likely to be fatal when it is made by an elderly man (Chapter 7).

14. Fewer than 100 human bodies have been placed in cryonic suspension worldwide, and no known attempts have been made to resuscitate (Chapter 6).

15. A death or other loss experience is most often the earliest childhood memory recalled by adults (Chapter 10).

16. Oregon and, more recently, Washington (Chapter 9).

17. Relief from pain is most often the top priority for palliative care or hospice programs. Relief from other symptoms is also provided as much as possible (Chapter 5).

18. The royal physicians replaced the heart with a scarab, a carved stone that represented the dung beetle, whose mysterious work of helping to bring life back from death was regarded as intrinsic to the great cycle of being (Chapter 12).

19. About one person in four in the United States now chooses cremation. There is much variation in frequency of choosing cremation within the United States and among nations (Chapter 12).

20. G-LOC is a sudden loss of normal consciousness that is experienced by pilots under acceleration stress. Tunnel vision and bright lights are among the perceptual changes that resemble near-death experiences (Chapter 13).

21. Less than a third of the patients whose lives Kevorkian helped to end were actually terminally ill at the time (Chapter 9).

22. Scientists now believe that asteroids were responsible for the three most recent mass die-offs or extinctions (Chapter 15).

23. The Harvard criteria have been applied to determine whether a nonresponsive person should be considered brain-dead (Chapter 2).

24. *Post-traumatic stress disorder* is a disabling condition that is related to overwhelming experiences, such as warfare and disaster (Chapter 3).

25. Socrates (Chapter 15).

Attitudes, Experiences, Beliefs, Feelings

Attitudes refer to our action tendencies. I am ready or not ready to act. I am ready to approach or to avoid this situation. *Beliefs* refer to our worldview.

Fatalism, already mentioned, is one type of belief. *Feelings* provide us with qualitative information, a status report on our sense of being. I feel safe or endangered, happy or sorrowful, aroused or lethargic. Two people may hold identical beliefs and attitudes but differ greatly in their feelings. On Inventory 2, question 10, for example, these two people may answer, "Yes, agree: The availability of handguns should be more tightly controlled to reduce accidental and impulsive shootings." However, one of these people may have relatively little feeling attached to this view. Perhaps this person thinks that it is risky to have a lot of handguns around on general principles. The other person might be the widow of a physician who was shot to death by an emotionally disturbed person who did not even know him. Her feelings could hardly be more intense. (This is a real person, the former owner of a home my wife and I purchased. Incredible as it may seem, the young widow herself became the recipient of death threats because she spoke up in favor of gun control.)

Personal experience influences our attitudes, beliefs, and feelings. For example, people who have had near-death experiences while in a life-threatening situation often develop a different perspective on life and death (Chapter 14). A paramedic who has responded to a thousand motor vehicle accidents is likely to have a stronger attitude and more intense feelings when noticing children without seat belts in a car. A person who has never suffered the death of a loved one may be more impatient with a bereaved colleague who does not seem to "snap back" right away.

There is a profound experiential difference between people who have had a personally significant death and those for whom death has remained a distant topic, or even just a word. Death stopped being just a word for a graduate student of social work when both her parents were killed in an automobile accident. She could not go on with her own life until she fully realized their deaths as well as her own mortality. "Before all this happened, it was just a word to me, death. I could hear death. I could say death. Really, though, it was just a word. Now it's like something under my own skin, if you know what I mean." Simply knowing intellectually that people die was not enough;

she now had to connect death with life in a very personal way.

This challenge is ours as well. If we have experienced a death that "got" to us—whether the death of a person or an animal companion—then we are also more likely to realize what other people have been going through. This is one of the most powerful dynamics at work in community support groups. Organizations such as Compassionate Friends and Widow-to-Widow provide emotional support for bereaved persons from those who have already experienced the sorrow and stress of loss. New support groups continue to be formed to help people with specific types of death-related stress (for parents whose child has been killed by a drunk driver or for persons with AIDS). However, there are limits to the value of experience. Just because a person has had a particular kind of loss experience does not necessarily enhance his or her ability to support others. Furthermore, some people have proven helpful to the dying, the grieving, and the suicidal even if they have not had very similar experiences in their lives. The basic point to consider is whether at this time in your life you are someone who has experienced death in an undeniably personal way, or whether you still have something of an outsider's perspective.

Some people have an inner relationship with death that goes beyond basic realization. The sense of being dominated or haunted by death can emerge from one critical experience or from a cluster of experiences. Perhaps you have mourned the deaths of so many people that you could not even list them in the space provided. Perhaps several people died unexpectedly at the same time. Perhaps you are still responding strongly to the death of one person who had been at the center of your life. The question of whether your life is being highly influenced by death-related experiences cannot be answered by examining a simple list. We would need to appreciate what these people meant to you, and what lingers in your mind regarding the deaths themselves, the funeral, and the memorialization process. Furthermore, we would need to examine your own involvement in the situation. Perhaps you have a vivid memory of your last visits with a person who was a very important part of your life. On the other hand, perhaps you were thousands of miles away when this person died and had no opportunity to be with your loved one. We may be much influenced by how a person has died as well as by the fact of death itself. A death by suicide, for example, has often been considered tainted, resulting in additional stress and social isolation for the bereaved family.

How Does State of Mind Affect Death-Related Behavior?

Much remains to be learned about the link between what goes on in our minds and how we actually behave in death-related situations. Here are a few studies that have addressed some of the questions:

- *The living will: why most of the living won't.*
  The document known as the *living will* (Chapter 6) has been available since 1968. Although this document was designed to meet the growing public interest in controlling end-of-life decisions, most people did not choose to use it. Why? VandeCreek and Frankowski (1996) found that most people had not thought much about their own deaths and also believed that their last days were a long way off. The authors conclude that "completing living wills connotes personal death, and this appears to be a substantial barrier to completing the document" (1996, p. 80). Over the past few years there has been an increase in the number of people signing an advance health care directive (a successor to the living will) because this option is now part of established hospital policy—but many hospital personnel still have not gotten around to completing their own document because, well, they'd rather not think about it. Ask your favorite health care provider if he or she has completed a living will or other advance directive: it could be an interesting conversation.
- *Should I sign an organ donation card?*
  All states, as well as the District of Columbia, have enacted some version of the *Uniform Anatomical Gift Act* (Chapter 6). Despite the widespread availability of the organ donation option in association with the driver's license, relatively few people sign and carry organ donor cards (Lock, 2002). Personal attitudes

"Briar Rose" (aka Sleeping Beauty) is only a kiss away from waking to Prince Charming's love, and living happily ever after. Fantasy to the rescue when we don't feel up to facing reality!

play a major role in this decision. Nondonors tend to be more anxious about death and to have the specific fear of being declared dead prematurely (Robbins, 1990). Additionally, people who think of themselves as effective and self-reliant are more likely to sign the donation cards. The decision to donate organs to save another person's life seems closely related to the individual's general attitude and personal fears and anxieties.

- *Stepping off the curb.*
  Is there a relationship between state of mind and risk-taking behavior in everyday life? Laura Briscoe and I (1975) observed 125 people as they crossed a busy street between the Detroit Art Institute and Wayne State University. There were equal numbers of

street crossers in five risk categories. People classified as Type A, the safest pedestrians, stood at the curb until the light changed in their favor, scanned traffic in both directions, entered the crosswalk, moved briskly across the street, and checked out traffic from the opposite direction lanes before reaching the halfway point. At the opposite extreme were Type E pedestrians who crossed in the middle of the block, stepped out from between parked cars with the traffic lights against them, and did not look at traffic in either direction (miraculously, all 25 in this study did survive their crossings). All street crossers were interviewed when they reached the other side. The observed street-crossing behavior was closely related to their general attitudes toward risk taking. For example, the high-risk pedestrians also classified themselves as high-risk drivers, and judged that they put their lives in jeopardy about 16 percent of the time in an average week, as compared with only 2 percent for Type A crossers. The Type E crossers were four times more likely than the Type A crossers to have contemplated or attempted suicide. They also reported a higher level of frustration with life. Within the limits of this study, it was clear that people's general attitudes and feelings can be expressed in behavior choices that either increase or decrease the probability of death.

- *In God they trust.*

Cardiovascular surgery has come a long way in recent years. Many distressing symptoms have been relieved, many lives extended. Nevertheless, the recovery and rehabilitation process is effortful and sometimes punctuated by medical complications or episodes of discouragement. A thought-provoking study (Ai et al., 2007) followed patients through their postoperative period and found that those with "positive religious coping styles" experienced less pain and distress. These people were secure in their faith, trusting in a higher and benevolent power. They were also able to draw on social support from other people who shared their faith and helped to sustain their hope. Other studies have also hinted at improved health outcomes, including reduced mortality, for people with secure

religious faith and peer support. Doubt and conflict in religious belief seems to have a negative effect on health outcomes, although more research is needed to firmly establish these findings.

MAN IS MORTAL: BUT WHAT DOES THAT HAVE TO DO WITH ME?

Our attitudes toward life and death are challenged when a person close to us dies. In *The Death of Ivan Ilych*, Leo Tolstoy provides an insightful portrait of the confusions and urgencies that can afflict everybody in the situation. Consider just one passage from a novel that has lost none of its pertinence and power over the last century:

> The thought of the sufferings of the man he had known so intimately, first as a schoolmate, and later as a grown-up colleague, suddenly struck Peter Ivanovich with horror . . . "Three days of frightful suffering, then death! Why, that might suddenly, at any moment, happen to me," he thought, and for a moment felt terrified. But— he himself did not know how—the customary reflection at once occurred to him, that this had happened to Ivan Ilych and not to him. . . . After which reflection Peter Ivanovich felt reassured, and began to ask with interest about the details of Ivan Ilych's death, as though death were an accident natural to Ivan Ilych, but certainly not to himself (pp. 101–102).

Peter Ivanovich knows that we are all called mortals for a good reason. Yet he is playing a desperate game of evasion. Consider some of the elements in Peter Ivanovich's response:

1. He already knows of Ivan Ilych's death, but it is only on viewing the corpse that the realization of death strikes him. There is a powerful difference between intellectual knowledge and emotional realization. For one panicked moment, Peter feels that he himself is vulnerable. How could that be!
2. Peter Ivanovich immediately becomes concerned for Peter Ivanovich. His feelings do not center on the man who has lost his life or the woman who has lost her husband.

Count Leo Tolstoy, author of The Death of Ivan Ilych *and other powerful novels, entrances his grandchildren with a more lighthearted story.*

3. Yet he cannot admit that his outer line of defenses has been penetrated. He is supposed to show concern for others, not let them see his own distress. Furthermore, he hopes to leave this house of death with the confidence that death has been left safely behind.

4. Peter Ivanovich's basic strategy here is to differentiate himself from Ivan Ilych. Yes, some people really do die, but not people like himself. The proof was in the fact that Peter was the vertical and mobile man while Ivan (that luckless, inferior specimen) was horizontal and immobile. We witness Peter Ivanovich, then, stretching and tormenting his logic in the hope of arriving at an anxiety-reducing conclusion.

5. Once Peter Ivanovich has quelled his momentary panic, he is able to discuss Ivan Ilych's death. Even so, he is more interested in factual details than in feelings and meanings. He has started to rebuild the barriers between himself and death. Whatever he learns about how his friend died will strengthen this barrier: all that was true of Ivan obviously is not applicable to him.

These evasive strategies, and others, are not confined to the pages of a Russian novel. You might see them in operation when people in your life are confronted by what researchers today refer to as mortality salience. How will you deal with these situations?

ANXIETY, DENIAL, AND ACCEPTANCE: THREE CORE CONCEPTS

Three concepts that are central to understanding death attitudes are interwoven through this excerpt from Tolstoy's masterpiece. Peter Ivanovich felt tense, distressed, unwell, and apprehensive. *Death anxiety* is the term most often applied to such responses. Anxiety is a condition that seeks its own relief. To reduce the painful tension, a person might try many different actions—taking drugs or alcohol, for example, or fleeing from the situation. One form of avoiding death anxiety has received most of the attention from counselors and researchers: *denial.* This is a response that rejects certain key features of reality in the attempt to avoid or reduce anxiety. Peter Ivanovich denies the basic fact that he is as mortal as Ivan Ilych in order to distance himself from the death.

Many writers have urged that we should accept death. However, it is not always clear what they mean by acceptance: How does this response differ from resignation or depression? Precisely what should we accept—and on whose authority? And what is it that makes acceptance the most desirable response? Does a "good death" (Chapter 15) require acceptance? In Tolstoy's novel, Ivan Ilych eventually does achieve a sense of acceptance, but Peter Ivanovich seems to be as self-deceived and befuddled as ever.

Anxiety, denial, and acceptance are not the only death attitudes that we encounter, although most research has concentrated on these concepts. People often experience depression and a sense of loss when death is near. Although sorrow and anxiety are both distressing states of being, neither can be reduced to the other, although both can be co-experienced (Kastenbaum & Heflick, in press). Sorrow is oriented toward the past, anxiety toward the future. Furthermore, neuroscientists (Izard, 2009; Mobbs et al., 2007 are finding that strong emotional states have differential pathways of operation. Still another strategy is to identify with death: Some people attempt to reduce their own death anxieties by joining forces with death and killing others, whether in reality or in games and fantasies. How much harm have people done to each other when they have tried to control their own anxiety by becoming instruments of death?

STUDIES AND THEORIES OF DEATH ANXIETY

Death anxiety has attracted much attention from researchers and theorists. What has been learned? We will review the main findings, and then acquaint ourselves with the theories and their implications.

Self-report questionnaires are widely used in studies of death anxiety. Self-report instruments have the advantage of brevity, convenience, and simple quantitative results. There are limitations to what we can learn from them, however (Kastenbaum, 2000b):

1. Low scores on death anxiety scales are difficult to interpret. Do they mean low anxiety or high denial?
2. How high is high anxiety, and what is a "normal" level? Little has been learned about the level of death anxiety that is most adaptive in various situations because little information is acquired about how the questionnaire responses relate to real life behavior.
3. Respondents often are selected opportunistically. College students continue to be overrepresented, and members of ethnic and racial minorities continue to be underrepresented.
4. The typical study is a one-shot affair. How the same respondents might express their attitudes at another time or in another situation is seldom explored.

Despite these limitations, some findings have been obtained repeatedly and are worth our attention. Death anxiety research has also become somewhat more sophisticated in recent years.

MAJOR FINDINGS FROM SELF-REPORTS OF DEATH ANXIETY

Several patterns have emerged from self-report studies of death anxiety.

How Much Do We Fear Death?

Self-report studies consistently find a low to moderate level of death anxiety. Should we take these results at face value? Or should we suspect that most people are trying to convince themselves and others that death holds no terror? However we interpret the results, it appears that most people do not consider themselves to be very anxious about death as they go about their everyday lives. I am inclined to believe that the self-report instruments measure death anxiety only when the scores are very high: when the respondent is in a genuine state of alarm—and that seldom is the situation when the questionnaire is presented.

The few studies that have used laboratory experiments find that people could be cool, calm, and collected on the verbal level while at the same time experiencing a strong emotional response on the neurophysiological level (e.g., Feifel & Branscomb, 1973). Most often, though, we can only speculate about what the respondents were feeling when they were providing their moderate replies.

Are There Gender Differences in Death Anxiety?

Women tend to have higher death anxiety scores on self-report scales. This pattern is confirmed by a survey of studies conducted in 15 nations (Lester et al., 2006–2007). Does this mean that women tend to be "too" anxious? Probably not. Women are more comfortable than men in dealing openly with their thoughts and feelings on many emotionally intense subjects, not only on those that are death-related.

Over the years, I have observed that women almost always outnumber men decisively in seminars and workshops that deal with dying, death, and grief. I have met many more women than men in hospice and other care-giving situations as well (also see Chapter 5). If this is anxiety, perhaps we should be grateful for it, since relatively few "low death anxiety" men have responded to these challenges. In any event, research findings reveal a gender difference, but do not demonstrate that women are "too" anxious. Most nurses reported a higher level of death anxiety than the general population, yet they also accepted death as an integral part of life. Furthermore, some of the anxiety could be attributed to their limited training in caring for people with life-threatening or terminal conditions (Brisley & Wood, 2004). Level of death anxiety tells us something, but not everything, about the way a person interprets and responds to death-related situations.

Are There Age Differences in Death Anxiety?

Do we become more anxious as the years pass and the distance from death decreases? If so, then elderly adults might be expected to express a higher level of death anxiety. Not so. Studies show either no age differences or somewhat lower death anxiety for elders. Having seen and learned much from life, many people have come to terms with death as they move through their later years. The fear of becoming helpless and dependent on others may increase, but with death itself regarded as a natural ending to their lives. Elderly participants in a cardiac fitness program were totally aware of their continuing risk, but had found their own individual ways to experience a meaningful life without the sharp edge of death anxiety (Kastenbaum, 2010).

Episodes of intense death anxiety in elderly people often are related to relationship loss, increased health concerns, or uncertainties and also often can be relieved when the person is helped to feel safe again (Kastenbaum, 2000a). There is still another side to death anxiety in the later adult years: Some people experience so much distress from bereavement, social isolation, financial concern, and physical ailments that they feel ready to have their lives come to an end (Kastenbaum, 2009). This attitude is also reflected in the high completed suicide rates for elderly white men. Low death anxiety might then be related to dissatisfaction with the quality and prospects of life.

Death anxiety tends to be relatively high in adolescence and early adulthood (Twelker, 2004). The younger respondents also had more specific worries about dying before they could do everything they wanted to do, dying alone, not being remembered, and what to expect after death. It is possible that such concerns are moderated as one's life becomes more settled and predictable. On the other hand, it is also possible that death anxiety goes underground through much of the adult life course, not so much overcome as sent back to the closet. Death anxiety is apt to rise again in later middle age, perhaps occasioned by the death of friends and family and signs of one's own aging. After this rise, there is a decline to a new low in death anxiety for people in their 70s.

A study by Russac et al. (2007) gives us something else to think about. Death anxiety peaked at around age 20 for both men and women. It was also found that women—but not men—experienced a secondary peak in death anxiety as they entered their fifties. Death anxiety decreases for women as they enter their sixties, and continues relatively low for men. Why? The researchers suggest that for women the age 50 spike is related to the end of their reproductive careers and therefore as a depressing reminder that they are growing older. They also note that the peak of death anxiety occurs at the same time that men and women reach the height of their reproductive capabilities. These are the researchers' speculations. What do you think?

Here Come the Boomers

Most of the studies reviewed here are cross-sectional. In the Russac et al. study, for example, they were not able to wait for 20-year-old respondents to become 50 or 80 years old. It is probable, that there are generational as well as age differences at work. The baby boomer generation is a case in point. The term has usually been applied to people in the United States and the United Kingdom who were born between 1946 and 1964. Experts, however, see two population waves with significantly different cultural experiences (e.g., Gillon, 2004). Those born soon after the end of World War II are the true boomers because there are so many of them, the product of a spike in the birthrate (roughly, 1945–1955). They became the first television-from-the-cradle and rock-and-roll generations and came of age during the Vietnam War era, with its tensions and dissensions. By the mid-1960s, the population increase had subsided, coincident with the newly available birth control pills.

Babies no more, boomers are becoming eligible for Social Security. Many have earned the right to be called the *sandwich generation* because they have had the challenge of caring for their long-lived parents as well as their children. Aging is not popular with this active and achieving generation. They are not the first generation with the preference to stay young and live forever (Grollman, 2000), but perhaps the most dynamic in trying to accomplish this feat.

Boomers are falling into the many nets laid about by researchers. Benton et al. (2007) have found a close connection between aging anxiety and existential death anxiety (see also below). Retirement can reduce social status and amputate part of one's identity. Other losses include the death of family members and friends and physical changes that the mirror impudently reports. There will be more research and more insights from the boomers themselves, but it is clear that belonging to a particular generation influences our view of death as well as our style of life.

Is Death Anxiety Related to Mental Health and Illness?

Death anxiety that is high enough to be disabling may warrant the attention of professional caregivers. Generally, self-reported death anxiety is higher in people with diagnosed psychiatric conditions. Death anxiety can rush to the surface when a person's ego defenses are weakened and can no longer inhibit the impulses, fears, and fantasies that are ordinarily suppressed. However, death concern is not limited to people who are emotionally disturbed. For example, it is not unusual to experience an upsurge of death anxiety when we realize how close we have come to being killed in a motor vehicle accident. The sudden, unexpected death of another person can have a similar effect. Situations in which people feel alone and unprotected can also arouse a passing sense of separation anxiety, which often is indistinguishable from death anxiety.

There are reasons to be both anxious about death and to keep our anxiety within bounds. People with a sound mental health status have learned to avoid the extremes of too much anxiety and too heavy a reliance on defenses against anxiety. It has also been found that people with a knack for regulating their thoughts in general are less likely to have anxious and defensive responses to death-related situations (Gailliot et al., 2006).

Does Religious Belief Lower or Raise Death Anxiety?

The influence of religion in death anxiety has been a subject of controversy for many years. Bronislaw Malinowski (1948), a pioneering anthropologist, concluded that religion has the basic function of reducing the individual's intense fear of death. A fellow anthropologist, A. R. Radcliffe-Brown (1952) came to just the opposite conclusion: Religion gives rise to fear of evil spirits, punishment, torment, and hell. Both sets of observations were based primarily on an outsider's observations of preliterate societies, and leave untouched the question of whether or not religion serves the same function in societies at a higher level of general development.

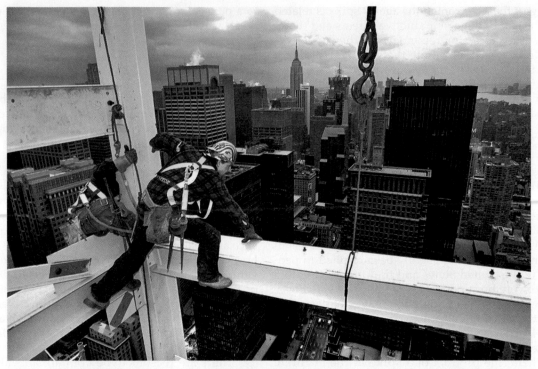

"High anxiety" has two meanings: fear of heights and a general state of elevated apprehension and dread. This steel worker 750 feet above New York City's famous Broadway district seems well equipped, mentally and equipment-wise to cope with at least the first type of high anxiety.

There are substantial differences in religious belief and practices. In many tribal societies, death is believed to be followed by a life similar to the one that has just been concluded (Chapter 13). There may be anxiety about the journey through death to the next life (Kastenbaum, 2004), but the outcome is neither annihilation nor some frightening new state of being. By contrast, spirit possession is a major component in some religions, so interactions between the living and the dead are vital concerns. Fear of the dead may be more intense than fear of death (Frazer (1933/1966)). People in one society may fear eternal damnation, while in another there might be an intense taboo against contact with a dead body.

A longitudinal study in the United States (Wink & Scott, 2005) found no support for the assumption that highly religious people would report the lowest level of death anxiety in their later adult years. Strong religious belief did not provide an effective buffer against fear of dying and death.

People who firmly believe or firmly disbelieve in religion and an afterlife report less anxiety than those with doubts or "moderate belief."

Religion seems to enter into our death orientations in a complex manner. From a practical perspective, we would probably be more effective by learning how religion and death are associated for a particular person or family. We would also become aware of the many ways in which people in the United States construct distinctive religious ideas and practices from a variety of sources instead of accepting one traditional view.

Situational Death Anxiety

The apprehension and restlessness we carry around with us in everyday life is sometimes called *trait anxiety*. Some of us are more "antsy" than others. However, there are also situations that tend to make most people more anxious. We are gradually learning more about situational factors in death anxiety (Kastenbaum, 2009).

Transitional situations often lead to a spike in death anxiety. A list of transitional situations might well begin with separation, divorce, and other types of relationship loss. Even the exercise of imagining separation from a relationship partner can lead to more death-related thoughts (Mikulincer, Florian, Birnbaum, & Malishkevich, 2002). Feeling abandoned increases our sense of vulnerability, which, on the emotional map, is not far from fear of mortality. Heightened death anxiety might pervade society during periods of financial distress, violent episodes, family separation because of military action, and whatever else can shake a society's confidence in its values and competence.

Exposure to death might seem to be a situation that will increase our anxiety. Often, though, we seal off such episodes before they can penetrate awareness. Most of us have strategies for limiting the impact of an exposure to death. For example, it's too bad about the neighbor who died of pulmonary disease, but we don't smoke the same brand of cigarettes, so, no worry. However, a delayed stress reaction often arises some time after the brush with death. We might have nightmares or sudden moments of distress without quite knowing why. Often, this is the death-related experience getting through to us. A severe response of this type is now recognized as post-traumatic stress disorder (PTSD).

The death of another person sometimes becomes the wake-up call that reminds us of our own mortality. Often it is the death of a parent, or some other significant person in our life, whom we had let ourselves assume always would be there. "When my father died, it was like Death had me next on his list," a colleague confided. The "pecking order of death" phenomenon is perhaps more common than realized.

Life-threatening illness can persist for weeks, months, even years. During this extended period, people are likely to have a variety of thoughts and feelings about their situations. The first jolt often occurs when people discover that illnesses are life-threatening or terminal. Suicidal thoughts might occur at this time. A second period of anxiety arousal may occur later, accompanied by depression, as a result of continuing physical decline and fatigue. At this point the anxiety may be focused more on the fear of abandonment and suffering, rather than on death itself. Other moments of anxiety can develop when a new complication arises or a new treatment is proposed. Nevertheless, drawing upon their own resources and support from family and friends, many people can cope with a life-threatening situation without experiencing intense anxiety. Effective communication, symptom relief, and a positive worldview contribute much to anxiety reduction.

THEORETICAL PERSPECTIVES ON DEATH ANXIETY

There are two classic theories of death anxiety, and they could hardly be more opposed to each other. Which one seems more convincing to you?

Early Psychoanalytic Theory

Sigmund Freud reasoned that we could not really be anxious about death:

> Our own death is indeed quite unimaginable, and whenever we make the attempt to imagine it we can perceive that we really survive as spectators . . . at bottom nobody believes in his own death, or to put the same thing in a different way, in the unconscious everyone of us is convinced of his own immortality (1913/1953, p. 304).

Our "unconscious system" does not respond to the passage of time, so the end of personal time through death would just not register. Again, on the unconscious level, we do not have the concept of negation, so there is no death to cancel out life. Furthermore, we have not actually experienced death. When we express death anxiety it is only a cover story. For many years psychoanalysts spoke of *thanatophobia* as the expressed fear of death that serves as a disguise for the actual source of discomfort. Their mission was to dig, dig, dig until unearthing the underlying fear.

What, then, do we fear, if it is not death? Freud's answer was not exactly his finest moment: thanatophobia derives from the castration anxiety experienced during our normally abnormal psychosexual development. Boy loves mother and fears that father will cut him down to size. Freud's description of the Oedipus complex has enjoyed a flourishing career in fiction, drama, and popular psychology, but not so much in the behavioral and social sciences. If people have not been dead before, it is also the case that very few have been castrated, so, to use Freud's own reasoning, how could they be afraid of this calamity? Castration anxiety is even more a stretch when applied to females. The assertion that girls feel they have already been castrated because they don't have what boys have deserves all the ridicule it has reaped.

However, Freud's castration–death anxiety theory could be interpreted more generously. He admitted to making up little stories as a way of getting new ideas across. Freud might have been suggesting that the source of death anxiety is the fear of losing value, love, and security by being less than a whole person. People who are losing their sense of security in the world might experience this generalized confusion and fear as death anxiety. This is an interpretation that does ring true with clinical observations. People who feel they cannot control the frightening things that are happening (or might happen) to them often do experience an upsurge in death anxiety (Kastenbaum, 2000a).

The bottom line for the early psychoanalytic position is clear, even if the explanation is open to question: Way down deep, we just cannot comprehend our own annihilation; therefore, our anxieties can only seem to be about death.

The Existential Challenge

The existential position takes the opposite approach. Awareness of our mortality is the basic source of anxiety. Our fears take many forms but can be traced back to our sense of vulnerability to death. Ernest Becker (1973) believed that people with *schizophrenia* suffer because they do not have enough insulation from the fear of death. The rest of us might share the schizophrenic's panic if our society did not work so hard to protect us from the *ontological confrontation*—the awareness that we are always and acutely mortal.

Society's primary function is to help us to maintain the illusion of continuity—that life will just go on and on. This is accomplished by a belief system supported by rituals and symbols that produce a sense of coherence, predictability, and meaning. It is a comforting illusion in which most

of us are willing to participate. We feel that we are part of something bigger, more powerful, and more durable than ourselves. Monumental edifices contribute to the illusion of invulnerability. The destruction of the World Trade Center towers would be thought to have had a profound, unsettling effect on all of us, allowing our death anxiety to break through the cracks in society's protective posture.

Becker's writings stimulated the development of *terror management theory* (Tomer, 2002), which suggests that we try to control our death anxiety by socially sanctioned evasions and fantasies. There are two facets to this strategy: Keep up our own self-esteem, and become an integral part of an entity greater than ourselves. Religious belief and practice can go a long way to meet this need. However, faith can be undermined by disasters that overtake society (e.g., virulent epidemics, famine) as well as by radically changing circumstances (e.g., the rise of science and technology). Fortunately, we have an alternative strategy available: let's feel so confident and competent that we can master death threats through our own strengths. We are doubly protected when we feel strong personally in a strong society. If one of these foundations is shaken, then it is time to make the most of the other.

A productive series of studies has refined and supported terror management theory (Pyszezynski et al., 2004 for a review of the pioneering research). Helping to strengthen people's self-esteem seems to decrease death anxiety. Other studies have found that people tend to become more defensive when reminded of their mortality and then try to control their anxiety by focusing on the worldviews from which they draw comfort (Schmeichel & Martens, 2005). Cultural worldviews buffer us from fearful preoccupation with our own impermanence, vulnerability, and mortality (p. 658).

Terror management theory has shown the flexibility to modify its working hypotheses as the results come in. There are several concerns, however (Kastenbaum, 2009). Are these studies actually tapping into the depths of existential terror—or just arousing a little discomfort in the usual suspects (college students) who are responding to the research cues within the relatively safe academic environment? It seems a long way from the anguish and despair of mortal terror to the controlled setting and circumstances of the research. Another concern is the assumption that society is devoted 100 percent to the amelioration of death anxiety. This proposition has been contradicted repeatedly by societies that have deliberately pumped up death anxiety, the better to incite the population into violence against a supposed demonic enemy, or for other power-control purpose. Terror management can be a tool either to raise or lower anxiety level.

Recent findings open a new chapter in understanding the relationship between terror and other responses to the prospect of personal death. Terror management studies have routinely asked their college student respondents to describe their thoughts and feelings at the time of their death. This probe was intended to arouse mortal terror, but the brief essays themselves were not analyzed. Working with more than 200 such narratives, Kastenbaum & Heflick (2010–2011) discovered a broad range of responses in addition to or instead of anxiety. Of these, none were more intense and pervasive than sorrow. And many of the sorrow responses focused on the feelings of family and friends, rather than self, e.g.:

> *"I'm not afraid of death. If I was to die, then it was my time to go. I would never commit suicide because that's just selfish. So absolutely no feelings about me dying. I'd miss everyone and feel sorry for the people who have to live with me gone."*
>
> *"The first thing that comes to mind is the feelings of my friends & families. Honestly the thought of death doesn't scare me but knowing how hard it would be on my family scares me."*
>
> *"Sorrow. I would most of all feel terrible for my family & friends. That would hurt the most."*

The insights pursued by terror management theory will be more useful when integrated into a broader understanding of how we respond to death threats. Even within the limits of the brief narratives, many respondents were already testing out and developing more effective ways of relating to their mortality.

Edge Theory

Both the Freudian and existential positions make basic assumptions that seem beyond empirical investigation. How can we know with any degree of certainty what the "unconscious system" knows or does not know? How can we prove all anxieties have their roots in the fear of nonbeing? Why is it that most people do not report a high and disabling level of death anxiety, but also do not completely deny such feelings? The typical report of a moderate level of death anxiety supports neither the psychoanalytic nor the existential positions. There are many useful observations in the writings of insightful psychoanalysts and existentialists, but their propositions remain open to question.

There is room for other theories as well. I have proposed an *edge theory* that distinguishes between our everyday low level of death anxiety and the vigilant state that is aroused when we encounter danger (Kastenbaum, 2000b). The experience of death anxiety is the self-awareness side of a complex organismic response to danger. Anxiety has its survival function; it is not always something to be sedated or rebuked. We feel ourselves to be at the very edge of the safe and known, perhaps just one step away from disaster. Edge theory emphasizes our survival and adaptation functions—the ability to detect sources of potential harm both through built-in biomechanisms and through the development of cognitive and social skills. There is no need to be anxious all the time; in fact, this would be an exhausting and ineffective way to function. However, there are dangerous situations in this world, and we might save our own or somebody else's life by moving quickly to an emergency footing when confronted by a significant threat.

The first responders to the World Trade Center attacks showed a remarkable blend of alarm and control. They neither ignored nor faltered in the face of an overwhelming threat to life. Most of us do not have their training and experience to cope with emergent disasters, but we can hone our own danger response systems to provide enough anxiety to provoke our attention but also exercise enough control and balance to see the situation through.

Whatever reduces our everyday stress level is likely to improve our ability to detect and respond to actual threats. A relaxed attitude is also more likely to free us to discover opportunities for adventure, creativity, and more rewarding relationships. Despite their differences, all the theories mentioned here agree that feeling at peace with ourselves and secure—but not overconfident—in our abilities can reduce death anxiety without compromising our ability to cope with threats.

ACCEPTING AND DENYING DEATH

What about death-related feelings, attitudes, and actions within our everyday lives?

> *Sitting in his favorite chair after dinner, the man suddenly went pale. He felt severe pain in his chest, and had to gasp for breath. His wife was by his side in a moment. "What's wrong? Oh! I'll get the doctor, the hospital." The man struggled for control and waved his hand feebly in a dismissive gesture. "It's nothing— really. . . . I'll just lie down till it goes away."*

This scene, with variations, has become familiar to health care professionals. The concept of denial comes to mind when a person has delayed seeking diagnosis and treatment for a life-threatening condition. Accepting the reality of serious illness can increase anxiety but also increase the

chances of survival. There is often a subtle interplay between our impulses to accept and deny death-related events.

Is It Really Denial?

"Acceptance" and "denial" are used in a variety of ways. Their meanings can become blurred and misleading. From a psychiatric standpoint, denial is regarded as a primitive defense. Denial rejects the existence of threat. This strategy may be effective for a short period of time and for situations in which there is an overwhelming threat. However, denial becomes increasingly ineffective when prolonged or used repeatedly. We do not survive long in this world when we ignore crucial aspects of reality. Denial is often associated with a psychotic reaction, or as any person's first response to crisis and catastrophe.

Denial in this fundamental sense is not usually part of our everyday repertoire of coping strategies. But we do engage in a number of behaviors that have some resemblance to denial. "Oh, she's just in denial!" people say, when the individual in question has only engaged in a strategic evasive action. By using this term as a buzzword, we often come to glib and premature conclusions. People may be coping with difficult situations in the most resourceful ways they can discover at the moment. This will become clearer as we distinguish among several processes, all of which can be mistaken for denial (Box 1-1):

1. *Selective attention.* Imagine a situation in which many stimuli and events are competing for our attention. We cannot give equal attention to everything that is going on. This often happens with children. The individual is not "in denial," but simply directing his or her attention to whatever seems most novel or salient in the immediate situation.

2. *Selective response.* A person exhibiting this behavior may have judged that this is not the time or place to express personal thoughts and feelings about death. The person may think, I'm not going to open up to this young doctor who looks more scared than I am, or, there is nothing effective I can do about the situation at this moment, so I will talk about something else, or just keep quiet. The person may also decide there is something very important

BOX 1-1

Denial and denial-like responses to death

- *Selective attention*

  "I will feel less anxious if I don't allow myself to notice some things."

- *Selective response*

  "It would be better if I did not let others know how I feel right now."

- *Compartmentalizing*

  "One subtracted from one will not be zero as long as I keep these two numbers separate from each other."

- *Deception*

  "I will deliberately mislead you in order to reduce your anxiety and mine."

- *Resistance*

  "Of course I know that my life is in danger— but I'm not going to give in to it in any way."

- *Denial*

  "A touch of indigestion, that's all."

I must accomplish while I still have the opportunity, and it must take priority. Therefore, the person who may seem to be denying death might actually be working very hard at completing tasks in full awareness that time is running out.

3. *Compartmentalizing.* The individual is aware of being in a life-threatening situation, and is responding to some of its aspects. But something is missing: the connection, the drawing of the line of realization between the scattered dots of information. For example, the person may know that the prognosis is poor, discuss the situation rationally, and cooperate with treatment, and yet may make future plans that involve travel or vigorous exercise, as if expecting to be around and in good health for years to come. In compartmentalizing, much of the dying and death reality is acknowledged, but the person stops just short of *realizing* the situation. All the pieces are there, but the individual resists putting them together to complete the whole picture.

4. *Deception.* People sometimes deliberately give false information to others. This can occur during the turmoil of a death-related situation. When people are telling each other lies (for whatever purpose), it makes sense to acknowledge this deceptive action for what it is and not confuse the issue with the buzzword *denial.*

5. *Resistance.* People who are in stressful situations may recognize their danger but decide not to "give in" to it. Some people in wartorn Bosnia, for example, decided to go about their daily rounds of shopping and visiting, although these activities increased their vulnerability to snipers. They were not denying the death risk. Rather, they had resolved to defy the war and keep their spirits up by not becoming prisoners to fear. A person who has been diagnosed with an incurable medical condition might become angry instead of anxious. ("I'll show them!") And sometimes, as we all know, a person with an apparently terminal condition does recover. There is a significant difference between the person who cannot accept the reality of his or her jeopardy and the person who comprehends the reality but decides to fight for life as long as possible.

6. *Denial* (the real thing). This is the basic defensive process that was defined earlier. The individual is not just selecting among possible perceptions and responses, limiting the logical connections between one phenomenon and the other, or engaging in conscious deception. Rather, the self appears to be totally organized

against recognizing death-laden reality. Such an orientation can be bizarre and may accompany a psychotic reaction. It does not have to be that extreme, however. There is also a more subtle denial process that weaves in and out of the individual's other ways of coping.

Temporary denial responses can be experienced by anybody who is under extreme stress. Denial responses are often seen in the wake of overwhelming catastrophes. For example, a woman was discovered intently sweeping the floor of her home after a tornado had passed through the city; the floor was practically all that was left of her home. Another woman was so debilitated by her long illness that she could no longer take nourishment by mouth or carry out other basic activities of everyday life. She had participated actively in decisions about her impending death: cremation, a simple memorial service, gifts to her church's youth program in lieu of flowers, and so forth. One morning, though, she astonished her visitors by showing them a set of travel brochures and her new sunglasses. She spoke of feeling so much better and was as eager as could be to take a long-delayed vacation. Two days later she was dead.

The Interpersonal Side of Acceptance and Denial

The purpose of denial, writes Weisman (1972), is not simply to avoid a danger, but to prevent the loss of a significant relationship. All of the adaptive processes that have been described here might be used, then, to help the other person feel comfortable enough to maintain a vitally needed relationship. The individual faced with death may have to struggle as much with the other person's anxiety as with his or her own. Instead of placing the negative label of denial upon these adaptive efforts, we might instead appreciate the care and sensitivity with which they are carried out.

One person may come from an ethnic background that treats dying and death in a straightforward manner (e.g., the traditional Amish). But suppose that person becomes enmeshed with a medical establishment where death is still a taboo topic. Here is a potential death accepter trapped

among the deniers. The reverse also happens. Consider a woman who grew up learning how to deny death, especially the deeper emotions that it evokes. Suppose she becomes a patient in a health care establishment where the staff relentlessly practices its belief that we must be open and sharing with each other. Here, then, is the denier confronted by the accepters. It is useful to be aware of the forces operating in the present situation and the individual's previous life pattern in order to understand what is taking place between the dying person and the caregiver.

Weisman has observed that a person does not usually deny everything about death to everybody. More often, a selective process is involved. We must go beyond the question, "Is this person denying death?" It is more useful to ask instead, "What aspects of dying or death are being shared with what other people, under what circumstances, and why?" The same questions could be asked about acceptance—a person might "deny" with one friend and "accept" with another. Apparent denial on the part of the patient may derive from a lack of responsive people in the environment.

Anxiety, Denial, and Acceptance: How Should We Respond?

Anxiety is an uncomfortable, at times almost unbearable, condition. Yet it has a function. Small doses of anxiety can alert us to danger: "Something's wrong here, what?" Anxiety can also prepare us for action: "I've been on stage a thousand times and a bundle of nerves a thousand times—but that's just how I want to feel before the curtain goes up!"

The response strategies of acceptance and denial likewise are not necessarily good or bad in themselves. We must examine the contexts in which these processes are used and the purposes they serve. An individual might be making a desperate stand against catastrophe. The person has been forced to fall back on a primitive defense process that rejects important aspects of reality. This individual needs psychological help and, quite possibly, other types of help as well.

On the other hand, the person may not be denying so much as selectively perceiving, linking, and responding to what is taking place.

The coping pattern might include evasion, but there is also method, judgment, and purpose at work. Even flashes of pure denial may contribute to overall adaptation, as when challenges come too swiftly, last too long, or are too overwhelming to meet in other ways. Later, the individual may find another way to deal with the challenge, once the first impact has been partially deflected and partially absorbed.

Consider the following set of premises:

1. Most of us have both acceptance and denial-type strategies that are available for coping with stressful situations. These strategies may operate within or outside our clear awareness, and one strategy or the other may dominate at various times.
2. States of total acceptance and total denial of death do occur, but usually in extreme circumstances: when the individual is letting go of life after achieving a sense of completion and having struggled as long as struggling seemed worthwhile, or when the individual is resisting the first onslaught of catastrophic reality. These experiences can have a profound spiritual resonance.
3. Much that is loosely called denial can be understood more adequately as adaptive processes through which the person responds selectively to various aspects of a difficult situation.
4. Our pattern of adaptation should be considered within the context of our interpersonal network. Do we interact mostly with people who share and listen, or who avoid conversations on difficult issues and are quick to pass judgment? Family, friends, and colleagues can make it either easier or more difficult to find our way through the anxiety of life-threatening situations.
5. Acceptance and denial can be evaluated only when we are in a position to understand what the person is trying to accomplish and what he or she is up against.

In the Shade of the Jambu Tree

At the start of this chapter, we made a brief visit to the exotic land of the Uttarakurus, where the magic Jambu tree grows and people live 1,000 or, perhaps, 11,000 years. Attempts to remove the sting from the prospect of death have stimulated more than beguiling legends. Influential worldviews have been formed around the core issue of what should be done with death. A significant example is *Taoism*, a major philosophical–religious system that developed in ancient and medieval China and continues to contribute to world thought and culture. Our eyes see a diversity of forms and activities as well as a relentless process of change. It is up to our minds to comprehend what cannot be so easily perceived: the basic unity of nature. Tao (pronounced "dow") is translated as *The Way*. It is the force that both moves and unites all that exists. We may be in the habit of separating mind from matter, for example, but both are in the flow of the Tao.

What we call life and what we call death are also facets of the Tao. The same reality underlies both. This sense of an affinity or communion between life and death is part of the Taoist answer to death. There is also a more activist dimension, though. Life can be prolonged by drawing upon the power of the Tao. In practical terms, this philosophy led to exercise, diet, and use of natural substances (such as herbs) that were thought to strengthen health and preserve life. Present-day fitness regimes were prefigured in Taoist philosophy and practice.

Chemistry, biology, pharmacology, metallurgy, and other sciences and technologies also were given impetus by Taoist philosophy (Gruman, 2003). Nature has secrets that might be divined by patient study and moments of inspired observation. We can live longer and better and therefore keep the simmering pot of death anxiety from boiling over. Chinese alchemy devoted much of its attention to life prolongation, and this also became one of the prime goals of alchemy when it developed in Western culture. Transforming base metals into precious metals was also an ardent pursuit, but a life free from death anxiety was the true gold standard.

Thinking of life, we are also at least implicitly thinking of death. Thinking of death, we are attracted to the idea of a life that somehow flourishes, continues, and renews despite a universe that seems to have other plans. Perhaps each of us can find our own comfort zone in which life can be enjoyed while death is given its due.

■ SUMMARY

Not thinking about death has been a failed experiment. Listening and communicating are far more helpful approaches. You monitored your own knowledge, attitudes, beliefs, and feelings about death in a series of self-inventories. These exercises provided you with a stronger base for looking at the way other people think about death and how state of mind can affect death-related behavior.

After a brief introduction to the history of death drawing largely on the work of Phillipe Aries, we reminded ourselves that our personal orientations toward death are far from simple. For example, although the survival motive is powerful, sometimes we delight in risk-taking behaviors. The dynamics of accepting and denying death were explored with the help of characters in Leo Tolstoy's probing novel *The Death of Ivan Ilych*. We then looked carefully at the core concepts of anxiety, denial, and acceptance. Freudian and existential theories offer competing ideas about death anxiety and its place in our lives. A series of studies has supported terror management theory, derived from Ernst Becker's existential approach. Cultural worldviews and personal self-esteem seem to be important buffers against the experience of intense death anxiety, but both sources of support are subject to breakdown. A recent study finds that anxiety is not always the dominant response, however, with sorrow about the anticipated grief of others often the primary concern. We respond differently when reminded of death (*mortality salience*), and even more so when our vulnerability to death is exposed by a threatening situation. Most people report themselves to have a low to moderate level of death anxiety, with women having somewhat higher scores.

The baby boomer generation is experiencing the challenges of aging and the prospect of death. It is probable that generational influences on the ways we negotiate life and death will become more evident from now on. We also saw that denial is a term that is often used too loosely in regards to death. Some responses that are misinterpreted as denial are better understood as selective attention, selective response, compartmentalizing, deception, or resistance. Attention was also given to the kind of interactions we have with each other in death-related situations, and some suggestions were offered. The ancient philosophical–religious system of Taoism provides an influential example of thinking about life and death as unified in the reality underlying all that exists.

■ REFERENCES

Abdel-Khalek, A. M. (2004). Does war affect death anxiety level? Seven readings of measurements (1988–2002) before and after the Iraqi invasion of Kuwait. *Omega, Journal of Death and Dying, 49*, 287–298.

Ackerman, D. (2007). *The zookeeper's wife*. New York: W.W. Norton, 2007.

Ai, L. A., Park, C. L., Huang, B., Rodgers, W., & Tice, T. N. (2007). Psychosocial mediation of religious coping styles: A study of short-term psychological distress following cardiac surgery. *Personality and Social Psychology Bulletin, 33*, 867–882.

Aries, P. (1981). *The hour of our death*. New York: Random House.

Aries, P. (1962). *Centuries of childhood: A social history of family life*. New York: Alfred A. Knopf.

Aries, P. (1987 reprint edition). *A history of family life*. (Vol. 5). Cambridge, MA: Belknap Press.

Becker, E. (1973). *The denial of death*. New York: Free Press.

Benson, J. F., Christopher, A. N., & Walter, M. I. (2007). Death anxiety as a function of aging anxiety. *Death Studies, 31*, 337–350.

Brisley, P., & Wood, L-M. (2004). The impact of education and experience on death anxiety in new graduate nurses. *Contemporary Nurse, 17*.

Choron, J. (1973). *Death and Western thought*. New York: Macmillan.

CNN (2004, July 7). Several trampled by Pamplona bulls. http://cnn.com/2004/WORLD/Europe/07/07/spain.Pamplona.

Dumont, M., Yzerbyt, V., Wigboldus, D., & Gordjin, E. H. (2003). Social categorization and fear reactions to the September 11 terrorist attacks. *Personality and Social Psychology Bulletin, 29*, 1509–1520.

Durkheim, E. (1951). *Suicide* (J. A. Spaulding & G. Simpson, Trans.). New York: Free Press. (Original work published 1859).

Epicurus. In Warren, J. (2004), *Epicurus and his critics*. New York: Oxford University Press.

Feifel, H., & Branscomb, A. B. (1973). Who's afraid of death? *Journal of Abnormal Psychology, 81*, 282–288.

Frager, G. (1996). Bearing witness. In C. K. Cassel (Ed.), *Caring for the dying. Identification and promotion of physician competency* (p. 41). Washington, DC: American Board of Internal Medicine.

Frazer, J. G. (1966). *The fear of the dead in primitive religion.* New York: Biblo & Tannen. (Original work published 1933.)

Freud, S. (1953). *Thoughts for the times on war and death.* In *Collected works* (Vol. 4, pp. 288–317). London: Hogarth. (Original work published 1913.)

Gailliot, M. T., Schmeichel, B. J., & Baumeister, R. F. (2006). Self-regulatory processes defend against the threat of death: Effects of self-control and trait self-control on thoughts and fears of dying. *Journal of Personality and Social Psychology, 91,* 49–62.

Gillon, S. (2004). *Boomer nation: The largest and richest generation ever and how it changed America.* Glencoe, Ill: Free Press.

Grossman, T. (2000) *The baby boomers' guide to living forever.* Golden, Colorado: Hubristic Press.

Gruman, G. J. (2003). *A history of ideas about the prolongation of life.* New York: Springer.

Hall, J. R. (2009). *Apocalypse. From antiquity to the empire of modernity.* Cambridge, MA: Polity Press.

Harmon-Jones, E., Simon, L., Greenberg, J., Pyszczynski, T., Solomon, S., & McGregor, H. (1997). Terror management theory and self-esteem: Evidence that increased self-esteem reduces mortality salience effects. *Journal of Personality and Social Psychology, 73,* 24–31.

Izard, C. E. (2009). Emotion theory and research: Highlights, unanswered questions, and emerging issues. *Annual Review of Psychology, 60,* 1–25.

Jacinto, L. (2002, December 11). Death by fire. Forced marriages are driving some women to self-immolation. ABCNEWS.com.

Johnson, J., & Williams, C. (October 7, 2007). Roller coaster still stalling, riders injured. *Washington Post,* p. CO3.

Kastenbaum, R. (2000a). Counseling the elderly dying patient. In V. Molinari (Ed.), *Professional psychology in long term care* (pp. 201–226). Long Island City, New York: Hatherleigh.

Kastenbaum, R. (2000b). *The psychology of death.* (3rd ed.). New York: Springer.

Kastenbaum, R. (2004). *On our way. The final passage through life and death.* Berkeley: University of California Press.

Kastenbaum, R. (2009a). Death anxiety. In G. Fink (Ed.), *Encyclopedia of stress.* (2nd ed.). New York: Academic Press.

Kastenbaum, R. (2009b). Should we manage terror—if we could? *Omega, Journal of Death and Dying, 59,* 271–304.

Kastenbaum, R. (2010). Treadmilling to the far side: An informal guide to coming of age with mortality. In T. R. Cole, R. E. Ray, & R. Kastenbaum (Eds.), *A guide to humanistic studies in aging* (pp. 343–362). Baltimore: Johns Hopkins University Press.

Kastenbaum, R., & Briscoe, L. (1975). The street corner. A laboratory for the study of life-threatening behavior. *Omega, Journal of Death and Dying, 7,* 351–359.

Kastenbaum, R., & Heflick, N. A. (2010–2011). Sad to say: Is it time for sorrow management theory? *Omega, Journal of Death and Dying, 62,* 305–327.

Kirkwood, T. (2010). Why can't we live forever? *Scientific American, 303,* 42–47.

Lee, W. E., Wadsworth, M. E. J., & Hotopf, M. (2006). The protective role of trait anxiety: A longitudinal study. *Psychological Medicine, 36,* 345–351.

Lester, D., Templer, D. I., & Abdel-Khalek, A. (2006-2007). A cross-cultural comparison of death anxiety: A brief note. *Omega, Journal of Death and Dying, 54,* 255–260.

Lock, M. (2002). *Twice dead. Organ transplants and the reinvention of death.* Berkeley: University of California Press.

Malinowski, B. (1948). *Magic, science, and religion and other essays.* Garden City, NJ: Doubleday.

McCaron, P., Gunnell, D., Harrison, G. L., Okasha, M., & Smith, G. D. (2003). Temperament in young adulthood and later mortality: Prospective observational study. *Journal of Epidemiology and Community Health, 57,* 888–892.

Mikulincer, M., Florian, V., Birnbaum, G., & Malishkevich, S. (2002). The death-buffering function of close relationships: Exploring the effects of separation reminders on death-thought accessibility. *Personality and Social Psychology Bulletin, 28,* 287–299.

Mobbs, D., Petrovic P., Marchant, J. L., & Hassabis, D. (2007). When fear is near: Threat imminence elicits prefrontal-periaqueductal gray shifts in humans. *Science, 317,* 1079–1082.

Peck, P. (November 16, 2005). American Heart Association: Thrill-a-minute roller coaster rides may be dangerous to our hearts. http://www.medpagetoday.com/Cardiology/Arrhythmias/2159.

Phillips, R. (2010). *A captain's duty: Somali pirates, Navy SEALS, and dangerous days at sea.* New York: Hyperion.

Quill, T. E. (1993). *Death and dignity*. New York: Free Press.

Radcliffe-Brown, A. R. (1952). *Structure and function in primitive society*. New York: Free Press.

Robbins, R. A. (1990). Signing an organ donor's card: Psychological factors. *Death Studies, 14,* 219–230.

Routledge, C., Arndt, J., & Goldenberg, J. L. (2004). A time to tan: Proximal and distal effects of mortality salience on sun exposure intentions. *Personality and Social Psychology Bulletin, 30,* 1347–1358.

Russac, R. J., Gotliff, C., Reece, M., & Spottswood, D. (2007). Death anxiety across the adult years: An examination of age and gender effects. *Death Studies, 31,* 549–561.

Schmeichel, B. J., & Martens, A. (2005). Self-affirmation and mortality salience: Affirming values reduces worldview defense and death-thought accessibility. *Personality and Social Psychology Bulletin, 31,* 658–667.

Stephens, J. R. (2006). *Weird history 101*. New York: Fall River Press.

Tolstoy, L. (1960). *The Death of Ivan Ilych*. New York: The New American Library. (Original work published 1886.)

Tomer, A. (2002). Terror management theory. In R. Kastenbaum (Ed.*),* *Macmillan encyclopedia of death and dying* (Vol. 2, pp. 885–887). New York: Macmillan.

Twelker, P. A. (2004). The relationship between death anxiety, sex, and age. http://www.tiu.edu/psychology/deathanxiety.htm.

VandeCreek, L., & Frankowski, D. (1996). Barriers that predict resistance to completing a living will. *Death Studies, 20,* 73–82.

Weisman, A. D. (1972). *On dying and denying*. New York: Behavioral Publications, Inc.

Wink, P., & Scott, J. (2005). Does religiousness buffer against the fear of death and dying in late adulthood? Findings from a longitudinal study. *Journal of Gerontology, 60B,* 207–214.

■ GLOSSARY

Uniform Anatomical Gift Act A law that permits people, upon their own deaths, to designate their bodily organs for transplantation to other people.

Death anxiety Emotional distress and insecurity aroused by encounters with dead bodies, grieving people, or other reminders of mortality, including one's own thoughts.

Denial An extreme response in which one attempts to cope with danger or loss by ignoring important features of reality.

Edge theory A theoretical approach that emphasizes the survival function of death-related anxiety.

Fatalism The belief that future events have already been determined; therefore, one is powerless to affect the future.

Living will A document that instructs medical personnel on an individual's wishes should a situation arise in which that person cannot communicate directly. Often involves the request for limiting the type of medical interventions. The living will is one of a class of documents known as advance directives (Chapter 6).

Mortality salience A situation that is likely to bring thoughts of death to mind. Related to ontological confrontation, but often not as threatening.

Ontological confrontation A situation that sharply reminds people of their personal vulnerabilities to death.

Post-traumatic stress disorder A delayed response to a death or other disturbing experience that has occurred under extremely stressful conditions. The traumatic event is reexperienced repeatedly, and other disturbances of feeling, thought, and behavior are also likely to occur.

Schizophrenia A form of mental, and perhaps biomedical, illness in which a person is out of contact with reality and emotionally alienated from others.

Taoism Chinese philosophical–religious system that sees life and death as linked in a fundamental reality that underlies the apparent diversity, change, and disorder of the observable world.

Thanatophobia Fear of death.

Terror management theory A theory based on the proposition that many of our sociocultural beliefs, symbols, and practices are intended to reduce our sense of vulnerability and helplessness in prospect of death.

■ ON FURTHER THOUGHT . . .

What of your generation? How would you describe the prevailing attitudes toward life and death among people of your age?

Useful Reference Books for Exploring Death-Related Topics

Bryant, C. D. (Ed.). (2009). *Encyclopedia of death & the human experience.* Two volumes. Thousand Oaks, CA: Sage.

Kastenbaum, R. (Ed.). (2002). *Macmillan encyclopedia of death and dying.* Two volumes. New York: Macmillan.

Taylor, R. P. (2000). *Death and the afterlife. A cultural encyclopedia.* Santa Barbara, CA: ABC-CLIO.

Scholarly and Professional Journals

Death Studies
   www.tandf.co.uk
Illness, Crisis, and Loss
   www.baywood.com
Mortality
   www.tandf.co.uk
Omega, Journal of Death and Dying
   www.baywood.com
Suicide and Life-Threatening Behavior
   www.guilford.com

What Is Death?

What Does Death Mean?

"Astronomers think white dwarfs must not be stars so much as the corpses of stars. Each was once much like our sun and shone with the same brilliance. But then it began to run out of fuel and entered its stormy death throes, swelling to 100 times its previous size and brightening 10,000-fold, before shedding its outer layers and shriveling to a glowing cinder the size of Earth. For the rest of eternity, it will sit inertly, slowly fading to blackness."
—Michael Werner & Michael A. Jura (2009, pp. 38–44)

Each day, following birth, and for the rest of our lives, we lose many thousands of cells in tissues and organs throughout our body. This cell loss occurs by a highly regulated process known as programmed cell death (PCD), a kind of death by design, . . . No one escapes this phenomenon. It occurs in both sexes, in all races, ethnic groups, and religions, in CEOs and blue-collar workers, and in individuals of all political persuasions.
—Robert R. Buss et al., 2006, p. 2

Even though a person may be "dead" because his heart stops working, some muscle, skin and bone cells may live on for many days. So, while the entire person as a functioning organism is dead, parts of the biologic organism live on for varying periods of time. The amount of time these cells and tissues live depends on their ability to survive without oxygen and other nutrients, and with an increasing amount of metabolic waste products building up within them. . . . Then when is a person dead?
—Kenneth V. Iserson, M.D. (2001, p. 3)

You are the nurse. Or the physician, hospital administrator, clergyperson, or lawyer. Perhaps instead you are the family member. The person in this bed does not seem responsive or able to survive without intensive care. Make your diagnosis:

Akinetic mutism?   *Brain damage?*
Brain-dead?   *Catatonia?*
Coma?   *Locked-in Syndrome?*
Minimally conscious state? *Permanent vegetative state?*
Transient vegetative state?

—A situation that is occurring more often

Death is NOT to be ruled by the mere lifting of life support until it is certain that the soul has departed the body.

—Dr. Bakr Abu Zaid (2002, p. 3)

There we have it! The "friendly skies" are littered with corpses. Stars gone dead are vulnerable to convulsive explosions, and astrophysicists sometimes charge their most intimate companions with murder, sucking the last good stuff from a fading partner. But what in the world does this have to do with us?

Plenty! Just a chapter ago we acknowledged that denial of death has been rampant throughout history and is still with us today. And now we find that astrophysicists choose death as the most enticing metaphor in discussing chunks of churning cosmic matter that never drew a breath or entertained a thought. In doing so, they revert to an ancient habit, namely, attributing anthropomorphic qualities to stars and planets. Perhaps we should not be surprised. It is the human mind that encompasses both its own mortality and the remote reaches of the universe. Nervous about facing mortality close up, we project death into distant time-space. And we are still triumphantly here as privileged observers of the celestial spectacle!

There's more. We live at a street address within an area code. Our lives are played out within a circle of family, friends, colleagues, and other people basically not that different from ourselves. But we also live in that strange universe that even astrophysicists find difficult to conceive. This Everythingness came from whence and, wherever it is going, seems unlikely to take us along. It has already become a cemetery for many elapsed offspring of the Big Bang. Life could be a passing miracle. Should we trouble ourselves about this unlovely scenario? Or should we just

These two hard-working Purkinje brain cells labor in the cerebellum to maintain our posture, balance, and muscle tone. The clock of programmed cell death is running, however.

whistle our way through our daily rounds? In other words: to what loomings of death should we pay attention?

And what of programmed cell death (PCD)? Here death is not in the stars, but in every cell of our bodies. *Isis* is one of many deities who have been linked with the continued commerce between life and death: the one is always passing to the other. Sigmund Freud (1920) brought the drama into our own being with his concept of a death instinct. He named this concept *Thanatos* after the Greek god who delivers a peaceful death. At one point, Thanatos was trapped in a sack by Sisyphus in a desperate attempt to avoid death. It didn't work. This Freudian concept was mostly rejected, but has been let out of the sack recently by neuroscientists who find it a heuristic idea to pair with PCD (Cole & Perez-Prado, 2004). Thanatos is regarded as part of the larger process that generates new cells and maintains organ function, though not forever. (There are other kinds of cell death as well. Accidents can destroy cells, and so can developmental, particularly genetic, factors.)

From this perspective, we die yearly, daily, and by the hour, and that's the plan. At the same time, though, we might be feeling vigorously alive. Life and death are intimates all the way.

There is still another challenge to received assumptions about life and death. Yes, cells are programmed to die within us—but might cells live when we are sort of dead? Iserson reminds us that our body is primed to fight for survival, so there can be local manifestations of life even if we have been pronounced dead. "Then, when is a *person* dead?" asks Iserson, and we might add, "What, then, is death?"

Consider now a second set of experiences and interpretations.

I shouldn't smoke. I need a smoke. I shouldn't smoke.
Why shouldn't you?
The burning is so painful. It hurts the tobacco so much.
Does the tobacco feel pain?
It has a soul. Everything has a soul. Everything feels pain.
But I need to smoke! (Tears of anguish in his eyes)
Are you feeling pain, too?
(Registering surprise at the question). Dead men don't feel pain.
I need a smoke

—Author's conversation with
psychiatric patient (1958)

Before he died he said that his skin had come on fire, with the feeling of insects crawling beneath it. A scar he bore on his right cheek just to the edge of his mouth had been caused by a nail driven through the coffin.

—Reported by Wade Davis (1988)

In all the darkest pages of the malign supernatural there is no more terrible tradition than that of the Vampire, a pariah even among demons. Foul are his ravages; gruesome and seemingly barbaric are the ancient and approved methods by which folk must rid themselves of this hideous pest.

—Montague Summers (1928)

I collected the instruments of life around me, that I might infuse a spark of being into the lifeless thing that lay at my feet. It was already one in the morning; the rain pattered dismally against the panes, and my candle was nearly burnt out, when, by the glimmer of the half-extinguished light, I saw the dull yellow eye of the creature open; it breathed hard, and convulsive motion agitated its limbs.

—Victor Frankenstein, in Mary
Shelley's *Frankenstein* (1818/1977, p. 72)

I carefully noted the simulated positions of seventeen different kinds of insects belonging to different genera, both poor and first-rate shammers. Afterwards I procured naturally dead specimens of some of these insects . . . others I killed with camphor by a slow easy death; the result was that in no instance was the attitude exactly the same, and in several instances the attitudes of the feigners and of the really dead were as unlike as they could possibly be.

—Charles Darwin's notebook as
quoted by Carrington & Meader (1921)

Plastination reveals the beauty beneath the skin, frozen in time between death and decay.

—Dr. Gunther von Hagens (2005)

Then, when lust hath conceived, it bringeth forth sin; and Sin, when it is finished, bringeth forth death.

—New Testament, James: 1:15

Death? It's a change of clothes. That's all!

—Interview respondent

Death? I see him as very patient and very polite. He waits for each of us some place, just around a corner or even at the foot of our bed. I think of him as being there all the time, but only when we can see him is he there for us. He doesn't have to say anything and neither do we. He knows what he's here for and he knows what we know.

—Respondent in a study of death personification.

IDEAS ABOUT THE NATURE AND MEANING OF DEATH

What do we know for sure? Some of us know for sure that death is the implacable enemy of life. Others of us know for sure that death is the portal through which we enter a higher form of existence. And, yes, some of us are capable of holding both these beliefs at the same time. We might have difficulty in realizing that life and death can be regarded differently by other people. In Hindu philosophy, for example, birth, death, rebirth, and, then again, death are linked in a constantly recurring cycle (Kramer, 2003). We are born to die, but die to be reborn.

What we mean by "death" becomes of practical importance when we communicate with others who have a different conception. What is this death that one person accepts and another person denies? That one person seeks and another person avoids? That one person cannot stop thinking about and another person believes is hardly worth thinking about?

Not only do individuals differ in their attitudes and feelings, but the same person may differ from situation to situation—as when I noticed that the starboard engine of the ancient DC-3 had burst into flames. *Death* was no longer a word for scholarly contemplation but the nerve-buzzing prospect of falling into the green hills of West Virginia. It was different years later as pretty much an inert lump on an intensive care unit, I felt death to be already with me. He was being slow and casual about his work and somehow not as interesting as I would have supposed (Kastenbaum, 2004). Many survivors of near-death experiences have reported an enduring change in their conceptions of death and life alike (Chapter 13). There are practical consequences resulting from the fact that death can mean different things to different people, or different things to the same person at different times. If you and I hold varying assumptions

about the nature of death, then we may also take different courses of action at decisive moments. We see this clearly in the variety of death interpretations previously quoted.

The psychiatric patient was housed in a high security building on the campus of a Veterans Administration Hospital. He had returned broken in body and mind from his World War II combat service as a lieutenant in the Pacific campaign. Now he had his health back, but was neither eating nor speaking. You could see he had been through hell and brought hell back with him. Somehow we bonded. The cigarette episode was one in which he expressed himself with a deeply wounded innocence.

I see tears in your eyes. You are feeling pain now.
Touch your cheeks,
Feel your tears.
Are those my tears?
It hurts so much to be alive.
(Pause. Lights cigarette. Pause.)
(With great deliberation, as though each word cost him something)
No more war.

This man felt deadened and sometimes dead. Nevertheless, there was still a roiling desperation that could erupt into violent action. Feeling dead is an exhausting way of going through life. Paradoxically, deadening can also be a way of protecting the self and giving it another chance.

The "dead man walking" condition can be a cultural as well as an individual phenomenon. Clairvius Narcisse is classified as a recovered zombi. He recovered first from being a corpse, and then from being a drudge laborer who only had the ability to follow simple orders. Narcisse had literally returned from the grave (if the evidence be trusted). He seemed to have taken something of death back with him, although eventually recovering his personality.

The vampire commutes between life and death. Today our image of the vampire is strongly conditioned by Hollywood and television versions, including an apparently unlimited supply of parodies. Montague Summers re-introduced the earlier and earthier version in his classic *The vampire and his kith and kin* (1928). Vampires still have something to teach us, and so we will be meeting them again, along with the revenant and the zombie in a section devoted to the undead.

Death in life, or life in death? The Archer is one of many three-dimensional figures created by anatomist Gunther von Hagens from corpse tissue. Plastination produces durable specimens for study by medical and nursing students. Museum tours of von Hagens' plastinates demonstrate technology's continuing adventuring across the boundaries between life and death.

Copyright: Gunther von Hagens, Institute for Plastination, Heidelberg, Germany (*www.bodyworlds.com*).

The hard-driving basketball player depicted in this chapter is a remarkable example of a new way to appreciate life through death. Anatomist Gunther von Hagens developed a tissue preservation technique known as *plastination*. Death has always been associated with decay. Plastination replaces the fluids and lipids in biological tissues with polymers (such as silicone, epoxy, and polyesters). The result is a dry, odorless and durable specimen that can be studied by generations of medical students. Often the focus is on a particular body part, such as a region of the nervous system. However, von Hagens also created a gallery of life-like figures from plastinated corpses. Like her companion figures, The Archer offers a distinctive opportunity to view both the human body in an action position and a special anatomical feature: Her brain is situated above the skull for easier viewing. Two traveling BodyWorlds exhibits attracted millions of museum visitors in Asia, Europe, and North America. Dr. von Hagens's stated objective, which includes respect for the human body in life and death, is also evident. It is in this context that he suggests, "Plastination reveals the beauty beneath the skin, frozen in time between death and decay."

DEATH AS OBSERVED, PROCLAIMED, AND IMAGINED

Both Victor Frankenstein and his monster were created by an 18-year-old woman who had been born through death. Mary Shelley's mother was an independent thinker who wrote powerfully about the rights of women 200 years ago. Mary Wollstonecraft's death soon after childbirth had an enduring effect on her daughter, who would later marry poet Percy Shelley and go on to live a creative, adventuresome, but tragedy-marked life. In addition to her own curiosity about death, Mary Shelley came of age at a time when "galvanic" (electrical) experiments were a conspicuous part of the new scientific enterprise; doctors were procuring corpses by suspicious means to improve the quality of medical education and knowledge, and reports were circulating about people having been buried alive (Bondeson, 2001).

Shelley's novel brought the growing excitement and fears into sharp focus. Perhaps the dead could be reanimated. Perhaps death is not necessarily permanent and irreversible. And perhaps the age of the "modern Prometheus" was about to begin. Just as Prometheus pilfered fire from the gods as a gift to humans, so a Victor Frankenstein might harness lightning to the alarming project of creating life. Mary Shelley knew, however, that Prometheus suffered a terrible punishment for his disobedience. Frankenstein's creation turned out to be profoundly flawed—a warning to future scientists that anticipates the gene splitters and cloners of today. Attitudes toward death and the dead became more complex with the introduction of Frankenstein, as well as Bram Stoker's *Dracula*

(1975) and other works of fiction that dared to test the boundaries.

Unlike Victor Frankenstein, Charles Darwin was a real scientist, and on his way to transforming our understanding of life on planet earth. When not making discoveries ashore, he conducted small experiments aboard his ship, *The Beagle*. Darwin learned to distinguish between spiders that were either feigning death or actually were dead. *Thanatomimesis* is the simulation of death, often to avoid being killed (Kastenbaum, 2003), and also is used in children's play to master death-related anxiety (Chapter 10). The lieutenant's conviction that he was dead had the function of protecting him from being killed again. Darwin's observations contributed to the unsettling realization that the dead may be only apparently so (Bondeson, 2001).

Medical Professor Kenneth V. Iserson does his part to keep us off balance by discussing death not as a sudden and massive event but as a complex process over time. Even as the physician signs a death certificate, there may still be biologic activity throughout the body. Tradition, society, and science have come up with criteria for pronouncing death, but nature does not entirely agree.

Islam does not agree either. A thousand years ago, the most learned and effective physicians were in Islamic lands, writing treatises that guided European doctors for centuries to come. Dr. Bakr Abu Zaid is well aware of current practices in the definition of death and life support systems. Nevertheless, he cautions against taking a purely materialistic or objective approach. According to Islamic teachings, death is certain and final only when the soul has left the body. Neither Dr. Zaid nor Islam is alone in this belief. The people of many world societies have long believed that death is marked by the separation of soul from body.

We enter still other realms of death perspectives when we open books of ancient philosophy or the *New Testament*. In the third century B.C., Epicurus offered a philosophy that has continued to influence many people. (A good way to become familiar with this view is to read *On the Nature of Things*, the narrative poem in which Lucretius articulates Epicurus's ideas.) Epicurus, agreeing with another philosopher, Democritus, argued that the universe comprises atoms in motion and that our own actions—indeed, our innermost thoughts and feelings—are shaped by the pattern of past events. We live and die in a materialistic universe. What,

then, is death? It's not much of anything—simply one more event in a long sequence of events that has no intrinsic meaning or value. We never actually experience death, and the fact of death does not violate any contract we might imagine that the gods have cosigned with us.

How, then, should one live, Epicurus? Wise people appreciate life and maintain a sense of balance and proportion. We are not major players in a great cosmic drama. We just happen to be here for a while, then again will become part of the vapor from which we arose. A depressing view? Not for Epicurus, at least. He formed a community known as The Garden, in which like-minded people—women as well as men, poor as well as rich, slaves as well as free citizens—lived in equality and friendship. Epicurus offered a model for harmonious living within a universe that does not seem to care about either our lives or our deaths. Nevertheless, most people have preferred a version in which the universe is rule abiding and purposeful, and in which human lives and deaths do count for something.

The Christian version was responsive to this need. The New Testament story is told somewhat differently from one gospel to the next. The faithful can encounter a bewildering variety of interpretations. The Christian message regarding death can be read as simple or complex. The quotation from James at the beginning of this chapter delivers one facet of this message. Lust—sexual feeling, thought, and activity—is intimately associated with death. Before the emergence of Christianity, other religions in the ancient world had emphasized a connection between withering away and fertility. Life was regenerated through death (was that a vampire slithering by?). Careful observance of rituals might persuade the gods to allow crops to succeed and babies to thrive. Sacrifices (animal or human) could also help matters along—a little death here and there as payment for life.

Christianity, however, specified that sexuality itself is sinful and carries the death penalty. Virginity and abstinence take on theological resonances. Suicide and *martyrdom*, especially in earlier eras, were seen by some Christians as preferred alternative to sexual indulgence. Not only the "deathification of sex," but also the "sexualization of death" have been consequences of the concept put forth in the gospel of James and other passages in the New Testament. Passionate and mystical union with God became an increasingly dominant theme in the version of Christianity that became known to the world through the interpretations of *Paul the Convert* (Segall, 1990). At the same time, sexual union between humans and their bonds of attachment were seen as less spiritual and worthy. Not all Christians favor this intertwining view of death and sexuality, but it is an influential part of the tradition.

The man who said death is "a change of clothes. That's all!" perhaps identifies himself with what was known as the New Age movement. Those within this movement view life as a journey through multiple lives. Death is a transition, a door through which one passes on the way to the next life. This conception clearly differs from the others. Unlike Epicurus and other atomists, life and death are regarded as purposeful—there is a point to it all and a progression. Unlike the New Testament view, death is not a punishment for sexuality or for anything else. A flat *EEG* is not impressive, because the life and death of the spirit are not seen as byproducts of brain activity. This view has some commonality with Islam and other religious traditions that believe in a soul principle that is not entirely dependent on the physical body.

Death becomes less abstract when represented as a person. The college student who envisioned death as "very patient and very polite" was stepping away from the more common American view of death as an enemy whose presence should be denied as long as possible. Instead, she pictured death as a kind of watchful companion who knows and respects us throughout our lives and whom we should not be surprised to see when the time comes. Is this how you would personify death?

Death as Symbolic Construction

What is death? An idea? A concept? Some scholars see death as a *symbolic construction*, something we have cobbled together from our experiences, guesswork, needs, and ignorance. Death is therefore subject to the same rules and limitations as any other concept. This does not mean that death is unreal or fictitious. Death is a concept we need because it has so many important referents, associations, and consequences. Water is also a concept. We look at ice, snow, mist, rain, standing pools, and flowing streams and write the formula H_2O on the board and call them all water, even though

their forms look so different. Water is not simply something that presents itself to our eyes, but a useful concept. When we try to determine the difference between "alive" and "dead" and to define death itself, we are dealing with symbolic constructions. We are working with the words, concepts, and ways of thinking that are available to us in a particular society at a particular time.

"Dead" and "death" are concepts that are still under construction—still subject to question, challenge, and revision. For example, I have often had to sort out my own impressions when at the bedside of an unresponsive person who is not expected to recover. If I judge that this person is dead (as a person), then why even try to communicate? If, however, I cannot be sure of this person's state of being, then I might try to attempt to communicate as best I can. Symbolic constructions of death can lead us either to increased or reduced interactions.

Some of the most influential constructions of death in our society come from movies and television, with the Internet also coming on strong. People today are less likely to have direct, unfiltered encounters with dying and death than in the past. At the same time, we are frequently exposed to constructed depictions of dying and death in the media and online. Schultz and Huet (2000/2001) examined popular and award-winning films. Most deaths were presented in a sensational and violent manner. Seldom were we shown the actual course of dying and death that is experienced by most people in our society. Encouragingly, perhaps, films that had received awards were much more likely to include expressions of sorrow and sadness. Gender differences were striking. Male characters were six times more likely to instigate death, and female characters were twice as likely to be the victims. The authors conclude that "in American film, death is distorted into a sensational stream of violent attacks by males, with fear, injury, further aggression and the absence of normal grief reactions as the most common response" (p. 149). The male as slayer and female as slain is consistent with homicide patterns in the United States (Chapter 9).

Fitsimmons (2009) paints an even darker picture of death as depicted in television and movies. Recent productions tend to present death as social disconnection and final abandonment. The meaning of the death to the individual is seldom the central issue. Fitzsimmons sees the philosophically depiction of death as related to:

> . . . *Our inability to articulate our understanding of existence . . . in answering the philosophical questions of who or what we are, and how we will end up. The concept of death is important to this understanding because it defines our end* (p. 359).

We will see (Chapter 10) that it takes a while for children to understand that death is not just intentional or accidental but will befall everybody in one way or another. The child's attempt to understand the nature and meaning of death is certainly not assisted by the aggressive and violent constructions of death in popular movies.

The ideas about death that we have sampled here have taken on a more urgent aspect in recent years. Is this person "dead enough" to have organs removed and transplanted to save another person's life? To have the life-support system removed? The ancient question, What is death? has been joined by an even more pressing concern—When is dead? We turn, then, to biomedical approaches to answer these related questions.

BIOMEDICAL APPROACHES TO THE DEFINITION OF DEATH

Death is "certified" thousands of times every day by physicians. This process meets society's need for verifying that one of its members has been lost. It is also a signal to the bereaved survivors and society. The survivors are now expected to start reorganizing their lives around the fact of this loss, while society makes its arrangements. Insurance benefits are to be paid, the deceased will not be eligible to vote at the next election, and this unique death will become part of mortality statistics. The "*When* is dead?" question takes a practical form: "Under what conditions should a person be considered dead?"

Traditional Determination of Death

The most common signs of death have been lack of respiration, pulse, and heartbeat, as well as failure to respond to stimuli such as light, movement, and pain. Lowered body temperature and stiffness are also expected to appear, followed later by bloating and signs of decomposition.

In the past, physicians usually had no need for technology, but errors could be made. Victims of drowning and lightning, for example, would sometimes be taken for dead, when in fact their vital functions had only been suspended. Those who suffered a stroke, epileptic seizure, or diabetic *coma* might also be pronounced dead instead of receiving treatment. The same fate could befall a person gifted in the once popular art of hysterical fainting. "Madame Fluffington fainted dead away at the distressing news!" (She might have kept one eye open.)

The possibility that people might be pronounced dead while still alive was an unsettling one, and Edgar Allan Poe seized upon this fear for some of his scariest writings. One of my favorite articles from the past was published in the land where, as popular mythology has it, the undead have been most active. Writing in the *Transylvanian Journal of Medicine* in 1835, Dr. Nathan Shrock reports that his own uncle had almost been buried alive until, at the last minute, he showed faint signs of life. Shrock then leads the reader through the traditional signs of death and explains how even the lack of moist breath on a mirror held in front of the nose and mouth, can be misleading.

Mark Twain (1883/1972) claimed to have visited a municipal "dead house" in Munich:

> *Around a finger of each of these fifty still forms, both great and small, was a ring; and from the ring a wire led to the ceiling, and thence to a bell in a watch-room yonder, where, day and night, a watchman sits always alert and ready to spring to the aid of any of that pallid company who, waking out of death, shall make a movement— for any, even the slightest movement will twitch the wire and rings that fearful bell. I imagined myself a death-sentinel, drowsing there alone, far into the dragging watches of some wailing, gusty night, and having in a twinkling all my body stricken to quivering jelly by the sudden clamor of that awful summons!* (p. 189).

A pathologist working in a Detroit hospital instructed nurses to call him when a patient's death was imminent. He wanted to be there at the moment of death. Jack Kevorkian, M.D., was already drawn to the mysterious transition between life and death (2000a). He was one of the few physicians who wrote about the status of the eye at death. He believed the condition of the eye provided the most reliable basis for determining whether or not the person was dead (and, if dead, for how long). Kevorkian reported his observations with 51 consecutive cases (1957) and discussed his method and overall findings in a later paper (1961). Specifically, he found that the status of the eye at death included (a) segmentation and interruption of blood circulation, (b) a haziness of the cornea, and (c) appearance of homogeneity and paleness. Kevorkian urged other physicians to follow his lead by examining dying patient's eyes with an ophthalmoscope. Few took up his suggestion. Health care providers as well as the general public were not ready to look death in the eye.

Ways of Being Dead

Medical advances have made it possible to maintain the body of a nonresponsive individual for an indefinite period of time. The heart continues to beat; the respiratory system continues to exchange its gases. Reflex responses may also be elicited. The *person*, however, no longer seems to be there. Under such circumstances, we may hesitate to evoke either category, alive or dead. Eventually, though, a decision might have to be made, and it will require a definition of "deadness," if not of death. Consider the following brief examples, each dependent on a firm definition of death:

1. Family members and the attending physician agree that the life-support system should be withdrawn because the patient is unresponsive and has no chance to recover. Would "pulling the plug" constitute murder?
2. Another patient is also comatose and unresponsive but vegetative processes continue even in the absence of an elaborate life-support system. (*Intravenous fluids* are being given, but there is no ventilator to maintain respiration.) Elsewhere in the hospital, an organ transplant team is urgently seeking a kidney that might keep somebody else alive for many years. The needed kidney could be liberated by ruling that the comatose patient is dead. The organ

must be removed while the host body is still relatively intact if it is to have its best chance to function in the other patient. Removal of the kidney is a procedure that will be fatal for the *comatose* patient. Would this operation be a crime, or is it laudable because it might help one person and cannot harm the one who is dead or all-but-dead?
3. The vegetative functioning of a comatose woman is being maintained by elaborate life-prolonging procedures. However, there is a living fetus within the woman. The fetus will not survive unless society decides to keep the woman's vegetative processes intact until it has become more viable. Does this mean that society is keeping a dead person alive? And should society knowingly kill that dead person in order to deliver a baby who has a fighting chance to survive?

Either the similarities or the differences among these conditions could be emphasized. How vital is the distinction between cessation of bodily processes and loss of the person as a person? What difference, if any, is there between the "deadness" of a body that continues to function on a vegetative level with or without an elaborate life support system? Who or what is it that no longer lives—perhaps still a person but not the same person? Answers to these questions are still being proposed—and challenged.

Brain Death and the Harvard Criteria

By the 1950s, it was recognized that some unresponsive patients were "beyond coma," that is, no electrophysiological activities could be detected from the brain. Postmortem examinations revealed extensive destruction of brain tissue. This condition came to be known as *respirator brain*. Some patients connected to ventilators had lost their brain function. At first, the concept of brain death served mainly to help physicians decide that additional medical procedures would be of no benefit to the patient. Soon, however, the concept was being used in a new and controversial way: ". . . the practice of undertaking organ removal from beating-heart donors rather than waiting upon the cessation of effective pumping of blood by the heart . . ." (McCullagh, 1993, p. 9).

Here was a remarkable change in the construction of deadness. The heart is still beating—in fact, physicians make sure the heart is still beating—but the patient might be "dead enough" to be classified as an appropriate organ donor. Biomedical advances had led us into a twilight zone in which ethical standards and value priorities became elusive. Both the health care and the justice systems felt the need for guidance. A committee of the Harvard Medical School faculty issued an opinion (Ad Hoc Committee, 1968) that has since served as primary guide for determination of brain death over the years. As we shall see, though, it is now subject to reconsideration. The first three Harvard criteria would have come as no surprise to physicians of an earlier generation. It is the last two criteria, utilizing technological advances, that introduce new considerations.

The Harvard Criteria

1. *Unreceptive and unresponsive.* No awareness is shown for external stimuli or inner need. The unresponsiveness is complete even when ordinarily painful stimuli are applied.
2. *No movements and no spontaneous respiration or other spontaneous muscular movement.*
3. *No reflexes.* The usual reflexes that can be elicited in a neurophysiological examination are absent (e.g., when a light is shined in the eye, the pupil does not constrict).
4. *A flat EEG.* Electrodes attached to the scalp elicit a printout of electrical activity from the living brain. These are popularly known as brain waves. The respirator brain does not demonstrate the usual pattern of peaks and valleys. Instead, the moving stylus records a flat line: the absence of electrophysiological activity.
5. *No circulation to or within the brain.* Without the oxygen and nutrition provided through blood circulation, brain functioning soon terminates.

The first three criteria—the traditional ones—usually serve the purpose. The Harvard report was not intended to require the use of the EEG in all cases, only those in which a question remains and the traditional criteria may not be sufficiently reliable. It was recommended that in such situations the tests of brain functioning should be repeated about 24 hours later.

The Current Scene

Today's issues about forgoing life support are more complex than those of the 1970s. They involve physician-assisted suicide, active killing for mercy, conflicts among plausible surrogates, forgoing implanted devices such as pacemakers that would require active intervention to remove, tensions over which treatments are futile, and controversies involving resource allocation (Veatch, 2009, p. 18).

This is the perspective of Robert Veatch, an ethicist who has monitored the definition of death controversy through the years. He traces controversy and confusion in decision-making to a still unstable definition of death.

Brain death became an official diagnostic category in 1981. It was defined as a condition in which irreversible known damage has permanently destroyed all functional brain activity, including loss of the brainstem's capacity to enable spontaneous breathing. The possibility that there is residual brain functioning that is "on hold" rather than destroyed must be ruled out. It must be established that the patient's condition had not been caused by drugs, severe metabolic or endocrine disturbances, or hypothermia (cold shock).

This is a conservative approach that gives benefit of doubt to the possibility of recovery. Some have argued that permanent loss of functioning in the cerebral cortex should be enough to diagnose brain death. The networks of highly differentiated cells in the upper reaches of the brain are considered essential for experience, thought, and personality. Massive and nonreversible damage to the cerebral cortex dissolves the person, even though flickerings and reflexive movements may continue to be produced by nerve centers in the brainstem. It is destruction of both cerebral cortex and brainstem, however, that has become established as the criterion for brain death. This condition has been known as *whole brain death.*

The Harvard Criteria and the decision to require whole brain failure as the criterion for brain death have provided useful structure and guidance. Complications have arisen, though, with the improvement of neurological assessment techniques and the recognition of variant states of brain dysfunction. Several additional phenomena have been identified and are the subject of ongoing

TABLE 2-1 *Brain Death and Related Concepts*

Akinetic Mutism	Sensorimotor pathways are preserved but cannot initiate actions or speak. Bilateral frontal lobe dysfunction and possibly other brain injuries are involved.
Brain Damage	General term that has become of limited usefulness.
Brain Death	Prolonged nonreversible cessation of all brain activity with complete absence of voluntary movements, response to stimuli, brain stem reflexes, and spontaneous respirations.
Catatonia	Immobility, muscular rigidity, mutism, posturing, grimacing, stupor; sometimes giving way to sudden outbursts of violence, panic, or hallucination. Considered to be a neuropsychiatric disorder.
Coma	A deep state of unconsciousness from which the individual cannot be aroused. Usually associated with injury or dysfunction involving both cerebral hemispheres or the brain stem.
Locked-In Syndrome	Neurological condition in which a person is conscious and able to think but cannot move any part of the body except the eyes, which can be used for communication.
Minimally Conscious State	Severe impairment that can be distinguished from coma or vegetative state by occasional and limited behavioral evidence of awareness.
Permanent Vegetative State	All cognitive functions, including awareness, are absent, even if eyes are open and sounds and nonpurposive movements are made. Sleep–wake cycles, autonomic control, and respiration continue. Condition is of long duration.
Persistent Vegetative State	(See transient and permanent vegetative states.) The condition is known to have been caused by brain damage that might be moderated or reversed.
Transient Vegetative State	(See persistent vegetative state.) However, condition has been caused by drugs, extreme cold, or injury with possibility of recovery.

Sources: Burns, Login, Bruno, Kimura, Crisci, Saosnik, Beslac-Bumbasirevic, Ercegovac, & Wijdicks (2004); Giacino, Ashwal, Childs, Cranford, Jennett, Katz, Kelly, Rosenberg, Whyte, Zafone, & Zasler; (2002); Iserson (2003); Jennett (2002); Wade & Johnston (1999); Wijdicks (2001).

research as exemplified in Table 2-1. As Veatch has pointed out, the situation seems to be getting more complicated all the time.

Each condition identified in Table 2-1 has its own implications for decision making, management, and outcome. Several of these conditions could be mistaken for brain death by uninformed observers. This could happen readily in observing patients with akinetic mutism, *catatonia, coma,* or the locked-in syndrome with its harrowing similarity to being buried alive. Each of these conditions is essentially different from the others, but all can give the impression of terminal nonresponsiveness. By contrast, we might be impressed by the nonpurposive

reflexes and grimaces of a person in a persistent or permanent *vegetative state* and thereby persuade ourselves that the person is still there.

The less familiar diagnosis of "*minimally conscious state*" is receiving increasing attention in the hope of identifying more cases in which recovery has some likelihood (Giacino et al., 2002). Success in identifying these cases depends much on the ability of physician or psychologist to identify behavioral clues to the patient's mental state. The diagnosis of persistent vegetative state can be set aside once a patient has shown the ability to follow simple commands, answer questions with word or gesture, and make a purposeful movement.

The phenomena surveyed here will be encountered again when we explore euthanasia and the right to die (Chapter 9).

"Total Brain Failure": An Emerging Concept

The quest for the best possible definition and determination of death continues to this day. Perhaps the most significant development is the report issued by the President's Council on Bioethics (2008). This report has achieved worldwide attention and respect because it was prepared by experts who attempted to look at all sides of the issue and not restrict their perspective to the status quo. Readers with a deep interest in this issue can access the full report. Here we focus on a few of the main points, as brought forward by Zamperetti & Bellome (2009).

- The term "total brain failure" excludes "death" because this condition should be verified, not assumed.
- More specifically, it questions the assumption that "a patient diagnosed with whole brain death is a mere group of artificially maintained subsystems" (Vamperetti & Bellome, p. 1306).
- Coordinated activities of bodily functioning can continue because the brain is not the only integrator.
- There have been enough observations made to take seriously the possibility that certain areas of the brain may remain intact even though failure seems total.
- The report offers a perhaps surprising alternative perspective to prevailing concepts and practices: "Determining whether an organism remains a whole depends on recognizing the persistence or cessation of the fundamental vital work of a living organism—the work of self-preservation, achieved through the organism's need-driven commerce with the surrounding world" (President's Council, p. 60).

  The surprise is that focus is no longer entirely on physical symptoms and systems, but reminds us that even the severely impaired person continues to interact with the world and can be fighting hard for survival.

How and how much will this new approach affect determination of death and decision-making?

EVENT VERSUS STATE

We create some of our own difficulties by using the same word for different ideas. Death is sometimes treated as though an event—that is, something that occurs in a specific way and at a specific time and place. When it is death as event that concerns us, it is often possible to be factual and precise. ("This is the room where the victim was found. There is the blunt instrument. The clock was toppled over and still shows the exact moment that this dastardly act was committed!"). Quite different is our use of the same word in referring to the state that follows the event. Life has ceased (death as event). What happens from now on? The answer to this question is much less accessible to ordinary sources of information. Some interpretations of death as a state follow, including a challenging new construction that is, well, still under construction.

WHAT DOES DEATH MEAN?

Let's take an example before looking systematically at the meanings that are summarized in Table 2-2.

The soloist in Bach's haunting Cantata No. 53 sings:

> *Schlage doch, gewunschte Stunde,*
> *brich doch an gewunschter Tag!*
> Strike, oh strike, awaited hour,
> approach thou happy day!

The hour that is awaited eventually will be displayed on the face of an ordinary clock. It belongs to public, shared, or mortal time.

TABLE 2-2 *Meanings That Have Been Given to Death*

- Death is an enfeebled form of life.
- Death is a continuation of life.
- Death is perpetual development.
- Death is waiting.
- Death is cycling and recycling.
- Death is nothing.
- Death is virtual and, therefore, not really death after all.

The hour and day of death will be entered into the community's vital statistics. What the devout singer anticipates, however, is entry into a new realm of being in which the time changes of terrestrial life no longer apply. The survivors will continue to measure their own lives by clock and calendar. They may remember that the deceased has been dead for six months, five years, and so on. But this conventional manner of marking time has no bearing upon the deceased. The hour that strikes refers to death as event; the heavenly blessing that follows refers to death as state.

This, however, is only one interpretation of death as a state. Other meanings have emerged throughout history.

INTERPRETATIONS OF THE DEATH STATE

Here are competing interpretations of the death state that have long been influential—plus an interpretation that has been emerging in our society and deserves consideration.

Enfeebled Life

Young children often think of death as a less vigorous form of life. The people who "live" in the cemetery don't get hungry, except once in a while. The dead are tired, sad, bored, and don't have much to do. A three-year-old girl, who was saving her comic books for grandmother, worried that she might have forgotten to take her bifocals with her to the grave.

The child of today who offers this interpretation is in a sense carrying forward the belief system common in Mesopotamia thousands of years ago. The deceased person is gradually submerged into the underworld. There the deceased is transformed into a repulsive and pitiable creature one might expect to find today in a horror movie. The mightiest ruler and the fairest maiden lose all power, all beauty. The dead become equal in their abysmally low estate.

This decremental model ruled throughout much of the ancient world. Abandonment, depletion, and endless misery were the lot of all mortals—with the possible exception of mighty rulers and a few other notables.

Continuation

The cessation of life is extraordinary, so it must also lead to something extraordinary. Or so it might seem. By contrast, tribal societies often have pictured the dead as going on with life pretty much as usual. One hunts, fishes, plays, makes love, becomes involved in jealousies and conflicts, behaves wisely or stupidly. The individual faces challenges and crises just as before, including the possibility of a final annihilation. For example, the Dayak of Borneo believed that the soul returns to earth after its seventh death and there enters a mushroom or fruit near the village. This returned soul invades the body of a woman who chances to eat the morsel, and one is therefore reborn. One may be less fortunate, however. A buffalo, deer, or monkey might find this delicacy first, and the soul will then be reborn as the munching animal. Many world peoples have projected their own life experiences into the realm of death.

Perpetual Development

Suppose that the universe is not completely determined. Suppose further that what we make of our lives is part of this universal process. What might be the death state in such a flowing, changing universe? This possibility emerged first from the prophets and philosophers of evolution. These visionaries either anticipated or built upon Darwin's discoveries in proposing a radically different view of life and its place in the universe. For example, philosophers Samuel Alexander (1920) and Lloyd Morgan (1923) suggested that evolution applied not only to species but to the universe as a whole. Life itself is an emergent quality from a universe that continues to transform itself. Mind is a further quality that has emerged from life. In Alexander's words, the universe itself is in the process of "flowering into deity": God is still being created. In this view, the relationship between life and death also continues to evolve. The basic law is continued development both for individual minds and for the universe at large. This vision now faces strong competition from the cosmic doom scenario previously noted.

One of the most striking conceptions was offered by a man who also made enduring contributions to scientific methodology. Back in 1836, Gustav Theodor Fechner proposed a

Hindu-influenced model of the death state itself as perpetual development. Death is a kind of birth into a freer mode of existence in which continued spiritual growth may occur. Death is not the same for everybody. Individuals differ in the stage of spiritual development they have achieved up to the moment of the death event. Furthermore, the death state not only varies for different people but is itself subject to change as the universe continues to evolve. In a sense, then, the death state provides everyone with at least the opportunity to become more alive than ever.

Evolutionary biologists today operate on the premise that the future state of a system cannot be entirely predicted from knowledge of its starting point (Goldsmith & Zimmer, 2001). In other words, change is real (or reality is change). Biological systems are subject to change within the larger system we call the universe, which is itself subject to change. Perhaps what we call life and death are not exceptions to the apparent transformation and unpredictability of the universe.

Waiting

What happens after the death event? We wait!

In Western society, this waiting period is regarded as having three phases: suspension, judgment, disposition. During the first phase, the souls or spirits are in a transitional state between the end of earthly life and entry into their new realms of being. The Day of Judgment arrives, the sleepers awaken, receive salvation or damnation, and take their places either for "eternity" or "for all times" (concepts that often are treated as though identical, although philosophers hold them to be sharply different). Some Christians emphasize the long rest phase. Others focus attention upon the moment of judgment. Still others contemplate that ultimate phase when sorrows and anxieties will have passed. Some believers have embellished this phase by predicting that their own redemptions will be accompanied by the punishment of unbelievers. In ancient Egypt, by contrast, the act of judgment occurred promptly after death, with less emphasis on the preceding state of suspended animation.

I have characterized this general conception of the death state as waiting in order to emphasize its implications for time, tension, and striving. A tension exists between the death event itself and the end state. The dead may seem to be at rest—but it is actually a time for watchful waiting.

Furthermore, the sense of waiting hovers on both sides of the grave. The aged and the critically ill are sometimes regarded as waiting for death. In this view, death is not simply the cessation of life, but a deliverance as well. From a broader perspective, all the living, healthy though they may be, are only "putting in time" until they too move through the event into the state of death. The waiting is not over until all souls have perished and then awakened for judgment and final disposition. Perhaps some of our daily tension derives from this apprehension that fate will not be determined until the end of the end . . . beyond death.

Leon-Dufour (1986) notes that the man who most forcefully interpreted Jesus's message himself wavered between radically different alternatives. Paul at first conceived that the Kingdom of Heaven would not open its gates until the end of time. Later, he expressed the belief that one would experience the gratifications of eternal life immediately after death. Paul regarded death both as welcome release and catastrophic event. However one chooses to interpret the interpretations, the concept of waiting both for death and for the final outcome of death might have more influence on us than we usually realize.

Cycling and Recycling

One of the most popular conceptions of the death state is also one of the most radical. Death comes and goes, wending in and out of life. This view is often expressed by children. Sure, the bird was dead Friday, but maybe it's been dead long enough. Some adults also regard death as a temporary condition that alternates with life. Death is just one position on a constantly revolving wheel, the great wheel of life and death. (The "Bankrupt" place on *The Wheel of Fortune* television program comes to mind.)

Philip Kapleau (1971) points out that the wheel is a core symbol of Buddhism. Another important symbol is a flame passing from lamp to candle. This signifies rebirth. Kapleau also reminds us of the phoenix, "a mythical bird of great beauty who lived for five hundred years in the desert. It immolated itself on a funeral pyre and then rose from its own ashes in the freshness of youth, living another cycle of years" (p. viii). The phoenix represents both death and regeneration. Some funeral rituals also encourage the regeneration or recycling of life through death (Block & Parry, 1996). Kapleau argues for the rationality of the cyclical view: why should we assume that nothing precedes birth or follows death?

Kapleau's comparison between the states of prebirth and postdeath reminds me of the all-too-bright 10-year-old who attended one of my classes with his mother. At the end of the class, I asked him if there was anything he would like to say. "Just a little question. I mean, what are we *before* life and where are we or is it only nothing and would that be the same nothing we are after life or a different kind of nothing and . . . ?" I have since grown more cautious in asking 10-year-olds for their questions!

The recycling of life through the death state was an article of faith for many peoples in the past. This idea regained popularity in recent years in the United States with the emergence of the Aquarian or New Age movement. A typical statement by a follower: "Death is simply a transition from one life to another. We all live many lives."

Nothing

Perhaps we are deceiving ourselves when we imagine death to be any kind of state. What kind of being is it to not-be? This self-deception is further encouraged when we fail to distinguish between dying and death. Dying is something. The death event is also something: the final cessation of life processes. But is death itself a *state*? One might think instead of death as total absence: absence of life, absence of process, absence of qualities. The more we say about death, the more we deceive ourselves and use language to falsify. Even when I say, "This person is dead," I may be slyly contradicting myself. This person *is*? No, the whole point is that this person *isn't*. Our language lures us repeatedly into subtle affirmations of being even when we are trying to acknowledge nonbeing.

It is difficult to cope with the concept of nothing. Calling it *nothingness* reifies a reification, making a bigger somethingness out of nothing. Our minds do not know what to do with themselves unless there is at least a little something to work with. Yet the difference between even a little something and the concept of nothing is enormous. Furthermore, we tend to become anxious when faced with formlessness and with experiences that do not fit into our usual fixed categories of thought. Sometimes we try to deal with this anxiety by calling death a "void" or a "great emptiness." It feels reassuring to give things a name: Perhaps any name for nothing would be better than nothing.

Virtual, Therefore Not Death

Many of us have become involved with people who are not exactly either here nor there. *Virtual reality* first came to general attention through audiovisual devices that delivered impressions so vivid that our brains were tempted to suppose them real. Virtual reality (although a fading term) has opened new opportunities for learning, experiencing, and achieving—and escapism.

Death has not been neglected. The joy of killing is featured in many popular games. People living, people dead, and people computer-generated can interact. Virtual cemeteries have blossomed on the Internet, where the dead can be accessed 24/7 by families, friends, and curious strangers. The body of the deceased has become less crucial to some funeral rites and memorialization.

The Internet now offers itself as either another dimension of remembrance or a possible replacement for traditional interactions with the dead. No exhausting and expensive trips to distant cemeteries. No complicated scheduling. No concern that the burial site will have deteriorated. No standing in the rain. No having to put up with certain relatives one does not especially cherish. No physical aura of death and decay. On the other hand, by not actually visiting the grave, there is less opportunity to speak privately to a deceased family member and no opportunity to place a flower on the actual gravesite.

The dead are "there," in whatever sense that cyberspace is a place. It is a different kind of dead, though, and takes some getting used to. The fact that younger generations grow up with computer skills increases the likelihood of increased virtual interaction with the dead. What will we have gained and what will we have lost when virtual interaction with the dead becomes a larger element in our death system?

The more we become accustomed to remote interactions, the less our senses and feelings are guided by the breath and presence of people who really live and can really die. The more we become engrossed in virtual reality, the greater may be the temptation to see death as also something that is without dimension and place. Virtual reality has the compelling characteristic of being everywhere and nowhere at the same time. It can also be shuttled back and forth between existence and nonexistence at our pleasure. The virtual universe can go dark at our command and return in all its glory whenever we choose to access it again. It is not as messy as real life and death, and offers the illusion of control without asking very much of us in return. Death can be kept where we like it best: somewhere else.

Implications of the Ways in Which We Interpret Death

How we interpret the state of death can influence our thoughts, feelings, and actions. A person may refuse to approach a corpse, even that of a much beloved individual. The ancient Babylonians, Egyptians, and Hebrews attempted to comfort their aged. But who among them would want to be contaminated by a body that was beyond the pale of life? Elaborate decontamination rituals were

prescribed for those who inadvertently or by necessity had touched a corpse:

> *Whoever touches the dead body of anyone will be unclean for seven days. He must purify himself with water on the third day and on the seventh day. . . . Whoever touches the dead body of anyone and fails to purify himself . . . must be cut off from Israel . . . (Old Testament: Num. 19)*

Two terminally ill people who are equally firm in their religious convictions might differ in their specific anticipations of death and therefore in their moods and behaviors. A terminally ill person who believes that death is simply a passage to the next reincarnation may be less concerned about the moment of judgment than either of the foregoing people; the terminally ill person may be more interested in what is to come than the life that will be left.

These are but a few implications of the ways in which we interpret death as a state. Because of the difficulty of trying to interpret death as any kind of state, humankind has often used a supplementary approach—comparing death to conditions with which we have more direct knowledge.

CONDITIONS THAT RESEMBLE DEATH

We can liken death to something else or we can liken something else to death. Exploring death analogies will help not only in defining death but will lead us into several problem areas that deserve further attention.

Inorganic and Unresponsive

Fire, lightning, whirlpools, floods, earthquakes, and other natural phenomena have always impressed humankind. But we can also be impressed by lack of activity in the world. Gaze at those everlasting mountains! They were here in the days of our ancestors and will continue to tower above our children's children! At other times, however, silent and inert surroundings can elicit a sense of deadness.

The hard, unyielding surface of a rock contrasts with our vulnerable flesh and sensitive feelings. A person accused of misdeed might "stonewall it," creating a shield of unresponsiveness that emulates the lifeless character of the rock. Stone was also used as a representation of death in mythology. Mythological unfortunates were transformed from flesh and blood into insensate rock by incident or unwise action—a glimpse of Medusa's terrifying visage on one of her "bad hair days," or that fatal backward glance made by Orpheus upon leaving Hades.

We live in an invented, as well as a natural, world. We say things like, "The motor has died" and "The battery went dead." We age, and our machines wear out. Ancestors who lived close to the rhythms of earth had fire and stone to inspire their representations of life and death. We have added the mechanical and electronic apparatus. For example, stand at the bedside of a critically ill person who is connected to an external support system with multiple lifelines. Is this a living person? Or is it a set of machines functioning? Or can the situation best be understood as an integrated psychobioelectromechanical process in which the human and nonhuman components have merged to form a special system of their own? While we are considering this situation, it ends. The monitor reveals a flat line: Life activity has ceased. But what has ended? Do we say the machines failed or the body, or—?

Sleep and Altered States of Consciousness

Sleep has long served as another natural analogy to death. The ancient Greeks pictured sleep (*Hypnos*) as twin brother to death (*Thanatus*). Sleep and death remain entwined with cultural traditions. Orthodox Jews, for example, on arising from sleep in the morning, thank God for restoring them to life again.

Some people today still replace the word *death* or *dead* with *sleep* when they speak to children. However, when children are told that a deceased person is "only sleeping," we may question what message is coming across. The young child is not likely to have a firm grasp on the distinction between sleep and death. Late in the evening, the child is told, "Go to sleep!" by the same parent who said that grandmother is asleep or that death is a long sleep. It should not be a surprise if the child has difficulty falling asleep that night.

Adults as well as children may experience insomnia when death intrudes in their lives. While working in a geriatric hospital, for example, experience taught me to expect nocturnal disturbances on any ward where a patient had died unexpectedly. An aged, patient might speak matter-of-factly about the death and seem not to have been personally affected but then awaken in terror and confusion that night, seeking a living face and a comforting word.

Whether used wisely or foolishly, however, sleep remains one of the most universal and easily communicated analogies to death. Myth and fairy tale abound in characters who, believed dead, are actually in a deep, enchanted sleep. Snow White and Sleeping Beauty are perhaps the best known examples.

Altered states of consciousness occurring in sleep or resembling sleep have also been used as analogies to death. People may dream they are dead and feel frozen, immobilized, powerless to act (see also Chapter 13):

> *My dream was going along OK, for a dream. Then it was suddenly not my dream. It was something that was happening, and I couldn't do anything. I couldn't move anything. Not my hand, not one finger. The more I thought about it, the worse it got. . . . I was frozen in a panic. My heart was pounding like mad and I still couldn't do anything. I remember thinking, "Yeah, maybe I'm dead in my grave and this is just what it's like, thinking you can do something, you should do something, but you can't"* (dream report from a client in counseling who was experiencing situational stress).

Beings Who Resemble or Represent Death

In Homer's epic, *The Odyssey*, Ulysses ties himself to the mast of his ship to protect himself from enormous bird-like creatures with the heads of women. Some are perched on a rock, trying to lure the sailors with sweet song; others circle near the vessel. The hybrid bird-person has been a compelling figure in art and mythology for many centuries. Often these winged creatures were associated with death, although as the stork has reminded us, also with birth. Post-Homeric Greeks had to contend with *sirens* who brought death, and *harpies* who obliterated memory.

The winged hybrid at other times was depicted as a soul bird. This represented the spirit leaving the body at the time of death, hinting at resurrection. Later the bird-people were joined by fish-people, many of whom were also associated with death. The hybrid death-beings usually were portrayed as females. There was a tendency for peaceful death to take masculine form, whereas painful and violent death came through female agents. This characterization hardly seems fair: consider how many people have died violently in man-made wars and how many have been comforted in their last days by women. The Muses, arriving a bit later in history than the sirens and harpies, were females who were depicted in a more kindly light. The Muses would sing at funerals and guide departed souls on their journeys through the underworld. Some also inspired artists, writers, and musicians in their creative ventures.

Orpheus was remarkable for his powers rather than his appearance. Orpheus represented power over death. He charmed the fearsome guardians of the underworld with his music. Orpheus not only liberated his beloved Eurydice from Hades through his song but also brought rocks and trees to life.

The skeleton has also enjoyed a long career as a deathly being. Examples can be found throughout the ancient world. Artifacts from the buried city of Pompeii include a modern-looking depiction of a skeleton boxed inside a black border, suggesting a symbolic depiction of death. The skeleton flourished in medieval Europe, appearing in numerous works of art from approximately the 13th through the 15th centuries. We see the skeleton, for example, bearing a scythe on its shoulder and confronting young men, with the world behind them and hell gaping open underneath. This depiction appears on the title page of one of many books of the time called *Ars Moriendi* (The Art of Dying). The skeleton is also a prominent figure in van Eyck's rendering of *The Last Judgment*.

The animate skeleton did not simply pose for pictures. It danced. One whirl was enough for any mortal. Images of the *Dance of Death* flourished during the 14th and 15th centuries when the effects of the bubonic plague (the "Black Death") were keenly felt. Skeletal death was a measured and sedate dancer; frenzy and terror were not depicted in its moves.

We have not entirely forgotten this representation of death even today. The skeleton still dangles from doors on Halloween, although with lessening frequency because it has been placed on the politically incorrect list. The image of skull and crossbones appears on bottles containing poisonous substances, highway safety brochures, and in old Errol Flynn, or newer Johnny Depp, pirate films. The skeleton is especially conspicuous on the *Day of the Dead*, celebrated in Mexico and in Mexican American communities in the United States. The living and the dead greet each other and renew old acquaintances on this day. Special religious services are held in private homes, churches, and graveyards, and skull-shaped candies are among the delicacies of the day (perhaps not what the pious quite had in mind when singing "Come sweet death").

These are but a few of the shapes that humans see as resembling and representing death. The next shape to consider is the human form itself.

DEATH AS A PERSON

The field glitters in the intense sunlight. A solitary worker is harvesting the crop with his scythe. He is:

> *a vague figure fighting like a devil in the midst of the heat to get to the end of his task—I see in him the image of death, in the sense that humanity might be the wheat he is reaping. So it is— if you like—the opposite to that sower I tried to do before. But there's nothing sad in this death; it goes its way in broad daylight with a sun flooding everything with a light of pure gold (as quoted by Gottlieb, 1959, p. 161).*

This was Vincent van Gogh's own interpretation of his painting. Other artists have also represented death as a person or person-like figure. Death has also had a starring role in movies. In two of death's most notable film appearances, we find the figure in a monk's robe in Ingmar Bergman's *The Seventh Seal* and as Mr. Brink in Paul Osborne's *On Borrowed Time*. In these films, a determined knight delays the death monk's victory in a chess match, and an elderly man captures Mr. Brink in a tree. Nobody can be taken by death while these serious games are in progress.

Personifications of death can be found throughout the spectrum of human expressive activity from ancient times to the present (Aries, 1981; Tamm, 2003). These days, death is most often

*"Happy fortieth. I'll take the muscle tone in your upper arms,
the girlish timbre of your voice, your amazing tolerance for caffeine,
and your ability to digest French fries. The rest of you can stay."*

personified as a male, if gender is personified. In the past, female personifications were less uncommon, such as the Slavic's woman in white who held an everlasting green sprout in her hand. Female personifications eventually gave way to the skeleton and grim reapers. Death has often participated in children's games through the centuries. Hide-and-seek is a game that has thrilled children the world over, possibly because the child who is "it" can be understood as a stand-in for death and will catch the unwary. The child who is tagged can later enjoy taking a turn as the impersonator of death (Opie & Opie, 1969).

Personifications can help individuals and societies cope with death by (a) objectifying an abstract concept; (b) expressing feelings that are difficult to put into words; (c) serving as a coin of communication among people who otherwise would hesitate to share their feelings; (d) absorbing some of the shock, pain, anger, and fear that is experienced as a result of traumatic events; and (e) providing symbols that can be repeatedly reshaped to stimulate emotional healing and cognitive integration.

How We Personify Death: The First Study

Studies of death personification can tell us something useful about the ways in which both the individual and society are interpreting death.

We are now in a position to compare young adults' personifications of death at two points in time: 1971 and 1996. Four types of personification were offered most frequently by participants in the first study. The *macabre* personification vividly depicted ugly, menacing, vicious, and repulsive characters. One undergraduate stated:

> *I see Death as something I don't want to see
> at all. He or she—I guess it's a he, but I'm not
> sure—has jagged, sharp features. Everything
> about how he looks is sharp and threatening, his
> bony fingers with something like claws on the
> end of all of them, even a sharp nose, long, sharp
> teeth, and eyes that seem as though they can tear
> and penetrate right into you. Yet all this sharp-
> ness is almost covered over by . . . hair, bloody,
> matted hair.*

A young nurse had difficulty in personifying death at first and then said:

> I can imagine him, Death, being nearby. It makes me feel trembly and weak, so I don't want to take a good look at him. I feel his presence more than actually see him. I think he would be strong, unbelievably strong, and powerful. It could make your heart sink if you really had to look at him. But if he wanted you, there wouldn't be anything you could do about it.

It was common for the respondents to express emotional reactions to their own macabre images—for example, "When I look at this person—don't think it isn't possible—a shivering and nausea overwhelm me." The macabre personification often was an old person and almost always a terrifying being who is the sworn enemy of life. The relationship between age and personification is not so simple, however, as the next image reveals.

The *gentle comforter* could hardly be more different. Although usually pictured as an aged person, there was little physical and no psychological resemblance to Mr. Macabre. The gentle comforter was the very model of serenity and welcome. People who gave this kind of personification generally were those who also found the task easiest and least threatening. The following typical example is from a registered nurse:

> A fairly old man with long white hair and a long beard. A man who would resemble a biblical figure with a long robe which is clean but shabby. He would have very strong features and despite his age would appear to have strength. His eyes would be very penetrating and his hands would be large. Death would be calm, soothing, and comforting. His voice would be of an alluring nature and, although kind, would hold the tone of the mysterious. Therefore, in general, he would be kind and understanding and yet be very firm and sure of his actions and attitudes.

Another depiction suggests the respondent has been working toward an accepting attitude regarding her mortality:

> Death, I see him as very patient and very polite. He waits for each of us some place, just around a corner or even at the foot of our bed. I think of

> him as being there all the time, but only when we can see him is he there for us. He doesn't have to say anything and neither do we. We know what he's here for and he knows we know.

The *gay deceiver* is usually seen as a young and fascinating individual. (The term does not refer to a homosexual orientation: Gay deceiver was applied to this form of death personification before gay became widely used as a synonym for male homosexuality.) The personification can be either male or female, often with sexual allure. The gay deceiver tends to be an elegant and worldly person who can guide one into a tempting adventure. But, as one study respondent noted, "One could not trust him. He would be elusive in his manners, hypocritical, dishonest, persuasive. Death would first gain your confidence. Then you would learn who he really is, and it would be too late."

One young woman described death in the following manner:

> She is beautiful, but in a strange way. Dark eyes and long dark hair, but her skin is pale. She is slender and she is sophisticated looking. . . . I imagine her beckoning me to come with her. She will take me to a new circle of people and places, a lot fancier, more exotic than what I have in my own life. I feel sort of flattered that she would want my company, and I sort of want to go with her, to discover what I may have been missing . . . . But I am scared, too. How will this evening end?

The gay deceiver is unique for its mixture of allure, excitement, and danger. Death remains the outcome, but at least the getting there is interesting.

The *automaton* does not look like anything special. He is undistinguished in appearance. One might pass him on the street and not really notice him. The automaton tends to be dressed conservatively. If there is any distinctive quality at all, it is a sort of matter-of-fact blandness, a blank expression. This "ordinariness" is an important facet of his personality and meaning. One woman, for example, characterized him as:

> having no feeling of emotion about his job— either positive or negative. He simply does his job. He doesn't think about what he is doing, and

there is no way to reason with him. There is no way to stop him or change his mind. When you look into his eyes you do not see a person. You see only death.

The automaton appears in human guise but lacks human qualities. He does not lure, comfort, or terrify; he just goes about his business like as might any bored functionary. It has always seemed to me that there is something rather modern about this depersonalized personification—Does he represent a quality of alienation in mass society?

Respondents were most likely to see death as "a gentle, well-meaning sort of person." The "grim, terrifying" image was the least frequently selected. Death usually was personified as a relatively old person. Masculine personifications were given much more frequently than feminine. In more recent samples, the percentage of feminine personifications has increased across all categories. Masculine representations continue to remain most common, however.

The Follow-Up Study

Much has changed in our society since the first study. For example, there are now many more death education courses, grief counselors, peer support groups, and hospice care programs—as well as a raging controversy over physician-assisted death. There are also larger societal changes, such as the reduction of a nuclear war menace, the increase in terrorism, transformations in electronic communication, and continued progress in the empowerment of women. Have our personifications of death also changed in some way?

In a follow-up study, Kastenbaum and Herman (1997) found that:

- Death is still represented predominantly as a male—but there is a sharp increase in female personifications from female respondents.
- Men and women now differ more in the type of personality they attribute to death. Women continue to favor the image of death as the gentle comforter. Men, however, now most often describe death as a "cold and remote" person. The men were also more likely than the women to see death as "grim and terrifying."

- There is still a tendency for the gentle comforter to be viewed as an elderly person, but this is no longer true of the other personifications.

After completing the death personification items, respondents were asked to identify Jack Kevorkian. He was at that time in the news almost every day for his advocacy and practice of physician-assisted death. Almost all respondents correctly reported that he is the physician who "puts people out of their misery." We had wondered if Dr. Kevorkian's central role in the public controversy on physician-assisted death might have produced a new or modified personification, one that might be modeled after him. The answer was clear. Nobody mentioned Dr. Kevorkian as a person who came to mind when they thought about their death personifications. Despite his media image as "Doctor Death," Kevorkian did not influence death personifications. Perhaps our personifications come from deeper levels of the mind, as discussed by Jung (1959) and Neumann (1971), and therefore cannot easily be moved aside by passing faces and events.

CONDITIONS THAT DEATH RESEMBLES

"That was an awfully dead party," we might say, or "Look how tired she is—she's dead on her feet!" These are examples of using death or dead as metaphors to describe other things. Here are some other ways in which deadness serves as an instructive way of acknowledging certain aspects of life.

Social Death

You are with other people but nobody is paying attention to you. You might as well not be there at all. *Social death* is identified by how a person is treated by others. The concept of social death recognizes that when we die in the eyes of others, we may become somewhat less of a person.

Social death can be seen in ways such as the following:

- A person has violated one of the group's taboos. As a result, the individual is "cut dead."

This could be the West Point cadet who is given the silent treatment or the child who married some body of the "wrong" religion, race, or socioeconomic echelon.

- A member of the tribe violates a taboo and is ritualistically expelled, a symbolic execution. In a bone-pointing ceremony, the tribal community certifies one of its errant members as dead. This public ritual does not harm a hair on the offender's head but terminates the individual's life as a group member. The offender's property may be redistributed, and his or her name may be discarded or assigned to somebody else after it has become decontaminated. A parallel process sometimes occurs in mainstream Western society. For example, when an agency supervisor was dismissed on the basis of sexual harassment charges, a corporate official issued a command that his name was never to be mentioned again. Here was bone pointing, minus the bone. The law may also strip a person of the rights of citizenship, and the church may excommunicate.

- The social transformation of a living person into a custodial object can occur in modern facilities with cheerful decor as well as grim and decrepit institutions. Even the old person who lives independently in the community can be a victim of the socially dead treatment (e.g., being passed over while trying to get the attention of a store clerk or being placed at the bottom of medical or educational priorities). Exclusionary actions have also operated against people who have developed feared diseases such as AIDS, or against those who make others uncomfortable because of scars or physical infirmities.

- A dying person may be treated as though already dead. An elaborate pattern of aversive and person-denying behavior may be generated around a living person whose demise is anticipated. This pattern is likely to include little or no eye contact, reluctance to touch, and talking to others in the presence of the person as though he or she were not there. What makes this kind of situation even more unfortunate is that the person taken for dead may still be very much alive, alert, and capable of meaningful interaction.

Phenomenological Death

Concentrate now on what is taking place inside the person. Regardless of society's attitudes and actions, is the individual alive to himself or herself? There are two types of phenomenological death. First, part of the person may die in the mind of the surviving or observing self. Partial death can range in personal significance from the trivial to the profound. Two examples follow:

- A young man undergoes surgery that saves his life but results in the loss of the capacity to father children. In his own mind, one part of his total self has died. He will never be a parent. There is now the challenge of working through the loss of one of his most valued potential roles and sources of satisfaction.

- A young athlete is physically fit by most standards. But she has suffered an injury in athletic competition that is just disabling enough to end her career. She is a runner with bad knees. She was an accomplished athlete both in her mind and in the minds of others. Now she has to remake her identity, while still mourning privately for the athlete who has perished.

In the first example there is a surviving self who recognizes the loss of one or more components of the total self. "I am still here, but I am not the person I once was or might have become." There is an element of mourning for the lost aspect of the self. The other type of phenomenological death is quite different. Here, the total self takes on a deadened tone. The person does not experience life as freshly or intensely as in the past. Pleasures do not really please. Even pain may fail to break through the feeling of dulled indifference.

Feeling dead to yourself is a quality of experience that can shade into depersonalization: "I have no body," or "This body is not mine." Some psychotic people present themselves as though they were dead. This may be accompanied by a depersonalized attitude toward other people as well. The person may be mute, slow moving, and given to maintaining a rigid posture for protracted periods (as in the catatonic form of schizophrenia).

The sense of inner deadness or fading out sometimes is experienced with the use of alcohol or other drugs. It can also accompany other alterations in bodily state. Whatever the cause, the circumstances, or the outcome, we must recognize a state of mind in which the person becomes dead to himself.

People sometimes choose pain over sedation to avoid the sense of being dead to themselves (Baider, 1975):

> Mrs. A. was a 62-year-old Puerto Rican woman who constantly refused to take any medicine, even when in great pain. Her rationale was that doctors don't know as much as they think they do about the person's body. Each body has a soul, and if the doctor cannot see the soul, then he cannot see the body. "I know, I know that my family does not want that I suffer . . . but suffering is part of life . . . No medicine can help with any pain . . . or, sometimes it could help putting all your body asleep . . . like a baby . . . and then it takes away my pain . . . but it also takes away all that I feel and see. If I could feel the pain I can also feel my body . . . and then I know I am still alive (p. 378).

One person, perhaps in good physical health, reduces the sense of aliveness in an effort to avoid emotional pain. Another person, perhaps in extremely poor health, accepts intense physical pain as a link to life itself. These differences in our relationships to phenomenological aliveness and deadness are but two of the variations that must be acknowledged as we continue our exploration into the human encounter with death.

THE UNDEAD

The borderline between "alive" and "dead" has been crossed many times by human imagination, escorted variously by hope, fear, curiosity, and downright thrill seeking. The vampire is one of the earliest and most enduring characters in this tradition. Although well represented in fiction, drama, and parody, the vampire also has had a featured role in fertility rites, religious thought, and world folk culture. The *revenant* and the *zombie* are other creatures who reside in the shadowlands between life and death. We have already seen

that biomedical developments sometimes blur the distinction between alive and dead. The Undead, then, are not quite as far out as they might seem to rational people like us. (We are rational, aren't we?)

In visiting The Undead it would be best to leave behind our media-saturated images and stereotypes. With all respects to Bela Lugosi, Vincent Price, George Montgomery, Vampira, Buffy, and the stars of the *Twilight* series, we really need to learn something more substantial about the birth, history, and perhaps the fate of The Undead.

The Fertile Dead

Life gives way to death. This stubborn fact was recognized by our most remote ancestors. But death also gives way to life. The dry, wilted field awakens to the bird song of spring. A soul passes out of this life, and a new—or recycled—soul appears. Agricultural people such as the ancient Egyptians were embedded in the procession of seasons, their survival dependent on renewal by sun and flood. Farmers encouraged their crops with deconstructed organic materials that became known as fertilizers. Rituals were performed to persuade the gods to keep the good times coming. Sacrifices were crucial to fertility rituals in many parts of the world: A particularly effective sacrifice involved elevating a member of the society into a transcendent role: "You are king! No, wait! You are god!" This promotion was, in the truest sense, short-lived. The hero-king-god would be ritually murdered, and his remains offered to that always ravenous mega-creature, *The Great Mother*. Neumann (1963, pp. 148–149) lays this out for us:

> In the myths and tales of all people, ages, and countries—and even in the nightmares of our own nights—witches and vampires, ghouls and specters, assail us, all terrifyingly alike. . . . This Terrible Mother is the hungry earth, which devours its own children.

Here we have come to the nub of what we might dub *The Undead Complex*. This is a culturally shared, emotionally charged belief configuration with the following components:

- Something mysterious happens between life and death and between death and life. What

Earth as The Terrible Mother who gives life and then demands death is one of the most ancient themes devised by the human mind.

was living loses breath and blood, becomes pale and stiff. What is buried under ground sprouts new life. People, too?

- This is scary stuff, because the decomposition of the body is so repulsive.
- This is also sacred stuff because gods control the life and death cycle. Somebody or something must be at work underground to digest and reconstruct the dead. The Egyptians identified the scarab (aka dung beetle) as a significant intermediary.
- We should therefore cherish the intermediaries between life and death, no matter how their work and their persons might offend our sensibilities. At the same time, it is prudent to beware of creatures that scuttle back and forth from the grave—especially when they sport human-like features, distorted, mocking images of ourselves.

From Beast to Dark Lover

Vampire is derived from a Slavic word that also meant werewolf (Perkowski, 1989). And, indeed, there was a bestial quality to the vampires who haunted the imagination of European peasants through many centuries. They were often crude, smelly creatures who were more likely to attack a cow than seduce a lady in her boudoir. This primitive vampire was at home in superstition and folk tale. The people of the village knew he was real, though: who else could account for those savage attacks, and look at how this grave has been disturbed!

An upgraded vampire started to emerge in the early eighteenth century, and a broader public took notice. This version was a lot more interesting, if for all the wrong reasons. He (and occasionally, she) had an inordinate craving for blood. This intensified obsession coincided with the introduction of transfusions that, in themselves, raised hopes, fears, and fantasies. Experiments with electricity were also starting to test the possibility of reanimating the dead—so the vampire now had a larger stage on which to slither. Now clearly more human than animal, the vampire was at home in two places where most were not: the night and the grave. The dark side of respectable non-vampires was weirdly receptive to this terrible, and also naughty creature.

The decisive step up the cultural ladder occurred when the vampire went literary. Several stories had already made the rounds, but it was Bram Stoker's *Dracula* (original 1897; in Wolf, 1975) that established the vampire as the model to whom all others must aspire. Count Dracula was a sophisticate of royal blood whose horrifying nocturnal activities included more than a hint of forbidden sexuality. Stoker fashioned Dracula from Slavic folk materials. Stage productions drew huge audiences who cringed with horrified delight. The film industry, when it arrived, made him into a star. Ordinary leading men, let alone the average fellow in the audience, were confronted by a rival who could outdo them in just about every department that counted. Women were properly appalled and improperly thrilled.

It did not take long, though, for nervous laughter to arise. Dracula proved to be a reliable source of comic material, from vaudeville to contemporary film and television. Even Halloween children could master the master of darkness by impersonating him with plastic fangs and cape. Scholars, bold creatures that they are, also ventured to net the vampire in their treatises (interesting examples include Auerbach's (1995) *Our Vampires, Ourselves*, and Wilcox's (2006), *Why Buffy Matters*). The vampire would now be deconstructed for us in feminist, political, and psychoanalytic terms. (A fate worse than death?)

The vintage vampire is not yet on the endangered list, but has to negotiate the complexities of postmodern life. The many novels by Anne Rice and other popular writers have invited us to perhaps feel little compassion for those who find it as hard to die as to live. In doing so, perhaps we might also accept the invitation to revisit the darker side of our own natures where life and death do not necessarily obey the rules of strict rationality.

Bringing the Vampire Down to Earth

We have bypassed the most obvious question about vampires in order to present this brief survey of their origins in the human mind and their reputed behaviors. This question is, of course: *are they real?* Paul Barber (1988) has offered a persuasive analysis. He notes that throughout history people have been mighty curious about what goes on in the grave. We see people die and we bury them—but then what? Hardly anybody knew in detail the sequence of changes that a buried corpse undergoes. Fantasies arise from this ignorance. Most of the reports that fostered the vampire legend came from rural areas of Eastern Europe and featured unnatural happenings (our cow's milk turned sour!) and untidy graves. Barber explains the untidy grave as follows:

- Animals dig up bodies from shallow graves: that's why it's empty!
- Flooding uncovers bodies from shallow graves: he didn't excavate himself!
- Grave robbers, well, they rob graves, looking for anything useful, including marketable body parts.
- The corpse probably did move a little. That's what happens when gasses expand.
- This corpse looks in better than expected condition, but check the temperature and the soil chemistry.

The null hypothesis is, as ever, a tough proposition to prove. Neither Barber nor anybody else can say—for sure—that there never was or never might be an authentic vampire, but positive evidence for their existence is not abundant. The situation is similar for revenants, sad, wandering spirits still in their human form. It is likely that figures matching that description have been encountered, but less likely that they are dead men walking. Zombies have been described in somewhat similar terms. A true zombie has returned from his grave with a diminished capacity for thought and feeling. Unlike revenants and vampires, zombies have been associated largely with the voodoo religion and Creole culture as practiced in Haiti, West Africa, and areas of the U.S. South. The available evidence invites conjecture, but is insufficient for firm conclusion. A leading hypothesis (Davis, 1988) is that so-called zombies are people who slipped into a nonresponsive trance after being deliberately poisoned with a serving of puffer fish (yes, that Japanese delicacy!). They might have been buried before recovering, or they might have interpreted their lapse of consciousness as death. Tradition has it that zombies can also be created through religious rituals that might or might not include drugs. Zombies have a secure place in our repertoire of fringe beings and continue to work steadily in the motion picture industry.

Today's Undead still bear some marks of their sacred, bestial, and gothic-romantic ancestry. It might only be in our nightmares, however, that we catch a whiff of their mysterious mission between the living and the dead.

DEATH AS AN AGENT OF PERSONAL, POLITICAL, AND SOCIAL CHANGE

How we interpret death can either support the status quo or hasten political and social change. Following are major examples of death at work within society.

The Great Leveler

Since ancient times, people have been sorting each other out by class, caste, sex, physique, race, geography—and whatever I've left out. The result is a structure of dominance and submission. For example, the latest wave of immigrants to the United States from "the old country" often were looked down upon by those who had made the same transition a little earlier. Those who have themselves been victims of discrimination on the basis of religious or racial identities sometimes discriminate against people within their own groups (e.g., as "too orthodox" or "too liberal" or as looking too much like, or too much different from, those in the mainstream). How far does the urge to discriminate go? Does it at least end with death?

On the eve of his execution in 1672, Peter Patrix (1910) wrote these lines in his dungeon cell. He would be thrilled if you would read them aloud with a proper sneer:

I dreamt that, buried in my fellow clay,
Close by a common beggar's side I lay.

And, as so mean a neighbor shock'd my pride,
Thus, like a corpse of quality, I cried,
"Away, thou scoundrel! Henceforth touch me not;
More manners learn, and at a distance rot!"
"Thou scoundrel!" in a louder tone, cried he,
"Proud lump of dirt! I scorn thy word and thee.
We're equal now, I'll not an inch resign;
This is my dunghill, as the next is thine." (p. 292)

Death has often been used in an ironic and forceful manner to support the cause of equal worth and rights during life. If death has equal power over the mighty and the lowly—but we have Shakespeare to say this for us in a speech he gives to King Richard II (dare you to give this speech yourself!):

Within the hollow crown
That rounds the mortal temples of a king
Keeps Death his court; and there the antick sits,
Mocking his state, and grinning at his pomp;
Allows him a breath, a little scene,
To monarchize, be fear'd, and kill with looks;
Infusing him with self and vain conceit—
As if this flesh, which walls about his life,
Were brass impregnable; and humor'd thus,
Comes at the last, and with a little pin
Bores through his castle wall, and— farewell king!
(III: 2)

This speech did not increase the comfort level of crowned heads the world over. With no weapon other than his pen, Shakespeare had advanced the cause of a society in which the living as well as the dead might regard each other as people with certain inalienable rights.

Works of art commissioned during medieval times often displayed the theme of death as the great leveler. Gallant knights and beauteous maidens are interrupted on their journeys by death, often in the form of a skeleton. Skulls stare sightlessly from tables, shelves, and nearly hidden corners of the room as scholars ponder their books or marriage rites are performed. In such ways did the elite remind themselves that pride and triumph are fragile commodities. Our lady of the mirror (cover illustration) represents the "all is vanity" component of the great leveler.

The enormous toll of lives taken by the bubonic plague during its major visitations temporarily unseated aristocracy church. Peasants observed how royalty and church officials either fell prey to the disease or scurried away in panic. The first clumsy revolutions were attempted, and a few reforms were achieved (only to be lost when the power establishment had recovered itself). Many years later, a new and more equitable social order would take hold. As the winds of social change swept through Europe, death the leveler had a distinctive role, emboldening the common person to resist the established system. Peter Patrix would have liked that.

The Great Validator

Society also uses death to measure the value of its deceased members. Funereal splendor is an obvious way of demonstrating the worth of individuals—and, perhaps more importantly, their survivors. A Midwestern funeral director described the situation as he sees it:

> I do what you want me to do. You come in here and say you want simple arrangements, and that is exactly what I will provide. You know what you want, and I am here to meet your needs . . . . But let me tell you why I sell some of the more expensive items—it's because the people themselves want it that way! . . . They are not satisfied until they feel they are getting the best funeral for their loved one that they can afford . . . . If everybody wanted bare-minimum funerals, that is what we would be providing. When you see a big, a magnificent funeral, you are seeing what the family felt it truly must have.

Interestingly, the tradition of a "big funeral" has its roots in early American tradition. In colonial days, families sometimes spent themselves to the verge of poverty. Religious leaders such as Cotton Mathers decried the lavish funerals much as critics do today, but many of his brethren remained intent on proving their piety and worth by funereal displays.

The opportunity for survivors to affirm their own worth through the funeral process (Chapter 10) has been seized upon throughout the centuries. The heroine in a Greek tragedy risks her own life by arranging for the proper burial of her outcast brother. Committees meet in closed session to decide whether a deceased person is distinguished enough to deserve burial in sacred soil. And the legendary cowboy simply implores, "Bury me not on the lone prairie."

We have found that obituary notices in Boston and New York newspapers give more space and more often use photographs in reporting the deaths of men as compared with women (Kastenbaum, Peyton, & Kastenbaum, 1977). Studies by other researchers in the United States and the United Kingdom have confirmed this finding (Moremen, 2003). It has also been found that most of the obituaries were written by men. However, the gender gap in honoring the dead is decreasing as more women become prominent for their own achievements.

Death Unites/Separates

Death radically alters our relationships with others. It can be seen either as the ultimate act of separation or the opportunity to rejoin others who have gone before us. Occasionally death has even been seen as a way of bringing friends and foes together. Alexander Pope wrote in the seventeenth century:

> The grave united, where even the great find rest
> And blended lie the oppressor and oppressed.
> (Lines 315–316)

Two centuries later, a British soldier imagined his own battlefield death—an event that soon thereafter actually happened as World War I neared its end. Wilfred Owen (1918) concluded his antiwar poem with this poignant stanza:

> I am the enemy you killed, my friend.
> I knew you in this dark, for so you frowned
> Yesterday through me as you jabbed and killed.
> I parried; but my hands were loath and cold.
> Let us sleep now. (p. 1)

The despairing or dying person may yearn to become united with God. This hope is expressed in many hymns and carols. Typical is this verse included in a popular collection of 1844, *The Original Sacred Heart*:

> *Northfield*
> How long, dear Savior, O how long
> Shall this bright hour delay?
> Fly swift around, ye wheels of time,
> And bring the promised day.

This promise, however, was not without its threatening aspect. The gravestone marker for Miss Polly Coombes of Bellingham, Massachusetts (dated 1785) takes a challenging tone:

> READER ATTEND: THIS STATE
> WILL SOON BE THINE

Perhaps the most common form of the union-through-death theme is the wish to be with loved ones who are "on the other side." An old woman dreams that she has become a little girl once again and is being welcomed by her father. A boy wrestles privately with thoughts of suicide so that he can join the big brother he misses so much. The survivor of a random, drive-by shooting consoles herself with the expectation of being reunited some day with her slain family member. Although some of us may find comfort in the prospect of reunion with loved ones through death, the immediate consequence is separation. The familiar face of someone who has died is not to be seen again. One has lost a treasured companion, and the pain of separation can be overwhelming.

"I felt like part of me had been pulled apart. Like I wasn't a whole person any more. And then I went numb. Like I was in shock, with loss of blood, just like I had lost an arm or a leg or worse." This is the way a young woman felt when she learned that her husband had been killed in Vietnam. He had been alive to his loved ones until the message came, although in objective fact he had been dead for an indeterminate period of time. The moment that his wife learned of their final separation is the moment when the death event occurred for her. The shock and pain of sudden loss was experienced again by thousands of Americans after the terrorist attacks of September 11, 2001. Family and friends of terrorist victims had some comfort in knowing that the nation shared in their grief: Those bereaved by the Vietnam War had much less support because the war itself had been opposed by many people.

This sense of separation can occur in advance of the actual death and linger long afterward. For example, some families face the probable death of their living children while still suffering from a previous loss.

The family were still grieving Ann's death when Roy began to exhibit symptoms of the same disease . . . . Adam has a similar form of the same illness . . . . "We know it all now—we shall be left with nothing—no children—nothing" (Atkin, 1974, p. 66).

Children also experience the sorrow of separation from each other, even if they do not fully understand the concept of death.

He had lost one sibling and was facing the experience a second time. His sister, in the latter stages of her illness, seemed unaware and unresponsive. Yet her little brother seemed to evoke some faint recognition. She appeared to smile with her eyes—a last window into the darkness. He said: "I don't mind if you don't talk to me. It's lonely without you. I can talk to you." He prattled on about his rabbit, his cars, and his wish to have a party on his birthday (p. 69).

Difficulty in understanding death, coupled with the strong need to continue the relationship, can lead both children and adults to behave at times as though final separation had not really taken place (see also Chapters 8 and 11). The deceased person may still be spoken of in the present tense ("Jimmy only likes smooth peanut butter"), and interaction patterns may seem to include the expectation that the deceased has been only temporarily detained.

Ultimate Problem or Ultimate Solution?

Death is sometimes regarded as either the ultimate problem or the ultimate solution. We may even hold both views at the same time.

A dark jest made the rounds in the aftermath of the French Revolution: "Come and see the wonderful new machine—a miracle! One treatment by the good Dr. Guillotine and—phoof!—never again a headache!" The Guillotine brothers were appalled by public executions and suggested the device as a replacement for slower and more painful methods. But why have public executions in the first place? Are there no other ways to resolve conflicts and protect the legitimate interests of society?

Death as ultimate solution has been applied on a mass level as well (Chapter 9). Hitler's "final solution of the Jewish problem" translated into the genocidal murder of more than 6 million men, women, and children—Jews, Romani (gypsies), and others despised as "non-Aryan."

Unfortunately, the attempt to solve a problem by killing others neither started nor ended with the Holocaust, nor even with Rwanda and Darfur. Never mind history; we need read only today's news.

Opposing this theme is the conviction that death is the ultimate problem because it ends our opportunity to achieve. This is certainly a threat in a society in which the need to achieve has been a dominant motive. ("I can't die just yet—I have so much to do!")

Death may also be seen as the ultimate problem because it brings the curtain down on the theater of inner experience. No more images, thoughts, or feelings. Still again, death may be seen as the ultimate problem because it defies understanding. Faith may be sufficient for some people, but others may be frustrated because the human intellect seems incapable of penetrating the mystery of death. The last words of the dying are sometimes given special attention in the hope that those who are closest to the mystery might also be closer to the answer and somehow able to impart this answer to us. Unfortunately, this logic is questionable (Kastenbaum, 1993; 2002a). We can learn much from the strength and resourcefulness of many people as they cope with the dying process, but they do not necessarily understand death any better than the rest of us.

The Ultimate Meaningless Event

Random, senseless death might be regarded as the ultimate meaningless event. A young man fires an automatic weapon into a group of people working out in a health-and-fitness facility. A person who will later be described as a "disgruntled former employee" returns to the workplace and fires at everybody who happens to be there. A retired man with a grudge against a homeowners' association blasts away at neighbors enjoying themselves at a community center. The family, friends, and colleagues of these victims suffer not only the grief of loss, but also the shock and confusion that accompany an event that is outside one's normal frame of reference. We can understand why violent death might occur in the course of criminal activities or dysfunctional relationships. Some deaths,

however, appear to make no sense at all, especially those in which the killer did not know the victim or have anything palpable to gain from the act of murder.

Fatal accidents can also raise the question of meaninglessness. A man survives hazardous battle situations but is killed by a neighbor backing her car out of the driveway. An infant is left unattended for a few minutes and drowns in a bathtub that contained only a few inches of water. Two children are playing quietly on a sidewalk near the school when a van swerves over the curb, strikes them dead, and then plows into another group of people. The consequences of a few minutes of inattention or disregard for safety seem so tremendously out of proportion to the "little" error that was involved. As with the victims of random killings, accidental deaths may seem to violate our basic expectations about life. This is not the way things are supposed to happen, not the way that lives are supposed to end.

Many of us are reluctant to conclude that there is no answer. It is difficult to accept the proposition that a death could be meaningless, because this implies that life, too, might not be part of a meaningful, rational, and coherent universal pattern. Perhaps we are misled at times by faith in rationality. There has to be a good explanation for everything—even death. Everything has to make sense; everything (even nothing) has to be logical.

But—maybe not!

■ SUMMARY

There are many competing answers to the related questions: What is death? What does death mean? Philosophers Democritus and Epicurus held that the universe consisted fundamentally of atoms in motion without any guiding principle or purpose. In this indifferent universe, neither life nor death had any special meaning. Christianity entered with a powerful message of hope—a sanctified life after death—but also with the belief that death itself as punishment for sin. For people who are often described as "New Agers," death is not meaningless, punishment, or salvation. It is simply one of the way stations in a long, perhaps infinite spiritual journey across many lives.

Fantasy (Victor Frankenstein) and actual (Charles Darwin) scientists of the past explored the uncertain boundaries between life and death, and this endeavor continues to flourish today. The competing ideas about death can be seen as symbolic constructions, drawn from our experiences, our needs, and our guesswork. It would be difficult to do without a concept of death, but it seems almost as difficult to agree on the specifics.

The biomedical approach is more complex and tends to focus on the question: When (under what conditions) is a person dead? The development of life-support systems and organ transplantation procedures has created more situations in which questions can arise. The Harvard Criteria for determining brain death have become useful guidelines to decision making. Nevertheless, it is a challenge to recognize such distinctions as persistent, permanent, and transient forms of vegetative state, as well as the minimally conscious syndrome and several other conditions, all of which have implications for decision making. Prevailing definitions and practices regarding brain death are now being challenged by a report from experts who contributed to the President's Council on Bioethics. The situation is therefore becoming even more complex and controversy unabated.

Several interpretations of the death state were examined. The traditional interpretations are: death as (1) enfeebled state, (2) continuation of life, (3) perpetual development, (4) waiting, (5) cycling and recycling, and (6) nothing. We also considered an emerging new interpretation: death as virtual and, therefore, not really death at all. We also explored objects and conditions that resemble death. These include inorganic and unresponsive objects, sleep and altered states of consciousness, and beings who resemble or seem to personify death. The most commonly given death personifications were identified and discussed. There are also conditions that death resembles, such as social and phenomenological death.

The Undead have flourished since ancient times as mysterious, frightening, yet perhaps essential components of the life-into-death-into-life cycle. The vampire's transition from bestial predator to dark lover reveals how society can do a make-over on its symbolic constructions. We are also reminded that a purely rational approach to the interplay of life and death would distort the reality of darkness and light.

Death has often served as an agent of personal, political, and social change. It has taken the form of the great validator that measures the social value of deceased people, but death has also been seen as uniting or separating people, representing the ultimate problem, the ultimate solution, or the ultimate meaningless event.

■ REFERENCES

Ad Hoc Committee of the Harvard Medical School to Examine the Definition of Brain Death. (1968). A definition of irreversible coma. *Journal of the American Medical Association, 205,* 337–340.

Alexander, S. (1920). *Space, time, and deity* (Vols. 1–2). London: Macmillan.

Aries, P. (1981). *The hour of our death.* New York: Knopf.

Atkin, M. (1974). The "doomed family": Observations on the lives of parents and children facing repeated child mortality. In L. Burton (Ed.), *Care of the child facing death.* London & Boston: Routledge & Kegan Paul.

Auerbach, N. (1995). *Our vampires, ourselves.* Chicago: University of Chicago Press.

Baider, L. (1975). Private experience and public expectations on the cancer ward. *Omega, Journal of Death and Dying, 6,* 373–382.

Barber, P. (1990). *Vampires, burial, and death: Folklore and reality.* New Haven, CT: Yale University Press.

Block, M., & Parry, J. (Eds.). (1996). *Death and the regeneration of life.* Cambridge, UK: Cambridge University Press.

Bondeson, J. (2001). *Buried alive.* New York: Norton.

Bunson, M. (1993). *The vampire encyclopedia.* New York: Gramercy.

Burns, J. M., Login, I. S., Bruno, M. K., Kimura, C., Crisci, G., Saposnik, L., Beslac-Bumbasirevic, S. G., Jovanic, D., Ercegovac, M., & Wijdicks, E. F. (2002). Brain death worldwide: Accepted fact but no global consensus in diagnostic criteria. *Neurology, 59,* 470–471.

Buss, R., Sun, W., & Oppenheim, R. W. (2006). Adaptive roles of programmed cell death during nervous system development. *Annual Review of Neuroscience, 29,* 1–35.

Cole, K., & Perez-Polo, J. R. (2004). Neuronal trauma model: In search of Thanatos. *International Journal for Development Neuroscience, 22*, 485–496.

Davis, W. (1988). *Passage of darkness: The ethnobiology of the Haitian zombie.* Chapel Hill: University of North Carolina Press.

Fechner, G. T. (1977). *The little book of life after death.* (Reprinted by New York: Arno.) (Original work published 1836.)

Fitsimmons, P. (2009). Depictions of death in television and the movies. In C. D. Bryant & D.L. Peck (Eds.) *Encyclopedia of death and the human experience* (Vol. 1, pp. 359–362). Los Angeles: Sage.

Freud, S. (1920/1960). *Beyond the pleasure principle.* New York: Norton.

Giacino, J. T., Ashwal, S., Childs, N., Cranford, R., Jennett, B., Katz, D. I., Kelly, J. P., Rosenberg, J. H., Whyte, J., Zafonte, D. O., & Zasler, N. D. (2002). The minimally conscious state. *Neurology, 58*, 349–353.

Goldsmith, T. H., & Zimmer, W. F. (2001). *Biology, evolution, and human nature.* New York: Wiley.

Gottlieb, C. (1959). Modern art and death. In H. Feifel (Ed.), *The meaning of death* (pp. 157–188). New York: McGraw-Hill.

International Society for Plastination. http://edis.at/plast.

Iserson, K. V. (2003). Persistent vegetative state. In R. Kastenbaum (Ed.), *Macmillan encyclopedia of death and dying* (Vol. 2, pp. 668–669). New York: Macmillan.

Jennett, B. (2003). *The vegetative state: Medical facts, ethical and legal dilemmas.* New York: Cambridge University Press.

Johnson, S. (2006). *The ghost map.* New York: Penguin.

Jung, C. G. (1959). *Four archetypes.* Princeton, NJ: Princeton University Press.

Kapleau, P. (1971). *The wheel of death.* New York: Harper & Row.

Kastenbaum, R. (1993). Last words. *The Monist. An International Journal of General Philosophical Inquiry, 76*, 270–290.

Kastenbaum, R. (2000a). Looking death in the eye: Another challenge from Doctor Kevorkian. In K. K. Kalman (Ed.), *Right to die versus sacredness of life* (pp. 279–286). Amityville, NY: Baywood.

Kastenbaum, R. (2000b). *The psychology of death.* (3rd ed.). New York: Springer Publishing Co.

Kastenbaum, R. (2002a). Last words. In R. Kastenbaum (Ed.), *Macmillan encyclopedia of death and dying* (Vol. 2, pp. 515–518). New York: Macmillan.

Kastenbaum, R. (2003). Thanatomimesis. In R. Kastenbaum (Ed.), *Macmillan encyclopedia of death and dying:* (Vol. 2, p. 888). New York: Macmillan.

Kastenbaum, R. (2004). *On our way. The final passage through life and death.* Berkeley: University of California Press.

Kastenbaum, R., & Herman, C. (1997). Death personification in the Kevorkian era. *Death Studies, 21*, 115–130.

Kastenbaum, R., Peyton, S., & Kastenbaum, B. (1977). Sex discrimination after death. *Omega, Journal of Death and Dying, 6*, 33–44.

Kevorkian, J. (1957). Rapid and accurate ophthalmoscopic determination of circulatory arrest. *Journal of the American Medical Association, 164*, 1660–1662.

Kevorkian, J. (1961). The eye in death. *CIBA Clinical Symposia, 13*, 51–62.

Koszer, S., & Moshe, S. L. (2001). Brain death in children. *www.medicine.cm/neuro/topic491.htm.*

Kramer, K. P. (2003). Hinduism. In R. Kastenbaum (Ed.), *Macmillan encyclopedia of death and dying* (Vol. 1, pp. 410–444). New York: Macmillan.

Leon-Dufour, X. (1986). *Life and death in the New Testament.* New York: Harper & Row.

McCullagh, P. (1993). *Brain dead, brain absent, brain donors.* New York: Wiley.

Moremen, R. D. (2003). Gender discrimination after death. In R. Kastenbaum (Ed.), *Macmillan encyclopedia of death and dying* (Vol. 1, pp. 311–314). New York: Macmillan.

Morgan, L. (1923). *Emergent evolution.* London: Williams & Norgate.

Neumann, E. (1971). *The origins and history of consciousness.* Princeton, N.J.: Princeton University Press.

Opie, I., & Opie, P. (1969). *Children's games in street and playground.* London: Oxford University Press.

Owen, W. (1918). Strange meeting. http://www.illyria.com/owenstr.html.

Patrix, P. (1910). In F. P. Weber (Ed.), *Aspects of death and correlated aspects of life in art, epigram, and poetry* (p. 292). London: H. K. Lewis & Co., Ltd.

Perkowski, J. L. (Ed.). (1976). *Vampires of the Slavs.* Cambridge, MA: Slavica Publishers.

Pope, A. (Original work published 1746). *Windsor-Forest.* http://andromeda.rutgers.edu/~jlynch/Texts/windsor.html.

President's Council on Bioethics (2008). Controversies in the determination of death. A white paper of the President's Council on Bioethics. Washington, DC. http://bioethics.georgetown.edu/pcbe/reports/death/index.html.

Schultz, N. W. & Huet, L. M. (2000/2001). Sensational! Violent! Popular! Death in American movies. *Omega, Journal of Death and Dying, 42,* 137–150.

ScienceSpace (no date). vrinfo@gmu.edu.

Segall, A. (1990). *Paul the convert.* New Haven: Yale University Press.

Seifert, J. (1993). Is "brain death" actually death? *The Monist. An International Journal of General Philosophical Inquiry, 76,* 175–202.

Shelley, M. (1977). Frankenstein, or the modern Prometheus. In L. Wolf (Ed.), *The annotated Frankenstein.* New York: Potter. (Original work published 1818.)

Shrock, N. M. (1835). On the signs that distinguish real from apparent death. *Transylvanian Journal of Medicine, 13,* 210–220.

Stoker, B. (1975). Dracula. In L. Wolf (Ed.), *The annotated Dracula.* New York: Potter.

Summers, M. (1928). *The vampire and his kith and kin.* New York: E. P. Dutton.

Talbot, M. (1992). *The holographic universe.* New York: HarperPerennial.

Tamm, M. E. (2003). Personifications of death. In R. Kastenbaum (Ed.), *Macmillan encyclopedia of death and dying:* (Vol. 2, pp. 669–671). New York: Macmillan.

Twain, M. (1972). *Life on the Mississippi.* Reprinted by Norwalk, CT: Heritage. (Original work published 1883.)

Veatch, R. (2009). The evolution of death and dying controversies. *Hastings Center Report, 39,* 16–19.

Von Hagens, G. (March 27, 2002) in Chris Hogg, Body Parts. http://news.bbc.co.uk/2/hi/talking_point/forum/1888662.stm.

Wade, D. T., & Johnston, C. (1999). The permanent vegetative state: Practical guidance on diagnosis and management. http://bmj.bmjjournals.com/cgi/content/full/319/7213/841.

Werner, M., & Werner, J. A. (2009). Improbable planets. *Scientific American, 300,* 38–44.

Wijdicks, E. F. M. (2001). The diagnosis of brain death. *New England Journal of Medicine, 344,* 1215–1221.

Wilcox, R. (2006). *Why Buffy matters.* London: I. B. Tauris.

Wolf, L. (1975). *The annotated Dracula.* New York: Clarkson N. Potter.

Zaid, B. A. (2002). The Islamic ruling on brain death and life support. TheModernReligion.com/misc/hh/braindeath.html.

Zamperetti. N., & Bellome, R. (2009). A new contribution to the President's Council on Bioethics on the definition of death related to the neurological standard. *Intensive Care Med., 35,* 1305–1307.

Zeman, A. (2001). Consciousness. *Brain, 124,* 1263–1289.

■ GLOSSARY

Brain Death A condition in which vegetative processes of the body may continue, although the capacity for thought, experience, and behavior has been destroyed.

Catatonia A neuropsychiatric disorder that at times takes the appearance of stupor, rigidity, immobility, and mutism.

Coma, Comatose A deep state of unconsciousness from which the individual cannot be aroused.

EEG The electroencephalogram presents a visual display of the ongoing electrical activity of the brain.

Intravenous Fluids Liquids that are introduced directly into the veins to restore metabolic balance and provide nutrition, avoid dehydration, or treat infections.

Martyrdom The heroic sacrifice of one's life for a cause or faith. *Respirator Brain:* Physical destruction of the brain as observed in postmortem examinations.

Minimally Conscious State Severe impairment distinguished from coma or *vegetative state* by occasional and limited evidence of awareness.

Revenant An undead wanderer who does not necessarily behave like a vampire.

Transient Vegetative State Characteristics are those of the VS (following entry) but caused by drugs, extreme cold, or injury that has some potential for recovery.

Vampire A nocturnally reanimated corpse who seeks fresh blood.

Vegetative State Sleep–wake cycles, respiration, and other vital autonomic activities continue, but awareness and thought are absent. A persistent vegetative state may be reclassified as a permanent VS after long duration.

Virtual Reality Computer-generated scenes, beings, and events that simulate actual or possible versions of the world.

Zombie A reanimated corpse whose death and resuscitation involved sacred rituals but perhaps also drugs. He or she now functions in a lifeless and automatic way. Associated primarily with West African, Haitian, and Creole voodoo practice.

ON FURTHER THOUGHT . . .

Argue against one of the main themes of this chapter! Under what conditions might we be better off if we did not think about death? Think about not thinking—and when you come up with something good, please pass it around!

The Death System

YOUR NEWSPAPER (Today)
The devastating _____ that brought death and destruction to _____ has
left _____ and _____ in its wake. The government response is said to
have been _____ and _____.
Some people attribute the extent of the catastrophe to _____
                              —A generic disaster report. Feel free to fill in the blanks.

Michael Jackson's estate earned $250 million dollars in the year since his
death in 2009, proving the "King of Pop" is still reigning at the top of the
charts. Before his death, the estate was more than $500 million in debt.

"You've come a long way, Baby!" (1968)
"It's a woman thing!" (1995)
                              —Virginia Slims advertising slogans

"Chatfield, there seems to be something wrong with our bloody ships today."
                    —British Vice-Admiral, quoted by Sharon Tosi Moore (2007)

"I'd have, like, seen this much ice and thought, 'Oh, my gosh, we're going to
crash.'"
                              —Co-pilot of Continental Flight 3407; quoted by
                                              Rebecca Shaw (2009, p. 21)

Dhanu, the single name of a young woman, is the most famous Tamil Tiger
suicide bomber. On May 21, 1991, she hid a girdle of grenades beneath her
gown, presented a garland to Rajiv Gandhi, India's top political figure, and
exploded, instantly killing them both. Dhanu has become a heroine to the
women of Sri Lanka's Hindu Tamil minority.
                              —Robert A. Pape (2005, p. 226)

The blood-stained cloak allegedly worn by Mary Todd Lincoln on the night of
the assassination. Locks from Elvis' GI haircut. Pieces of Beethoven's corpse.

Albert Einstein's brain. This odd array of historical artifacts is at the center of a new ethical conflict for life scientists.

—Lori B. Andrews et al. (2004, p. 215)

I watch Fellers creep around the pond, his beard dripping, his burly form crouched over his waders, a net in his hand and a flashlight in his mouth. Taking care not to let the frog see his moon shadow, Fellers inches forward, pauses, inches closer— and then whips the net down in a splash. It comes up full of slimy stuff that he pulls out, a handful at a time, until he reaches the frog at the bottom.

—W. Wayt Gibbs (2002)

A vulture die-off throughout India was first documented in the 1990s. It was a bizarre sight to see them with heads bent so low. Death's select birds were themselves dropping away.

—Stephen Bodio (2001)

Seven newborn boys, six of whom were black, were injected with radioactive iodide *in the early 1950s at a hospital in Memphis, Tenn., as part of a study funded by the federal government . . . it was one of at least five done around the country on a total of 235 newborns and older infants.*

—Scripps Howard, December 22, 1993

Simon was the family angel. He was handsome. He was perfect. Everybody loved him. Of course, he got more attention than I did, but you couldn't get angry at him. Then he died. It was diphtheria. Most people today don't even know that word. Diphtheria was just terrible. My mother's sister died about the same time after delivering her second baby. That baby died, too, or was born dead, I don't know which. Ellie came down with rheumatic fever. She made it to her 15th birthday, and couldn't even blow out the candle; that's a fact. The graveyard kept filling up with family. When I was about 10 or so, I remember coming back from the graveyard and thinking: "Why, there are as many of us here as home." Maybe that's why I've always felt at home at graveyards.

—A man of 93, reflecting on his childhood

Everything that makes a collection of individuals into a society and keeps that society going has implications for our relationship to death. In this chapter, we will be looking more systematically at the *death system*. First, however, we will take these diverse examples as our introduction.

Death and survivor grief often are experienced with the loss of one family member or friend. But sometimes deaths come en masse and threaten to overwhelm a community, or even a nation. Nobody has to tell us about the profound and disturbing effects if we have ourselves been part of a disaster scene or its aftermath. Mostly, though, we learn about disasters from television, and, if we are "old school," from newspapers and news magazines. We might feel compassion for the victims and survivors; perhaps we also contribute what we can to disaster relief. As time goes on, however, one disaster seems to replace another. How often can we respond intensely to still another disaster in the news? And aren't they all much the same—as far as media coverage and discussion are concerned? The definitive answer: well, yes, and no.

The sequence of effects and societal response often has similarities from one disaster to another (as discussed later in this chapter and Chapter 8). Nevertheless, there are also consequential differences, depending on the type of disaster and the geopolitical situation in which it has occurred. Are we capable of understanding what is distinctive about a particular disaster as well as what it has in common with others? Or have we become so inured to media representations that with little effort we could write up our own generic news story? Here is one way we might have filled in the blanks. How did you do it?

> The devastating flood that brought death and destruction to Pakistan has left chaos and hunger in its wake. The government response is said to have been slow and ineffective. Some people attribute the extent of the catastrophe to a weak and corrupt government. There is growing concern about the use of the funds donated for care and rehabilitation.

- Michael Jackson is not the first celebrity to reap a postmortem financial harvest. In his case, the estate was in debt until his market value increased after his sudden and unexpected death. Dead, Elvis Presley continues to makes way more money each year than most hard-working people earn in a lifetime (*www.forbes.com*). Elvis's $37 million per year was followed by *Peanuts* cartoonist Charles Schulz ($28 million), Beatle John Lennon ($20 million), race car driver Dale Earnhardt ($20 million), and "Dr. Seuss" (Theodore Geisel; $19 million). Some people have been so valued by society that they continue to flourish in economy as well as memory. Other people have also gained in esteem and earning power after their deaths. For example, during his life, Vincent van Gogh's paintings could have been purchased for the cost of dinner and a bottle of inexpensive wine. While society forgets some people almost instantly upon their deaths—or even before—others become even treasured. Discovering how and why these choices are made could tell us much about the way in which society uses, abuses, or dismisses its dead.

- A few women smoked a few cigarettes in the first half of the twentieth century. They would light up a single cigarette once or twice a week as part of a social occasion, and seldom if ever inhale. Many more women started smoking many more cigarettes in the post–World War II years, largely as the result of advertising campaigns that associated this activity with what they were assured was the new, liberated woman. The women would be advertising their own emancipation every time they flamed up an Eve, Virginia Slim, or one of the rugged male brands. The impressive increase in female smoking was soon shadowed by an equally impressive rise in their lung cancer rates and mortality (Cancer Facts & Figures, 2009). There is no doubt that the manipulation of cultural symbols in a saturated advertising campaign has cost many women their health and lives. The end-of-life experiences for each of these women can be studied from medical palliative care, and spiritual perspectives, as can the grief of family and friends. But we would be missing a big part of the picture if we neglected the way in which the tobacco industry penetrated our society's death system, and was allowed to do so.

- Vice Admiral David Beatty had made an accurate observation. There certainly was something wrong with his bloody ships. Two of England's greatest battle cruisers had just exploded within minutes of each other under German fire and plunged into the North Sea. His own flagship, *Lion,* was on the verge of the same fate, but saved by an officer's quick-thinking heroism. Beatty's response was a classic understatement. It also revealed the world of difference that often exists between people in command and control positions, and those who are embedded in the actual situations. Military commanders, ranking governmental officials, corporate directors, and theoreticians tend to have different perceptions and priorities than people who are fully occupied with living their

CRAVEN "A"

Will not affect your throat

Good news, indeed! Cigarettes are not only an attractive symbol of the liberated woman, but never, ever, will do harm. Not so! The post World War II tobacco advertisement campaign resulted in a continuing high lung cancer mortality among women who emulated role models such as depicted here.

own lives. Beatty could not afford to think of all the lives that had just been lost.

The copilot was commenting on her own inexperience as the flight from the Denver airport attempted to take off after a weather delay. It over-rotated, struck the ground, and turned upside down. Of the people aboard, 28 of 82 were crushed to death. Air travel is one facet of a mass society in which decisions made by a particular individual in a particular situation can have life-or-death implications for many others. What kind of mindset leads to both the admiral's incomprehension of a naval disaster and a young aviator's hesitation to act on her own perceptions of risk?

- Dhanu, described as a "remarkably beautiful young woman in her late twenties" (Pape, p. 226),

is thought to have been the first attacker to use a suicide belt—years before this tactic became part of Middle East and North African violence. How? Through a long period of training and practice. With what kind of mindset? Patient, disciplined, not impulsive. But why? Two powerful and related motivations. Dhanu was active in a political movement that had taken up terrorist methods in an effort to establish independence from India. There was also something intensely personal involved. Dhanu was gang-raped by Indian soldiers who had killed her four brothers. Rape and murder have since become even familiar terror techniques where populations are sharply divided on political, economic, ethnic, and religious issues. Dhanu and other members of the Black Tigress unit have broken from a nearly universal cultural tradition in which women are regarded as the bearers of fertility and protectors/nurturers of life. It remains to be seen whether a society can revert to traditional gender expectations after killing has become an accepted mission for women as well as men.

- Being dead does not automatically exclude a person from a society's desires and motives. There are numerous cultural traditions of invoking the dead and attempting to communicate with them (Chapter 13). Lori Andrews and her colleagues (2004) call attention to the need for ethical guidelines for studying the dead. Does our curiosity justify any and all inquiries into the dead? The authors urge that research on human remains be conducted in consultation with all relevant people and organizations, certainly including family members and descendants, and should also conform to all applicable state, federal, and international regulations regarding the treatment of the dead. They also suggest requiring researchers to make a case that the (deceased) individual would have agreed to testing for that purpose. Would Beethoven have wanted to find out if some of his odd behavior late in life, and perhaps even his deafness, had been caused by sipping wine from a favorite lead cup? Should our scientific impulse or simple curiosity end at the grave site?

- Frogs and vultures. We think of these creatures as belonging to the natural order of things. They don't have Social Security numbers and e-mail addresses, and they don't pay taxes (at least, not yet). Nevertheless, they are very much a part of the death system in every nation where they flick their tongues for flying insects or keep watch for carrion. The connection has turned lethal in recent years. Many ponds where the lusty songs of frogs were a sure sign of spring have gone silent. Grossly deformed frogs have also turned up in great numbers, and some species seem to have disappeared from their habitats.

Meanwhile, vultures have also been dropping to their own deaths in alarming numbers. Why "alarming"? For centuries in India, vultures have been relied upon to strip the corpses of humans as well as animals. Tibetan Buddhists have also assigned vultures a key role in "sky burial".

With vultures now in short supply, India's sacred cattle—living and dying on the streets—are being left to rot because Hindus are forbidden to touch these corpses. The remains of other dead animals will also remain longer. Outbreaks of tuberculosis, anthrax, and other diseases can occur under these circumstances, and the situation could also spread to Africa.

Two elements are especially significant in the frog and vulture die-off: (1) the most probable cause is pesticides, especially DDT; and (2) religious attitudes and practices that have enhanced the role of vultures. The possible impact of frog extinction is less obvious but perhaps even more significant in the long run, because it could be part of a much broader pattern of endangerment to many biological species, a cascading process with effects of unknown breadth and magnitude.

What should we make of the deaths of the creatures who themselves seem to have been designed by nature to assist the dead in recycling new life forms?

- Injecting newborn infants with radioactive iodide as part of a government-funded study met with severe criticism by physicians and ethicists as soon as the facts came out (after nearly 40 years of silence). John Gofman, a leading expert on the dangers of low-level radiation, observed that "It's like saying, 'We're going to visit cancer on some of you—not necessarily all of you—but we have increased the risk individually and some of you will get it.' It's not a nice thing to do with children" (Scripps Howard, 1993). The fact that this was an official government project exposes still another type of conflict within our society's death system. Here was the government playing an active role in increasing the probability of illness and death—and for newborns! Furthermore, the Memphis study was disturbing in its revelation that "liberty and justice for all" seemed not to have been applied to infants of color. Racism in life prepares for racism in death.

- The man of 93 is part of a disappearing generation that remembers when childhood was a time of ever-present risk for disabling illness and death. The local cemetery was an extension

Vultures await their next assignment as part of nature's program of recycling life through death. Pesticides are threatening the lives of vultures in India, arousing public health concerns as well as disrupting the established order of life-death transition.

of the neighborhood where so many promising and cherished family resided. Dramatic changes in longevity and life expectation are usually expressed in statistics, but we will not want to forget that advances in public health are really about giving individuals the opportunity to survive well into their adult years.

• Infancy has been an exceptionally risky time of life through much of history. It is the major reason why the average life expectancy has been estimated at about 30 or 40 years in many past societies: so many did not make it beyond infancy and early childhood. As O'Connor (2004) notes, the United States has become an increasingly safer place to be born, so the most recent statistics were not generally expected. The explanation that has been offered calls for further reflection. The slightly elevated infant mortality rate is attributed to more high-risk pregnancies and births. Multiple births, low birth weights, and other complications have increased as more women make use of fertility treatment and/or become pregnant at an older age. Improved fertility techniques and more effective care for at-risk infants are resulting in more live and viable births—but also in more deaths.

These are but a few of the conflicts and complications that are found in any society's death system. Perhaps we should make things simpler for ourselves—why don't we just get rid of death?

A WORLD WITHOUT DEATH

Suppose that the world is just as we know it, with one exception: Death is no longer inevitable. Disease and aging have been conquered. How would

BOX 3-1

GENERAL AND PERSONAL CONSEQUENCES OF A WORLD WITHOUT DEATH

Consequences for Me	Consequences for the World

people respond to this situation, individually and as a society? How would the quality of life change?

Think first of the effects of the no-death scenario on the world at large. In the left side of Box 3-1, write down the changes you think would be likely to happen.

Think next of how the no-death scenario would influence your own life. In the right side of the box, describe some of the major ways the no-death situation would be likely to influence you. None of us can know for sure what would actually happen if this hypothetical situation became reality. Nevertheless, many plausible and interesting predictions can be offered. Compare your ideas with those that follow, as given by other students who have completed this exercise.

General Consequences

- Overcrowding would lead to infringements on privacy, mobility, and other individual liberties. "Space would be incredibly precious." "People would develop new mental and physical habits to keep others at an emotional distance." "Turf mentality would be all-powerful." "After a while, nobody would feel comfortable being alone even if you could be." "I don't see how people could still be individuals."
- Birth control would be enforced. This control would be an exercise of power and prestige. "It will all depend on what the elite want people

bred for." "If basketball coaches get control, they'd want to breed for 7-foot centers." "Every group of crackpots and bigots would try to use selective birth control to exterminate the kind of people they don't happen to like."
- New laws would be needed because relationships between people will have changed so much. "Inheritance might not mean anything anymore." "I think that babies with genetic or with birth defects might not be allowed to survive because there would be room for so few babies when adults are not dying off."
- Society would become very conservative and slow to change its ways. "Old people would outnumber young people so much that anything new would hardly have a chance." "The world wouldn't really have a future. There'd only be a terrific bias to keep things as they are or even to roll things back to the past."
- The economic structure of society would be seriously impacted: "Life insurance—who would need it? And then, what would happen to that whole industry?" "People wouldn't have to put money away for their funerals. In fact, there would be hardly any money to be made on the dead." "Doctors might not make as much money because there wouldn't be all this fear of death. But maybe they'd make even more money with plastic surgery and fancy ways to try to keep people looking young. Who knows?"

- Moral beliefs and practices could change in many ways. "That would be just about the end of marriage, and maybe of divorce, too. People would think, hey, what's the point of being married to just one person forever and ever? Everybody'd either screw around a lot with everybody else or maybe just get tired of it after a couple of thousand years and play video games instead."
- Death might take on a radically different aspect. "Religion is mostly getting people to shape up or go to Hell. If we're not going to die, then who's going to listen and what's going to happen to religion?" "Death has always been the enemy. Now it might be the biggest friend ever. We might hire people to kill us in some really decisive way, like blowing us to pieces. I think I would buy shares in the Mafia. Or maybe governments would arrange special wars only for the purpose of getting a lot of people killed." "I really don't think we can do without death psychologically. Society would find some way to make death possible, and this would be considered the right thing, not an evil thing."

Personal Consequences

- We would organize our lives differently. "I don't know if I would have the same ambitions and make any progress on them. As it is now, about the only way I get anything done is when a deadline is staring me in the face, which happens all the time in my classes. If there's all the time in the world, there wouldn't be any pressure, and I might not ever get anything done." "I would just give up trying to plan ahead. There would be just too much ahead, so much that it would be very hard to comprehend." "I'd be really afraid of making some terrible mistake in what I do, because the consequences could follow me I guess forever, for centuries anyhow."
- We would be free from the fear of death. "If I found out that there really and truly wasn't going to be any more death, I would feel light and free for the first time and I could really enjoy life. I hope I'm not kidding myself either, but even the thought of a no-death world makes me feel wonderfully free." "My brother's got himself almost killed at least three

times. He's into being a macho risk-taker. I'm a lot more careful. I would probably take more chances with my life, and do some more exciting things, because it really wouldn't be taking such a chance, would it? I wonder what my brother would do?"
- Our personal relationships would extend indefinitely, creating new opportunities and new challenges. "It's a crazy idea, but I like it. The people I care about would always be with me." "I find it hard to think of becoming an old person and being an old person right along with my parents and grandparents. Would I still feel like a child? What would become of generations if we all spent most of our lives being old together?"
- Our ideas about the purpose and meaning of life might change. "It would be a hard idea to get used to, especially with all that I have always believed as a Christian. I would want to keep my beliefs—I would have to—but it might make some difference, there not being natural death and therefore not being eternity and heaven. Or would there still be? It could be confusing." "I have to wonder what value anything would have anymore. Maybe the only thing I would value is how to fill all that time . . . how to fill all that time."

A world without death would differ in many ways from the world we know today. You may have thought of some consequences that go beyond those presented here, and the list certainly could be extended. *The main point is that our individual and societal patterns of functioning are connected with death in one way or another.* Life insurance, for example, depends on the profit motive, and the profit motive in turn arises from complex ideological and social conditions. Yet, as respondents often observed, no death means no life insurance. Consider also what some respondents have predicted: other establishment of stringent birth control measures. "If nobody dies, then nobody can get born." This relationship has now taken on new dimensions with the development of reproductive assistance strategies (e.g., sperm and eggs frozen for later use). How might this intensify the anxiety—even the desperation—of people who are highly motivated to have children of their own?

Individual implications of our relationship to death cannot easily be separated from the general consequences. Consider, for example, those who fear they would lose their drive for accomplishment if time were endless. This is a personal matter, but connected with a cultural ethos in which the achievement motive is highly valued. Social philosophers have argued that one of the most powerful driving forces in Western society is the need to achieve a kind of salvation through achievement. We accumulate material goods and acquire status to demonstrate that we should be among the blessed. A bumper sticker that had its day in the sun once advised us that "The winner is the one who dies with the most toys."

Lessen the need to achieve and acquire and we alter our relationship with time and death. The lifestyle oriented toward work and achievement has been increasingly challenged by enthusiasm for a leisure lifestyle. Baby boomers sometimes work very hard at play as signs of aging and the shadow of mortality arise. One boomer may have spoken for many others when he confided to me, "If I work any harder at playing and staying young, I'll be old before my time and kill myself for sure." And then he was off jogging again under brilliant Arizona skies.

This no-death thought experiment raises many questions that require us to think of society as well as the individual. The death system concept provides a way of doing so.

BASIC CHARACTERISTICS OF THE DEATH SYSTEM

How serious is my health problem? What should I say to my neighbor whose child was killed in an automobile accident yesterday? Would I be better off dead than old? These personal challenges take place within a dynamic society. It is true that we live and die as individuals, but it is also true that we are linked with each other by language, expectations, customs, and needs. In this section, we shift our focus to the ways in which our confrontations with death are systematically influenced by our participation in society.

The concept of the death system invites our attention to interconnections, to the subtle network of relationships and meanings through which one sphere of action influences another. We face death

alone in one sense, but in another and equally valid sense, we face death as part of a society whose expectations, rules, motives, and symbols influence our individual encounters. This will become clearer as we turn our attention now to the components and functions of the death system.

COMPONENTS OF THE DEATH SYSTEM

The death system is made up of people, places, times, objects, and symbols.

People

All of us are potential components of the death system. Tomorrow I might be called on suddenly to use the techniques I learned in a cardiopulmonary resuscitation course, or somebody else may be called on to use these skills on me. (I hope we've both learned well!) Most of us phase in and out of the death system as circumstances dictate. Some of us though, such as people working in the funeral and memorial industry, serve as core participants. How they are perceived by others is often strongly influenced by their profession.

One funeral director described the typical situation members of this trade must contend with: "When I walk into a room, Death walks in with me. That is how people react to me." The fact that many of us find it difficult to think of a funeral director as a normal and distinct individual testifies to this individual's embeddedness in the death system.

The agent who sells life insurance is also very much part of the death system. The same may be said for all the clerks, adjusters, marketing people, and executives involved in life insurance. The members of the custodial staff who clean up the high-rise offices of MegaMoolah Insurance Company late in the evening are unlikely to reflect on their role in the death system, but their paychecks have their origin in somebody's decision to make a financial investment in anticipation of death. The premiums we pay to guarantee death benefits are part of a complex network of investments. The death money may be used to create new jobs or abolish old ones, support a local business, challenge it with a competitor, or simply to further enrich the investors.

The florist is also part of the death system. "Floral tributes" help flower growers and merchants stay in business. The lawyer who meets clients to draw up wills and living trusts is another involved person. This is one of the few situations in which a healthy adult is likely to sit down and discuss personal death-related issues. Even so, many lawyers report that their clients often prefer to delay making a will or living trust as long as possible because of the obvious connection with death.

People working in a variety of occupations earn their livelihoods from death-related services. A consumer movement that encourages less elaborate and costly funerals (Chapter 12) affects the funeral director, the florist, and the cemetery association. The trend toward merged families with "his, her, and our" children can complicate the inheritance process. The increasing availability of life care retirement communities can reduce the amount of money that can be passed along to children and therefore also alter estate planning and will making.

Other people associated with the death system might not come so readily to mind. Think, for example, of the big truck you saw pull up behind a supermarket the other day. It was filled with pet food, case after case. Every can in every case depicts a contented dog or cat, while the inside contains a meat product. All that meat, of course, came from what once were living creatures. The truck driver, the person who shelves the cans, the assistant store manager who makes sure they are priced correctly, and the clerk at the checkout register are but a few of the people who participate in the death system through their processing of pet food. Those who raise, those who slaughter, and those who process a variety of living animals to become food for pets also should be included. The people in the canning factory should be included, as should the accountants, the executives, and the advertising agency. The cat that meows so convincingly for its favorite brand on television is also part of the death system—as is the cat at home who, unimpressed by the advertising programs, sniffs disdainfully at the food dish, turns up his or her tail, and walks away with an offended air. As purchasers of this product, are we not all part of this complex network as well, a network that requires the death of animals to feed other animals?

Still unmentioned are the health professions and the clergy, all of whom have important roles in the death system. It would not do to leave out the scientists who are designing lethal weapons or tinkering with life and death through cloning techniques. Dolly the cloned sheep was preceded and has been followed by many attempts on a variety of species. (Most attempts have failed to produce a healthy, viable mammal specimen). Should we also clone the extinct Tasmanian tiger (Tinkler, 2002) to keep it company, or perhaps rescue the wooly mammoth from the dead as a theme park feature? Trying to create new forms of life or reversing extinction is on the growing edge of science today, although imagined in the past (as in Frankenstein, Chapter 2). Today, some scientists are again trying to retro-evolve the auroch, a massive and formidable animal from which domestic cattle developed (hunted to extinction in the seventeenth century). One of the motivations: to again hunt the great beast!

What other occupations have an important bearing on death, and might not even exist otherwise? This open list is in your hands to extend as you like.

Places

Certain places have become identified with death. The cemetery and the funeral home are obvious examples. There are other places whose associations with death depend on the ideas and experiences we carry around with us. Today, people come and go from the hospital all the time. It is the place where babies are born, routine surgical procedures are performed, accident victims are treated, and clinics are available for outpatient care. It is also the place where people die sometimes, but that is only one facet of the modern medical center. People with long memories, however, give a different perspective. A spry woman of 93 explained:

> The doctors would say, "We're taking you to the hospital, Mike." And Mike he would directly close his eyes and turn his face to the wall. Then the doctor would say, "Now, now Mike. Don't take on like that. We're going to make you well at the hospital." And Mike, he wouldn't say a word. But when the doctor walked out the room, Mike, he would say, "I'm a dead man." Everybody knew it. You went to the hospital to die. . . . And even to walk by the hospital, you would shudder right down to your shoes. And you walk a little faster.

In a modern hospital, death is often granted its small, isolated territory in return for promising to stay within those bounds. Here the patients with the most severe life-threatening conditions reside. However, any room on any unit can become a death place when a patient unexpectedly "goes sour." It can take months before the ward feels safe again. In the meantime, you can see a variety of decontamination rituals as those associated with the ward attempt to rid the environment of its newly acquired "deathness." Similar measures have been taken in private homes as well: a bed may be given away because it is the one in which Uncle Otto "expired," and its continued presence somehow keeps the unwelcome aura of "deathness" in the household atmosphere.

Historical battlefields often are thought of as death places for centuries, as is the Tower of London, that grim edifice by the banks of the Thames where royal murders occurred. The Ford Theater in Washington, DC, is remembered mostly as the place where Lincoln was assassinated. A pathway in the woods may be spoken of in hushed tones by the schoolchildren who discovered a human corpse while on a nature walk. Even a familiar house across the street can be a death place in the minds of neighbors who now feel uncomfortable as they pass by. Once a place has become associated with death, we no longer think and feel the same way about it. We have but to think of Oklahoma City and New York City, where people perished and buildings collapsed as a result of domestic and foreign terrorism. The people of Oklahoma City will long remember how a major downtown building suddenly became a place of death.

Times

Death also has its times or occasions. Memorial Day, for example, is a regularly occurring time set aside in the United States to honor those who have fallen in defense of the nation. In some tribal societies, several days are devoted to communal mourning for all who have died during the preceding year. (Simpler burial rituals are held immediately after the deaths.) The Mexican tradition of *el día de los muertos* (the Day of the Dead) (Rosales, 2003), with its public carnival atmosphere, suggests an easy familiarity with the dead. The visitor might not be aware of the more reflective and somber rituals that are conducted at the family level. Family and friends return from the dead for a brief sociable visit. This celebration has roots in Aztec and other native festivals, further shaped by Roman Catholic belief and practice, and in some places by Halloween (Taylor, 2000). Many societies have established periodic occasions when death is granted dominance over everybody's thoughts and feelings. Just as we might grant death its own space in return for death not invading ours, so we might set aside special times for death, hoping that death will not steal the time of our lives.

Prayers for the dead are offered on regular occasions—for example, by Jewish and Japanese Americans who are keeping the faith, and by Catholics who are celebrating Mass. December 29 is observed in honor of the Sioux annihilated by the Seventh Cavalry at Wounded Knee, South Dakota, in 1890. Anniversaries of the disasters in Waco, Texas, Oklahoma City, and the three sites of the September 11, 2001, terrorist attacks are observed by many of those who were affected. Some of us also acknowledge a death time that has deep personal significance that may not be shared by others. This can be a private spiritual reflection but also take the form of what psychiatrists call an anniversary reaction, in which the survivor falls ill, behaves erratically, or suffers an "accident."

The clock and the calendar treat each passing moment, each passing day, with equal disinterest. For the individual and for society, however, certain times seem to fall under the particular auspices of death, and we tend to treat these times in a special manner.

Objects

Death has its objects and things as well as its people, places, and times. The hearse and the death certificate are among the conspicuous objects in the American death system. Death notices have their own separate section in newspapers. Taxidermists have converted hunting trophies and beloved animal companions into still life (or still death) souvenirs. Freeze-drying could be the technique of the future (Bryant & Shoemaker, 2003). The noose, the gallows, and the electric chair are also among our more obvious images of death, as are the nuclear "devices" that we have aimed at potential enemies for years while they aimed theirs back at us.

Objects whose intended uses have little to do with death may produce lethal effects through accidents or misuse. Both the automobile and the cigarette have been spoken of as instruments of death, although not conceived for that purpose. Alcoholic beverages and other pharmacological substances have also been viewed as instruments of death, although, again, not intended for such a purpose. Things, like people, places, and times, can be recruited into the death system, and when this happens their meanings are transformed, even though the objects themselves remain the same.

Symbols and Images

Language, other symbols, and images play a major role in death systems. In Western culture, the black armband tells a story. Funeral directors generally provide limousines for the funeral procession and garb themselves in similar colors. Not all societies symbolize death with dark colors, but we soon learn to recognize the particular colors and other symbols meant to convey death-related messages. In some neighborhoods, closing the shutters has been a traditional signal of a death within, although this practice continues to fade. Administration of the priestly ritual for the sick often is associated with impending death, although not officially described as "last rites."

Death symbols tell us something about a culture's attitudes toward death. The choice of music is one example (Kastenbaum, 2003). Slow, solemn music intoned on an organ suggests an orientation different from that of a simple folk song with guitar accompaniment and is different again from a brass band strutting down the street playing "When the Saints Go Marching in." The Catholic requiem mass encompasses both a plea for the Lord to grant the dead eternal rest in His perpetual light, and, in the *Dies irae* section, a terrifying evocation of the Day of Wrath and its call to judgment. When gang members decided to organize the funeral for a slain member, they included a rap song written in his memory (Holveck, 1991). By contrast, when Queen Mother Elizabeth died in her 101st year:

> *Slow drumbeats punctuated the shrill bagpipe lament of nearly 200 regimental musicians. Soldiers of the Royal Horse Artillery in gold-trimmed black tunics rode six black horses pulling a gun carriage that bore the coffin (Associated Press, 2002, April 10).*

That soldiers and a gun carriage should be so integral to the funeral services also tells us something about a society's associations with death.

The words we use and those we refrain from using also reveal much about the nature of the culture's death system. For many years in our society, people "passed on," "expired," or "went to their reward." I have noticed a decrease in euphemisms and an increase in dismissive expressions such as, "She OD'd" (overdosed) and "He croaked." Both the euphemistic and the dysphemistic approach serve to keep a distance between the speaker and the raw reality of death. Currently, health care professionals prefer the objectivistic "terminally ill" to the still uncomfortably emotional "dying." (Yesterday I heard one refer to death as "end-state event." What next?)

Cultural representations of death have often included deities who take lives and deal with the dead. The dynastic Egyptians had *Anubis*. Jackal-headed Anubis judged the dead and decided what was to become of them. Up north, *Freya* was one of the most powerful of Norse gods. She looked after fertility and abundance but was also the warrior deity who was devoted to war and collected some of the fallen to reside and rejoice with her in *Folkvangr*. (Possibly it was the fortunate dead who first said, "Thank god, it's Freyaday!" But maybe not.) Morrighan served similar purposes for the Celts, but Meng Po had a different specialty. In the guise of an old woman, she would provide the tea of forgetting so the newly dead would be free from memories of their lives. We will meet up with the twin Greek deities, Hypnos and Thanatos, in Chapter 15. Many other gods of death have flourished throughout the world as re-introduced in Ernest L. Abel's (2009) *Encyclopedia of the rulers, evil spirits, and geographies of the dead*. Is our mainstream society liberated from or deprived of death gods?

Although today more people discuss death openly, we still tend to code the topic with indirect, symbolic, and sometimes downright evasive language. I know of one major hospital system, for example, in which a deceased patient is still spoken of as having been transferred to "Tower Nine." There are eight towers or units in this hospital; the ninth is not of this world. Notice with what linguistic garments people clothe their communications about dying and death, and you will also be observing something important about their underlying attitudes.

FUNCTIONS OF THE DEATH SYSTEM

We have surveyed the components of the death system. Next we will become acquainted with its major functions.

Warnings and Predictions

A core function of society is to protect its members. All societies issue warnings and predictions intended to stave off threats to life. These cautions can be based on folk customs, science, pseudoscience, organized religion, or individual revelation. The threats that are forecast may be accurate, exaggerated, or completely imaginary. Society may choose either to respond to or to ignore the alarms. Cassandra's plea to destroy the horse that the Greeks left as a gift at the gates of Troy is a classic example of a warning unheeded and its disastrous consequences. Investigation of the FBI and CIA responses to warnings of a terrorist attack are more recent examples (National Commission on Terrorist Attacks, 2004).

It can be difficult to determine which warnings should be taken seriously. A central problem for our times is how to navigate between the extremes of hypervigilance and smug neglect. How much of our attention should be devoted to the recently surfaced threats posed by terrorism, and how much to the continuing problem of air and water pollution and climate change? To the possible effects of overhead high-voltage wires? To radon, asbestos, and lead in our homes and workplaces? Are we tempting death if we drive across one of the nation's many bridges that are considered hazardous?

"Small-craft warning" and "tornado watch" are familiar phrases in some parts of the United States. In Arizona, we hear occasional "flash flood" warnings: it is not easy to imagine that a dry ravine might suddenly resound to the roar of a raging current of water. We expect to be advised of impending floods, blizzards, avalanche conditions, and dust storms. There are also frequent announcements of possible hazards associated with consumer goods and services. Evaluating all these warnings would be more than a full-time job in itself.

The death system provides warnings and predictions to specific individuals as well as to larger units of society. The physician may hesitate before interpreting that laboratory report to us.

The mechanic may fix us with a hard look: "Your car is an accident ready to happen."

Hearing that there is a threat to our well-being does not end the story. We must still decide what we are going to do about it. Mr. Macho Guy and Ms. Lucky Goose might ignore all the warnings, as might those who live life by the numbers and figure that there is nothing they can do when their own numbers come up.

Preventing Death

All death systems have strategies that are intended to prevent death. In Western society, there are health professionals, firefighters, police, and researchers striving for preventions, cures, or safety improvements. One of the great accomplishments of the past few generations has been the control of contagious diseases that once took a high toll, especially among the very young and the very old. Efforts are being made to prevent other causes of death, such as cancer and heart disease, and to minimize hardships associated with aging. But hard-won medical victories create rising expectations. As one physician with more than 40 years of experience explained:

> People don't want much these days. All they expect is to live forever and, well, maybe to be young forever, too. . . . I guess it's our fault for knocking off typhoid, scarlet fever, diphtheria, tuberculosis and whatever. They expect us to cure everything now. I guess we almost expect it, too.

We seem to enjoy the idea of "making war" on death and disease. There are problems with this conception, however. The war against death often is conducted in a selective manner, following society's general paths of discrimination and unequal opportunity. Whatever makes some people appear to have high social value in general makes them more favored candidates for death-prevention efforts. "If you are going to have a heart attack, make sure you are wearing a good suit and are in the right part of town—also, try to be young and white!"

Cynical comments of this type unfortunately retain a core of truth even today, as disclosure of the radioactive iodide studies has reminded us. For example, poor women in the United States are still less likely to be diagnosed and treated for breast cancer and are therefore more likely to die from this ailment (Associated Press, 2002, April 3). It could also be said that the war against death includes a war against ourselves because many lives now end as a result of lifestyle practices and decisions (e.g., using tobacco and alcohol or engaging in practices that increase the risk of HIV-AIDS transmission).

Caring for the Dying

A staff member in one of the world's most sophisticated medical research centers was describing her work to me in a completely professional manner. Suddenly, tears of sorrow and frustration intruded as she tried to explain what happens when the decision is made to shift from "cure" to "comfort" care:

> *Sometimes the point comes when the doctors decide that's it. There's nothing we can do—or should do—all the cards have been played, and there's just no way we can really hope to arrest the illness. The brakes screech! We all have to come to a full and sudden stop. We may have been doing everything in the world to keep this person alive for months and now we have to stop all that and change what we do, but it is a lot harder to change how we feel about the patient and ourselves, about what we're doing. I don't think human thoughts and feelings were made for such sudden stops and starts!*

Fortunately, the transition between trying to prevent death and providing care to a dying person is not always this drastic. Prevention and comforting can be encompassed within the same philosophy and carried out by the same people in many situations. Patients and their families may play an active part in the decision making, and health care providers may function as a team (e.g., hospice care; see Chapter 5).

How can health professionals (each with distinctive skills, points of view, and needs), the family, and the life-threatened person work together harmoniously if some of them persist in life-prolonging measures while others believe that there is a time when comfort and relief should take precedence?

Advocates of both positions can be found in the ranks of all those associated with terminal care. There are physicians who take quite literally the never-say-die orientation—so long as life has any chance, it is the physician's responsibility to do all within his or her power to support this chance. Other physicians accommodate their efforts to the signs of impending and inexorable death. This attitude seems to be more in keeping with earlier medical practices when physicians had fewer options to work with and were inclined to see themselves as nature's assistant.

Disposing of the Dead

"Disposing of the dead" is a heartless-sounding phrase, but it refers to a task that all societies must perform. At the very minimum, there is a need to dispose of the physical remains. Seldom, however, is a society content with the minimum. The funeral and memorialization process (Chapter 12) tells much about the overall stability and cohesiveness of a culture as well as what that society makes of death.

Here are a few examples from American society:

- A minister dies unexpectedly. His wife and children are stunned, then grief stricken. Forced to think of funeral arrangements, they find themselves in perfect agreement. The minister had been a family-oriented person who preferred the simple, the intimate, the natural. The funeral, then, should be without ostentation. Only the family and a few special friends should be involved. But this plan offends the congregation. A small, simple, private commemoration would fail to symbolize the deceased's significant place in the community and diminish the status of the congregation itself. No, it just wouldn't be right to let this death pass without a conspicuous public ceremony. The power of the many prevailed in this instance. The disposal of this man's body and the accompanying ritual became a public event. It was a "beautiful" funeral, with participation from community leaders as well as the congregation.

How did the family feel? They reacted as though not only the husband and father had been taken away from them but his death as well. What they experienced deeply as private loss and grief had become a public exhibit. And yet the community felt that it, too, had strong rights and needs. Just as much of this man's life had been devoted to the public sphere, so his death should be shared. This is one of many examples that could be given of the contest between private and public "ownership" of the deceased. Some death systems emphasize one side, some the other, but the private-versus-public dialectic seems to be present in all of them.

- Two young men are pushing a gurney through the corridors of a large modern hospital. This action has been planned to attract as little attention as possible. Soon they have reached the service elevator and the door closes behind them. The casual observer will have noticed only an empty stretcher. A more sophisticated observer will recognize that this is a false-bottomed device that is designed expressly for disguised transportation of the dead. A society whose health care establishment goes out of its way to wrap a cloak of invisibility around the dead is telling us something about its fundamental attitudes toward the meaning of life. Do we think of the dead as fearful, disgusting, or dirty? Are we as afraid of being "contaminated" as members of any preliterate society? Such questions arise when we observe avoidance-of-the-corpse rituals even within the corridors of the modern hospital system.

- An old man has died. Family converge from everywhere. There is a problem, however. The oldest generation, including the widow, expects a traditional observation of the death. The younger generations, however, are more Americanized and consider the old way too formal, too consuming of time and money, and generally not to their liking. The funeral director is caught squarely in the middle. The death of a respected family patriarch, then, threatens to bring a bitter intergenerational conflict to the surface.

Our death system undergoes change with every new generation. And, since three- and four-generation families are becoming increasingly common in the United States, we face the challenge of understanding each other's viewpoints when dealing with body disposal and other death-related decisions. Whatever improves intergenerational communication and understanding will help our death system to function in a more harmonious and effective manner.

- The rain and floods that devastated large sections of the United States in the summer of 1993 created problems for the dead as well as the living. In Hardin, Missouri, flood waters churned through the local cemetery. This burial ground had been used for about 200 years and was a core of the community's history. Hundreds of bodies were unearthed from their graves. Despite the pressing need to deal with flood recovery, the community showed no less concern for making things right with the dead. They did all they could to identify the corpses and return them to their designated burial places. Anthropologists, *pathologists*, and other outside experts offered their assistance. Eventually, approximately 100 bodies were identified; the others, still anonymous, were provided with caskets and given a mass burial. Members of the community spoke of their relief in helping their loved ones "rest in peace."

The Amish Way of Life and Death

Our diverse American society includes subgroups with distinctive lifestyles. The Amish way of life and death provides an instructive example of alternative approaches (Bryer, 1977; Clark, 2010;

Hostetler, 1993). There are approximately 80,000 Amish people in the United States, descendants of Swiss Anabaptists who were persecuted for their beliefs until granted refuge and religious liberty by William Penn in 1727. The Amish maintain a family-oriented society that emphasizes religious values, a simple agrarian lifestyle, separation from the non-Amish world, and a strong doctrine of mutual assistance (Amish Country News, 2010). The infirm and the mentally ill are looked after in the community rather than in institutions. The Amish people function "at the same unhurried pace as . . . their forefathers, using horses instead of automobiles, windmills instead of electricity, and facing death with the same religious tenets and steadfast faith of their fathers" (Bryer, 1977, p. 256).

The Amish way of life and death is clearly expressed in behavior associated with body disposal. Family members dress the deceased in white garments (Bryer, 1977):

> It is only at her death that an Amish woman wears a white dress with the cape and apron which were put away by her for the occasion of her death. This is an example of the lifelong preparation for the facing of death, as sanctioned by Amish society. The wearing of all white clothes signifies the high ceremonial emphasis on the death event as the final rite of passage into a new and better life (p. 254).

The funeral is very much a home-oriented event. A large room is cleared for the simple wooden coffin and the hundreds of friends, neighbors, and relatives who will soon visit. The coffin is placed in the center of the room; there are no adornments to distract from the basic fact of death. The funeral service is held in the house or barn, a practice of the Amish for many generations. Neighbors dig the grave, and all watch in silent prayer as the coffin is lowered and the grave filled with earth. Other families see to it that the mourners are fed. The Amish response to death is very much in keeping with the Amish way of life. This is expressed, for example, by the old woman who carefully washes, starches, and irons her own funeral clothing so it will be ready when the time comes. A death may occasion grief and lead to hardships for an Amish family like any others, but many of the doubts, tensions, and conflicts that have become commonplace in the

larger death system seem to be absent for these people, who have developed and perpetuated a distinctive lifestyle of their own.

Social Consolidation After Death

Death does not merely subtract an individual from society. It can also challenge society's ability to survive. In small societies, the impact of every death challenges the integrity of the entire group. In a mass society, this challenge becomes obvious only when death unexpectedly strikes down a powerful leader.

The terrorist attacks of September 11, 2001, had the short-term effect of bringing people together in grief, compassion, and determination. Before the terrorist attacks, there were the assassinations of John F. Kennedy, Martin Luther King Jr., and Robert Kennedy, which exemplified the types of death that shake even the largest and most powerful nations. Each of these men represented political power as well as something on a more personal and emotional level to millions of others. The manner of their deaths intensified the impact. The sudden, unexpected death of a significant person makes ordinary people feel vulnerable. Furthermore, each of these deaths was not only sudden but also violent, and not only violent but also intentional. People were shaken by the realization that even the most powerful among us were vulnerable.

One major function of the death system, then, is to meet the challenges posed to the individual and the group by loss of a member. This challenge may be of broad scope, as in a terrorist attack or the violent death of a powerful leader, or it can be as personal as a death in the family:

> The realtor's illness didn't appear serious, but he died a day after entering the hospital, even before testing could be completed. From that point on the family hardly seemed to be a family anymore. They went their own ways, found things to do that kept them from being home at the same time, and seldom took a meal together. At first the 16-year-old son appeared to be the least affected. He continued his usual routines, although he did spend even more time behind the closed door of his room. Within a few months, though, it was obvious that the young man was

really not doing so well after all. Most of the time he barely spoke, but then he would explode in anger without known reason and stalk away. An observant teacher noticed that the only time he mentioned his father he used the present tense, as though he were still alive.

This is an example of the temporary failure of social consolidation after a death. The family had fragmented, and relatives, friends, and neighbors had also failed to provide useful support. For contrast, consider again the Amish. Consistent with their general orientations toward life and death, the Amish provide direct and long-term support to those whose lives have been disrupted by the death of a loved one. It is not a case of many people coming by to express sympathy for a short period and subsequently disappearing; instead, relatives or friends may take over vital functions in the home for months, until the family can get back on its feet. Social consolidation after death is vital if the survivors are to continue as confident and competent members of the culture.

Making Sense of Death

Our efforts to explain death to each other represent another important function of the death system. Some explanations are handed down from generation to generation in the form of philosophical statements, poetry, and commentaries on holy scriptures. There are also famous last words and scenes that have been attributed (and often misattributed) to heroes, leaders, and other celebrated people of the past. Authentic last words seldom meet the listener's need to discover or affirm a coherent meaning of death (Kastenbaum, 1993a; 2002a).

Still other explanations are passed along informally within a particular subculture or family, or through successive *cohorts* in the military service or schools of nursing or medicine. "This is what we say and this is what we think and this is what we do." Nurses, physicians, clergy, funeral directors, insurance agents, and terrorists are socialized to express the attitudes and explanations of death that come with the trade.

Laconic statements such as "Nobody lives forever!" hardly qualify as explanations. However, much of our discourse on the subject of death is on this superficial level. Such statements might reduce the anxiety of the person who makes them through bridging what would otherwise be a tense and awkward silence. Perhaps hearing any words at all on the subject has some value to the recipient.

I spent several days in a hospital waiting area unobtrusively listening to conversations among visitors of terminally ill friends and relatives. The conversation was usually on other matters, and most of the death-oriented talk was limited to clichés. The visitors seldom, if ever, seemed to say anything new or thought provoking to each other—as if by mutual agreement. Nevertheless, there was some comfort taken and some comfort given, however, in exchanging words.

Consider the alternative. Not to have words spoken might confirm the fear that death is unspeakable, and, therefore, perhaps unthinkable as well. We would feel more helpless and alienated than ever. When we can at least go through the motions of exchanging words in this difficult situation, then we are showing the ability to function under stress. We are trying to make sense of death, and this mental and emotional activity helps keep us going.

At other times, however, we are not searching for just any words about death. We are looking for the most cogent and powerful understanding possible. The kind of explanation is related to the particular questions we have in mind. A child, a young adult, and an aged adult might have different questions in mind as well as different ways of evaluating possible answers. So, too, a person deeply rooted in Asian tradition and one with equally strong roots in the Western world are likely to differ in their approaches.

Making sense of death becomes an especially high-priority activity for us when a death undermines the basic way in which we interpret the world. Unexpected death, especially of a child, might shake our guiding assumptions about life. Most of us can easily call upon the range of explanations that are available to us within our particular death systems. It is more challenging, however, to examine the credentials of these various explanations and more challenging still to work toward our own explanations. Studies (Idler et al., 2009; Krause, 2009) are now finding support for the proposition that people who have a sense of meaning and purpose in their lives cope more effectively with stress and loss.

Killing

All death systems have another major function: killing. This function is carried out in many ways. *Capital punishment* has been practiced by many, but not all, cultures, with widely varying criteria for the conditions under which a person should be put to death. In recent years, there has been a general trend in Western nations to eliminate capital punishment. Ordinarily, only a few people have had their lives ended by this mode, although there have been episodes during which execution became a salient mode of death (e.g., the procession to the guillotine in the aftermath of the French Revolution). English criminal law, upon which much of our own legal system is founded, made death the punishment for an astonishing array of offenses—but, in practice, relatively few were actually executed. The death penalty conveys a mighty theme even when it is responsible for few deaths: This same society that on many occasions functions to protect and prolong life will on certain occasions act on behalf of death. Capital punishment is as susceptible to local circumstances and general social forces as any other function of the death system.

Individual states have varied both in the crimes that are punishable by death and the methods of execution. Hanging, once a common form of execution, is legal now only as an option in Montana and Washington. The firing squad, a dramatic remnant from the past, is still on the books in Idaho and Utah. There is no capital punishment at all in the District of Columbia, American Samoa, Guam, Puerto Rico, and the Virgin Islands, nor in the states of Alaska, Hawaii, Iowa, Maine, Massachusetts, Michigan, Minnesota, North Dakota, Rhode Island, Vermont, West Virginia, and Wisconsin. Some states have abolished capital punishment while their neighboring states have not (e.g., North Dakota and South Dakota). Additionally, there are differences in the types of crime that are punishable by death. In Missouri, for example, capital punishment applies to those who commit murder in the hijacking of public conveyances or who murder employees of correctional facilities. Maryland has a concise rule: Subject to the death penalty are those who commit "first degree murder,

either premeditated or during the commission of a felony." In contrast, Alabama lists "murder during kidnapping, robbery, rape, sodomy, burglary, sexual assault or arson; murder of a peace officer, correctional officer, or public official; murder while under a life sentence; contract murder; murder by a defendant with a previous murder conviction; murder of a witness to a crime."

A series of Supreme Court decisions from 1977 to 2005 had a strong impact on application of the death penalty in the United States (*http://www.law.cornell.edu/topics/death_penalty.html*):

- The death penalty is excessive punishment for the rape of an adult woman.
- Retarded criminals should not be executed because this practice constitutes "cruel and unusual punishment," as prohibited by the Eighth Amendment to the Bill of Rights.
- The death penalty can no longer be applied to juvenile offenders: teenagers have diminished culpability for their crimes because of their assumed lack of maturity, incomplete character development, and vulnerability to negative influences.
- The jury rather than the judge must make a finding of "aggravated factors" that would justify imposition of the death penalty rather than a lesser punishment.

The death penalty is only the most obvious example of the death system as killer. Any culture that is not thoroughly vegetarian is involved to some extent in killing for food. (And isn't pulling a turnip up by its roots also a form of killing?)

Living creatures may be killed for other reasons as well. The quest for fur and feathers has brought several species to the edge of extinction. The belief that the horn of the rhinoceros can bestow sexual powers has led to the profitable slaughter of many a beast. Hunting may be pursued as an exercise in skill, a proof of manhood, or just an excuse to be outdoors. There are also consequences when hunting is restricted or banned. The Inuits native to Canada were forced to abandon their long tradition of seal hunting and have since experienced significant difficulties as a society even though they have received some benefits in compensation: Their way of life has been undermined. It is probable that all societies have many adjustments to make when they decide to alter the killing function in their death systems.

Two forms of killing deserve special attention: warfare, and sacrifice.

War as a Function of Society

Warfare has brought death to millions through the centuries. Fundamental questions are raised about human nature. Are we killers at heart? Is there a deep-rooted aggressive instinct that must find expression in bloody triumphs? Or does war arise from situational pressures that could be reduced by improved knowledge, skills, and social organization? Does the commandment "Thou shalt not kill" express our real moral position, or is it undermined by a more basic conviction that we have the right to take the lives of others?

War has often been considered the natural state of affairs. It was taken for granted that one group would raid another's lands to steal the cattle and other valuables, and that the other group would retaliate as opportunities arose. Much of the routine fighting would take the form of raids and skirmishes. Killing and being killed were possible outcomes but not necessarily the main objectives. It was so much easier if we could surprise and scatter the enemy in order to loot at our leisure and return unharmed. However, there would also be raids of reprisal in which a previous death on one side would have to be avenged by killing somebody on the other side.

War also held true as a normal fact of life for the most sophisticated civilizations. The ancient Greek city-states were following the examples of their own gods when they took the field to sack and subdue another people. Had not their own deities triumphed over the Titans after the most awesome battles? Rome sent its legions on missions of conquest, and its successors, the Holy Roman Empire and the Byzantine Empire, both excelled in the military arts. Their holy men generally affirmed that deadly force was a right, indeed a responsibility, of the state. When the devout Thomas More published *Utopia* (1516) many centuries later, he affirmed the legitimacy of war and its attendant taking of life: The Utopian must simply perform in a thoughtful and cost-effective manner.

By the eighteenth century, a great philosopher, Immanuel Kant, wrote *Perpetual Peace* (1795/1932), convinced that peace is an absolute necessity and could be achieved by international organization and cooperation. Years later, however, Karl von Clausewitz (1832/1984) could still persuade many that the capacity to make war is vital to a nation's success. The psychological dimensions of war were examined in a memorable exchange of correspondence between Albert Einstein and Sigmund Freud (1933). The physicist believed that the most critical problem facing humanity was not the nature of the physical universe but our own propensity for violence. The psychoanalyst agreed that an aggressive instinct did exist and was not likely to be rooted out of our nature. He suggested, however, that we might learn to love the other in ourselves and ourselves in the other person—in other words, to experience and respect our common humanity.

Having survived "the war to end all wars," Freud believed that civilization had one more chance to channel its aggressive tendencies to constructive use. Alas, a few years later he was an old man dying in a foreign land (England) because the unthinkable Second World War had already flamed out from his own country to engulf the world. The physicist who had feared so deeply for our ability to survive our own warlike nature would soon be known as godfather of the nuclear bomb.

Examples can be found to support almost any theory of war and human violence. Religion, for example, has provided visions of universal human kinship and perpetual harmony—but also incitement for the most relentless and pitiless slaughter. War has taken the aspect of a rational instrument of state policy but also of a catastrophe we blunder into from time to time for any number of trivial reasons. No simple answer encompasses all the themes, motives, and events that have issued from warfare.

A DEADLY SPECIES

We have become ever more a deadly species as we have become more "civilized." The invention of the standing army, for example, made it possible to wage war in any season and extend the duration of the hostilities. The application of assembly line tactics for raising livestock ensures that astounding numbers of chickens are hatched each day (17 million is one estimate) and rapidly moved along from egg to fast food sandwich without ever having seen a barnyard. Improved technology has made it possible to conduct night warfare against each other and, as a spin-off, to increase the hunter's advantage over his prey. Killing on behalf of society or special interest groups is a function of the death system that thrives on organizational expertise.

The state's systematization of killing can be seen in the specification of precisely how executions are to be conducted in relationship to the crime. Consider the following verdict passed on a thirteenth-century Englishman (cited in Jankofsky, 1979):

> Hugh Dispenser the Younger . . . you are found as a thief, and therefore shall be hanged; and are found as a traitor, and therefore shall be drawn and quartered; and for that you have been outlawed by the king, and . . . returned to the court without warrant, you shall be beheaded and for that you abetted and procured discord between the king and queen, and others of the realm, you shall be embowelled, and your bowels burnt. Withdraw traitor, tyrant and so go take your judgment, attained wicked traitor (p. 49).

This example of "overkill" was not a random emotional outburst but a deliberate attempt to strengthen those in power. A respected individual who had taken the wrong (losing) side in a conflict or who was a member of the aristocracy might simply have his head severed. As a special privilege, the head of the executed might not be placed on a spike of the city gates. Capital punishment, then, could either inflict agony and heap disgrace on the condemned or be content with taking life but not reputation.

Killing by the death system—or, to put it another way, society turned killer—can take more subtle forms, and it is these forms that actually result in more deaths than capital punishment. Infant mortality in the United States, for example, has consistently been higher in families who live below the poverty level. Nonwhite subpopulations have an exceptionally higher risk, with respiratory illnesses being the most frequent specific cause of death. Excessive risk of death follows impoverished and socially disadvantaged people throughout their lives. For example, toxic waste dumps are often placed in areas whose residents are people who are already at greater than average risk for death because of poverty and discrimination. Whether or not the term kill is used, the outcome of systematic deprivation may be premature death.

Sacrifice: Killing for Life

Seldom if ever does a single function of the death system operate by itself. Sacrifice is a major example of several functions coming together with both death and life the intended outcomes.

Blood sacrifice has been an integral part of many world societies for about as long as historical record can tell us. Ancient sites in Asia, Europe, North Africa, and South America bear evidence of human sacrifice (Benson & Cook, 2001; Carrasco, 1999; Davies, 1981; Eliade, 1978; Green, 2001). Sacrifice was intended to persuade the gods to look with favor on their people. Often sacrifice was at the core of rituals to encourage fertile crops or protect against disaster. Sometimes the sacrifices were in the service of expeditions for conquest, war, or trade. Food, drink, objects, and animals were commonly dedicated to the gods, but human sacrifice was the most compelling offering.

Each society had its own configuration of beliefs and circumstances for sacrifice. Nevertheless, the core belief was that life can be traded for life if this transaction is mediated by death. Give the gods the vibrant lives they seek, and in return they may award continued life to society.

One of the most disturbing facets of human sacrifice was also one of the more common: the ritual murder of children. Skeletal remains of sacrificed children have been found enclosed within gates, walls, fortresses, and other structures. Child sacrifice is specified in Judeo-Christian history as well. The Book of Kings tells us that when Joshua destroyed Jericho he made an ominous prophecy. The man who dares to rebuild that city "shall lay the foundation stones thereof upon the body of his first born and in his youngest son shall he set up the gates thereof." This is precisely what happened, again, according to scriptures, when Heil sacrificed his oldest and youngest sons as he rebuilt Jericho. A central episode in religious history is Abraham's preparation to obey god by sacrificing his son, Isaac (who, at the last moment, is replaced by an animal). Less often discussed is the fate of Jephtha's daughter. Jephtha asked God for victory in battle, vowing that he would sacrifice the first living creature he saw when returning home. Upon his victorious return, Jephtha was greeted by his daughter. His daughter (whose name is not mentioned) became a burnt offering to God: No last-minute reprieve here.

Inca and Aztec rituals centered on the sacrifice of a great many people; new findings continue to be discovered (notably in Peru and northern Argentina). Young females were frequently the victims in Inca ceremonies; Aztec practices required such a large supply that their warriors were kept busy bringing back captives. Drinking the blood and eating the flesh of sacrificial victims were thought to transfer the vital energies of one person to another, while the heart and other choice offerings were dedicated to the gods. In other cultures, such as ancient China and Egypt, family, government officials, and household servants were entombed along with a deceased royal personage of the first rank, the better to continue their service and companionship in the next life.

Human sacrifice has diminished through the centuries. Human victims were replaced by animals and, then, often, by symbols, such as the small figurines placed in the later Egyptian tombs. How recently human sacrifices have been conducted and by whom is a matter of controversy. It is possible that occasional murder/sacrifices are still occurring at the hands of deranged people rather than established societies (Kastenbaum, 2002b).

DISASTERS AND THE DEATH SYSTEM

Was there a clear and timely *warning*? Had diligent measures been taken to *prevent* or limit the effects? These and all other functions of a society's death system are challenged when disaster threatens and strikes. Not least of the issues: what is the *meaning* of this disaster for who we are and how we move ahead? Every disaster has its unique aspects, but many disasters also have common features. Here we explore, review several of the many disasters that have stressed individuals and their societies.

The tsunami of December 26, 2004, resulted in enormous loss of life. The death toll has been estimated as within the 200,000 to 300,000 range. Furthermore, more than a million survivors were burdened with grief, and entire communities found themselves without residences and means of earning income. On August 23, 2005, the National Hurricane Center in Miami, Florida, issued an advisory about a weather system forming over the Bahamas, about 350 miles east. It was the twelfth tropical depression of the turbulent season. The storm strengthened to become Hurricane Katrina. It made land on the Gulf Coast the next day. In the midst of widespread destruction, New Orleans mayor Ray Nagin estimated that as many as 10,000 people might have died.

How did these two societies attempt to cope with these onslaughts? Tables 3-1 and 3-2 summarize the events.

Tsunami: A Stealth Wave and Its Impact

Tsunami comes from the pairing of the Japanese words for harbor (*tsu*) and wave (*nami*). It has often been described as a "tidal wave" but has little to do with tidal rhythms. A peculiarity of the tsunami is that it can pass without notice in the sea because of its very long wavelength, but it becomes a powerful destructive force as it becomes concentrated in the shallows approaching landfall.

There was no general warning of the killer tsunami of December 26, 2004, although at least one villager recognized the danger at the last moment and was able to save almost all his neighbors (Herman, 2005). This could be regarded as a major failure of the death system in nations bordering the Indian Ocean: Indonesia, India, Sri Lanka, Thailand, Malaysia, Somalia, Kenya, and Tanzania. This would not be a fair assessment, however. Devastating tsunamis are rare. It is difficult to maintain a high state of alertness for a rare catastrophe. Learning from disaster is perhaps a more appropriate measure of a death system's effectiveness. Within six months of the tsunami, plans were well advanced for an early warning system (Kettlewell, 2005, June 24). A network of monitoring technology for the Indian Ocean has been linked to an international web of warning centers. It should be possible to provide quick alarms and communications.

The tsunami itself could not have been prevented by any known technology. The fishing villages and occasional tourist destinations along the Indian Ocean coast have relied primarily on

TABLE 3-1 *The Tsunami and the Death System*

Function	Comment
Warning and predicting	No general warning or prediction and no preparation for same.
Preventing	The tsunami could not have been prevented, but thousands of lives could have been saved by an effective warning system.
Caring for the dying	Most died within a few minutes or escaped. Few were dying after the sudden catastrophe.
Disposing of the dead	Finding and identifying the dead were difficult and frustrating efforts, only partially successful.
Social consolidation after death	Total or near loss of entire families and communities limited intimate support, as did prevalence of other survivors with their own grief and needs.
Making sense of death	Generally recognized as an act of nature and a risk associated with coastal living.
Killing	No killing directly associated with the tsunami, but preexisting political violence continued in some areas.

TABLE 3-2 *Hurricane Katrina and the Death System*

Function	Comment
Warning and predicting	• Long-standing recognition of vulnerability. • Clear advance warning of impending disaster.
Preventing	• Hurricane itself could not be prevented. • Loss of life, social disorganization, and massive property destruction could have been sharply reduced by improved advance planning and emergency response.
Caring for the dying	• Medical care interrupted and undermined by damage to hospitals and communications.
Disposing of the dead	• Delay in recovering bodies; major problems in identifying corpses.
Social consolidation after death	• Community support shattered by evacuation, scattering of family members, limited response by overwhelmed human service agencies.
Making sense of death	• Intense criticism of governmental agencies whose alleged failures contributed to death and destruction.
Killing	• Reports of a spike in lethal violence were later found to be inaccurate.

their own traditional efforts with less expectation of technological solutions, and survivors did not blame anybody for the failure to predict or prevent the disaster. Although the tsunami could not have been prevented, improved recognition and communication could have saved many lives, and emergency education programs have since been established.

Care of the dying is a crucial function of the death system. However, although many people were killed by the tsunami, few people were injured or dying. The tsunami was ruthlessly exact in its selection of victims; most people either drowned or escaped unhurt.

The 9/11 terrorist attacks on the United States (Chapter 8) also resulted in swift death, with very few injured or dying survivors. In both instances, much of the effort turned immediately to identifying victims and disposing appropriately of their remains. Many victims of the tsunami and of 9/11 could not be identified, although for different reasons. The bodies of tsunami victims that were found could have been the source of dangerous contagions. Additionally, the lack of safe drinking water and adequate sanitation could have opened the way to epidemics of life-threatening diseases, such as cholera and typhoid. Local authorities and international assistance averted these threats with prompt attention to the human remains, provision of safe drinking water, and immunizations. Competent attention to the dead almost certainly saved lives.

The memorialization process was limited by the fact that so many family and friends who would have participated in these events had themselves perished. The overall process of social consolidation after death could not readily follow traditional practices because the local communities with their support potential had been seriously damaged and, in some cases, completely destroyed.

Another challenge: how could the survivors again become part of a viable community? Displaced children, many of them orphaned, were given a place in schools that immediately offered emotional support and a sense of belongingness, along with useful activity. Often the men from the affected areas were either farming in high country or fishing well offshore when the tsunami occurred. In either case, they were spared the disaster. Their wives, sisters, and mothers, along with many children, were in the tsunami path. Husbands suddenly found themselves widowers. They experienced intense grief—but also a sense of disorientation. These were "family men." Life without their wives and other family members was terribly incomplete and baffling: These rugged men had to grapple with unfamiliar roles, dependent on one another and uncertain about what would come next. With their families gone, some said their lives lost purpose (Nakashima, 2005, January 25, p. A01). Nevertheless, many of the men did find ways to reconstitute their lives. This process involved more bonding and sharing with each other and also a gradual reaching out to find other possible wives and construct other families.

Making sense of death is sometimes the most difficult challenge. Genocide and other acts of violence have often caused people to question their basic assumptions about God, justice, and their fellow humans. This existential anxiety does not seem to have afflicted most of the tsunami survivors. They know the disaster was not devised by enemies, nor was it God's punishment for some sin or failing. It was just a terrible thing that happened to happen. The fact that many people were in the same situation had some supportive value.

The tsunami took many lives, but the death system itself did not become a killer. Or did it? There have been charges that much of the international aid was siphoned off by rich and powerful people, seldom reaching the poverty stricken and those most in need. What is clear is that violence did continue between governmental and rebel factions in some of the affected regions, even though efforts were made to call a truce until the crisis had been controlled.

The fact that the international community did respond with human services and supplies after the tsunami suggests that compassion does continue to cross boundaries in this world, despite all the personal agendas and competing interests.

Hurricane Katrina

Fortunately, the death toll from Hurricane Katrina was well below the early estimates, which are often unreliable in disaster reports. Even so, many died. Louisiana suffered 1,035 storm-related fatalities, Mississippi had 228, Florida 14, Alabama 2, Georgia 2 (AP MAINSTREAM, 2005). Conflicting interpretations of the disaster and intense criticism of government response became the dominant story in national media.

Experts in atmospheric disturbances were alarmed about the possibility of this particular tropical depression transforming itself into a colossal hurricane a month before it struck the Gulf Coast (Revkin, 2005). A week before the impact, local, state, and federal agencies heard reports that Katrina could be the long-feared "big one" that could destroy New Orleans. Nonstop conference calls were made to confirm that all emergency plans were in place, and National Guard troops outside of Louisiana were placed on ready alert (Zwerling & Sullivan, 2005). Some observers would later comment that Hurricane Katrina was the most predicted natural disaster in history.

The storm reached the Gulf Coast on August 29. The levees protecting New Orleans had been rated as able to withstand up to a category 3 hurricane (i.e., one with sustained winds up to 130 miles per hour). Katrina was widely reported to be a category 4 hurricane when it hit New Orleans: sustained winds up to 155 miles per hour. Actually, though, data later showed that Katrina's diminished power made it a category 3 storm when it reached landfall, and that it might have further weakened when it punched through New Orleans' levees and flooded most of the city (Kaye, 2005). St. Bernard Parish was quickly under 10 feet of water.

Most residents of New Orleans tried to obey the mayor's announcement of mandatory evacuation. Roads were jammed. Some people chose not to leave, however, and others had no means of transportation. Residents of low-income areas were the most likely to become trapped. The media raised the issue of racism: persistent conditions that were seen as marginalizing blacks were blamed for blacks' higher risk in a disaster situation.

Over the next several days, it became evident that the situation within New Orleans was out of control. Efforts to plug the levee breaches were not successful, so the flood continued. A patchwork of rescue teams in boats and helicopters was working hard to find and liberate people trapped by the toxic waters with their mix of biological and chemical pollutants. Thousands of people found their way to the Superdome. A typical report of the situation that developed there:

> They had flocked to the arena seeking sanctuary from the winds and waters of Hurricane Katrina. But understaffed, undersupplied, and without air conditioning or even much lighting, the domed stadium quickly became a sweltering and surreal vault, a place of overflowing toilets and no showers. Food and water, blankets and sheets, were in short supply. . . . By Wednesday, the stink was staggering. Heaps of rotting garbage in bulging white plastic bags baked under a blazing Louisiana sun on the main entry plaza, choking new arrivals as they made their way into the stadium after being plucked off rooftops and balconies. "They're housing us like animals," said an Army veteran, dripping with perspiration, unable to contain her fury and disappointment (Treaster, 2005, p. 1).

The extensive media coverage documented rooftop rescues, but also corpses that nobody had time to remove. Police and other security personnel were seldom on the scene. It would later be confirmed that 249 of the city's 1,500 police officers had abandoned their posts during the emergency (Bolstad & Spangler, 2005). There were also alarming reports of widespread violence—snipers firing at rescue helicopters, murderous gangs, child rape. These reports proved to be unfounded, suggesting that the media had accepted rumors without adequate investigation (Tribune Wire Services, 2005; Wester, 2005). The news cameras repeatedly documented an apparent disconnect between the distress and outrage of people trapped in the city and the bland and hesitant response of local and federal officials. It would be nearly a week before personnel and supplies arrived in force to the shattered city. Questions of who was to blame for what soon became leading political issues. There was no question, however, about the inefficiency of the overall response effort in the critical first week. "Crisis and Chaos: New Orleans' Descent into Despair" (Thomas, 2005) was not an exaggerated title for a magazine article. The people caught up in the catastrophe had reason to believe that bureaucracy itself had contributed much to the risk and suffering.

Many survivors of the storm remained anxious about the fate of family and friends whose safety and whereabouts were still unknown. Parents sought out their children, and children searched for their parents. Many had deaths to mourn. Many had lost homes, neighbors, schooling, church, employment—so much of what had connected them to their personal worlds. Post-traumatic stress disorder (Chapter 11) afflicted some of people who were exposed to extreme stress.

Hurricane Katrina and the Death System

The response of the U.S. death system to the threat and then the reality of a massive Gulf Coast hurricane is hinted at in Table 3-2. It would take a book of its own to describe and draw lessons from this catastrophe. I offer three key points that are worth keeping in mind:

- *Frame of reference*—everyday or emergency? Most of us most of the time operate within our everyday frame of reference. We sort of know what to expect and what to do. Paramedics, firefighters, and other people who have training and experience in coping with life-or-death situations often have domesticated the emergency frame of reference. They can switch quickly and efficiently into emergency mode. People in a fragile emotional condition tend to operate as though "ordinary" situations are threats and emergencies—and sometimes they are more perceptive than those who are dulled into routine. Organizations as well as individuals tend to slip into a self-perpetuating everyday frame of reference. ("This is how we always do things.")

- *Switching into emergency mode has its cost.* We must put aside our routines, obligations, and pleasures. Furthermore, we are also admitting to vulnerability, as well as taking the risk that it is really not much of an emergency at all, so we will just look foolish. It is also difficult to sustain the vigilance and activation over a period of time. A crucial question, therefore, is: Who will switch to an emergency framework under what circumstances? For residents of New Orleans, there had been hurricanes and hurricanes, and people kept surviving them. Officials had often taken this attitude as well. It would be expensive to upgrade the levees and upgrade other protective measures. The very fact that one had not yet fallen victim to catastrophe deadened the survival impulse. Previously, many Galveston, Texas, residents also had ignored evacuation announcements, and on one day—September 8, 1900—8,000 died as a result. When should we hold onto our everyday frame of reference, and when should we switch to emergency mode?

- *Turf issues: Who is in charge here?* Survivors of the tsunami for the most part had to rely on themselves. By contrast, the response to Hurricane Katrina involved a large number of local, state, and federal agencies. Each of these agencies had its own mission and internal hierarchy. Ongoing relationships among the agencies were not necessarily close and amiable. Many of the documented failures to respond promptly and effectively were related to the drag of the bureaucratic process and to uncertainty and conflict regarding each agency's responsibilities and authority. As organizations increase in size and become arrayed in hierarchic ranks, it becomes difficult to respond to emerging situations. How can organizations intended to protect lives learn to

cooperate for the common cause instead of becoming caught up in turf wars? This is another question that deserves better answers, as well as more application of knowledge that has already been gained.

- *Community and place can make the critical difference in emergency situations.* New Orleans, for example, is not a generic Any City. It is distinctive for its location, history, ethnic mix, and vibrant culture. Outsiders can make significant errors, as in assuming that low-income people experience themselves as victims mired in poverty, when in fact they have a secure sense of place and meaning. Scholar and New Orleans native Judith Wester (2005) offers the example of military crashing through front doors to rescue the inhabitants for their own good.

Why did they not simply knock on the door and say: "We do not understand this area, we need your help in saving it. Can you guide us?" In this way they could have engaged the inhabitants in their own salvation rather than condemn them with their beliefs and attitudes about poverty.

Fortunately, there were also many instances of compassionate and effective response in both societies. Volunteer nurses and Red Cross workers were among those who worked tirelessly under stressful circumstances to help injured and distraught survivors. Cities across the nation provided housing and other assistance, including employment and schooling opportunities, for people forced out of their communities. Some lessons were learned—and quickly (Gibbs, 2005).

A Cyclone and Two Earthquakes

Thousands died on May 8, 2008, as a powerful earthquake destroyed schools and other structures in the Chengdu region of China. On the same day, a cyclone ravaged the west coast of Myanmar (Burma), also taking thousands of lives. In both disasters, many deaths were swift; other victims needed to be rescued and given medical treatment if they were to survive. The Chinese government responded immediately and in-depth. More than 100,000 soldiers were sent for rescue efforts. Hospitals and other local service providers quickly moved into action, supported by throngs of

An impoverished Pakistani family struggles through flood waters after torrential rains force them to leave their homes.

volunteers and generous donations. Coming to the aid of the earthquake victims was clearly the number one national priority. By contrast, the ruling military regime of Myanmar ignored the catastrophe and instead went ahead with a dubious election to extend and strengthen its power. Orphaned and homeless children were evicted from shelters so they could be used for the referendum. There followed weeks of frustration and anguish as the regime blocked most relief efforts while victims struggled for survival. Preventing death, caring for the suffering, and reconstructing a damaged society was a much lower priority than a dictatorial regime's self-interest.

Still another type of situation developed when Haiti was devastated by an earthquake on January 10, 2010. The death toll has been estimated at 200,000. The capital city of Port-au-Prince was reduced to ruins, and an estimated 3 million people lost their homes and livelihoods. This catastrophe happened in a nation that was already impoverished, crime-ridden, and without effective government (Smith, 2010). There were pressing needs: evacuating and feeding the survivors, and burying the dead. A safe water supply was also of high priority to prevent widespread disease. It soon became evident that heightened security was also required: earthquake victims were becoming targets for kidnapping and rape. Leaders emerged within Haiti and the international response was vigorous at first, but then faded as the media moved on to other events. The earthquake and its aftershocks were the primary source of trauma, but an already dysfunctional nation had to rely on the compassion of others to make it through the immediate crisis and support the rebuilding.

Flood: Pakistan

Floods are seasonal expectations in Pakistan and many other places, but few people, if any were prepared for the slow, relentless, and all-encompassing onslaught that started early in August 2010:

> The water came in the morning, quietly sweeping across the rice paddies and into the village. Within hours, it was as high as a man's shoulder and Abdul Nabi had lost his harvest, his mud home, and all 10 of his buffalo. It had barely been raining at all. Weeks after massive downpours first battered northern Pakistan, submerging tens of thousands of square miles, killing about 1,500 people and leaving millions homeless, those floodwaters are still sweeping downriver and through the south, adding one more layer of misery to people long accustomed to hardship (Sullivan, 2010).

The misery referred to by Sullivan includes oppression and neglect from a corrupt political establishment, a succession of bloody insurgencies, and military coups. About a third of its 170 million people lived in poverty, and the farmers had just spent years of exhaustive struggle with low rainfall that threatened crops and survival. That popular term "infrastructure" scarcely applied to a largely illiterate and abandoned population. Practically all they had managed to save was being swept away by the flood.

How did the world community respond to this disaster? In some ways the response was immediate and vigorous, e.g., international aid groups moved into position and did what they could with the resources at hand; fund-raising campaigns were launched. There was, however, a huge disconnect between public perception and actual magnitude of the disaster. Much of the hesitation to respond fully had to do with the nature of the disaster itself. Storms and earthquakes strike immediately and are readily visualized. Floods also can strike quickly, but they are also inclined to continue for some time, as was the case in Pakistan. Lethal effects can also occur after the flood has retreated from its crest, e.g., water-borne disease, malnutrition, and the erosion of social support systems.

Many of us had difficulty in comprehending the scope of the disaster—miles and miles of land now covered by deep water; whole villages vanished. We might also have resisted aiding a nation that was so often in the news for its reputed ties to terrorists and inclination to siphon away funds given for humanitarian purposes. Disasters take many forms and all societies are vulnerable, but the "same" event can have profoundly different consequences, depending on tradition, resources, reputation, and spirit. Japan, devastated by earthquake, tsunami, and nuclear radiation hazard on March 11, 2011 , is still on the difficult road toward recovery. This includes not only the massive needs for physical reconstruction, but also the long-cherished worldview that has seen Japan through the centuries.

Disaster Research

There is much more to be learned about disaster prevention and short- and long-term response. Fortunately, this has become a committed topic for international research (e.g., Gulberson, 2010; Hyndman & Hyndman, 2010; Keller & Blodgett, 2010). One of the most promising areas of research focuses on best treatment for disaster victims. For example, a team of Chinese bioscientists (Wen et al., 2009) has improved the identification of infection risk, and others (e.g., Kahn et al., 2009) have demonstrated the need for improved evaluation of the triage procedure in prioritizing victims to be treated. It remains to be seen how readily health and social service providers will make use of the emerging findings and insights.

HOW OUR DEATH SYSTEM HAS BEEN CHANGING— AND THE "DEATHNIKS" WHO ARE MAKING A DIFFERENCE

We have completed an overview of the death system, with particular attention to the United States. Now we ask where this system has been and where it is going. We begin with the kinds of people who have emerged as counselors, educators, researchers, and change agents in the death system.

Changing Ways of Life, Changing Ways of Death

There is a strong connection between ways of life and ways of death in every culture in every epoch. (For useful historical examples, see Aries, 1981; Eire, 1995; Huizinga, 1926/1996; Laungani,1996.)

Here we use a more narrow focus. First, we will identify one of the main influences on death systems throughout history—the ways in which people died. In the next section, we see how the deathniks and thanatology (the study of death) have emerged and contributed to the current death system.

Many societies have been dominated by a particular image of death. I have noticed that these images of death are influenced by the types of catastrophic dying with which a society has become intimately familiar. Table 3-3 presents some of the major forms of catastrophic dying that human societies have been experiencing through the centuries, along with the markers and signifiers associated with each (Kastenbaum, 1993b).

For example, tuberculosis was a realistic source of intense anxiety from the nineteenth century and well into the twentieth century. People who felt helpless as loved ones lost their vitality, suffered, became emaciated, and died also had reason to fear that they might have the same fate as a result of a disease that is more readily contagious than AIDS. The avoidance of death that became so entrenched

in our culture was certainly influenced by experiences with people who died the harrowing death of a tuberculosis victim. We have already touched on one of the forms of dying that is making an impact on our current death system—the persistent vegetative state (Chapter 1). Our feelings and ideas about death often are influenced by what we know or think we know about how people die. As one or another mode of dying becomes more prominent in society, the death system is likely to change in response. Similarly, as sociocultural conditions change, the types of death that are most prominent are also likely to change. There may be no logical connection between how people die and what death means. Nevertheless, we are all likely to be influenced by the circumstances that surround death.

Yesterday, the death systems of most societies were organized around the prospect of death at an early age as a result of contagious diseases and infections. Many did not survive childhood (Lundgren & Houseman, 2010). The dead were also more of a presence, as corpse, as ancestor participating in everyday life, and as ghost. Kearl

TABLE 3-3 *Modes of Dying and the Images of Death They Have Encouraged*

Condition	Markers and Signifiers
The Black Death	Agony, disfiguration, partial decomposition while still alive, putrefaction > human vanity and pride, punished and abandoned by God.
Syphilis	Facial disfiguration, dementia, moral degradation > wages of sin.
Tuberculosis	Death steals our breath; blood flows from our bodies, which increasingly become skeletonized > curse of the cities and factories, but also romantic exit for beautiful, brilliant, doomed youth.
Live Burial	Imagined and occasionally actual fate of some who fainted, seized, or otherwise lost consciousness > terror of life in death.
Cancer	Pain, anxiety, body damage, and distortion >insidious attack by an enemy from within.
Persistent Vegetative State	Profound helplessness, inability to think or act on one's own behalf > terror of death in life.
AIDS	Symptoms and stigma of many of the earlier forms of catastrophic dying—blood and body fluid related, disfiguration, dementia, skeletonization, respiratory distress, plus linkage with taboo sexuality > Death encompasses the most frightening experiences and outcomes that have ever haunted the imagination.

Source: Kastenbaum (1993b, pp. 84–85).

(2010, p. 48) reflects on how the dead have been banished from symbolic partnership with the living and from active memory.

> With lives no longer ending "prematurely" to the unprepared, the ghostly embodiments of social frustrations occasioned by incompletely lived lives have largely disappeared. The dead, like the contemporary old, supposedly occupy a "roleless role."

Nevertheless, Kearl suggests that at least a few of the dead, notably celebrities, or those who have died in interesting ways, have been embraced by the media:

> Prime-time television is full of programs and commercials featuring spirits, channeling mediums, angels, and dissected corpses (p. 47).

Today many deaths are related to lifestyle (smoking, drinking, murder, suicide, motor vehicle accidents). Conditions associated with advanced age have also become salient.

Rising expectations for a long life can lead to a moment of shock and confusion when people do die "before their time." In the past, it was living the long life that seemed remarkable.

The Beginnings of Death Education, Research, and Counseling

The death system in the United States (and in many other nations) was once devoted to avoiding even the thought of death. This situation started to change after the end of World War II. The reality of violent death could not easily be denied, nor the loss and grief experienced by survivors. Reflective people wondered anew about this strange race known as *Homo sapiens* that periodically devotes its resources and passions to killing each other. People of religious faith were hard-pressed to discover purpose, redeeming value, and God's love and mercy in a slaughterhouse world. There arose insistent questions about the meaning of life, death, and personal responsibility. Perhaps we had to come to terms with death in order to live a coherent and positive life.

There was also an increasing awareness of the private sorrows many people experienced. Many had to remain silent about their grief because there were few people who were willing and able to listen. Mental health specialists started to recognize that unresolved grief was a major factor in some behavioral and emotional problems.

Meanwhile, another massive problem was also working its way to the surface. People who would have died quickly of virulent diseases and uncontrolled infections made prompt recoveries with the newly developed antibiotic and other "wonder drugs." However, biomedical advances had achieved only limited results with other life-threatening conditions, such as many types of cancer and progressive neurological disorders. More and more people were therefore being maintained in the borderlands between life and death, often suffering pain, social isolation, and despair. The state of the art in medicine could not restore health, but it could keep people alive in stressful circumstances. Some health care professionals and members of the general public became distressed and outraged by this situation. Why should people be made to suffer in this way—especially in a society that considers itself humane and technologically competent?

These were some of the issues that forced themselves into public and professional awareness. Instrumental in this movement were people from various backgrounds who broke through the taboo against acknowledging death. There were few if any "experts" in death half a century ago (although there were people with skills in specific areas, such as the funeral director). The people who taught the first classes on dying and death had never taken such courses themselves. The people who provided counseling to dying or grieving people had never received professional training for these services. The people who designed and conducted the first research projects likewise had to develop their own methods, theories, and databases. Included among these people were anthropologists, clergy, nurses, physicians, psychologists, sociologists, and social workers. Many had to overcome deeply entrenched resistances before they could offer educational or therapeutic services or gain entry for research. These pioneers of thanatology were hardy people, however, and gradually made themselves understood and welcome in many quarters. Some described themselves as thanatologists (from the Greek, *thanatos*, for death); others smiled and accepted the appellation deathnik. Mostly, they did not believe that a whole new profession had to be created. Instead, the mission was to bring concern for the human encounter with mortality into the awareness of caregivers, educators, and researchers within existing disciplines. The "nurse-thanatologist," for example, must first be a knowledgeable and skillful nurse. Few workers in this field would claim that the mission has been fully accomplished, but there is a growing cadre of people with expertise to give a hand. We will catch up again with the deathniks in later chapters.

CAUSES OF DEATH: YESTERDAY, TODAY, AND TOMORROW

A child born in the United States in 1900 had a life expectancy of about 47 years, a little more if a female, but considerably less (about 33 years) if "Black and other." By the middle of the twentieth century, life expectancy at birth had increased about another 20 years for citizens of all racial backgrounds. We offer here a digestible helping of statistics that also includes life expectancy information at several other ages. Table 3-4 displays two patterns that have existed since the modern era of population statistics:

- Females have a longer life expectancy than males from birth onward.
- Whites have a longer life expectancy than blacks from birth onward.
  Other significant patterns:
- Life expectancy continues to increase in the United States at all age levels—even at 100!—and for both race categories that are in common use. (The broad white/black categorization is flawed but still often relied on.)

What about the rest of the world? By the start of the twenty-first century, newborns in developed nations had a life expectancy of about 75 years and upward, increasing at various ages, as in the United States. Unfortunately, life expectancy in less developed nations has remained significantly lower, as documented in Table 3-5. The outlook could worsen even further if HIV-AIDS continues to spread, not only claiming lives directly but also contributing to the breakdown of societal and family functioning. Obviously, conditions of life have much to do with length of life.

TABLE 3-4 *Life Expectancy in the United States by Age, Sex, and Race*

Life expectancy at birth	White	Black	All races
Female	.5	76.1	80.1
Male	.4	69.2	74.8
Both Sexes	.0	72.8	77.6
Life expectancy at age 20			
Female	.9	57.5	
Male	.9	50.9	
Both Sexes	.5	54.3	
Life expectancy at age 40			
Female	.7	38.6	
Male	.3	33.1	
Both Sexes	.6	36.0	
Life expectancy at age 80			
Female	9.6	9.8	
Male	.0	8.0	
Both Sexes	.0	9.2	

Source: National Vital Statistics Reports (2005). "All races" data for years other than birth not presently available.

TABLE 3-5 *Life Expectancy at Birth in World Regions*

Area	All	Females	Males
Africa		55	52
Asia	67	68	65
Developed nations		79	72
Europe		78	74
Latin America (and Caribbean)		74	68
Less developed nations		66	63
North America		80	74
World		69	65

Source: World Health Organization, Population Reference Bureau (2004).

It has been estimated that 1.5 billion people live in poverty, 830 million are chronically malnourished, a billion lack clean drinking water, and 3 billion lack adequate sanitation—nearly half the world's population (Turner, 2003). Malaria remains a scourge in tropical nations, but perhaps will be controlled by preventive measures that are gradually taking effect. Political instability and violence could be added to that list of conditions that foreshorten the lives of a great many people throughout the world.

BASIC TERMS AND CONCEPTS

Several terms and concepts are used frequently in presenting mortality data. *Mortality* refers to deaths, as distinguished from *morbidity*, which refers to illness. Here are several other key terms and concepts:

Life expectancy: The estimated number of years remaining in a person's life at a particular time. It is usually computed from date of birth, but any other time period can be substituted (e.g., life expectancy after retirement) Keep in mind that half of the population is expected to live longer and half is expected to live shorter lives than, say, the mythical average person.

Longevity: The average number of years between birth and death. This statistic is based on lives that have ended, as distinguished from life expectancy, an estimate of years yet to be lived. From the standpoint of geneticists, longevity is also regarded as the upper limit for survival for a particular species.

Cause of death: This determination is made by a physician and recorded on the death certificate. There are three general categories: degenerative biological conditions, disease, and socioenvironmental (such as accident, suicide, and murder). In practice, these categories may overlap, and the completeness and accuracy of cause of death information is subject to question.

Mortality rate (also known as death rate): This is a measure of the proportion of people who have died within a particular time period to the number of people in the population. The mortality rate is calculated on the basis of number of deaths either per 1,000 individuals or per 100,000 individuals within a one-year period unless otherwise specified. It is important not to confuse the mortality rate with a percentage. For example, in 2003, the mortality rate for motor vehicle accidents in the United States was 16.1. This does not mean that 16.1 percent of the population died in motor vehicle accidents in that year—that would be death on a catastrophic scale. It means that in a population of more than 250 million, there were 41,426 deaths from this cause: still alarming, but very different from the toll that would have been exacted from a percentage of 15.2. *Crude death rate (CDR):* A measure that does not control for age. It is simply the total number of deaths divided by the number of people in a population. Much of the readily available data are in the form of CDR—the easiest and least expensive kind of information to obtain. It is also the easiest kind of information to misinterpret. The number of deaths in a population is affected by the age structure. The United States today, for example, has a much higher proportion of long-lived people today than was the case at the turn of the century. The CDR in the United States has continued to decline.

Age-standardized mortality rate (ASMR): The ASMR does make adjustments for age. When data are presented in this form, we can make more reliable comparisons between the death rates of various populations, or even the same nation, at different times. Developing nations, for example, often have a higher proportion of younger people because fewer reach the advanced adult years. Their death rate from cancer is likely to be lower but mainly because many die of other causes first.

For the United States, census data provide the most comprehensive and accurate information on causes and rates of death. These data themselves age somewhat in the 10 years between census reports; so the most recent data available often go back about several years.

With this background information in mind, we can now look at changing patterns of mortality.

Leading Causes of Death in the United States Today

There have been changes not only in the death rate but also in the most common causes of death. In 1900, pneumonia and influenza (considered together) and tuberculosis were the two leading causes of death, almost equal in their toll. The third most common cause of death at this time was a set of intestinal illnesses in which diarrhea and enteritis were frequent symptoms. Twenty years later, these intestinal maladies vanished from the list of major causes of death and never returned. Pneumonia/influenza still topped the list—in fact, the nation and much of the world were still trying to recover from a devastating epidemic of influenza. Tuberculosis was still a major threat to life, but its death toll had declined markedly (from 194.4 to 113.1 per 100,000 between 1900 and 1920).

By 1940, heart disease had become the leading cause of death in the United States, and so it has remained. Why? Fewer people are dying young of infectious diseases. This means that more people are living long enough to develop physical problems in various organ systems, many of these problems having an impact on the functioning of the heart and of the entire cardiovascular system. Additionally, changes in the diet, activity, and stress patterns put more people at risk for heart problems—a risk that in more recent years is being reduced by increased attention to diet and exercise.

Cancer is another condition that people become more vulnerable to with increasing adult age. By 1940, cancer had become the second most common cause of death in the United States, and this also remains true today. The emergence of cancer cannot be attributed entirely to the "graying" of the population, however. For example, the use of tobacco products is linked to lung cancer as well as to a variety of other life-threatening conditions. Lung cancer is the number one cause of cancer deaths. Nearly 100,000 men and more than 60,000 women die of lung cancer each year. Cancer death rates for children have been reduced by an estimated 60 percent since 1950, with slighter declines for young and middle-aged adults. The death rate has increased somewhat for older adults and is increasing markedly for African American males for reasons not yet determined.

From Crisis to Lingering Trajectory

The pathway from health to death has lengthened for many people. Biographies, memoirs, and novels written a hundred or more years ago often depict people going through intense life-or-death crises. People would either die or pull through within a matter of days, and there was not much the physician could do in most cases, except to join in the prayers. In our own times, people often live for years with a life-threatening condition (see "The Lingering Trajectory," Chapter 4). The protracted and uncertain course of heart disease and cancer has even unsettled the way in which we speak of the at-risk person. Is this woman "dying" if, in fact, she operates a business from her home and continues to do much of the child care? Is this man "terminally ill" if he gets by with just a little assistance here and there and still enjoys a rewarding family life? Both people are afflicted with the condition that will probably be cited eventually as cause of death. Although it is likely that their lives are being foreshortened, they do not function from day to day as "terminally ill" or "dying" persons. Essentially, they are people who are trying to make the best of their lives under difficult circumstances.

We may also think of people in their late 80s or 90s who are alert and active yet frail. These people also are not terminally ill or dying, and it would be inappropriate to apply these terms to them. They, too, are trying to make the best of each day for as long as they can. We need to develop a new vocabulary and new concepts for describing the slow procession from vigorous life to death. A simple dying/not dying distinction is not very useful in a society in which so many people move through life resourcefully despite a variety of stresses and constraints.

Changes in causes of death and mortality rates have many implications for the way we interpret and respond to people who are at a particular risk for their lives. With these considerations in mind, we now check on major causes of death in the United States (Table 3-6).

Alzheimer's disease has become one of the leading causes of death as the population continues to age. Heart disease, cancer, stroke, influenza and pneumonia, and homicide have become somewhat less frequent causes of death. It should be kept in mind, however, that many people live with Alzheimer's for years, at various levels of functioning.

What Will Be the Cause of My Death?

This is a question we might prefer not to ask. However, as students of thanatology, perhaps we should inform ourselves regarding the leading causes of death at a particular time of life. The three leading causes of death for young adults are

TABLE 3-6 *The 12 Leading Causes of Death in the United States*

Cause	Rate	Deaths
1. Heart disease	247.8	700,142
2. Cancer	196.0	553,768
3. Cerebrovascular*	57.9	163,538
4. COPD**	43.7	123,013
5. Accidents	35.7	101,537
6. Diabetes mellitus	25.3	71,372
7. Pneumonia, Flu	22.0	62,034
8. Alzheimer's disease	19.1	53,852
9. Kidney disease	14.0	39,480
10. Septicemia	11.4	32,238
11. Suicide	10.7	30,622
12. Liver disease	9.5	27,035

*"Stroke" and related conditions.
**Chronic obstructive pulmonary disease.
Source: National Vital Statistics Reports (2005).

the result of human decisions and actions. Here is a golden opportunity for reducing the risk of death by improving our decision making. Accidents and suicide continue to be among the highest death risks for adults who are 25 to 44 years old. Teen drivers and their passengers are at special risk: nine teens a day die as a result of motor vehicle accidents (CDC, 2010). From that point on, heart disease and cancer become the leading causes of death. Young adults might take a moment to appreciate their low overall death rate: a look ahead makes it clear that the risk increases markedly in future years.

Causes of Death in the Future?

Public health advances have tamed some of the threats to life that ravaged world populations throughout history. Antibiotics have saved many lives from infections that previously would have been fatal. Yellow fever, malaria, cholera, typhoid, plague, diphtheria, tuberculosis, and small pox are among the contagions repeatedly afflicting society, especially deadly for infants, young children,

and elders. These diseases have been brought under various levels of control in developed nations. However, people in some regions remain highly vulnerable to epidemics. Malnutrition, unsafe water, lack of medical services, and the stress of violence often lower resistance to a wide variety of illnesses.

Diseases can now spread rapidly through the world, so that an illness once restricted to a small and isolated area can rapidly enter the mainstream. It is not only familiar conditions such as malaria that remain active in local areas and therefore potentially a worldwide threat. Previously unknown conditions have also been emerging. Many health authorities believe that the organism responsible for AIDS found a few human hosts and was quickly on its way to becoming a worldwide scourge. The prevention function of the death system was alerted by the emergence of AIDS and has since given heightened attention to other potential threats. The Ebola virus, spread by blood, saliva, and feces, was discovered in 1976 when a lethal outbreak occurred in a small community in Zaire. This virus is fast working, deadly, and, at present, without a definitive form of treatment. It reappeared in Zaire in 1995 in another brief and contained episode—but there are fears that it might occur again and spread to large population centers.

Indigenous people have been vulnerable to diseases brought to them by "discoverers," conquerers and settlers. This process is still ongoing and likely to continue. For example, the Yanomami of the Amazon have been decimated by pathogens carried by gold miners (Davis, 2010). There is two-way traffic in lethal diseases: to and from relatively undeveloped nations.

There is still another prospect that has public health authorities very much concerned: The antibiotics that have been so valuable in subduing infections are starting to lose their effectiveness. Some viruses and other microorganisms have developed resistances to the most frequently used antibiotics. The unwise use of antibiotics for minor ailments and the public's more-than-occasional failure to use them as directed may also be responsible for the loss of effectiveness. Perhaps we will be lucky. But perhaps the evolution of infectious diseases (Ewald, 1994) and emerging viruses (Morse, 1993) will result in a catastrophic increase in death rates. There have already been bioterrorism alarms that focus on the dangers of anthrax and smallpox, diseases with a lethal history that have been controlled by medical research and public health practices. But these diseases could be unleashed again by those who identify with the killing rather than the preventing and healing functions of the death system.

■ SUMMARY

Everything that makes a collection of individuals into a society and keeps that society going has implications for our relationship to death, as we have seen through many examples. At first we tried to imagine a world without death. This helped us to freshen our perspective on the world in which we do live as mortals and the death system in which we participate. We may think of the death system as the interpersonal, sociophysical, and symbolic network through which an individual's relationship to mortality is mediated by society. The death system of any society can be analyzed in terms of its components and functions. The components include people, places, times, objects, and symbols (including language) that have special death-related meanings. The functions include warnings and predictions, preventing death, caring for the dying, disposing of the dead, social consolidation after death, making sense of death, and killing. Each of these functions was illustrated with key examples that often revealed conflicts, biases, and strains in society (e.g., unequal protection from life-threatening conditions, the influence of lifestyle on vulnerability to death, war, and blood sacrifice). Recent storm, flood, and earthquake disasters revealed the strengths and limitations of the death systems within the affected societies.

A brief historical review showed how various modes of dying (e.g., the Black Death, syphilis, and tuberculosis) have influenced society's images of death itself. We also became familiar with the beginnings of death education, research, and counseling.

Leading causes of death were examined after we solidified our knowledge of terms such as mortality and morbidity, and the various ways in which mortality (death) rates are reported. We saw that the general mortality (death) rate in the United States continues to decrease, decreased throughout the twentieth century, and was accompanied, as we would expect, by increases in life expectancy.

Females and whites continue to have higher life expectancies than males and blacks. The leading general causes of death were identified (heart disease is still number one), as well as leading causes of death for various age groups. It was noted that the three leading causes of death for youth (ages 15–24) in the United States are related more to lifestyle than to medical factors. New risks to life may be on the horizon, particularly emerging viruses with the potential for causing worldwide epidemics.

■ REFERENCES

Abel, E. L. (2009). *Death gods*. Westport, CT: Greenwood.

Amish Country News. (retrieved 2010). Amish religious tradition. http://www.amishnews.com/amisharticles/religioustraditions.htm.

Andrews, L. B., Buenger, N., Bridge, J., Rosenow, L., Stoney, D., Gaensslen, R., et al. (2004). Enhanced: Constructing ethical guidelines for biohistory. *Science, 304*, 215–216.

Aries, P. (1981). *The hour of our death*. New York: Knopf.

Associated Press. (2002, April 3). Poor called more likely to die of breast cancer. *The Arizona Republic*.

Associated Press. (2002, April 10). Thousands pay solemn respects to Queen Mother. *The Arizona Republic*. http://www.digitaljournal.com/article/34093

Benson, E. P., & Cook, A. G. (2001). *Ritual sacrifice in ancient Peru: New discoveries and interpretations*. Austin: University of Texas Press.

Bodio, S. (2001, September). India's disappearing vultures. *The Atlantic Monthly, 288*, 25–27.

Bolstad, E., & Spangler, N. (2005, September 28). Embattled New Orleans police leader calls it quits. *East Valley Tribune*, p. A8.

Bryant, C. D., & Shoemaker, D. J. (2003). Dead zoo chic. Some conceptual notes on taxidermy in American social life. In C. D. Bryant (Ed.), *Handbook of death and dying* (Vol. 2, pp. 1019–1026). Thousand Oaks: Sage.

Bryer, K. B. (1977). The Amish way of death. *American Psychologist, 12*, 167–174, 254–256.

Carrasco, D. L. (1999). *City of sacrifice: The Aztec empire and the role of violence in civilization*. Boston: Beacon.

Center for Disease Control and Prevention (2010). Teen drivers: Fact sheet. http://www.cdc.gov/Motor vehiclesafety/teen_drivers/teendrivers_factsheet.html.

Clark, M. S. (2010). *A pocket guide to Amish life*. Peabody, MA: Harvest House.

Clausewitz, K. V. (1984). *On war*. Princeton, NJ: Princeton University Press. (Original work published 1832.)

Davies, N. (1981). *Human sacrifice in history and today*. New York: Morrow.

Davis, W. (2010). Last of their kind. *Scientific American, 303*, 60–67.

Einstein, A., & Freud, S. (1933). Why war? In C. James & S. Grachen (Eds.), *Collected papers of Sigmund Freud* (Vol. 4, pp. 273–287). London: Hogarth.

Eire, C. M. N. (1995*). From Madrid to purgatory: The art and craft of dying in sixteenth-century Spain*. Cambridge, UK: Cambridge University Press.

Eliade, M. (1978). *A history of religious ideas*. Chicago: University of Chicago Press.

Ewald, P. W. (1994). *Evolution of infectious disease*. Oxford, New York: Oxford University Press.

Gibbs, N. (2005, October 3). Act two: Hurricane Rita. *Time*, pp. 30–42.

Gibbs, W. W. (2002). On Cemetery Pond. www.sciam .com.

Goodman, P. S. (2005, February 3). Tsunami's unpredictable outcome: Few injuries. *Washington Post*, p. A01.

Green, M. A. (2001). *Dying for the gods: Human sacrifice in Iron Age and Roman Europe*. Charleston, SC: Tempus.

Guiberson, B. Z. (2010*). Disasters: Natural and man-made catastrophes through the centuries*. Henry & Holt.

Herman, W. (2005, January 14). The man who saved his village. *Arizona Republic*, p. A2, 18.

Holveck, J. (1991). Grief reactions within the adolescent gang system (project paper). Tempe: Arizona State University. Department of Communication.

Hostetler, J. A. (1993). *Amish society*. (4th ed.). Baltimore: Johns Hopkins University Press.

Huizinga, J. (1996). *The autumn of the Middle Ages*. (Corrected version). Chicago: The University of Chicago Press. (Original work published 1926.)

Hyndman, D. W., & Hyndman, D. (2010). *Natural hazards and disasters*. (3rd ed.). Brooks/Cole.

Idler, E. L., McLaughlin, J., & Kasl, S. (2009). Religion and the quality of life in the last year of life. *Journal of Gerontology, Social Sciences, 64*, 528–537.

Jankofsky, K. (1979). Public execution in England in the late Middle Ages: The indignity and dignity of death. *Omega, Journal of Death and Dying, 10*, 433–458.

Kahn, C.A., Schultz, C. H., Miller, K. T., & Anderson, C. A. (2009). Does START Triage work? An outcomes assessment after a disaster. *Annals of Emergency Medicine, 54*, 424–430.

Kamman, J. (2005, September 10). Did Bush do the right thing? *Arizona Republic*, p. A9.

Kant, I. (1932). *Perpetual peace*. Los Angeles: U. S. Library Associates. (Original work published 1795.)

Kastenbaum, R. (1993a). Last words. *The Monist, an International Quarterly Journal of General Philosophical Inquiry, 76*, 270–290.

Kastenbaum, R. (1993b). Reconstructing death in postmodern society. *Omega, Journal of Death and Dying, 27*, 75–89.

Kastenbaum, R. (2002a). Last words. In R. Kastenbaum (Ed.), *Macmillan encyclopedia of death and dying* (Vol. 2, pp. 515–518). New York: Macmillan.

Kastenbaum, R. (2002b). Sacrifice. In R. Kastenbaum (Ed.), *Macmillan encyclopedia of death and dying* (Vol. 1, pp. 733–737). New York: Macmillan.

Kastenbaum, R. (2003). "Arise, ye more than dead!" Culture, music, and death. In C.D. Bryant (Ed.), *Handbook of thanatology* (Vol. 2, pp. 1008–1018). Thousand Oaks, CA: Sage.

Kaye, K. (2005, October 4). New data suggests Katrina was a less intense category 3 storm. *South Florida Sun-Sentinel*, p. 1.

Kearl, M. C. (2010). The proliferation of postselves in American civic and popular culture. *Mortality, 15*, 47–63.

Keller, E., & Blodgett, P. H. (2010). *Natural hazards, disasters, and catastrophes*. Englewood Cliffs, NJ: Prentice Hall.

Kettlewell, J. (2005, June 24). Tsunami alert system takes shape. http://news.bbc.co.uk/1/hi/sci/tech/4619069.hstm.

Kettlewell, J. (2005, June 25). Tsunami aid "went to the richest." http://news.bbc.co.uk/hi/world/south_asia/4621365.stm.

Knight-Ridder Newspapers. (2005, September 11). Katrina: Anatomy of a disaster. *East Valley Tribune*, p. A1, A8.

Krause, N. (2009). Meaning in life and mortality. *Journal of Gerontology, Social Sciences, 64*, 527–537.

LaFraneiere, S. (2005, April 11). Health workers race to block deadly virus in Angolan town. http://www.nytimes.com/learning/teachers/featured_articles/20050412tuesday.html.

Laungani, P. (1996). Death and bereavement in India and England: A comparative analysis. *Mortality, 1*, 191–212.

Lundgren, B. S., & Houseman, C.A. (2010). Banishing death: The disappearance of the appreciation of mortality. *Omega, Journal of Death and Dying, 61*, 223–250.

Manning, A. (2005, July 7). Bird flu could spread to humans. *Arizona Republic*, p. A7.

Marvin, C., & Ingle, D. W. (1999). *Blood sacrifice and the nation. Totem rituals and the American flag.* Cambridge, UK: Cambridge University Press.

More, T. (1975). *Utopia.* New York: Norton. (Original work published 1516.)

Morse, S. S. (Ed.). (1993). *Emerging viruses.* Oxford, New York: Oxford University Press.

Nakashima, E. (2005, January 12). Indonesian children go back to school. *Washington Post*, p. A14.

Nakashima, E. (2005, January 25). For men of seaside village, lonely and unfamiliar roles. *Washington Post*, p. A01.

Nakashima, E. (2005, January 28). Indonesia offering "olive branch" to rebels. http://www.washingtonpost.com/wp-dyn/articles/A42800-2005Jan27.html.

National Commission on Terrorist Attacks Upon the United States. (2004). *The 9/11 Commission report.* New York: Norton.

National Vital Statistics Reports. (2005).

O'Connor, A. (2004). U.S. infant mortality rate rises slightly. http://www.nytimes.com/2004/02/12/us/us-infant-mortality-rate-rises-slightly.html.

Pape, R. A. (2005). *Dying to win.* New York: Random House.

Revkin, A. C. (2005, September 27). Gulf currents that turn storms into monsters. http://www.nytimes.com/2005/09/27/science/earth/27loop.html.

Rosales, F. A. (2003). Days of the dead. In R. Kastenbaum (Ed.), *Macmillan encyclopedia of death and dying* (Vol. 1, pp. 204–206). New York: Macmillan.

Scripps Howard (1993, December 22). Babies in U. S. study got radioactive shots. www.shns.com/shns/g/index.

Smith, A. (2010, July 9). Haiti donations: $1.3 billion. CNNMoney.com.

Sullivan, T. (2010, August 18). Pakistan flood shapes an archipelago of misery.

Taylor, R. P. (2000). *Death and the afterlife. A cultural encyclopedia.* Santa Barbara: ABC-CLIO.

Thomas, E. (2005, September 12). Crisis and chaos: New Orleans' descent into despair. *Newsweek*, pp. 42–46.

Tinkler, E. (2002, May 29). Extinct tiger tapped for cloning. *The Arizona Republic*, p. A15.

Treaster, J. B. (2005, September 1). Superdome: Haven quickly becomes an ordeal. http://www.nytimes.com/2005/09/01/national/nationalspecial/01dome.html.

Tribune Wire Services (2005, September 28). Reports of rape, murder at Katrina evacuation sites may be overblown. *East Valley Tribune*, p. A7.

Turner, B. (Ed.). (2003). *The statesman's yearbook.* New York: Palgrave Macmillan.

Wen, J., Shi, Y. K., Li, Y. P., Wang, L. I., Cheng, L., Gao, Z., Lio, L. (2009). Risk factors of earthquake inpatient death: A case control study. *Critical Care, 13*, 24–34.

Wester, J. R. (2005). To help or harm: Misperceptions of the relief worker in Post-Katrina New Orleans. Paper presented at Death, Dying, and Deposition Conference, Bath, England.

Wildlife park to add mammoth attraction. (2002, August 21). www.cnn.com/2002/TECH/8/21/clone.mammoth.

Yardley, J., & Altman, L. K. (2004, April 24). China is scrambling to curb SARS cases after a death. http://www.nytimes.com/2004/04/24/world/china-is-scrambling-to-curb-sars-cases-after-a-death.html.

Zwerdling, D., & Sullivan, L. (2005, September 26). Katrina timeline: Unexecuted plans. http://www.npr.org/templates/story/story.php?storyId=4839666.

■ GLOSSARY

Age-Standardized Death Rate A mortality rate in which the age of a population is statistically controlled so that it does not affect interpretation of the numbers.

Capital Punishment Execution carried out by the legal system in accordance with the death penalty.

Cardiovascular Resuscitation (CPR) The process of reestablishing respiration and heart action by opening the airway, rescue breathing, and compression of the chest, as required by the circumstances.

Cerebrovascular Accident (CVA) Commonly known as a stroke. Primary effects on speech and voluntary movement. Can be fatal.

Cohort The name given to a set of people who were born at the same time (birth cohort) or entered a particular situation at the same time (e.g., students entering college in 2006).

COPD Chronic obstructive pulmonary disease. Includes emphysema and chronic bronchitis, both of which progressively create "air hunger" (dypsnea).

Crude Death Rate (CDR) Death rate not corrected for age (see Mortality Rate).

Life Expectancy Estimated length of time between a specified point in time (e.g., birth and death).

Death System The interpersonal, sociophysical, and symbolic network through which society mediates the individual's relationship to mortality.

Excess Death Rate A measure of the extent to which the death rate of a particular population is higher than the rate that would have been expected for the population as a whole.

Longevity Number of years between birth and death.

Microbial Agents Bacteria and viruses.

Morbidity Illness.

Mortality Death. Also: the condition of being vulnerable to death.

Mortality Rate Proportion of people in a particular population who die within one year, based on number of deaths per 1,000 or 100,000. Also known as death rate.

Pathologists Physicians who specialize in the study of living or dead cells and *tissues*.

Radioactive Iodide A substance used in diagnosing and treating disorders of the thyroid gland.

Thanatology The study of death and death-related phenomena.

Tsunami A series of extremely long waves generated by earthquakes, landslides, or underwater volcanic eruption. Previously known erroneously as "tidal wave."

■ ON FURTHER THOUGHT . . .

- Does your state have a death penalty? If so, for what offenses? www.deathpenalty.org For further information: Bureau of Justice Statistics, http://www.ojp.usdodj.gov/bjs/pubal2.htm#C.

Other Useful Online Resources

CDC National Prevention Information Network
    www.cdcnpin.org
DeathNet
    www.rights.org/deathnet/open.html
Ethics Updates
    http://ethics.sandiego.edu/Applied/DeathPenalty/index.asp
Kearl's Guide to Sociology of Death andDying
    http://www.trinity.edu/mkearl/death.html
Sociology Online Library
    http://www.fisk.edu/vl/Sociology/Overview.html
Thanatolinks
Webster
    www.katsden.com/death/index.html
World Health Organization
    www.who.int
Yahoo's Death Page
    www.yahoo.com/Society_andCulture/Death

4

Dying

Transition from Life

Time comes, I'll be passing on, fading away, expiring, checking out, cashing in my chips, buying the farm, and/or biting the dust. Perhaps also giving up the ghost and shuttling off this mortal coil. But that would be all so second millennium! Update me as life-limited, life-threatened, terminal, chronic complex condition, end-stage, end-event prone, or hospice Medicare-option eligible. Heck, I'm already guarded prognosis. Just don't say "dying."

—The author's mind, meandering again

I thought deeply as to how I should discuss her status. Although I believe she knew that her disease is progressing, I was fearful of her reaction as she just renewed her marriage vows three weeks prior and was determined to "beat" this cancer.

—Chadi Nabhan, M.D. (2009, p. 239)

Civil War soldiers had many opportunities to die and a variety of ways in which to do so. . . . As men became soldiers and contemplated battle, they confronted the very real possibility of death. They needed to be both willing and ready to die, and as they departed for war, they turned to the resources of their culture, codes of masculinity, patriotism, and religion to prepare themselves for what lay ahead.

—Drew Gilpin Faust (2008, pp. 4–5)

Woe is me. I think I am becoming a god.

—Vespasian (A.D. 79)

Don't let it end like this. Tell them I said something.

—Pancho Villa (1923)

This is going to sound terrible. It is terrible. I wanted to shake her. Shake her and say, "Are you in there? Are you IN there?" I didn't, but I wanted to: that's still terrible, isn't it?
— Daughter whose aged mother had died in a geriatric facility

On average, patients spent 18 hours, 39 minutes per day alone. These seriously ill patients with poor prognoses spent most of their time in the hospital alone. Staff visits were frequent but brief . . . . Patients with advanced dementia and minority patients appear to have less bedside contact.
— Daniel P. Sulmasy (2000, p. 289)

When a person looks at you and says, "I'm going to die," they usually do die. That's what my experience has been. Somehow they know that their life is going to pass. . . . Sometimes you're the last person they're talking to. What I've learned is: get that family member, get that husband, get the wife, get the daughter, get the grandson, whoever that significant person who's waiting in that waiting room so anxiously, get them in there. So their last few breaths can be with that family member—not with someone who doesn't really know them.
— Noreen Levison, told to Studs Turkel (2001, p. 42)

My father died in his ninety-third year. He was alert, comfortable, and still very much himself. What he said most often to everybody was, "Thank you, thank you, thank you."
— Yohei Sasakawa, M.D., private communication (1996)

"DYING": PRIMPED AND MEDICALIZED

The rules have changed since Feifel (1959) called attention to society's taboo-ridden attitude toward death, dying, and grief. Death education, hospice care, grief counseling, and media coverage have challenged the taboo with a fair degree of success. However, we are perhaps as evasive as ever when "dying" would seem to be the appropriate word. These substituted terms often are branded as a denial response. I don't see it that way. Denial, properly understood, is a radical blank-out of reality. It does happen, and can be expressed both verbally and nonverbally. Much of the time, though, we *primp* dying. This is accomplished by various linguistic maneuvers. "Expiration date" has become a readily available metaphor, thanks to the credit card industry. It's kind of funny and kind of serious at the same time. For older generations, "buying the farm" adds a sense of nostalgia and continuity with its dry humor. Most common and once-common euphemisms for dying are ways of primping the hearse. The stark reality is not denied, but made more presentable by a comparison with more familiar and less threatening processes. The inexorable often is graced with the suggestion of voluntary participation, e.g., did I ever kick that bucket!

The medicalization of dying is quite a different matter. The passage from life has become increasingly under the surveillance of the medical–bureaucratic complex. "Dying" is seldom heard, even though end-of-life communication and regulation have proliferated. There are practical reasons for devising an alternative rhetoric. "Dying" is too vague and general to describe all the distinctive pathways to death (as we will see, for example, in the study of "trajectories." Concepts such as "life-limited" and "Medicare hospice-eligible" can seem more useful in health care management.

But medicalization also serves the purpose of insulating physicians and bureaucrats from the mortal realities. "Dying" is the word that most clearly expresses the universal mortal predicament that we share with all who have gone before us. A steady barrage of substituted terms has the potential to narrow perspective and downsize the mortal move. So that's why this chapter on dying is still called dying.

Patients are often fearful when contending with a life-threatening condition. Professional caregivers have their own share of anxiety. Nabhan, an oncologist, overcome his own uneasiness to lay out the facts to his patient. He explained that additional therapeutic interventions would only increase her discomfort. Nabhan made it clear that he was not abandoning her, but will call on a full range of palliative services to provide her with better care. "As I was ending my meeting with her she asked with tearful eyes: 'How could you do this?' I was taken aback by that question. 'How could I do what?' 'How could you do this job?' She said, as the tears started coming down faster. 'How could you go to bed every night after telling so much bad news to so many patients?'" Here was a moment of deep communication between two humans aware of their common mortality—not just another exercise in evasion between caregiver and patient.

Soldiers in the American Civil War were for the most part young and healthy. The longer the bloodshed and debilitating war-related illnesses continued, the less meaningful it all seemed. Was "doing your duty" enough reason to die miserably far too soon and far too away from home? They faced the prospect of ending their lives in the company of strangers.

Today there are significant changes taking place in the conditions of both life and death. What lessons we should keep from the past and what new lessons might need to be learned? A useful place to begin is at the end: the moment of death where philosophical issues of meaning come down to the here and now of a unique individual's unique situation.

Charles A. Leal, then a young army surgeon, held Lincoln's hand as the assassinated president lay dying "to let him in his blindness know that he had a friend."

THE MOMENT OF DEATH: IS IT VANISHING?

The moment when life passes into death has long been charged with passionate meanings. In Irish folklore, a death invoked a spirit known as the *banshee* pierced the air with its wild lament. Among the Lugbara of central Africa, it was a designated member of the community who uttered the *cere*, a whooping kind of melody that was sounded only at the moment of a death. For centuries, the deathbed scene was regarded as the climax of the Christian drama on earth, with salvation or damnation suspended in the balance. In a modern hospital room, a wife transformed into widow hurled herself onto the body of her husband with screams and racking sobs.

Each of these responses is linked to a distinctive aspect of the dying person's situation.

The banshee's cry announced the painful transition of a soul to the realm of the spirits. In contrast, the Lugbara's *cere* signaled a shift in communal arrangements: the deceased person's assets and obligation were now to be redistributed according to tradition. The Christian deathbed scene attempted to provide a model for righteous living and faith that might earn salvation in the afterlife (Bell, 2005; Paxton, 2003). The numerous family members I observed overcrowded in their dying patriarch's hospital room were of Romani (gypsy) heritage. Here it was the anguish of loss and separation from a loved one that dominated the scene. The fiercely expressed sorrow was alarming to some of the staff but an essential response on the part of the family.

Last words have often been seized upon as emblems of meaning. Vespasian was an up-from-the ranks general who succeeded Nero as Roman emperor and attempted to restore integrity to the regime. Becoming a god was the hope of every Roman emperor, but Vespasian did not welcome this transformation because he still had so much work to do. Pancho Villa was both a notorious Mexican bandit and a beloved folk hero who retired in good graces, only to be assassinated by a rival. A media favorite, Villa was chagrined to realize that he had nothing "famous" to say as he lay dying, hence his request that reporters invent something interesting that he might have said. Vespasian and Villa felt the need to offer spontaneous "exit interviews" from their lives. The emperor left us with a glimpse of a reluctant god; the bandit left us with the anxiety of a person who was for once at a loss for words while the world was waiting to listen.

These examples demonstrate the impulse to draw meaning from the last moment of life. It could be inspiring to hear, for example, that the person "passed away peacefully," that loving words were exchanged, that it was felt to be "the right time." A positive memory image might also help the survivors come to terms more easily with their own mortality. What we would not want to hear is that "all that suffering was for nothing" or "What's life if it ends like this?"

Up to this point we have been reviewing tradition—but what is happening today? The woman whose mother died in a geriatric facility had an experience that is becoming increasingly common. The aged woman had slipped deeper and deeper into a nonresponsive condition. She no longer recognized her daughter. Was her mother still somewhere "inside" that passive form on the bed? There was no obvious transition from life to death when the end did come. No deathbed scene. No last words. No ceremony. No ripple through society.

The Slipping Away

This is how many aged people ended their lives in geriatric facilities from about the middle of the twentieth century onward. Even more lives are now ending with an almost imperceptible slipping away. Our traditional ideas about the dying process are becoming less descriptive of today's. Why is this so?

- Medical advances help people to survive longer with conditions that formerly had been considered terminal. The person now has a "life-threatening" or "life-limiting" condition. It has become more difficult to determine when the progression of a long-term illness should be considered dying. Ask not for whom the bell tolls: It is probably the beep of a monitor when vital signs cease.
- There is still a tendency for physicians to experience a patient's death as their own failure and therefore distance themselves.
- Alzheimer's disease and related dementias more often accompany people in their last phase of life. Afflicted individuals might not seem present at their deaths.
- Sedation can reduce awareness. Communication is also impaired and the passage from life becomes less conspicuous. There is also a zone of indeterminancy in which a person might be unable to respond to the family or staff member, yet still be cognizant of the situation.
- Often the person dies alone. Family might have visited, but do not happen to be there at the last moment. Being with a minimally responsive terminal patient is seldom a high priority for hospital systems. The nurses who have provided attentive care might be strongly motivated to be with the patient through the end phase but will probably be under pressure to serve other patients. Sulmasy (2000) and others have documented the limited amount of personal contact a hospitalized patient is likely to experience. I have tried repeatedly to obtain accurate statistics about presence or absence of a staff member at the time

This is George Washington's other deathbed scene—here surrounded by family in portrait appropriate formal clothing, including wigs for the gentlemen. This version, carefully staged for posterity, takes liberties with the actual deathbed scene. Both verbal and pictorial constructions of deathbed scenes are subject to influence by societal values.

of death, only to be defeated by bureaucratic resistance. As a former hospital administrator myself, I can understand why few people really want to know how many people in our society exit from life without another person in attendance.

The "moment of death" is still being nurtured by compassionate health care providers Valentine (2007) reports that few of the terminally ill patients in her study were known to have offered last words. However, some patients "took charge of their own dying and leave-taking" and "recovered their own characteristic selfhood . . . in some cases becoming more than themselves, to assume an enhanced aliveness, presence, and relatedness to loved ones" (p. 233). Yohei Sasakawa, executive director of one of Japan's major philanthropic organizations, has the cherished memory of his

aged father's last words. His simple but eloquent "Thank you, thank you, thank you" has become a family treasure.

In this chapter, we consider dying not so much as an abstraction but as an experience that takes many forms, depending on the nature and management of the illness, the social support system available, and the unique person whose life is in jeopardy. How and when we die is influenced by societal practices as well as physical disorders. For example, it has been found that hospitalized patients are more likely to die when members of either an understaffed nursing (Aiken et al., 2002) or medical (Provonost et al., 2002) service have excessive demands on their time and energies. But why do hospitals often have fewer nurses and physicians available? Furthermore, why do some of the best academic teaching hospitals provide only minimal care for patients in end-of-life situations and fail to provide end-of-life education for the next generation of physicians (Meier, 2005)? To answer questions such as these we will become more familiar with the American death system. We will also be touching on how personal lifestyles affect the timing and manner of our deaths. For example, negative emotions have been found to endanger health by undermining or overwhelming our immune systems (Kiecolt-Glaser, McGuire, Robles, & Glaser, 2002). If negative emotions are part of our daily experiences, we are more likely to encounter life-threatening experiences, and more likely to lose that battle. It is unlikely that we can understand dying by focusing only on dying: We must also consider the total pattern and meaning of the life that is coming to an end.

Dying as Transition

Dying is one of many transitions that we experience in our lives. This means that we can call upon what we already know from other transitional situations. We are already "practicing death" with bedtime rituals in childhood and in other temporary separations of daily life (Kastenbaum, 2004; Chapter 10). In growing up, we experience our first day of school, our first romantic adventure, our first solo ride behind the wheel of a car, our first day on the job. Many of us move on to such other memorable transitions as the first time we hold our baby or discover a gray hair on our own head. Some transitions are long awaited ("At last, I'm old enough for my driver's license!"). Some may have been dreaded ("Do I actually have to support myself now?"). Many transitions are tinged with ambivalence ("I'm kinda ready to get married, sort of, but sort of not").

The transition from life includes interactions that can either be disturbing or be comforting, communications that can either inform or confuse, and self-evaluations that can either undermine or strengthen one's sense of identity. No two people bring the same thoughts, feelings, accomplishments, and illness-related experiences. Furthermore, no two people have the same set of relationships. The quality of life during the final illness depends much on the quality and availability of the individual's most valued relationships.

We give attention first to the basic question of what dying is and when it begins, following up on our opening discussion. Next, we look at some of the "trajectories" that the dying process can take and their consequences for patients, family, and staff. The challenge of communicating well throughout the dying process is then explored, including problems that have been well documented in the health care system. The influences of age, gender, interpersonal relationships, disease, treatment, and environment are considered. This is followed by an exploration of stage theories and other models of the dying process, including a multiple perspective approach that identifies important parallels between dying and other experiences with which most of us are more familiar. We conclude with attention to ongoing efforts intended to improve care of the dying.

This is a good time to pause and consider dying from a very personal perspective. I suggest that you give your attention now to the thought exercise outlined in Box 4-1. Why not try this exercise right now? It has proved helpful to other people who were also starting to study dying and terminal care. The questions raised in this exercise are taken up later in the text, and your instructor will have other observations to add.

WHAT IS DYING, AND WHEN DOES IT BEGIN?

Individual and Interpersonal Responses

What is dying, and when does it begin? The knowledge that "I am dying" can transform the individual's view of self and world.

New England artist Kate Lesses (1982/1983) described the comfortable familiarity of her home during her terminal illness:

> I live with an oak coffee table
> beside my bed where
> my silver-framed clock ticks hard
> through the night
> like my cat when she purrs.

But this sense of comfort could not disguise the fact that her life had changed decisively:

> I hate every morning
> hating it
> with my stomach jumping

BOX 4-1

Your Deathbed Scene

A Thought Exercise

They are planning a movie about your life. This film is intended to be as faithful as possible to the facts. Help them plan the deathbed scene. Describe the ending of your life in as much detail as you can, based upon what you expect is most likely to happen. It would be best if this description is complete enough to help locate the setting, the time, who else might be on the scene, and anything else that is needed. (Yes, of course—they're giving you lots of money for your cooperation, but you are in control of planning this scene according to your best guess at what the future will bring.)

Please use a separate sheet of paper for this exercise.

before I've had a chance to think
of anything I awake non-thinking and I am
like a small animal backed into the corner
of a cage to escape from the hand clutching,
reaching through the wire door
I feel the power of the hand's grasp
and fear it
without knowing what the power is.

Greg

Other terminally ill people have different experiences to report, but the feeling that "How I live now is not as I lived before" is hard to escape. Friends and relatives also are affected, and their responses in turn affect the terminally ill person. Consider Greg, for example, a college student I remember well through the years. Greg lived more than two years with the knowledge that he would probably die in the near future. He suffered from a form of leukemia that was unusually puzzling to his physicians. Greg recognized that the disease was his central problem, but often he was more concerned about how other people related to him:

I have had to develop almost a whole new set of friends. My good old buddies just felt awfully uncomfortable around me. They couldn't be themselves anymore. I realized they'd be relieved if I would just sort of drift away from them.

What disturbed Greg's friends most was the discrepancy and ambiguity. His sturdy appearance made it difficult to accept that he was in the grip of a life-threatening disease. None of the "good old buddies" could relate to both facts: that Greg looked healthy and functioned well and that he was also terminally ill. Most of his friends and family chose to relate only to the healthy young man.

When something new happened, or I started feeling shaky about it, I would say something. Oh, man—they just couldn't handle it!

When Greg had an acute episode, he would be in the hospital. Afterward he would keep to himself for a while. "I didn't like to show my face around when I felt rotten," he said. This pattern crossed his friends' expectations. Everybody knew that a dying person looks different, so Greg should have looked different. A young man also might be expected to protect his macho image by concealing signs of pain, weakness, or fear. Greg was a deviant, then, in behaving as a dying young man should not.

Matilda

By contrast, Matilda D. was depleted by many years of illness and seemed too frail to survive much longer (Kastenbaum, Barber, Wilson, Ryder, & Hathaway, 1981). She was admitted to a geriatric hospital at age 86, suffering from painfully advanced rheumatoid arthritis, anemia, and difficulty in eating and drinking. Attentive nursing care enabled her to remain relatively stable for several months, but Matilda's condition gradually worsened. Most of her time was spent in bed, with considerable discomfort. At this point, she was regarded as failing but not dying. This was a meaningful distinction to staff members because it indicated what pattern of care would be most appropriate. They did not face the ambiguity that Greg's friends had to contend with. Furthermore, the staff and Matilda's daughter also expected that dying and death would soon follow for Matilda. This again contrasts with Greg, for whom there was some hope of remission.

Matilda was officially considered a dying person when her lungs started to fill with fluid and her general condition weakened. The next "proper" action was to relocate Matilda to the intensive care unit (ICU). Some patients are treated successfully for a medical crisis on the ICU, but it also serves as the exit ward. Matilda's status change to a dying person meant that she would be moved to a death place. When a facility has an agreed-upon death place, then it is possible to maintain the illusion that death will not visit elsewhere. Her new status could also be seen in an altered pattern of staff interactions. Basic care was still provided in a conscientious, professional manner, but the contacts were now briefer and more mechanical. The subtle change from a living to a dying person had taken place in the perceptions and actions of staff members. The certainty of her death made it easier for staff to shift their patterns.

Fortunately, Matilda's life did not end with isolation and dehumanization. My hospital colleagues and I had started a therapeutic companion program to help provide residents with a core relationship through which they might regain their sense of personhood and control. Andrea George (a folk singer by profession) had formed a close relationship with Matilda. There had been time to discover Matilda's personal qualities and values. Her therapeutic companion and her daughter continued to relate to Matilda as a distinctive human being, even when she could no longer respond in words. Matilda's favorite song (*Edelweiss*) was sung and played to her, and she died literally in touch with two people for whom she had remained a unique and valued person.

We often treat people differently when they are perceived as dying, even if we are not aware of this difference. A classic study by LeShan (1982) found that nurses delayed going to the bedside of a dying patient as compared with other patients on their unit. The nurses were surprised when told of this differential response pattern, and resolved to respond promptly to terminally ill patients. After a few weeks, however, the original pattern reinstated itself. As much as they wanted to treat all patients equally, the nurses found it difficult to avoid being influenced by society's ingrained fear of contact with dying people.

Onset of the Dying Process: Alternative Perspectives

The point when dying begins depends on our frame of reference. The proposition that *we die from the moment we are born* might be useful in developing a personal philosophy of life, but also encourages evasion. Furthermore, it is also questionable as fact. It is true that programmed cellular death (*apoptosis*) expresses itself in the life course from the perinatal phase onward. The loss of the umbilical cord after birth is an obvious example. It would be misleading, however, to insist that the normal turnover of cells and the atrophy of unnecessary structures constitute a process of dying for the organism as a whole. Unperturbed by losing its once-indispensable umbilical cord, the infant surges ahead at a dazzling developmental rate.

A related concept has been with us for many years. Three centuries ago, Jeremy Taylor, chaplain to King Charles I of England (Taylor, 1651/1977), suggested that *aging might be regarded as slow dying and dying as fast aging*. However, elderly people cannot be described as dying without ignoring the vigor and vitality that many continue to express at an advanced age.

Dying usually begins as a psychosocial event. Organ systems fail, but it is in the realm of personal and social life that dying occurs. Let us now consider some of the contexts in which the onset of dying is discovered or certified.

1. *Dying begins when the facts are recognized.* A doctor's waiting room might include essentially healthy people who have been convinced for years that they are dying, but also people showing up for a routine checkup who are not yet aware of their life-threatening conditions. Perhaps, then, the dying process begins when a physician concludes that the patient is afflicted with a terminal illness. This might be a reasonable basis for establishing the onset of dying, but it excludes people with the same terminal illness who have not consulted a physician. Furthermore, a person might have a terminal disease but still remain relatively symptom free and functional for some time to come.

2. *Dying begins when the facts are communicated.* Perhaps we should date the onset of the dying process from the moment at which the physician informs the patient. This can be a complicated situation. Physicians seldom break the news at the same instant that they reach their conclusions. There may be a delay of days, weeks, or even months before the physician tells the patient what has been found. Furthermore, sometimes the physician never does tell the patient—or the patient does not "hear" the unwelcome information.

3. *Dying begins when the patient realizes or accepts the facts.* More than one nurse has returned from the bedside of a patient almost bursting with anger at the physician. "Why hasn't he leveled with this patient? This man is dying, and nobody has told him what's going on!" At times this concern is well justified. At other times, however, the patient was told but "didn't stay told." Somehow the patient was able to forget or misinterpret the central facts, or the physician said one thing with words and something else with facial expression and tone of voice. Studies reviewed by Kaufman (2005) find that patients tend to overestimate their probability of survival and are therefore not dying to themselves. Weisman (1972) adds that our realization of a terminal illness often is partial and floating, what he calls *middle knowledge*. What we think we understand about the patient's state of mind might apply only to a particular moment in time as the situation and interpretation continue to alter.

The physician's communication can be subtle or direct, couched in clear language or obscured by technical jargon. The patient may go away either with a clear understanding or in a state of uncertainty and confusion. There can be another time lag, then, between communication and realization of terminal illness. For examples of poor and competent physician–patient communication, see Box 4-2.

BOX 4-2

"BREAKING THE BAD NEWS": PHYSICIAN–PATIENT COMMUNICATION

How Not To

Give the bad news right away and get it over with.

Give all facts at one time.

Impress patients and family with your medical knowledge.

Tell the diagnosis, then move on.

End the session after you have told what you patient/consider enough.

Make sure you have broken through denial.

Stretch the truth if necessary to cheer up the patient.

Make it clear that there is nothing more we can for the patient.

✔ A Better Way

✔ Take the time to establish a relationship with the patient and family.

✔ Share a fact, see how the patient responds, and wait until one fact is digested before going on.

✔ Keep it simple. Don't "snow" them with details unless they ask for more details.

✔ Take the time to discover what this diagnosis means to the patient: Explain and educate.

✔ Allow pauses, breathing spaces, so family can ask questions.

✔ Respect what might seem like denial: The message will be heard when the patient is ready.

✔ Do not say anything that is not true; this destroys trust and sets up later anger and sorrow.

✔ Make it clear that you will be with the patient and respond to his or her needs.

It can be difficult to determine how much the patient does understand. Some aged patients who appeared to be completely unresponsive proved capable of responding when approached with patience and touch-enhanced communication (Kastenbaum, 2000). People with advanced Alzheimer's disease may not be able to understand that they are dying but nevertheless appreciate compassionate human contact. Hurley and Volicer (2002) urge that family and other caregivers of people with Alzheimer's prepare them to cope with the progression of the disease in the early stages; those with the disease should learn ways of asking for help so they may best understand what is being communicated. Improved family–physician communication is also being urged (Associated Press, 2008) in deciding what treatment and comfort measures should be selected as a demented person approaches the end of life.

4. *Dying begins when nothing more can be done to preserve life.* The physician might not have classified the person as dying, despite the diagnostic signs, because "I haven't tried all possible combinations of drugs," or "Building the patient up with transfusions might make her a better candidate for another surgical procedure." This often happens when the medical and nursing staff have an exceptionally strong motivation to keep the patient alive (e.g., a child or a person of their own age and background). Reluctance to define a patient as dying can stand in the way of discussing the possibility of hospice care; (see Chapter 5). Furthermore, the family physician may have an opinion that is different from that of the specialist—and one specialist might differ from another. When to shift from "prevention of death" to "care of the dying" is a question that hinges in part upon our definition of dying.

TRAJECTORIES OF DYING: FROM BEGINNING TO END

We have been exploring the onset of the dying process as interpreted by the various people involved. Chapter 5 examines in detail the hospice approach, with its emphasis on the home and family. Here the emphasis is on what are still the most common pathways to death—those that end in a health care facility.

A series of pioneering studies by Barney Glaser, Anselm Strauss, and Jean Quint Benoleil (1966, 1968) observed interactions with dying people in six medical facilities in the San Francisco area. Keep in mind that field researchers did not have the responsibility for patient care that occupies the energies of the hospital staff. Furthermore, the researchers were not the husbands, wives, or children of a dying patient. This emotional distance gives field researchers a limited but unique perspective.

The research team organized many of its observations according to the concept of *trajectories of dying*. All dying processes take time; all have certain paths through time. For one person, the trajectory could be represented as a straight downward line. For another, it might be represented more accurately as slowly fluctuating, going down, leveling off, declining again, climbing a little, and so on. Be patient with the description of these varying trajectories: they represent the real life and real death circumstances in which most of us will find (or lose) ourselves.

Certainty and Time

Staff members are faced with two questions about every patient whose life is in jeopardy: Will this patient die? If so, when? These are the questions of certainty and time. The attitudes and actions of the health care staff are based largely on what they take to be the answers. It is uncomfortable when a patient's condition does not lend itself to straightforward expectations such as "This man will recover" or "This woman will die, but not for some time." In the emergency room, the staff's initial uncertainty can change to certainty in less than a minute. The fate of a premature baby may be determined in a few hours or a few days, but the outlook for a cancer patient may remain indeterminate for months.

Together, certainty and time yield four types of death expectation:

1. Certain death at a known time.
2. Certain death at an unknown time.
3. Uncertain death, but a known time when certainty will be established.
4. Uncertain death and an unknown time when the question will be resolved.

Isabel Spinoza was placed on dialysis when her kidneys failed. She is not a U.S. citizen and faced termination of her life-prolonging treatment because of budget problems in the Arizona health care system. The state did continue to fund her treatment, but economic issues continue to influence the care of life-threatened people throughout the nation (see also Chapter 5).

Especially important are situations in which expectations change. One of the staff members' examples is a physician's decision to discontinue blood transfusions. The subtle pattern of communication among staff in such a case affects everybody (Glaser & Strauss, 1968):

> Since the doctor had said nothing official, even nurses who believe the patient is dying can still give him an outside chance and stand ready to save him. They remain constantly alert to counterclues. "Everybody is simply waiting," said one nurse. If the doctor had indicated that the patient would die within the day, nurses would have ceased their efforts to save him, concentrating instead on giving comfort to the last, with no undue prolonging of life (p. 11).

This physician did not carelessly forget to instruct the nurses to alter their approach. By putting nothing into words, the physician allowed a little leeway for others to continue their efforts to maintain life against the odds. We can become more familiar with the patterns of communication that accompany the dying process by considering three of the dying trajectories identified by the Glaser–Strauss–Benoleil research team: lingering trajectory, expected quick trajectory, and unexpected quick trajectory.

The Lingering Trajectory

The caregivers display a characteristic pattern when a patient's life is slowly fading. Seldom is there a dramatic rescue scene. Staff members try to keep the patient comfortable but feel that they have already done "all that we can" and that the patient has "earned" death after a long struggle. It would be unusual to find a team of specialists rushing into the geriatric ward to perform heroic measures.

Perhaps a lingering trajectory is more acceptable because the person was considered socially dead. The more responsive patients are considered more alive. More people on the lingering trajectory are aware of their social death than might be realized. "You're as good as dead when they put you behind the fence. That's why they went and put up the fence!" That observation was made to me by the resident of a large geriatric facility that, in fact, had recently been fenced off from the community. "Life's on that side. We're on the other." From what I was starting to see for myself, he was filing an accurate report.

Visits from family members often fall off sharply with the lingering trajectory. The slowly dying person seldom speaks of final things to family and friends—or to anybody:

> These patients drift out of the world, sometimes almost like imperceptibly melting snowflakes. The organization of work emphasizes comfort, care and custodial routine, and is complemented by a sentimental order emphasizing patience and inevitability (Glaser & Strauss, p. 64).

But the picture is not always so tranquil. Somebody in the situation might deny or resist the impending death. This can be a temporary reaction as, for example, when an adult son has a difficult time realizing that the mother he has known as a vigorous, can-do person is now debilitated, exhausted, and inching toward death (Kaufman, 2005). There can also be a more aggressive attitude. As Proulx and Jacelon (2004) observe, there can be "tremendous societal pressure on a dying person to be a 'good patient' while trying to experience the 'good death'" (p. 119). Glaser, Strauss, and Benoleil noticed incidents in which a next of kin would upset the staff by showing "too much emotion" after the patient died. Strong reactions to a patient's death can challenge the staff's assumption that there is little social loss in the passing of a "lingerer."

The patience of family and/or staff may be strained when a patient fails to die on schedule. I remember the daughter of an aged patient who strode angrily back from his ward and complained, "They said he was on the death list, so I came here as soon as I could. And there he was—you can see for yourself! Sitting up in bed and playing cards.

And winning!" There had been a misunderstanding. A nurse had informed the daughter that her father was on the "D. L.," a term that actually means *danger list*. The daughter did have reason to believe that her father was close to death and had organized her emotions accordingly. After cooling off, she made it clear that she did not really want her father dead but that it was difficult to keep thinking of him as all but dead and waiting "for the other shoe to drop."

The lingering trajectory allows both the patient and the family time to grow accustomed to the idea of dying, make plans, work through old conflicts and misunderstandings, and review the kind of life that has been lived. But it also can attenuate relationships and create situations in which the person is perceived as being in limbo— not quite alive and not quite dead.

The Expected Quick Trajectory

Time is truly of the essence on an expected quick trajectory. The staff organizes itself to make the most effective use of the time that remains. Classifications of the situation can change rapidly. For example, "He is out of immediate danger but probably will not survive very long" changes to "I think he has passed the crisis point and has a real chance of pulling through."

Several types of expected quick trajectories were observed, each accompanied by a different pattern of staff interaction. In a *pointed trajectory*, the patients are exposed to risky procedures that might either save their lives or result in death. The staff often has enough advance time to organize its efforts properly. The patient may also have the opportunity to exercise some control and options (e.g., share precious minutes with a loved one, see that certain personal matters are acted upon). By contrast, the *danger-period trajectory* requires more watching and waiting. The question is whether the patient will be able to survive a stressful experience such as high-risk surgery or a major heart attack. The patient may be unconscious or only partially aware of the surroundings as compared with the alert state of a patient with a pointed trajectory. The danger period can vary from hours to days. The family may remain at bedside or in the corridor, with doctors, nurses, and monitoring devices maintaining their vigilance.

The *crisis trajectory* imposes still another state of tension. The patient is not in acute danger at the moment, but the individual's life might suddenly be threatened at any time. The tension will persist until the patient's condition improves enough so that the danger passes or until the crisis does arrive and rescue efforts can be made.

Different from all of these is the *will-probably-die trajectory*. The staff believes that nothing effective can be done. The aim is to keep the patient as comfortable as possible and wait for the end to come, usually within hours or days. There can be intense administrative pressure to move will-probably-die patients to facilities that require less expensive resources. People who are not quite ready to die may be perceived as taking up expensive space in a cure-oriented medical center. Unfortunately, this pressure can result in transferring an aged person to a geriatric facility that lacks the staff to offer expert preterminal care.

And what should those people in the waiting room be told? Who should tell them? Is this the time to prepare them for the bad news, or can it be postponed a little longer? Should all the family be told at once, or is there one person who should be relied on to grasp the situation first? What should we do if the family itself is in disagreement, making conflicting requests and demands? This situation challenges the staff's stamina, judgment, and communication skills. However, the presence of the family can also make a positive difference to a person for whom death seems to be in near prospect.

The most salient features of the expected quick trajectory are time urgency; intense organization of treatment efforts; rapidly shifting expectations; and volatile, sensitive staff–family interactions. In the midst of this pressure, errors can be made. For example, there may be attempts to save patients from medical problems they do not have. A person may arrive at the hospital in critical condition with no medical history available to guide the staff. The pressure of time may then force medical personnel to proceed on the basis of educated guess rather than secure knowledge.

Whether there is a chance to save the patient's life sometimes depends on the resources that are available at the crucial time in a particular hospital or unit. The lack of a trauma response team or advanced diagnostic equipment could make the difference between the will-probably-die trajectory

and one with more hope. Ask around in your own area: *Where would health care professionals themselves prefer to be taken if they were in a serious accident or had some other type of medical emergency?* They will probably identify significant differences in equipment and staffing that could make a life-or-death difference. The perceived social value of the endangered person can also spell the difference between an all-out rescue attempt and a do-nothing orientation. "When a patient is not 'worth' having a chance," say Glaser and Strauss (1968), "he may in effect be given none." Social stereotypes that hold that one person is more important than another (whether on the basis of age, gender, race, occupation, economic status, or whatever) can play a decisive role in the death system when quick decisions must be made about priority and extent of life-sustaining effort.

The Unexpected Quick Trajectory

The significance of the interpersonal setting in which dying takes place is emphasized again by the *unexpected quick trajectory*. The experienced emergency room team adjusts quickly to situations that might immobilize most other people. However, the emergence of the unexpected quick trajectory on other units of the same hospital can spark a crisis. On these wards, there is less preparation for emergency, and personnel may experience a "blow up" (Glaser & Strauss, 1968, p. 121). The staff in nonemergency areas know but do not believe that a life-or-death situation might arise at any moment. In this sense, something really does blow up when a patient unexpectedly enters a crisis phase on the "wrong" ward—the staff's comforting myth of an orderly and manageable universe.

Some unexpected deaths are more disturbing than others. The staff is more likely to be upset by the death of a "medically interesting case," a patient who presented unusual features and challenges. Personnel also tend to be affected more by the death of a patient whose life they had tried especially hard to save. Glaser and Strauss report that it is the "poor physician who tried so hard" who receives the sympathy of other staff members rather than the patient. The patient may have never seemed like an individual human being to the staff during their intensive life-saving efforts. The patient who dies for the wrong reasons also dismays and alarms the staff. Treatment may have been focused on one critical aspect of the patient's condition, while death was stealthing through a different route. The staff's need to shield itself against surprise is a major theme that runs through the unexpected quick trajectory. There can be persistent efforts to maintain the illusion of control. Patients have reported how hard they have worked to bolster the doctors' impressions that they have everything under control (Kastenbaum, 1978). The well-practiced defenses of the hospital staff may become dangerously exaggerated or suddenly give way when reality punctures illusion.

The hospital itself can precipitate an unexpected quick trajectory. Glaser and Strauss observed confusion in the mobilization of treatment resources, the turning of attention away from other patients to concentrate on an urgent case, accidents attributable to carelessness or poor safety practices, and a variety of problems that can arise when a hospital is understaffed. Problems attributable to understaffing and staff turnover have become even greater in the years following the pioneering studies carried out by Glaser and Strauss.

The combination of time pressure and surprise can lead to what Glaser and Strauss term *institutional evasions*. For example, there may not be time to bring a physician to the bedside. If nurses carry out the potentially life-saving procedures without direct medical supervision, then they will have exposed themselves to the possibility of criticism and liability action—but if they do not act promptly, the patient may die before the physician arrives. Evasions of institutional rules may be minor or substantial. The institution itself may choose either to notice or to carefully ignore the infractions. One extra source of tension within the unexpected quick trajectory, then, is the conflict between doing what seems to be best for the patient without delay and abiding strictly by the regulations.

Life-or-Death Emergencies

There is another type of "quick trajectory" that can occur any time, any place. A person in good health may suddenly become the victim of an automobile accident, a small child may fall into a swimming pool, an "unloaded gun" may discharge, a restaurant patron may choke, a person with a history of heart disease may sustain another attack. These are just a few of the emergency situations that can result in death.

Several types of problems are more likely to arise when there is a life-or-death emergency in a community setting as compared with a health care facility:

- *Panic:* "This can't be happening! What should we do?"
- *Inappropriate action:* "Let's get him on his feet."
- *Misinterpreting the situation:* "Stop whining and go back to bed!"
- *Minimizing the danger:* "I don't need a doctor. It's just a little indigestion."
- *Preoccupied by own concerns:* "I'd better clean this place up before I call anybody."

There have been many examples of prompt and competent response from family members, neighbors, colleagues, and passersby. For example, a man in his 80s had the presence of mind and the skill to perform cardiac pulmonary resuscitation (CPR) on a toddler who had fallen into a pool—an all too frequent occurrence in Arizona. This child recovered, but many others have died or suffered permanent injury. Emergency medical technicians and paramedics are often called upon when life-endangering situations arise in the community. Trained to provide front-line response to emergent health crises, they may have more encounters with disaster in two or three days than most people do in a lifetime. Dale Gladden recalls one of his first experiences as a paramedic (Kastenbaum, 1993–1994, pp. 6–7):

> It was at a (community fraternal club). There was a dance going on—lots of loud music, dim lights. No one was dancing. Everyone was just standing around. An elderly man had collapsed . . . . The man had gone into ventricular fibrillation. I intubated him, and the RN with me tried to get an IV in him—it was hard for her because of the bad lighting. He was a diabetic. IV (intravenous) was hooked up and we started defibrillation. There was that smell of burning hair associated with defib machines. We got a pulse and blood pressure back. Got an ambulance. The man was breathing fine so I took the tube out and we transported him to the hospital. He survived and was very thankful to me.

This man almost certainly would have died without the prompt and skilled intervention. Sometimes, however, no amount of skill and effort can save a life. It is not unusual for paramedics to find one or more people already dead on the scene. Even though the paramedic knows that a person is beyond resuscitation, it may be necessary to carry out CPR and other procedures in order to conform with regulations. At such times, the paramedic is likely to feel—as Gladden did after responding to another call—that it is wrong "to go through all this trouble for a dead person, why not let her be at peace? I had lots of questions why we went through the whole routine when she was already dead."

There is another odd situation that can arise when a person dies suddenly in a community setting. Although paramedics or nurses on the scene may know that the person is dead, the legal declaration of death may not be made until the body has been transported to a medical facility. This means that some of the deaths that are reported as having occurred in a hospital actually occurred elsewhere. Hospital physicians simply confirmed the ER team's assessment that the patient was beyond resuscitation. In many communities, emergency response personnel are now following "Field Termination of Resuscitation Guidelines" that enable them to forego useless procedures when it is obvious that the person has no chance of survival. Such an incident was reported soon after the new provisions were approved in Mesa, Arizona. A chronically ill 90-year-old woman refused breakfast one morning, sat in her favorite chair, and stopped breathing. Her son later commented that "We didn't know what to do. She wanted to die at home. We wanted to handle it as quietly as we could." The paramedics who came to the home honored the family's wishes. Instead of performing unwanted and ineffective resuscitation procedures, they stayed to talk with the family and help them deal with their first wave of grief and make arrangements for disposition of the body. The Mesa paramedics also receive training in the basics of grief support—certainly a good idea for police officers as well and all people who may be called upon when a death occurs.

Where the law applies, we can complete a medical care directive that forbids resuscitation measures. Paramedics and EMTs then can refrain from performing resuscitation procedures without exposing themselves to legal risk. What is the law in your state and community? Your local department of health, hospital, or medical association can answer this question for you.

GUARDED FEELINGS, SUBTLE COMMUNICATIONS

Most of us do not say everything on our minds to whomever we happen to be with in every situation. How we communicate with another person depends on our own personality style, who that other person is, and what's at stake in the immediate situation.

Difficulties in Communication

We should not be surprised, then, to find that feelings may be guarded and communications subtle among people faced with the prospect of death. One might assume—mistakenly—that the dying person does not know what is happening or is unwilling to discuss it. Often the implicit rules make honest communication very difficult. For example, while working in a geriatric hospital, I found that personnel usually responded to patients' direct communications about death in a manner that quickly ended the interaction. The odds were about three to one against the staff member being willing to listen to what the patient had to say. Giving false reassurance ("Oh, you'll outlive me, Charlie!"), changing the subject, and a variety of other evasive responses were more common than an openness to what the dying person really wanted to communicate.

This attitude is still prevalent in many places. Aged patients on a lingering trajectory frequently are treated as though socially dead and are therefore denied even the opportunity to die as a person. I have heard staff members make remarks such as the following in the presence of the patients (Kastenbaum, 1984):

"This one, she can't talk. She doesn't know what you are saying."

"You should have seen her when she first came here, but look at her now!"

"The poor thing would be better off going in her sleep" (p. 6).

These remarks were not only degrading but erroneous. There was independent evidence that these patients, although vulnerable and failing, did understand what was being said over their (socially) dead bodies. One example that I will always remember occurred during an inspection of an extended care facility that was under court orders to improve its physical plant and its treatment program. The whistle had already been blown, time had been provided to improve care, and my visit as a consultant for the federal government was expected. However, there was no evidence of improvement, or motivation to do so. I was told that "these people (the patients) don't understand anything, anyhow."

I asked the staff to show me the most impaired, uncomprehending patient on the ward. This request seemed to throw them into confusion, so I walked to the farthest corner of this large, dark, and filthy ward. An old, pale, scrunched-up woman was lying in bed, her hair tangled and untended, her body smelling of neglect. I asked for the patient's name and information about her background. Did she have a husband, children, visitors? What had been her interests, activities, and achievements before she came here? All the staff knew was her name, and the fact that her husband or somebody visited once in a great while.

I stood by the woman's bed, took her hand, and spoke to her, using the small bits of information I had been given. In less than a minute she had painfully faced around and squeezed my hand in return. In another few minutes she was speaking and moaning. I could not make out all the words, but there was no mistaking that she knew somebody was trying to communicate with her and that she wanted to respond. She was still there as a person. The staff observed this interaction and silently retreated. But at the end of the inspection visit, the charge nurse turned to me and muttered, "If you're going to write anything about this, I'd better tell you that this is not the patient I told you it was. I mixed the patients up somehow. That was Mrs. ___, not Mrs. ___."

This story is not told to criticize geriatric facilities in general. The situation on this particular unit was the outcome of systematic neglect of the frail elderly and of those who provide care for them. Having their own sense of horror to contend with, the staff responded by erasing the patients' individuality and humanity. This woman had almost no opportunity to communicate to anybody about anything. It is not simply that we often have difficulty communicating about "mortal matters": There are many people close to death who are deprived of the opportunity for normal social interaction of any kind. And how unnecessary!

Doctor–Patient Communication: The Support Study

The health care system is still resonating from the results of a major study conducted back in 1998. This project is known by the acronym SUPPORT: Study to Understand Prognoses and Preferences for Outcomes and Risks of Treatment (SUPPORT, 1995). The SUPPORT project was intended to help physicians make better decisions about end-of-life issues and to prevent "a mechanically supported, painful, and prolonged process of dying." The results could hardly have been more discouraging. More than 9,000 adult patients with life-threatening diseases were studied in five teaching hospitals. Half the patients and their doctors were observed for two years; the other half were included in a two-year intervention phase that attempted to improve communication and care. Box 4-3 summarizes the unsettling results of both phases.

The observation phase found that physicians seldom showed interest in the patients' own preferences. *Cardiopulmonary resuscitation (CPR)* would be performed regardless of the patient's stated preference. Giving patients the opportunity to express their preferences seemed to be only an empty gesture. Pain control was also ineffective. Many patients therefore were exposed to unrelieved pain and aggressive treatment, and spent at least 10 days on life support systems in the ICU.

The intervention phase of the study attempted to improve this situation by providing the physicians with more information about their patients' preferences as well as their physical status. Nurses with special training made multiple contacts with patient, family, physician, and hospital staff. They encouraged attention to pain control and to better physician–patient communication to contribute to better decisions in planning the course of treatment. Unfortunately, these interventions did not work. Communication remained flawed; physicians continued aggressive treatment despite patients' preferences; pain control was as poor as before.

The findings prompted an immediate editorial response from the *Journal of the American Medical Association* ("Improving Care," 1995). The anonymous editorial writer urged other physicians:

> *Don't project our concept of a good death onto patients. . . . Respect for patient autonomy*

BOX 4-3

THE SUPPORT STUDY OF SERIOUSLY AND TERMINALLY ILL HOSPITALIZED PATIENTS: MAJOR FINDINGS

I. The Observation Study

1. Half of the patients who died during the course of the study had moderate or severe pain during their final three days of life.
2. Physicians often used jargon that the patient did not understand when talking about cardiopulmonary resuscitation (CPR) and often (41 percent) never even discussed this subject with their patients.
3. In 80 percent of the cases, physicians misunderstood what the patients wanted with respect to the use of CPR.
4. Physicians often did not follow the patients' stated preference to avoid the use of CPR: In about 50 percent of the cases, the physician did not write a do-not-resuscitate (DNR) order.

II. The Intervention Study

1. There was no increase in discussions between physicians and patients.
2. Physicians often continued to disregard patients' preferences to have CPR withheld, even when these preferences were known to them.
3. There was no improvement in pain control.
4. Computer projections of the patients' prognoses were no more accurate than those made by the attending physicians.
5. Much of the patient information generated during the intervention phase failed to reach the physicians because of various communication problems.

means that physicians must allow informed patients to determine what value they place on such a chance of survival and what risks they are willing to undergo (p. 1635).

Since publication of the SUPPORT findings, there have been additional efforts to encourage physician respect for the preferences of terminally ill people and to provide more effective pain relief. This process continues to face resistance from entrenched attitudes and habits. Encouragement is to be found in the rapid growth of palliative care programs within hospitals (Meier, 2005) and in the more receptive approach to patient communication by the current generation of medical students on their way to becoming physicians.

Improving Communication

It has been known for years that most people in a life-threatening situation would prefer to have open discussions with their physicians and family members (Hayslip & Peveto, 2005). This need for honest communication was expressed by most of the terminally ill people whose outcomes were followed in the SUPPORT study. The need for improved communication is expressed by terminally ill people who prefer the continuation of active treatment as well as those who prefer that aggressive treatment be discontinued as death approaches. This is often accompanied by the urgent request for alleviation of pain (Laakkonen, Pitkala, & Strandberg, 2004). For example, one woman who realized that the end of her life was near wished that the doctors would communicate with her so that

I would get the information, whether there is anything that can help. Even though I have lived this long and seen quite enough, it's amazing how one wants to cling to life. That's how it is always (p. 121).

Physicians Emanuel, Fairclough, Wolfe, & Emanuel (2004) concluded that it is misguided practice to discourage or even forbid people from discussing death with terminally ill patients. This is not exactly breaking news, however. That many dying people welcome the opportunity to discuss this situation was established by Herman Feifel (1959) in the early days of the death awareness movement. Apparently, we still need to keep making this discovery.

Nevertheless, an open awareness communication approach (Glaser & Strauss, 1966) should be made available, not imposed. Timmermans (2008) draws on personal and research experience to remind us that some of the people involved in an end-of-life situation might not be ready to communicate openly. He concludes that:

> There is not one optimal or appropriate response to a terminal diagnosis. Acceptance of the impending death may be appropriate for some patients and family members in certain conditions, and it may be more functional for the hospital staff, but open awareness cannot be imposed upon all patients or family members (p. 336).

Suggestions for Communicating with People in Life-Threatening Situations

Here are a few other suggestions about communicating with people who are in life-threatening situations.

First, be alert to symbolic and indirect communications, as illustrated by the following examples:

1. *Sharing dreams.* People may prepare themselves for their final separation through dream work before conscious thoughts and direct interpersonal communications occur. Dreams reported by terminally ill cancer patients have been found to have a higher frequency of death contents than healthy older people (Coolidge & Fish, 1983/1984). The dreamer usually saw somebody else as dead. The dreamer often attempted to discover the identity of this person:

> I dreamt of a funeral and in the funeral was a little girl going to be buried in her coffin. I couldn't get to her so I tried to open it to see who it was and it was one of my daughters. Little Antoinette. She was lying on her side and the lid was falling in the coffin . . . . I went to fix the lid . . . . I kept on doing things that would upset the coffin. I felt like a criminal that didn't belong there (p. 3).

It is not essential that the patient or the listener come up with the "right" interpretation of these dreams. Simply being able to share these inner experiences with another person can provide an additional supportive line of communication.

2. *Symbolic and indirect language.* Here is an example that came to our attention during a research project in a geriatric hospital (Weisman & Kastenbaum, 1968).

> The 75-year-old former stonemason had lost some of the vigor he had shown earlier in his hospital stay, but otherwise appeared to be in stable condition and doing well. One morning he asked for directions to a cemetery near his former home. He announced that he was expecting the undertaker. This statement was not taken up by the staff as a clue to impending death. It was just a statement that didn't make much sense. The next day, he told several people that his boss (going back many years, in reality) had called for him: he was supposed to help dig graves for eight people. The delusion now became persistent. He insisted on staying around the ward so he could be available to the people who would come to take him back to the cemetery.
>
> Two days before he died, the patient had several teeth extracted (a procedure that was seen as having little risk because of his good condition). He then told staff that it was time to call his sisters—about whom he had never before said a word. His death came as a surprise to the staff although, apparently, not to himself. Cause of death was determined to be cerebral thrombosis. Despite all the clues this man had given, no notice had been taken. His "crazy talk" seemed even less crazy when a subsequent review indicated that the old stonemason had outlived seven siblings—his reference to digging a grave for eight people no longer seemed to be arbitrary (p. 16).

After a number of such experiences, both our clinical and research staffs improved their ability to identify patients whose death was more imminent than might have been expected and learned to pay closer attention to what was said, whether in direct or symbolic language.

Much of physician–patient–family communication about death is indirect. This tendency was made clear again in a study that found discussions of a terminally ill patient's condition often avoided direct mention of death and instead touched on what will probably be happening in the future (Rodriguez et al., 2006). This apparently slight difference in language allows each of the participants to comprehend the situation in their own way but within the bounds of reality.

3. *Leave-taking actions.* People who sense that their lives are nearing the end often engage in behaviors such as sorting through and giving away possessions, creating the occasion for one last interaction of a familiar kind, such as playing checkers or going fishing together; and terminating mutual obligations and expectations (e.g., "Thanks for the loan of the bowling ball. I won't be needing it anymore"). Most people who are aware of their terminal illnesses do hope to bid farewell to the important people in their lives—but not necessarily all in the same way. It is wise to take our cue from the dying person rather than impose a

particular kind of farewell scene that happens to appeal to us.

Second, *help to make competent and effective behavior possible.* Illness, fatigue, and reduced mobility undermine competent functioning. This is true whether or not the individual is suffering from a terminal condition. The progressive nature of terminal illness, however, increases the individual's dependency on others and limits the range of spontaneous action. Family, friends, and other caregivers cannot only improve communication but also help to support the dying person's sense of self-esteem by striking a balance between meeting the realistic needs associated with dependency and creating an environment in which the person can continue to exercise some initiative and control.

Timely and appropriate support is needed, not a total takeover of the dying person's life. By accomplishing one side of the communication

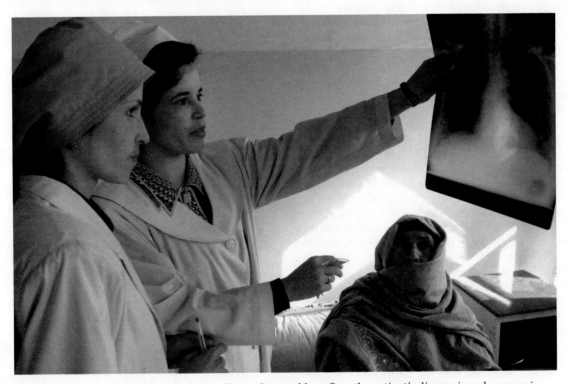

Two Afghanistan physicians examine an X-ray that could confirm the patient's diagnosis and prognosis. The patient anxiously endures her waiting time. What are her chances? Will the doctors tell her everything? Communication is often difficult for everybody in a life-or-death situation.

process—listening and observing—it becomes more probable that the patient can maintain a core of competent and effective behavior and continue to communicate needs and attentions.

Third, *allow the dying person to set the pace and the agenda.* There is no schedule that has to be met, no set of tasks that the dying person must accomplish—unless clearly established by the dying person. This is no time for listeners to impose their own needs or preconceived ideas of just what it is that a dying person is supposed to do. Although the patient will usually introduce thoughts concerned with dying and death, there are individual differences regarding when and how this topic is brought up. For example, during a particular interaction the patient may choose to say nothing about death. This does not necessarily mean that the patient is "denying" or "behind schedule." The patient may just be taking a little "vacation" from this overwhelming topic or be more concerned at the moment with some other matter. Furthermore, one terminally ill person might choose to discuss specific death-related issues (e.g., reviewing funeral plans or the distribution of property) while another is more focused on feelings and relationships. I have known many dying people who had not much left to say about death because they had already had all the time they needed to settle their thoughts and communicate their concerns and desires. These people still had need for supportive everyday communication but did not need to be reminded that they were dying!

Fourth, *do not confuse the dying person's values and goals with our own.* Communication can be distorted or even broken off when others project their own needs on the dying person. Requiring the dying person to move along from one "stage" to another, for example, imposes an additional burden on everybody in the situation. Another stress is introduced if we insist that the patient give up "denial." As noted earlier (Chapter 1), denial has become an overused and often misused term. There are many reasons why people might not acknowledge their terminal condition at a particular time and to a particular individual. Furthermore, denial-like behaviors may be useful strategies. Connor's (1992) research with terminally ill cancer patients confirmed that the supposed "deniers" were downplaying the seriousness of their illness because this strategy was helping them to maintain their most significant interpersonal relationships.

Connor also reminds us that some people have had a dysfunctional lifestyle for many years and continue to make excessive use of denial-like behaviors in their terminal illness. Other people have functioned well until confronted with the loss, stress, and uncertainties associated with a life-threatening illness. To say that a person is denying seldom tells us all that would be useful to understand and may, in fact, misrepresent the situation.

INDIVIDUALITY AND UNIVERSALITY IN THE EXPERIENCE OF DYING

Does everybody die in the same way? If so, then it might be possible to discover general laws or regularities upon which care and management can be based. Or does everybody die in a unique way, depending on many different factors? We are more likely to be good observers and useful caregivers if we understand the specifics of each situation. The discussion begins, then, with respect for both universal factors and individual dimensions of dying.

Factors That Influence the Experience of Dying

Here some of the ways in which age, gender, interpersonal relationships, disease, treatment, and environmental context influence the experience of dying.

Age Age by itself is an empty variable. Nevertheless, chronological age guides us through a variety of factors that influence our lives and deaths.

- *Comprehension of dying and death.* Our intellectual grasp of death is related both to the level of development we have achieved and to our life experiences (see Chapter 10). At one extreme is the young child who is keenly sensitive to separation but who does not yet comprehend the finality and irreversibility of death. At the other extreme is an aged adult who not only recognizes the core facts of death but has seen many close friends and relations die through the years. The "same" experience will be different for people with varying life histories and cognitive structures.

- *Opportunity to exercise control over the situation.* Children are accorded fewer enfranchised rights than adults. Even the "natural death" acts passed by state legislatures do not directly strengthen the child's position as a participant in decision making. The traumatic experiences of young Marie (Chapter 5) illustrate a serious problem that has not yet been entirely remedied.
- *Perception and treatment by others.* Perceived social value differs with age. Elderly patients often are victimized by the assumptions that (a) they are ready to die and (b) nobody would miss them much. For example, doctors are much more likely to withhold resuscitation efforts in patients older than the age of 75, even though they are likely to force CPR on younger patients. It is all too easy to mistake a depressive reaction for a terminal course. Many circumstances can lead to depression among elderly adults, including bereavement, social isolation, fatigue, and chronic though not life-threatening conditions. Expertise in assessing and treating depression is required, along with the independence of mind to break free of the "ready to die" stereotype and look carefully at each individual's situation.

Misperceptions also occur at the other extreme of the age range. For example, some physicians continue to believe that infants do not experience pain to any appreciable extent. Bone marrow samples are taken, needles are inserted into the spine, and burn dressings are changed without adequate analgesia. A life-threatened infant may undergo very painful procedures repeatedly. This discredited belief can serve anxiety-reduction purposes for physicians and nurses who are responsible for their treatment.

Gender A man with cancer of the prostate may be concerned with the threat of becoming impotent as well as with the risk to his life. Cervical cancer may disturb a woman not only because of the life risk but hysterectomy would leave her unable to become pregnant. Both the man and the woman may be troubled about the future of their intimate relationships even if the threat to their lives is lifted. Some people interpret physical trauma affecting their sexual organs as punishment for real or imagined transgressions. Others become preoccupied with their physical condition in a way that interferes with affectionate and sexual relationships. "I'm no good any more" may be a self-tormenting thought for either the man or the woman, each. These examples simply illustrate some of the many possible interactions between sex role and disease.

When a woman is faced with a life-threatening illness, she is likely to have concerns about the well-being of her family. Will the children eat well? Can her husband manage the household? What most troubles the woman/wife/mother may be the fate of her family as much, or even more than, her own. The man/husband/father in the traditional family is likely to have distinctive concerns of his own. Has the illness destroyed his career prospects? Will he lose his job or his chance for advancement even if he makes a good recovery? Has he provided well enough for his family in case he doesn't pull through? Is he, in effect, a "good man" and a "real man" if he cannot continue to work and bring in the money? There may be a crisis in self-esteem if he is confined to hospital or home for a protracted time, away from the work situations that support his sense of identity. The changing patterns of gender and occupation could, in turn, introduce new challenges when a life-threatening condition develops.

Gender differences are also important from the standpoint of professional caregivers. Direct care to the dying person is usually provided by women, often nurses, licensed practical nurses, aides, or technicians. Responsibility for the total care plan, however, still is often in the hands of a male physician. The physician may be more time conscious and personal-achievement oriented, characteristics that favor survival of the rigors of medical training, and therefore be more persistent in cure-oriented treatments and quicker to withdraw when death is in prospect. The nurse may be more sensitive to the patient's relationship with significant people in his or her life and less apt to regard impending death as a failure.

Nursing, traditionally one of the few careers readily open to women, now is but one choice among others. Furthermore, as women enter or reenter the workforce, the number of people available to serve as volunteers and informal helpers may decline, unless more men step up.

Interpersonal Relationships It is difficult to overestimate the importance of interpersonal relationships in the terminal phase of life. Clinical experience continues to support the findings of an influential early study (Weisman & Worden, 1975). Among hospitalized patients who were likely to die within a few months, those who maintained active and mutually responsive relationships survived longer than those with poor social relationships. The patients who died rapidly also had fewer friends, more distant relationships with their families, and more ambivalent relationships with colleagues and associates. They became more depressed as treatment failed. The patients with poor relationships often expressed the wish to die, but that this did not represent an actual acceptance of death: It was a product of their frustration and disappointment with life. The same investigators (Weisman & Worden, 1976) later found that the terminally ill patients who were experiencing the most distress also were those with the most interpersonal difficulties. Not only the length of survival, then, but also the quality of life was associated with the kind of interpersonal relationship enjoyed or suffered by the patient. Fortunately, there is now more recognition of the role of family relationships in a person's end-of-life experiences (e.g., Hickman, Tilden, & Tolle, 2004).

Sometimes it is the family who needs the most support. For example, an elderly man on a lingering trajectory toward death was at home, under the care of his wife. Mr. Tchinsky was in a semicomatose state, not suffering either physical or emotional distress. His wife, however, was struggling with anxiety and guilt. Mrs. Tchinsky was a loving and attentive caregiver, but had difficulty in controlling the leakage from her husband's *colostomy bag*. This relatively small problem was the source of great distress because to Mrs. Tchinsky it meant that she was failing her husband in his time of need. A visiting nurse identified and responded tactfully and effectively to this problem. Within a short time, Mrs. Tchinsky was again secure in her role as loving wife and caregiver, and the rest of the family was also relieved. This intervention did not involve the application of either high technology or counseling: A caring family just needed a little timely help to fulfill its obligations toward the dying man (Kastenbaum & Thuell, 1995).

Final conversations between people in close relationships can be profoundly valuable both for the dying person and the survivor. Keeley's (2007) interviews with family members or friends reveal parting messages that confirmed love, strengthened identity, validating religious or spiritual beliefs, achieved reconciliation, or emphasized the depth of their abiding relationship. Sometimes the messages were simple and direct, e.g., "I love you," repeated several times during the conversation. A daughter and her dying father used American Sign Language to communicate "I love you" when he lost his ability to speak. Words of affection often were accompanied by nonverbal actions, such as taking the dying person's hand and looking at each other. Final conversations often helped the survivor to have a sense of closure and completion. Keeley's study and the experience of many end-of-life caregivers make it clear that opportunity for final conversations should be made available, even in situations that are not conducive to intimate personal interactions.

Where and How We Die—From the Abstract to the Particular

We die in a particular place that contributes to our comfort, misery, or both. Similarly, the particular services we receive also have a significant effect on our experience. Discussions of the dying process sometimes become so abstract and generalized that we neglect the specific medical problems involved. Think, for example, of the difference between a person whose likely cause of death will be kidney failure and a person experiencing severe respiratory distress. As waste products accumulate in the body, the patient with kidney failure is likely to become more lethargic and less able to sustain attention and intention. There may be intermittent periods of better functioning when the patient seems more like his or her old self, but the final hours or days may be spent in a comatose condition.

By contrast, a degenerative respiratory condition is likely to produce more alarming symptoms and experiences. Perhaps you have seen a person with advanced emphysema struggle for breath. An episode of acute respiratory failure is frightening to the individual and arouses the anxiety of others. Once a person has experienced this kind of distress, it is difficult to avoid apprehension about future episodes.

Some conditions are accompanied by persistent pain and discomfort unless very carefully managed. Other conditions can reach peaks of agony that test the limits both of the individual and the state of medical comfort giving. Nausea, weakness, and a generalized sense of ill-being may be more dominant than pain for some terminally ill people. It is difficult to be serene when wracked by vomiting or diarrhea. *The point is that we do not die abstractly.* We bring our distinctive life history to the situation, and the situation itself is distinctive and almost certain to change over time. As we consider theoretical models of the dying process, then, it is useful to keep in mind that death comes down to the unique individual within a complex and shifting situation. Abstract perspectives can be useful, but we will always want to keep the actual person and situation well in mind.

THEORETICAL MODELS OF THE DYING PROCESS

People hesitate to interact with dying people for many reasons. One of these reasons can be the lack of a coherent and useful perspective. What does it mean to be dying? What can be expected? Several conceptual approaches have attempted to deal with questions of this kind (Corr, Doka, & Kastenbaum, 1999). In this section, you are invited to consider several additional perspectives.

Do We Die in Stages?

Two stage models of the dying process have been especially influential. Another model has not (yet) returned from the past to claim its share of current attention. All three models regard dying as a sequence of psychological or spiritual stages. The differences are also substantial, however.

A Buddhist Perspective Buddhists have long been aware of individual differences in the way people die. Some people are killed instantly in an accident, and others slowly decline and outlive their mental powers. In such situations, there is no opportunity to progress through the stages. Furthermore, some people are anxious and beset by emotional conflict as death nears. These people are also unlikely

to proceed through the stages of spiritual enlightenment. His Holiness, Tenzin Glyatso, the fourteenth Dalai Lama, states that not all people move through the stages as they die (Gyatos, 1985). One must have sufficient time and be in a state of mind that is conducive to spiritual development. Those who have developed spiritual discipline throughout their lives are more likely to experience the entire cycle of stages.

For Buddhists, there is a complex relationship between mind and body. At death, the coarse connections between mind and body are severed—but the very subtle connections continue. There is also a broad philosophical conception that becomes especially significant as death approaches. As the Dalai Lama expresses it: "When you are able to keep impermanence in mind—seeing that the very nature of things is that they disintegrate—most likely you will not be greatly shocked by death when it actually comes" (p. 170).

There are eight stages in the Buddhist journey toward death. Perhaps our first surprise is that these stages occur in ordinary life as well. "In more subtle form, the eight transpire each time one goes in or out of sleep or dream, sneezes, faints, or has an orgasm" (Gyatos, 1985, p. 98). Only the sensitive and disciplined person is aware of these subtle forms of dying that occur in everyday life.

What are the fundamental changes that occur as one moves from the first to the final stage of dying?

Stage 1. Eyesight dims, but one begins to have mirage-like visions.

Stage 2. Hearing diminishes. There is a new internal vision: of smoke.

Stage 3. The sense of smell disappears, and there is now an internal vision that is "likened to fireflies in smoke." The dying person is no longer mindful of other people.

Stage 4. Sensation is lost from the tongue and the body. The dying person is no longer mindful of his or her own concerns. Breathing ceases. (At this point the person would be considered dead by a Western physician, but not so to the Buddhist.)

Stage 5. This is the first of the pure visionary stages. White moonlight is perceived.

Stage 6. The person experiences visions of red sunlight.

Stage 7. The person experiences visions of darkness, faints, and then awakens into the final stage.

Stage 8. The clear light of death appears. This unique state of consciousness persists until death.

The Buddhist stages, then, focus on the experiential state or phenomenology of the dying person. They are divided equally between those that occur while the person is still alive by ordinary standards and those that occur when the person would appear to be dead to most observers. This model of dying served as a guide to Buddhists for many centuries before the current death-awareness movement arose in Western society. (There is also a somewhat less elaborate stage theory of dying within the Islamic tradition [Kramer, 1988].)

Saint John Bosco: The Throes of the Dying Man
John Bosco (1815–1888) was a priest known for his work with disadvantaged children. He was canonized as saint by Pope Pius XI in 1934. He was a remarkable person—acrobat, juggler, magician, and, according to some, miracle worker. He also reported dreams and visions that attracted attention throughout all the ranks of the Church. Bosco described stages of dying for the edification of young men so they would live on faith and virtue. Here is the last part of his 14 stages (Eco, 2004, p. 391) from a document still under wraps in the Vatican library (Bosco, undated):

> Mercy, have pity on me.
> When my eyes, darkened and stricken with
> horror by death's imminence, shall fix
> Their enfeebled and moribund glances at You,
> merciful Jesus, have pity on me.
> When my pale, leaden cheeks shall inspire
> compassion and terror in onlookers.
> And my hair, damp with death's sweat, shall
> stand erect, announcing the
> nearness of my end, merciful Jesus, have pity on me.
> When my imagination, agitated by terrible,
> fearsome specters, shall be immersed
> in mortal sorrows, merciful Jesus, have pity
> on me.
> When I shall have lost the use of all my senses,
> and the entire world shall have
> vanished from me, and I shall moan in death's
> final, anguished throes,
> merciful Jesus, have pity on me.

> The saint's stages or throes are up close and
> personal, vivid, alarming,
> unremitting and unmistakably prescriptive: live
> in faith and hope of salvation.
> The end of life is all about our relationship to
> God, not to each other.

We turn now to the stage theory that has become most familiar to readers in the Americas and Western Europe.

Kübler-Ross: The Five Stages Five stages of dying were introduced by Elisabeth Kübler-Ross in *On Death and Dying* (1969). These stages are said to begin when a person becomes aware of his or her terminal condition. The stages are presented as normal ways of responding to the prospect of death and the experience of dying. The patient in denial moves through the remaining stages of anger, bargaining, depression, and acceptance. Some people do not make it all the way to acceptance. Progress may become arrested at any stage along the way. Furthermore, there is often some slipping back and forth between stages, and each individual has a distinctive tempo of movement through the stages. This conceptualization, then, emphasizes a universal process that allows for a certain amount of individual variation.

Stage 1. Denial is the first response to the bad news. "No, not me, it can't be true." The denial stage is fueled by anxiety and usually runs its course in a short time. It could also be described as a "state of shock from which he recuperates gradually" (p. 37).

Stage 2. Anger wells up and may boil over after the initial shock and denial response has passed. "Why me?" is the characteristic feeling at this time. Rage and resentment can be expressed in many directions—God not excluded. The patient is likely to become more difficult to relate to at this time because of the struggle with frustration and fury.

Stage 3. Bargaining emerges as the middle stage. The dying person attempts to make a deal with fate. "Let me live just long enough to see my son graduate from high school, my daughter's wedding . . . ." The bargaining process may go on between the patient and caregivers, friends, family, or God.

Stage 4. Depression eventually follows as the person experiences increasing weakness, discomfort, and physical deterioration. "I'm not getting better. I won't get better!" Along with stress, strain, and feelings of guilt and unworthiness, there may be explicit fear of dying at this stage. The person becomes less responsive and his or her thoughts and feelings are pervaded by a sense of great loss.

Stage 5. Acceptance, the final stage, represents the end of the struggle. The patient is letting go. Despite the name, it is not a blissful state. "It is almost void of feelings. It is as if the pain had gone, the struggle is over, and there comes a time for 'the final rest before the long journey' as one patient phrased it" (Kübler-Ross, 1969, p. 100).

Interwoven through all five stages is the strand of hope. Realistic acknowledgment of impending death may suddenly give way to hope for a miraculous recovery. In addition to describing these stages, Kübler-Ross indicates some of the typical problems that arise at each point and suggests ways of approaching them. She emphasizes, for example, the need to understand the patient's anger during the second stage rather than to retaliate and punish the patient for it.

Evaluating the Kübler-Ross Stage Theory We first consider shortcomings of the stage theory, followed by observations that are more supportive.

First, *the existence of the stages as such has not been demonstrated.* Although four decades have passed since this model was introduced, there is no clear evidence for the establishment of stages in general, for the stages being five in number, to be those specified, or aligned in the sequence specified. Dying people sometimes do use denial, become angry, try to bargain with fate, or lapse into depression or a depleted, beyond-the-struggle way of being. However, the reality of these moods or response sets has nothing necessarily to do with stages. Dying people have many other moods and responses as well. These include, for example, expressions of the need to control what is happening and to preserve continuity between themselves and those who survive them. For a particular person at a particular moment, any of these needs may take highest priority. The few studies that have examined facets of stage theory have not supported this model. Textbooks in allied health fields as well as the media continue to perpetuate the five stages despite the lack of evidence, and often to the exclusion of other aspects of the dying process.

This casual attitude regarding the factual basis of a theory suggests that it meets social or emotional needs rather than scientific criteria.

Second, *no evidence has been presented that people actually do move from Stage 1 through Stage 5.* Brief clinical descriptions of various patients are given in the Kübler-Ross book, but evidence that the same person passed through all the stages was not offered either at that time or subsequently. One might as well offer snapshots of five different people in five different moods as proof that these moods occur in a particular sequence.

Third, *the limitations of the method have not been acknowledged.* The conclusion that there are five stages in the terminal process was based on psychiatric-type interviews conducted by one person and interpreted by the same person. This is a reasonable way to gather information, gain insights, and develop hypotheses, a potentially useful beginning. However, the research effort never moved past this beginning, and its inherent flaws and limitations were never transcended. Furthermore, what the dying person says and does in the presence of a psychiatrist is a highly selective behavior sample. The nurse who cares regularly for the patient's physical functioning often sees other aspects of the personality that do not show up in an interview, and the same may be said of physicians, ministers, family members, and friends. Behavioral studies might reveal still another different perspective, as might a diary kept by the patient. One limited source of information about the experiences and needs of the dying patient has taken the place of extensive, multilevel, cross-validated approaches.

Fourth, *the line is blurred between description and prescription.* Kübler-Ross repeatedly cautioned against trying to rush a person through the stages. Nevertheless, many people did assume that the patient should be hustled "on schedule" from denial right through to acceptance, and that it is a mark of failure for everyone concerned if the timing is off. This expectation added unnecessary pressure and enshrined "acceptance" as the universally desired outcome of the dying person's ordeal. The concept of universal stages lends itself to misuse by those who prefer their tasks simplified and anxieties reduced through a standardized approach to the dying person.

Fifth, *the totality of the person's life is neglected in favor of the supposed stages of dying.* The supposed universality of the stages sometimes leads to the dying person being treated as a specimen moving along predetermined paths rather than as a complete human being with a distinctive identity. However, each dying person is male or female, of one ethnic background or another, and at a particular point in his or her life. The nature of the disease, its symptoms, and its treatment can all have a profound effect on what the dying person experiences. Who the person *is* deserves prime consideration in this situation as in any other. Even if the stage theory were clarified and proved, it would not account for as much of the dying person's experience as has been widely assumed. We take the entire course of our lives with us into the final months and weeks. Emphasis on the hypothetical stages of reaction to terminal illness tends to drain away individuality or at least our perception of it.

Finally, *the resources, pressures, and characteristics of the immediate environment can also make a tremendous difference.* There are still communication networks in which almost everybody denies death almost all of the time. The terminally ill person who seems to be "in denial" may be following the implicit social rules of the situation rather than a manifestation of either individual personality or the hypothetical sequence of stages. Why waste one's depleted energies by fighting the system? The same terminally ill person might respond quite differently in a community hospital, a major medical center, an Amish community, or a hospice program. Environmental dynamics, mostly neglected in stage theory, have much to do with the experiences and responses of terminally ill people.

Nevertheless, Kübler-Ross did much to awaken society's sensitivity to the needs of the dying person. Accepting the stage theory is not essential for appreciation of her many useful observations and insights. Some of the practical problems that have arisen in the wake of Kübler-Ross's presentations should be attributed to their hasty and uncritical application by others. Kübler-Ross's contributions might be most valuable for their emphasis on communicational interactions. She demonstrated that it is possible, and helpful, to converse with terminally ill people. Many nurses and social workers were inspired by her lectures and workshops. With these examples in mind, they were able to overcome the prevailing societal taboos against open and honest communication with dying people.

Psychiatrist Elizabeth Kübler-Ross did much to overcome the isolation of dying people.

A Developmental Coping Model of the Dying Process

Charles A. Corr (1993) has proposed an alternative perspective that is intended to move beyond the flaws and limitations of the stage theory. He believes that "an adequate model for coping with dying will need to be as agile, malleable, and dynamic as is the behavior of each individual" (p. 77). People may try out certain coping strategies only to reject them firmly, or may pursue several strategies at the same time, even if they are not compatible. Furthermore, people will differ in the tasks and needs that are important to them as well as in their methods of coping.

Corr identifies four challenges that dying people encounter: the physical (satisfying body needs and reducing stress), the psychological (feeling secure, in control, and still having a life to live), the social (keeping valued attachments to other individuals and to groups and causes), and the spiritual (finding or affirming meaning, having a sense of connectedness, transcendence, and hope). We face challenges throughout the course of our lives, so we can draw upon what we have already learned and achieved when we must cope with the challenges of the dying process.

Above all, Corr advocates greater empowerment for the dying person and caregivers. With open communication and trusting relationships, we might feel less need for simple theories of the dying process. It is also a useful approach for recognizing that the dying person remains a living person who is attempting to cope as resourcefully as possible with challenges and stresses, and for including the full range of factors that influence the experience and course of the dying process.

The Dying Person's Own Reality as the Model

The patient's own reality is at the heart of another theory. The emphasis here shifts from the observer's frame of reference. Instead, the challenge is to learn how dying people interpret their own situation. In this view, there may be as many theoretical models of dying as there are dying people. Interest in the way terminally ill people interpret their experiences has been growing in recent years. For example, Debbie Messer Zlatin (1995) found that terminally ill people had a variety of different life themes to share. She also observed that there are important differences between people who do and who do not have integrated life themes to call upon as they face the stress of the dying process. Neris Diaz-Cabello (2004) found that within Hispanic culture there are a variety of individual and family perspectives on dying and death. Xolani Kacela (2004) identified significant differences between "religiously mature" and less mature people in interpreting their end-of-life experiences. Patient narratives collected by Barnard (2000) and Lawton (2000) offer additional examples of the ways in which terminally ill people interpret their own experiences.

An in-depth example has been provided through the journal kept by a distinguished researcher during the last weeks of his life (Kastenbaum, 1995/1996). William McDougall, a British-born physician, was a founder of the field of social psychology and an influential thinker in several other areas of scholarly activity. His terminal illness in 1938 was a painful ordeal, years before palliative care techniques became widely available. The last weeks of his life centered on a confrontation between the relief of pain and his determination to exercise his will power as long as possible. When his pain was at its most intense, the exercise of his intellect was also at its most inspired. He could avoid becoming what he perceived as a passive and defeated victim as long as he could maintain his intellectual effort against pain. Occasionally, McDougall and his will power were victorious: "How far can an intellectual effort diminish pain? It can throw fairly severe pain into the background and keep it there pretty steadily for an hour or two. And I think one gains confidence and success in the effort" (p. 142).

McDougall's intellectual approach to the dying process is at odds with the current emphasis on emotions, relationships, and peaceful acceptance, and he does not subscribe to any standard list of "developmental tasks." Such reliance on intellectualism and will power would have made McDougall guilty of a politically incorrect response, if we apply the "shoulds" that became popular when the death awareness movement emerged in the 1970s. McDougall, though, continued to be McDougall—even more so—as he called upon all his knowledge and skills to integrate dying and death into his overall view of self and world. A person who decided to treat McDougall from an outsider's perspective would have very likely failed to understand and, therefore, respond usefully to this man's rock-solid and distinctive interpretation of the dying process.

A Multiple Perspective Approach

For many years I was focused on what might be unique about the dying process. Eventually, though, I realized that much of what the dying person experiences has its counterpart in other situations. The more clearly we recognize the similarities, the more we can draw upon knowledge of more familiar phenomena to help us understand and support the dying person. This multiple perspective approach suggests that we identify these other processes one at a time and then to gradually put them together to form both a more comprehensive and a more detailed understanding of the dying person's situation. The central fact that

BOX 4-4

Partial Models of the Dying Person's Situation

Model	Brief Description
1. Restricted activity	I can do less and less.
2. Limited energy	I must conserve what is left of my strength.
3. Damaged body image	I do not look and feel as I should.
4. Contagion	You act like you would catch something bad from me.
5. Disempowerment	I have lost the ability to influence you.
6. Attributional incompetency	You think I can't do anything right.
7. Ineffectuance	I can't make things happen the way I want them to.
8. Stress response overload	My defenses have become so intense that they are causing problems of their own.
9. Time anxiety	I fear it's too late to do all I must do.
10. Performance anxiety	How am I doing? How do you think I am doing?
11. Loss and separation	I am losing contact with everything that is most important to me.
12. Disengagement	I feel like withdrawing from interactions and responsibilities.
13. Journey	I am going some place I have never been before.
14. Closing the book	I am doing everything for the last time; it will soon be over.
15. Endangered relationship	I fear I am losing your love and respect.
16. Struggling brain	My mind is not working as it should; the world is slipping away from me.
17. Storying	I must come up with the best possible story of all that has happened, is happening, will happen.

the person is terminally ill would then be added to complete the picture (Kastenbaum, 2000).

Seventeen partial models of the dying process are identified in Box 4-4. By "partial model" I mean that each offers a framework for observing and responding to one aspect of the dying person's situation. Which of these partial models would be most useful for understanding what a particular person is experiencing will depend on that particular person and his or her situation.

It would be unusual to go through life without experiencing some of these situations, perhaps repeatedly. A person with a progressively life-threatening condition is almost certain to have many of these sources of concern—in addition to the prospect of death. We can draw upon our own life experiences and observations to help us understand and respond effectively to what a dying person is experiencing, although we will not assume

that the other person must be interpreting the situation the same way we did. Here are brief comments regarding a few of the partial models. Draw upon your own observations and reflections to go beyond what space permits us to present here (see also Kastenbaum, 2000 and "practicing death," Kastenbaum, 2004).

1. *The restricted activity model.* We are likely to become frustrated, angry, and depressed when circumstances prevent us from doing what we usually do and feel very much needs doing. Some people become tense and agitated when confined to bed for just a few days. Some people in perfect physical health either stew or feel helpless when their activities are restricted by external circumstances (such as bad weather, bureaucratic delay, or insufficient funds). Part of the tension and frustration experienced by

dying people can be attributed to restricted activity. Everything we know and everything we can devise to help people deal with a restricted activity situation could relieve some of the dying person's stress.

2. *The damaged or altered body image model.* You have never been upset because the mirror suggests you might be too thin or too heavy. You have never had a bad hair day. You will certainly not be concerned when wrinkles curl in and age spots blossom out. And certainly you felt just as good about yourself as ever when you had that runny nose or outbreak of zits. Most of us, though, do respond with concern when our body no longer looks the same. Our anxiety tends to increase further when our body no longer performs the same. We experience anything from mild to severe distress when what we see and feel suggests we are not now as we were. (By the way, who is that old guy in the mirror, and what am I supposed to do with him?) The dying person is subject to prolonged and intensifying feedback that challenges self-image and confidence. What do we know about coping with distorted and altered body image? How might we help?

3. *The disempowerment model.* Experiences of powerlessness and helplessness can afflict us in many life situations. "I couldn't do anything. I couldn't say anything," as she was evicted from her home on a sudden foreclosure. "The two of them would take my lunch money just like that, or my lunch, if I had one. Anything I'd try to do would only make it worse." These experiences are devastating during a life-threatening illness. Sand et al. (2008) found these feelings among dying cancer patients, but also found something else. Sudden symptoms and events and uncertainty about the outcome intensified the sense of powerlessness and helplessness. Discovering ways to protect and renew the sense of empowerment throughout the broad range of life situations could be especially valuable at the end of life.

4. *The time anxiety model.* Will you get it done in time? How will you write all those term papers and prepare for all those exams with so little time left? Schedules and deadlines are ever present in the lives of many people. It is not unusual to face several sets of schedules and deadlines at the same time as personal, family, social, and work demands converge on us. Everything seems to be moving too fast, and we feel tense and irritable as we look for a way out of the dilemma. The situation is intensified when we have too little time to accomplish something that is of great importance to us. Dying people sometimes find themselves in precisely that situation. They may have such crucial end-of-life issues as making financial arrangements to benefit the family or rescuing an intimate relationship that had come apart. We might be more helpful if we recognized that a dying person might be struggling with a foreshortened future and pressing needs to accomplish some things. Gibson et al. (2009) confirm the anxiety experienced by "futureless people" who wonder if the next day will be their last. How can we learn to reorient ourselves to a foreshortened future and continue to find value and meaning in life? This is another question we might consider when we encounter less formidable examples throughout life.

5. *The journey model.* The idea of journey is embedded in many world cultures (Cole, 1992). Galen, Aristotle, and other voices from ancient times described the life course as a journey from one age or stage to the next. Christian theologians spoke of "spiritual ages." Erik H. Erikson's (1950) "Eight Ages of Man" is among the more influential updatings of the journey idea. Rituals have long been closely associated with journeys. It is risky to leave our present situation and venture forth. The real and symbolic distance between where we are and where we are going is full of danger. Ritual protects. Anybody who has ever moved into a new relationship, new job, or new community has probably experienced something of the anxiety that can be associated with even a positive change. Dying people are in transition from the world they have known (Kastenbaum, 2004). Some of their thoughts and feelings might well be understood in these terms. Are there forms of ritual that would be meaningful and supportive to this person on the final journey?

Most of us do not come to the dying process as complete strangers. We have had experiences such as those identified in Box 4-4, and perhaps we have learned something useful from them.

Your Deathbed Scene

Perhaps you took a crack at the deathbed scene exercise suggested in Box 4-1. Following is some information on the way that other people participating in death-related classes have depicted their own deaths (Kastenbaum & Normand, 1990). The typical respondent:

- Expected to die in old age
- At home
- Quickly
- With the companionship of loved ones
- While remaining alert and
- Not experiencing pain or any other symptoms.

What was the most common alternative response? Those who did not expect to die in the manner summarized instead saw themselves as perishing in an accident, usually on the highway and in the near future while they were still young. Almost all thought they would be alert and experience no pain or other symptoms as they neared death, whether death happened at home in old age or on the road in youth.

These deathbed scene expectations by mostly young college students will take on more meaning when we continue our exploration of the dying process in the next chapter with the focus on hospice care. You can enhance the personal meaning of the next chapter by pausing to answer the questions raised in Box 4-5.

Improving End-of-Life Care

That too many people die in pain, isolation, and despair has been known for a long time by those close to the situation. The hospice and palliative care movement (Chapter 5) developed in response to this need. There is now more widespread recognition of the need to improve end-of-life care, although policy decision makers and major societal institutions still have responded somewhat laggardly. Unfortunately, the evidence of inadequate symptom relief continues to be troubling. A study of nearly 500 elderly people in a university hospital finds that care planning and symptom palliation often was deficient in the last days of their lives. Pain, agitation, and stressful breathing were prevalent. Welling et al. (2010) note that this distress could have been prevented or alleviated by more attentive clinical assessment and charting.

A national survey (Last Acts, 2002) found that Americans judge that end-of-life care is inadequate and should be improved. There was a disconnect between the way in which most Americans wanted their lives to end and what usually did happen. For example, 7 of 10 people said they would prefer to die at home, surrounded by family and friends—but more than 7 in 10 died in a hospital.

The National Institutes of Health (NIH) (2005) also inquired into the status of care for terminally ill people in the United States. The NIH report notes that very little has been learned about

---

BOX 4-5

A THOUGHT EXERCISE

The following questions were included in the National Hospice Demonstration Study (in a slightly different form). In the next chapter, you will learn how terminally ill people responded to these questions and some of the implications for hospice care.

Now, imagine yourself nearing the end of your life. Give the answers that best describe your own thoughts and feelings. Write your answers on a separate piece of paper.

1. Describe the last three days of your life as you would like them to be. Include whatever aspects of the situation seem to be of greatest importance.
2. What will be your greatest sources of strength and support during these last days of your life?

the end-of-life situations for children and their caregivers and for persons with severe cognitive or other communication disorders. Minorities have remained underrepresented in end-of-life research as well as in access to and use of health care options. There is also little evidence on the management of symptoms other than pain. Furthermore, most of the research has focused on people with terminal cancer, so relatively little has been learned about the experiences of people with other types of terminal conditions. Congestive heart failure, end-stage renal disease, chronic obstructive pulmonary disease, and liver failure are among the life-limiting conditions that have rarely been studied from the end-of-life perspective. The experiences and stresses of professional caregivers at the end of life have also not been studied sufficiently.

Several of the conclusions and recommendations especially deserve our attention here (National Institutes of Health, 2005):

- Spiritual well-being has achieved recognition as a goal in end-of-life care. The information currently available suggests that families as well as patients benefit from programs that support dignity, purpose, and meaning. There is much yet to do if such programs are to be developed throughout the nation and their positive outcomes confirmed.
- The level of staff training varies across settings of care (e.g., nursing, homes, community hospitals, university hospitals, and hospices). More attention is needed on identifying the types of care that are most beneficial in each setting and on providing adequate end-of-life training for all care providers.
- There is a need to heighten awareness of ethical questions "regarding such things as the concept of a good death, and identify and resolve ethical problems in end-of-life care that arise from conflicting needs of care givers and care receivers" (p. 6).
- "Current end-of-life care is often fragmented among providers and provider settings, leading to a lack of continuity of care and impeding the ability to provide high-quality, interdisciplinary care" (p. 7).
- "Enhanced communication among patients, families, and providers is crucial to high-quality end-of-life care" (p. 7).

The positive is that there is now enough experience and accomplishment to make end-of-life care a national priority. Whether there will be enough support to reach the next level of quality care remains to be seen. Meanwhile, care providers and researchers are reporting success with patient contacts that explore deeper levels of communication. Some people seem to benefit greatly from the opportunity to prepare themselves by exploring their "life completion" (Steinhauser et al. 2009), as well as a related approach for professional caregivers to enable them to "be with" the dying in a more resourceful and helpful manner (Rushton et al. 2009).

■ SUMMARY

This chapter has considered dying as part of our total life experience while at the same time attending to what is distinctive about living with terminal illness. We have noted that the process of dying has been changing along with broader changes in society and medical technology. The "last moment," for example, is less likely to pass as a salient and memorable occasion (though see Chapter 5 for the hospice approach). You were given the opportunity to imagine your own deathbed scene before we turned to the fundamental questions: What is dying, and when does it begin? How we answer these questions is consequential because a person is often treated very differently by others when defined as dying or terminally ill. Several competing alternatives were identified. Dying might be said to begin when (1) the physician draws this conclusion, (2) the physician informs the patient, (3) the patient accepts this conclusion, or (4) nothing more can be done to preserve life.

The transition from life to death can take one of several different trajectories, as described by Glaser and Strauss. We gave particular attention to the lingering trajectory, the expected quick trajectory, and the unexpected quick trajectory. Hospital staff members usually feel and respond differently to people who are on different trajectories. Awareness of these differences can help us to provide more effective support to patients, family, and staff. Familiar terms such as healthy, dying, and terminally ill do not apply to all individuals.

Some people end their lives in social isolation because of inadequate communication with others. Studies have documented continuing gaps in communication between many physicians and their terminally ill patients. A physician's inability or unwillingness to listen to a patient's statements all too often leaves the patient with uncontrolled pain and violates the patient's preferences for end-of-life management. Suggestions are made for improving communication with dying family members and friends.

We reminded ourselves that dying is both a universal and an individual experience. Age, gender, interpersonal relationships, the nature of the disease and its treatment, and the environmental setting were considered as influences on the individual's experience of dying.

Theoretical models of the dying process include three stage theories that have originated in markedly different contexts: the ancient Buddhist conception of passages, a saint's vision of "the throes of dying," and the clinical observations made by Kübler-Ross. The eight-stage Buddhist model is intimately related to that religion's view of the ever-changing and disintegrating process we call everyday life. The last four of these stages are said to occur past the point at which a physician would have certified death. The Kübler-Ross model consists of a sequence of responses that moves through denial, anger, bargaining, depression, and acceptance. Individuals do not always proceed through all the stages in either of these models. The Kübler-Ross stage theory is carefully evaluated. Attention is also given to three more recent theoretical approaches: a developmental coping model, accepting the dying person's own reality as the model, and a multiple perspective model in which many different physical, personal, and interpersonal processes are considered separately and then brought together. We then revisited the deathbed scene you created and invited you to consider some further questions about how you might feel in the last days of your life.

In conclusion, we drew upon reports from Last Acts and the National Institutes of Health that documented continuing challenges to the improvement of end-of-life care in the United States.

■ REFERENCES

Aiken, L. H., Clarke, S. P., Sloane, D. M., Sochalski, J., & Silber, J. H. (2002). Hospital nurse staffing and patient mortality, nurse burnout, and job dissatisfaction. *Journal of the American Medical Association, 288,* 1987–1993.

Associated Press (February 2, 2008). Fatal dementia cases raise ethical issues. *Arizona Republic,* p. A9.

Barnard, D. (2000). *Crossing over: Narratives of palliative care.* New York: Oxford University Press.

Bell, R. J. (2005). "Our people die well": Deathbed scenes in Methodist magazines in nineteenth-century Britain. *Mortality, 10,* 210–223.

Bosco, J. (undated). Il giovane provveduto (The Provident Young Man). In *Opera Edite' II.* Rome: Libreria Ateneo Salesiano.

Cole, T. R. (1992). *The journey of life.* Cambridge: Cambridge University Press.

Connor, S. R. (1992). Denial in terminal illness: To intervene or not to intervene. *The Hospice Journal, 8,* 1–15.

Coolidge, F. L., & Fish, C. E. (1983/1984). Dreams of the dying. *Omega, Journal of Death and Dying, 14,* 1–8.

Corr, C. A. (1993). Coping with dying: Lessons that we should and should not learn from the work of Elisabeth Kübler-Ross. *Death Studies, 17,* 69–84.

Corr, C. A., Doka, K. J., & Kastenbaum, R. (1999). Dying and its interpreters: A review of selected literature and some comments on the state of the field. *Omega, Journal of Death and Dying, 39,* 239–261.

Diaz-Cabello, N. (2004). The Hispanic way of dying: Three families, three perspectives, three cultures. *Illness, Crisis, & Loss, 12,* 239–255.

Eco, U. l (2004*). The mysterious flame of Queen Loana.* New York: Harcourt.

Emanuel, E. J., Fairclough, D. L., Wolfe, P., & Emanuel, L. L. (2004). Talking with terminally ill patients and their caregivers about death, dying, and bereavement. *Archives of Internal Medicine, 164,* 1999–2004.

Erikson, E. H. (1950). *Childhood and society.* New York: Norton.

Faust, D. G. (2008). *This republic of suffering. Death and the American Civil War.* New York: Alfred A. Knopf.

Feifel, H. (Ed.). (1959). *The meaning of death.* New York: McGraw-Hill.

Gibson, B. G., Zitzelsberger, H., & McKeever, P. (2009). "Futureless persons": Shifting life expectancies and the vicissitudes of progressive illness. *Sociology of Health and Illness, 31,* 554–568.

Glaser, B. G., & Strauss, A. (1966). *Awareness of dying.* Chicago: Aldine.

Glaser, B. G., & Strauss, A. (1968). *Time for dying.* Chicago: Aldine.

Gyatos, Tenzin, the fourteenth Dali Lama. (1985). *Kindness, clarity, and insight.* (J. Hopkins, Trans.). Ithaca: Snow Lions.

Hayslip, B., Jr., & Peveto, C. A. (2005). *Cultural changes in attitudes toward death, dying, and bereavement.* New York: Springer.

Hickman, S. E., Tilden, V. P., & Tolle, S. W. (2004). Family perceptions of worry, symptoms, and suffering in the dying. *Journal of Palliative Care, 20,* 20–27.

Hurley, A. C., & Volicer, L. (2002). Alzheimer's disease. "It's okay, Mama, if you want to go, it's okay." *Journal of the American Medical Association, 288,* 2324–2331.

Improving care near the end of life: Why is it so hard? [Editorial] (1995). *Journal of the American Medical Association, 274,* 1634–1636.

Kacela, X. (2004). Religious maturity in the midst of death and dying. *American Journal of Hospice & Palliative Medicine, 21,* 203–208.

Kastenbaum, R. (1978). In control. In C. A. Garfield (Ed.), *Psychosocial care of the dying patient* (pp. 227–244). New York: McGraw-Hill.

Kastenbaum, R. (1984). The changing role of the physician with the terminally ill elderly. In I. Rossman (Ed.), *Clinical geriatrics* (3rd ed., pp. 618–620). New York: Lippincott.

Kastenbaum, R. (1993/1994). Dale Gladden: An Omega interview. *Omega, Journal of Death and Dying, 28,* 1–16.

Kastenbaum, R. (1995/1996). "How far can an intellectual effort diminish pain?" William McDougall's journal as a model for facing death. *Omega, Journal of Death and Dying, 32,* 123–164.

Kastenbaum, R. (2003). *The psychology of death* (3rd ed.). New York: Springer.

Kastenbaum, R. (2004). *On our way: The final passage through life and death.* Berkeley: University of California Press.

Kastenbaum, R., Barber, T., Wilson, S., Ryder, B., & Hathaway, L. (1981). *Old, sick, and helpless.* Cambridge, MA: Ballinger.

Kastenbaum, R., & Normand, C. (1990). Deathbed scenes as expected by the young and experienced by the old. *Death Studies, 14,* 201–218.

Kastenbaum, R., & Thuell, S. (1995). Cookies baking, coffee brewing: Toward a contextual theory of dying. *Omega, Journal of Death and Dying, 31,* 175–188.

Keeley, M. P. (2007). "Turning toward death together": The functions of messages during final conversations in close relationships. *Journal of Social and Personal Relationships, 24,* 225–253.

Kellehear, A. (2009). Dying old—and *preferably* alone? Agency, resistance and dissent at the end of life. *International Journal of Ageing and Later Life, 4,* 5–21.

Kiecolt-Glaser, J. K., McGuire, L., Robles, T. F., & Glaser, R. (2002). Emotions, morbidity, and mortality: New perspectives from psychoneuroimmunology. *Annual Review of Psychology, 53,* 83–107.

Kramer, K. (1988). *The sacred art of dying.* New York: The Paulist Press.

Kaufman, S. R. (2005). *. . . And a time to die. How American hospitals shape the end of life.* New York: Scribner.

Kübler-Ross, E. (1969). *On death and dying.* New York: Macmillan.

Laakkonen, M. L., Pitkala, K. H., & Strandberg, T. E. (2004). Terminally ill elderly patients' experiences, attitudes, and needs: A qualitative study. *Omega, Journal of Death and Dying, 49,* 117–130.

Last Acts (2002). *Means to a better end: A report on dying in America today.* Princeton, NJ: Robert Woods Johnson Foundation.

Lawton, J. (2000). *The dying process. Patients' experiences of palliative care.* London: Routledge.

Leale, C. A. (2010). *Lincoln's last hours.* Amazon Kindle.

LeShan, L. (1982). In M. N. Bowers, E. N. Jackson, J. A. Knight, & L. LeShan (Eds.), *Counseling the dying* (pp. 6–7). New York: Nelson.

Lesses, K. (1982/1983). How I live now. *Omega, Journal of Death and Dying, 13,* 75–78.

Mamo, L. (2008). Death and dying: Confluences of emotion and awareness. *Sociology of Health & Illness, 30,* 13–36.

Meier, D. E. (2005). Variability in end of life care. http://www.bmj.com/content/328/7449/E296.full.

Nabhan, C. (2009). How could you do this, Doctor . . . ? *American Journal of Hospice & Palliative Medicine, 26,* 239–240.

National Institutes of Health. (2005). Improving end of life care. http://consensus.nih.gov/2004/2004EndOfLifeCareSOS024html.htm.

Paxton, F. S. (2003). Christian death rites, history of. In R. Kastenbaum (Ed.), *Macmillan encyclopedia of death and dying* (Vol. 1, pp. 163–167). New York: Macmillan.

Proulx, K., & Jacelon, C. (2004). Dying with dignity: The good patient versus the good death. *American Journal of Hospice and Palliative Medicine, 21,* 116–120.

Provonost, P. J., Angus, D. C., Dorman, T., Robinson, K. A., Dremisov, T. T., & Young, T. L. (2002). Physician staffing patterns and clinical outcomes in critically ill patients, *Journal of the American Medical Association, 288,* 2151–2162.

Rodriguez, K. L., Gambio, F. J., Butow, W., Hagerty, R., & Arnold, R. M. (2006). Pushing up daisies: Implicit and euphemistic language in oncologist-patient *Communication. Supportive Care in Cancer, 15,* 153–161.

Rushton, C. H., Sellers, D. E., Heller, K. S. Spring, B., Dossey, B.M., & Halifax, J. (2009). Impact of a contemplative end-of-life training program: Being with dying. *Palliative and Supportive Care, 7,* 405–414.

Sand, L., Strang, P., & Milberg, A. (2008). Dying cancer patients' experiences of powerlessness and helplessness. *Support Care Cancer, 16,* 853–892.

Steinhauser, K. E., Alexander, S. C., Byock, I. R., George, L. K., & Tulsky, J. A. (2009). Seriously ill patients' discussions of preparation and life completion: An intervention to assist with transition at the end of life. *Palliative and Supportive, Care 7,* 393–405.

Sulmasy, D. P. (2002). I was sick and you came to visit me: Time spent at the bedsides of seriously ill patients with poor prognoses. *American Journal of Medicine, 111,* 385–389.

SUPPORT. (1995). A controlled trial to improve care for seriously ill hospitalized patients. *Journal of the American Medical Association, 274,* 1591–1599.

Taylor, J. (1977). *Holy dying.* New York: Arno Press. (Original work published 1651.)

Timmermans, S. (2008).Dying of awareness: The theory of awareness contexts revisited. *Sociology of Health & Illness, 31,* 322–339.

Vespasian (A.D. 79) In last words of real people. .

Villa, P. In last words of real people. http://www.geocities.com/Athens/Acropolis/6537/realt.hm.

Walling, A. M., Asch, S.M, Lorenz, K. A., Roth, C. P., Kahn, B. T, & Wenger, N. S. (2010). The quality of care provided to hospitalized patients at the end of life. *Archives of Internal Medicine, 170,* 1057–1063.

Weisman, A. D. (1993). Avery D. Weisman: An Omega interview. *Omega, Journal of Death and Dying, 27,* 97–104.

Weisman, A. D., & Kastenbaum, R. (1968). *The psychological autopsy: A study of the terminal phase of life.* New York: Behavioral Publications.

Weisman, A. D., & Worden, J. W. (1975). Psychosocial analysis of cancer deaths. *Omega, Journal of Death and Dying, 6,* 61–65.

Weisman, A. D., & Worden, J. W. (1976). The existential plight in cancer. Significance of the first 100 days. *International Journal of Psychiatry in Medicine, 7,* 1–16.

Zlatin, D. M. (1995). Life themes: A method to understand terminal illness. *Omega, Journal of Death and Dying, 31,* 189–206.

■ GLOSSARY

Apoptosis Cell death that is programmed into the biology of the life course.

Cardiopulmonary Resuscitation (CPR) Massage, injection, or electrical stimulation intended to restore heart and breath.

Colostomy Bag A container for the collection of feces, attached to an abdominal opening following a surgical procedure on the bowel.

Danger List (D.L.) A classification used by some health care systems to indicate that a patient is at risk for death.

Institutional Evasions Techniques used by staff members to bypass the rules in order to get through a difficult situation.

Middle Knowledge A state of mind in which the person has some awareness of death but shifts from time to time in acknowledging and expressing this awareness.

Stage Theory Holds that the phenomena in question occur in a fixed sequence of qualitatively different forms. *Trajectories of Dying:* The distinctive patterns through time that can be taken by the dying process, for example, a long fading away (lingering trajectory) or unexpected (quick trajectory).

■ ON FURTHER THOUGHT . . .

Useful online resources:

AIDS Caregivers Support Network
   www.wolfenet.com/acsn
The ALS Association*
   www.alsa.org
   (*amyotrophic lateral sclerosis, also known as Lou Gehrig's disease)

American Cancer Society
   www.cancer.org
American Lung Association
   www.lungusa.org
Last Acts
   www.lastacts.org
Leukemia and Lymphoma Society
   www.leukemia.org
National Alliance for Children with Life-Threatening
   Conditions
   www.nacwltc.org
National Association of People with AIDS
   www.napwa.org
National Stroke Association
   www.stroke.org
Partnership for Caring
   www.partnershipforcaring.org

A Challenge: Dying Alone, Preferably?
Sociologist Allan Kellehear (2009) contends that negative value judgments on dying alone are off base. "Dying alone is viewed either as an outcome of antisocial behavior or the result of family, neighborhood or social services neglect. The idea that people may be exercising agency resistance or dissent at the end of life and that they do not want attention from services or the wider community receives little or no consideration" (p. 5). Is this a valid point, or itself off base? What do your experience and judgment tell you?

Hospice and Palliative Care

For those that argue that there are symptoms more important than pain, I disagree. Pain is a demon and a disabler and affects more than a subjective sense of suffering. It also affects immune status cognitive and functional abilities affective states, and psychoemotional health, all of which increase morbidity and reduce quality of life.

—Paul Rousseau M.D., 2010, p. 97

I was his caregiver but I was his wife first . . . you know, that was our relationship. I mean I looked after him, not in the sense that I was a caregiver, but because I was his wife and I wanted to do it.

—Quoted by Brazil et al., 2010, p. 114

They're just the most caring, loving, compassionate group of people I've ever known, and they can talk to me openly about death, and they can use the word "terminal" and look me in the eye . . . and I mean, we're able to talk about it.

—A woman with heart disease describing her hospice experience (Caroline Pevey, 2005, p. 131)

Hundreds of hospice providers across the country are facing the catastrophic consequences of what would otherwise seem a positive development: their patients are living longer than expected.

—Kevin Sack, 2007 (p. 3)

. . . it's that which is so frightening . . . it feels . . . it feels roughly like . . . running on a treadmill . . . and there right at the front on the treadmill . . . there' it's like death . . . you fight and you fight but . . . but you don't get away, and, well, I can't explain it in a better way.

—A woman with terminal cancer describing her fatigue (Olav Lindqvist, Anders Widmark, & Brigit H. Rasmussen, 2004, p. 241).

To feel safe. To be with people who know and care about you. To have the attention of expert caregivers who respect your values and wishes. Palliative care offered an alternative to the typical medical management approach to terminally ill people when it was established in the United Kingdom and introduced to North America with the New Haven Hospice (later renamed Connecticut Hospice in 1974).

Through its relatively short history, modern hospice care has been changing as well as expanding. Even the terminology has shifted. *Hospice* too often suggested a place, not a program of care. We now hear more of *palliative care*. This term was suggested by Canadian physician Balfour Mount (2003) in the 1970s and has continued to gain favor. As Mount notes, this word derives from *pallium*, the Latin for cloak. The term now refers to interventions that reduce suffering.

Hospice has come a long way toward fulfilling its promise. The National Hospice and Palliative Care Organization (NHPCO, 2010) estimates that currently about 1.45 million people a year in the United States receive services through a hospice program. Nearly two out of five terminally ill people select hospice care—a remarkable development. There are now almost 5,000 hospice programs throughout the United States. Enrollment in a palliative care program is not always concluded by death. Each year more than 200,000 recover sufficiently to be discharged. Hospice has been found to protect and enhance patients' quality of life as well as to provide cost savings for Medicare when compared with traditional medical management (Enck, 2009; Raduluvic, 2007). In fact, federal support of hospice programs has been contingent on cost savings from the very start.

Nevertheless, palliative care remains very much a work in progress. It has to deal with the complexities of the overall human services system and meet all the needs of all the people who might benefit. This chapter identifies the obstacles, limitations, and challenges of palliative care as well as its achievements.

Why, for example, should a physician need to remind his colleagues that pain is "a demon and a disabler?" This is what compassionate physicians and nurses were saying 50 years ago, and was one of the prime reasons for developing palliative care

programs. But Paul Rousseau, a leader in geriatric and terminal care, still encounters everyday examples of physicians who withhold effective pain relief medications. Rousseau is troubled by:

> *The apparent fear of opioids and the stark ability of many physicians to emotionally detach themselves and look past the suffering of a fellow human being in pain. . . . Perhaps they themselves or their family have never experienced the anguish of pain. . . perhaps they lack education in pain management [and] do not value a "new" specialty such as palliative care—or perhaps they truly do fear the very remote possibility of regulatory scrutiny and penalty (op. cit., p. 97).*

Relief of pain—the crux of the palliative care movement—has yet to become a prevailing value in the health care system, although progress has been made.

The woman quoted by Brazil et al. had long been both wife and caregiver. Now, however, she had to adjust to a different type of caregiving and somehow maintain yet alter her relationship with her terminally ill husband. Hospice programs rely much on family caregivers. In every instance, though, there are particular challenges to the family member who is taking on this responsibility. Hospice personnel must teach, and family caregivers must learn effectively and find the emotional strength to carry through.

Another challenge? Consider, for example, the shifting configuration of conditions with which people enter hospice care. Terminal cancer was by far the most common illness among hospice patients from the beginning. Now, however, palliative care is also being provided for an increasing number of people with life-threatening heart conditions. Betty Specter, the woman quoted above who so warmly appreciated hospice care, is among those with a cardiac condition. Hospice services are proving helpful. But there is a catch, as noted by Sack (2007) and others. Hospice patients with cardiac conditions often live longer than expected by Medicare regulations and budgeting provisions. Should patients with terminal heart disease be ejected from hospice care even if they are receiving a superior level of care? If forced out of hospice, the cardiac patients would still require care, and that care would still cost money. Effectively meeting human needs at the end of life does not guarantee a hospice organization that it will be given realistic support by the health care bureaucracy.

This ongoing situation reminds us that hospice care is more than an arrangement between terminally ill people, their families, and compassionate caregivers: it is part of a complex health management system in which political and economic agendas play a powerful role. Palliative care made it into this system quickly, but thereby became vulnerable to a massive bureaucracy. Continued public advocacy for palliative care could make the difference. On the positive side, the medical establishment, after a period of hesitation, is making significant contributions to the palliative care movement. A subspecialty in palliative medicine was approved in 2006, and major programs have been launched to educate physicians and nurses in terminal care (e.g., Harvard Medical School, 2008), though there is still a long way to go across the nation.

Back to Kim, the woman with terminal cancer who was experiencing a debilitating sense of fatigue:

> If I can have a reasonably tolerable life . . . but
> to take one step and then you have to rest
> and then one step and then it hurts in your
> chest . . . and . . . well then then then I can feel it
> sometimes that . . . yes, if you could just, bang,
> fall asleep then . . . and it was all over (sigh)
> although I don't really want that (sad) (p. 241).

The palliative care movement recognizes that many of us eventually find ourselves in situations at the edge of hope and endurance. There is a continuing effort to develop improved care techniques. Hospice must also keep itself alive and well even when confronted by daunting challenges. The vitality and resourcefulness of the hospice movement is itself an achievement worth celebrating.

HOSPICE: A NEW FLOWERING FROM ANCIENT ROOTS

Temples of healing ministered to the psychological and physical ailments of the Greeks. Priests and other healers recognized that health and illness involved the whole person. The temples were designed to soothe and encourage the anxious and ailing people who journeyed to them. Every effort was made to restore the patients through an appealing physical environment, music, therapeutic conversation, positive imagery, bathing, massage, and walks in the countryside. Later, imperial Rome established hospitals for military personnel. However, neither the temple nor the hospital was designed primarily for the care of the dying person.

Some compassionate people did provide comfort to the dying. In the *harem* of a Byzantine ruler there were women with special skill in caring for the dying. Some wealthy families in Syria and Athens saw to it that the poor were treated well in their last days of life. The documentary trail becomes clearer with the advent of the Christian era. Public infirmaries (*nosocomeia*) were established in Greek-speaking areas of Christianity during the fourth century. These facilities cared for people dying of epidemics as well as those who were likely to recover. Roman Emperor Julian, an opponent of the upstart Christian movement, acknowledged that these hospices had made a very favorable impression on everybody "owing to the humanity evinced by Christians toward outsiders" (Phipps, 1988). Julian resolved to establish hospices in every city, but his own death aborted this plan.

The hospice movement spread to Western Europe near the end of the fourth century through the influence of Fabiola, a wealthy Roman widow who was inspired by the care for the sick that she had witnessed in monasteries in the Holy Land (Phipps, 1988). Fabiola brought this concept back with her to Italy, not only supporting hospices financially but also serving as a nurse herself. St. Jerome knew Fabiola and honored her contributions, writing that "Often too she washed away the matter discharged from wounds which others, even though men, could not hear to behold . . . She gave food with her own hand and even when a patient was but a breathing corpse she would moisten his lips with liquid" (cited by Phipps, p. 93). And so Fabiola, this woman who lived and died about 1,600 years ago, may have given an enduring gift to humankind that in our own time has been renewed as the modern hospice program.

A type of hospice became well established in the fifth century. The term itself derives from the Latin *hospitium*, which has also given us the words *host* and *hostess*. The medieval hospice was

It is a woman who provides care for disabled and life-threatened men in this thirteenth-century illustration, and it is still most often women who serve at the bedside of terminally ill people.

usually a house in which people in need could find comfort under Christian auspices. Care of the homeless dying was but one function; it also served those undertaking the arduous pilgrimage to the Holy Land. Established by Benedictine monks in the sixth century, the Monte Cassino monastery was one of the most noted hospices (unfortunately, destroyed during World War II). Throughout the medieval period, the hospice functioned as one of the purest expressions of Christian piety: here the hungry were fed, the thirsty given water, the naked clothed, the homeless sheltered, and the sick provided with care and comfort. Medical treatment was minimal—which was probably just as well, considering how ineffective or even dangerous most "remedies" were at that time.

Unfortunately, something went very much wrong between the time that the early hospices flourished and the beginning of the modern hospice movement. During the intervening centuries the original hospice tradition clung to life in only a few scattered facilities. Phipps suggests that hospices became an innocent casualty of the Protestant Reformation, and were replaced by state-run institutions. Bureaucracy and technology-oriented medicine gradually took over the scene. Modernization of health care had neither a strong religious foundation nor an interest in people who persisted in dying even though favored with the latest miracle treatments.

A renewed hospice approach made its appearance in the nineteenth century. Again, the leaders were women who recognized the need to provide compassionate and effective care for people at the end of their lives. Jeanne Garnier inspired other young widows to establish L'Association des Dames du Calvaire in Lyon, France, in 1842.

Her influence spread to other cities, where organizations were established that anticipated modern hospice care (Clark, 2000). Another major step forward was Mary Aikenhead's establishment of St. Vincent's Hospital in London. In her memory, Our Lady's Hospice for the Dying started in 1879 at a nearby convent. In 1905, St. Joseph's Hospital introduced improvements in pain relief and general medical care. The worldwide hospice movement today owes much to the women who created such caregiving institutions, despite their initial lack of financial resources and political influence. For some time, however, these programs remained small and isolated as industrial and technological developments continued to transform society. They were also deeply embedded in religious belief systems and church practices (Humphreys, 2001).

The hospice movement took its next major step forward when a medical officer at St. Joseph's Hospice, Dr. Cicely Saunders, improved pain control for dying people. In 1967, Saunders founded St. Christopher's Hospice in London, which has since served as inspiration and model for many others. Starting out as a student of philosophy, politics, and economics, Saunders enrolled in a nurse training program during World War II. A back injury made it difficult for her to continue as a nurse, so she became a social worker, and then a physician. This triple perspective liberated Saunders from seeing the dying person from the limitations of any one health provider standpoint. Her vision of hospice care emphasized contributions from people of diverse backgrounds.

I asked Dame Saunders about the circumstances that led to her introduction of modern hospice care. The inspiration provided by two people were especially important. Lillian Pipkin, a Salvation Army matron, taught her the basics of pain management for and communication with terminally ill patients. The other person was David Tasma, a dying man who (Saunders, 1993)

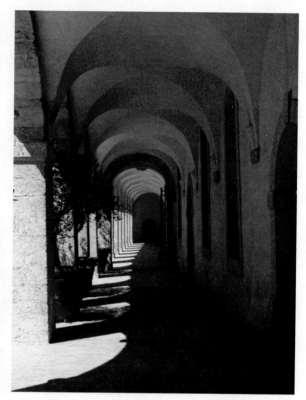

Now a cultural landmark, Marsielle's La Vielle Charite provided hospice care to dying and other desperate people a thousand years ago.

needed not only symptom relief, but also the time, space, and atmosphere in which to come to his own terms with his life. At this point, David was feeling that his life had been unfulfilled and perhaps meaningless. Something emerged during our long conversations that not only sparked the inspiration for hospice but also made possible his own quiet peace. . . . David had made

a personal peace with the God of his forefathers before he died, and he left me with the assurance that he had found his answers—and with the belief that all our caring must give total freedom to others to make their own way into meaning" *(Saunders, 1993).*

Tasma also contributed his small legacy to Saunders for what would become the hospice project.

And what was the first response of physicians and nurses to Saunders's innovations? Would they be dubious and resistant?

I was therefore soon able to demonstrate to an increasing number of visitors that dying patients could be alert, as well as free from pain, and very able to do the teaching themselves. Without this opportunity, I do not think the modern hospice movement would have been established and I am

Dame Cicely Saunders (1918–2005), founder of the international hospice movement.

everlastingly grateful to the patients and Sisters of St. Joseph's who, together with David Tasma and the patients of St. Luke's, I see as the true founders (Saunders, 1993).

Although hospice leaders often are people with strong religious belief, the emphasis is on giving "total freedom to others to make their own way into meaning." This was evident at the start in the interaction between a Christian physician and her agnostic Jewish patient (Tasma).

STANDARDS OF CARE FOR THE TERMINALLY ILL

An International Work Group on Death and Dying (IWG) recognized the need to develop guidelines for hospice care. I suggested that first we identify the unspoken assumptions that governed the care of the terminally ill. These were the hidden rules that hospice intended to replace (Kastenbaum, 1975a: Kastenbaum, 1975b).

Hidden or Implicit Standards of Care

1. The successful death is quiet and uneventful. The death slips by with as little notice as possible; nobody is disturbed.
2. Few people are on the scene. There is, in effect, no scene. Staff is spared the discomfort of interacting with family and other visitors whose needs might upset the well-routined equilibrium.
3. Leave-taking behavior is at a minimum: there are no awkward, painful, or emotional goodbyes to raise the staff's anxiety level.
4. The physician does not have to involve him- or herself intimately in terminal care, especially as the end approaches.

5. The staff makes few technical errors throughout the terminal care process and few mistakes in medical etiquette.

6. Attention is focused on the body during the caregiving process. Little effort is wasted on the unique personality of the terminally ill individual.

7. The patient expresses gratitude for the excellent care received.

8. The person dies at the right time, that is, after the full range of medical interventions has been tried out before the onset of a long period of lingering on.

9. After the patient's death, the family expresses gratitude for the excellent care received.

10. The staff is able to conclude that "we did everything we could for this patient."

11. Physical remains of the patient are made available to the hospital for clinical, research, or administrative purposes (via autopsy permission or organ donations).

12. A memorial (financial) gift is made to the hospital in the name of the deceased.

13. Money was not wasted on a person whose life was beyond saving or, even better, the hospital came out ahead.

The task force itself proposed a very different set of standards!

Proposed Standards Recommended by the International Task Force

- Patients, family, and staff all have legitimate needs and interests.
- The terminally ill person's own preferences and lifestyle must be taken into account in all decision making.

These were the basic guidelines. Examples of more specific standards include the following (Kastenbaum, 1976):

Patient-Oriented Standards

1. *Remission of symptoms is a treatment goal.* Even if the patient is expected to die within hours or days, efforts should be continued to maintain functional capacity and relieve pain and anguish. A dying person should not be made to endure thirst, for example, or gasp for breath when a change of position might afford relief.

2. *The patient's intentions will be respected as one of the main determinants of the total pattern of care.* The rights and responsibilities of family, staff, and society as represented by the legal system must also be taken into account. (Advance directives, see Chapter 7, would later come into being.)

3. *Patients should feel safe.* They should not have to live in apprehension of unexpected diagnostic or treatment procedures, brusque interactions, or a breakdown in medication and meal routines.

4. *Opportunities should be provided for leave-takings with the people most important to the patient, and for experiencing the final moments in a way that is meaningful to the patient.* This requires flexibility in visiting hours and rules. There should be privacy, and freedom from interruption. The patient should also have the opportunity to take leave of other patients and staff members if desired.

Family-Oriented Standards

1. *Families should have the opportunity to discuss dying, death, and related emotional needs with the staff.* It is not acceptable for the staff to disregard requests for information or expressions of the need to share feelings.

2. *Families should have the opportunity for privacy with the dying person both while living and immediately after death.* This might include their participation in dressing the corpse and escorting it to the funeral home. Or it might include simply being alone with the dead spouse, sibling, or parent for an hour or so without interruption by staff.

Staff-Oriented Standards

1. *Caregivers should have adequate time to form and maintain personal relationships with the patient.* This is not a priority in most medical facilities. Hospital scheduling practices seldom make it possible for a nurse or other staff member to maintain a steady relationship with a patient.

2. *A mutual support network should exist among the staff.* Care for the terminally ill can become an emotionally depleting experience, especially if staff are given little opportunity to share their experiences and feelings.

These guidelines were subsequently incorporated into the Medicare specifications for a full-service hospice and the standards adopted by the National Hospice and Palliative Care Organization. A more detailed version was later developed in a cooperative project by several organizations concerned with improving end-of-life care. An executive summary and the full text are available through Info@NationalConsensusProject.org.

THE HOSPICE IN ACTION

"Should we choose hospice or traditional care?" is a key question. We will be in a better position to consider this question after exploring how a hospice actually works. Here are a few examples.

Entering St. Christopher's

The first example is an observation I had the opportunity to make during a visit to St. Christopher's. A station wagon had just pulled up to an entrance facing the hospice's attractive garden plaza. The patient-to-be was a frail, emaciated woman who looked to be in her 60s. She was accompanied by a younger man. Dr. Saunders and the woman greeted each other as sunlight propitiously broke through the cloudy London skies. The woman smiled and said, "Well, I finally made it!" On her face there was the mark of physical ordeal, but no indication of anxiety, anger, depression, or confusion.

The patient was immediately introduced to the nurse who would be responsible for much of her care. The nurse then assisted her to what would be her own bed (which had been transported by elevator to the ground entrance). Just a few minutes later, while touring the hospice, we came upon this woman again. She was already settled into her own place, sipping tea with the man who had driven her to the hospice. As it turned out, he was her husband. The debilitating effects of advanced cancer had given her an aged and emaciated appearance.

This simple incident tells us something about the aims and techniques of the hospice. The patient and her family had already been well acquainted with the hospice before time of admission. Consequently, there was a sense of having made the next logical stop on her journey through life rather than a jarring transition from home to an impersonal institution. Much of St. Christopher's effort is

devoted to its home-care program. With the guidance of hospice personnel, some families are able to provide high-quality care to their terminally ill members throughout the course of the illness. Patient and family know that the inpatient facility is there when and if they need it.

A hospice can be thought of more aptly as a process and as a spirit of mutual concern rather than as a place. The sociophysical environment of the palliative care facility is designed for life as well as death. For example, staff recognized the importance of the first few minutes of the admission process. Efficiency was improved by having the patient's own bed ready for her, an innovation at that time. Most important was the affirmation of human contact by both the medical director and the nurse. Welcoming the husband through the tea service further encouraged the maintenance of interpersonal relationships and comforting habits.

The philosophy of care encompasses the entire family unit. Many family members not only visit with their own kin but also befriend other patients. This reduces social isolation for the patient and the sense of helplessness for the family. It does raise the possibility, however, that the family might spend so much time and effort at the inpatient facility that they neglect their own needs. To place a friendly limit on family involvement, St. Christopher's established a weekly "family's day off." This allows the family a brief vacation without any sense of guilt attached. At the end of this day I finally noticed what was missing among the residents of St. Christopher's: anxiety, shame, or despair. Their dignity and security were intact.

Mother's Last Moments: A Daughter's Experience

Another example comes from an American hospice program and expresses the viewpoint of the young adult daughter of a woman who had been terminally ill for several months. The woman was being cared for at home during what proved to be the final phase of her illness.

> *The next day I woke up and went in to see my mother. I noticed the difference immediately. She had this rattle in her throat. She kept trying to talk, but her words were garbled by the mucus in her throat. . . . I called the doctor and he gave me a good idea of what was happening. It was very*

hard for me to believe that she was so close ["to death" were the words implied but not spoken by the daughter]. She looked so calm and serene in her room and among all her things. She looked really okay. She didn't look like she was in distress. She looked like she was just glowing. And my sister came over . . . and left a picture of her little boy so my mother could see him. And it was just as if everything was in preparation.

I got out her makeup and lotion and started to make her up. I put lotion all over her skin. She knew what I was doing, because she held out her arms, and moved a little here and there to make it easier to make her up. But I was afraid to touch her body. She was so frail. Before this, she hadn't wanted to be touched because it hurt. But now it didn't seem to hurt her at all; her pain had diminished. I put blush on her face . . . and lipstick on . . . and I brushed her hair.

As I bent down to hug her, she—her body, I don't know how to describe it—she opened her mouth as I was holding her, and blood came out. I thought at first, "What's wrong, what's happening?" And Emma, our temporary housekeeper, said, "It's okay, it's nothing. She'll be okay. Why don't you go out? A break would be good for you." But it was hard for me to let go of her. A part of me felt like "that was it," but oh, no, it couldn't have happened. When I looked at her again, she looked beautiful. She was glowing. She was just beautiful. It was the only time I saw her look so beautiful during her whole illness.

When I came back, the hearse was in front of our house. I said, "Oh, no! You're not going to take my mother away!" My father was there, and all the people who were supposed to be there; the things that were supposed to happen . . . I resented it all. I wanted to touch her. I wanted to be alone with her. I went in and closed the door. And I touched her all over, and took her all in. And then I realized . . . she had gone without a struggle. It was really right, it was all right, you know? She looked very good. She looked as if it was right. It wasn't painful. It was the right time, and she was ready to go.

This is part of just one person's experience with death. Other family members responded in their own distinctive ways. The father, for example, did much planning and managing—his way of coping with the impending loss. Family

members could respond in ways true to themselves, instead of being constricted by a traditional hospital situation.

This woman died free of pain and suffering. She felt safe. The final impression that "it was right" helped the daughter integrate her mother's death into her own ongoing life. She would not have to live with regret, self-recrimination, or anger about her own actions. Would she have felt comfortable applying lotion and make up to her mother if they had been in a hospital? Would this even have been permitted? Would she have been allowed to return for a few minutes of privacy with her mother after death?

The Hospice of Miami was an important source of support, but there was also strength in the intact and affectionate family itself. This does not mean, however, that the relationship between hospice and family was smooth at all times. At first there was resistance because the introduction of palliative care forced them to realize that they would soon lose the mother/wife to death.

The daughter's life had changed at the moment she first learned of her mother's *terminal illness* some months before. The circumstances of her mother's death and dying influenced her so much that she selected a career in human services so she can provide care and comfort to others.

Dying from Two Worlds

Hospice had its primary roots in white Christian tradition. Today, many people in the United States draw on multiple traditions. How hospice can respond to these diverse and individual situations is exemplified by Barbara, a woman who had lived an active and useful life in two worlds. She was deeply rooted in her Native American culture and also a distinguished university faculty member. Barbara was diagnosed with ovarian cancer at the age of 46 and within a few years would lose the battle for her life (Staton, Shuy, & Byock, 2001). Her friends and family helped her end her days in a way that respected both of her traditions as well as her unique personality. During most of her final illness, Barbara received care either at her or her sister Irene's home. She would go to Missoula's Hospice House when needed.

One day Barbara stopped eating and drinking. She now had a faraway look in her eyes. Irene asked her: "Have you started your journey to the other side?" Barbara replied with a smile "so big. And I told her, 'I'm here with you. I'm not going to leave you. You don't have anything to be afraid of. I want to thank you for this opportunity to see through your eyes to the other side.'" The sisters shared Native American traditional beliefs in which ancestors would come to escort them to the other side, but also drew comfort from the Bible, which Irene read to her near the end.

> I always read her the Psalms—Psalm 23—and then I would burn smudge for her. I hung my eagle fan above her head because our belief is that's the dream world. And that when you lay down to rest, that eagle spirit is going to help you to have good dreams (op. cit., p. 276).

From the hospice's first contact with Barbara through the memorial services, there was a natural meld of Native American culture with Christian tradition and modern palliative care techniques. No religious spokesperson on either side demanded an exclusionary approach. The Bible and the eagle feather, the hospice and the home were meaningfully related through the life of Barbara and her friends.

Adult Respite Care

Hospice programs usually provide care at the patient's home and in medical care facilities, as needed. There is a third alternative: respite care. At some point in the course of a terminal illness, the patient may feel more comfortable in a respite care setting than either at home or in a hospital. For example, Walter, a robust businessman with "never a sick day in his life," experienced a persistent feeling of fatigue and discomfort. When finally persuaded by his family to see a doctor, he learned that he had an advanced and incurable cancer.

Once it was clear that there was no realistic hope for recovery, the family agreed to select the hospice alternative. Walter's condition was stabilized for several weeks. He took advantage of this time to work out a satisfactory business deal with his partner, say his good-byes to old friends, and immerse himself in the daily life of his very supportive family. His functional capacity then declined sharply. With great tact, Walter suggested that he be given "a few days off" until he recovered his strength. In retrospect, the family and the

hospice nurse realized that he had wanted to relieve the unremitting pressure on his family—and that he sensed his death was imminent.

At his suggestion, Walter was taken to a respite care center, housed in a comfortable home-like setting. He thanked his wife and son and gently ordered them to take good care of each other and the rest of the family until he perked up a little and could come home. About an hour later the hospice nurse came by to see how he was doing. "I can go now," he smiled, "and so can you." He died peacefully within a few minutes.

In this instance, the respite care center did not have to offer any special services. What Walter needed was a way of establishing a little distance between himself and his loving family at the very end of his life. It is not unusual for a dying person to feel that he or she has "taken care of business" and expressing personal feelings to the people who most matter. The availability of an adult respite care center can give family members a valuable relief from constant responsibility, even though this may be for only a few days. These brief "vacations" can be useful to the terminally ill person as well as the family. As one woman confided within a week of her death: "I try my best to keep their spirits up, but it's getting harder and harder. I don't like to be alone either, but at least when I'm alone I don't have to perform." A few days with caregivers who are not part of one's interpersonal network can liberate the dying person from investing the limited available energy in meeting the needs and expectations of others.

Hospice-Inspired Care for Children

Consider this description of an episode in the life of Marie, "a ghostlike seven-year old" who had already undergone three unsuccessful kidney transplants from cadavers and was being kept on dialysis treatment until a fourth transplantable organ could be located:

> As Marie sat on the child-life worker's lap, she ground her teeth with great intensity and anxiously shifted the position of her blood-pressure cuff. She incessantly scratched and picked at the gauze pads which guarded her old abdominal wounds. 'My tummy hurts! My tummy hurts!' she announced, in hope that she would be permitted a day off. After Marie's blood pressure was read, she reenacted the procedure, detail by

detail, with the child-life worker. Marie methodically placed the cuff on the child-worker's arm, pumped forcefully, and, stethoscope in hand, engagingly admonished her to be still and not to cry. She took the child-life worker's hand and hesitantly hobbled toward the scale where she was weighed. . . .

When the preparations for dialysis were over, reality robbed Marie of her tenuous control over her experience. Her dialysis rituals could no longer protect her, and her fear was apparent in her eyes. As the staff placed Marie's papoose, or restraint, under her back, she frantically pleased, 'Have to make pee-pee. . . Mommy coming?. . . Bleeding! Give me something to put me to sleep!' Three adults . . . wrestled with Marie as in panic she squirmed and fought to release herself from the papoose. Marie's right hand, the only part of her body free of restraint, blindly gripped the child-life worker's fingers. . . . Marie's mother would not be waiting for her after the ordeal had ended. Sedatives would not be used to ease the passage of time (Meagher & Leff, 1989–1990).

This was a recurring experience in Marie's life. She suffered physical and emotional pain throughout her final hospital stay—abandoned by her family because they could no longer tolerate the stress themselves. Astoundingly, the medical staff systematically denied Marie the partial relief she might have experienced from pain-killing medication. Instead they attempted to deceive her by pretending to inject medications into her tubing. Why? So that she would not become a drug addict!

Marie experienced the torment of pain and abandonment in addition to the ravages of her disease. Her caregivers were not evil or unfeeling people, but they were working within the framework of aggressive, cure-oriented medicine. This "pull out all the stops" approach often reaches its peak of intensity when the patient is a child. The death of a child is an exceptionally powerful blow and violates our expectations in a society where so many people survive into advanced adult years.

It is very difficult in the case of a child to say, "let her go with love and comfort" as long as there seems to be any chance at all to prolong her life. This is probably the main reason that hospice care

for dying children has not become more common. The decision to select hospice care involves recognition of impending death, a recognition that is usually avoided by family and caregivers as long as possible (and even a little longer).

Fortunately, pediatric palliative and hospice care is now becoming more available (Friebert, 2009). It is a challenging enterprise because the palliative teams most care for patients with a wide variety of conditions and who do not have an adult's perspective to interpret their experiences. Pediatric caregivers often speak of life-limiting or life-threatening conditions because of the varied trajectories associated with so many different diagnostic circumstances. There are still only a few life-limited children receiving pediatric hospice and palliative care, perhaps one of ten. There is also limited information about opportunities for program access.

Nevertheless, many general hospices do accept children, and there is a growing advocacy for including children in discussions about hospice and other medical care situations (Hinds, Bradshaw, Oakes, & Pritchard, 2002). Home care can be arranged for many terminally ill children. The opportunity to stay at home may be even more important for children than adults, avoiding the anxiety of separation. Care might be furnished either by a hospice organization, or by a growing number of hospitals that have introduced palliative care into their own programs. These comprehensive, patient-and-family palliative programs are not only improving the quality of life for seriously ill children but also enabling many to survive longer than expected (Ward, 2007).

Hospice Care for People with AIDS

A person whose HIV infection has converted to an active case of AIDS might encounter the same sources of stress as does any person afflicted with a terminal illness. These include (1) The progressive loss of functions; (2) pain, fatigue, and other symptoms; (3) disruption and potential loss of interpersonal relationships; and (4) a future in which hopes, plans, and ambitions become replaced by the prospect of death. Palliative care and effective management often reduce the stress level and maintain a higher degree of comfort and individual lifestyle during the final phase of the illness.

There were barriers, however, to hospice care for persons with AIDS, when this condition became recognized as a major public health hazard in the 1980s. These barriers included:

- Willingness of the community to support hospice operations through volunteer services and fundraising if hospice programs accept AIDS patients.
- Willingness of hospice staff and administrators to provide services to AIDS patients.
- Willingness of AIDS patients to select the hospice option and willingness of their families to serve as participating caregivers.
- Willingness of the health care system to make whatever adjustments might be necessary in admission and management of AIDS patients.

Hospice programs did quickly made themselves available to AIDS patients. There was at first the risk that volunteers and other forms of community support would fall away if AIDS patients were accepted. By and large, though, the community maintained its support, although troubled by the association between AIDS and a promiscuous lifestyle. More accustomed to helping patients with terminal cancer, hospice programs had to devise new procedures for dealing with AIDS, a complex condition with many *symptoms* to treat and difficult treatment decisions to make. As time went on, almost all hospice programs reported that people with AIDS were receiving their full range of palliative care and support services.

HIV/AIDS remains a significant cause of illness and death in the United States and throughout much of the world. However, more people with HIV now live for years without symptoms. New drugs have made important contributions to this development. Some people with AIDS are reluctant to enter hospice care because they either hold out hope for *remission* or have been denying the severity of their illness. There is a zone of uncertainty about individual prognosis, so people differ in how they evaluate their situations. Nevertheless, hospice care often can manage their complex physical and emotional needs more adequately than traditional medical practice.

Hospice Care on the International Scene

Desperate refugees flooded the nation by the hundreds of thousands. Hospitals and rehabilitation centers were overwhelmed by the

number of wounded people. The mass media was filled with reports of killing, torture, and extreme suffering. The question was raised: does it make any sense to speak about "dying with dignity" amid so many terrible and extremely humiliating deaths? Is it realistic to speak about dying decently in a country where so many persons now cannot live decently (Jusic, 1997, p. 126).

Anica Jusic, M.D., was founder of the first palliative care unit in Croatia just before his country was invaded by the Serbian/Yugoslav army. Hospice pioneers in other nations have also encountered chaotic and dangerous situations, along with a lack of understanding and responsiveness from the ruling establishment. In Colombia, for example, the authorities were intent on denying morphine derivatives to ease the pain of terminally ill patients—at the same time that the illicit drug trade was the nation's most prosperous industry. Every hospice established within a particular cultural and geographical setting has its story to tell. Humane and effective care for dying people is a universal challenge, and people are finding ways to develop palliative care service that is realistic and acceptable in a particular setting.

An international survey of hospice programs (Wilson & Kastenbaum, 1997) found that:

- Hospice programs are growing rapidly throughout much of the world.
- The programs vary greatly. Some hospices serve small populations in a sprawling rural area with difficult road access, few telephones, and limited health care facilities. Other hospices serve a large but compact population in a technologically developed urban area. What works well for one hospice organization may not be feasible for another.
- Throughout the world the largest number of hospice patients fall within the 60–79 age group, with only about one patient in nine being under the age of 40. Men and women are using hospice services more or less equally, with some local variations.
- Home care is the type of service most often received by hospice clients in every world region—often in nations or areas in which there had been no previous home care services of any type.

- All world cultures are proving to have traditional strengths that can contribute to the success of a palliative care program. Traditional cultures may at first resist hospice services, but reports indicate that love and concern for dying members of the family eventually bring forth a warm and caring response.
- The early phases of hospice development invariably encounter resistance from some medical practitioners and governmental officials as well as a public that has long avoided open discussion of the "taboo" topics of dying and death. The United States has not been alone in its reluctance to deal with death. Similar response have been reported by hospice pioneers in Africa, Asia, Near and Middle East, and South America.
- Pain relief remains the central objective of palliative care, no matter how the program is structured or what cultural group it serves. Most hospice programs around the world have had to work strenuously to persuade physicians and law makers that it is possible to relieve the suffering of terminally ill people without creating drug addicts or causing premature death. Unfortunately, there is still considerable resistance to effective pain relief from people who have not informed themselves about the actual facts of palliative care.
- Education of the general public, human service professionals, and governmental decision-makers has been recognized as a high priority by hospice programs around the world. Palliative care requires a host society that is able to integrate dying and death into its conception of the life course.

Despite notable progress, many people throughout the world continue to suffer for lack of palliative care. David Clark (2007–2008, p. 107) characterizes the situation as "desperate. Where the need is the greatest, the fewest hospice and palliative care services exist. There is unrelieved suffering on a mass scale and the efforts of a handful of activists to promote palliative care globally are often ignored and unsupported. One million people die each week. It is estimated by the World Health Organization that 60 percent of these could benefit from palliative care. Yet at present only a tiny proportion of dying people ever receive the support of hospice and palliative care services."

RELIEF OF PAIN AND SUFFERING

Alleviation of pain and suffering is the primary goal of palliative care programs. Why is pain control so important?

- Pain is, by definition, a stressful experience.
- Pain reduces the ability to give attention to other matters, thereby isolating the sufferers and reducing their opportunities to reflect, interact, and accomplish.
- Pain can intensify other symptoms such as weight loss, insomnia, pressure sores, and nausea.
- Fear and anticipation of pain can also be demoralizing. "Will the pain return?" "Will it get worse?" "Will I be able to endure it?" For many people, anxiety about the level of pain that might be yet to come can be even more disturbing than the pain that is already being experienced.
- Pain contributes much to anxiety about the dying process. Some people assume that dying is "all pain" and unavoidable. This expectation can generate emotional distress, impair communication, and lead to thoughts of suicide. ("I'd kill myself first!")

Temperature, pulse, respiration, and blood pressure. Those are the four *vital signs* that physicians and nurses throughout the world have been monitoring for many years. Recently, a fifth vital sign: *pain.* The hospice movement has made pain control a major priority in terminal care. More health care providers are also trying to determine the level of pain experienced by patients with any medical condition. Although not yet universally practiced, the establishment of pain as the fifth vital sign is a significant contribution from the palliative care movement. it remains difficult to assess level of pain—and, therefore, level of relief, because it is essentially a qualitative and subjective experience. Nevertheless, progress is being made in pain assessment, and there is a gradual increase in the number of health care providers who are skilled in this process.

Much of the hospice success in pain control derives from superior knowledge of available medications and their optimal use. This effectiveness accords with hospice philosophy: people should be as pain-free as possible as the end of life approaches, to allow them the opportunity to complete projects, engage in leave-takings, or just to find some enjoyment and meaning in each remaining day. Patients and their families should not have to endure pain as long as possible until forced to beg for relief.

The hospice team has particular expertise in controlling what otherwise would be unremitting pain. Traditionally, the medical profession has had only intermittent focus on pain relief, often limited to short-term or acute pain situations. This approach is seldom effective with terminally ill cancer patients (Davis, 2004). Hospice practice and research have demonstrated that most people can receive significant relief from pain throughout the dying process. There are still times, however, when the available techniques do not bring adequate pain control, so innovation and research remain a key priority.

Many of the failures in pain relief throughout the health care system are failures to apply knowledge that is already available (Davis & Walsh, 2004). For example, it has been found that hospital-based nurses and physicians did not have the correct facts about pain relief in terminally ill people even though they held generally favorable attitudes toward hospice (Kinzel, Askew, & Goldbole, 1992).

> *Only 35 percent of nurses and 56 percent of physicians recognized that the total dose of narcotic to provide equivalent pain relief would be less with a regular dosing schedule than on an as-needed basis in this (a palliative care) setting. Only 10 percent of nurses and 38 percent of physicians were able to correctly order four narcotic analgesics according to potency. None of the physicians or nurses correctly identified "more than 960 milligrams" as the correct response on a multiple choice question regarding the maximum safe dose of morphine sulfate that can be given orally over 24 hours (p. 88).*

Physicians have reported that they do not have adequate education and training in providing relief from pain. They did not prescribe adequate medication to relieve the acute suffering of dypsnea (difficulties in breathing); and erred seriously by ordering forced feedings for patients with lack of appetite. Patients with advanced cancer under the care of these physicians would have suffered the anxiety of dypsnea without relief because of the widespread fear in the medical profession

that opioids, the drug of choice for this problem, would turn the patients into addicts. Inflicting forced feeding on a person with advanced cancer would add another torment without providing real benefit. Physicians with more experience were no more competent than those with less experience. Unfortunately, physicians who themselves were not skilled in managing pain and other symptoms were the models for younger physicians.

Effective pain management requires more than a textbook knowledge of drug effects (especially since some of the textbooks themselves are out of compliance with clinical experience). The needs and pain tolerance of the particular individual must be considered, and the course of treatment must be subject to prompt review whenever problems arise.

Knowledgeable caregivers acquaint themselves with the family's concerns and show them how they can be part of the pain relief effort. Family-oriented care can reduce their stress, and therefore the patient's as well. Attention to the family's needs has also been shown to help them cope with grief after the death has occurred (Kissane, Lichtenthal, & Zaider, 2007–2008). Another key to alleviating pain in terminally ill patients is to reduce the mental distress that is associated with illness, dependency, loss of function, and concern about the future. The personality and mental state of the patients and the interpersonal setting in which they are located can influence sensitivity to pain. Some people have difficulty with the concept that pain can be all too real and at the same time related to one's mental and emotional state. A related tradition also can interfere with adequate pain relief. Since the middle of the twentieth century it has been fairly common practice for physicians to use a set of specific observations to distinguish "real" (organic) from "fake" (psychological) pain. It turns out that the frequently used Waddell observational signs *do not* reliably distinguish organic from psychological pain but do underestimate the amount of pain that is actually experienced (Fishbain, Cole, Cutler, Rosomoff, & Rosomoff, 2003).

Other techniques for relieving pain have included massage, application of heat, cold, menthol and electrical nerve stimulation to the skin, careful positioning and exercising, hypnosis, guided imagery, and aroma therapy. These methods, reminiscent of the ancient Greek temples of healing, have been applied along with drugs and surgery.

The comforting presence of companion animals has also been found helpful (Geisler, 2004). Most of these techniques can be used safely by informed caregivers and provide comfort without themselves producing stress or side effects. Some people whose distress has led them to contemplate suicide or physician-assisted death have responded well to noninvasive pain alleviation techniques and respite care programs.

Other Symptoms and Problems

Pain is not the only problem that can beset a dying person. Other symptoms include:

- Nausea
- Vomiting
- Dypsnea (respiratory difficulties)
- Pressure sores
- Insomnia
- Incontinence
- Weakness
- Fatigue
- Confusion and dementia
- Depression

Effective care requires attention to the prevention or alleviation of all these problems. A patient-centered approach with frequent interactions is required for palliation. For example, Foubert and Vaessen (2005) consider nausea to be a much neglected symptom, although it is often a side effect of chemotherapy. Despite the best care, however, the terminally ill person is likely to become weaker and more fatigued as the end approaches. Fatigue to the point of exhaustion is a symptom of terminal decline that often has not received the attention it deserves. Little is known about the relationship between a patient's experience of exhaustion and the accompanying physical condition, nor has there yet been much development of palliative measures. Furthermore, symptoms that might be noted separately on a check list often are interlinked. A woman struggling with terminal cancer was quoted earlier in this chapter: ". . . but to take one step and then you have to rest and then one step and then it hurts in your chest." Exhaustion, pain, and depression are all part of this experience.

There is another common symptom that is only now starting to receive the attention it deserves. "Confusion," "delirium," and "dementia" are the terms most often applied to the disordered mental states that appear in some terminally ill patients as well as in other situations. The terms are sometimes used interchangeably, but it is useful to recognize the differences. *Confusion* (from the Middle English for "mingled together") is a state of mind in which there is a lack of clarity and organization, along with a difficulty in making accurate judgments. A person can be confused momentarily because of circumstances. Effective communication (e. g., explaining a medical procedure in a way the patient can understand) is sometimes sufficient to dispel the confusion. *Delirium* is an agitated and incoherent state of mind that could be described as a fit of madness. It is often associated with intoxication and other physical disorders. Wildly fluctuating moods often occur. Careful evaluation of medical status is essential. Delirium can be part of an acute life-threatening episode. It is a common, though far from universal, syndrome in the last few days of life. Unlike the other terms, *dementia* signifies a long-term, perhaps permanent mental-and-brain decline that cripples memory and renders the person unable to provide competent self-care. Alzheimer's disease has become the most widely known type of dementia.

Effective care for one symptom can help reduce the stress of other symptoms, but the direction will continue toward less energy and functional ability. Palliative care is ongoing, resourceful, and realistic in its expectations. Hospice patients are less likely to be restricted to their beds until death is very close, but eventual decline must be expected. Findings from the landmark *National Hospice Study* (Mor, Greer, & Kastenbaum, 1988) indicate that the social quality of life remained high for hospice patients during their final weeks and days as compared with patients receiving traditional medical care. Despite the inescapable fact of continued physical deterioration, patients receiving hospice care maintained their intimate relationships and avoided the social isolation that has often befallen the dying person. The data also suggested that the personality and values of the person before becoming terminally ill also had a major influence on experiences during the last weeks of life. The difference between hospice and traditional types of care is significant, but so are individual differences in personality and social support system.

The Last Three Days of Life: From Patients' Perspective

Recall the thought questions raised at the end of Chapter 4. You were asked to describe the last three days of your life as you would like them to be. Reflect on your own responses as you learn how terminally ill people participating in the NHDS answered the same questions (suggested by Beatrice Kastenbaum). The following types of answers were most common (in order of frequency):

- I want certain people to be here with me.
- I want to be physically able to do things.
- I want to feel at peace.
- I want to be free from pain.
- I want the last three days of my life to be like any other days.

The support offered by hospice care makes it possible for many patients to be at home and enjoy the company of the "certain people" who mean the most to them. Similarly, with the advice and support of hospice volunteers and staff, the patient could still control some activities of daily life. Remaining in their environment provided a context for feeling at peace and having each day keep something of the feeling of a comforting routine. The patients' goals and the goals of hospice care were identical.

It is interesting to note some of the *least* frequently mentioned wishes for the last three days of life. Only about 1 person in 20 cared about "completing a task" or being "mentally alert." Even fewer hoped to "accept death," and fewer still wanted to "know when death is imminent, "to be able to bear pain," or "live until a certain time or event." This collection of low-incidence items includes many of the most dramatic wishes that are sometimes attributed to the dying person. By far the greater number of terminally ill people simply wanted the comfort of familiar faces, the ability to continue to do a little for themselves, and to have a sense of peaceful routine. The goal of accepting death philosophically or demonstrating the ability to tolerate pain was seldom stated.

These findings invite reflections such as the following: (1) what most people wanted was no more and no different from what hospice care tries to achieve and (2) it is wiser to learn from each individual what really matters than to attribute motives and themes picked up elsewhere. The question on *sources of strength* was also included in the NHDS survey. Following are the most frequent responses.

- Supportive family or friends
- Religion
- Being needed
- Confidence in self
- Satisfied with the help received

There appears to be a good match in general between what terminally ill cancer patients hopes for their last days and what hospice is designed to provide. The dying person's quality of life depends much on the social support that has been available to that person. Competent management of pain and compassionate attention from both family and hospice caregivers is helping many a terminally ill person to find continuing meaning and value in life. Palliative care can address the "partial models of the dying person's situation" (Kastenbaum, 2000) reviewed in Chapter 4. Terminally ill people will still experience, for example, restricted activity, limited energy, damaged body image, but they can also experience the support and understanding of professional and family caregivers who can help them continue to feel secure and valued.

Your Deathbed Scene, Revisited

Think again about the personal deathbed scene you imagined while reading the preceding chapter. Now that you have read more about the dying process and terminal care, it might be instructive to review your own expectations. Was your deathbed scene similar to those of most students? If so, then you came up with a sanitized image that is at odds with the way that most people actually die. Most dying people have pain and a variety of other symptoms (perhaps fortunately controlled by skilled and compassionate caregivers). Most college students portray themselves as dying without pain and without other symptoms (Kastenbaum & Normand, 1990). Additionally, most students indicated that they wanted to and actually *would* "go quickly." By contrast, most people actually die over a longer period of time. Some terminally ill people do "slip away quietly" in their sleep, but preceded by months of declining health and increased functional limitations. Realistically, most of us will live for sometime with our final illness, and so will our loved ones. How should we balance wishful fantasy and reality?

What does it mean if even those self-selected people who have chosen to enroll in a death-focused class have unrealistic ideas about their probable condition at the end of life? Your reflections are invited.

HOSPICE ACCESS, DECISION MAKING, AND CHALLENGES

Palliative care takes place within a complex and shifting mix of circumstances: cultural, political, and economic, as well as medical. It's not at all simple. Here we summarize the basic procedure for hospice access, and then identify several ongoing issues of concern to service providers, patients, and their families.

Choosing the Hospice Option

Hospice care in the United States is available as an optional program under Medicare Part A. A person with what is described as a "life-limiting illness" can choose to receive traditional hospital-based medical care, or enroll instead in an approved hospice organization. To be certified and reimbursed, a hospice must meet a firm set of standards. These include having its services available 24/7, staffed by a team of qualified professionals and trained volunteers. There are also patient eligibility requirements.

Gaining access to a hospice program is most direct for patients who are eligible for Medicare (Part A) hospital insurance. A physician is required to certify that the patient has a life expectancy of six months or less. Most physicians are troubled by this requirement, which often does not take into consideration the ambiguities of the medical situation. When this certification has been made, the patient signs a statement that confirms selection of hospice care for the terminal illness. This *hospice Medicare benefit* then replaces the standard Medicare benefit. The coverage is quite extensive. The services of physicians, nurses, home health aide, homemaker, and pastoral counselor are all included, as are rentals of medical equipment and medications. Generally, at-home expenses are fully covered, but there may be some expenses associated with in-hospital stays. Unfortunately, bereavement services are seldom adequately funded, so individual hospices vary in the support they can offer to families after the death.

Access to hospice can be more difficult if a patient does not have a primary physician with whom a strong trusting relationship has been established, or is not eligible for Medicare hospital benefits. These and other possible obstacles often can be overcome after discussion with a hospice director or social worker. It is useful to allow some time to explore the situation, have one's questions answered, and solve problems that might stand in the way of access. The most common barriers to hospice service include:

- Physicians' difficulty with hospice admission criteria, reluctance to lose control of their patients, and, in some cases, restrictions on the number of pain control prescriptions they are allowed to write.
- Insufficient family cooperation with hospice. As one nurse commented: "Many times, the patient is ready for hospice and the family is not."
- Inadequate communication between managed care health staff and terminally ill patients and their families. As expressed by another hospice nurse:

  Doctors don't take the time to discuss with patients and families. This is particularly true for the County system and HMOs. Patients have seen so many doctors, they don't have a particular doctor. They feel so trashed, because they feel like they've been bumped from person to person, and now they have to choose hospice.

A recent study (Guo et al., 2010) identified several areas in which caregivers reported that the health care providers neglected patient needs, such as:

- Protecting patients' privacy. This is important to their dignity, human rights, and self-esteem. Caregivers were unhappy about health care providers' insensitivity to patients' privacy such as unnecessary exposure of the patient's body: "At the hospital they just let him lay there. And every time we came in . . . he was always exposed" (Guo, p. 337).
- Late referral of patients to hospice care. This is a persistent problem throughout most of the world. Patients are sometimes referred to hospice when they have only a few days to live, thereby severely restricting the ability of palliative care providers to help them. At its most extreme, patients are not referred for

hospice care until death is only hours away. Most often, it is the physician who is criticized for reluctance to admit "failure" and to acknowledge that the time for comfort care has come, or resists transferring a patient. Sometimes, though, it is the family that is not ready to accept the proximity of death and continues to demand that the physician do everything possible (Sanders, Burkett, Dickinson, & Tournier, 2004).

- Availability of family support. The basic hospice model involves a dying person, that person's family and home, and the services provided by professional and volunteer caregivers. Ideally, there is an intact family that wants the dying person to be at home as much as possible and whose members are ready and willing to participate in the daily care. That each hospice patient must have a primary family caregiver (e.g., spouse or child) has became a requirement in the federal regulatory and funding system. There are a growing number of exceptions, however, and regulatory agencies appear to a little more flexible in this regard. Hospices, neighbors, and others can sometimes be very creative in coming up with a primary caregiver and a home environment. In deciding about hospice care, then it is useful to give attention to the availability of family and, if necessary, additional caregiver support.

Unequal Access to Hospice Care

It has already been noted that the international hospice movement, for all its effort, reaches only a very small proportion of terminally ill people throughout the world. There are significant access problems within the United States as well. Gorospe (2006) judges palliative care to be an essential public health intervention that is seldom available to ethnic minorities. His focus is on Native Americans whose general health services have long been rated as insufficient. Public health advances have contributed to lengthening of life, but also to lengthy periods of decline and suffering. Other people rarely given the opportunity for palliative care include impoverished residents of both inner-city and rural areas, and migrants. The "have-nots" in society are likely to be excluded from palliative care as well as from other services and opportunities.

Studies have shown that there is not equal access to and utilization of palliative care. Homeless people encounter discrimination from many sources, and are seldom consulted about their end of life preferences by health care providers. "Relationship-centered care, characterized by compassion and respectful, two-way communication, was . . . absent" (Tarzian, Neal, & O'Neil, 2005, p. 36). Members of racial and ethnic minorities less frequently choose hospice care (Lyke & Colon, 2004). Other people, such as the homeless, have very little contact with the health care system throughout their lives. Still others do not meet the Medicare requirements for participation.

The end of life takes place in a nursing home for about one person in five, and this frequency has been increasing in recent years. Unfortunately:

> *Dying residents experience high rates of untreated pain and other symptoms. They and their family members are isolated from social and spiritual support. Hospice improves end-of-life care for dying nursing home residents by improving pain control, reducing hospitalization, and reducing use of tube feeding, but it is rarely used (Zerezan, Stearns, & Hanson, 2000).*

The "done-bads" have also been neglected. The population of prison inmates has continued to age, along with the general population. Hospice programs—especially those that provide comprehensive and high quality services—are still a rarity in prisons, although awareness of this problem is gradually increasing.

Patient Care Issues

Palliative care providers, attuned to individuals and their distinctive circumstances, cope with a variety of challenges every day. There are some concerns, however, that have not yet been given sufficient attention.

Continuity of care is one of these issues. Ward & Gordon (2006–2007) observe that the intimate bond so important in hospice care is jeopardized by economic and organizational pressures. The patient and family sense of safety, security, and comfort depends much on the establishment and maintenance of trusting relationships. Hospice philosophy has consistently emphasized the value of compassionate and dependable relationships at the end of life. A changing cast of care providers, all under time pressure, makes it very difficult for intimate bonds to form and endure. In their case study of a nonprofit, stand-alone hospice, Ward & Gordon find that forced organizational restructuring has jeopardized the organization's ability to continue with its labor-intensive, high staff to patient ratio. The restructurings were forced by Medicare regulations and intensifying competition from large, profit-making health care organizations. The result was a renewed "medicalization of death" that allowed little latitude for supportive interactions and a spiritual perspective. Many other hospice organizations have been experiencing the same pressured shift from original purpose and method to "a more businesslike and clinical culture" (Ward & Gordon, p. 10). One of the defining characteristics of palliative care—a situation of safety and trust with continuity of relationships—is at considerable risk today.

Spirituality, already mentioned, has been a cherished theme for many hospice pioneers. It was often rooted in Christian belief, but not limited to any one faith. St. Christopher's Hospice, for example, was alert to the spiritual needs of all its patients and families, including those with agnostic or atheistic worldviews. Today, in the "more businesslike and clinical culture" of health care organizations, hospices are having some difficulty in protecting the spiritual core of their mission. But what is spiritual care in practice? Pulchaski (2007–2008, p. 42) offers this example:

> To be able to sit in silence as someone grapples with the unknown, and through the silence and the compassionate presence facilitate healing of that person, that is a profound act of love and of honoring the dignity of each person we treat.

It remains to be seen whether spirituality can be integrated into the care of seriously and terminally ill people within a mega-health care system that has other priorities and processes.

Two other issues challenge hospice philosophy and practice. The "difficult patient" is well known to health care providers. Nurses are often skilful in dealing with resistant and ill-tempered patients. The really difficult patient can test caregivers to their limits; however, this is a situation that one does not ordinarily associate with hospice service. "Mr. A." is an example discussed by Reeves,

Douglas, Garner, and Reynolds (2007). As a nursing home resident, he insulted the staff, frequently with racial and sexual slurs. He disrupted the facility, accused the staff of neglect, and hassled the other residents. If his behavior pattern is still in doubt, we learn that "On eight occasions he has tried to assault people with his motorized wheelchair, once leaving the facility and attempting to hit people on a busy street until police intervened" (p. 13).

Palliative care programs believe in giving everybody a chance, so a person such as Mr. A. can sometimes bring his behavioral problems into a hospice. The added stress of just one person with a significant behavior problem can be a significant burden. Additionally, there is a challenge to the basic hospice principle of patient autonomy. Terminally ill people are not to be over-managed, not made to conform with standard operating procedure. What should be done when a patient's abusive behavior affects the care of other patients and demoralizes compassionate care providers? The conflict between rights of the individual and the rights of other people occurs in many situations. Hospice, with its intensive service to seriously ill people and their families, is still seeking ways to approach and resolve this challenge.

There is another situation that also can be unsettling. Theoretically, terminally ill people enroll in hospice care for expert symptom relief and comprehensive care, as distinguished from continued, all-out aggressive treatment. In practice, though, some people change their minds. A person, feeling stronger through hospice care, might transfer to the basic Medicare benefit for another round of cure-oriented treatment. This choice does not run counter to hospice philosophy and practice. What does generate concern is a patient's wish to hasten death. Palliative care is intended to help people through their last days, not to shorten their lives. It has taken years of public education to dispel the fear that hospice is not an agency of euthanasia or assisted suicide. There are special circumstances in Oregon and Washington, which are the only states in which *physician-assisted suicide (PAS)* is legal (see Chapter 9). Hospice staff might be divided in their personal attitudes toward a PAS request, but the existence of an established process at least removes concern about possible violation of the law (Harvarth, Miller, Smith, Clark, Jackson, & Ganzini, 2006). In all other states, a hospice patient who expresses the wish to hasten death thereby raises the acute issue of individual autonomy versus communal law and established practice. The ethical and public opinion standing of hospice could be endangered whatever response is made. Patients sometimes resolve the dilemma for themselves, either by working past the impulse to hasten death, or voluntarily refusing food and fluids.

Experienced care providers understand that a person's mindset can shift significantly as he or she copes with the physical, mental, and spiritual challenges of the final passage.

A simple but fundamental piece of advice is offered by Dr. Robert Twycross, (2007–2008, p. 13) a pioneer in the development of pain relief procedures for terminally ill people: *"Truth may hurt but deceit hurts more. Being sensitively honest with one's patients has always been a key characteristic of palliative care."*

DAME CICELY SAUNDER'S REFLECTIONS ON HOSPICE

The founder of the international hospice movement inspired to palliative care programs worldwide. Dame Cicely Saunders (1918–2005) agreed to respond to some fairly personal questions about her own experiences.

Q: *How do you get used to death and to losing people you have cared for—and then having to do it all over again the next day?*

A: An auxiliary nurse who has worked in St. Christopher's told me recently, "You miss some people a lot, but next day there is a new patient and family to get to know and help." Both of us, and everyone else I have talked with, have mentioned "team" or "community" as a major positive as well as the continued learning of new ways to help. Above all, the patients remain the inspiration. Meeting people of great maturity facing life's end with endurance, humanity, and faith in various forms is a great encouragement.

Q: *How do hospice caregivers renew their own spirits? What do you do in your own life to keep going? What are your sources of strength and commitment?*

A: For myself, my Christian commitment, together with constant learning, reading, and traveling to other teams/units have been forms of renewal.

I also have a great support system of friends and colleagues. A physiotherapist (after 30 years working in the field) says, "We know we cannot cure our patients but we can still maximize their remaining potential . . . the patients keep me sane and focused. We are pioneers in an unexplored field." My colleagues all have an indefatigable capacity for new thinking and developing together as a team.

Q: *Women provide direct care to terminally ill people in the United States far more often than men…*

A: The preponderance of women in the field seems to be common around the world. But some men have made invaluable contributions to caring. Many have a spiritual dimension as a basis for their commitment.

Q: *Two situations are often highly stressful both to caregivers and family—the patient who has no realistic hope of survival but wants to keep fighting, and the family who insists on having "everything done," although there is really nothing effective yet to be done. . .*

A: This is not such a desperate dilemma. Patients who want to go on fighting are likely to return to their oncologist, who will advise and counsel. Otherwise, really skilled listening and discussion with the palliative care specialist may resolve a situation. We find most people will gradually learn to let go. Cultural differences require explanation and understanding. Families likewise need careful communication from the first contact. Once trust is established, these problems can be approached if and when the time comes.

Q: *What is the "worst" death you have come across, and what made it so?*

A: A patient refused all pain control on principle and died slowly and painfully over several weeks. The doctors and nurses anguished over this. When he was semi-conscious and groaning, the psychiatrist maintained he was not suffering from any psychiatric symptoms and was competent to make that choice. It was felt ethically correct to respect the patient's decision, although the nurses were most unhappy and the team was split.

Q: *How does a "good death" affect the family survivors and the health care providers?*

A: I think my husband (aged 93) achieved a good death. After many years of caring as he went from one life-threatening illness to another, we had to accept his statement that "I have done what I had to do in my life and now I am ready to die." But when he was desperately breathless with a chest infection he asked me, "Can't you help me to die? I said, "It will be in God's time" and he then replies, "I agree." A few days later the breathlessness passed and he had two peaceful weeks, still alert and gradually less talkative, except for flirting with the nurses! On the last afternoon, two of his former art pupils visited him. One wrote to me afterwards. "He seemed very peaceful but as if he was in touch with something beyond where we were." He slipped away just before I returned from home that night, but that was all right for me too, because I knew he was not alone.

Q: *Dr. Kevorkian…*

A: What Dr. Kevorkian did seemed to me to be totally unprofessional and careless of true human compassion and skill.

Q: *The international hospice movement has come a very long way in a short time. What can we all do to help the hospice philosophy fulfill its potential?*

A: We need people to conduct more research into palliative care for people dying of other diseases, more research, more skills development, more education of health care professionals outside of hospice specialists, and more understanding of the values and commitment of developing countries.

Many people have discovered a way to become active in the hospice movement by serving as volunteers. Interested? See Box 5-1.

BOX 5-1

Should I Become a Hospice Volunteer? A Dialogue

- **Does my local hospice need volunteers?**

  Probably so. A hospice usually has a director of volunteers and will welcome your call.

- **What should I expect when I meet the director of volunteers?**

  A friendly but professional interview. The hospice has responsibility for exercising good judgment in the selection of volunteers.

- **You mean they might not accept me?**

  This is a possibility. Has someone very close to you died recently? Many hospices ask people who have had a recent bereavement to wait a while before becoming a volunteer. Or the interviewer may judge that you have a disorganized life style. . . .

- **Hey, I'm going to get organized, starting tomorrow!**

  Fine! But the volunteer director will need to be convinced that you are a reliable person who keeps appointments. And should you come

across like a person who needs to impose your own religious beliefs on others—or use hospice in the service of your own fantasies and problems—then you might receive a polite but firm refusal.

- **That won't happen to me. I'm taking this great class on death and dying, and reading this really terrific textbook. So after I'm accepted as a volunteer, will they give me some guidance and supervision?**

  Definitely. You will be asked to attend a series of training sessions before you are activated as a volunteer. Most people find this to be a valuable learning experience. You will receive guidance and supervision all the way along the line, and you will always have somebody to call if problems arise.

- **What kind of things would I do as a volunteer?**

  There are many possibilities. You might be a companion for a patient in his or her home for a few hours so that others in the household have

(Continued)

BOX 5-1 (*Continued*)

the opportunity to shop or take care of business. You might drive the patient to an appointment or to visit an old friend. You might help the patient write letters. You might help prepare a meal when family or friends visit. You might help the patient or a family member complete a special project. And at times you might just "be there." A hospice volunteer can wind up doing many different things, depending upon the needs of the individual families (Willis, 1989). And some volunteers devote themselves to keeping the hospice system going, rather than working with patients. They do office work, fund-raising, and other things depending upon the needs of the individual families. And some devote themselves to keeping the hospice system going, rather than working with patients. They do office work, fund-raising, and other things that do not necessarily involve direct patient or family contact.

• **What are the other volunteers like?**

I've been fortunate enough to know many hospice volunteers. As a rule, they are bright, mature, and neighborly people who have been rather successful in life. Many feel that through

hospice they can give something back to other people. Some are health care professionals who believe strongly in the hospice philosophy.

• **Like nurses and medical social workers?**

Yes, some volunteers are well-qualified professionals. Some have been very successful in other lines of work, but are new to health and social care. And you will find other students as well—looking for an opportunity to help others while acquiring valuable personal experience.

• **Anything else I should know?**

Before you contact hospice, reflect on your own motivation: a passing curiosity or a firm resolve to help others? Will you be available to serve as a volunteer after you complete the course? Even though hospice may ask you to give only a few hours of your time per week, people will be counting on you to come through. If you have further questions at this time, you might ask your local hospice to put you into contact with several of their experienced volunteers.

• **See you at the hospice office!**

Go easy on those donuts.

■ SUMMARY

Hospice care is intended to provide comfort, relief, and a sense of security for terminally ill people and their families. It differs from traditional medical management in several important ways: (1) it offers expertise in the control of pain and other symptoms; (2) it is centered around the situation, needs, and desires of the particular dying person and family; and (3) it includes family members and volunteers as part of the caregiving system. The hospice approach to terminal care has its roots in shelter houses established in the fourth century for the comfort of pilgrims, the ill, and the dying. After a period of neglect, hospice activity started again in the late nineteenth century and took its modern form with the establishment of St. Christopher's Hospice (London) in 1967. Connecticut Hospice (New Haven) was the first such program in the U.S. (1974). About one person in three in the United States now selects the hospice care option for end-of-life care. Standards of care for hospice

programs include the well-being of the patient, family, and staff. Adult respite programs can provide a useful temporary alternative to hospital and home care. Palliative care for children is becoming increasingly available. Case histories offered some idea of how hospice care is offered and its benefits for dying persons and their families.

Hospice programs have most often served adults with advanced cancer or progressive neurological dysfunction. Today, though, increasing numbers of people with life-threatening heart disease are selecting palliative care. Hospice is adapting well to providing care for cardiac patients, but this is producing a disconnect with Medicare: patients are living "too long." An open question is whether the health care system will adjust to changing circumstances or endanger hospice's ability to continue its high-quality programs. There is also concern that the original hospice mission, with its emphasis on enduring and trusting relationships, spirituality, and patient-oriented care, might be at risk from a more business-like and clinical orientation. We looked at several other applications of hospice philosophy and practice: for children, people with AIDS, and people of diverse ethnic backgrounds. Hospice programs are developing rapidly throughout the world, finding welcome in nations with very different cultural and religious patterns. Nevertheless, only a very small number of terminally ill people can turn to palliative care in developing nations.

Research and clinical experience indicate that hospice care often does prevent and relieve suffering. Pain relief is most often the highest priority. The gradual acceptance of pain as the fifth vital sign in health care contacts with all patients is one of the remarkable achievements of the hospice movement. Unfortunately, though, what has been discovered about effective pain relief in palliative programs has not always been applied by physicians operating outside of the hospice framework. Many physicians are still inadequately trained to provide effective pain relief for dying people, and many still have unrealistic anxieties about turning a person into a drug addict through the administration of morphine and related medications. Fatigue and nausea are among the other distressing symptoms that require attention in palliative care. The relief of suffering also requires attention to the mental distress that can be associated with illness, dependency, loss of function, and concern about the future.

We concluded by sharing an interview with international hospice movement pioneer Dame Cicely Saunders, a brief revisit to your imagined deathbed scene, and an introduction to the volunteer's role in hospice care.

■ REFERENCES

Brazil, K., Bainbridge, D., & Rodriguez, C. (2010). The stress process in palliative cancer care: A qualitative study on informal caregiving and its implication for the delivery of care. *American Journal Hospice & Palliative Medicine, 27,* 111–116.

Centers for Disease Control and Prevention (2001). *HIV/AIDS surveillance supplemental report, 2000.* Rockville, MD: CDCP.

Clark, D. (2000). Palliative care history: A ritual process. *European Journal of Palliative Care, 7,* 50–55.

Clark, D. (2007–2008). End-of-life-care around the world: Achievements to date and challenges remaining. *Omega, Journal of Death & Dying, 56,* 101–110.

Dabbs, B., Butterworth, L., & Hall, E. (2007). "Tender mercies": Increasing access to hospice services for children with life-threatening conditions. *American Journal of Maternal/Child Nursing, 32,* 311–319.

Davis, M. P. (2004). Acute pain in advanced cancer. *American Journal of Hospice & Palliative Medicine, 21,* 47–50.

Davis, M. P., & Walsh, D. (2004). Epidemiology of cancer pain and factors influencing poor pain control. *American Journal of Hospice & Palliative Medicine, 21,* 137–142.

Doorenbos, A. Z., & Schim, S. M. (2004). Cultural competence in hospice. *American Journal of Hospice & Palliative Medicine, 21,* 28–32.

Durhan, J. D. (2002). AIDS. In R. Kastenbaum (Ed.), *Macmillan encyclopedia of death and dying* (Vol. 1, pp. 16–24). New York: Macmillan Reference USA.

Field, J. J., & Behrman, R. (Eds.). (2003*). When children die: Improving palliative and end-of-life care for children and their families.* Washington, DC: National Academies Press.

Fishbain, D. A., Cole, B., Cutler, R. B., Lewis, J., Rosomoff, H. L., & Rosomoff, R. S. (2003). A structured evidence-based review on the meaning of nonorganic physical signs: Waddell signs. *Pain Medicine, 4,* 141–181.

Foubert, J., & Vaessen, G. (2005). Nausea: The neglected symptom. *European Journal of Oncology Nursing, 9,* 21–32.

Freibert, S. (2009). *Pediatric palliative and hospice care in America.* National Hospice and Palliative Care Organization. www.nhpco.org.

Geisler, A. N. (2004). Companion animals in palliative care: Stories from the bedside. *American Journal of Hospice & Palliative Medicine, 21,* 285–88.

Goldman, A., Hain, R., & Liben, S. (2006). *Oxford textbook of palliative care for children.* New York: Oxford University Press.

Gorospe, E. C. (2006). Establishing palliative care for American Indians as a public health agenda. *Internet Journal of Pain, Symptom Control, & Palliative Care, 4,* 1528–8227.

Guo, G., Phillips, L. E., & Reed, P. (2010). End-of-life caregiving interactions with health care providers. Learning from the bad. *J. Nursing Care Quart, 25,* 334–343.

Harvard Medical School (2008). Harvard Medical School Center for Palliative Care. Pallcare@partners.org.

Harvarth, T. A., Miller, L. L., Smith, K. A., Clark, L. D., Jackson, A., & Ganzini, L. (2006). Dilemmas encountered by hospice workers when patients wish to hasten death. *Journal of Hospice and Palliative Nursing, 8,* 200–209.

Hinds, P. S., Bradshaw, G., Oakes, L. L., & Pritchard. M. (2002). Children and their rights in life and death situations. In R. Kastenbaum (Ed.), *Macmillan encyclopedia of death and dying* (Vol. 1, pp. 139–147). New York: Macmillan.

Humphreys, C. (2001). "Waiting for the last summons": The establishment of the first hospices in England 1878–1914. *Mortality, 6*, 146–166.

Jusic, A. (1997) Palliative medicine's first steps in Croatia. In C. Saunders & R. Kastenbaum (Eds.), *Hospice care on the international scene* (pp. 125–129). New York: Springer Publishing Co., Inc.

Kassine, D., Lichtenthao, W., & Zaider, T. (2007–2008). Family care before and after bereavement. *Omega, Journal of Death & Dying, 56*, 21–32.

Kastenbaum, R. (1975a). Toward standards of care for the terminally ill: That a need exists. *Omega, Journal of Death and Dying, 6*, 77–78.

Kastenbaum, R. (1975b). Toward standards of care for the terminally ill. II: What standards exist today? *Omega, Journal of Death and Dying 6*, 289–290.

Kastenbaum, R. (1976). Toward standards of care for the terminally ill. III: A few guiding principles. *Omega, Journal of Death and Dying, 7*, 191–194.

Kastenbaum, R. (2000). *The psychology of death* (3rd ed.). New York: Springer Publishing Co.

Kastenbaum, R., & Normand, C. (1990). Deathbed scenes as expected by the young and experienced by the old. *Death Studies, 14*, 201–218.

Kastenbaum, R., & Wilson, M. (1997). Hospice care on the international scene: Today and tomorrow. In C. Saunders & R. Kastenbaum (Eds.), *Hospice care on the international scene* (pp. 262–272). New York: Springer Publishing Co., Inc.

Kinzel, T., Askew, M., & Goldbole, K. (1992). Palliative care: Attitudes and knowledge of hospital-based nurses and physicians. *Loss, Grief & Care, 6*, 85–95.

Lindqvist, L., Widmark, A., & Rasmussen, B. H. (2004). Meanings of the phenomenon of fatigue as narrated by 4 patients with cancer in palliative care. *Cancer Nursing, 27*, 237–243.

Lyke, J., & Colon, M. (2004). Practical recommendations for ethnically and racially sensitive hospice services. *American Journal of Hospice & Palliative Medicine, 21*, 131–133.

Meagher, D. K., & Leff, P. T. (1989–1990). In Marie's memory: The rights of the child with life-threatening or terminal illness. *Omega, Journal of Death and Dying, 20*, 177–191.

Mor, V., Greer, D., & Kastenbaum, R. (1988). *The hospice experiment*. Baltimore: Johns Hopkins University Press.

Mount, B. (2003). Palliative care: A personal odyssey. *Illness, Crisis, & Loss, 11*, 90–103.

Movementbuilding. (Nd). Understanding prison health care: Elder & end-of-life. Care. http://etgec .utmb.edu/ETGEC_Documents/Elder_and_End-of-Life_Care.htm.

National Hospice and Palliative Care Organization. (2008). NHPCO facts and figures: Hospice care in America. http://www.mass.gov/Ihqcc/docs/expert_panel/2008_NHPCO_Facts%20and%20Figures.pdf

Pevey, C. (2005). Patient speaking: Hospice patients discuss their care. *American Journal of Hospice & Palliative Medicine, 22*, 129–133.

Phipps, W. E. (1988). The origin of hospices/hospitals. *Death Studies, 12*, 91–100.

Puchalski, C. M. (2007–2008). Spirituality and the care of patients at the end-of-life: An essential component of care. *Omega, Journal of Death and Dying, 56*, 33–46.

Radulovic, J. (2007). Hospice care saves money for Medicare, new study shows. http://nhpco.org/i4a/pages/Index.cfm?pageID=5386.

Reeves, R. R., Douglas, S. P., Garner, R. t., & Reynolds, M. D. (2007). The individual rights of the difficult patient. *The Hastings Center Report, 37*, 13–15.

Rousseau, P. (2010). The neglect of pain: The sad tale of opioids at the end of life. *American Journal Hospice & Palliative Medicine, 27*, 97–99.

Sack, K. (2007). Hospice care: Longer lives mean money lost. *New York Times.* http://www.nytimes.com/2007/11/27/us/27hospice.html.

Sanders, B. S., Burkett, T. L., Dickinson, G. E., & Tournier, R. E. (2004). Hospice referral decisions: The role of physicians. *American Journal of Hospice & Palliative Medicine, 21*, 196–202.

Saunders, C. (1993). Dame Cicely Saunders: An Omega interview. *Omega, Journal of Death & Dying.*

Staton, J., Shuy, R., & Byock, I. (2001). *A few months to live. Different paths to life's end.* Washington, DC: Georgetown University Press.

Tarzian, A. J., Neal, M. T., & O'Neill J. A. (2005). Attitudes, experiences, and beliefs affecting end-of-life decision-making among homeless individuals, *Journal of Palliative Medicine, 8*, 36–48.

Twycross, R. (2007–2008). Patient care: Past, present, and future. *Omega, Journal of Death & Dying, 56*, 7–20.

Ward, E. G., & Gordon, A. K. (2006–2007). Looming threats to the intimate bond in hospice care? Economic and organizational pressures in the case study of a hospice. *Omega, Journal of Death & Dying, 54*, 1–18.

Ward, G. (2007). More hospitals offering sensitive end-of-life care. *Daily News Journal* (Murfreesboro,

Tenn). http://dnj.midsouthnews.com/apps/pbcs. Dll/article?AID=/20071228/BUSINESS.

Willis, J. (1989). Hospice volunteers. In R. Kastenbaum & B. K. Kastenbaum (Eds.), *Encyclopedia of death* (pp. 147–149). Phoenix: The Oryx Press.

Wilson, M., & Kastenbaum, R. (1997). Worldwide developments in hospice care: Survey results. In C. Saunders & R. Kastenbaum (Eds.), *Hospice care on the international scene.* New York: Springer Publishing Co., Inc.

Zerzan, J., Stearns, S., & Hanson, L. (2000). Access to palliative care and hospice in nursing homes. *Journal of the American Medical Association, 248,* 2489–2494.

■ GLOSSARY

Amyotropic lateral sclerosis A neuromuscular disorder in which there is a progression of weakness and paralysis until vital functions are inoperative. Also known as "Lou Gehrig's disease" after the New York Yankees Hall of Fame first baseman, and in Europe as motor neurone disease.

Cachement area The geographical region served by a health care agency.

Hospice (1) A program of care devoted to providing comfort to terminally ill people through a team approach with participation by family members. (2) A facility in which such care is provided.

Medicare Hospice Benefit A federal reimbursement program that enables eligible people to select hospice care as an alternative to traditional medical management during their terminal illness.

National Hospice Study A major project (1982–1983) that compared traditional and hospice care for terminally ill people in the U.S. The Medicare Hospice Benefit was established as a result of this study.

Palliative care Health services intended to reduce pain and other symptoms to protect the patient's quality of life.

Physician-assisted suicide (PAS) Termination of a person's life by a physician through lethal injection or other means, at that person's request. (Illegal except in Oregon when in compliance with the state's Death with Dignity Act).

Remission The disappearance or relief of symptoms

Symptom An observable sign of dysfunction and/or distress (e.g., pain, fever).

Terminal illness Defined in the Medicare Hospice Benefit as an illness that is expected to end in death within 6 months or less. In other contexts, the specific definition of terminal illness is open to discussion and controversy.

Vital signs Body functions that are routinely assessed by physicians and nurses. Traditionally included signs are temperature, pulse, respiration, and blood pressure. Now also includes patient's experience of pain.

■ ON FURTHER THOUGHT . . .

Useful online resources:

American Academy of Hospice and Palliative Medicine
   http://www.aahpm.org/
Hospice Association
   www.americanhospice.org
Canadian Palliative Care Association
   http://www.chpca.net/index
Children's Hospice International
   http://www.chionline.org/
Association for Palliative Care
   http://www.apmonline.org/page.php?pageid=1
Hospice and Palliative Nurses Association
   www.hpna.org
National Association for Home Care & Hospice
   www.nahc.org
Hospice Foundation of America
   www.hospicefoundation.org
Hospice Information (international)
   http://www.helpthehospices.org.uk/
   hospiceinformation/
National Hospice and Palliative Care Organization
   http://www.nhpco.org
National Hospice Work Group
   www.nhwg.org
Stop Pain.Org (Department of Pain Medicine & Palliative Care at Beth Israel Medicine Center)
   www.stoppain.org

An Unsettled Question

The modern hospice movement was incubated by caregivers with a strong religious orientation, largely Christian. What should be the role of religion in palliative care today? In thinking about this question, take into account people with a terminal illness whose religious orientations differ from mainstream Christianity, have no religious affiliations, or belong to ethnic and racial groups that have not expressed much interest or comfort with the idea of hospice care. Can hospice care fulfill its promise without a strong religious orientation? Is "spirituality" identical with or significantly different from association with an established religion?

How risky is it to cross this street? Perhaps such everyday
decisions help prepare for difficult end-of-life issues.

BOX 6-1

THE LIVING WILL

My Living Will

To My Family, My Physician, My Lawyer and All Others Whom It May Concern:

Death is as much a reality as birth, growth, maturity, and old age. If the time comes when I can no longer take part in decisions for my own future, let this statement stand as an expression of my wishes and directions, while I am still of sound mind.

If at such a time the situation should arise in which there is no reasonable expectation of my recovery from extreme physical or mental disability, I direct that I be allowed to die and not be kept alive by medications, artificial means, or "heroic measures." I do, however, ask that medication be mercifully administered to me to alleviate suffering even though this may shorten my remaining life.

This statement is made after careful consideration and is in accordance with my strong convictions and beliefs. I want the wishes and directions here expressed carried out to the extent permitted by law. Insofar as they are not legally enforceable, I hope that those to whom this will is addressed will regard themselves as morally bound by these provisions.

DURABLE POWER OF ATTORNEY (optional)

I hereby designate _____ to serve as my attorney-in-fact for the purpose of making medical treatment decisions. This power of attorney shall remain effective in the event that I become incompetent or otherwise unable to make such decisions for myself.

Signed _____

Optional Notarization: Date _____

"Sworn and subscribed to Witness before me this _____ day of _____ 20_____"

Witness Address _____

Notary Seal Address _____

(Optional). My Living Will is registered with Concern for Dying

(Number _____).

RIGHT-TO-DIE DECISIONS THAT WE CAN MAKE

The living will stirred up interest, hope, and anxiety. As we will see in Chapter 9, troubling questions arose about the right to refuse treatment and the kind of evidence that should be required as proof of the person's intentions. The right to refuse treatment gained support as courts upheld the principle of informed consent, which requires that in all situations patients receive adequate information about the nature of the procedures and the potential risks as well as benefits. It was no longer a process limited to life-threatened or terminally ill individuals.

We consider now some of the major developments in advance directives since the introduction of the original living will.

From Living Will to Patient Self-Determination Act

State legislatures hesitated, then complied with, the public's request to place a legal foundation under the living will. Starting with California in 1976, every state has passed a "natural death act" (also known as "death with dignity" and "living will acts"). Two significant transfers of power from the state to the individual are embodied in these measures:

- The law recognizes a mentally competent adult's right to refuse life support procedures (such as machines to assist respiration and circulation).
- Individuals are entitled to select representatives who will see that their instructions are carried out if the individual is not able to do so. A patient who can no longer speak, for example, should be able to count upon his or her appointed health care agent to safeguard the terms of the advance directive. These agents are often known as health care proxies. The responsibility assigned to this person is usually known as *durable power of attorney for health care*. It is not required, however, that the agent or proxy actually be an attorney.

These significant new laws, however, did not guarantee that the intentions would be respected in practice. Physicians and hospital administrators were not accustomed to having patients tell them what they could and could not do. There was also the problem of integrating an advance directive into the health care communication system. Where should the document itself be located? How many copies should be made? How can patients be sure that anybody will actually look at their living wills when the time comes? These problems were especially common in the early days of the living will and are still encountered today.

Newer advance directive forms encourage people to be more specific. This requires a willingness to think about end-of-life issues and also to gain some familiarity with medical concepts and issues. It has become clear that many people (including professional care providers) do not complete advance directives. Members of ethnic groups with a tendency to distrust the health care system and a reluctance to disclose their feelings to strangers have a low rate of participation in the advance directive process (Barnato et al., 20009; Searight & Gafford, 2005).

Cultural traditions of avoiding discussion of death and dying also contribute to this reluctance. People with decisional incapacity often have difficulty in comprehending advance directives and, therefore, do not participate in the process (Hardin & Yusufaly, 2004). Useful suggestions have been offered for making advance directives easier to comprehend, including the substitution of oral statements to physicians in place of written directives. Whatever the decision we reach, we will probably know ourselves better and be in a better position to help family and friends who may also be considering this option.

We can begin the process immediately by responding to the questions presented in Table 6-1. These questions explore our readiness to consider and discuss end-of-life issues in general.

In prefacing *The Rules and Exercises of Holy Dying* (1651/1970), Jeremy Taylor observed that:

> *It is a great art to die well, and to be learned by men in health, by them that can discourse and consider, by whose understanding and acts of reason are not abated with fear or pains: and as the greatest part of death is passed by the preceding years of our life, so also in those years are the greatest preparations to it . . . (p. iv–v).*

Taylor's advice is perhaps even more relevant today because the options for technological prolongation of life have so greatly increased and, as we have seen, the legal and moral dimensions have also become more complex.

We are ready now for Table 6-2, which presents several of the key decision points that should be specified in an advance health care directive if we want to convey specific instructions to health care providers. It might be stressful to think our way through each of these decision points, but doing so will reduce ambiguity for the health care service providers who we depend upon to honor our requests. We need to take responsibility to make and communicate our own decisions in the clearest possible manner if we expect others to take responsibility for respecting these decisions.

College Students' Attitudes Toward End-of-Life Issues

The last item in Table 6-2 is taken from a study of college students in history of medicine and sociology classes at the University of

TABLE 6-1 *My Readiness to Explore and Discuss Personal End-of-Life Issues*

Open heart surgery is one of the many options that was not available until recent years. When should all possible treatments be tried, and when should attention turn instead to comfort care?

Yes   No

____ ____   1.   I feel ready to consider all the issues that are related to the end of my life.

____ ____   2.   I intend to discuss at least some of these issues thoroughly with at least one other person whose views matter to me.

____ ____   3.   I intend to require of my physicians that they provide me with all the information I need to guide my decision making in a prompt, comprehensive, and honest manner.

____ ____   4.   I intend to select or create a document that communicates my preferences regarding treatment during the terminal phase of life.

____ ____   5.   I intend to designate a person to represent my preferences and interests in the event that I become incapacitated.

____ ____   6.   I intend to review and, if appropriate, modify my will and other legal instruments to ensure that they represent my final wishes in an effective way.

____ ____   7.   I intend to review my most significant relationships and take whatever steps are needed to resolve lingering problems and to renew and strengthen mutual ties.

____ ____   8.   I intend to do all that is possible to provide the opportunity for meaningful leave-taking interactions with the people in my life.

____ ____   9.   I intend to convey my preferences regarding burial/cremation and funeral services to those who will be responsible for making the arrangements.

____ ____ 10.   I intend to review and reflect upon what is of most importance to me in life and to devote much of my remaining time and energies to these core values.

TABLE 6-2 *Advance Directive Requests*

Yes   No

____ ____   1.   I want all life-sustaining treatments to be discontinued if I become terminally ill and permanently incompetent.

____ ____   2.   I want all life-sustaining treatments to be discontinued if I become permanently unconscious, whether terminally ill or not.

____ ____   3.   I want all life-sustaining treatments to be discontinued if I become unconscious and have very little chance of ever recovering consciousness or avoiding permanent brain injury.

____ ____   4.   I want to be kept alive if I become gravely ill and have only a slight chance of recovery (5 percent or less) and would probably require weeks or months of further treatment before the outcome became clear.

____ ____   5.   I want to have fluids and nutrition discontinued if other life support measures are discontinued.

____ ____   6.   Five types of possible life-sustaining options are listed below. If you were seriously ill, which of these options would you choose? (You can choose more than one).

Rochester (Karnik, Kamel, & Harper, 2002). Most of the respondents did choose one or more of the life-sustaining options. Major surgery, perhaps the most familiar of the choices, was also the choice most frequently made. There were no significant differences in choices made by the women and the men. There were differences, though, in relationship to ethnic background. African Americans (72 percent) were the most likely to request life-sustaining measures in general—and least likely to ask for a do not resuscitate (DNR) order. Hispanics (47 percent) were the least likely to request life-sustaining measures, with whites (59 percent) in the middle. There was also an Asian sample but from such diverse nations and cultures that it did not seem appropriate to consider them as a unitary group.

What about religious faith? Atheists were the least likely to request a DNR order. They preferred to take advantage of a last chance to continue this life. There were only small differences in life-sustaining option choices among Catholics, Jews, and Protestants.

The researchers offer additional comments as they draw upon interviews with the participants and results of other studies. African Americans tend to receive less intense medical care than whites and to be more negatively stereotyped than other patients. They express concern that the quality of care would be further diminished if a DNR were posted. Mexican American families are reported as having more hope for recovery, so families would feel guilty if they declined any life support measure.

Students of nursing were the most reluctant to accept life-prolonging treatments and the most supportive of DNR orders. "Nursing students were probably the most familiar with the concept of DNR . . . and the limits of modern medicine, and thus approached the questions more from a health care provider's point of view" (p. 5).

Advance Medical Directives: What Should We Do?

Many people think an advance medical directive is a good idea, but relatively few have actually taken this step.

Useful guidance to advance directives is offered by attorney Charles P. Sabatino (2005). He sets several pertinent facts in front of us:

- Advance directives are legal in every state.
- An advance directive legal in one state generally will be legal in all others. There may be some difference in terminology between the versions, but adjustments are made so that the basic expressed wish of the patient is respected.
- Advance medical directives do not restrict treatment efforts within generally accepted medical standards. Pain control and comfort care are continued, as is any treatment that does not attempt to keep patients alive against their wishes.
- We can use a form approved by our home states or can revise it to better express our own concerns and preferences. Sabatino (2005) declares that "it is a mistake to pick up an 'official' form and just sign it unchanged, without first being sure that it truly reflects one's specific wishes" (p. 1).
- A lawyer is not needed to complete a legal and effective form, though could be a useful resource if questions arise.
- Doctors and other health care providers are legally obligated to follow an advance directive. This was not the case in the past, notably with the living will. Medical providers cannot treat us against our wishes. Having said this, we should recognize that there are complexities and ambiguities in the link between preparing a directive and guaranteeing that it will be honored. We can improve the chances by expressing ourselves precisely and selecting a competent *health care proxy*. Even so, a sudden life-or-death crisis might not make it possible to retrieve and apply the directive. In many states, paramedics are still required to resuscitate and stabilize accident victims to rush them to the hospital. It would be wise to check the status in your own locality.

Sometimes the patient and family must take the initiative to encourage health care personnel to discuss end-of-life experiences with them. There is a lingering fear in the medical tradition that people just cannot deal with dying and death. Research says otherwise (e.g., Emanuel, Fairclough, Wolfe, & Emanuel, 2004), as does more than four decades of experience in the death awareness movement.

Sabatino and others recommend that our first decisive step should be the selection of a *health care proxy*, a person with the ability to represent our wishes and see that they are fulfilled if we are unable to do so ourselves. The next formal step is completion of the advance directive itself. You can obtain a valid form by contacting the American Bar Association or its local chapter, your state's department of health services, or your medical service provider. You might also visit the Aging with Dignity website (http://www.agingwithdignity. org) and become familiar with its version of the advance directive. Although not legally binding in all states, this document is instructive for the opportunities it offers to consider our options and preferences.

The Combined Advance Directive

A promising new development might encourage more people to complete an AD and also improve the chances that it will be readily available when needed. The combined advance directive (CAD) is more comprehensive than the forms previously available. It therefore provides the opportunity for people to consider the full range of end-of-life options and share their questions and views with their families, friends, and professional service providers. Because all the individual's preferences are included in a single document, it is easier to put on record and distribute.

Several versions of the CAD have been developed by concerned and informed citizens, and additional versions can be expected. The instrument articulated by the Vermont Ethics Network (2006) is particularly worth considering for clarity and accessibility. The complete form with instructions is available as a download.

The first of five sections offers a guide to select an agent and alternative for making health care decisions if the situation should arise. The second section presents treatment wishes: preferences for accepting or stopping treatment to keep one alive under certain circumstances. The items are clear and detailed, an improvement over the vague language in some previous documents. The basic list is augmented by "specific care wishes near the end of my life." Here one can address three significant issues: (1) "I want sufficient pain medication even though it may hasten my death; (2) I want hospice care when I am dying, if possible and appropriate; (3) I prefer to die at home, if this is possible." A person can check any, all or none of these

options. Another feature of this section is the opportunity to share one's spiritual and other care concerns. This has been somewhat neglected in previous documents.

Organ donation is the subject of the third section. It is not as detailed as some documents that have been devised specifically for organ donation, but is concise and informative. Section four takes us to "My wishes for disposition of my remains after my death," and the concluding section presents the "signed declaration of wishes." It also includes the important reminder to list people and locations that will have a copy of this document.

With and Without an Advance Directive

The SUPPORT study (1995) delivered a double dose of disappointment for those concerned with advance directives and the larger issue of patient-physician communication. As summarized in Chapter 5, the study first documented a pervasive pattern of medical indifference to the wishes of life-threatened and terminally ill people. An intervention was then conducted to improve medical responsivity, but it failed miserably. A research team has recently examined the role of advance directives more than a decade after both the SUPPORT study and introduction of the Patient Self-Determination Act (Teno, Gruneir, Schwartz, Nanda, & Wetle, 2007). The focus was on people who died in a nursing home, hospital, or at home with hospice, a total sample of more than fifteen hundred. The follow-up information was obtained from bereaved family members or other knowledgeable informants.

Most of these people—about 7 out of 10—did have an advance directive (AD). Those who died in a hospital were the least likely to have an AD. There were two clear differences in the experiences of people with and without an AD during their end-of-life period. Fewer people with an AD were on a respirator or intubated for feeding. This differential can be interpreted as more compliance with a patient's wish to limit medical interventions; it can also be interpreted as receiving more efficient care to avoid the need for respirator and feeding tube. Physician communication with patient and family was perceived as more problematic when no AD had been prepared. Bereaved family members in these situations more often felt that the physicians were not keeping them well informed.

This study suggests that there are advantages in completing and presenting an AD. Nevertheless, even with an AD, about one of four patients experienced inadequate pain control, and half were reported to have received inadequate emotional support. There is still work to be done.

Informed Consent and Advance Directives: How Effective?

It is clear that the PSDA, informed consent, and advance directives are contributing to improved end-of-life care for many people. However, it is also clear that these provisions have not been used as frequently as expected and, when used, have sometimes stumbled over problems such as the following:

- Patients are too often rushed to make an informed consent decision, especially when the health care providers are themselves under time pressure, and when the overall quality of care has been inadequate (Rhodes & Teno, 2008). A person who is not truly informed and given an opportunity to think through the situation is not really in a position to make a cogent self-determination. Unfortunately, physicians sometimes "doctor" the information they share with the patient, misrepresenting the situation (Minkoff & Marshall, 2009).
- Fifteen years after passage of the PSDA, many physicians continue to ignore the patient's stated wishes (Morrell et al., 2008). The discrepancy is overwhelmingly in the direction of proceeding with resuscitation even though the patient has chosen DNR. Morrell's research team notes that one could hardly tell that advance directives had been made, so limited was their effect on physician behavior. When DNR orders were respected, their implementation often was delayed.
- Communication about end-of-life care among patient, family, and doctor remains limited. It is not unusual for the patients never to have discussed their decision and wishes with either physician or family—thereby reducing the probability that these wishes will actually be effective when the time comes.
- More than a few people have difficulty making well-thought-through decisions as health and cognitive functioning declines (Silveira et al., 2010). This problem arises most often among

older adults with significant health problems, but also with younger people who do not have command of their mental facilities. People undergoing a chronic critical illness at any age can enter a sort of twilight zone between "still hanging in" and dying.

Enlightened family involvement and an open-minded physician can help to arrive at the best possible way to manage the situation (Camhi et al., 2009).

The PSDA is more or less effective, depending on how well we use it.

A RIGHT *NOT* TO DIE? THE CRYONICS ALTERNATIVE

Do we have a right *not* to die? Even if we are dead? Did Walt Disney make this choice, and should "The Splendid Splinter" have been given the opportunity to stand again in the late-inning shadows of Fenway Park and glare at a nervous pitcher? The answer to the first question is clear: Disney was not placed in *cryostasis*, despite rumors to the contrary. The second question runs afoul of the persistent issue of who deserves a second chance at life, and who should make that decision.

The *cryonics* alternative has been available since 1967, when the first person chose to have his certified dead body placed in a hypothermic (frozen) condition for possible resuscitation at a later time. I did not meet Dr. James H. Bedford personally, but paused for a moment by the aluminum chamber that holds his physical remains at the Alcor Life Extension Foundation in Scottsdale, Arizona. Bedford, a psychologist, was the first person to test the possibilities of cryonic preservation and restoration with his own body. Stephen Bridge, former Alcor director, helped transfer Bedford from his original cylinder to a newer model in 1984. He observes that Bedford looked as "healthy" as when first placed into cryostasis. Bedford is 1 of about 80 at that facility (precise numbers are difficult to pry from cryonic sources). Another is the mother of R. C. W. Ettinger, whose best-selling book, *The Prospect of Immortality* (1966), brought keen but fleeting attention to the subject. Most people in cryostasis with Alcor or other facilities have requested that their identities be kept confidential.

Relatively few people were aware of the cryonics movement until the controversy following Ted Williams's death in 2002. There were conflicting reports about Williams's own intentions, and dissension within his family. The sports community was appalled by the image of the near-legendary baseball player's body being "kept on ice," as some erroneously characterized the process. The situation took a bizarre turn in 2003, when a former Alcor employee charged that Williams's head had been damaged by careless treatment. These charges were denied and not clearly resolved, but the president of the organization resigned and the state of Arizona imposed additional regulatory authority over Alcor. This episode damaged the reputation of the cryonics alternative, and accusations and counteraccusations continue to do so.

Nevertheless, the cryonics alternative is worth considering here as a counterbalance to the prevailing emphasis on the right to die. It is also instructive only for what the public's response might tell us about our attitudes toward life and death.

A Longer Life? Historical Background

The desire to extend our lives is one of the most enduring themes in human history. In pretechnological times it was attempted through physical ordeals, magical spells, secret rituals, and experiments with a variety of substances and concoctions. The impulse for life extension has often been associated with the quest for eternal or restored youth (Gruman, 1966; Kastenbaum, 1995). An ancient Egyptian papyrus offers instructions on how to transform a person of 80 into a youth of 20 (reportedly, some of the suggestions have become incorporated into the modern cosmetic industry). Alchemists whose work eventually prepared the way for the physical sciences dreamed of converting base metals such as lead into gold—but hoped even more fervently that they could find the elixir to keep people alive and healthy for many more years. Importing the essence of monkey glands into one's body or having a coil or two of one's intestines removed was the leading edge of medical optimism well into the twentieth century; and was no more successful than the ancient maneuvers. We are now on the cusp of genetic/stem cell

sorcery that might or might not do the trick. So—what does the cryonic approach have on offer?

Rationale and Method

Advocates of the cryonic approach believe it possible to maintain "deceased" people at very low temperatures for long periods of time. Eventually, medical breakthroughs will cure the conditions that led to their "death" (Drexler, 1991). Some believe that resuscitation should wait even longer—until science has turned off or reversed the aging process. Until recently there were two levels of vision: (a) restoring "dead" people to continue their lives where they had left off and (b) not only raising the dead but equipping them with bodies that will be resistant to aging and mortality. An even more ambitious scenario is now being explored: growing new bodies from "neuro" preparations (brains only).

This scenario has often been introduced in movies and works of fiction. Nevertheless, there is some connection to demonstrable reality. Surgeons routinely lower the patient's body temperature, especially for lengthy operations. Human sperm and embryos have been maintained in a frozen condition until use—perhaps some readers of this book were given their lives in this manner. There has been some success in preserving body parts and even whole animals in a hypothermic state. In short, cryonic procedures have a significant place in biomedical procedures. These applications, however, are a long way from preservation and revival of a certifiably dead human being.

Cryonicists are sensitive about the criticism that it is selfish to desire a second chance at life. The fact that this alternative seems limited to people with adequate financial resources is troubling from the ethical standpoint: perhaps cryonics would turn out to be another example of elitism and discrimination. Is the cryonic alternative a legitimate exercise of individual rights, or a demonstration of excessive ego?

The cryonics procedure cannot begin until a physician has certified the patient as dead. To begin the procedure earlier could be considered homicide. Cryonicists immediately lower the body temperature and give injections to protect vital organs, while a heart–lung machine circulates the cryoprotectant agents that are intended

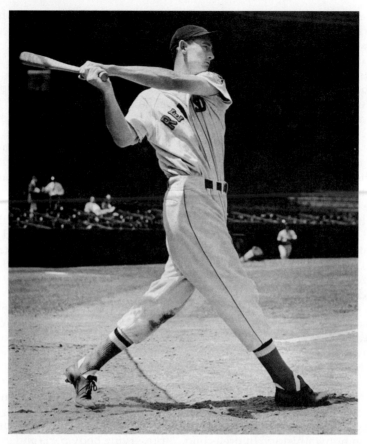

Baseball great Ted William's death was followed by controversy and outrage when his head was separated from his body and placed in liquid nitrogen storage.

to protect against the hypothermic process. The body is brought to the nearest cryonics facility, where further preparations are made and the cooled and wrapped body is placed into a cylinder filled with liquid nitrogen. The cryonic organization is under contract to maintain the level of liquid nitrogen (which is subject to evaporation over time) and ensure the integrity of the protective chamber. And sooner or later, or perhaps never, biomedical advances will make it possible to thaw, resuscitate, and cure the person of "temporary death."

No such attempts have yet been reported at Alcor, the largest of the life extension foundations, or any other facility. Medical and scientific advisors to the cryonic movement state that resuscitation techniques have not yet advanced to the point where such an attempt would be feasible.

Heads of Stone: A Radical New Development

The methods already described have been improved somewhat over time, notably in the effectiveness of the cryoprotectants to prevent formation of crystals as a result of freezing. It is not clear, however, whether these improvements are adequate for the challenge. More recently, there have been two major changes: (a) neural (head-only) preservation has replaced whole-body preservation, and (b) the cooled tissues are vitrified (transformed into a stone-like substance).

Why preserve only the head? Less cost, takes less space. And it is the brain, not the head, that is the focus.

Vitrification? It's a process that replaces the fluid inside cells with antifreeze compounds. The temperature is then dropped way down, to –130°C. The result is a rigid stone-like structure that is actually a form of glass. The vitrified tissues are considered to be no longer subject to biochemical processes and are expected to remain stable indefinitely. Vitrification has had other uses in medical research and education (including Dr. von Hagen's plastinates, Chapter 2). It is a new application rather than a new process. Like earlier forms of cryostatis, though, no attempts have yet been made to reverse the process.

Vitrification requires an extra leap of faith. Two leaps, actually—first, that an entire body can be regenerated from neural DNA and, second, that glass can again become flesh. Cryonicists believe that whole-body regeneration will become feasible as cloning experiments continue. In the past, people who considered the cryonic alternative could at least envision a whole body (head and all) keeping cool until the time came for resuscitation. It is asking much more of people to imagine a glass–stone head that will morph into a new or renewed person.

The switch to vitrification has been defended as a more refined, as well as less expensive, procedure. Alexander (2003), however, offers a critical perspective. He reports that by the end of the twentieth century, cryonicists admitted to themselves that:

> People frozen before the late 1990s were goners. The old methods were just too crude. Alcor and the other cryonic outfits kept them frozen out of a sense of sacred duty, respect for the pioneers, and the slim chance that in some great technological leap, all the cells popped by ice crystals, all the cracked, mushy organs could somehow be repaired. . . . But when they weren't putting on a brave face, even the boundless optimism of the most ardent cryonicist gave way to the recognition that the prospects for even the more recently chilled were pretty iffy (pp. 232–233).

More Questions

Here are some other questions that are far from settled. What do you think? Should we regard cryostasis:

1. As body preservation, like mummification?
2. As body disposal (cryo-remains)?
3. As an affront to God and Nature or just one more life-prolongation effort among others? As *denial* of, or *resistance* to, death?
4. As the potential realization of a long-cherished human desire, or just a fantasy that affluent people can afford?
5. As a new chapter in the ancient mythology of the journeys of the dead, or in the related stories of a sleeping beauty waiting to be warmed by a lover's kiss?
6. As a fantasy addition to a category of "sleepers" who are neither living nor dead in the traditional senses of the terms?

Having left so many questions for your own consideration, I will venture an observation on one more issue. Counting all of Alcor's guests, there seem to be not much more than 100 cremains in the entire world. Although several hundred have reportedly signed up for possible cryostasis, this is an astoundingly small number of people who have attempted to overcome death with this technological option. Few of the cryonic organizations that were established in the early days of the movement seem to be operational today. Social and behavioral scientists have given little attention to this phenomenon. I must rely upon a study I conducted back in the 1960s, in which most respondents firmly rejected cryonic suspension even though they were open to other end-of-life possibilities. "Freeze—wait—reanimate!," the slogan of the time, was a scary idea. Often mentioned was the fear of overstepping the human domain: It's not for us to challenge the mortality to which God has consigned us. There was also much concern about loss and distortion of relationships. ("If I come back young, and my wife is old. . . .; "I wouldn't want to come back alone, without my people.") Others were distressed by the idea of losing so much control, along with being distrustful of how their fate would be managed by others. Although few said so explicitly, there was also a fear akin to being buried alive. It must also be said that five decades after Dr. Bradford venture into cryospace, there has still not been anything resembling a breakthrough in demonstrating the effectiveness of this procedure.

ORGAN DONATION

Organ donation stands in marked contrast to the hope of cryonic resuscitation. Registering one's self as an organ donor improves the chances of another person's survival. The organs most sought for transplantation are kidneys and livers. Hearts, heart–lung sets, intestines, and pancreases are also on the waiting list. In 2009, there were 8,021 deceased organ donors and 6,610 living organ donors, resulting in 28,465 organ transplants. Unfortunately, the demand is far greater than the supply. Many people wait anxiously for their turn—which might or might not come in time. Approximately 100,000 people are on the waiting list in the United States at any point in time, and approximately 18 die each year while waiting (United Network for Organ Sharing, 2010). More detail is provided by Tuttle-Newhall et al., 2009, and the websites are listed at the end of this chapter.

Successful Organ Transplantation

Five factors restrict the number of successful transplantations: (a) willingness of people to donate; (b) condition of the donated organs; (c) biological match between donor and recipient to avoid rejection; (d) whether the overall condition of the recipient is strong enough to ensure survival with the new organ; even if it is not rejected; and (e) expense and timely delivery. Furthermore, health care professionals may be caught in a stressful situation: required by federal regulations to ask families for permission, yet hesitant to impose on the grieving survivors, especially when the death occurred in a sudden and unexpected manner.

Organs are sometimes donated by living people who are likely to survive their anatomical gift (often a kidney). In these circumstances, it is possible to plan carefully for the future. Most often, living people donate organs to family members or others they know, but anonymous donations to unknown recipients are becoming more common. Cadaveric donations remain the most common source for transplants. Victims of fatal motor vehicle accidents are some of the most available sources. Organ donations by the living have increased over time, but the dead still contribute a little more than half of the organs transplanted each year (United Network for Organ Sharing, 2010). The situation is further complicated by the revelation that about a third of the people listed as waiting for an organ transplant are not eligible because of health or other complications (Stein, 2008).

Competition, Tension, Controversy

Competition has spurred conflict. Should an available organ go to the person who is in the most need and has the highest probability of surviving with it—or to a person who resides in the local area from which the donation was received? There is also concern that some potential recipients face discrimination. Discrimination against recipients on the basis of ethnicity or race would violate accepted standards of care.

As already noted, there is also concern about disadvantaged people selling their organs for use by those who are more affluent. Authorities in India remain concerned about the illegal but prospering sale of organs from living human donors (Devraj, 2002). Pakistan hosts a lively market for kidney vendors and their mostly foreign consumers. Moazam et al. (2009) found that most of those who sold a kidney were illiterate and hard-pressed financially. They felt weak, as though bloodless, and unable to continue with the manual labor they had been doing before the organ harvesting.

> Pointing to the left half of his body, one vendor told us that mehsoos hota hay kay khalee jaga hay (I feel there is an empty space here), and that he was now an adhoora banda (incomplete or half a man). This curious sense of feeling "half" being "empty," somehow having been transformed into "incomplete" person, was among the most common statements we heard (p. 33).

Authorities condemn this practice both on ethical and biomedical grounds: the donors, already suffering hardships and deprivations, increase their own risks of death.

Organ donation by Chinese prisoners who face execution presents a different situation, and need to be understood within that nation's philosophy and traditions. From the Confucian perspective, the rightful order of society can find it "as a morally praiseworthy act of the prisoner who is willing to make the final effort to repent and correct his/her evil conduct and to leave something good to the world" (Wang & Wang, 2010, p. 197). (Note the comments of an American transplant surgeon below.)

Marrow rich in blood stem cells can be a life-saving donation and has been relatively free of controversy. Harvesting organs shortly after death, however, has raised issues difficult to resolve.

Anthropologist Margaret Lock offers a penetrating analysis of organ transplantation from a sociocultural standpoint in *Twice Dead* (2002). In Japan, for example, the exchange of gifts is closely woven into the social fabric. Although a kidney is a distinctive and nontraditional gift, the offer nevertheless occurs within a strong pattern of exchange and therefore might constitute an expected kind of behavior. Within Christianity, organ donation can accord with "the biblical sense of charity." There are aspects of organ donation, however, that can create confusion and frustration. For example, many Americans prefer having the opportunity to choose who will receive their organs. This desire runs counter to the needs and practices of the

health care system. Prejudices can also complicate a prospective transplantation gift. People may have difficulty, for example, accepting voluntary organ donations from death-row prisoners. Lock quotes a transplant surgeon regarding this situation:

> *He said to me, with some embarrassment, "I wouldn't like to have a murderer's heart put into my body," then added hastily, glancing at my tape recorder and trying to make a joke out of the situation, "I might find myself starting to change" (p. 320).*

Most recipients are matter-of-fact about the source of their organs, but some feel emotionally linked to the donors and believe that their lives have changed because of this intimate connection with another person.

Another challenging issue is the relationship between organ donation and the diagnosis of brain death. This has been a subject of concern for years (Chapter 2): Would the pressure for quick harvesting of organs lead to premature certification of death? This issue has become more salient in recent years because of a practice known as "donation after cardiac death" (DCD). Previously, most organs were removed only after a patient was certified as brain dead. The new procedure, advocated by federal health officials, transplant surgeons, and organ banks, involves removal within minutes after the heart stops beating (de Groot et al., 2010; Stein, 2007). It is used most frequently when family members have agreed to have life-support efforts terminated after a motor vehicle accident or stroke.

The number of DCD procedures is rapidly increasing. Health care organizations are faced with the question of whether this practice should be allowed in their facilities. Advocates point to the opportunity for harvesting more usable organs and distributing them more rapidly to those who so urgently need them. However, some doctors and bioethicists fear that transplant surgeons might pressure families to discontinue treatment, thereby compromising their terminal care, or even hastening their deaths. At present, many hospital organizations are in process of deciding about the advisability of using the DCD procedure.

Another approach was mentioned at start of this chapter: how about operating a survival lottery for people in need of an organ or issue transplant? Several types of lottery have been proposed since the mid 1970s. In its most dramatic form, everyone in the waiting pool would be a potential donor for everybody else (Harris, 1994). This donor would be selected by a random and presumably fair process, the anatomical gift then made available to another person in the waiting pool, again by random drawing. Perhaps needless to say, this plan has not yet been put into action (as far as is known). It has remained, though as a stimulus to bioethicists who are searching for some fair way out of the supply/demand dilemma. Overland (2007) has recently taken up this challenge. He suggests there is still merit in the survival lottery proposal, though there are prickly details to be resolved. Is this a direction that should be encouraged? Would you welcome a survival lottery for yourself or your loved ones if on a list for organ transplantation?

Becoming a Donor

"Should I register as a prospective organ or tissue donor?" This is obviously a personal decision that is likely to be influenced by our life experiences and worldview. Sometimes, though, the decision is clouded by uncertainties regarding the process. Fortunately, there is detailed and reliable information readily available. It is widely recognized that acquiring and distributing anatomical gifts is a sensitive process that needs to be regulated in the best interests of everybody involved. You will find an authoritative presentation of the Revised Uniform Anatomical Gift Act (2006, revised 2007) available for download (http://law.upenn.edu and at other sites). It is also worth checking out the version of this act that has been adopted by your state government (e.g., State of Arizona, 2007). It is probable that most of your questions will be answered by these documents; if not, inquiries can be made to your local government and organ banks.

One point is particularly worth noting: The participation of a *disinterested witness* is required when a person "makes, amends, revokes or refuses to make an anatomical gift" (State of Arizona, p. 1). This is a person who is not eligible to receive an anatomical gift and is not a relative or guardian of the person making the decision. This provision is among the safeguards to protect the independence of decision making.

It is useful to think ahead of time regarding details of the donation. Do you wish to donate any and all organs or tissues, or are there some you would prefer to exclude? Do you wish to make this anatomical gift available for whatever purpose it proves to be most suitable for: therapy, education, or research? Or would you prefer to limit the use? These can be difficult questions to consider, but a little easier to deal with when given advance thought.

FUNERAL-RELATED DECISIONS

The funeral and memorialization process is discussed in Chapter 12. Individual decision making, though, can benefit from acquiring specific information, exploring alternatives, and discussing the situation with the important people in our lives. We will focus on the practical matters of funeral and burial costs and arrangements.

It sounds rather cold to think of ourselves as "consumers" of funeral and burial services, but this is part of the reality. Here are several useful suggestions that have been passed along by AARP as well as other public interest groups:

- Funeral homes are required to provide price lists at their place of business and some will mail the information. Although prices can also be disclosed by telephone, it is a good idea to have a written list that includes all options.
- Do thorough comparison shopping. The differences can be significant. Look at separate price lists for general services, caskets, and outer burial containers, rather than only at an overall cost estimate.
- Be aware of additional charges for additional services and products. For example, many funeral homes will prepare obituary notices or provide music, but for an additional charge.
- Do not hesitate to inquire about simple and immediate burials or about cremation. Again, check to learn what services are included in the basic fee.
- The most expensive single item in a traditional funeral is the casket. Be aware that you can choose to purchase a casket from the Internet or other outside source and that a funeral home cannot charge you extra for this.
- Resist agreeing to add-on services or products unless these are what you and your family really want.

There has been increasing pressure on the public in recent years to plan funerals well in advance and often to commit their money in advance as well. This development is part of a major change in the funeral industry. The family-owned community funeral home is rapidly being taken over or displaced by corporate expansion. Even though a familiar family name might still be seen on signs and advertisements, it could be that your local funeral home has become a franchise operation with national or international headquarters elsewhere. Funeral director Thomas Lynch (1997) is among the critics of this trend:

> The firm in the next town was bought out last year by Service Corporation International (SCI)— The Big Mac of the mortuary trade. They own most of Paris and Australia, a lot of London and Manhattan. They buy guys like me. They want the brick and mortar, the fifty years of trading on the family name. They want to be like one of the family, mine and yours. At the moment these multinational firms own a fifth of the mortuary dollar volume in the United States. They are in a hurry to own more and more (pp. 174–175).

Many others are concerned about the mega-corporate influence on funeral services. Funeral directors were once among the most respected citizens in small town America (Holloway, 2002). Their families did know the families who came to them in time of need. Prepaid funeral and burial arrangements can be useful to some people, but caution is recommended.

A Perspective on End-of-Life Decisions

Society is actively engaged in restructuring the ways in which we treat each other near the end of life. Both the general public and health care professionals may at times feel uncomfortable because the rules have been changing. We are now being asked to make decisions that usually seemed to have made themselves. The physician generally was in the position of an unquestioned decision maker. These decisions often flowed from the belief that one should do everything that might be done to extend life, even if there was little or no hope of success. On occasion the decision could be made (quietly, unobtrusively) to withhold or withdraw cure-oriented treatment to spare the patient further suffering. Now the physician is expected to share decision making with patient and family and to be responsive as well to other health care professionals and legislative measures.

The new social and medical climate for end-of-life decisions favors strengthened participation, communication, and patients' rights. More physicians themselves have become active in this cause. And Millie Morrisey's distress was soon alleviated. The nursing home staff did become aware of her wishes; they quickly removed the ventilator and offered her comfort care that resulted in a peaceful death a few days later (Field & Cassel, 1997). Furthermore, shaken by this experience, the nursing home made changes in its policies and practices to prevent such a situation from happening again.

We are in a difficult but promising situation: More people are concerned about making end-of-life decisions that respect patient and family wishes, but how to do this in an effective and timely way is a challenge that still must be addressed by the health care system as well as individuals. There may also be crucial personal situations to resolve. Should the terminally ill person try to overcome years of grudges and negative feelings toward a family member or friend? Is it better to hold onto the anger or to seek resolution? Or is it the terminally ill person's relationship with God that needs to find resolution one way or another?

Still again, there may be a strong need to complete a project or mission. Near the end of his life, J. S. Bach (1685–1750) was so weakened by illness that his family tried to persuade him to remain in bed. He wouldn't have that. Instead he devoted practically every waking hour to *Art of Fugue,* one of the most remarkable compositions from one of the world's most remarkable composers. His mental and emotional powers remained at their peak despite his rapidly failing health. There are not many J. S. Bachs with such a monumental project to complete near the end of their lives, but there are others among us who have endeavors they are deeply committed to seeing through as long as possible. End-of-life decisions can take many forms, so we are well advised to be sensitive to the special needs of every individual.

Johann Sebastian Bach continued to compose his monumental Art of Fugue *until very nearly his last breath.*

■ SUMMARY

The responsibility for end-of-life decisions was once largely in the hands of physicians and the health care system. Today there is more opportunity for patients and their families to participate in decision making. However, not everybody feels prepared to exercise control over the medical interventions that should be attempted near the end of their lives. Some people most highly value the option of individual choice; others function within a tradition that favors family or faith-based decision making. There is growing awareness that more attention should be given to patient and family ethnic background and values.

The *living will* was the first advance directive to gain wide attention. This document stimulated widespread discussion of end-of-life issues. All states now have enacted legislation based upon the living will concept that people should have the right to limit the kind of treatment they receive near the end of their lives. Courts established the principle of *informed consent,* which supports individual choice. The federal government subsequently enacted the *Patient Self-Determination Act,* with the intention of increasing patient participation and hospital compliance. All these measures have had some success in providing patients and families with more choice in end-of-life health care options, but difficulties still persist. Research indicates that people who have prepared an advance directive do receive a pattern of terminal care that is closer to their own preferences. The *combined advance directive* is a new development that enables a person to express end-of-life preferences across a comprehensive range of issues: treatment wishes (including spiritual concerns), organ donation, and funeral arrangements. This document holds promise for encouraging more reflection and discussion of the end-of-life situation, as well as providing a single source for those who will be responsible for carrying out the individual's wishes.

The right to request limitation or termination of treatment was contrasted with the desire to do everything possible that might extend or renew life. The cryonic approach (earlier carrying the slogan, "Freeze—wait—reanimate!") was discussed as a salient and extreme example.

Organ donations (also known as anatomical gifts) are a much more demonstrably effective end-of-life option and have contributed directly and indirectly to the survival of many people. However, there is a chronic shortage of organs and tissues. People in need can wait only so long for the organ or tissue that could keep them going. The limited supply of available organs and tissues has generated intense anxieties and controversies. One example is the accelerated process for removing organs immediately after cardiac failure: this is praised for its efficiency, and criticized for a possible bias toward "premature harvesting" and disregard for the dying person. Proposals for a "survival lottery" are receiving a mixed reception, but many people are seeking ways to improve the current stressful situation of organ transplant distribution.

■ REFERENCES

Aging with Dignity. http://www.agingwithdignity.org/

Alexander, B. (2003). *Rapture.* New York: Basic Books.

Barnato, A. E., Anthony, D. L., Skinner, J., Gallagher, P. M., & Fisher E. S. (2009). Racial and ethnic differences in preferences for end-of-life treatment. *Journal of General Internal Medicine, 24,* 1497–1525.

Camhi, S. L., Mercado, A. F., Morrison R., Du, Q., Platt, D. M., August, G. L., & Nelson, J. E. (2009). Deciding in the dark: Advance directives and continuation of treatment in chronic critical illness. *Critical Care Medicine, 37,* 919–925.

Clements, J. M. (2009). Patient perceptions on the use of advance directives and life-prolonging technology. *American Journal of Hospice and Palliative Medicine, 26,* 270–276.

Cohen, I. G. (2010). Medical tourism: The view from ten thousand feet. *Hastings Center Report, 40,* 11–12.

de Groot, Y. J., Jansen, N. E., Bakker, J., Aerdts, S., & Maas, A.I. R. (2010). Imminent brain death: Point of departure for potential heart-beating organ donor recognition. *Intensive Care Medicine, 36,* 1–7.

Devraj, R. (2002). HEALTH-INDIA: Legal ban fails to check kidney "exports." http://ipsnews.net/news.asp?idnews=82807.

Drexler, K. E. (1991). *Unbounding the future.* New York: Morrow.

Emanuel, E. J., Fairclough, D. L., Wolfe, P., & Emanuel, L. L. (2004). Talking with terminally ill patients and their caregivers about death, dying, and bereavement. *Archives of Internal Medicine, 164,* 1999–2004.

Ettinger, R. C. W. (1966). *The prospect of immortality.* New York: Mcfadden–Bartell.

Field, M. J., & Cassel, C. K. (Eds.). (1997). *Approaching death: Improving care at the end of life.* Washington, DC: National Academy Press.

Go, R. S., Hammes, B. A., Lee, J. A., & Mathiason, M. A. (2007). Advance directives among health care professionals at a community-based cancer center. *Mayo Clinic Proceedings, 82,* 1487–1490.

Golmakani, M. M., Niknam, M. H., & Hedayat, K. M. (2005). Transplantation ethics from the Islamic point of view. *Medical Science Monitor, 11,* RA105–109.

Gresham, S. D., & Gresham, G. E. (2005, June 1). Preparing for the end. http://www.highbeam.com/doc/1G1-133007110.html.

Gruman, G. J. (1966). *A history of ideas about the prolongation of life.* Philadelphia: The American Philosophical Society.

Hardin, S. B., & Yusufaly, Y. A. (2004). Difficult end-of-life treatment decisions. *Archives of Internal Medicine, 164,* 1531–1533.

Harris, J. (1994). The survival lottery. In B. Steinbock & A. Norcross (Eds.), *Killing and letting die* (pp. 257–265). New York: Fordham University Press.

Holloway, K. F. C. (2002). *Passed on, African American mourning stories.* Durham, NC: Duke University Press.

Karnik, A. A., Kamel, H. K., & Harper, D. (2002). Attitudes of college students toward end-of-life issues. *Internet Journal of Pain, Symptom Control, & Palliative Care, 2,* 1–7.

Kastenbaum, R. (1995). *Dorian, graying: Is youth the only thing worth having?* Amityville, New York: Baywood.

Lock, M. (2002). *Twice dead. Organ transplants and the reinvention of death.* Berkeley: University of California Press.

Lynch, T. (1997). *The undertaking. Life studies from the dismal trade.* New York: Penguin.

Mathisen, L. (2005, March 1). Use of physical restraint in adult critical care: A bicultural study. *American Journal of Critical Care.*

Minkoff, H., & Marshall, M. F. (2009). Government-scripted consent: When medical ethics and law collide. *Hastings Center Report, 39,* 21–23.

Moazam, R., Zaman, R. M., & Jafarey, A. R. (2009). Conversations with kidney vendors in Pakistan: An ethnographic study. *Hastings Center Report, 39,* 29–44.

Morrell, E. D., Brown, B. P., Drabiak, R. Q., & Helft, P. R. (2008). The do-not-resuscitate order: Associations with advance directives, physician specialty and documentation of discussion 15 years after the

Patient Self-Determination Act. *Journal of Medical Ethics, 34,* 642–647.

National Conference of Commissioners on Uniform State Laws (2007). Revised Uniform Anatomical Gift Act (2006, revised 2007). www.nccusl.org.

Overland, G. (2007). Survival lotteries reconsidered. *Bioethics, 21,* 355–363.

Rhodes, R., & Tenn, J. M. (2009). What's race got to do with it? *Journal of Clinical Oncology, 27,* 5496–5498.

Sabatino, C. P. (2005, June 11). Ten legal myths about advance medical directives. http://www.abanet. org/aging/ myths.html.

Salmond, S. W., & David, E. (2005). Attitudes toward advance directives and advance directive completion rates. *Orthopaedic Nursing, 24,* 117–127.

Schneiderman, L. J., Kaplan, R. M., Rosenberg, E., & Teetzel, H. (1997). Do Physicians' Own Preferences for Life-Sustaining Treatment Influence Their Perceptions of Patients' Preferences? A Second Look. *Cambridge Quarterly of Healthcare Ethics, 6,* 131–137.

Searight, H. R., & Gafford, J. (2005). Cultural diversity at the end of life: Issues and guidelines for family physicians. *American Family Physician, 71,* 515–522.

Shewmon, D. A. (2009). And she's not only merely dead, she's really most sincerely dead. *Hastings Center Report, 39,* 6–7.

Silveira, M. J., Kim, S. U. H., & Langa K.M. (2010). Advance directives and outcomes of surrogate decision making before death. *New England Journal of Medicine, 362,* 1211–1218.

State of Arizona (2007). Senate Bill 1099. Relating to the Revised Uniform Anatomical Gift Act. www. dnaz.org.

Stein, R. (March 18, 2007). New trend in organ donation raises questions. *Arizona Republic,* p. A03.

Stein, R. (March 22, 2008). A third of patients on transplant list are not eligible. *Washington Post,* p. A01.

Taylor, J. (1651/1977). The rules and exercises of holy dying. New York: Arno. (Original work published in 1651.)

Teno, J. M. Gruneir, A. Schwartz, Z., Nanda, A., & Wetle, T. (2007). Association between advance directives and quality of end-of-life care: A national study. *Journal of the American Geriatric Society, 55,* 189–194.

Tuttle-Newhall, J. E., Krishnan, S. M., Levy, M. F., Orfowski, J. P., & Sung, R. S. (2009). Organ donation and utilization in the United States: 1998–2007. *American Journal of Transplantation, 9,* 879–893.

Veatch, R. M. (2009). The evolution of death and dying controversies. *Hastings Center Report, 39,* 16–19.

Vermont Ethics Network (2006). Vermont Advance Directive for Health Care. www.vtethicsnetwork.org.

United Network for Organ Sharing. (2004). http:// www.unos.org.

Wang, M., & Wang, X. (2010). Organ donation by capital prisoners in China: Reflections in Confucian ethics. *Journal of Medicine & Philosophy, 35,* 197–212.

Wu, A. M. S., & Tang, C. (2009). The negative impact of death anxiety and willingness to donate organs among Chinese adults. *Death Studies, 33,* 51–72.

■ GLOSSARY

Advance Directive A legal document that specifies the type of health care an individual wishes to receive should that individual not be in a position to express his or her wishes in a critical situation.

Anatomical Gift A donation of all or part of a human body after the donor's death for the purpose of transplantation, therapy, education, or research.

Cryonics An approach that attempts to preserve a body at very low temperatures until medical advances have made it possible to cure the fatal condition.

Combined advanced health care directive A single document in which the individual can address the full range of decision-making options.

Cryostasis The condition of a body being maintained at a very low temperature.

Disinterested witness A person who is not related to the individual making or revoking an organ donation decision and who would not be a recipient.

Durable Power of Attorney for Health Care The transfer of legal authority to a person who would make health care decisions for a person who at that time is unable to make or communicate his or her own decision.

Health Care Proxy A person officially designated to make end-of-life and other health care decisions for an individual, should that individual be unable to make decisions because of illness or other incapacity.

Informed Consent The principle that patients should be provided with sufficient information to make decisions for or against accepting a treatment.

Living Will The first type of advance directive to be introduced, requesting that no aggressive treatments be attempted if the individual is in the end phase of life.

Patient Self-Determination Act A federal law that requires health care organizations to provide patients with the informed opportunity to establish an advance directive to limit medical treatment in specified situations.

Physical Restraints Devices such as mitts, bulky dressings, leather wrist straps, and restrictive vests that are sometimes used in hospitals to prevent patients from removing life support connections, falling out of bed, or otherwise injuring themselves.

■ ON FURTHER THOUGHT . . .

Useful online resources:

Aging with Dignity
   agingwithdignity.org
Death with Dignity National Center
   www.deathwithdignity.org
Duke Institute on Care at the End of Life
   www.iceol.duke.edu
Growthhouse
   www.growthhouse.org
National Alliance for Caregiving
   www.caregiving.org

Organ donation regulations
   www.organdonor.gov/
Promoting Excellence in End-of-Life Care
   www.promotingexcellence.org
Center for Practical Bioethics
   www.practicalbioethics.org

Useful books:

Goldman, C. (2002). *The gifts of caregiving: Stories of hardship, hope, and healing* (with CD of radio program on same subject). Minneapolis, MN: Fairview Press.

Staton, J., Shuy, R., & Byock, I. (2001). *A few months to live: Different paths to life's end.* Washington, DC: Georgetown University Press.

Zaner, R. B. (2004). *Conversations on the edge: Narratives of ethics and illness.* Washington, DC: Georgetown University Press.

Organ Donation: Knowledge, Fears, Values:

Go ahead. Stir up some trouble, or perhaps just some lively conversation with family and friends. Who would donate an organ? Why or why not? Who has already signed a directive to make organs available: Why or why not? What ideas, experiences, or feelings have encouraged each person to either accept or reject the option of organ donation? Check your facts with such publications as Lack's *Twice Dead* (see reference list), or visit an informative online site such as Living Bank International (www.livingbank.org).

Suicide

She had a whirlwind romance—a marriage proposal on the first date. The Disney World wedding fulfilled that part of her fantasy, but not the part where her favorite singer would agree to make a special appearance. Karen Carpenter had succumbed to a severe eating disorder. Terri's own eating disorder would soon place her on extended life support, and on the front page of newspapers and television news and talk shows.

—Chapter 9 of this book

If you're reading this, you're no doubt asking yourself, "Why did this have to happen?" The simple truth is that it is complicated and has been coming for a long time.

—Joe Stack (2010)

He enlisted in the Navy at age 16 and became the first to rise through the ranks to become chief of naval operations. ". . . journalists made an appointment to question him about a small brass V, which he had worn on the ribbon of one of his medals."

—Saxby Pridmore (2010)

Glycogen synthase kinase levels "were significantly higher in the prefrontal cortex (PFC) and hippocampus of teenage suicide but not in adult suicide victims. [This] may represent a neurodevelopmentally associated decrease and may be important in the pathophysiology of teenage suicide."

—Pandey et al. (2008a)

And if we can't remember who attended our son's funeral or forget the directions to our home or even our sister's name, we begin to understand that we are not suffering from a sudden onset of Alzheimer's—we are having memory lapses that are probably shielding us in some way from the full impact of our loved one's suicide.

—Michael F. Myers & Carla Fine (2007)

133 B.C. The inhabitants of the Spanish city Numance, after being besieged for eight years by the Romans, rather than surrender, chose to slit the throats of their women and children. Afterward they set fire to the city and challenged each other to death; the last survivor threw himself off the ramparts.

—Mancinelli, Comparelli, Girardi, & Tatarelli (2002)

Emmy, Susie, Tammy—My Dear Ones

Don't think badly of me. I am finally doing the right thing. I did so many things that were wrong or just plain stupid. Please remember one thing. That I love you and always have and always will. None of this was your fault. It was just time for me to get out of everybody's life so you can all have a life. Love you, love you, love you.

Mom

The bills are all paid.

—Suicide note of a 37-year-old woman

I remember sitting at this adding machine in this insurance office. These ladies were bossing me around and I'm adding numbers. . . . I decided right then: I already felt dead. Everything I did, I felt more dead. Nothing felt alive and nothing would help. I just felt it would be more congruent to be dead. Just not to have this body to keep being in.

—Karen, quoted by Richard A. Heckler (1994, p. 67)

His third try was to move out of the apartment that reminded him too much of Sadie and the life they had once shared. Max relocated to a Sunbelt state, but he hated it. Surrounded by strangers and an alien environment, he felt more isolated and lonely than ever. He finally went out and bought a handgun and spent an evening staring at it.

—Kastenbaum (1994)

A young woman who seemed to be living her romantic dream. A frustrated engineer who focused on the Internal Revenue Service as his nemesis. A distinguished admiral who had one of his honors called into question. A postmortem study of human adolescent brains. Family members alarmed by disturbed thoughts and unnerving experiences. An ancient city's resort to mass suicide with an enemy at its gates. A mother assuring her children that the bills have been paid before she takes her life. Another woman feeling that she is not really alive decides "it would be more congruent to be dead." An elderly widower feeling that life no longer seems worth living.

People who contemplate, attempt, and sometimes complete suicide cannot be reduced to a simple stereotype: The facts say otherwise, as suggested by the opening examples. The notion that only a certain kind of person commits suicide is a distancing strategy. Nevertheless, there are general risk factors for suicide. It is our challenge to understand the relationships between the impulses of individuals and the forces operating within their worlds. In this chapter, we explore suicide in many of its individual and societal circumstances. We include statistical information and large-scale phenomena but keep in mind that suicide is not an abstraction.

Karen Carpenter and Terri Schiavo both suffered from the eating disorder *bulimia nervosa*. Repeated suicide attempts are more frequent among people who drastically reduce their food intake over a period of time (Brausch & Gutierrez, 2009). Neither Carpenter nor Schiavo ended their lives with a direct suicide attempt. Their intention was to achieve and maintain what they considered to be the perfect—exceptionally slender—body image. Suicide is regarded as intended self-termination. Unfortunately, a pattern of self-destructive behavior in the service of an illusory ideal self can have a fatal outcome. The warning signs both for suicide and catastrophic organ failure are the same: the eating disorder itself, a distorted body image, impulsivity, low self-directedness, and a history of childhood obesity. There is an emerging principle that will be taken up again in this chapter: whatever helps to navigate people through physical, psychological, or socioenvironmental stress also helps to reduce suicidality.

Joe Stack expressed his rage in a lengthy letter that was found after he had piloted his small plane into an office building housing a branch of the Internal Revenue Service (Austin, Texas, February 18, 2010). That he fully intended to end his life was made clear from his opening statement: "Well, Mr. Big Brother IRA man . . . take my pound of flesh and sleep well." Stack felt victimized by the government, particularly the justice and tax systems. A sense of helplessness and hopelessness can motivate an end-all transformation from passivity to action. Might Stack have found a different, nonlethal way to recover his sense of efficacy?

Is suicide in the brain? Over the years there have been numerous attempts to discover biological markers for suicide risk. Several lines of research were explored, but with limited results. Neuroscientists now have more advanced methods at their disposal. Recent and ongoing studies provide much more detailed information (e.g., Ernst et al., 2009). It is too early to put these findings in perspective and to determine the actual relationships between biological markers and suicidal behavior. One point, though, is difficult to ignore: the differences found in the prefrontal cortex between suicidal and nonsuicidal

adolescents. Do these findings suggest that teens at higher risk for suicide have a biologically associated inability to predict the consequences of their actions? And, if so, is there anything that can be done about it?

Suicide has both immediate and long-term effects on other people. Immediate responses can include anxiety and guilt: "Was there something I could have done to prevent this?" Survivors' grief after a suicide is often more complicated and disturbing than after a natural death (American Association of Suicidology, 2010a). The family who experienced memory lapses and transient hallucinations was relieved to learn that this is a common response to traumatic bereavement by suicide (Myers & Fine, 2007). Survivors' attitudes toward their own lives can also be profoundly influenced. For example, a suicide in the family history is known to be a risk factor for additional suicides. The American Association of Suicidology estimates that nearly 200,000 people are closely affected by a suicidal death each year, and that about 6 million people in the United States have lost a family member or friend to suicide.

Suicide can be the outcome of an individual's stressful and frustrating experiences, often lubricated by alcohol or other drugs. However, suicide has sometimes been a collective response to an unbearable situation. For example, mass suicide has occurred repeatedly in Jewish history, with the Masada episode (A.D. 73) followed by others during persecution throughout Europe from the eleventh to the thirteenth centuries. In recent times, cult suicides such as those at Jonestown and Heaven's Gate have again demonstrated that a group of people can self-destruct for reasons that do not seem rational to others. Mass suicide also can include acts of homicide, as demonstrated by the besieged people of Numance and members of the Jonestown community who were forced to drink poisoned Kool-Aid.

Can a dead woman kill herself? Yes, and dead men, too; it happens many times every year. Karen became emotionally numb to protect herself from her sorrows and stresses. Nobody seemed to notice. Feeling as though one were already dead may be protection from both life and death in the short term, but it can also be another step closer to a suicide attempt (Heckler, 1994).

The media paid no attention to Max during his more than 60 years of meeting his occupational, social, and family obligations. Little notice would have been taken had Max ended his life with his new handgun. He would have become just one more statistic: older white males have the highest suicide rate in the United States.

The woman who wrote a farewell note to her children had made two previous suicide attempts before taking a fatal overdose. She had been quiet and uncomplaining as she went about her responsibilities, so the family also went about its business. On the first anniversary of her death, the oldest daughter (age 13) made a serious but nonfatal suicide attempt. Self-destruction frequently is a family matter.

Suicide occurs at every age, from childhood onward. The victims are males and females, the affluent and the impoverished, the seeming failures and the apparently successful. People take their own lives in rural Vermont and urban San Francisco, and in crowded Tokyo and sparsely populated Lapland. The scope of the problem is worldwide and not limited to any particular class of person, although some groups are more at risk than others. Furthermore, the casualties of suicide include parents, children, spouses, lovers, and friends, all of whom are at risk for traumatic grief (Chapter 12).

We begin with a statistical profile of suicide attempts (also known as *parasuicide*) and completed suicides. More detailed attention will then be given to gender differences, suicide among children, youth, elders, ethnic and racially diverse populations, and the military. Circumstances in which there is a higher risk of self-destruction will also be considered. We will then examine both cultural and individual meanings of suicide, with special attention to the descent into suicide and the attempt itself. This background will prepare us to consider the challenge of suicide prevention, and emerging issues.

WHAT DO THE STATISTICS TELL US?

Many people exit this life by their own hand each year. The World Health Organization estimates there are about 1 million suicides, encompassing all continents and peoples in widely varying situations (WHO 2010). It is the thirteenth leading cause of death worldwide, and tenth leading cause in developed nations. Suicide is even more prevalent among the youth (15–24) of the world and the fourth most common cause of death. There is reason to believe that the global phenomenon of modernization has been a major factor in the surge of attempted and completed suicides. Reduced to its essence, modernization makes it more difficult for people to feel connected and secure within a familiar and predictable society. We will return to modernization—and add postmodernization—as we consider emerging issues at the end of this chapter.

In the United States, suicide has been among the leading causes of death ever since reliable statistics have been available. It remains the eleventh most common cause of death in the general population. In recent years there have been more than 33, 000 certified suicides (almost 90 a day). Experts believe that the actual toll is even greater. It is not unusual for a death to be classified as accidental, natural, or indeterminate if the suicidal component has not been established beyond a doubt. Furthermore, many people still find it difficult to believe that a child might be capable of committing suicide, so the reported statistics among the very young could be underestimates. The suicides of ailing and socially isolated old men sometimes go into the records as arteriosclerosis or heart disease. Sympathetic medical examiners have also been known to shade the facts when there is any ambiguity as to cause of death at any age. The statistical profile, then, tends to underrepresent the actual incidence of suicide.

The *suicide rate* is determined by the formula:

$$Suicide\ rate = \frac{Number\ of\ suicides}{Population} \times 100,000$$

It is easy to make a mistake here. We are more accustomed to thinking of percentages than of rates. The U.S. suicide rate of 11.1 would seem catastrophic if we mistreated the number as though it were a percentage. There would be close to 30 million suicides in the United States each year, instead of the 33,300 reported in the most recent data! The rate actually means that 11 people out of every 100,000 took their lives during the year. The rate is also different from the number of total deaths by suicide. The larger the population, the higher the number of deaths if the rate is held constant. It is possible, for example, to have more suicides per year as a population expands, even if the rate

The "soup kitchen" became a fact of American life during the Great Depression that started in 1929. Unemployed men, unable to support their families and stressed by loss of occupation and self-esteem were vulnerable to thoughts of suicide, as were those who had made and lost fortunes.

remains constant or even declines slightly. Now—on to the data themselves, bearing in mind that national data sets lag several years behind, and world data even more so.

Suicide Patterns in the United States

Suicide risk varies by age, gender, and race/ethnicity (Table 7-1). We will see that completed suicides also vary by geography, and in what is perhaps an expected way.

Basic Facts

Most of the information in Table 7-1 indicates consistency throughout the decades in which comparable data has been collected, e.g., the higher rates for males at all ages.

1. *Completed suicides occur most often among white males.* At every age, white males are at greater risk for suicide than females or black/nonwhite males. The difference is substantial: Four of five suicides are by males, and predominantly white males.
2. *The white male suicide rate increases with age, but females and nonwhite males reach their peak vulnerability earlier in adult life.* Although the rate is highest among older white men, the actual number of suicidal deaths is higher for middle-aged men because there are more of them. Even a lower rate represents more fatalities.
3. *The male suicide burden encompasses American Indian, Alaskan Native, and Hispanic populations—but not Black, Asian, and Pacific Islanders.*
4. *Suicide remains the third leading cause of death among youth (ages 15–24).* The impact of

TABLE 7-1 *U.S. Death Rates from Suicide by Selected Characteristics*

Nation		11.1
Ages		
5 to 14		0.5
15 to 24		9.9
25 to 34		12.3
35 to 44		15.1
45 to 54		17.9
55 to 64		14.5
65 to 74		12.6
75 to 84		15.9
85 & over		15.9
Gender		
Male		16.0
Female		4.5
Race/Ethnicity	*Males*	*Females*
White	19.6	5.1
Black male	9.4	1.4
Hispanic	8.8	1.8
American Indian, Alaska Native	18.3	5.1
Pacific Islander	7.9	3.4

Source: U.S. National Center for Health Statistics, www.cdc.gov/nchs/hus/htm.

suicide is so powerful on adolescents and young adults because for the most part they are spared of heart disease, cancer, stroke, and chronic respiratory diseases that are major contributors to death among people in their middle and later adult years.

5. *Bad economic times are usually associated with an increase in suicide rates.* The suicide peak in the United States occurred during the Great Depression of the 1930s, and a later period of recession produced another rise in suicide. There are case reports that suggest a rise in suicide since the Wall Street/foreclosure financial calamity that began in 2007, but definitive data are not yet available.

6. *The suicide rate is higher among people who: (a) suffer from depression or other psychiatric problems; (b) use alcohol while depressed; (c) suffer from physical, especially irreversible, illness; (d) deal with challenges and frustrations in an impulsive way; (e) are divorced; (f) have lost an important relationship through death or break-up; and (g) live in certain areas of the country.*

Depression and a sense of hopelessness often precede suicide attempts. Suicide is often an impulsive act, especially among young people, and alcohol is a contributing factor at all adult ages. Prolonged discomfort, increasing disability, and fear of further physical deterioration become more frequent situations in the later adult years and therefore contribute more to suicidality.

A Geography of Suicide

Scenic and spacious Wyoming, Alaska, Montana, and Nevada have suicide rates about three times as high as competitive, crowded, fast-moving places such as Massachusetts, New Jersey, New York, and the District of Columbia (National Center for Health Care Statistics, 2009). A lack of social support and connectedness seem to be key factors in the differential suicide rates within the same nation. The highest suicide rates in the United States are found in Western states, especially in rural areas that offer relatively few opportunities for social interaction and support. The lowest rates occur in high-density states where it is very difficult not to bump into people all the time.

But who chooses to live in Nevada and who in New Jersey? Are stresses greater in the "most suicidal" states, or are social support systems less available there? Clearly, we need studies that are more up close and personal. We also see that homicide and suicide rates do not necessarily keep company: For example, the District of Columbia is notorious for its consistently high murder rates but has a lower suicide rate than any of the 50 states. What should we make of that?

WHAT ABOUT SUICIDE ATTEMPTS?

Up to this point, we have focused on completed suicides. It is more difficult to determine the frequency of suicide attempts, many of which never show up in official documents. A number of small studies through the years have indicated that suicidal thoughts are not uncommon in the general population. These findings have now been confirmed and extended by the first national survey of suicidal thoughts in the United States (SAMSHA, 2009). It was found that:

- Nearly 8.3 million adults reported having serious thoughts of suicide in the past year alone.
- More than a million had actually made a suicide attempt.
- Younger adults (aged 18 to 25) were the most likely to have seriously considered suicide.
- Substance abuse added a major risk factor as expressed in suicidal thoughts, planning, and attempts.
- Suicide attempts differ in lethality. This is true even within the same modality—an overdose could have either a marginal or an almost certain probability of fatal outcome. However, it is not unusual for a marginal attempt to end in death, nor for the victim of a severe self-inflicted trauma to struggle all-out for survival. Mental health experts have learned to take all suicide attempts seriously.

The Human Side

The impact of suicide cannot be gauged by numbers alone. Even attempts that do not result in death can have significant consequences. For example, family and friends are put on alert and respond either by renewed efforts to help the individual or by further emotional isolation of the attempter because of their own heightened anxiety. The suicide attempt might win temporary attention and concessions—or it might make things worse by being interpreted as manipulative and thereby leading to further resentment and withdrawal by others.

I have observed a tremendous range of responses to suicide attempts. In one instance, colleagues became more sensitive to the individual's despair and were able to provide life-enhancing support. In another instance, however, the parents refused to be "impressed" by their adolescent daughter's near-fatal attempt and in effect challenged her to "finish the job." She did.

The social cost of suicide is high, although impossible to calculate precisely. When the suicide of a young celebrity is reported vividly by the media, there may be a short-term increase in suicide attempts and completions by people who have identified with the star and who have been having problems of their own. "Copycat suicide" has been shown to occur in many nations following the suicide of a person with whom some people closely identify, but these effects are usually limited and discontinue after a short time (Stack, 2000).

The human side of suicide also includes children who are left without parents and therefore made more vulnerable to stress and self-doubts that can haunt them throughout their lives. Children with family members who attempted or completed suicide are more likely to make suicide attempts themselves at some point in their lives. Behind each number in the suicide statistics there are families, friends, and colleagues who will never be quite the same again.

FOUR PROBLEM AREAS

A more detailed look at suicide among children and youth, elderly persons, ethnic/racial minorities, and active or veteran members will illustrate the relationships between individual self-destruction and society.

Do Children Commit Suicide?

It has often been assumed that few if any children commit suicide. Unfortunately, this assumption is not true. Children do think about death (Chapter 10) and are affected by uncertainties and frustrations of life. Third graders have a clear understanding of suicide and even some younger children realize that people sometimes take their own lives (Mishara, 2002). It is rare that children see suicidal persons receiving help or any form of prevention.

Israel Orbach and his colleagues (1988) studied "children who don't want to live." They identified a typical progression toward a potentially lethal suicide attempt:

> *The process starts with a harmless attempt, by which children can assess the effect it has on their surroundings. At the same time, this attempt represents a test of their ability to cope with their fear of death. A second attempt often follows*

the first—especially if there is only a minimal response from the social environment. This second attempt is a little more bold and dangerous, and has more serious consequences (p. 27).

Children often give a number of verbal and non-verbal messages about their desperation and their intent prior to a lethal suicide attempt. Adults simply do not believe the children mean what they say.

Recognition of suicidal thoughts and actions in childhood becomes even more important when we realize that this is also the foundation from which many suicides in adult life originate. For example, a young child who considers himself or herself un-wanted and unloved may have thought of suicide repeatedly and even make one or more attempts that escape notice. In adolescence or young adult-hood, this person may encounter new experiences of rejection and disappointment that resonate with the earlier anxiety and self-destructive tendencies. This child whose suicidal orientation was ignored years before may become part of the suicide statis-tics in adolescence or the early adult years.

Yang and Clum (2000) find that stressful experiences in childhood can increase the risk of suicide in adult life by distorting the way the child thinks about self and world. The development of suicidal behavior in children and adults follows the same general pattern. The earlier phases of this pattern include a sense of intolerable pressure from the family, a depressed attitude, and various coping attempts that do not work very well and result in accumulated frustrations and loss of self-confidence. If this stressful situation is not altered, the idea of suicide appears and the child or adult now attempts to cope through some type of self-destructive behavior. If others still do not respond in a helpful and effective manner, the individual feels increasing pressure and a sense of failure that confirms the feeling that suicide is the only solution. Self-destructive behavior is often set into motion as early as childhood, but may claim its casualty at any later developmental level as well. A recent study confirms that suicidal thoughts can be active with sixth graders (Stoep et al., 2009). Seldom are these thoughts shared and discussed with adults. It is also clear that a fragmented and dysfunctional home life in childhood later becomes an elevated suicide risk factor (Sourander et al., 2009).

Do children commit suicide? In returning to this question, we must reply, Yes, sometimes, but it is just as important to recognize that suicidal orientations may develop early in childhood and have their fatal outcomes later in life. Having faced this harsh reality, we are in a better position to be helpful both to the children who are at particu-lar risk for development of a suicidal orientation and to the troubled families whose own anxieties are represented in the child's distress. Lives can be saved by preventing the establishment of self-destructive thoughts and tendencies in childhood. As Orbach and others have observed, even those children who are experiencing high levels of stress still have a desire to grow, to flourish, to live.

Youth Suicide

Suicide is the third leading cause of death between the ages of 15 and 24, exceeded only by car crashes and homicide. The suicide rate among adolescents and young adults had nearly tripled between the mid-1960s and mid-1980s. It then decreased and become more stable—until "a dramatic and huge increase," according to the Centers for Disease Control (Bluestein, 2007, p. 1). Much of this unex-pected increase occurred with preteen and teen-age females, though males also had a higher rate. Hanging and, to a lesser degree, suffocation had become the most common suicide methods for preteen and teen females.

Consider these additional facts:

1. *Academic pressure seems related to suicide among college students but not in a simple way.* Many undergraduates who commit suicide had a higher grade point average than their peers. However, they had performed below what they took to be their parents' expectations. "I couldn't face Dad and that big scene there would be after all the money he had spent on my education and how he had wanted to be proud of me and blah, blah, blah!" This is how one student explained his near-fatal suicide attempt to a counselor. Many others have had similar experiences.

2. *Most of those who have gone on to commit suicide expressed their despondency to others and made explicit comments about their intentions.* Unfortu-nately, few youths who were at risk for suicide received mental health treatment or counseling (National Household Survey on Drug Abuse [NHSD], 2002). Clinicians have long held that

many suicidal people do issue a cry for help. Every expression of suicidal intent provides an opportunity for a helpful intervention.

3. *Counseling is often effective in preventing youth suicide.* Many colleges and universities now offer counseling services for students experiencing loss, depression, and frustration. Suicidal thoughts, feelings, threats, and gestures can be recognized before they turn into self-destructive action. An increasing number of college students are making use of this resource and finding their way back to a more positive state of mind (Schwartz, 2006).

4. *Alcohol is a frequent contributor to suicide at all ages.* A sudden change in drinking habits may be a particularly important factor because the risk of suicide increases when a person goes on a "jag." Alcohol and drug abuse have been identified as especially important factors in youth suicide. Adolescent males who consume alcohol are estimated to be 17 times more likely to attempt suicide, and females 3 times more likely (Groves, Stanley, & Sher, 2007). It has also been found that many adolescent alcohol abusers are from families with the same problem (Sher, 2007). Furthermore, those who drink to excess also have more cognitive and language deficits. It is possible that neuropsychological dysfunction might have a role in the development of adolescent alcohol disorders as well as become an effect. Teens who drink when they are feeling "down" are especially vulnerable to impulsive suicide attempts (Schilling et al., 2009).

5. *The loss of a valued relationship is one of the most common triggering events for youth suicide.* This can involve the death of a parent, breaking up with a lover, having a quarrel with a close friend, being disappointed in a role model, or learning that one's favorite dog or cat has died. Many people experience these kinds of losses and stresses without becoming suicidal. However, past experiences of loss, rejection, and unworthiness make some youths more vulnerable to suicide when new interpersonal problems arise.

Katie

Risk is especially high when an emotionally needy young person seeks salvation through a relationship that is not likely to endure. Katie, a bright and articulate college student, was trying to make a life for herself after a stressful childhood in a dysfunctional family. Academic achievement provided one life-support line, but it was difficult for Katie to meet her own expectations for "that next A." More crucial was Katie's relationship with Mark, her sometimes attentive, sometimes elusive, boyfriend. On the first page of her first diary, Katie wrote:

> *I am depressed and suicidal. My body feels restless and tired. I don't know who to turn to for help. I don't want to bother anyone with my battle. I've been acting out in all sorts of ways. I just feel like crying. . . . I love Mark so deeply, but I don't know if it's True love for him. . . . I really want to marry him so badly. . . . I really hate my life where it is, with everything I am. . . . God give me strength. Help me today. I feel so unbelievably lonely and battered (quoted in Pennebaker & Stone, 2004, pp. 101–102).*

On the last page of the last of five diaries, she turned again to God:

> *Please, dear God, bring some wonderful, encouraging, unbiased, loving, respecting people in my life. . . . I want to feel whole inside, instead of being severed in hundreds of little pieces. . . . Please help me through this and next week . . . things are so hard now (Pennebaker & Stone, p. 73).*

Soon after writing that entry, Katie committed suicide by hanging herself in her dormitory room. She had tried hard to escape from an anguished childhood and make a go of her life. The fear of being abandoned by Mark was literally a life-and-death matter for her. She did not experience herself as a whole person with intrinsic strength and value. Unfortunately, every day other youths also experience upsurges of suicidal thought when a relationship critical to their sense of self-worth has ended or become jeopardized.

6. *Heavy metal music attracts depressed youth—it does not cause suicide.* Many heavy metal fans come from dysfunctional families, experience difficulties in coping with the world, and have low self-esteem. The angry, pounding rhythms resonate with their feelings, but have not been shown to contribute directly to suicide. An informal history of death

The high decibel, pounding rhythms of heavy metal music do not cause suicide, but do attract angry, depressed, and suicidal youth.

metal and grindcore (Mudrian & Peel, 2004) discusses bands such as "Napalm Death, Death, Morbid Angel, Carcass, Obituary, Deicide, Entombed, and Cannibal Corpse" (p. 22). Many other groups could be added to this list. This intense identification with death probably has contributed to some youth suicides, but perhaps the opportunity for self-expression and the storm of violent sound has also provided a safe release for some young people. With or without heavy metal music, depression creates an elevated risk for suicide among both youth and adults.

7. *Teens and adolescents who frequently change their place of residence are at a higher risk for suicide.* Geographical mobility weakens interpersonal support as well as the comfort of a familiar environment.

8. Family patterns often have a role in youth suicide. Leenaars and Wenckstern (1991) have found that families with rigid rules and poor communication ("Nobody ever listens to anybody") are more likely to be associated with youth suicidality. Father or mother absence, alcoholism, mental illness, and incest are other contributing factors. Suicidal youths, then, may represent distress within the entire family on the part of their entire families.

All of us may have the opportunity to help an adolescent or young adult find an alternative to suicide. This process begins with our willingness to take this measure of concern and responsibility. The next step is to become familiar with some of the most typical signs of suicide risk in this age group (Table 7-2). Often the same person is caught in a multiple risk pattern that includes recent smoking, drinking, threatened at school, unsafe sexual behavior, and exploratory suicidal actions such as glue sniffing (Epstein & Spirito, 2009).

Many suicidal youths are misguided by vague and wishful thoughts about death. There is often the

TABLE 7-2 *Youth Suicide: Factors Associated with Higher Risk*

- There have been suicidal attempts by other members of the family.
- The person himself or herself has made a previous suicide attempt.
- There have been recent changes in this person's behavior, including level of social activity, sleeping, eating, choice of clothes, and use of alcohol or drugs. The behavior change can take either the direction of withdrawal from previous interests and activities, or a sudden burst of pleasure-seeking and risk-taking activities. The clue is that in either case this person is acting very much differently than usual.
- A sense of hopelessness, apathy, and/or dread is expressed. "What's the point of trying again?" "There's nothing I can do about nothing." "So, who cares anyway? I don't!"
- Explicit or implicit statements are made about ending his or her life. "I've had enough of this crap!" "You're going to see me on the ten o' clock news!" "I want to get it all over with, and I will!"
- The thought process has narrowed to the point that everything seems open or closed; there is little or no ability to acknowledge shades of meaning and only extreme courses of action are envisioned. "I'll kill her, or I'll kill myself." "I can never get anything right." "He was the only person who understood me and I can't live without him." "There's only one way out of this mess."
- Abrupt flashes of anger interfere with activities and interactions. He or she becomes touchy and unpredictable and seems to overreact to small frustrations or provocations. There may also be an increase in glowering resentment and uncooperativeness, even if this does not explode into overt displays of anger. Aggressive and antisocial behavior occurs more often among males than females as a forerunner of a suicide attempt.

assumption that the person will be able to witness the response of survivors. "Look how upset they will be!" "They'll be sorry they treated me so bad." "They'll know I really meant it." I have also heard many expressions of the assumption that death is "just a trip," perhaps similar to a pleasant alcohol or drug high. Another common presuicidal belief is that death is better than life (as compared with the alternative view that death refers to the absence of life). Envisioning death as more rewarding than life can take one that much closer to a suicidal action.

It is useful to remember that suicidal impulses do not have free reign. People of all ages also have strong reasons not to take their lives, despite episodes of discouragement and frustration. One of the keys to suicide resistance among youth is the fact that they have powerful reasons for wanting to live, such as the desire to experience more of life, discovering their own special purpose in life, wanting to grow together with friends, and not wanting to hurt family.

Suicide Among Elderly Persons

We left Max staring at his newly purchased handgun (see page 192). The elderly white man remains the person most vulnerable to suicide. In recent decades, the largest increase in the suicide rate

has been among people 85 years of age and older; combine the increasing suicide rate with age and the fact that more people are living into the later adult years and we can see that there is a powerful trend toward self-termination as the world population ages. Suicide rates among white men increase from middle age onward. Despite this elevated risk, suicide among the elderly often fails to receive sufficient attention. The victim may have been socially isolated for some time before death, or the community may be less disturbed by the act than when a young person is involved. Nevertheless, suicide in later life not only represents the premature death of a fellow citizen but an implicit commentary on the place of the elderly person in society.

Physical illness and other sources of distress do not necessarily make self-destruction the inevitable plan of choice. My colleagues and I have worked with many older people who had reason to despair over the harsh realities of life. Often these people were able to draw upon their own personal resources and rediscover their will to live. The key in some cases was a short reprieve from a stressful situation or objective changes to improve their quality of life; in other cases, it was a therapeutic alliance and counseling. Stress and despair can be experienced at any age—and the same is true of recovery. Several other findings about suicide in later life follow:

1. *The major demographic risk factors include being white, male, older than the age of 65, living alone, and residing either in a rural area or a transient inner-city zone* (Grek, 2007). Social isolation is the underlying theme. The "oldest old" (over the age of 85) white males are at greater risk than any other age–gender–race group (American Association of Suicidology, 2010b).
2. *Elderly suicide rates are higher in areas where divorce rates and interstate migration are also higher* (Conwell, 2001).
3. *Depression increases the risk of suicide.* Mood disorders are the strongest predictors of suicide attempts in elderly people (Beautrais, 2002). This is not the same as concluding that depression "causes" suicide. People cope with depression in many ways and not all suicidal elders show an obvious picture of clinical depression.
4. *Physical illness is a major risk factor for suicide among elderly adults.* Attention is now being given to suicidality associated with specific physical conditions, such as living with diabetes of experiencing a heart attack (Abbas et al., 2009; American Association of Suicidology, 2010c). Again, it should be kept in mind that (a) many elders cope with physical problems without becoming depressed and (b) depression may occur without a basis in significant physical problems.
5. *Alcohol use increases the risk of suicide among elderly adults.* Alcohol abuse is approximately twice as frequent among suicidal adults than among the population in general. Increased use of alcohol is often intended to ward off depression and suicidal thoughts, but eventually, however, alcohol and/or drug abuse tends to increase the probability of suicide because of the impact on social isolation, health, and clarity of thought.
6. *Failure to cope with stress increases the risk of suicide among elderly adults.* Persistent stress syndromes (see also Chapter 12) can develop when an individual's coping responses are overwhelmed by life changes and crises encountered in the later adult years. The lack of adequate social support systems intensifies the stress. Once it has started, the psychophysiological stress reaction tends to keep going, generating anxiety and exhaustion.
7. *Loss of relationships increases the risk of suicide among elderly adults.* Bereavement and divorce are the most common types of relationship loss for elderly adults. Some older adults also experience a particularly harrowing kind of loss of relationship when the spouse is afflicted with Alzheimer's disease or a similar condition of dementia. The spouse is still there, but the relationship has altered radically.

The Lethality of Suicide Attempts in the Later Adult Years

Suicide attempts by older adults are more often completed than with younger age groups. This is especially so for men. Overall, elders have a 4:1 ratio of attempts to completions, as compared with the young adults' ratio of 20:1. Elderly males and females most often choose firearms as their mode of suicide. This is true for adults in general in the United States. However, the proportion of firearms use is even higher among elders: about three of every four elderly male suicides involve the use of firearms.

Elderly males are less likely to give clear warnings of their suicidal intent, especially if they live alone and have little participation in community activities. The lethality of the suicide attempts is also increased by avoiding discovery or interference. Furthermore, elders are less likely to recover from suicide attempts that produce serious trauma but from which a younger person might survive. Older adults who are an elevated risk for suicide often show several of the characteristics identified in Table 7-3.

Preventing Suicide in the Later Adult Years

"I'd rather kill myself than get to be that way." Some people express a fear of aging that rivals or exceeds fear of death. Our first priority, then, is to come to terms with our own "inner elder." Becoming familiar with people who are enjoying life in their later adult years is perhaps the most natural and readily available approach.

It is possible to identify high suicide risk in elders and provide alternatives. Human service

TABLE 7-3 *Elderly Adults: 10 Indicators of Possible Suicide Risk*

1. Sad, dejected, or emotionally flat mood
2. Stooped, withdrawn, fatigued, lack of eye contact
3. Careless in grooming and dress
4. Restlessness, handwringing, constant motor activity
5. Inattention, lack of concentration, losing the thread of the conversation
6. Loss of appetite/weight
7. Sleep disturbance (insomnia or oversleeping)
8. Loss of interest in activities that previously were pleasurable
9. Loss of interest in other people
10. Preoccupied with vague and shifting physical complaints

providers often have interactions with elders who are one step away from suicide. Nearly half of the people who commit suicide had seen a physician within a month of their death (Murphy, 1995). It is probable that elders are overrepresented in this group because relatively few physicians are trained in detecting depression and suicidality. Fortunately, increased awareness of this risk on the part of service providers can result in timely and effective interventions.

There is reason for optimism in the prevention of elder suicide. By and large, people do not reach their later adult years unless they have both resilience and skill. Max, for example, had demonstrated competence in school, work, and interpersonal relationships throughout his life. He had overcome challenges, savored success, and adjusted to disappointment. The death of his wife was a severe loss to him. Along with the sorrow there was the question of how—and why—he should go on with his life.

Max decided to try a solution that is deeply engrained in the tradition of this nation: When all else fails, kill somebody (see Chapter 8). However, after staring at that gun, Max realized that this was not his solution. Just as he was not a person who was made for sitting around in the sun, so he was not a person who dealt with problems in an explosive and violent manner. And so Max returned to his old neighborhood and drifted naturally over to the library that had been his home away from home

in childhood. He soon became first an unofficial assistant to the librarian and a person sought out for advice and companionship by neighborhood children and youth. Max not only felt useful and connected again—he *was* useful and connected. He took the money he received from selling the gun and plunked it into the library's fund to help low-income children purchase their own books.

We have been focusing on elder male suicide because this is the subpopulation that is most at risk. As we have seen, though, elderly women also tend to use lethal means when they attempt suicide. It is also probable that an undocumented number of elderly women hasten their deaths by not looking after their health and gradually withdrawing from social contact. Deaths of this type are known as *subintentional*. They are not certified as suicides, but those who are familiar with the situation often believe that the person contributed to the death in a significant although indirect manner.

Baby Boomers at Risk?

On its way to elderdom, the baby boomers generation is showing indications of stress and vulnerability to suicide. It is too early to draw conclusions, but there are alarming statistics. The Centers for Disease Control and Prevention have found a 20 percent increase in the suicide rate for 45- to 54-year-olds in a recent five-year period. This is an increase much greater than for any other age group. It is possible that this precipitate rise in suicide among middle-aged people—women substantially more than men—will turn out to be a statistical blip, but it is also possible that boomers are experiencing significant difficulty in adjusting to the challenges of life transition. As Patricia Cohen (2008) notes: "Just why thousands of men and women have crossed the line between enduring life's burdens and surrendering to them is a painful question for their loved ones. But for officials, it is a surprising and baffling public health mystery."

Suicide Among Ethnic and Racial Minorities

The conditions of life—and, therefore, of death—differ greatly within a nation as large and diverse as the United States. There are many differences within ethnic and racial minorities, including specific heritage, lifestyle, education, and socioeconomic status. Recent immigrants from chaos and violence in their homelands, for example, have markedly different experiences from families with several generations of residence in the United States.

Native Americans

In Native Alaskan villages, a culture of sorrow. The older brother killed himself. The younger one used a gun. They died 38 days apart. . . . They've lost their culture, they don't have a way to support their family, and then what we see is a lot of alcohol use. There's such a feeling of hopelessness, particularly for young men (Yardley, 2007, p, 2).

Throughout much of the world, the people native to a region have given way to forces from other lands who were equipped with more advanced military and technological resources. Outsiders often call native people "indigenous populations." In recent years, they have often characterized themselves as "first people." By whatever name, they have often been deprived of their previous means of existence, been victimized by discrimination, and faced systematic campaigns to destroy their cultural heritage (Hunter & Harvey, 2002).

Elevated suicide rates are often among the consequences, with the indigenous people of Australia, Canada, and New Zealand, as prime examples. The Royal Commission on Aboriginal Peoples (1995) left no doubt as to the basic cause: "collective despair or lack of hope" (p. 38). The white man's conquest and development of the New World was also catastrophic to the ancestors of many of those who are now known as Native Americans. It is equally troubling to think that the present high suicide rate among Native Americans is a continuing part of that heritage.

The basic facts about suicide among Native Americans:

1. *The rate is exceptionally high.* Native Americans have the highest suicide rate of any ethnic or racial subpopulation. The suicide rate of 19.3 is more than a third higher than that of the general population.
2. *Tribal differences in suicide rates are large and also vary over time.*
3. *Alcohol is a major factor in Native American suicide.* Although there is a strong association

between alcohol and suicide for the general population, it is even more so with Native Americans. Heavy alcohol consumption has been found to be associated with about two thirds of the suicides among American Indians in New Mexico over a 10-year period (May et al., 2002). Alcohol abuse has been related to high unemployment, prejudice, cultural conflict, and the loss of heritage, among other factors. Suicide is clearly a symptom of social stress and disorganization as well as a tragic outcome for the individuals and their survivors.

4. *Unlike the general population, it is among the young Native Alaskans that depression, alcoholism, and suicide are at peak levels: they are caught between two cultures, neither of which are is adequately supportive.* Women seem to have suicidal thoughts over a longer period of time but are also more likely to share these feelings with others (LeMaster, Beals, Novins, & Manson, 2004).
5. *The average life expectancy remains relatively low for Native Americans.* Those who survive into their later adult years seem to be highly resistant to suicide—quite the opposite of the lifespan risk for suicide among whites.

Programs that provide realistic opportunities for youth to pursue their goals and dreams and that strengthen tribal values are likely to result in a sharp decrease in suicide.

African Americans

Deprivation, stress, and racial discrimination were visited upon African Americans from their earliest years as "property," and this was followed by more long years of seeking equality and justice. We might therefore expect that suicide rates would also be very high among African Americans. This is not the case, however. The suicide rate has consistently been markedly lower than it is in the white majority. The most recent data are presented in Table 7-4.

Why do African American women demonstrate such remarkable resistance to suicide? A plausible answer is starting to emerge. Two sets of researchers have come up with findings that are essentially in agreement (Marion & Range, 2003; Willis, Coombs, Drentea, & Cockerham, 2003).

TABLE 7-4 *African American and White Suicide Rates**

Females	
African American	1.5
White	4.8
Males	
African American	9.1
White	19.9

*National Vital Statistics, 2004 [Report 53 (5)].

Religious belief and social support contribute to a problem-solving style of acting together that provides a strong buffer against suicidality. Suicide is often regarded as a failure of faith and an offense against God. Close emotional support from family, friends, neighborhood, and church help to prevent feelings of being alone, abandoned, and helpless in the midst of life's struggles.

Hispanic suicide has only recently started to receive systematic attention—perhaps because of the rapid growth of this population in the U.S.: currently estimated at about 40 million. It is difficult to define {this shortcoming is related to difficulties in defining "Hispanic" clearly enough to establish firm precise populations statistics and classify health outcomes. ('Latino" is often used interchangeably.) The estimated suicide rate has been very low through the years, but there is now a reported increase in feelings of distress and suicidality among Hispanic youth (Del Pilar, 2009; Garcia et al., 2008). Ninth-grade girls had an alarmingly high frequency of reported suicidality; 40 percent reported thinking of ending their lives and almost one in five reported an actual attempt in the past year. Suicidality is also most likely to be experienced by youth with a sense of mixed ethnic identity. Researchers speak to the need for identifying and supporting family strengths to reduce anxiety and protect against suicidality.

Asian Americans/Pacific Islanders collectively now constitute about 6 percent of the total population, and this percentage is continuing to grow. This population represents a remarkably diverse heritage, with more than 40 ethnic groups and 100 languages and dialects (Trujillo, 2009). Statistical data regarding suicide and other mental health issues are still meager. People with Chinese, Filipino, and Japanese heritage are estimated to have lower suicide rates than Caucasians—but elderly Asian American women have higher rates. PTSD is estimated to be extremely high—about 70 percent—for recent Southeast Asian refugees who had survived deprivation, loss, and terror. There is much we still do not know about the Asian Americans/Pacific Islanders who enrich our population.

Military Suicide

People who serve the nation in the armed forces are at heightened risk for suicide, both during and after their war experiences. This added threat to life became evident through the study of Vietnam War veterans. The stress of engaging in a confusing war in a remote land was often followed, upon returning home, by a sense of being shunned by a public that had become increasingly critical of the purpose and conduct of the conflict. Post-traumatic stress disorder (PTSD) was common. Many of the combatants could not help but take the war home with them, and it proved difficult to return to their previous relationships and life patterns. Years later, the Vietnam Memorial Wall would remind the nation of the sacrifices made by fellow Americans during the war and arouse more compassion (Chapter 12). In the meantime, there was often a sense of estrangement and depression—and, for some, suicide.

The actual number of suicides and attempts associated with the Vietnam War will probably never be determined. Alexander Paul, himself a Vietnam veteran, in his fact-based novel, *Suicide Wall* (Paul, 1996), and Chuck Dean (1990), also a veteran, found that estimates of suicide by Vietnam veterans ranged from 20,000 to 200,000. The highest figures include indirect suicide through single-car accidents and other deaths that were not officially classified as suicides. Many veterans struggled with suicidal thoughts at some point during their reintegration into society. Perhaps many lives were saved by good friends, loving family, and the returning veteran's own personality strengths. There is little doubt, however, that society's discomfort with the Vietnam War increased the stress upon men and women returning from the horrors of war.

Suicide among members of the U.S. armed forces in Iraq during the Gulf War became an additional concern. A major study followed 320,890

Attempted and completed suicides have become much more frequent among active military personnel and veterans. Physical rehabilitation can also help to restore confidence and hope for the future. Here, the assistance is provided by Lt. Melissa Stockwell and physical therapist Bob Bahr who work together at the Walter Reed Army Medical Center.

men over a 12-year period (Kaplan, Huguet, McFarland, & Newsom, 2007). The suicide risk of these veterans was twice as high as men who were not veterans. At highest risk were white and college-educated veterans. Severely wounded soldiers (Underwood, 2008), and members of the National Guard or Reserves who were on active duty (Associated Press, 2008) were also at particularly high risk. Other causes of death did not differentiate between veterans and nonveterans.

The ongoing military actions in Afghanistan and Iraq have been associated with even higher suicide rates. Suicides among military personnel on active duty have reached their highest level since records have been compiled. The number of attempted suicides has increased sixfold since the start of the Iraq and Afghanistan wars, with the army unprepared either for the markedly increased suicidality or PTSDs (Priest, 2008).

Substantial increases in suicide rates have been found among National Guard units both on active and inactive status (Zoroya 2011a). The suicide rate of female soldiers has tripled as they have been deployed in war zones, and the rate for men also increases (Zoroya, 2011b).

Congress reacted quickly to public outrage over the disclosure of the Veterans Administration's inadequate response to the needs of veterans returning with mental and physical disabilities. The Joshua Omvig Veterans Suicide Prevention Act (named for an Iraq War veteran who suffered from posttraumatic stress disorder and committed suicide) required the Veterans Administration to upgrade its counseling and other services to reduce suicidality. It remains to be seen whether this measure will have the intended effect. Unfortunately, there have been charges of systematic misinformation on the part of the Veterans Administration regarding the frequency of military suicides and suicide attempts. In 2007, The VA reported 800 attempts, while independent sources estimated the actual number at about 12,000 (McClatchy, 2008). A VA official apologized, saying he did not think there was a deliberate attempt to mislead Congress or the public.

It is clear that more attention is being given to military-related suicide, but the results are not yet so clear. The higher risk for members of the military could have a longer history than usually recognized, as a large-scale study by McCarthy et al. (2009) suggests. The stress associated with military life can persist for many years. The record high number of military suicides has also been found to be associated with excessive risk-taking in their personal lives, according to a recent Army report (Zoroya, 2010). These risk-taking behaviors include drinking, drug use, and criminal activity. The Army expressed concern about a permissive environment that allows these behavior patterns to develop, sometimes with lethal outcomes.

High-Risk Situations for Suicide

The risk of suicide is increased in some situations other than war. Here are several important examples:

1. *Suicides often increase after a natural or man-made disaster.* This pattern has been found among victims of floods, earthquakes, and hurricanes in 377 nations (Krug et al., 2003). Suicidal and other self-injurious behaviors increased after the September 11, 2001 terrorist attacks, and these effects might still be continuing (Wouter de Lange & Needleman, 2004). Anxiety, depression, and suicidality are frequent responses to these traumatic losses. Mental health services, offered both immediately and over a period of time, could prevent many acts of self-destruction.
2. *People with HIV/AIDS are at a higher risk for suicide.* The American Foundation for Suicide Prevention estimates that the risk of suicide is up to 20 times greater for people with HIV/AIDS than for the general population. The feeling of being isolated and rejected can contribute more to suicidality than the disease itself. However, as with other life crises, people with HIV/AIDS often have come to terms with their situation and continued to live meaningful and useful

lives. Furthermore, the improved survival outlook for people with HIV/AIDS in recent years is another protection against suicide.
3. *Gambling is associated with a higher risk of suicide.* "Las Vegas, the premier U. S. gambling setting, displays the highest levels of suicide in the nation, both for residents of Las Vegas and for visitors to that setting. In general, visitors to and residents of major gambling communities experience elevated suicide rates. In Atlantic City, abnormally high suicide levels for visitors and residents appeared only after gambling casinos were opened. The findings do not seem to result merely because gaming settings attract suicidal individuals. Pathological gamblers, beset with depression, are at particular risk for suicide" (Wong et al., 2009).
4. *Schoolyard bullies increase the suicide risk of their victims and often are themselves more vulnerable because of their own depression and insecurity* (Klonek et al., 2009). This situation becomes even more dangerous when victims feel they have no social support from family, teachers, or friends (Herba et al., 2008). Bully and harassment victims report more suicide ideation. Homicidal thoughts may also occur. For example, the Columbine High School killers felt that they had been rejected and mocked by classmates and/or teachers. Cyberbullying has recently emerged as a new avenue of harassment that can increase the victims' suicidality (Drogin et al., 2008; Kowalski, 2008).

"Suicide by cop" refers to incidents in which an armed suicidal person confronts a police officer with the intention of forcing the officer to shoot in self-defense. This type of encounter is very stressful for officers before and after the shooting. Police departments now often provide specific training for dealing with these situations. Those seeking suicide by cop often have been found to have strong homicidal as well as self-destructive impulses and will be considered in the following chapter. Suicide terrorists are also considered in the next chapter.

Gender and Suicide

In the United States and most other nations, women are less likely than men to commit suicide. How should we interpret this fact? First, we might remind ourselves that the death rate for males generally is higher at all age levels for all causes except those specific to females (e.g., pregnancy and birth). Sex differences in life expectancy have favored females ever since records have been kept (Stillion & McDowell, 2001/2002). Females born in 1850 had an average life expectancy of about 40 years—2 years more than males. A century later, this gap had expanded: Females born in 1950 had a life expectancy of 72 years, more than 5 years longer than their male peers. This differential in life expectancy continues to increase. Lower male life expectancies also occur in most other nations, including those in which fewer people survive into the middle and later adult years. Suicide might then be part of male's greater vulnerability to life-threatening conditions and stresses.

There is, however, a major exception to the rule. It has been estimated that China has 21 percent of the world's population but 44 percent of suicides—and 56 percent of the world's female suicides (Canetto, 2002). Most of these suicides seem to be motivated by a sense of hopelessness. Painful and frustrating experiences have led many Chinese women to feel that they have little or no chance of a good life. The situation is especially desperate in rural areas, where government policies—including limiting married couples to having one child—have disrupted traditional family patterns and increased the stress of life (Jianlin, 2000). Abortion and infanticide (Chapter 10) have also increased under the intolerable pressure. Again, we remind ourselves that a high suicide rate is not only alarming in and of itself, but that it also represents an even more widespread sense of anxiety and desperation because some sufferers stop short of suicide.

Most of the female suicides in China seem to be of the type that sociologist Émile Durkheim classified as fatalistic: death as a way to escape an oppressed and hopeless life. (We will be considering Durkheim's influential theory later in this chapter.) Another approach has been articulated recently by psychologist Silvia Sara Canetto. She notes that each society has its own models and rules for suicidal behavior. It is as though there are scripts to follow in the performance of self-destructive behavior. There is some evidence that suicide is one of the more culturally acceptable scripts for desperate Chinese women who have few other choices available. Canetto (2002) applies the same concept to the gender–suicide link in the United States:

> Nonfatal suicidal behavior is considered less masculine than fatal suicidal behavior. . . . Males are particularly critical of other males who survive a suicidal act. Studies also show that killing oneself is seen as a masculine and relatively strong act. . . . Men who kill themselves are viewed as better adjusted than women who kill themselves, independent of the reasons for the suicide (p. 817).

If the cultural script depicts completed suicide as masculine, then females may have less inclination to perform this role. A suicidal threat or nonfatal attempt would be more in accord with cultural expectations. The gender–suicide connection is still a long way from being understood, however, and we would not want to apply any general theory to all individual situations.

Balancing Individual and Cultural Influences on Suicide

The realities of everyday life and prospects for the future differ appreciably for a white, Anglo-Saxon, Protestant undergraduate; an elderly African American widow; and a youth living on a poverty-stricken reservation. The same act of desperation can flow from many sources. Prevention and intervention efforts will be more effective in some circumstances if they are focused on the individual; in other circumstances, a broader social policy approach may be necessary. We now examine some major cultural and individual influences on suicide.

SOME CULTURAL MEANINGS OF SUICIDE

The act of suicide has been interpreted in many different ways throughout human history (Minois, 1999; Murray, 1998, 2000). Most of these earlier conceptions are with us. We are also faced with newer situations, such as persistent vegetative states and the intensified advocacy for "death on demand" and physician-assisted death (see Chapter 10). New interpretations of suicide may emerge from such new challenges.

Suicide as Sinful

The Catholic Church has condemned suicide since at least the fifth century. St. Augustine established the Catholic position with two fundamental objections: (1) suicide precludes the opportunity to repent of other sins, and (2) the Sixth Commandment tells us, "Thou shalt not kill." Self-murder is not exempt from this commandment, according to St. Augustine. He did, however, volunteer a few exceptions to his own rule (426/1971):

> Abraham indeed was not merely deemed guiltless of cruelty, but was even applauded for his piety, because he was ready to slay his son in obedience to God, not to his own passion. . . . Samson, too, who drew down the house on himself and his foes together, is justified only on this ground, that the Spirit who wrought wonders by him had given him secret instructions to do this (Book I, Chapter XXI).

St. Augustine, so hard on suicide, condoned Jephthah's execution of his daughter because he had promised God he would sacrifice "whatever first met him as he returned victorious from the battle." This church father's pronouncement has troubled some believers through the century by ruling against suicide yet justifying a father's killing of his daughter in order to keep his own reckless promise. St. Thomas Aquinas (1279/1971) added another objection to suicide. Only God has the power to grant life and death. The self-murderer is engaging in the sin of pride. This self-assertion shames the whole family. Some regimes through the centuries seized upon this belief as an excuse for confiscating the property of families in which such a dishonorable death had occurred.

Condemnation of suicide as a violation of the Sixth Commandment is difficult to square with the warfare and violent death that has at times been actively pursued by defenders of the faith. Religious wars and the persecution of heretics repeatedly have violated the Sixth Commandment edict, "Thou shalt not kill." As Jacques Choron (1972) observes, "during the Middle Ages, mass suicide was frequent among persecuted sects of Christian heretics and non-Christian minorities. . . . The category of non-Christians included Moslems and Jews, who refused to be converted to Christianity and preferred to commit suicide" (pp. 25–26).

The persecuted victims were sinners for committing suicide, but their persecutors were lauded for inflicting torture and death in the name of their religion. Nevertheless, The Old and New Testaments do not directly prohibit suicide, nor do they even seem to find this action particularly remarkable. Some of the early Christian thinkers regarded the death of Jesus as suicide (Brown, 1998), as did deeply reflecting Christians of later times, such as John Donne (1646/1977).

Other influential voices within the Christian tradition have offered alternative interpretations. For example, philosopher David Hume (as quoted in Colt, 1991) reasoned along these lines:

> If upon account of age and infirmities, I may lawfully resign any office, and employ my time altogether in fencing against these calamities, and alleviating as much as possible the miseries of my future life; why may I not cut short these miseries at once by an action which is no more prejudicial to society? (p. 43).

Islam also forbids suicide, and nations in which that faith prevails have relatively low suicide rates.

Suicide as Criminal

The intertwining of church and state once made it easy to regard suicide as both criminal and sinful. Through the years, however, the civil and sacred realms of authority have become more independent of each other. The word *suicide* itself seems first to have entered use in about the middle of the seventeenth century. The Oxford English Dictionary attributes the following statement to Walter Charleton in 1651: "To vindicate ones self from . . . inevitable Calamity, by Suicide is not . . . a Crime." Suicide is more apt to be punished when it is interpreted as a crime as well as a sin. Suicide attempts have often brought severe punishment on top of the moral condemnation. This has included torture, defamation, and impoverishment.

The interpretation of suicide as crime is waning. Criminal laws have been erased from the books. It was once common for insurance companies to treat suicide as a crime intended to defraud the underwriters. It is now possible to have death benefits associated with suicide, although with limitations and restrictions built into the contract. Decriminalization of suicide is based upon the realization that penalties have not served as effective deterrents, and that few people were willing to enforce the laws. Law enforcement agencies have become more effective frontline resources for suicide prevention in some communities, liberated from the obligation of treating the attempter as a criminal.

Suicide as Weakness or Madness

Some people who commit suicide can be classified as psychotic or severely disturbed, but this is not true of all who attempt to take their own lives. Individuals with diagnosed psychiatric conditions have a higher suicide rate than the population at large. People diagnosed as depressive psychotics tend to have the highest rates of completed suicides. They are also more likely to have made one or more suicide attempts. Prevention of suicide does require diagnostic and therapeutic attention to people suffering from depression or other psychiatric disorders. However, psychiatric disorder does not by itself adequately explain or predict suicide. Many people go through disturbed periods without attempting suicide. It might be tempting to believe that a person has to be crazy to commit suicide, but this is simply not true.

What about the related belief that suicide is the outcome of weakness? This view became salient as a dubious spin-off of the survival-of-the-fittest doctrine (Darwin, 1859/1971). Suicide was regarded by some as one of nature's ways to preserve the species by weeding out the less fit, an interpretation not endorsed by Darwin himself. This position is not taken as prominent today as it was in the heyday of rugged individualism. Nevertheless, we can still see it in operation. "If you can't stand the heat, get out of the kitchen!" was one type of comment heard after an executive leaped to his death from offices high above Manhattan. Media coverage emphasized the length of time that his fallen body tied up traffic! Little attention was given then or later to his state of mind, the meaning of his suicide, or the impact upon survivors.

Suicide as "The Great Death"

The Buddhist tradition in China and Japan includes the image of *daishi,* which translates roughly as "The Great Death." Zen masters demonstrated

how a person might pass admirably from this life. The discipline of the master also appealed to the warrior. The *samurai* would seek *daishi* on the battlefield. This influence remained strong enough through the centuries to enlist the self sacrifices of *kamikaze* pilots in World War II.

Suicide has been honored as a form of daishi. *Seppuku* was a traditional form of suicide in Japan, better known in the West as *hara-kiri.* The act itself consisted of disembowelment, usually with a sword. By opening his abdomen, the individual showed the world that his center of being was pure. The sword was inserted into the *hara,* home of the breath that is a link to both life and divinity. The terminal act therefore involved a network of physiological, individual, social, and religious referents.

People condemned to death might be given the privilege of becoming their own executioner. Voluntary *seppuku,* by contrast, might flow from a number of different motives on the part of the individual (e.g., to follow a master into the great beyond or to protest an injustice). Placing one's life at the disposal of an honorable motive was a much admired action. In our own time, the self-immolation of Buddhist monks in Southeast Asia to emphasize their religious and political protests made a deep impression on observers.

The ancient Greeks and Romans also considered suicide to be an honorable death (Colt, 1991):

> *In Alexandria in the third century* B.C., *the philosopher Hegesias taught that life was so fleeting and full of cares that death was man's happiest lot. He lectured so eloquently that . . . many of his listeners committed suicide. Two centuries later, during the reign of Cleopatra, herself a suicide, there seems to have existed . . . a school that taught the best ways of committing suicide. Some "students" were rumored to have killed themselves during sumptuous banquets. Such excess anticipated the Roman Empire. For if the Greeks rationalized suicide, the Romans made it a fashion, even a sport (p. 148).*

Suicide as a Rational Alternative

The belief that suicide can bring a glorious death has a more subdued echo in another cultural tradition that dates from ancient times: suicide as a

One of the founders of modern sociology, Émile Durkheim identified failures in social integration as a major influence on suicide.

rational alternative to continuing a miserable existence. Individuals do not destroy themselves to achieve a noble postmortem reputation or a place among the eternally blessed. Instead they wish to escape a life whose quality seems a worse evil than death.

Stoicism, a philosophical position that was enunciated in ancient Athens and Rome, has since become virtually a synonym for rational control. Alvarez (1970) explains that stoicism was:

> *a last defense against the murderous squalor*
> *of Rome itself. When those calm heroes looked*
> *around them they saw a life so unspeakable,*
> *cruel, wanton, corrupt, and apparently un-*
> *valued that they clung to their ideas of reason*
> *much as the Christian poor used to cling to their*
> *belief in Paradise and the goodness of God. . . .*
> *Stoicism, in short, was a philosophy of despair;*
> *it was not a coincidence that Seneca, who was its*

> *most powerful and influential spokesman, was*
> *also the teacher of the most vicious of all Roman*
> *emperors, Nero (p. 66).*

Renaissance thinkers often praised death as refuge from the cruelties and disappointments of life. Erasmus (1509) observed what a distance there is between our aspirations for the human race and the failings discovered on every side in daily life. The Renaissance spirit of hope and progress soon became shadowed by so profound a disappointment that it sometimes seemed it could be cured only by death.

There have been many times in human history when misery was so pervasive that it seemed natural to think seriously of suicide. However, some people, also thinking rationally, have devoted themselves to improve the conditions, while others have "irrationally" persisted with life, guided by faith, hope, and obligation to others.

A POWERFUL SOCIOLOGICAL THEORY OF SUICIDE

Theories of suicide have been challenging traditional attitudes. Émile Durkheim provided the comprehensive perspective. *Le Suicide* (1897/1951) became a cornerstone for the emerging science of sociology. His approach was audacious for its time. Suicide was not a matter of the individual's relationship to God, nor were moral values the primary focus. Instead, suicide could be viewed most effectively as an outcome of interaction patterns between individuals and their societies.

The Importance of Social Integration

We are all more or less integrated into our societies. Society itself may be stable, consistent, and supportive, or it may be falling apart under stress—or even morphed into a destructive force. The individual, then, may be weakly or strongly integrated into a high- or low-solidarity culture, as shown in Table 7-5.

The type of relationship between integration and solidarity is considered to be crucial for suicidal risk. The weakly integrated person in a cohesive society (Low-High in Table 7-5) and the person

TABLE 7-5 *Types of Connection Between Individual and Society*

Individual's integration into society	Society's solidarity
High	High
High	Low
Low	High
Low	Low

trapped in a disorganized culture (High-Low) both are endangered because there is not enough group control. Inadequate group control increases the possibility of suicide, as individuals are left to their own impulses and resources. However, suicide can also result from too much control by society, as we will see. Durkheim's theory, then, invites attention both to the cohesiveness of society and the *social integration* of any particular individual.

All cultures also have *collective representations* that convey their spirit or personality. These are expressed through the guiding symbols, themes, and rituals. Unfortunately, this group spirit can turn morose and self-destructive. Individuals who are highly integrated into such a culture are more likely to absorb the pessimistic mood of the larger society and may act it out with fatal results. The very forces that should hold a society together can take on the opposite character and lead to what we might call *sociocide*. The mass suicide and homicide in Jonestown, Guyana, that resulted in the eradication of a unique community and more than 900 lives is one such example.

Four Types of Suicide

Durkheim identified four types of suicide. Each represents a distinctive relationship between individual and society. The *egoistic suicide* is committed by people who do not have enough involvement with society. They are not under sufficient cultural control. The executive who literally fell from on high is one probable example. Celebrities in the entertainment field, creative artists who follow their own stars, and people who make their own rules on the basis of their wealth and power can put themselves beyond the reach of cultural

constraints. Intellectuals are also common within the category of egoistic suicide. Sensitive to underlying currents of melancholy and despair in the culture and drifting in their own thoughts, they have little outside themselves to grasp when the suicide impulse arises.

Very different is the *altruistic suicide*. Already mentioned were such examples as the *seppuku* tradition and the *kamikaze* combat death. Altruistic suicide occurs when the individual has what might be considered an excessive concern for the community. This is usually the strongly integrated person in a high solidarity culture (High-High, Table 7-5). Altruistic suicides tend to be less common in Western societies but admired when they do occur. The soldier who volunteers for a "suicide mission" to protect comrades or achieve a military objective can be considered both a hero and an altruistic suicide. Durkheim does not mention physicians and medical researchers who voluntarily expose themselves to fatal illness in order to help others, nor first responders who put their own lives at risk.

Durkheim's third type is called *anomic suicide*. Social breakdown is reflected most directly in the anomic suicide. People are cast adrift by the failure of social institutions. Unemployment is an important example. The person thrown out of work has lost a significant tie to society. Bad times, unemployment, suicide—a predictable sequence. Similarly, people who are forced to leave their occupation because of age may enter an anomic condition that leads to suicide. When the rupture between individual and society is sudden and unexpected, then the probability of suicide is thought to be especially high. This situation arises, for example, when the death of a spouse or other important person downgrades the survivor's place in society.

This set of three suicide types dominated the picture for many years. Recently, however, more attention has been given to a fourth type that Durkheim introduced but treated more as a curiosity. In *fatalistic suicide*, a person is overcontrolled by society. The individual feels stifled and oppressed; all opportunities and prospects seem to be blocked. Durkheim spoke of slavery as a condition that engenders fatalistic suicide but thought that civilization had put this kind of oppression well into the past. Oppression and subjugation have not disappeared from the human condition, however, as tyrannical regimes persist into the twenty-first century, and people are still held captive as slaves.

Both the altruistic and the fatalistic suicide involve excessive control of the individual by society. In altruistic suicide, the individuals appear to share wholeheartedly in the collective representations. They die for their people. In fatalistic suicide, they die in despair of ever being able to actualize themselves in a culture that affords little opportunity for self-esteem and satisfaction.

We move now from a sociological approach to the individual's own thoughts, motives, and life style as factors in suicide.

SOME INDIVIDUAL MEANINGS OF SUICIDE

Just as the preceding discussion did not exhaust all the cultural and sociological meanings of suicide, so this section can only sample some of the individual meanings. The intent is to convey something of the various states of mind with which people approach a suicidal action.

Suicide for Reunion

The loss of a loved one can be experienced as so unbearable that the survivor is tempted to "join" the deceased. Recently bereaved people often experience the "presence" of the dead, as did the family interviewed by Myers and Fine (2007) mentioned in the opening of this chapter. But desperate longing may impel a person to follow the dead all the way to the other side if the relationship has been marked by extreme dependency. "I can't go on without him." "I am not complete without her." "What's to become of me?" "I can't manage by myself." Sometimes these feelings are accompanied by suicidal thoughts. Reunion fantasies may have some temporary value while bereaved individuals reconstruct their lives, but they can also lead to suicidal actions.

Children are particularly vulnerable to reunion fantasies. The parent or older sibling who has "gone off to heaven" has left the survivor with painful feelings of incompleteness and yearning. Some adults remain relatively childlike in their dependency on others and feel very much the same

way when separated by death. Suicide to achieve reunion seems most likely when the person lacks a fully developed sense of selfhood; when death has removed a significant source of support; and when cultural influences make death appear unreal and the afterlife inviting.

Suicide for Rest and Refuge

Worn down by tribulations, a person may long for a "good rest" or a "secure harbor." A vacation far away from the grinding routine may restore energy and confidence. Life may be experienced as too exhausting and burdensome. The miracle of an ordinary good night's sleep can seem out of reach as depression deepens. Under such circumstances, the fantasy of a prolonged, uninterrupted sleep can take on a heightened allure. The sleep–death analogy is readily available in America as in most other cultures (Chapter 3). It is tempting to take a few more pills than *usual and just drift away.*

Advertisements instruct us to solve problems by taking something into our mouths (puff on a cigarette; swallow pills for headaches, indigestion, or any form of distress). People with oral escapist tendencies in their personalities are especially vulnerable to these lures of suicide, but the risk is there for anybody who has sat in front of a television set. Why not make ourselves a little more comfortable, take that one more something that can help us sleep away all our troubles permanently? Death is not that much different from a peaceful snooze, right?

Suicide for Revenge

The lover is rejected. The employee is passed over for promotion. Another child is preferred and pampered. Some people are burdened by the feeling that they go through life being treated unfairly. No matter how hard they try, love and appreciation are withheld. A college student had firsthand experience of this kind of situation:

> *I felt crushed. Absolutely crushed. It was my first really good semester. No incompletes. No withdrawals. All A's and B's. And no "episodes." I kept myself going all semester. I really felt strong and independent. I knew I shouldn't expect too much when I went home, but I*

guess . . . I mean I know I expected a little appre-
ciation. You know, like maybe Mother just smil-
ing and saying, "Had a good semester, didn't
you? I'm happy for you" or "I'm proud of you,"
though she would never say that.

This young woman felt that her achievement
passed without notice: in fact, the family hardly
noticed that she had come back home. If her family would not pay attention when she did something right, maybe they would when she did
something dramatically wrong. "I wanted to hurt
them—and hurt me—just enough." She slashed
away at her wrist and arm. The self-wounding temporarily released some of her despair. She had not injured herself seriously, so she wrapped the wounded
area in a bulky bandage. Nobody seemed to notice.
A few days later she removed the bandage, exposing the patchwork of fresh scars. Still no response.
Instead, the family was enthusiastically anticipating
the upcoming marriage of one of her cousins.

She felt crushed again when she was passed
over in the wedding arrangements:

I couldn't even be part of somebody else's hap-
piness. . . . I knew that revenge was stupid. But
I felt like doing something stupid. Listen every-
body: you're 100 percent right! I am a stupid
person. And here is something really stupid to
prove it!

She hurled herself from a rooftop.

I wanted to kill myself then. I think I did. But I
also wanted to see the look on their faces when
they saw that bloody mess on the sidewalk. I
could see myself standing alongside the rest
of them, looking at that bloody mess of myself
on the sidewalk, and looking at their shocked
looks. . . . I didn't think what it would be like if I
half-killed myself and had to live with a crushed
body. Maybe that was the really stupid part of it.

This talented young woman survived a suicide attempt that might have been fatal or crip-
pling. The pain and trauma provided temporary
relief of her emotional tension. Yet she felt that
she might "have to" do it again, perhaps "next
time for keeps." She did not need a psychologist
to suggest that her suicide attempts were efforts to
punish others by punishing herself. (This woman
survived and became a stronger person for the ordeals she had undergone.)

The example given here illustrates several
other characteristics often shown by the person
who is on a self-destructive footing. This woman's
fantasy included the virtual witnessing of her suicide. She had divided herself into murderer and
victim. People who attempt suicide for any reason
sometimes act upon the dubious assumption that
they will somehow survive their deaths in order to
observe the effects.

She also experienced some tension release
through the self-destructive action itself. It is not
unusual for the sight of one's own blood to relieve
built-up emotional pressures, if only for a while.
Another woman who had slashed her wrists on
several occasions told me, "I felt as if I had done
something finally. I wasn't paralyzed any more. I
wasn't suffering helplessly. I took action into my
own hands, and that felt good." Perhaps the experience of surviving this type of suicide attempt encourages the fantasy that one would still be around
to feel better after a fatal attempt as well.

The low self-esteem of many suicide attempters is also evident in the instance given here as
well as in Katie's troubled life and death. The combination of revenge fantasy and low self-esteem
appears to be a particularly dangerous one.

Suicide as the Penalty for Failure

The victim of suicide may also be the victim of
unfulfilled self-expectations. The person acts as
accuser, jury, judge, and executioner. Some take
the alternative of lowering expectations to close
the gap. Some find other ways to cope. However,
for other people a critical moment arrives when
the discrepancy feels too painful to be tolerated.
If something has to be sacrificed, it must be themselves, not the rigid goals or excessively high
standards.

A sense of failure is prominent among
many people who take their own lives. The
psychological autopsy technique (a special
kind of case review) often finds that adult male
suicides have occurred after the person was fired,
demoted, or passed over for promotion. Female
suicides are more often related to real or perceived
failures in relationships. Young female suicides
often had a history of persistent troubles with
men. Those who were married with children had
difficulties in meeting the responsibilities of the
maternal role. Older women who took their lives

German artist Fran Masereel's woodcuts convey the impersonality and alienation that some individuals experience in big city life—despair and suicidality can breed in such circumstances. (Untitled picture from The City, *1925).*

often seem to have lost or given up most of their social roles and obligations. For women younger than 50 years old, work failure does not seem to be nearly as salient a factor in suicide as it is for men. The suicidal person often has experienced repeated failure in both personal relationships and occupational success.

Fortunately, not every person who experiences failure commits suicide. This has led to Warren Breed's (1972) description of a basic suicidal syndrome. The syndrome includes rigidity, shame, and isolation. There is only one goal, one level of expectation, and only one way to achieve it. A person who has come up short today might succeed tomorrow—but people with Breed's suicidal syndrome are shadowed by a sense of shame and cannot let themselves off so easily. "I am no good. Never will be. I am nothing." This syndrome has been found by Breed and his colleagues most conspicuously in white, middle-class adults, both men and women. It does not seem to hold for lower-class black men who kill themselves.

It is going too far to speak of this as *the* basic suicidal syndrome. Breed readily acknowledges that there are also other patterns associated with suicide. But the high-aspiration, shame-of-failure dynamics revealed by his research do come close to the meaning of suicide for many in American society today. It does not tell us, however, why some people with a basic suicidal syndrome take their own lives while others find different solutions for their problems.

Suicide as a Mistake

People sometimes survive their potentially fatal suicide attempts. An unexpected rescuer appears on the scene, a determined self-mutilator misses a vital spot, an overdose induces vomiting instead of coma, a loaded gun fails to fire. Victims may also "betray" themselves, as in the case of the rare bridge jumper who survives the usually fatal fall and then swims desperately for life.

However, there can be a discrepancy in the other direction as well. Some people kill themselves even though there is good reason to believe that they had not meant to do so. The victim had counted on being rescued. The wound or overdose was not supposed to be lethal. Precaution had been exercised to limit the effect, and yet the outcome was death. The person may have wanted very much to survive and enjoy a better life, but a mood, a desperate maneuver, and a misjudgment brought that life to a sudden close.

The individual contemplating a self-destructive act often is of two minds. This is the impression, for example, of volunteers who pick up the phone when a call is made to a suicide prevention hotline. The very fact that a person would reach out for human contact in this way suggests a continuing advocacy for life. Suicidality is often an ambivalent state of mind, as impulses toward life and death contest for supremacy. Ambivalence can reveal itself in the details of a life-threatening act. Why would she have taken the overdose just a few minutes before her husband was due home if she was entirely of a mind to take her life? And yet she did take the pills and has wagered her life on the assumption that her husband will return home at the usual time.

Helping people to survive their mistakes is an important part not only of suicide prevention but of public health safety in general. Access to lethal means of self-destruction could be made more difficult, thereby placing some time and distance between a momentary intention and a permanent error. For example, suicide rates dropped significantly in England when coke gas was no longer widely available as a mode of suicide in the home and when its toxicity was reduced.

A Psychoanalytical Approach to Suicide

Since life seeks to preserve itself, how could any of us pursue self-destruction? Sigmund Freud first suggested (1917/1959) that suicidal individuals turn a murderous wish against themselves. What looks to the world like a suicide may be the symbolic murder of a person whose dominating image has remained lodged in the mind since childhood when the distinction between self and other was not fully developed. (There is some evidence for this hypothesis: suicidal adolescents had particular difficulty in differentiating between negative aspects of themselves and their parents [Brunstein, Zaisman, Apter, Meged, Har-Even, Diller, & Orbach, 2007]).

Freud did not remain satisfied with this startling theory. Later (1923/1961) he offered a more philosophical concept. Each of us has a pair of instinctual drives that have different goals. There is a life instinct, *Eros,* and a death instinct, *Thanatos.* Eros is the force leading to expansion, growth, adventure, and pleasure. Thanatos is the biological force that tempts us to withdraw from the field of action, shut down our lives, and seek silence and death. These drives constantly interact. When Thanatos gains the upper hand, we are more likely to engage in a self-destructive action. Why self-destructive? Because much of our aggression has been forced inward as first our parents and then the world punish outward aggression. Everybody is vulnerable to suicide because there are obstacles in our pathway to gratification (Eros) and much of our aggression is forced inward.

This twin-instinct theory still has something to offer (Kastenbaum, 2000) but has not earned much application to day-by-day interactions with people at suicidal risk. However, the psychoanalytical approach does alert us to the long developmental career that precedes a self-destructive action. A young child, for example, may internalize the negative attitudes conveyed by parents. This burdens the child with a *superego* that is excessively oriented toward criticism and self-destructive action. Chaotic and inadequate parenting may also jeopardize children by leaving them with a brittle ego that fragments and shatters under pressure.

Present-day clinicians and researchers take more account of sociocultural factors. As we have seen, for example, some Native Americans are at exceptionally high risk for suicide and other self-destructive actions. Their sense of low self-esteem comes from the deprivation and discrimination experienced in their contacts with mainstream U.S. society. Native American children are in danger of growing up with a severe lack of confidence in their identities and worth as well as with tendencies to keep aggressive impulses locked up under high pressure until efforts at control fail. This is in contrast with the pride and satisfaction children would have taken in preceding generations when the people were independent and possessed a favorable group self-image. These dynamics of low self-esteem and self-directed aggression can lead to fatal outcomes other than suicide, as witnessed by the high alcohol-related death rates on the same Native American reservation. The psychoanalytical approach, then, remains useful today, but its interpretation must be tested against experience, and other relevant factors should also be considered.

The Descent Toward Suicide

How do people move toward suicide? Richard A. Heckler (1994) offers a useful description of experiences that often occur along the way to a suicide attempt and its potentially fatal outcome:

- An experience of loss and/or trauma that deprives the person of emotional support and leads to the expectation of further losses. These hurtful experiences often occur early in life when the person is most vulnerable. For example, the father may have abandoned the family, followed by the mother's depression and drug addiction, and then her death.

- The experience of losing hope for a satisfying life and losing the belief that the world is a coherent and rational place where good intentions have good consequences.

- The sense of descending, sinking, falling slowly into a subhuman kind of existence. This is accompanied by low self-esteem and a feeling of helplessness—like trying to run through quicksand.

- Withdrawal and communication breakdown increasingly isolate the individual from others. There is often a mutual withdrawal from significant emotional interactions as family members and friends also find themselves unable to cope.

- The presuicidal person now constructs a facade as protection against further emotional pain. Karen, as quoted in the beginning of this chapter, built a robot-like facade around her doubts, fears, and vulnerabilities. She was just there, doing her work, trying to be invisible to avoid interactions. In a sense, though, she was not there at all. Karen experienced the deadening effect of this protective strategy and "just felt it would be more congruent to be dead. Just not to have this body to keep being in."

- The person now descends into what Heckler calls the *suicidal trance*. There is a greatly restricted range of thoughts and feelings. One is aware of one's suffering but of little else. There is a deepening conviction that the only options available are to continue suffering or to escape through death.

- The person now exists as though trapped in a tunnel. Death increasingly seems to be the only logical and possible exit.

- The movement toward suicide is likely to be accelerated by the impression that death is somehow beckoning to the individual, offering release, even commanding the act of self-destruction (for some people, this takes the form of hallucinatory voices, but others are aware that it is their own minds at work).

- A precipitating event can trigger the actual suicide attempt when the person is already primed toward death as release. Often this precipitating event is some form of rejection from another person.

The descent toward suicide can be halted at any of these points by understanding and helpful interactions, as well as by the individual's own resourceful efforts. The deeper the person has descended into the presuicidal sequence, however, the more difficult the challenge. Nevertheless, it is an encouraging fact that Heckler's case sample is drawn from people who did "wake up, alive." I was impressed by the courage and resourcefulness of many of the people Heckler described who fought uphill battles against despair before making suicide attempts. I have also known some people like this, and perhaps you have, too. The private hells they have had to survive often were not at all of their own making.

FACTS AND MYTHS ABOUT SUICIDE

Some of the major social and individual meanings of suicide have been considered. Now we consider myths that have grown around the subject over the years.

- *People who talk about suicide will not actually take their own lives.* This statement is not true. Approximately three out of every four people who eventually kill themselves give some detectable hint ahead of time, whether by less serious attempts or by verbal statements. This is one of the most dangerous myths because it encourages us to ignore cries for help. The rejection of the communication can itself become the last straw for people contemplating suicide.
- *Only a specific class of people commit suicide.* It is sometimes held that suicide is a particular risk of either the poor or the rich. The poor are supposed to feel helpless and deprived, the rich to be bored and aimless. These simplifications fail to consider the complexity of the individual's relationship with society. People in all income brackets and social echelons commit suicide.
- *Suicide has simple causes that are easily established.* It would be closer to the truth to say that many of us are satisfied with simple explanations. This chapter has emphasized meanings and situations rather than causes of suicide, which are often far from simple.

- *Asking people about suicide will put that thought in their minds and encourage suicide attempts.* This is one of the most common of the mistaken assumptions. Many lives have been saved by opening communication on the prospect of suicide.
- *Only depressed people commit suicide.* People with a diagnosis of depression do have a higher suicide rate than those with other psychiatric syndromes or those without known syndromes. But suicide may occur in any type of psychiatric disorder. People may not even seem to be especially unhappy immediately before fatal actions. It is dangerous, then, to overlook suicidal potential on the basis of the assumption that only depressed people take their lives.
- *Only crazy or insane people commit suicide.* This mistaken proposition is related to the one just described. Many suicides are associated with obvious mental disorder, but rational people can also feel overwhelmed by circumstances and without effective means of coping.
- *Suicidal tendencies are inherited.* Some families do have suicidal traditions that seem to perpetuate themselves. But there is little evidence for a hereditary basis, even in studies made of identical twins. The explanation for suicide must be sought elsewhere—with particular attention to family patterns of communication.
- *When suicidal people show improvement, the danger is over.* The period following apparent improvement is actually one of special danger. Sometimes this is because clients have improved enough to be discharged from mental hospitals and therefore have more opportunity to commit suicide. It may also be related to a recovery of enough energy to take action. Sensitivity and interpersonal support are especially needed when people seem to be pulling out of suicidal crises.
- *People who are under a physician's care or who are hospitalized are not suicidal risks.* This is wishful thinking. Many people who commit suicide have received some form of medical or psychiatric attention within six months preceding the act. Suicides can and do occur in hospitals. Furthermore, the institutional situation itself can contribute to anxiety, low self-esteem, and other conditions conducive to suicide (Kastenbaum, 1995).

- *Suicide can be prevented only by a psychiatrist or mental hospital.* Some of the most successful suicide prevention efforts are being made by a variety of people in the community who bring concern, stamina, and sensitivity to the challenge.

SUICIDE PREVENTION

We have already touched on suicide prevention in several ways. Improving our ability to observe signs of possible heightened suicidal risk in children, youth, and adults is a useful first step. Recognizing that a number of common assumptions about suicide are not supported by fact is another useful step. Now we will consider some other contributions that we can make to suicide prevention as individuals and as a society.

Individual Guidelines to Suicide Prevention

Many suicides can be prevented. Perhaps you have already played a role in preventing suicide without realizing it. The companionship you offered a person during a crucial period or the confidence you displayed in a friend after he or she suffered a failure experience might have provided just enough support to dissolve a self-destructive pattern in the making. Whenever we bring sensitivity and a genuinely caring attitude to our relationships with other people, we may be decisively strengthening their life-affirming spirit.

How best to proceed depends upon who the suicidal person is, who we are, and what kind of relationship we have to go on together. A few general guidelines can be offered, however:

- *Take the suicidal concern seriously.* This does not mean panic or an exaggerated, unnatural response. It does mean time, attention, and active listening.
- *Do not issue a provocation to suicide.* Do not be one of those "friends" who dares this person to carry out the threat or who intimates that he or she is too "chicken" to do so. Do not belittle or joke away the suicidal state of mind— this might intensify the need to do something desperate so that others will appreciate how bad the individual really feels.

- *Go easy on value judgments.* "You can't do that— it's wrong!" This is seldom a useful response. It is not very helpful to inject value judgments when a troubled person is confiding self-destructive thoughts.
- *Do not get carried away by the "good reasons" a person has for suicide.* We may think, "If all of that were going wrong with my life, I'd want to kill myself too!" It is possible to respect the reality factors in the suicidal individual's situation without lining up on the side of self-murder. This respectful, nonevaluative approach is taken by the people who pick up the phone when a crisis hotline call is put through.
- *Know what resources are available in the community.* Who else can help this person? What kind of help might this person find most acceptable? What services are available through local schools, religious groups, mental health centers? Does your community have a crisis intervention service? How does it operate? Learn about, and if possible participate in, your community's efforts to help those who are in periods of special vulnerability.
- *Listen.* This is the advice you will hear again and again from people who have devoted themselves to suicide prevention. It is good advice. Effective listening is not passive. It is an intent, self-giving action that shows the troubled person that you are there and provides an opportunity for the person to start rebuilding trust and self-confidence.

Systematic Approaches to Suicide Prevention

I could not dial 911 when I saw that runaway horse crash through the window of the corner barbershop. My aunt could not call for comfort and advice when she again had an impulse to end of her life. That was then. Now we do have 911, and throughout most of the nation we also have crisis hot lines, and a variety of peer support groups. Add the immense connectivity of Facebook and other platforms for social messaging. The contemporary suicide prevention endeavor has both contributed to and benefitted from this continuing wave of communication development. We consider here suicide prevention centers, school education and gatekeeping programs, and targeted efforts such as Native American youth, the suicide risk of smoking cessation, sleep disturbances, and the lure of the bridge.

Suicide Prevention Centers

Many communities have 24/7 crisis hotlines and other services that can be useful both to a suicidal person and to the individual's worried family, friends, and colleagues. Large metropolitan areas have centers and mental health specialists dedicated to suicide prevention. Further information can be obtained through local human service directories and the American Association of Suicidology.

Suicide prevention centers usually offer 24-hour telephone counseling services. Some also provide walk-in clinics. Many who make use of these services are able to work through their crises without resorting to suicide. However, there are also many people with high suicidality who do not contact a center. Younger adults and women are more likely to seek help through a suicide prevention center than are older adults and men. Suicide prevention centers try various types of public information and outreach programs to encourage contacts from older adults and men. It is not easy to bring some of the people at greatest risk into the orbit of the suicide prevention center, so alternative ways of reducing suicide must also be pursued.

The community may decide to take other actions to reduce suicide risk, for example, by supporting recreational and employment programs for youth. Reducing access to guns could be a particularly effective component of a community's suicide prevention because elders are less likely to shift to other modes of self-destruction. It has been found that restricting the availability of firearms is associated with a reduction in suicides (Maris, 2003).

School Education and Gatekeeping Programs

One of the most promising systematic approaches to suicide prevention is through educational programs. School-based programs are developing in the United States (King, 2009; Miller et al., 2009) and Europe (Mishara & Ystgaard, 2000). Educators and parents must first work through their own anxieties and become more familiar with the facts of suicide. Gatekeeper training is another approach that shows promise. Clergy, teachers, school staff members, police officers, bartenders, and physicians are among the people who often have contact with people who are in suicidal crises. Improving their ability to recognize and respond to the crises can save many lives. "One day the light went on," a physician serving retirement community told me. "So many patients were starved for hope and understanding, and I was just sitting there with my prescription pad. We are all recovering from that." Educational programs all the way through to professional training are starting to prove their effectiveness.

Targeted Programs: Four Examples

Native-American communities are painfully aware of the high suicide risk among youth. The White Mountain Apaches are among those who have devised an effective action plan (Mullany et al., 2009). Tribal council took the leadership in a study to identify the specific risks and most promising prevention and intervention efforts. It was found that family and other relationship conflicts were the most common precipitating cause, and hanging the most common method. The tribal community is now targeting its resources to prevent a youth's crisis moment from ending with self-destruction.

Researchers concerned with suicide prevention are continuing to identify situations where people are at higher risk than usually supposed. The Federal Drug Administration has issued an alert that links a smoke-cessation drug with increased suicide risk (Kuehl, 2008). Other researchers have found that sleep disturbances in adolescents often occur shortly before a suicide attempt. Specific findings such as these can guide systematic, targeted suicide prevention efforts.

The Lure of the Bridge

San Francisco's Golden Gate Bridge has long been admired for its eye-catching architecture. Unfortunately, it also has long been a lure for people in the grips of a suicidal impulse. Authorities resisted updating the number of deaths after it reached 1,000, and the most recent official figure of 1,330 has surely been surpassed by several hundred. In a typical month about a hundred people arrive at the bridge with suicidal intention. Most change their minds or are so persuaded—but two dozen or more leap to their deaths.

Year after year, citizen groups have advocated for installation of a safety feature that would prevent most if not all of these suicides. Mental health experts have supported these efforts, making the point that removing a convenient or attractive method often will result in the passing of a suicide crisis without a fatal outcome. Seiden (1977) followed up on more than 700 people who had approached either the Golden Gate Bridge or Bay Bridge with suicidal intentions and who were intercepted by alert citizens or police before completing the action. Ninety-six percent of these people did not make subsequent fatal attempts, and all the survivors favored construction of a barrier, Seiden found. "If there had been a barrier every one of them reports they would have reconsidered" (p. 274). The suicidal intention had been strong but ambivalent. The attempters had given society a chance to catch them before making a fatal mistake.

Society as well as the individual has demonstrated mixed feelings about self-destruction. Municipal authorities consistently resisted the bridge modification efforts. Despite evidence to the contrary, the argument has been that a suicidal person would just find another way. The expense of the modifications and concern about tampering with the celebrated looks of the Golden Gate Bridge were also frequently mentioned objections.

Now there seems to be a resolution. San Francisco authorities have approved construction of a suicide barrier that can be smoothly integrated into the architecture (Prado 2010). Long-time advocates will be holding their collective breath until the plan becomes reality. Other suicide-allure bridges have their own parallel stories, notably Seattle's Aurora and San Diego's Coronado (Baker 2010).

Public education is a vital component of systematic suicide prevention. Bridge suicide, for example, owes much of its allure to the wish for a dramatic, meaningful, and perhaps beautiful exit from an unhappy life. John Koopman (2005), a reporter who has been covering Golden Gate Bridge suicides for many years, offers a dose of reality:

> Suicide by bridge is gruesome. . . . The impact is tremendous. The body goes from roughly 75 to 85 mph to nearly zero in a nanosecond.

> The physics of inertia being what they are, internal organs tend to keep going. The force of impact causes them to tear loose. . . the jumpers have lacerated aortas, livers, spleens and hearts. Ribs are often broken, and the impact shoves them into the heart or lungs. You breathe in salt water and asphyxiate (p. 1).

Bridges are not the only focal points for suicide. Other landmarks also are used for this purpose. The Empire State Building has a high safety fence and is patrolled by security guards; nevertheless, desperate people have sometimes found a way to leap to their death from this iconic structure. Each year in New York City alone, hundreds of people threaten and some carry through with jumping from buildings and bridges (Salazar, 2010).

EMERGING ISSUES AND CHALLENGES

There has been encouraging progress in the understanding and prevention of self-destruction, but new issues and challenges continue to emerge. We begin with two developments that draw on advances in the neurosciences, and then consider survivor vulnerability, internet suicide pacts, and the big picture of modernization and its accelerating successor, postmodernization.

Antidepressants: Prevention or Added Risk?

Our first visit is to the unsettling controversy regarding antidepressants. Medication that reduces depression should also reduce self-destructive actions. Suicide rates have indeed fallen since the use of antidepressants became more common in the 1980s. It is not clear how much of the credit should be attributed to antidepressives because much else has been happening in society, but people with severe depression who take Prozac or other antidepressants generally are at less risk for suicide.

However, warning flags have been raised about possible adverse effects. The media have given substantial coverage to clinical trials that found an increase in suicide in children and adolescents who were taking antidepressants. There are now cautions on the labels of antidepressants regarding their use by minors as a result of a Food and Drug Administration warning (Olfson et al., 2009). The pharmaceutical industry and many health care providers have come to the defense of antidepressants (Zarembo, 2005). It is generally agreed, though, that more research is needed, for example, on whether antidepressants have different actions on the brains of children and adults (Frantz, 2004).

Furthermore, people who receive antidepressants sometimes experience a feeling of panic—and this can set a self-destructive course in action There is an increasing call for the development of more effective antidepressants that will not have adverse reactions. Eventually, finding and disabling a possible "genetic trigger" for depression might be the answer that is sought.

Wong and Licinio (2004) note that "depression is one of the world's most lucrative drug targets" (p. 136). It is advisable to keep careful watch when big money as well as lives are at stake. Furthermore, emphasis on a drug fix for suicide can divert attention from a broader range of preventive actions, including enlightened and effective human contact.

Young Brains

Neuroscientists have been making good use of the sophisticated new methods available to them. Our understanding of the human brain and its quirks is undergoing a remarkable transformation (for a brief introduction: Insel, 2010). Some of the most interesting results center on characteristics of the brain in adolescence. In our teens, we are still very much a work in progress. What are the implications for suicide?

Rap your forehead and you are knocking on the door of your prefrontal cortex. Don't rap too hard, because this area is vital to the higher mental functions. We activate this area when planning for the future and working out complex thought sequences. It has now been shown that this function generally does not mature until adulthood (Ernst et al., 2009). This limitation makes itself known in predicting the consequences of our actions—risky and self-destructive behavior, for example. Another way to say this: impulsive actions are not adequately restrained because one does not really grasp their potentially catastrophic outcomes.

There is more to this picture. Casey et al. (2007) observe that adolescence brings with it a new and enticing array of incentives and rewards: things that the teen very much wants to happen. Neurologically, it's the limbic system that's steaming away while the executive control and decision making of the prefrontal cortex is not yet up to the job. Teens who are already disposed toward risk taking are now in a heightened danger zone.

Another significant factor has been noted by Davey et al. (2007) and Pandy et al. (2009), among others. Adolescents seem to be especially vulnerable to depression. In daily life, rejection, failure, frustration, and confusion can induce depression—but there is already a sensitivity that is linked to the incomplete development of an integrated nervous system.

New findings will continue to refine this picture. It is already clear, however, that depression and suicidality in adolescence have a neural basis that should not be ignored. This opens rather than closes the matter: how can teens be helped to negotiate past this susceptibility, learn effective coping techniques, enhance self-esteem? We can probably pick up some good advice from those who have overcome the perils of impulsivity and inexperience.

Survivor Vulnerability

The stress that family members and friends experience after a suicide deserves more attention. Their suffering and risk has been confirmed by a comprehensive review of the literature. They are likely to become more vulnerable to

> heightened levels of guilt, shame, anger, family dysfunction, and social stigmatization. Survivors of any sudden, traumatic death of a loved one have an increased chance of developing disorders such as traumatic grief. . . . Perhaps most tragically, evidence suggests that suicide survivors may be at elevated risk for someday completing suicide themselves (Jordan & McMenamy, 2004, p. 337).

Mental health experts recommend that more assistance be made available to suicide survivors. Useful information from as well as about suicide survivors is available from the American Association of Suicidology.

Internet Suicide Pacts

Naoki is a 34-year-old Japanese bank employee who has been laid off work because of stress-related problems for six months. He explained to BBC correspondent Andrew Harding (2004) why he was considering joining a suicide group:

> Well, I'm depressed—and that's a disease. But to be honest, I think I've always been interested in killing myself. . . . then I visited a website and thought—ah, if I join this, I won't have to go through with it on my own. It's like crossing the road when the traffic light is red. . . . It's not so scary when you're with others (p. 2).

In the two-week period before this interview, three groups of three people and two groups of four had been found dead by carbon monoxide poisoning in cars on remote mountain roads. They were among the increasing number of Japanese who were planning, and sometimes completing, suicide through the many Internet websites and chat rooms devoted to suicide. Another BBC report (2004) suggests that the continuing rise in youth suicide is related to economic problems and an increasing sense of isolation. (Durkheim's alienation form of suicidality seems applicable to the phenomenon Japanese call *hikomorei*: dropouts from society who stay in their rooms and interact mostly with the Internet.)

Will Internet suicide ventures among young people become a significant problem in the United States as well? Consideration might be given to supporting websites that offer more constructive ways of approaching life crises. Naoki, in fact, has started his own website to help other people work through their difficulties without resorting to suicide.

More Than Modern—More or Less Suicidal?

Steven Stack (2009) lays it out for us:

> Modernization comprises three interrelated dimensions: economic development, urbanization, and secularization. Each tends to break down the ties between the individual and society. Migration from the countryside to urban centers erodes ties to ancestral farmland, friends, and kin. Industrialization . . . requires mass

education [and] thrives on a large mass of consumers. Religiosity is weakened . . . and replaced by an ever-changing, questioned, and diverse culture and social order. . . . The greater the economic development, the greater the suicide rate (p. 915).

Durkheim's (1951) concept of *anomie* resonates with *modernization*'s effect of reducing the ties between an individual and society. From a spiritual standpoint, the desperate victims could also be regarded as lost souls—no longer feeling at home in society, and less certain of salvation in an afterlife. Durkheim's less familiar concept of *fatalistic* suicide also applies. The mass impersonality of a modernizing society can crush the individual's sense of hope and meaning: what's the point of going on?

But wait—there is a paradox here. Many lives improved with advances in technology and shifts in social structure. There was a new sense of opportunity. Perhaps we were no longer bound to our meager and onerous place in society, but could make something more of ourselves and our family—look at those who were doing it. In other words, the level of expectation had risen and, therefore, also the risk of frustration and disappointment.

Modernization is still in progress, but jostled and often overtaken by postmodernization. Perhaps the Columbia Encyclopedia (2008) best captures the tone:

> In general, the postmodern view is cool, ironic, and accepting of the fragmentation of contemporary existence. It tends to concentrate on surfaces rather than depths, to blur the distinctions between high and low culture and, as a whole to challenge a wide range of cultural values.

Postmodernism is often seen as a reaction against an ordered and rational view of the world. Causes are not simple; "truths" are situational. Authorities are merely claims that compete with other claims. As individuals, we multitask select the stuff of our lives from any time, place, or belief system that appeals. If thoroughly postmodernized, we are likely to feel more involved with never-met Internet partners than with our next door neighbors.

What are the implications of postmodernism for suicide? We don't know. Perhaps there will be more lost souls than ever. Or perhaps more people will become agile acrobats in the Wi-Fi circus and acquire new levels of survival skills. Those connected and those not connected with the communication network might well experience different types and levels of suicide risk.

■ SUMMARY

Suicide takes many forms. Research continues to find that both thoughts and attempts are more common than we might have supposed. Suicide is the eleventh most common cause of death in the general population of the United States, but even higher for adolescents and young adults. Male suicide rates are higher than female rates almost everywhere; however, the pattern is reversed in China, where many women, especially in rural areas, suffer from oppression and hopelessness. Special attention was given to youth suicide, and particularly to risks experienced by college students. Suicide rates are highest among elderly people, especially white males. An unexplained increase in suicide among middle-aged adults suggests that the baby boomer generation might be experiencing significant difficulties in adjusting to life transitions. Suicide rates are alarmingly high among young Native Americans and Alaskan Natives, as well as indigenous people throughout the world. African Americans, especially women, consistently have a lower suicide rate than whites, perhaps because of their social support network and active religiosity. Hispanic suicide rates have been relatively low, but there is growing concern about the risk among youth. Members of the armed forces and veterans are at much higher risk for suicide than others of their age. More attention is urgently needed for traumatized military personnel returning from deployment in Afghanistan and Iraq.

Rival meanings of suicide have been promulgated in society: suicide as sinful, as criminal, as weakness or madness, as "The Great Death," and as a rational alternative. Sociobehavioral scientists and clinicians have offered their own explanations. Durkheim introduced the sociological concepts of social integration, collective representations, and the altruistic, anomic, egoistic, and fatalistic types of suicide. Several individual meanings of suicide were then discussed: suicide as reunion, rest and refuge, revenge, penalty for failure, and mistake.

Freud's first theory explained suicide as anger toward others that has been turned inward; his second theory proposed warring life (Eros) and death (Thanatos) instincts in which self-destructive tendencies may dominate because of problems experienced in early development. Richard Heckler's description of "the descent toward suicide" added to our understanding of the failed attempts at coping that can lead first to suicidal thoughts, then to attempts and, finally, to death.

Common myths about suicide were identified and critiqued (e.g., that people who talk about suicide will not actually take their own lives). We then considered what we can do to prevent suicide as individuals and as citizens. Attention was given to a variety of higher risks and prevention efforts, including the lure of the bridge, benefits and risks of antidepressant medication, the vulnerability of suicide survivors, and the Internet as a staging ground for youths making suicide pacts. Advances in brain research have identified biological markers for depression and elevated suicide risk, and the ongoing shift from modernism to postmodernism raises questions about self-destructive behavior in the years ahead.

■ REFERENCES

Alvarez, A. (1970). *The savage god.* New York: Random House.

Associated Press. (2005, January 14). Suicide rate among soldiers up in Iraq. http://msnbc.msn.com/id/3956787.

Associated Press. (2008, March 16). Most suicides in Guard, Reserves. *Arizona Republic,* p. B4.

Baker, M.V. (2010, March 18). The *L.A. Times* on the Aurora Suicide Bridge barrier. http://thesunbreak.com/2010/03/08/the-la-times-on-the-aurorabridge-suicidebarrier.

Beautrais, A. L. (2002). A case control study of suicide and attempted suicide in older adults. *Suicide and Life-Threatening Behavior, 32,* 1–9.

Beautrais, A. L. (2004). Further suicidal behavior among medically serious suicide attempters. *Suicide and Life-Threatening Behavior, 14,* 1–11.

BBC News. (2004, October 12). Nine die in Japan "suicide pacts." http://news.bbc.co.uk/2/hi/asia-pacific/3735372.stm.

Bluestein, G. (September 6, 2007). American girls' suicide rates rise. *Arizona Republic,* p. A7.

Breed, W. (1972). Five components of a basic suicide syndrome. *Life-Threatening Behavior, 3,* 3–18.

Brown, R. E. (1998). *The death of the messiah* (Vol. 2). New York: Doubleday.

Casey, B. J., Getz, S., & Galvan, D. (2008). The adolescent brain. *Current Directions in Risk and Decision Making, 26,* 62–77.

Canetto, S. S. (2002). Suicide influence and factors: Gender. In R. Kastenbaum (Ed.), *Macmillan encyclopedia of death and dying* (Vol. 2, pp. 815–818). New York: Macmillan.

Choron, J. (1972). *Suicide.* New York: Scribner.

Cohen, P. (February 19, 2008). Midlife suicide rises, puzzling researchers. http://www.nytimes.com/2008/02/19/us/19suicide.html.

Colt, G. H. (1991). *The enigma of suicide.* New York: Simon & Schuster. *Columbia Encyclopedia* (2008) (6th ed.). Chicago: Gale.

Conwell, Y. (2001). Suicide in later life: A review and recommendation for prevention. *Suicide and Life-Threatening Behavior, 31* (Suppl.), 32–47.

Daly, R. (2007). VA told to establish multiple suicide prevention programs. *Psychiatric News, 42,* 4–5.

Darwin, C. (1971). *Origin of the species.* Cambridge: Harvard University Press. (Original work published 1859.)

Davey, C. G., Yucel, M., & Allen N. B. (2008). The emergence of depression in adolescence: Development of the prefrontal cortex and the representation of reward. *Neuroscience & Biobehavioral Reviews, 32,* 1–19.

Dean, C. (1990). *Nam vet.* Portland, OR: Multnomah Press.

De Groot, M. H., de Keijser, J., & Neeleman, J. (2006). Grief shortly after suicide and natural death. *Suicide and Life-Threatening Behavior, 36,* 418–432.

Donne, J. (1977). *Biathanatos.* New York: Arno Press. (Original work published 1646.)

Drogin, E. Y., & Young, K. (2009). Forensic mental health aspects of adolescent "cyber bullying": A jurisprudence science perspective. *Journal of Psychiatry & Law, 36,* 679.

Durkheim, É. (1951). *Suicide.* (J. A. Spaulding & G. Simpson, Trans.). New York: Free Press. (Original work published 1897.)

Erasmus. (1994). *The praise of folly.* New York: Penguin (Original work published 1509.)

Ernst, C., Mechawar, N. M., & Turecki, G. (2009). Suicide neurobiology. *Progress in Neurobiology, 89,* 316–333.

Frantz, S. (2004). Hunt on to explain antidepressant risk. *Nature Reviews Drug Discovery, 3,* 1–2.

Freud, S. (1959). *Mourning and melancholia.* Collected papers (Vol. 4, pp. 152–172). New York: Basic Books. (Original work published 1917.)

Freud, S. (1961). *The ego and the id.* New York: Norton (Original work published 1923.)

Garcia, C., Skay, C., Sieving, R., Novokton, S., & Bearinger, L. H. (2008). Family and racial factors associated with suicide and emotional distress among Latino students. *Journal School Health, 79,* 478–495.

Goldstein, T. R., & Bridge, J. A. (2008). Sleep difficulties preceding adolescent suicides. *Journal of Counseling & Clinical Psychology, 76,* 84–91.

Grek, A. (2007). Clinical management of suicidality in the elderly: An opportunity for involvement in the lives of older patients. *Canadian Journal of Psychiatry, 52,* (Suppl. 1), 1–14.

Groves, S. A., Stanley, B. H., & Sher, L. (2007). Ethnicity and the relationship between adolescent alcohol use and suicidal behavior. *International Journal of Adolescent Medical Health, 19,* 19–25.

Harding, A. (2004, December 7). Japan's internet "suicide clubs." http://news.bbc.co.uk/hi/programmes/newsnight/4071805.stm.

Heckler, R. A. (1994). *Waking up, alive.* New York: Ballantine.

Hendin, H. (1995). *Suicide in America* (rev. ed.). New York: Norton.

Herba, C. M., Ferdinand, R. F., Oldehinkel, A. J., & Ormad, J. (2009). Victimization and suicide ideation in the TRAILS study. *Journal of Child Psychology and Psychiatry, 49,* 867–876.

Hunter, E., & Harvey, D. (2002). Suicide influences and practices: Indigenous populations. In R. Kastenbaum (Ed.), *Macmillan encyclopedia of death and dying* (Vol. 2, pp. 818–821). New York: Macmillan.

Ikeda, R. Mahendra, R., Saltzman, L., Crosby, A., Willis, L., Mercy, J., Holmgreen, P., & Annest, J. L. (2002). Nonfatal self-inflicted injuries treated in hospital emergency departments—United States, 2000. www.cdc.gov/mmwr/preview/mmwrhtml/mm5120a3.htm.

Insel, T. R. (2010). Faulty circuits. *Scientific American,* (April), 44–51.

Jianlin, J. (2000). Suicide rates and mental health services in modern China. *Crisis, 21,* 118–121.

Jordan, J. R., & McMenamy, J. (2004). Interventions for suicide survivors: A review of the literature. *Suicide and Life-Threatening Behavior, 34,* 337–349.

Kaplan, M. S., Huguet, N., McFarland, B. H., & Newsome, J. T. (2007). Suicide among male veterans: A prospective population-based study. *Journal of Epidemiology & Community Health, 61*, 619–624.

Kastenbaum, R. (1994). Alternatives to suicide. In L. Tallmer & D. Lester (Eds.), *Now I lay me down. Suicide in the elderly* (pp. 196– 213). Philadelphia: The Charles Press.

Kastenbaum, R. (1995). The impact of suicide on society. In B. L. Mishara (Ed.), *The impact of suicide* (pp. 169–186). New York: Springer.

Kastenbaum, R. (2000). *The psychology of death* (3rd ed.). New York: Springer.

Kim, Y. S., Leventhal, B., Koh, Y-J, & Boyce, W. T. (2009). Bullying increased suicide risk; Prospective study of Korean adolescents. *Archives of Suicide Research, 13*, 15–30.

King, K. A. (2009). Developing a comprehensive school suicide prevention program. *Journal of School Health, 71*, 132–137.

Klomek, A., Sourander, K., Kumpulaien, J., Piha, T., Tamminen, I., Mollannen, F., & Gould, M. (2009). Childhood bullying as a risk for later depression and suicidal ideation among Finnish males. *Journal of Affective Disorders, 109*, 47–55.

Koopman, J. (2005, November 2). Lethal beauty: No easy death: Suicide is gruesome and death is almost certain. http://articles.sfgate.com/200511-02/news.

Kowalski, R. M. (2008). Cyber bullying. Recognizing and treating victim and aggressor. *Psychiatric Times, 25*, 1–4.

Krug, E. G., Kresnow, M. J., Peddicord, J. P., Dahlberg, L. L., Powell, K. E., Crosby, A. E., & Annest, J. L. (2003). Suicide after natural disasters. www.nejm.org.

Kuehn, B.M. (2009). Studies linking smoking cessation drugs with suicide risk spark concern. *Journal of the American Medical Association, 30*, 108–11.

Leenaars, A. A., & Wenckstern, S. (1991). *Suicide prevention in schools.* New York: Hemisphere.

LeMaster. P. E., Beals, J., Novins, D. K., & Manson, S. P. (2004). The prevalence of suicidal behaviors among Northern Plains American Indians. *Suicide and Life-Threatening Behavior, 34*, 242–254.

Mancinelli, I., Comparelli, A. Girardi, P., & Tatarelli, R. (2002). Mass suicide: Historical and psychodynamic considerations. *Suicide and Life-Threatening Behavior, 32*, 91–100.

Marion, M. S., & Range, L. M. (2003). African American college women's suicide buffers. *Suicide and Life-Threatening Behavior, 33*, 33–43.

Maris, W. W. (2003). Understanding suicide in the 21st century. *Preventing Suicide, 2*, 4–7.

May, P. A., Van Winkle, N. W., Williams, M. B., McFeeley, P. R., DeBruyn, L. M., & Serna, P. (2002). Alcohol and suicide death among American Indians of New Mexico: 1980–1998. *Suicide and Life-Threatening Behavior, 32*, 240–255.

McCraig, L. F., & Burt, C. W. (2001). National Hospice Ambulatory Medical Care Survey: Advance data from vital and health statistics; no. 320. Hyattsville, MD: U.S. Department of Health and Human Services. CDC, National Center for Health Statistics.

McCarthy, J. F., Valenstein, M., Kim, J. M, Hgem, M., Zivin, K., & Blow, F. C. (2009). Suicide mortality among patients receiving care in the Veterans Health Administration System, *American Journal of Epidemiology, 169*, 1033–1038.

McClatchy Newspapers. (2008, April 24). Senator: VA hid suicide tries. *Arizona Republic*, p. A1.

Miller, D. N., Eckert, T. L., & Mazza, J. (2009). Suicide prevention programs in the schools: A review of public health programs. *School Psychology Review, 38*, 168–188.

Minois, G. (1999). *History of suicide. Voluntary death in Western culture.* Baltimore: Johns Hopkins University Press.

Mishara, B. L. (2002). Suicide over the life span: Adolescents and youths. In R. Kastenbaum (Ed.), *Macmillan encyclopedia of death and dying* (Vol. 2, pp. 832–835). New York: Macmillan.

Mishara, B. L., & M. Ystgaard (2000). Exploring the potential of primary prevention: Evaluation of the Befrienders International Reaching Young Europe Pilot Programme in Denmark. *Crisis, 21*, 4–7.

Mudrian, A., & Peel, J. (2004). *Choosing death. The improbable history of death metal and grindcore.* Los Angeles: Feral House.

Mullany, B., Barlow, A., Goklish, N. Larzelere-Hinton, F., Gwik, M., Craig, M., Walkup, J. T. (2009). Toward understanding suicide among youths: Results from the White Mountain Tribally Mandated Suicide Surveillance System, 2001–2006. *American Journal of Public Health, 99*, 1840–1849.

Murphy, G. E. (1995). 39 years of suicide research. *Suicide and Life-Threatening Behavior, 25*, 450–457.

Murray, A. (1998). *Suicide in the Middle Ages: Vol. 1. The violent against themselves.* New York: Oxford University Press.

Murray, A. (2000). *Suicide in the Middle Ages: Vol. 2. The curse on self-murder.* New York: Oxford University Press.

Myers, M. F., & Fine, C. (2007). Touched by suicide: Bridging the perspectives of survivors and clinicians. *Suicide and Life-Threatening Behavior, 37,* 119–126.

National Household Survey on Drug Abuse. (2002). Substance use and the risk of suicide among youths. www.samhsa.gov/oas/2k2/suicide/suicide/html.

Olfson, M., Marcus, S. C., & Druss, B. G. (2008). Effects of Food and Drug Administration warning on antidepressant use in a national sample. *Archives of General Psychiatry, 65,* 94–101.

Orbach, I. (1988). *Children who don't want to live.* San Francisco: Jossey-Bass.

Orbach, I., Mikulinger, M., Gilboa-Schechtman, E., & Sirota, P. (2003). Mental pain and its relationship to suicidality and life meanings. *Suicide and Life-Threatening Behavior, 33,* 231–244.

Osgood, N. J. (1992). *Suicide in later life.* New York: Lexington.

Pandy, G. N., Dwivedi, Y., Rizavi, H. S., Teppen, T., Gaszner, G. L., Roberts, R. C., & Conley, R. R. (2009). GSK-3B gene expression in human postmortem brain: Regional distribution, effects of age and suicide. *Neurochemical Research, 34,* 274–285.

Paul, A. (1996). *Suicide wall.* Portland, OR: PakDonald Publishing.

Peck, D. L. (2003). Suicide and suicide trends in the United States, 1900–1999. In C. Bryant (Ed.), *Handbook of death and dying* (Vol. 1, pp. 319–338). Los Angeles: Sage

Pennybaker, J. S., & Stone, L. D. (2004). What was she trying to say? A linguistic analysis of Katie's diaries. In D. Lester (Ed.), *Katie's Diary* (pp. 55–80). New York: Brunner-Routledge.

Potter, L. B., Kesnow, M., Powell, K., Simon, T. R., Mercy, J. A., Lee, R. K., et al. (2001). The influence of geographic mobility on nearly lethal suicide attempts. *Suicide and Life-Threatening Behavior, 32* (Suppl.), 42–48.

Prado, M. (2010, February 23). Golden Gate Bridge suicide barrier ready to go, money needed. http://www.marinij.com/marinnews/ci_14392213.

Pridmore, S., & McArthur, M. (2008). Suicide and reputation damage. *Australasian Psychiatry, 16,* 312–316.

Priest, D. (January 31, 2008). Soldier suicides at record level. *Washington Post,* p. A01.

Royal Commission on Aboriginal Peoples. (1995). *Choosing life: Special report on suicide among Aboriginal Peoples.* Ottawa: Royal Commission on Aboriginal Peoples.

Rudd, M. D., Joiner, T., & Rajab, M. H. (2004). *Treating suicidal behavior.* New York: Guilford Publications.

Rustad, R. A., Small, J. E., Jobes, D. A., Safer, M. A., & Petterson, R. J. (2003). The impact of rock videos and music with suicidal content on thoughts and attitudes about suicide. *Suicide and Life-Threatening Behavior, 33,* 120–131.

Salazar, C. (October 4, 2010). Authorities seek to stop suicides at U.S. landmarks. *Arizona Republic,* p. A98.

SAMSHA. (2009). First-of-a-kind national study reveals that 8.3 million adults in the U.S. had serious thoughts of committing suicide in the past year. http://www.samhsa.gov/newsroom/advisories/090917suicide0907.aspx.

Schilling, E., Aseltine, Jr., R., Glanovsky, A., & Jacobs, J. D. (2009). Adolescent alcohol use, suicide ideation, and suicide attempts. *Journal of Adolescent Health, 44,* 335–341.

Schwartz, A. J, (2006). College student suicide in the United States: 1990–1991 through 2003–2004. *Journal of American College Health, 54,* 341–352.

Seiden, R. H. (1977). A tale of two bridges: Comparing suicide incidences on the Golden Gate and San Francisco-Oakland Bay bridges. *Crisis, 13,* 32–40.

Sher, L. (2007). Functional magnetic resonance imaging in studies of the neurobiology of suicidal behavior in adolescents with alcohol use disorders. *International Journal of Adolescence Medical Health, 19,* 11–18.

Smith, L. (1997). *Fools, martyrs, traitors: The story of martyrdom in the Western world.* New York: Knopf.

Sourander, A., Klomek, A. B., Niemela, S., Haavisto, A., Gyllenberg, D., Helenius, H., Sillanmaki, L., Ristkari, T., Kumpalaien, K., Tamminen, T., Piha, J., Almqvist, F., & Gould, S. (2009). Childhood predictors of completed and severe suicide attempts. *Archives of General Psychiatry, 66,* 398–406.

Stack, J. (2010, March 17). Plane crash suspect's online diatribe. http://www.thesmokinggun.com/documents/crime/plane-crash-suspects-online-diatribe.

St. Augustine. (1971). *The city of God.* In R. M. Hutchins (Ed.), *Great books of the Western world* (Vol. 18, pp. 129–620). Chicago: Encyclopedia Britannica. (Original work published 426.)

St. Thomas Aquinas. (1971). *Summa theologica.* In R. M. Hutchins (Ed.), *Great books of the Western world* (Vol. 19). Chicago: Encyclopedia Brittanica. (Original work published 1279.)

Stack, S. (2000). The heavy metal subculture and suicide. *Suicide and Life-Threatening Behavior, 24,* 15–23.

Stack, S. (2009). Suicide, cross-cultural perspectives. In C. Bryant & D. Peck (Eds.), *Encyclopedia of death and the human experience* (Vol. 2, pp. 913–919). Los Angeles: Sage.

Stillion, J. M., & McDowell, E. E. (2001/2002). The early demise of the "stronger" sex: Gender-related causes of sex differences in longevity. *Omega, Journal of Death and Dying, 44,* 301–318.

Stoep, A. V., McCauley, C. A., & Stone, A. (2009). Thoughts on death and suicide in early adolescence. *Suicide and Life-Threatening Behavior, 39,* 599–615.

Trujillo, M. (2008). Multicultural aspects of mental health. *Primary Psychiatry, 15,* 77–84.

Underwood, A. (2008, May 29). War on wounds. *Newsweek,* p. 44.

Valenstein, M., Kim, H. M., Ganuczy, D. J., & McCarthy, J. F. (2009). Higher risk for suicide among Veterans Administrations patients receiving depression treatment. *Journal of Affective Disorders, 112,* 50–58.

Willis, L. A., Coombs, D. W., Drentea, P., & Cockerham, W. C. (2003). Uncovering the mystery: Factors of African American suicide. *Suicide and Life-Threatening Behavior, 33,* 412–419.

Wong, P., Chan, W., Conwell, Y., Conner, K., & Yip, P. (2009). A psychological autopsy study of gamblers who died by suicide. *Journal of Affective Disorders, 120,* 213–216.

Wong, M-L, & Licinio, J. (2004). From monoamines to genomic targets: A paradigm shift for drug discovery in depression. *Nature Reviews Drug Discovery, 3,* 136–151.

Wouter de Lange, A., & Needleman, J. (2004). The effect of the September 11th terrorist attacks on suicide and deliberate self-harm: A time trend study. *Suicide and Life-Threatening Behavior, 34,* 439–447.

Yang, B., & Clum, G. A. (2000). Childhood stress leads to suicidality via its effects on cognitive functioning. *Suicide and Life-Threatening Behavior, 30,* 183–198.

Yardley, W. (2007, May 14). In Alaskan villages, a culture of sorrow. *New York Times.* http://www.nytimes.com/2007/05/14/us/14alaska.html.

Zarembo, A. (2005, February 3). Study links Prozac to lower suicide rate. *East Valley Tribune,* A12.

Zoroya, G. (2010, September 19). Army suicides tied to risky behavior. *Arizona Republic,* p. A10.

Zoroya, G (2011a, January 20). More Army Guard, Reserve soldiers committing Suicide. *USA Today,* E-mail newsletter.

Zoroya, G.(2011b, March 16). Female soldiers' suicide rate triples when at war *USA Today,* e-mail newsletter.

■ GLOSSARY

Altruistic suicide Committed by people who have extremely high or excessive concern for society (Durkheim).

Anomic suicide Committed by people who fail to receive support and meaning from society (Durkheim).

Collective representations The symbols and themes that convey the spirit and mood of a culture (Durkheim).

Daishi An ideal or "great death" in Buddhist tradition.

Egoistic suicide Committed by people who are not under sufficient control by societal norms and obligations (Durkheim).

Fatalistic suicide Committed by people who are stifled and oppressed by society (Durkheim).

Modernization The transformation of a traditional, agriculture-based culture through technology and industrialization, leading to increased productivity, specialization, individuality, and a corresponding decline in social integration.

Parasuicide Attempted suicide.

Postmodernization A follow-up process of societal change after modernization in which individuals move further away from traditional forms of religion politics, and lifestyle and explore a variety of other possibilities.

Samurai Warrior who follows a strong code of honor (in Japanese tradition).

Seppuku Suicide by ritualistic disembowelment (in Japanese tradition). Also known in the West as *hara-kiri*.

Social integration The extent to which individuals are connected to a society that is more or less cohesive (Durkheim).

Stoicism A philosophical tradition that emphasizes rationality and the ability to withstand despair, provocations, and temptations.

Suicidal trance A state of mind in which a person sees death as the only way to relieve suffering and gives little attention to anything else.

Suicide Self-murder.

Suicide rate A measure that is computed by multiplying the number of suicides by 100,000 and dividing by the population number. The suicide rate is not to be mistaken for a percentage.

■ ON FURTHER THOUGHT . . .

Useful online resources:

American Association of Suicidology
   www.suicidology.org
Canadian Association for Suicide Prevention
   http://www.suicideprevention.ca/
International Association for Suicide Prevention
   http://www.iasp.info/
Suicide Aftercare Association
   http://www.suicideaftercare.org/

Sibling Survivors
   www.siblingsurvivors.com
Suicide Information & Education
   www.siec.ca

Specialist journal:

Suicide and Life-Threatening Behavior
   WileyOnlineLibrary.comJournal/SLSTB

Danger Zones:

There are times when people are at particular risk for suicide. At least two of these danger zones have been identified: (1) soon after learning that one has a progressive and life-threatening illness; (2) soon after the death (especially if unexpected) of a close family member. Most people who do not turn to suicide while in these danger zones find other ways to cope with their situations. Here is the challenge: How can people be helped or protected during these times without having their lives invaded or restricted by well-meaning family, friends, or professional caregivers? What should be the guiding principles? How should we go about it—or should we not go about it at all?

The first murder? The Book of Genesis tells us it was a case of domestic violence. Today's crime log is sure to include many further examples. This illustration of Cain's killing of his brother, Abel, was created by 16th century artist Tiziano Vecellio.

Violent Death: Murder, Terrorism, Genocide, Disaster, and Accident

Three-year-old Jaylyn was given a sleeping pill by her mother, Tysann Celestain. Then the woman placed a pillow over her daughter's face until the girl did not kick anymore and placed her in a plastic bag. After that, Celestain tried to commit suicide by smothering herself; however, because that didn't work, she took rat poison and sleeping pills.

—Alt & Wells (2010, p. 33).

The impersonal and bureaucratic nature of their jobs . . . and the controlled communicative exchanges expected of them contributed to "cold intimacy." Their concern with order and detail, their self-restraint, their discipline, and their commitment to routine meant they had an edge in their authoritative jobs as financiers, bankers, schoolteachers, businessmen, accountants, police officers, independent farmers, engineers, and doctors. However, for many, their inflexibility, compulsiveness, inability to fit in, seeming lack of creativity, and despondency undermined and diminished them as human beings.

—Neil Websdale (2010, p. 233).

Fifteen of the Indians had come to the camp and offered peace. He (Francisco Vázquez) ordered them tied to posts and that dry willow canes be placed around them with which to burn them. . . . They set fire to them, and burned them all alive.

—Juan de Contreras, 1544, translated by Richard Flint (2002, p. 113)

Berlin. Death came for Hatun Surucu at a cold bus stop here three years ago. The 23-year-old was the sixth Muslim woman murdered by a relative in Berlin in as many months for being "too Western."

—Joanne Jowan (2008)

It is the leading cause of death in people ages 10 to 24 around the world. Most of these deaths could have been prevented.
—World Health Organization (2008).

On December 26th, I was down by the ocean, talking to a friend, and I saw that the water was shaking. I thought, there is some problem in the middle of the sea.
—Victor Desosa, quoted by William Herman (2005, p. A18)

MESA, ARIZONA: A 16-year-old Mesa student was arrested Wednesday night after police uncovered a list of 53 students he wanted to kill with a rifle he was saving money to buy, Mesa police said Thursday. The teen also detailed how he planned to make a mask and gloves from the skin of his first victim, and then go to the school and kill everybody on the list while he was disguised as the dead student.
—Kristina Davis (2004, p. A3)

s the world as a safe place? Not for those who fall victim to *murder, terrorism, genocide,* disaster, or accident. How can people do such things to each other? In this chapter we consider deaths that stun and enrage, deaths that increase our fear of disorder and vulnerability. Violent deaths of human origin traditionally are separated into such categories as murder, infanticide, war, genocide, and terrorism. Other catastrophic events are labeled as accidents and disasters. The distinctions are not always that clear-cut, however. One person's terrorism, for example, might be another person's legitimate war. An accident might have been set up by negligence and disregard for safety.

It is painful to reflect on the tragedies encompassed by this chapter, but we would learn nothing by turning away. Consider, for example, the events already mentioned.

Tysann Celestain still did not die, so she cut her wrist, crawled out a window, and trudged through the snow to a garage where, huddling in the cold, she was found by the police. She explained that she had intended to kill herself because her life had become hopeless. Her daughter would be left without a mother in this mean-spirited world, so the best thing she could do for Jaylyn was to spare her a life as miserable as her own. Many child murders are committed by desperate parents who felt unable to protect themselves from the misfortunes of life, and even less able to do so for their children.

Alt & Wells (2010) identify many motives and influences in child murder, though the belief that it is in the child's best interests often is part of the decision.

Who kills? The media offers several compelling images, e.g., one criminal blasting away another in a drug deal gone wrong, a hotheaded young man with a gun and a grudge, a spouse who has been abused one time too many. Websdale (2010) finds that entire families are sometimes murdered coldly and systematically by one of their own quiet, respectable members (most often a parent). These are deliberate killings, sometimes planned down to the smallest details. The public is often shocked and shaken by these lethal outbursts from a "good citizen."

Oh, that sixteenth century! The Spanish monarchy was well along in its quest to conquer lands and peoples from Italy to Africa, and from the Philippines to South, Central, and North America. It was their divine right—indeed, their responsibility to do so. They brandished the One True Religion, and their ships could hold vast acquisitions of gold and other valuables. Burning alive 15 unarmed Indians was but one episode in one expedition—that of Francisco Vázquez de Coronado. He was under direct orders from the king to engage in no improper acts such as murder, plundering, and enslavement. All of these improper acts did occur—frequently, although perhaps less so than in earlier, even bloodier expeditions. Flint's (2002) commentary and translation of eyewitness reports exposes a radical split in the monarchy's worldview. Many leaders and their mercenary soldiers committed atrocities as part of their standard operating procedure. Yet the devout king and his palace administrators valued the idea that the subjected people would be well treated and welcomed to the faith. And so history has preserved remarkably candid and compassionate reports from padres who witnessed but were unable to prevent the atrocities. The same campaign bred greed and atrocity, but also uncompromising witness and censure.

Hatun Surucu was the victim of an *honor killing*. It is estimated by the United Nations that more than 5,000 such murders occur each year (Lederer, 2007). Who are the victims? Always females. Who are the killers? Members of their own family. Why? Because the sister, daughter, wife or mother was accused or suspected of bringing shame on the family. These murders take place within cultural traditions that severely constrain the rights and opportunities of women. This practice is so deeply entrenched and widespread that United Nations Secretary-General Ban Ki-moon has urged that all nations end the pandemic of violence against girls and women. Most nations have passed laws against beatings and sexual attacks as well as honor killings, but often the crimes continue and are not prosecuted. According to the U.N. leader, violence against women is

> tolerated under the fallacious cover of cultural practices and norms, within the walls of the home. Or it is used as a weapon in armed conflict, condoned through tacit silence and passivity by the state and the law enforcement community (Lederer, op. cit., p. A-13).

Constant surveillance, forced marriages, abduction, false imprisonment, and genital mutilation are often part of the pattern within which honor killings occur. Suicides are also part of the pattern. Shafiliea swallowed bleach after being kidnapped, forced to marry a chosen husband who, along with his entire family, exploited and abused her. It is possible that this was a combined suicide/murder because she dared complain about her treatment (Payton, 2008b). Torpekay, also pressed into forced marriage and a life of abuse, poured gasoline on herself and set herself on fire. She did survive that agonizing attempt (Payton, 2008b). Some of the most horrific in-family murders have more to do with money than with even a stretched concept of honor. Reports from India continue to describe "dowry killings" that are

> so common that there is even a commonly used term for the phenomenon, "bride burning," because many newly wed women die from being doused with kerosene and set on fire. The husband's family then reports the death as a "kitchen accident (Chu, 2007, p. A-26).

Hatun had won a divorce from her forced marriage at age 16. She had stopped wearing a headscarf, was now training to become an electrician, and was dating a German man. Her 18-year-old brother killed her for having a boyfriend, and bragged to his girlfriend about what he'd done. (Because this crime occurred in a "too Western" nation, the brother was convicted and imprisoned.)

Honor killings and other abuses against women invoke long-standing questions about moral relativism. Should all cultural practices be tolerated and accepted? And, if so, who should make the adjustment: the Western nation into which honor killing has been imported, or the female-as-property practitioners when they relocate themselves into an equalitarian country? Or are there basic human rights that should be protected in all cultures?

For many of us, *Darfur* was an unfamiliar name that we might have had difficulty locating on a map. Kristof (2004a, September 11) challenged us to witness the horrendous results of genocide in a distant land. How many have died of violence, starvation, and untended disease in the Darfur area of Sudan? Nobody will ever know for sure, but 200,000 is often the estimate. *Genocide* is a term introduced by Raphael Lemkin (1944) when he escaped from Nazi Germany. *Genos* is a Greek word signifying race or tribe. The Latin suffix *cide* signifies killing. Genocide therefore refers to the deliberate and systematic destruction of an ethnic or racial group or a nation. The Darfur massacre fits this definition. Janjaweed mercenaries massacred the inhabitants of this fertile area of Sudan so they could appropriate their property. The invaders' merciless assault was intensified by their beliefs that the black African inhabitants could be destroyed with impunity because they were regarded both as an inferior race and as people who did not share their religious faith. Rape, disfiguration, and slaughter were commonplace. Violence against women was an especially merciless component of the onslaught. Astoundingly, in a return visit, Kristof discovered that the two widows and their surviving children he had found under adjoining trees were still alive, had become close friends, and were recovering in a United Nations refugee camp (Kristof, 2004, October 16).

Are road traffic crashes "accidents?" The World Health Organization believes otherwise. Their statistics indicate that traffic injuries are the leading cause of death for people between the ages of 10 and 24—worldwide (Brown, 2007)! These deaths are still classified as accidents in standard mortality reports. Nevertheless, WHO experts hesitate to speak of an "accident" when the risk of injury and death has been heightened by environmental circumstance and/or public attitudes. The death toll among the young is especially high in developing countries in which many roads and vehicles are unsafe, and prosecution for speeders and drunken drivers minimal. Motorcyclists, operating often without helmets, are particularly vulnerable in both developed and developing nations. Improvements in public education—for pedestrians as well as motorists—and a higher priority for road safety could sharply reduce the death toll.

Sometimes it is nature that threatens peaceful lives with sudden and violent death. The *tsunami* that devastated coastal areas of southern Asia on December 26, 2004, is thought to have resulted in more than 175,000 deaths. The village of Galbokka was in an area of Sri Lanka that was engulfed by the massive wave. The people of Galbokka, however, escaped the fate of most other settlements. Victor Desosa, its headman, immediately noticed the strange behavior of the ocean and remembered having seen a similar situation many years previously while a merchant marine. He hooted and shouted to his people: "Go! Go!" The inhabitants of Galbokka and neighboring towns scrambled uphill—just before a 20-foot wall of water smashed into their village. Approximately 5,000 people were in danger, yet only one person died. The Haiti earthquake of January 12, 2010, resulted in an estimated 23,000 deaths, along with catastrophic destruction. Here, there was even less warning and opportunity to escape.

In recent years, there has been progress in understanding natural disasters and developing ways to prevent, or at least reduce, death and destruction. Disaster preparedness is becoming a significant facet of the death system.

The nation was shocked in 1999 when four students and a teacher were massacred by two students at Columbine High School in Littleton, Colorado. The students' plan could have resulted in many more deaths, including those of police officers and other rescuers (Meloy, Hempel, Mohandie, Shiva, & Gray, 2001). This violent episode lit a fuse on other high school campuses in various parts of the nation. The 16-year-old with a list of 53 fellow students he wanted to kill was taken very seriously by authorities. A few months later, another Arizona high school student was taken into custody after she prepared a detailed plan to kill teachers and security guards. Rifles, semiautomatic pistols, and boxes of ammunition were found in her home. The girl had a history of self-mutilation and suicidal thought (Davis, 2005). Mass murder on campus erupted again on April 16, 2007, when a sophomore biology major at Virginia Tech University shot 32 students and teachers before killing himself. Cho Seung-Hui was later described as a loner with eccentric habits whose occasional statements were hard to understand (Thomas, 2007). This explosion of violence was followed by grief and vulnerability. Blame was quickly leveled (justified or not) at law enforcement, university authorities, the ready availability of guns for mentally disturbed people, and the mental health system.

We are ready now to consider death by violence more systematically. We begin with murder, then continue to war, genocide, terrorism, disaster, and accident. Along the way, we will learn not only about violent death but also about some characteristics of the society in which we live.

MURDER

One brother kills the other. Something about who should be the favorite. Or something about the expression of pure evil against an innocent.

Or perhaps something about competition between farmers and herdsmen. Again, the root cause may have been the parent's inability to moderate the sibling rivalry: it had to end in violence. Whatever the preferred explanation, Qayin's (Cain's) murder of Havel (Abel) is the first but by no means the last homicide described in the Bible. Both the Old and New Testaments tell of violent endings at the hands of family as well as enemies. Sounding a note of caution, Rudoff and Esselstyn (2000) comment that if all the killings actually happened, there would have been no Palestine, Israel, or Judah. Furthermore, the most prominent murders, such as Abel by Cain, are used as lessons in morality. Nevertheless, murder has been common enough through human history, well beyond the pages of the Bible. Along with the achievements of many cultures, we also inherit a formidable rap sheet: we are the usual suspects.

A person who takes the life of another has committed homicide. It becomes murder if a court rules the killing intentional and unlawful. All murders are homicides; some homicides are murders. You may have committed "justifiable homicide" if you used lethal force to protect your own life; or you may be guilty of "negligent homicide" if your carelessness resulted in the death of another person. "Manslaughter" is another distinction used in the criminal justice system when a person is accused of contributing to a death without intending to have done so. For the purposes of this chapter, however, we will use the simplest and most direct word, murder.

Murder: The Statistical Picture

A college student from a Middle Eastern nation confided to me that on his first visit to the United States he had locked himself inside his Chicago hotel room. Why? "We loved American movies, but people were always getting shot or blown up. I wanted to come to America, but I didn't want to get killed." He soon discovered that the United States is not nearly as violent as portrayed in some of its most popular movies. Nevertheless, he had chosen to study in the nation with possibly the highest murder rate in the Western world. (Vital statistics are either unavailable or unreliable for some nations.) Who are the killers in the United States? Who are the victims, and what are the trends? Unless otherwise noted, our

data are based on the most recent available comprehensive information provided by the Bureau of Justice Statistics of the U. S. Department of Justice (2008):

- In 1950 the murder rate was 4.0 per 100,000 in the population. By 1980 the rate had soared to 10.2, the all-time high. The rate started to dip in 1995. The rate declined even more sharply as we moved into the twenty-first century. By 2002 there was a remarkable further drop to 5.6 (although there were still more than 16,000 homicides at that level). This decline was variously attributed to a healthy economy, more efficient police work, and a slightly smaller percentage of young males in the population. The murder rate and violent crime in general have continued to decline, despite the recession (FBI, 2010). This seems to break from the usual pattern of economic downturn and violent crime. Some experts suggest that it's because unemployment is keeping people at home and therefore out of trouble. (I don't know about that!)
- Firearms (especially handguns) are used in about two of every three homicides. Knives are the next most common weapons. The pattern of weapon use has remained about the same in recent years. Teenage killers are particularly likely to use a gun.
- Southern states continue to have the highest homicide rates, the northeastern states the lowest. Metropolitan areas consistently have higher murder rates than smaller cities and rural counties. Drug and gang-related activities are more common in large cities and are responsible for many of the homicides. The risk of murder often varies markedly within the same state and even within the same community. People living in impoverished areas are more likely to be victims of crime, including murder. For the U.S. cities with the highest and lowest murder rates, see Table 8-1.
- Men are most often both the killers and the victims. When a female is the victim, the murderer is male in 9 of 10 cases. When the victim is male, the killer is male in 8 of 10 cases. About three of every four murder victims is male.
- People between the ages of 25 and 44 are most at risk to become a murder victim. Racial differences do exist: homicide victimization rates

TABLE 8-1 *Murder and the City*

U.S cities with the highest and lowest murder rates (per 100,000 population)

Highest		Lowest	
New Orleans	63.6	Lincoln, Nebraska	1.8
St. Louis	46.9	Chandler, Arizona	2.0
Baltimore	36.9	Honolulu	2.0
Detroit	33.8	Henderson, Nebraska	2.3
Washington, D.C.	314	El Paso	2.8

Source: FBI (2008) gov/fbi/data.

for blacks are six times higher than for whites, most overrepresented in drug-related deaths, though less often as victims of sexual assault or workplace killings.

- Murders most often are committed by killers who are of the same race as the victims. This fact is worth emphasizing because interracial murders often arouse more fear and anger.
- At least three of five murders are committed by people who are relatives, lovers, friends, neighbors, or colleagues of the victims. The media tends to spotlight killings by strangers, but the killer and the victim are usually acquaintances, relatives or intimate companions. Homicides classified as "intimate," "family," "infanticide," and "eldercide" are much more common in large cities (Bureau of Justice Statistics, 2008).
- Murder has become the leading cause of death for women in the workplace. Men are usually the killers. Some observers believe that male insecurity and rage may be intensified by increasing competition from women, especially during a time of high unemployment. Another possibility is that the workplace has become more dangerous for everybody because of the overall social climate of violence and ready access to firearms. Both men and women can become frustrated and angry in a variety of workplace situations, but men are more likely to respond with a lethal outburst.

Patterns of Murder in the United States

A man with a long criminal record ambushes and executes another criminal; this was his day's work. Another man nervously attempts his first holdup. Something goes wrong and he fires his gun at the clerk, then flees in panic. After a bout of drinking, a rejected lover breaks in upon the woman, her children, and her new friend. He sprays the room with bullets from a semiautomatic rifle. A deranged woman strangles her child to obey the voices in her head. She then attempts to take her own life. There is no one explanation for murder. It is more useful to look at some of the specific patterns that murder takes in the United States. We will examine (1) violence and abuse in the home, involving spouse, children, or parents as victims; (2) young men's use of guns, including use in school shootings; (3) mass and serial killers; and (4) political murders (assassinations).

Domestic Violence Law enforcement officers are well aware that they themselves are at peril when they respond to calls about a family disturbance. Fortunately, fewer officers have lost their lives since improvements in tactical and communicational training, and the use of bulletproof vests (Batton & Wilson, 2006). Nevertheless, many police officers are stressed by their encounters with violence (Henry, 2004). Their anxiety and grief may persist long after the events:

> I knew I had to make the notification, and that was the hardest notification of my life because I knew this was an innocent victim. . . . and I said to [my partner], "Man, I don't want to do this." As I'm walking in I didn't know what I was going to say, and I said a prayer. Unrehearsed I took her [the mother's] hand and I said, "Do you believe in God?" "Yes." "Sit down." I'm holding her hand and she started to shake and I started to shake and I said, "What I'm about to tell you is the worst thing you can tell a mother." She picked up an ashtray and threw it across the room and shattered a mirror. She went crazy. She was hugging me and crying, "Is she dead" Is she dead?" I said, "Yes" (p. 236).

In domestic violence, the killer is usually a man, whether the murder develops from a domestic or criminal situation. Wives are the most common victims of intrafamilial killings, followed by husbands, sons, daughters, fathers, brothers, mothers, and sisters.

Men and Women Who Kill Their Partners Many women are subjected to repeated abuse and violence from their male partners (Gracia, 2004). More than a thousand women are killed each month, even if they had previously sought help from the police or the courts. Often the police had been called to the home on previous occasions. Unfortunately, battered women who resist abuse or fight back are more likely to be killed than those who suffer in silence (Ewing, 1997). Ewing adds that:

> control is the ultimate issue in most of these relationships. Batterers have an obsessive if not a pathological need to control the lives of the women with whom they share intimate relationships (p. 22).

Cultural traditions have given men enormous latitude for controlling the lives of their wives and children. Wife beating was seldom treated as a criminal offense through the long years when women were required to abide by their husbands' decisions and denied the right to vote or own property. There are women today who remember when they were refused a credit card unless it was registered in the name of husband or father—even though they were themselves employed. The approximately 1.5 million physical assaults upon women by their male partners are part of a lingering tradition of male dominance with few consequences for abusive behavior. Women may also kill, however, especially when they have suffered long-term humiliation, abuse, and injury at the hands of a man.

> "I'm going to kill you, you bitch. I'm going to kill you this night!" Bella ran from side to side in the room, but couldn't get to the door because Isaac had blocked it off. Isaac forced her into a corner, holding her up with a hand in her hair, and began hitting her repeatedly with his fist. Bella could hear the children screaming and kept crying to get them help. She was sure Isaac would kill her if no one intervened. Then he began to bang her head against the wall. Bella was too dizzy to resist anymore, and just hung on. The attack ended a few minutes later when a relative stopped by and restrained him (Browne, 1987, pp. 61–62).

This violent episode is typical of many others experienced by the battered women in Angela Browne's pioneering study. The rages were often sudden, unprovoked, and savage. Many women described their husbands as having become entirely different people during the assaults (e.g., "He'd get a look in his eyes and start to breathe differently . . . ." "It was like dealing with a stranger." In Bella's case, she endured 20 years of severe abuse until one night Isaac threatened to kill their oldest daughter when she came home. Isaac fell asleep first, however, and Bella and another daughter shot him and then set the house on fire. Although permanently disabled as a result of the repeated attacks, Bella was found guilty of murder in the first degree and sentenced to life in prison.

Legal protection and social support for battered women is still a work in progress in the United States (Zink, Elder, Jacobson, & Klosterman, 2004). There is more public awareness, peer support, and shelters, though often not enough to meet the need. A significant development in Israel offers a possible model for implementation in the U.S. and elsewhere. The highly publicized case of a wife killing her husband after many years of physical and psychological abuse led to the passage of a law that differs from the standard pattern in Western countries (Herzog, 2006). Judges now have the right to impose a more lenient penalty when a person who suffers prolonged abuse by a domestic partner takes that partner's life. This consequential change in the justice system was strongly influenced by the society's condemnation of spousal abuse.

People Who Kill Children A grade school teacher may have been speaking for many others when she told me:

> We don't want to notice. We don't want to suspect. We don't want to believe . . . But we have to notice, we have to suspect, and, more and more we have to believe that this child is being very badly mistreated and is at risk for . . . everything, including death. Including death.

It is no longer unusual to find police officers on the pediatric unit of a hospital. They have been called by a physician or nurse who recognizes a young child's injuries as being the results of abuse (beating, shaking, burning, throwing against a wall or down a flight of stairs) or neglect (starvation,

Child abuse and neglect sometimes ends only with death, a pattern that has become all too familiar to social workers, and health care providers.

dehydration, lack of physical care). From a nurse on a unit devoted to the care of infants:

> The worst thing is that it happens at all. The next worst thing is that it is becoming almost routine. You see this incredibly beautiful baby. And you see what has happened to it. And you know that even though the baby makes it through this time, you know there very likely will be a next time. Some cases, as soon as we have our first look, we're on the phone to the police. Let me tell you, they hate it, too, maybe as much as we do.

Most observers attribute the rising abuse and murder of children to dysfunctional families. The inability of families to care for their children is in turn attributed to such factors as unemployment, alcohol and drug use, and the abandonment of mothers and children by the father. Most infant/child homicides occur at home, using weapons of opportunity that include household objects. The killers are usually parents or other caregivers. African American children are at significantly higher risk

(Bennett, Hall, Frazier, Patel, Barker, & Shaw, 2006). There are at least three additional factors:

Lack of parenting skills. Many people who become threats to their own children have themselves had little opportunity to learn how to be caring and effective parents. Fortunately, these same people often are motivated to improve their parenting skills when given the opportunity through education and counseling.

Mental disorders. Postpartum psychosis is often involved in the murder of infants by their mothers. Male as well as female adults can have mood swings and impulse-control deficits that lead to violent acts against their children.

The replacement father syndrome. This is my name for a situation that is responsible for many instances of severe and repeated child abuse, all too often with a fatal outcome. A woman is left to cope alone with her children. She takes a new lover. For this man, the children are just in the way, unwanted distractions and responsibilities. In a surprisingly high number of instances, the man is set off by the infant's crying or young child's "disobedience." But there is something else here as well: There is an impulse to destroy the children of the previous husband or lover. During an episode of stress or alcohol- or drug-clouded thinking, the new lover attacks the child or children. These attacks may also be premeditated and carried out in a deliberate way—sometimes with the passive acceptance, or even the cooperation of, the woman who does not want to lose her new man.

Neonaticide (the killing of a newborn baby) requires special attention. Most women who commit this act are young, white, unmarried, uneducated, and poor. They have very little in the way of social support and are suffering from depression. Sometimes they conceal their pregnancy from others until the last moment. Usually they have made no plans for either the birth or the care of the child—they are simply overwhelmed and trying to make the problem go away, and do not expect anyone to help them. Most of these young women do not feel sufficiently connected to society to explore the alternative of adoption. Some young women in this predicament do leave the baby at a clinic or child care center. However, many of the unwanted infants are placed in a plastic bag and tossed in a trash or garbage bin to lessen the chance of a connection being made with the mother, and because the symbolism of trash and garbage resonates with the young woman's own feelings of worthlessness and horror.

Children Who Kill Parents Each year, about 300 parents are killed by their children in the United States. *Parricides* are much more often committed by sons than daughters (Moeller, 2001), and by adolescents rather than younger children. The overall pattern:

- Most of the murdered parents and stepparents are white and non-Hispanic.
- The victims are usually in their late 40s or 50s.
- Most of the killers are white, non-Hispanic males.
- Most of the juveniles who kill their parents had been victims of severe abuse by those parents.

Characteristics of adolescents who kill their parents are listed in Box 8-1.

It has often been observed that abuse and violence beget more abuse and violence. This proposition has been well documented in the study of parricide.

Young Men with Guns

The guns that kill are almost always in the hands of men, and most of the men are young. The role of the murderer has been passing to even younger

---

BOX 8-1

ADOLESCENTS WHO KILL THEIR PARENTS

1. A pattern of family violence
2. Failed efforts by the adolescents to get help
3. Failed efforts by the adolescents to escape from the family situation
4. Isolation and few social outlets
5. A family situation that became increasingly intolerable
6. Increasing feelings of helplessness
7. Inability to cope with increasing stress, leading to a loss of self-control
8. Little or no previous involvement with the criminal justice system
9. Ready availability of a gun
10. Alcohol abuse and/or alcoholism in the home
11. Evidence that the adolescent may have been in a dissociative state at or near the time of the killing
12. Evidence that the adolescent offender and other family members felt relieved by the victim's death.

Source: Moeller (2001).

men in recent years: those of ages 15–24 now have the highest rate of committing homicides—as well as the highest rate for becoming a victim of homicide. Nine out of 10 law enforcement officers who are killed in the line of duty are victims of guns in the hands of young men.

Many killings occur during drug-related transactions; others occur as part of gang rivalries. The public tends to pay less attention to these deaths than to murders that seem to be casual, random, and unpredictable. The belief that such killings are becoming more common has contributed to the present state of anxiety in which schools, public offices, merchants, and private individuals feel the need for increased security—a need that has resulted in more purchases of guns for self-protection.

Drive-by shootings have been responsible for much fear and grief. Law enforcement agencies generally have not tracked drive-by shootings as a special class of crime. Many of these episodes are gang-related, and not a few include the use of alcohol or other drugs. Substance-impaired judgment, however, is not enough to account for such attacks on people unknown to the men holding the guns. How, then, can we understand these incidents?

Consider the following hypotheses:

1. Young males who engage in drive-by and other forms of gun violence have not developed a sense of identification with the human race at large. There is little awareness of how others think and feel, little empathy. In their own lives they might have been treated without understanding and compassion.
2. Peer acceptance, important for most young adults, is a dominating motivation when plans and prospects for the future seem bleak. "I had no idea of who I could really be," recalls a former member of a violent gang. "So I did for today and waited to get dead."
3. Guns—and automobiles—provide remote devices for dealing death. One can be a "man" by killing another human being as easily as one operates a remote control for the television set.

Every generation known to history has faced the challenge of socializing its young males and

directing their spirit and energies into constructive uses. Our generation certainly has its work cut out for it.

School Shootings

In recent years there has been a marked increase in the fear of lethal violence on campuses, from middle school to university. Security concerns now compete for attention and funding with the basic educational mission. Many students, parents, and educators sense that schools are losing their special place in the community. Threat and disorder seem to have less respect for the school zone. The protective response to this perceived threat also could have its effects. Chances are that your local school boards and law enforcement agencies have been considering ways of strengthening security, while some members of the community resist measures that might induce an atmosphere of excessive control. The school campus is becoming a microcosm of U.S. society at large since 9/11. What should be the priority of homeland security as compared with continuing to live as expected and desired?

There is a need to sort out realistic concern from excessive fear. David Altheide's *Creating Fear: News and the Construction of Crisis* (2002) and *Terrorism and the Politics of Fear* (2006) describe how the media manipulates our emotions when a possible threat emerges. Fear, once unleashed and guided by mass media and political interest, can become self-sustaining and dominant. But there is also another side to the media coverage, which now is strongly abetted through Internet postings. Students who feel rejected, mistreated, and misunderstood have the temptation to make themselves "somebody" through an act of violence.

The ready availability of guns and recipes for bomb making has opened a dangerous avenue of expression for grievances. Furthermore, the victims are no longer limited to a particular person who is perceived as having mocked and rejected the killers. A pair of angry adolescents might choose an entire set of fellow students (e.g., athletes, people of a different race) or just let loose on anybody unfortunate enough to be on the scene. One "quiet kid, pretty much like the others" might bring a rifle and a backup pistol to school one day and fire at his classmates. But why?

- Killing has gained more acceptance as a way of solving problems. This belief flourishes in the media and popular culture, with particular attraction for young males. Killing of self or others has often been regarded as the "manly" response to insult and stress. Manhood and guns can have a powerful emotional linkage. The higher rate of male suicide is related to the lethality of the most frequently chosen method—guns. Students who plan or carry out school shootings often intend to complete the death work by turning their guns on themselves.

- There is no other way to deal with rejection, frustration, and loss. This belief is mistaken. Nevertheless, some teenagers become killers because they have not yet learned other ways to deal with a threat to their relationship with their girlfriends, schoolmates, or teachers. The thought process is therefore likely to be reduced to the fatal either/or: "Either she comes back to me or I have to kill—somebody, maybe everybody." A 15-year-old arrested for killing his parents and two classmates and wounding 20 others explained: "I had no other choice." Take frustration, inexperience, and oversimplified thought processes and add the availability of weapons—the potential for a lethal outcome is there.

- The world is divided between Us and Them (or just Me and All of You). Anybody who has survived adolescence is likely to remember the "in groups," the students who seemed to get all the attention and all the breaks. Even people who were among the most popular students later report that they often suffered from feelings of uncertainty, anxiety, and being left out. Furthermore, all the prejudices that have been nurtured in society have the opportunity to play themselves out in the high school years. The Columbine High School shootings, for example, had a racist component that has been associated with the influence of skinhead organizations. There are always others to blame and attack when things go wrong in one's own life.

A neglected question: why do so many students *not* turn to violence when they are angry, frustrated, and depressed? What in themselves, their families, the schools, and the communities serves as protection and alternative? Improved identification and cultivation of positive self-esteem potential and community resources could provided significant protection against outbursts of lethal violence.

Mass and Serial Killers: Who Are They and Why Do They Do It?

The *mass killer* is alarming to society both because of the many lives destroyed and because his very existence confounds our expectations of human feeling and conduct. A mass killing is one in which several people die in a single episode. Typically, mass murders in the United States involve firearms and are the work of a lone killer (a male); most involve firearms. Most often, the killer knows few if any of his victims. He may have wanted to get back at a particular person but had no compunction about slaying others as well. As with the school shootings, mass murderers in general often have a strong suicidal streak, willing even to die at the scene of their crimes. This is in contrast to most *serial killers*, who intend to keep on killing as long as they can.

The public perception of the mass murderer has generally proved to be accurate—a person who feels rejected by society, angry at real or imagined mistreatment, and motivated to "get back" at all that has oppressed him. James Oliver Huberty personifies this description. He had lost his long-time job as a skilled worker when the plant had to be downsized. He moved to another state, found another job, but lost it. Over the years, he had often practiced shooting his rifles into the basement wall and occasionally frightened his neighbors by brandishing a weapon. One afternoon he told his wife he was going to "hunt humans." She assumed that James was just trying to get her upset again. He kissed her good-bye and walked back to the McDonald's where he and his family had lunched a few hours earlier. He opened fire, killing 21 and wounding another 19 before he was felled by a police sharpshooter.

Some mass murderers are psychotic, but most psychotic people do not become mass murderers. In general, mass murderers and serial

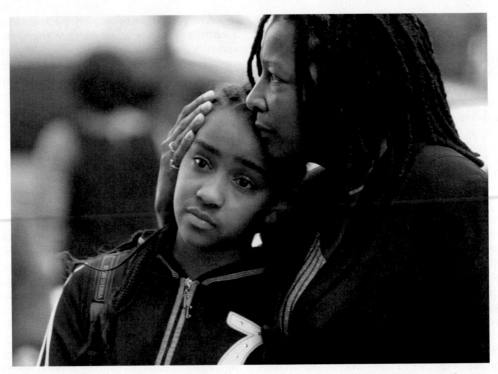

A mother comforts her daughter after one of the D.C.—area sniper killings that targeted people at random.

killers do not attract much attention until they are apprehended or shot. Others have little sense of their own identities and are willing to become disciples of a charismatic person—such was the situation with Charles Manson and several of his followers. Their mass killing episodes may also be compared with the hate group dynamics expressed by Nazis and emulated by others. Rarely is the mass murderer a hardened criminal, although a spotty history of property crime is common (Fox & Levin, 2001). The killings sometimes follow a period of frustration when a particular event triggers sudden rage; yet, in other cases, the killer is coolly pursuing some goal he cannot otherwise attain.

The mass murderer is typically a white male in his late 20s or 30s. However, media coverage through the years underestimated the frequency of African American serial killers. Walsh (2005) examined United States homicide data from 1945 to 2004. He found that 90 of the 413 serial killers were African American. This translates to a two to one overrepresentation of African Americans among serial killers. Fear of being accused of racism is one possible reason for avoiding mention of African American serial killings, but Walsh suggests that the more significant factor is that the victims usually are African Americans as well—and, therefore, not as "newsworthy." A thorough reevaluation of the relationship between race and serial killing remains to be done.

Several additional facts about mass killers are worth keeping in mind:

1. Mass killers do not draw their violence from the Southern tradition of homicide, although homicide is most common there. It is possible Southerners have continued to provide more support for each other through neighborhoods, churches, and other community organizations, thereby reducing the sense of alienation that can lead to violence against others.

2. Boom cities attract many people whose high hopes fail to be fulfilled. They become bitter, disillusioned, and ready to try something different to get rid of their frustrations and anger (as was the case with Huberty).

3. Most mass murderers are not psychotic but have an antisocial personality (also known as "sociopath" or "psychopath"). This type of killer does not hear voices that order him to kill. The antisocial personality does not feel affection or empathy for other people. This is the person who uses other people without remorse. The antisocial personality is likely to have a low tolerance for frustration and to explode in rage when things go wrong.

Nineteenth-century London's "Jack the Ripper" was a male who chose women for his victims. Prostitutes have long been at special risk for serial killing. Other serial killers, however, have attacked children or hospital patients, while others have selected almost any available target. Female serial killers come to attention less often because they use poison and other "quiet" methods and often have a financial motive (Hickey, 2005).

It is probable that the most lethal serial killer in U.S. history was an opportunistic physician who was active in Chicago just a few years after the depredations of Jack the Ripper in London. H. H. Holmes was skillful in attracting lonely women, gaining access to their sexual favors and funds, then making them disappear in the bustling chaos surrounding the 1893 Chicago World's Fair (Larson, 2004). When Holmes was through with a woman, he most often tricked her into entering a gas chamber he had constructed in his hotel. He would then dispose of the woman's remains in another unit not often found in hotels: a crematorium. He might have killed a hundred women—or twice or three times that number—before being apprehended. His persona as a charming and considerate physician concealed a person who believed that other people existed only to serve his needs.

Experts caution against reducing all serial killers to a single stereotype. Selerian (2002) notes that "serial killer" is not a medical diagnosis or scientific concept: it only refers to a person who murders repeatedly. Some serial killers are delusional, others are sexual predators, and still others experience periodic impulses to hunt and kill. There often are early warning signs, however. The child who takes pleasure in tormenting animals could be on the watch list for future serial killers.

Political Murder: Assassination in the United States

Abraham Lincoln, John F. Kennedy, Robert F. Kennedy, and Martin Luther King, Jr.—the *assassinations* of these four leaders are a disturbing part of American history. The murder of a political leader has both its private and its public side. A child loses a father, and a wife her husband. Mental illness accounts for only some of the assassination attempts. Some of the most prominent political assassinations and assassination attempts in the United States are listed in Table 8-2.

The public stereotype of the crazed assassin is represented by the men who threatened the lives of Andrew Jackson, James Garfield, and Theodore Roosevelt. These people were delusional. Guiteau, for example, had a friendly attitude toward Garfield but convinced himself that the president must be killed to "save the Republic." He would later say that God had made him do it. The recent assassination attempt in Tucson (January 8, 2011) that wounded Arizona Congresswoman Gabriele Giffords and killed six bystanders was made by a young man later determined to have been incompetent to defend himself on trial because of his paranoid schizophrenia.

Other assassins were extremists motivated by political objectives. Booth, Collazo, Torresola, and Sirhan identified themselves with nationalistic causes. Czolgosz thought that by killing McKinley he would be striking a blow for "the good working people." None of these men were insane (within a legal framework) or psychotic (within a psychiatric framework).

The antisocial personalities include Bremer, Byck, and Zangara. Unable to express feelings other than helplessness or rage, they cast about for a symbolic target. They did not have personal animosity toward their intended victims. Like the mass murderers, they showed assassins showed no remorse. Although not all mass murderers are "crazy," each has a fundamental character flaw in the ability to feel and express ordinary human feeling.

TABLE 8-2 *Political Assassination Attempts, United States*

Year	Intended Victim	Assassin	Outcome
1835	Andrew Jackson	Richard Lawrence	Unharmed
1865	Abraham Lincoln	John Wilkes Booth	Killed
1881	James Garfield	Charles Guiteau	Killed
1901	William McKinley	Leon Czolgosz	Killed
1912	Theodore Roosevelt	John Schrank	Wounded
1933	Franklin Roosevelt	Giuseppe Zangara	Unharmed[a]
1935	Huey Long	Carl Weiss	Killed
1950	Harry S. Truman	Oscar Collazo & Griselio Torresola	Unharmed[b]
1963	John F. Kennedy	Lee Harvey Oswald	Killed
1968	Martin Luther King, Jr.	James Earl Ray	Killed
1968	Robert Kennedy	Sirhan Sirhan	Killed
1972	George Wallace	Arthur Bremer	Wounded
1974	Richard Nixon	Samuel Byck	Unharmed[c]
1975	Gerald Ford	Lynette Fromm	Unharmed
1975	Gerald Ford	Sara Moore	Unharmed
1981	Ronald Reagan	John W. Hinckley, Jr.	Wounded

Sources: Clarke (1982) and Crissman and Parkin (2002).
[a]Chicago Mayor Anton Cermak was killed and four others were wounded in the volley of shots fired at President Roosevelt.
[b]Security guards Leslie Coffelt and Joseph Downs were wounded; Coffelt died as he returned fire and killed Torresola.
[c]Byck killed two Delta pilots and wounded a cabin attendant in a failed attempt to crash the plane into the White House.

TERRORISM

Terrorism did not begin with the attacks of September 11, 2001. What did begin was a mixed sense of vulnerability, anxiety, grief, and rage that continues to this day. Once a rather distant concept—terrorism was something that happened sometimes to other people in other places—it now became salient in American life. A previous bombing of the New York's World Trade Center had killed six people and injured hundreds of others, but left the massive establishment intact. The explosion that killed 168 people and demolished the Alfred P. Murrah Federal Building in Oklahoma City on April 15, 1996, was an alarming event whose national impact was eventually reduced when it was learned that domestic rather than foreign terrorists were to blame. Then came 9/11. Here, we will size up terrorism at large and then discuss events and concerns in the United States.

Terrorism in History

Terrorism has a long and diverse history that can only be sampled here.

Suicidal Killers in the Middle East: The Originals The Assassins were members of an eleventh-century Middle Eastern religious sect devoted to bringing about a new millennium. They carried out expert terrorist operations for about 200 years. Disguising themselves and armed with hidden daggers, they killed powerful leaders and created a climate of terror. The Assassins expected to die as they completed their missions.

During this same period, Christian Crusaders fought for possession of the Holy Sepulchre (which actually no longer existed). The Crusaders were not primarily terrorists, but did abandon themselves to episodes of massacre and atrocity. For example, they slaughtered many of the inhabitants

A distinguished physician and journalist, Jean-Paul Marat was also a fanatic who sent many of his French compatriots to the guillotine during the reign of terror. His own blood joined the flow when he was assassinated in his bathtub. The artist, Jacque-Louis David, also signed many execution warrants.

of Jerusalem, including women and children. The Jews of this city, who had played no role in the hostilities, were herded into a *mosque* and burned alive. The Inquisition, established in 1231 by the Catholic Church, persecuted suspected heretics through much of Western Europe. Thousands were burned alive, and many others died under torture. The later Protestant version of religious persecution was no less deadly. Suspected Catholic priests and sympathizers were subjected to elaborate torture before execution. Many conquerors have used terror tactics to undermine the will to resist. Tamerlane, for example, buried thousands of his victims alive, and a Transylvanian ruler was known as Vlad the Impaler for that reason.

For the word *terrorism* itself, we must turn to the French Revolution. About 30,000 suspected "enemies of the people" were sent to the newly invented guillotine in 1793–1794. Robespierre believed that slicing off heads that contained politically incorrect thoughts would create a society of love and harmony. Like most other terrorist campaigns, it failed to achieve its objectives, and Robespierre himself went to the guillotine.

An enduring image of this reign of terror was created by the artist, Jacque-Louis David. The pale man drooping over the side of a wooden tub in the nearby image was a physician and the most influential French journalist of his time. He was also a fanatic who was not satisfied with the bloody work already in process: the beheading of members of the aristocracy. He insisted that all traitors be slaughtered—and Jean-Paul Marat would provide list after list. Panic ensued as anybody who was disliked by anybody else became at risk for the guillotine. Another keen advocate of the revolution was a young woman by the name of Charlotte Corday. She came to Paris, where she bought herself a green hat and a kitchen knife. Corday gained entrance to Marat on the pretext of having a fresh list of traitors for him. Marat assured her, "Don't worry, in a few days I will have them all guillotined." And then she stabbed him to death. It was Marat she considered the most vile traitor for turning the "Liberty, Equality, Fraternity" movement into a horror show. (And, yes, she was soon beheaded.) The great artist David had blood as well as paint on his hands: he himself had signed about 300 death warrants.

Terrorism remained afoot throughout the nineteenth century. For example, the Thugs (or Thuggees) of India robbed and strangled travelers. The Thugs regarded these killings as acts of religious devotion. Like many other terrorists, they professed to hold death in contempt.

Terrorism then, and terrorism now: it has a way of escaping everybody's control, no matter what its supposed original purpose and scope.

Home-Grown Terrorism in the United States The Ku Klux Klan (KKK) and the Molly Maguires exemplify terrorist groups that formed in the United States shortly before and after the War Between the States. Started in 1867, at first the KKK attempted to protect Southern whites from threats to their accustomed way of life. Before long, however, the KKK had become a terrorist organization intended to keep the freed African Americans "in their place." The KKK engaged in property destructions, threats, beatings, and lynchings. The KKK often had the support of the local establishment (or actually was the local establishment under its robes). Thousands of African Americans were lynched; however, the actual number cannot be determined, in large part because these murders usually were covered up and no records were kept. Historian Philip Dray (2003) observes that:

> Atrocities in isolated Southern backwaters often went completely unremarked upon, as did race-riot killings of blacks by mobs or police officers in cities. Almost every black American family has a story in its history of an ancestor who "come up missing," who vanished into that empty place— the rural crossroads or rail siding, the bayou or jail cell. It is a living memory to most black Americans that their forebears were lynched and routinely subjected to violence and intimidation, and that they lived in almost constant fear of seeing a loved one lynched or of being targeted themselves (p. xi).

The Molly Maguires first made themselves known in the 1860s as many Irish Americans faced oppressive and dangerous circumstances. Wakin (1984) describes one of these situations:

> In Pennsylvania, the oppressors were mine owners who brutalized the miners and their families. The miners went down into the dangerous hell of the mines, often with their children along, digging up wealth for the owners and a marginal living for themselves. New waves of immigrants enabled the owners to keep wages low; workers were forced to live in company houses and buy at company stores. Even while working, many a miner received, instead of his monthly pay, a "bobtail check" showing that he owed the company money (p. 147).

The Molly Maguires were victims turned terrorists. They threatened and beat mine owners, then used bombs to create an atmosphere of terror, killing several people they considered to be oppressors. Like many other organizations that resorted to terror, it failed to achieve its basic objectives. Nineteen of its own members were executed, and it would be many hard years before conditions for miners would be somewhat improved.

Terrorism and Genocide in the Twentieth Century and Beyond What will historians say about

A Cambodian survivor prays for Khmer Rouge victims in front of a map made from their skulls.

the recently elapsed twentieth century? One fact will be impossible to overlook: the infliction of deprivation, cruelty, and death upon millions of people. Never before were there so many victims of human violence. How many people died as a result of persecutions and massacres in the twentieth century? Twenty-five million deaths would be a conservative estimate (and does not include direct war casualties). Fanatic Khmer Rouge battalions slaughtered more than a million Cambodians in their attempt to impose a Communist reign on a traditional society. Stalin became the most blood-stained mass killer of all time when he supervised the massacre and starvation of 11 million of his own citizens in 1929–1932, and then took another 600,000 lives in the purge of 1937–1938. Haynes and Husan (2003) are not exaggerating when they depict twentieth-century Russia as "a century of state murder." In a supposedly "classless" Communist society, the people of the land were systematically persecuted and destroyed. During the partition of India in 1946,

Hindus and Sikhs moving east were slaughtered by Muslims, and Muslims moving west were slaughtered by Hindus and Sikhs: about a million died. A million!

The list goes on, each entry presenting its distinctive version of inhumanity. Japanese soldiers tortured, bayoneted, burned, and buried alive perhaps as many as 400,000 Chinese civilians in Nanking. Additionally, Japanese physicians and scientists conducted lethal experiments on Chinese civilians. *The Secret Genocide of Axis Japan's Germ Warfare Operation* is the subtitle of historian Daniel Barenblatt's (2003) disturbing book. Japanese Unit 731 tested methods of spreading man-made epidemics of anthrax, cholera, dysentery, and other pestilences. It is estimated that its biological warfare campaign killed about 600,000 people. Water supplies were contaminated and disease-bearing rats and fleas were released into the population. Survivors recall that smiling doctors also handed out contaminated food to hungry children.

In 1994, Hutu extremists in Rwanda conducted a systematic genocide campaign against their Tutsi countrymen. Death squads killed about 50,000 Tutsis in just a few days. Families were hacked to death with machetes or burned alive. It was estimated that about 300,000 died while the international community was "evaluating the situation." The most frequently cited programs of mass terrorism do not even include government-sponsored massacres in Pakistan and North Korea that have seemed to vanish from collective memory.

Numbers can be numbing. We can grasp and respond to the death of one person, to the death of a family, perhaps to the death of all occupants of a jetliner. It is much harder to grasp catastrophe in which the victims are numbered in thousands or in millions. Meet a survivor, though, and the reality starts to come through. For example, an aged woman in Arizona never forgot how her childhood and very nearly her life were destroyed when Turkey launched a campaign to eliminate its Armenian population. In her own neighborhood, the men were rounded up for "routine questioning" that turned out to be excruciating torture, followed by killing. She and her family barely managed to escape: about 800,000 other Armenian women, men, and children did not. Peter Balakian (2003) reminds us that most of the Armenian intellectual and cultural leaders were imprisoned, tortured, and killed in the capital city of Constantinople on one night (April 24, 1915). They could not believe such a thing could be happening to them.

As World War I raged, relatively little attention was given to the slaughter of civilians in Armenia. Unimpeded by international pressure or dissension in their own land, the Turks proceeded to massacre Syrians, Assyrian Christians, and Greeks as well. Adolph Hitler would later observe that the international community had barely seemed to these massacres; perhaps they wouldn't much care if he did the same with Jews, Romani (Gypsies), and other people who did not deserve to live.

It is not within the scope of this book to examine these events in detail. However, we can offer a few observations that are based securely upon the available evidence:

1. Terror has often been unleashed against people who share the same land, but are *perceived as different*. Most German Jews, for example, were law-abiding and patriotic. However, when Hitler pushed the anti-Semitism button, Germans who also happened to be Jewish were first ostracized, then slaughtered. Hindus, Sikhs, and Muslims alike had shared the hardships of drought, famine, and colonial subjugation, but the mutual perception that their religious differences were all-important led to widespread atrocities and killings during the partition of India and creation of Pakistan—and hostilities have again resumed.

2. Killing is often preceded by *denying the other person's fundamental reality as a human being*. In this sense, the murder takes place first in the mind. In his penetrating analysis of genocidal terror, Eric Weitz (2003) documents the connection with fallacious beliefs in racial or ethnic "purity" and equally fallacious interpretations of the post-Darwinian "survival of the fittest" doctrine. One superior race is truly human; the others are to be exploited or eliminated because they are flawed subhumans. Declare that a threat or crisis exists, and one's logical course is to destroy or enslave those unworthy Others.

3. *Fear kills.* Reigns of terror have often been triggered because those in power have feared overthrow. The Stalinist purge of 1937–1938, for example, was directed almost exclusively at Soviet citizens suspected of harboring politically unreliable thoughts. These regime-sponsored murders had the effect of seriously weakening Soviet military capabilities in advance of the Nazi invasion. An alleged plot against the government of Indonesia aroused fear-driven hysteria of such magnitude that 600,000 fellow citizens were slaughtered in a short period of time, most of them innocent of any crime or criminal intention.

4. *Cold-blooded "rationalism" kills.* There have been many episodes of terrorism in which the attackers were frenzied by high passions. However, some of the most destructive terrorist operations have been systematically planned as "rational" ways to achieve political objectives. Stalin again comes to mind with the systematic starvation, as well as murder, of millions of peasants who supposedly were to be liberated by the Communist revolution.

Liberating allied armies at the end of World War II were stunned to see evidence for themselves of the Nazi-perpetuated Holocaust that took the lives of millions of men, women, and children. General Dwight Eisenhower, commander of American forces, wept.

5. *Religious intolerance instigates and justifies terrorism.* Many people live harmoniously with people of other faiths. Nevertheless, some of the bloodiest reigns of terror have been launched by people who were convinced both that they alone have the true religion and that they therefore must convert or destroy all others. There is no hesitation, no reflection, no compassion. True believers often appear on both sides of religious/ethnic issues. For example, the "ethnic cleansing" in Kosovo drew much of its virulence from religious intolerance. The actual differences in religious belief and practice might seem insignificant when compared with what is held in common, but to the people involved it can be sufficient cause for bloodshed.

I have known mental patients who heard voices urging them to kill another person. They suffered terribly because they did not want to kill and yet could not stand the pressure—so they sought help. I have yet to learn of a religious cult that asked for help to rid itself of murderous impulses.

6. *Terrorism fails.* Seldom has a terrorist organization or movement achieved its objectives. The Nazis' "final solution," for example, was not only brutal to the extreme, but also contributed significantly to Germany's defeat. *Germany without Jews* (Engelmann, 1984) was a weakened nation, having lost many of its leading scientists, physicians, and other professionals. Furthermore, Germany was left with a heritage of guilt and shame over the

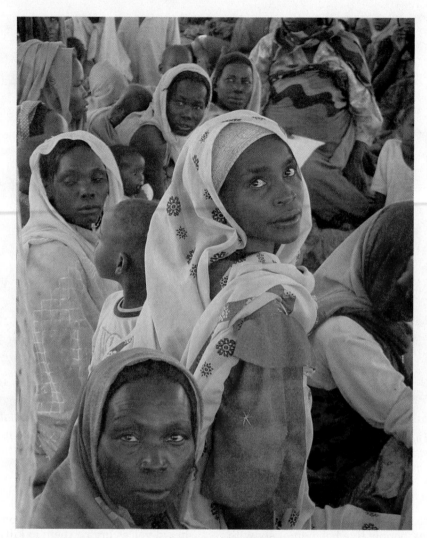

Thousands of people were massacred and thousands more succumbed to starvation and disease as they fled their homes in Darfur (Sudan).

participation of many people who became *Hitler's Willing Executioners* (Goldhagen, 1996). In an earlier epoch, an arrogant Spanish monarch banished the Moors who had been contributing much to the Spanish culture for centuries. The harsh conditions of this banishment led to a great many deaths. This "purification" or "ethnic cleansing" plan dealt Spain a self-inflicted blow from which it never recovered. Repeatedly, terrorism has failed to achieve lasting success; most often it has led to violent discord among the terrorists themselves, retaliation from others, and the loss of opportunities for improving one's conditions by positive efforts.

7. *Silence nurtures the expansion of terrorism and genocide.* Samantha Power has characterized genocide as "A problem from hell" in her disturbing (2002) examination of the muffled American response to mass violence

throughout the twentieth century. "Official knowledge, official silence" has been a recurrent theme. How much responsibility should one nation take for the horrors being inflicted in another land? How much responsibility, if any, should we have as individuals? What guidance should we draw from religious values? Ethical issues become matters of urgency whenever the specter of genocide arises.

9/11 AND ITS CONSEQUENCES

The transition to the twenty-first century brought no relief from terrorism and genocide. September 11, 2001, became a date that divides past and future in the United States. Commercial jets, hijacked by terrorists, crashed into the World Trade Center (WTC), the Pentagon, and a field in Shanksville, Pennsylvania. The death toll is given in Table 8-3.

The Day of the Attacks

That day, the sense of immunity from mass violence came to an abrupt end. Survivors, first responders, and witnesses quickly realized that things would never again be the same. The words of first responders to the World Trade Center attacks (Libaw & Goldman, 2002) express the shock when all that was solid and familiar suddenly dissolved. New York City fire captain Dennis Tadia: "It did happen, right? It's not something I'm going to close my eyes and open again and I'm going to see the tower again? It's not there." Jose Casaliggi, another member of the fire department, reports:

> You have two 110-story buildings. You don't find a desk, a chair, a phone, a computer. The biggest piece of a phone I found was half a keypad. The buildings are dust. How are we supposed to find people? (p. 2)

Witnesses of the World Trade Center attack were appalled as they watched people leap to their deaths rather than perish in flame and smoke. Firefighters who had experienced many previous disasters were overwhelmed by the sight and sound of bodies hitting the pavement.

TABLE 8-3 *Deaths from the Terrorist Attacks of 9/11*

	WTC	Pentagon	Shanksville
Jetliner	92	65	64
Ground	2,801	184	0
Total	**2,893**	**249**	**64**

The Japanese surprise attack on Pearl Harbor on December 7, 1941, had a powerful and enduring impact on American attitudes; the events of 9/11 had an even more profound effect. The casualties were mostly civilians, the destruction occurred on the mainland, the skyline of a great city was altered, and millions of people could watch the events on their television sets as they occurred. Smoke continued to rise from the World Trade Center disaster site (Ground Zero) for another six months, and body recovery efforts persisted long after hope of rescuing a live victim had vanished. The attack was also repeated in video reports on a daily basis, etching it into the consciousness of children as well as adults.

The valiant rescue effort earned worldwide respect and admiration. Nevertheless, chaos had won. Thousands had died. The towers had fallen. Death—raw, unpredictable, unfair—could still break loose in a society that had established so many levels of physical, symbolic, and ritualistic protections against mortal danger. We were not supposed to die young, violently, and in public, especially in a place where international commerce flourished. Our society's apparent victories over death anxiety had been snatched away in one morning of terror, to be replaced by a long wave of grief and stress that continues to this day.

The two other terrorist attacks of 9/11 were just as deadly to jetliner passengers and crew—all died. The fate of United Airlines Flight 93 differed from the other hijacked airliners. Modern communication technology—telephones in the sky—made it possible for some passengers and crew to learn of the two earlier attacks. Assaulting the hijackers, they prevented the airliner from completing its mission of destroying another major target and killing many more people on the ground. This disaster will long be remembered for the poignancy of the last telephone conversations between several passengers and their family members and the quick thinking and resolve with which they responded against the hijackers.

Immediate Response to the Loss and Trauma

Doctors and nurses rushed to New York City hospitals and clinics, and the call went out for blood donations. The health care system demonstrated its ability to overcome bureaucratic tangles and make its resources quickly available during a crisis. But where were the patients? Gradually, the almost unbelievable situation became clear: Those directly affected by the attack were beyond medical assistance. The absence of survivors merged with the silence at Ground Zero: All those active, lively people had vanished in just a few minutes.

Firefighters and other first responders had also expected to save people. There would be much exhausting labor and frustration before the volunteers were forced to conclude that there were no lives to be saved. There was another important objective to achieve, however: recovering and identifying the victims. It was recognized that the affected families could not put their lives back together until they had a sense of closure, which included a funeral and memorial service for the persons they had lost. The firefighters also felt strongly for their comrades who had not returned from the WTC; together they also had been a kind of family. The men and women searching through the debris developed their own spontaneous rituals when a body was found. All in the vicinity would pause in their work, kneel, and observe a moment of silence. Then—back to work. Eventually, memorial services were held for families who were left without the physical remains of their loved ones.

Memorial services and media coverage were exceptional in their recognition of individuals who lost their lives at all of the attack sites. At first, the high number of fatalities dominated national response. Soon, though, attention became focused on the individuality of the victims. The care taken to remember individuals probably served as a significant step in the long process of healing. Compassion arose not only throughout the United States but also throughout many other nations. Many people elsewhere had visited New York City or knew people who lived and worked there. The sorrow of bereaved family members resonated with the personal experiences of those who had experienced traumatic loss in their own lives.

Soon after the disaster, there was a perceptible increase in overt religiosity and patriotism. Churches reported higher attendance, and flags went on display throughout the nation. This large-scale emotional response to a large-scale disaster brings to mind the terror management theory of death anxiety that we considered in Chapter 1: arousal of individual death anxiety might prompt people to seek intensified support from the pillars of society.

The courage and determination of rescue workers inspired the public. First responders replaced celebrities as cultural heroes, recalling days past when volunteer firefighters were among the most admired people in society. A new generation now realized that there are "real-life" heroes among us.

The first phase of response was marked by sorrow and pain but also by a sense of national unity and compassion. It was a feeling-oriented and self-reflective phase. Many people experienced vicarious grief (Chapter 11), sorrowing for other people's sorrow. There was concern for the trauma experienced by bereaved family members, especially the possible impact on children. And when NYC Mayor Rudolph Giuliani mentioned that these events had forced him to think about his own mortality, it is probable that many others agreed: perhaps it was time to reflect upon our own lives, with a renewed awareness of death in mind.

The Mood Changes

Compassion, altruism, and a sense of unity are often prominent in the early response to a disaster, as we have seen, for example, with the earthquake in Haiti in 2010. This was certainly the case with 9/11, but, as in many other postdisaster situations, the early mood and response had limited staying power (Weaver, 2002).

Feeling-orientation and personal reflection soon gave way to military rhetoric and the call to arms against terrorism. It would be national policy to destroy the terrorist and improve protective measures against further attacks. Airport and border security would be tightened—and tightened again and again. Congress would establish a new cabinet-level Department of Homeland Security. Funding priorities would shift to deal with terrorism. Government agencies would be granted additional powers of surveillance and investigations, detain suspects, and use lethal force when deemed necessary.

The national image was transformed from passive victim to aggressive crusader. Preparation for action turned attention away from the quest for meaning, reflection, and emotional healing. People who had lost family members and friends in the terrorist attacks would continue to struggle with the trauma and the recovery process. The general public, though, was being instructed to set aside the inner challenge of feelings and reflections and dedicate itself instead to the external threat of terrorism (Kastenbaum, 2002).

Within a few months of the terrorist attacks. church attendance declined to its previous level (Rose, 2002). American flags were less frequently displayed. An early proposal to establish 9/11 as an official national day of mourning was tabled for lack of support (CNN, 2002), and the public went back to ignoring news of the world (Tribune Wire Services, 2002). People were still affected by the attacks, some very much so. Life in the United States, however, was trying very hard to return to normal.

The shifting national mood now allowed criticisms to be expressed. Bereaved families organized in protest against the bureaucracy that had been established to provide death benefits. Recovery workers engaged in disputes with the City of New York. Criticisms swirled around the design and construction of the WTC and the possibility that federal law enforcement agencies had missed opportunities to prevent the attacks. These and other concerns were addressed in detail by the *National Commission on Terrorist Attacks Upon the United States. The 9/11 Commission Report* (2004) is one of the most forceful and instructive books ever to emerge from a governmental committee, and is recommended for all with an interest in learning what did and did not happen on 9/11, along with suggestions for avoiding future catastrophes.

Is 9/11 Still Happening?

The catastrophic day is still happening in memories and attitudes. But research continues to indicate that 9/11 also has ongoing effects in stress-related symptoms that influence individuals, families, and the workplace. The passage of time seems more to have revealed rather than to have attenuated the effects. A national survey found a broad increase in stress-related symptoms among most Americans immediately after the terrorist attacks (Schuster et al., 2001). Their findings included:

- Nine of ten adults reported at least one stress-related symptom.
- Nearly half the adults reported one or more "substantial" symptoms of stress, that is, a disorder that interfered significantly with their lives.
- Nearly half the children were worried about their own or their loved ones' safety, and one in three were experiencing stress symptoms.

Children with existing psychiatric vulnerabilities were at heightened risk for a severe stress response after the attacks (Panda & Weiden, 2001). People without a previous psychiatric vulnerability became more at risk for post-traumatic stress disorder (Stephenson, 2001; see also Chapter 11) if they had witnessed the disaster first hand (e.g., seeing people leap from a tower, discovering a mutilated body).

Six months after the attack, workers in the vicinity of the WTC reported substantial rates of physical symptoms, especially problems with breathing and irritation of mucous membranes (Bernard et al., 2002). A new term came into existence: "World Trade Center cough" (Prezant et al., 2002). Even a brief exposure to the smoke and dust at Ground Zero was enough to jeopardize the health and imperil the life expectancies of previously healthy people. Accident researchers report that since the attacks, more people have been driving while drowsy because they decided against air travel. More people driving while exhausted and stressed have, in turn, contributed to motor vehicle accidents (Brody, 2002). Those who have increased their use of alcohol as a result of the stress would also be at a higher risk for involvement in accidents.

More recent studies continue to find evidence of 9/11-related terror. Children who lost a family member in the 9/11 attacks remain at increased risk for emotional and stress-related problems (Chemtob et al., 2007). Reviewing the research literature, Comer and Kendall (2007) conclude that children exposed to terrorist events and media coverage experience elevated levels of separation anxiety along with other symptoms of disturbance. Comer and Kendall introduced the term *secondhand terrorism* with respect to possible media excess in raising anxieties about future attacks [a conclusion reached independently by Altheide (2002; 2006)]. Adult vulnerability was most severe among those who had direct exposure to the attacks, lived or worked nearby, or consumed much of the media coverage. Several studies indicate that many people are showing a resilient response—getting on with their lives with energy and purpose—and yet, at the same time, still experiencing an alteration in their physiologic reactivity (Tucker et al., 2007). It is possible that our survival response systems have adapted to a more vigilant level out of concern for possible future dangers.

The terrorist attacks of 9/11 differed in almost every way from the everyday operation of our society's death system. Death came without warning, leaving no time to prepare and little time to respond. There was no opportunity to provide care for the dying and, therefore, no opportunity to affirm relationships until the end. The horrific circumstances at Ground Zero deprived families of the opportunity to conduct funeral and memorial services in a timely and acceptable way. On the positive side, the family survivors were not alone in their grief: The nation mourned with them. Social consolidation after death similarly was a challenge for the entire nation. Making sense of death remains a continuing challenge because our assumption that a familiar world is a safe world was shown to be mistaken, and for other psychological, philosophical, and religious reasons. Killing, often an overlooked facet of the death system, claimed prominence. We were forcefully reminded of the potential for violence within both individuals and their societies.

The impact of 9/11 has also continued in the form of widespread efforts to improve prevention, intervention, and postvention in the event of terrorist attacks. Many nations have been developing emergency plans and resources. In the United States it is no longer unusual for health professionals and other care providers to collaborate in training programs. *Planning Medical Care for High-Risk Mass Gatherings* (Leonard, Winslow, & Bozeman, 2007) is an example of the ongoing attention to minimize casualties of a terrorist attack.

For a more global perspective, sociological analysis (Spilerman & Stecklov, 2009) reveals that nations under frequent terrorist attack suffer more adverse changes than a nation recovering from a one-time massive trauma.

A death system summary is offered in Table 8-4. (Chapter 3).

Does Killing Beget Killing?

The idea that killing might "feed" on itself—that is, instigate motivations for further killing—is illustrated in instances of predominantly one-sided killing, such as genocide, in which initially limited killings escalate into progressively bigger massacres (Marten et al., 2007, p. 1251).

A research team explored this idea in a set of social psychological experiments. Their methodology is a long way from the brutal reality of terrorism and genocide. The participants (introductory psychology students, of course) were asked a question that one does not encounter very often: "Please rate how similar/different you think you are to small insects." Participants also had their consented to do some bug killing for science. The "extermination machine" was a modified stainless steel coffee grinder with a protruding tube and a funnel. A bug would be placed in the funnel, the participant would press a button, and sounds of whirling blades and grinding bugs would be heard. In actuality, no bugs were harmed during the study and the participants were later informed that they had not been killers after all.

Fewer bugs were killed by participants who perceived themselves as relatively more similar to the bugs. But wait—if high similarity participants were given a "practice period," they became enthusiastic killers when performing at their own discretion. In this sense, killing seemed to beget killing. Participants who killed more bugs also reported a positive change in their mood. The evidence, limited though it is, supports the proposition that violence feeds on itself. After the first abuse, assault, or killing, the others are easier. Martens et al. are well aware that their

TABLE 8-4 *Functions of the Death System and the 9/11 Attacks on America*

Function	Comment
Warning and predicting	Warnings not evaluated, given priority, or followed up effectively; attacks come as surprise.
Preventing	Failed to prevent deaths on airliners; failed to prevent loss of life on ground, but design features of WTC towers and courageous actions by first responders reduced the number of casualties.
Caring for the dying	Victims either died on the scene or escaped without life-threatening injuries.
Disposing of the dead	Exceptionally long and arduous efforts to recover bodies of victims; identified remains not found for all believed to have died at WTC.
Social consolidation after death	Delay and stress in grief recovery for bereaved families because so many bodies not found or identified; the cities attacked and the nation as a whole responded strongly and compassionately.
Making sense of death	Major issue immediately after the unexpected trauma; temporary stimulus to personal reflections on life and death.
Killing	National shift to killing (war on terrorism) orientation after assault by an external death system.

experimental model is far distant from real life atrocities, but their work can also make us aware of some of the dynamics that might impel good people to do astonishingly bad things.

How to break the cycle of violence? Colin Murray Parkes (2008) offers a concise analysis that takes us across individual, family, and cultural zones to improve our recognition of how violence originates and how it can be prevented. I highly recommend it!

ACCIDENT AND DISASTER

The deaths caused by both accidents and disasters are not intentioned. Unfortunately, intentionality can be difficult to establish. Often, we cannot be sure of another person's state of mind, and sometimes we may not be clear about our own intentions. Furthermore, people may have a degree of responsibility for accident or disaster deaths, even if they had no intention of doing harm. Here is one of many examples in which a sequence of behaviors can lead to an "accidental" death:

An 8-year-old girl became trapped by fire in her second-floor bedroom. Firefighters rushed to the scene but (Farmer, 2002):

Could not make the turn onto the girl's narrow street because of illegally parked cars. So they knocked down fences and plowed cars out of the way in a frantic effort to reach the dwelling. Officials say the delay in reaching the girl almost certainly contributed to her death, "When we say seconds count, it sounds cornball, but it's true," Fire Lt. William Dewan said yesterday at the station (p. B1).

Illegally parked vehicles are commonplace in Boston. Many other lives have probably been put at heightened risk over the years because of illegally parked vehicles. Those who had made Bowen Street nearly impassable did not foresee or intend the death of Katie Orr, but it might be said that they had some responsibility for this outcome.

There was even more to this situation. The fire was started by the young girl's father in the early morning hours. He was in bed, using an oxygen tank and smoking a cigarette. He had been repeatedly warned against smoking while using oxygen. It is probable that his respiratory illness had been caused by smoking. The agonized death of his daughter was not intentional, but the "accident" certainly was set up by his nonresponsible behavior as well as that of the drivers who illegally congested the street. Many other accidents result from a sequence of decisions and behaviors that have a share of the responsibility even if they were not intentioned to result in injury or death.

Despite these difficulties, the concept of unintended death provides a useful pathway through the kinds of death that are customarily called accidents or disasters.

Accidents

We begin with a statistical overview of accidents. We will then look more closely at the contexts and dynamics that are often associated with accidental deaths.

The Statistical Picture Accidents have always been a major cause of death. What might be surprising is the fact that the rate of accidental deaths has declined through the years. The number of unintentional-injury deaths has stayed fairly constant, though, because the population has continued to increase while the rate has decreased.

National Center for Health Statistics data reveal that more than 100,000 accidental deaths occur in the United States annually. The National Safety Council estimates that an injury accident occurs every two seconds, and a death every six minutes. Motor vehicular injury accidents, the most common type, occur every 16 seconds, and a motor vehicular death every 13 minutes. Alcohol intoxication remains a major factor in motor vehicular fatalities, and is involved in about two of every five deaths. Motor vehicular fatalities are the most common type of accidental death from age 1 to 75, and, as we have seen, are the number one cause of all deaths between the ages of 10 and 24. Infants are most vulnerable to suffocation, elders to life-threatening falls. The vulnerability of elderly men and women is often increased by preexisting health factors. They may also have more limited powers of recuperation from trauma and stress. Therefore, an accident

TABLE 8-5 *The Odds of Accidental Death in the United States*

Type of Accident	One-Year Odds	Lifetime Odds
Air	440,951	5,704
Boating	697,194	9,019
Bus occupant	6,696,307	86,628
Car occupant	17,625	228
Cave-in, falling earth	5,505,600	55,551
Contact with machinery	441,628	5,713
Contact with sharp objects	2,742,297	35,476
Drowning	83,534	1,081
Earthquake	9,288,426	120,161
Electric current	634,232	8,205
Excessive cold	445,729	5,776
Excessive heat	822,689	10,643
Falls	17,712	229
Firearms (accidental)	377,876	4,888
Fireworks display	57,588,244	744,997
Flood	31,993,469	413,887
Lightning	4,362,746	56,439
Motorcycle rider	89,562	1,159
Off-road motor vehicle	371,058	4,800
Overexertion & privation	2,617,647	29,102
Pedestrian	47,273	612
Poisoning	16,407	212
Smoke, fire, flames	91,149	1,179
Streetcar occupant	71,985,305	931,246
Venomous animal	3,788,700	40,013

Source: National Center for Health Statistics. www.cdc.gov/nchs/fastats/acc-inj.html.

that a younger person might recover from is more likely to prove fatal to an elderly person.

The National Safety Council (2005) has given us something to think about in its calculation of the odds of death by accident in the United States (using the most recent available data, 2002). Table 8-5 presents excerpts from a longer list that includes disasters as well as accidents. Two types of information are provided: the odds of becoming an accidental death victim in one year, and the lifetime odds.

The odds of dying from any kind of injury are 1 in 1,755. The odds of a person born in 2000 ending his or her life by accident is 1 in 23. There is an impressive difference between one-year and lifetime odds of a fatal accident throughout the listings.

We have placed "occupant of streetcar" in a conspicuous place to remind us that many factors go into determining risk of death. The low streetcar risk obviously has something to do with the fact that there are very few streetcars still in operation. When they were numerous and shared the road with horse-drawn vehicles and automobiles, streetcars were sometimes a high risk, as memorialized by the baseball team known as the Los Angeles (formerly Brooklyn) Dodgers. The odds are shaped by the frequency of the events as well as the risk per event.

The Human Side of Accident Fatalities The automobile passenger who is killed when the car in which he is traveling is broadsided by another vehicle is in a much different situation than the elderly pedestrian who slips on an icy sidewalk or the young child who drowns in the family pool when, for one tragic moment, nobody is standing watch. There can also be important differences within the same type of fatal accident. For example, reckless driving is often to blame for fatal motor vehicle accidents in which a young person is behind the wheel—poor maintenance of the vehicle is often a contributing cause as well. By contrast, failure to take sufficient note of traffic conditions and slow reaction times are more often associated with fatal accidents caused by elderly drivers. Additionally, the single-car accident is often associated with use of alcohol or drugs, and sometimes also with a self-destructive intention (in which case the "accident" is not entirely an accident).

The victim's contribution to a fatal accident has long been recognized. People of a certain age will remember the verses posted on a series of roadside signs around the United States. There were hundreds of verses, some of which were intended to keep the sponsor's customers alive, as in the following example:

SPRING

HAS SPRUNG

THE GRASS HAS RIZ

WHERE LAST YEAR'S

CARELESS DRIVER IS . . .

BURMA-SHAVE

A recent study supports and extends earlier research about the risky driver: this is most likely to be an angry person with the impulse to seek arousing sensations (Schwebel, Severson, Ball, & Rizzo, 2006, p. 809). The authors draw implications for prevention:

> Most current interventions to reduce motor vehicle crashes target engineering of the road environment or the motor vehicle. Prevention programs designed to change driver behavior are less common; when they are implemented, they tend to focus broadly on all drivers. Results from this study indicate interventions targeting sensation-seeking, unconscientious, and angry drivers might be more theoretically and economically sensible.

Some of the most devastating accidents have been primed by human error, indifference, or greed. In these instances, it is more accurate to speak of the lethal episode not as an accident but as a probable outcome.

Consider one of the most tragic examples in U.S. history. On April 27, 1865, the steamship *Sultana* started its voyage north from Vicksburg, Mississippi. Almost all the passengers were Union soldiers, including hundreds who had been incarcerated in prison camps under conditions of extreme stress and deprivation. They were exhausted survivors of a long and bitter conflict, finally on their way home. Early the next morning, the steam boilers exploded, the ship splintered, and passengers and crew were hurled into the cold waters of the Mississippi River. Of the 2,200 people aboard, 1,700 died almost immediately, and another 200 died of exposure and injuries later. The casualties exceeded even those of the Titanic.

An accident? The Sultana was built to accommodate 376 people. About six times as many people were crowded aboard. Furthermore, there

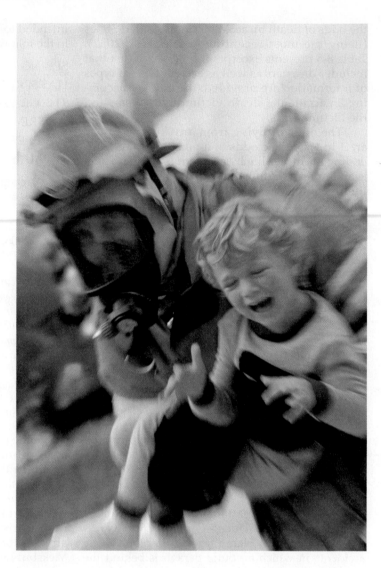

Firefighters are among the crucial first responders when accidents or disasters strike. Failure of safety precautions too often lead to life-and-death emergencies.

had been clear indications that the boilers were failing (Salecker, 1996). Greed and indifference to the safety of human lives had created a situation that markedly increased the probability of catastrophe. The tragic outcome is classified officially as an "accident," but this was far from an unpredictable event. The death toll was also increased by the fact that few of the passengers knew how to swim—largely because relatively few people in the United States at that time were proficient swimmers. There have been numerous other examples throughout the world in which ships have gone down with a heavy loss of life because of overcrowding and neglect of safety measures. It is a dangerous misrepresentation to classify as accidents fatal events that were shaped by human error and greed. "Accident" implies that nothing could have been done to prevent the loss of life—thereby contributing to lack of prevention in the future.

The failure to learn from experience has haunted many other types of accident-prone situations. In 1942, the nation was shocked when a very avoidable fire in Boston's Cocoanut Grove nightclub killed 492 people. The circumstances and practices that led to this holocaust were analyzed and condemned. From this point on, it was vowed, fire safety in night clubs and other gathering places would be much improved. But in 1977 it did happen again, and almost the same way, 165 people perished in a fire at the swank Beverly Hills Supper Club in Southgate, Kentucky. So stricken was the local community that to this day it has refused to allow any new building on the site—except for a memorial cross (Kurtzman & Wartman, 2007). Safety inspectors today will routinely fine violations of rules that have been put in place to prevent the next fire.

Airline catastrophes provide many examples in which human error has contributed significantly. For example:

> *The captain of an American Airlines jet that crashed in Colombia last December entered an incorrect one-letter computer command that sent the plane into a mountain, the airline said Friday. The crash killed all but 4 of the 163 people aboard (Associated Press, August 24, 1996).*

The pilot had not made a careless error. He thought he was entering the coordinates for Calí. But on most South American aeronautical charts, the one-letter code for Calí is the same as the one for Bogotá, 132 miles in the opposite direction. The coordinates for Bogotá directed the plane toward the mountain.

The lack of standardization among computer databases led the captain to make one fatal keystroke. For all the efficiency and potential of computerized processes, there is also the risk of fatal error.

Cushing (1994) found dozens of other instances in which inadequate communication resulted either in fatal accidents or near misses. Improved awareness of the communication process and its hazards could sharply reduce the possibility of accidents in aviation and other transportation situations. The automatic assumption that we have understood what the other person meant and that the other person has understood what we meant can produce what Cushing has aptly titled, *Fatal Words* (1994). We reduce the probabilities of a fatal accident happening to others or ourselves every time we check out our assumptions, monitor our communications, and resist the temptation to rush full speed ahead without charting the waters.

Laws of Accident Causation? Accidents are often the outcome of multiple causes. Nevertheless, it might be possible to identify common factors. Elvik (2006) has made a case for a set of four laws of accident causation within the realm of traffic injuries and deaths. He draws on a large range of statistical data. *The universal law of learning* states that detection and control of traffic hazards increase with the driver's experience. *The law of rare events* takes surprise into account. We are more likely to become involved in a type of accident that we did not happen to have in our cautionary expectations. An example would be suddenly encountering an icy slick on the road at a time and place that it is seldom expected. *The law of complexity* is related to a driver's tendency to allow only a small margin for safety. This minimal hedge against disaster can combine with other factors, such as road design and traffic, to develop a situation whose many elements can be too difficult to sort out and control. Finally, *the law of cognitive capacity* focuses on the driver's "surplus" attention: the ability to think and talk about other things while operating the vehicle. A driver's mental capacity can become overtaxed by physical or psychological impairment, and/or excessive attention to other matters. Alcohol is one of the common contributors to a critical decline in cognitive capacity while operating a motor vehicle.

Natural Disasters

> *Seventeen minutes before noon, the ground started to roll gently . . . people froze and marveled at the feeling of the earth turning oceanlike, but they were not panicked; the town had suffered these rollings ever since the English had been on Jamaica . . . . "It is an earthquake. Don't be afraid; it will soon be over" (Talty, 2007, p. 291).*

It was Port Royal that was soon over. The flourishing city (home to some of the world's most illustrious pirates as well as merchants and planters) was essentially liquefied within a few minutes of its 1692 disaster. The church steeple slammed into the crowd, a "hollow rumbling noise" sounded from all directions, and earth became water, streets rising and falling, and citizens swept along like corks on a wave. Some people were trapped in rapidly hardening sand until suffocated or swarmed upon by wild dogs. Notorious and flamboyant Port Royal became a lost city.

This catastrophe was certainly a natural disaster. However, it also bore the mark of human motivation and quirk. Many people knew it was an unstable and dangerous location, but also one that was terrific for business opportunity and indulgence in one's pleasures of choice. Warnings of catastrophic disaster were shrugged off as the party went on.

Today in the United States and elsewhere, locations at high risk for natural disaster are more popular than ever. These are not pirate hang-outs, but they are among the most attractive places to live—as long as one ignores nature's warnings. Disaster experts routinely warn the public about settling into high-risk locations, but these spoilsport messages have had little effect.

Occasionally the term *hybrid disaster* is used to make this point. The changes we make in our physical environment can either increase or decrease the probability of a disaster. Soil erosion as a result of poor farming practices is among the historical examples; global warming as a partial result of technology and consumerism is a current and future example.

"Natural disaster" customarily refers to an episode that occurs within a limited period of time. Earthquakes, storms, floods, and fires are the most common types, although the less common volcanic eruptions can also be deadly.

Through the centuries, earthquakes have been responsible for some of the most devastating disasters. In all likelihood, the most lethal earthquake occurred in 1556 when an estimated 830,000 died in Shaanxi, China. Tangshan, China, also suffered a quake that claimed 242,000 lives in 1976. The Chinese earthquake of 2008 was responsible for more than 50,000 deaths. Japan and India have had quakes with more than 200,000 fatalities. The tsunami that struck coastal areas of Southeast Asia in 2004 might have been generated by an underwater quake, if not a volcanic eruption. The 2010 Haiti earthquake and its aftershocks might have caused the death of more than the estimated 23, 000 people; in major disasters, the actual number of casualties often cannot be determined.

There is now a significant literature on prevention of natural disasters, enhanced by growing attention to postvention: care for bereaved survivors who need material and emotional support. Much can be learned from the human dysfunctions that contributed to such disasters as the Great Chicago Fire of 1871 and the historic flood experienced in 1889 by Johnstown, Pennsylvania, as a result of a dam break. Measures that can be taken include design, construction, and maintenance of disaster-resistant buildings and preparation for effective response by a broad spectrum of agencies that can provide immediate and continued assistance (Wallace, & Webber; 2004; Weaver, 2002). Increased attention to communication processes before, during, and after a disaster is also advocated. Health care professionals and other community organizations have become more aware of the need to develop a clear chain of command and an efficient emergency management system to make best uses of their combined resources (Shover, 2007).

■ SUMMARY

Sudden and violent deaths take the forms of murder, war, terrorism, disaster, and accident. We have seen that the boundaries between these forms of violent death are not always firm and stable. When is armed attack war, and when is it terrorism? When is an accident actually homicide? We have also observed connections between individual actions that result in death and societal beliefs and practices.

We first acquainted ourselves with characteristics of the people who are most likely to be killers and victims. For example, most murders are committed by people who are of the same race as the victims, and in most cases the victims and the killers knew each other. We then explored several types of murder. Domestic violence includes abusive men who kill their partners and women who kill the men who have been abusing them. The tragedy of adults who kill children—even newborn babies—was also examined, including the rising incidence of child abuse and neglect, the lack of parenting skills, and the replacement father syndrome. Domestic violence also includes parricide: children who kill their parents. These murders are often preceded by years of abuse at the hands of the parents. Young men with guns account for the largest number of murders, and school shootings have added another dimension to youth violence.

A mass killing is one in which several people die in a single episode. The killer is typically a white male, and his weapon a firearm. There is often a suicidal component: the killer is motivated to die at the scene of his crimes. Mass killers tend to feel rejected and mistreated by society. They often fit the profile of an antisocial personality, also known as a sociopath. Serial killers take the lives of three or more people over a period of time. Almost all identified serial killers are male, although some experts believe female serial killers have also operated, using poison and other "quiet" methods that are less likely to be detected. Political assassins have included some people who were delusional and incoherent, but others resemble mass killers in their frustration and anger against society. Still another type of political assassin is the person who hopes to redeem a life of failure and misery with an act of violence that will make him "famous."

Terrorism and genocide were rampant throughout the twentieth century and have crossed over into the twenty-first without missing a beat. The 9/11 terrorists attacks on the United States, and the genocidal massacres in the Darfur region of the Sudan are the most prominent; however, they are not the only examples of mass killing to challenge the wisdom and resources of the world in the third millennium. We also pondered a study that suggests that killing begets killing.

Finally, we learned about disasters and accidents as the causes of violent death. The accident rate in the United States has decreased over the years but could be sharply reduced if there were fewer intoxicated drivers at the wheel.

■ REFERENCES

Alt, B. L., & Wells, S. K. (2010). *When caregivers kill. Understanding child murder by parents & other guardians.* Plymouth UK: Rowman & Littlefield.

Altheide, D. L. (2006). *Terrorism and the politics of fear.* New York: Rowman & Littlefield.

Altheide, D. L. (2002). *Creating fear. News and the construction of crisis.* Hawthorne, NY: Aldine de Gruyter.

Associated Press. (1996, August 24). *Columbia crash linked to pilot error.*

Balakian, P. (2003). *The burning Tigris. The Armenian genocide and America's response.* New York: HarperCollins.

Barenblatt, D. (2003). *A plague upon humanity. The secret genocide of Axis Japan's germ warfare operation.* New York: HarperCollins.

Batton, C., & Wilson, S. (2006). An examination of historical trends in the killing of law enforcement officers in the United States, 1947–1998. *Homicide Studies, 10,* 79–97.

Bauder, D. (2002, August 20). *NBC seeks psychiatric help on 9/11 coverage.* New York: Associated Press.

Bennett, M. D., Hall, J., Frazier, L., Patel, N., Barker, L., & Shaw, K. (2006). Homicide of children aged 0–4 years, 2003–04: results from the National Violent Death Reporting System. http://injuryprevention. bmj.com/content/12/suppl_2/ii39.full.

Bernard, B. P., Baron, S. L., Mueller, C. A., Driscoll, R. J., Tapp, L. C., Wallingford, K. M., & Tepper, A. L. (2002). Impact of September 11 attacks on workers in the vicinity of the World Trade Center. [Special issue]. *Monthly Mortality & Morbidity Report, 51,* 8–10.

Breed, A. G. (2005, March 5). Number of U. S. serial killers unknown. Associated Press Online. http://s6.zetaboards.com/Horror_Fans_World/topic/987176/1/.

Brody, J. E. (2002, January 17). Driving while drowsy on rise. Traffic experts struggle to find solutions, *Arizona Republic,* B1.

Browne, A. (1987). *When battered women kill.* New York: The Free Press.

Bureau of Justice Statistics. (2005). Homicide data. http://bjs.ojp.usdoj.gov/content/homicide/homtrnd.cfm.

Bureau of Justice Studies. (2008). Homicide trends in the U.S. http://bjs.ojp.usdoj.gov/content/homicide/homtrnd.cfm.

Chemtob, C. M., Conroy, D. L., Hochauser, C. J., & Laraque, D. (2007). Children who lost a parent as a result of the terrorist attacks of September 11, 2001: Registry construction and population description. *Death Studies, 31,* 87–100.

Chu, H. (2007, November 22). Indian brides terrorized by in-laws over dowries. *Arizona Republic,* p. A26.

Clarke, J. W. (1982). *American assassins.* Princeton, NJ: Princeton University Press.

CNN news.com (2002, September 2). Poll: Support for 9/11 holiday/IPS.

Comer, J. S., & Kendall, P. C. (2007). Terrorism: The psychological impact on Youth. *Clinical Psychology: Science and Practice, 14,* 179–212.

Condon, P. (2005, April 1). Teen suspect saw film on school shooting. http://www.highbeam.com/library/doc3.asp?DOCID11P1:106949812.

Crissman, J. K., & Parkin, J. (2002). Homicide. In R. Kastenbaum (Ed.), *Macmillan encyclopedia of death and dying* (Vol. 1, pp. 423–426). New York: Macmillan.

Cushing, S. (1994). *Fatal words.* Chicago: University of Chicago Press.

Davis, K. (2004, April 9). Police arrest teen after "kill list" found. *Arizona Republic,* p. 3.

Davis, K. (2005, May 5). E. V. girl had script for school rampage. East Valley Tribune, p. A1–2.

Dray, P. (2003). *At the hands of persons unknown. The lynching of black America.* New York: Modern Library.

Einstein, A., & Freud, S. (1933). Why war? In C. James & S. Grachen (Eds.), *Collected papers of Sigmund Freud* (Vol. 4, pp. 273–287). London: Hogarth.

Elvik, R. (2006). Laws of accident causation. *Accident Analysis and Prevention, 38,* 742–747.

Enders, W., & Sandler, T. (2006). *The political economy of terrorism.* New York: Cambridge University Press.

Engelmann, B. (1984). *Germany without Jews.* New York: Bantam.

Evans, T. (April 30, 2007). Making of a massacre. *Newsweek,* pp. 22–31.

Ewing, C. P. (1997). *Fatal families. The dynamics of intra familial homicide.* Thousand Oaks, CA: Sage.

Farmer, T. (2002, November 12). Clear out: Menino launches parking crackdown after fatal fire. *Boston Herald,* p. B1.

Federal Bureau of Investigation. (2010). Murder rates in U. S. drop to lowest levels for four decades—despite the recession. http: govt.fbi/violentcrime/murder rates.

Flint, R. (2002). *Great cruelties have been reported.* Dallas: Southern Methodist University Press.

Fox, J. A., & Levin, J. (2001). *The will to kill.* Boston: Allyn & Bacon.

Freed, J. (2005, April 16). High dropout rate at U.S. school that was site of shooting seems to worsen. www.highbeam.com/library/doc3.asp?DOCID11P1:107487106.

Freud, S. (1923/1961). *The Ego and the Id.* New York: Norton.

Gabriel, R., Ferrando, L., Corton, E. S., Mingote, C., Garcia-Camba, E., Liria, A. F., & Galea, S. (2007). Psychyopathological consequences after a terrorist attack: An epidemiological study among victims, the general population, and police officers. *European Psychiatry, 22,* 339–346.

Goldhagen, D. J. (1996). *Hitler's willing executioners.* New York: Knopf.

Gracia, E. (2004). Unreported cases of domestic violence against women: Towards an epidemiology of social science, toleration, and inhibition. *Journal of Epidemiological Community Health, 58,* 536–537.

Haynes, M., & Husan, R. (2003). *A century of state murder? Death and policy in twentieth-century Russia.* London: Pluto Press.

Heide, K. M. (1992). *Why kids kill parents: Child abuse and adolescent homicide.* Columbus: Ohio State Press.

Henry, V. E. (2004). *Death work. Police trauma and the psychology of survival.* Oxford: Oxford University Press.

Herman, W. (2005, January 14). The man who saved his village. *Arizona Republic,* pp. A2, A18.

Herzog, S. (2006). Battered women who kill. An empirical analysis of public perceptions of seriousness in Israel from a consensus theoretical perspective. *Homicide Studies, 10,* 293–319.

Holcomb, K. (2005, April 21). 12 News. Child drowns in gated backyard. .

Jowan, J. (January 18, 2008). Caught in the clash of civilizations. http://stophonourkillings.com.

Kast, S. (2005, February 27). Interview: Eric Hickey discusses the behavior and characteristics of serial killers. (National Public Radio Weekend Edition).

Kastenbaum, R. (2002). Terrorist attacks on America. In R. Kastenbaum (Ed.), *Macmillan encyclopedia of death and dying* (Vol. 2, pp. 881–885). New York: Macmillan.

Kristof, N. D. (2004, September 11). Reign of terror. *The New York Times.* http://www.nytimes.com/2004/09/11/opinion/11kristol.html.

Kristof, N. D. (2004, October 16). The dead walk. *The New York Times.* http://whttp://ww.nytimes.com/2004/10/16/opinion/16kristof.html.

Kullman, T. (2008). Religious violence and weapons of mass destruction. In R. G Stevenson &

G. R. Cox (Eds.), *Perspectives on violence and violent death* (pp. 79–96). Amityville, NY: Baywood.

Kuper, L. (1981). *Genocide.* New Haven & London: Yale University Press.

Kurtzman, L., & Wartman, S. (May 27, 2007). Survivors relieve the horrors of fatal Nightclub fire in '77. *Arizona Republic*, p. A22.

Larson, E. (2004). *The devil in the white city: Murder, magic, and madness at the fair that changed America.* New York: Vintage.

Laughame, J., Janca, A, & Widiger, B. (2007). Posttraumatic stress disorder and terrorism: 5 years after 9/11. Personality disorders and neuroses. *Current Opinion in Psychiatry, 20,* 36–41.

Lederer, D. M. (March 9, 2007). U. N. chief urges end to violence against women. *East Valley Tribune*, p. A18.

Lemkin, R. (1944). *Axis rule in occupied Europe: Laws of occupation, analysis of government, proposals for redress.* Washington, DC: Carnegie Endowment for International Peace, Division of International Law.

Leonard, R. B., Winslow, J. E., & Bozeman, W. P. (2007). Planning medical care for high-risk mass gatherings. *The Internet Journal of Rescue and Disaster Medicine, 6,* 1–12.

Libaw, L., & Goldman, M. C. (2002, September 12). Unspeakable horror. Eyewitness accounts of N. Y. attacks. ABC.NEWS.com.

Lipstadt, Deborah (1994). *Denying the Holocaust. The growing assault on truth and memory.* New York: Plume.

Loewen, J. S. (1995). *Lies my teacher told me.* New York: The New Press.

Martens, A., Kosloff, S., Greenberg, J., Landau, M. J., & Schmader, T. (2007). Killing begets killing: Evidence from a bug-killing paradigm that initial killing fuels subsequent killing. *Personality and Social Psychology Bulletin, 33,* 1251–1264.

Meloy, J., R., Hempel, A. G., Mohandie, K., Shiva, A. A., & Gray, B. T. (2001). Offender and offense characteristics of a nonrandom sample of adolescent mass murderers. *Journal of the American Academy of Child and Adolescent Mass Murderers, 40,* 719–728.

Moeller, T. G. (2001). *Youth aggression and violence.* Mahwah, NJ: Lawrence Erlbaum Associates.

National Commission on Terrorist Attacks Upon the United States. (2004). *The 9/11 commission report.* New York: Norton.

National Safety Council (2005). What are the odds of dying? http://www.purewatergazette.net/oddsofdying.htm.

Oshinsky, D. M. (2009). *Capital punishment on trial: Furman v. Georgia and the death penalty in modern America.* University of Kansas Press.

Panda, A. U., & Weiden, M. (2001). Trauma and disaster in psychiatrically vulnerable populations. *Journal of Psychiatric Practice, 7,* 426–431.

Parkes, C. M. (2008). Making and breaking cycles of violence. In R. G. Stevenson & G. R. Cox (Eds.), *Perspectives on violence and violent death* (pp. 223–239). Amityville, NY.

Payton, J. (January 10, 2008a). "Picket the homes of honour killings." http://stophonourkillings.com.

Payton, J. (January 16, 2008b). Marriage practice victimizes young girls. http://stophonourkillings.com.

Power, S. (2002). "A problem from hell." *America and the age of genocide.* New York: Basic Books.

Prezant, D. J., Weiden, M., Banauch, G. I., McGuinness, G., Rom, W. D., Aldrich, T. K., & Kelly, K. J. (2002). Cough and bronchial responsiveness in firefighters at the World Trade Center site. *New England Journal of Medicine, 347,* 806–815.

Robinson, B. A. (2001). Mass crimes against humanity and genocides: A list of atrocities 1450 CE to the present. Kingston, Ontario Consultants on Religious Tolerance. http://www.religioustolerance.org/genocide/2.htm.

Rosario, R. (2005, April 25). School-shooting study delves into peers who knew attacks were coming. http://www.accessmylibrary.com/article-1G1-131860917/school-shooting-study-delves.html.

Rose, J. (2002, September 4). From fear to reality. A year after 9/11, a look at America's predictions of change. *Arizona Republic*, B1.

Rudoff, A., & Esselstyn, T. C. (2000). *Homicide in fact and fiction.* Bristol, IN: Wyndham Hall Press.

Salecker, G. E. (1996). *Disaster on the Mississippi.* Annapolis, MD: Naval Institute Press.

Salerian, A. J. (2002, October 24). What makes a serial killer tick? United Press International. www.upi.com.

Schustus, M. Z., Stein, B. D., Jancov, L. H., Collins, R. L., Marshall, G. N., Elliot, M. N., Zhnye, A. J., Kanoose, D. E. Morrison, J. L., & Bern, S. H. (2001). A national survey of stress reactions after the September 11 attack, *New England Journal of Medicine, 345,* 1507–1512.

Schwebel, D. C., Severson, J., Ball, K. K., & Rizzo, M. (2006). Individual differences in risky driving: The roles of anger/hostility, conscientiousness, and sensation-seeking. *Accident Analysis and Prevention, 38,* 801–810.

Shover, H. (2007). Understanding the chain of communication during a disaster. *Perspectives on Psychiatric Care, 43,* 4–14.

Spilerman, S., & Stecklov, G. (2009). Societal responses to terrorist attacks. *American Review of Sociology, 35,* 167–189.

Stephenson, J. (2001). Medical, mental health communities mobilize to cope with terror's psychological aftermath. *Journal of the American Medical Association, 286,* 1823–1825.

Talty, S. (2007*). Empire of blue water.* New York: Crown.

Tribune wire services (2002, June 10). Foreign news still foreign to U.S. after September 11.

Tucker, P. M., Pfefferbam, B., North, C. S., Kent, A., Burgih, C. E., Parker, D. E., & Hossain, A. (2007). Physiologic reactivity despite emotional resilience several years after direct exposure to terrorism. *American Journal of Psychiatry, 164,* 230–235.

Wakin, E. (1984). *Enter the Irish-American.* New York: Thomas V. Crowell.

Wallace, M., & Webber, L. (2004). *Disaster recovery handbook: A step-by-step plan to ensure business continuity and protect vital operations, facilities, and assets.* New York: AMACOM.

Walsh, A. (2005). African Americans and serial killing in the media. *Homicide Studies, 9,* 271–291.

Walsh, J. (1996, September 9). Killings down but 'crime storm' looms. *Arizona Republic,* pp. A1, A24.

Weaver, J. D. (2002). Disasters. In R. Kastenbaum (Ed.), *Macmillan encyclopedia of death and dying* (Vol. 1, pp. 231–240). New York: Macmillan.

Websdale, N. (2010). *Familicidal hearts. The emotional style of 211 killers.* Oxford: Oxford University Press.

Wegner, G.P. (2009). *Violence and the dehumanization of victims in Auschwitz and beyond: Remembering through literature.* In R. G. Stevenson & G. R. Cox (Eds.), *Perspectives on violence and violent death* (pp. 59–77). Amityville NY: Baywood.

Weitz, E. D. (2003). *A century of genocide. Utopias of race and nation.* Princeton, NJ: Princeton University Press.

Zink, T., Elder, N., Jacobson, J., & Klosterman, B. (2004). Medical management of intimate partner violence considering the stages of change: Precontemplation and contemplation. *Annals of Family Medicine, 2,* 231–239.

■ GLOSSARY

Assassination The murder of a public official or other political figure.

Branch Davidians A Christian sect, some of whose members died in its compound near Waco, Texas, during an attack by federal agents.

Genocide Mass killing intended to destroy an ethnic, religious, or racial group.

Homicide The act of killing a human being.

Interpol International Police Organization, primarily an information-sharing agency.

Mass killer A person who murders a large (but not fixed) number of people in a single episode.

Mosque An Islamic place of worship, a temple.

Murder The criminal act of killing a human being.

Parricide Murder of a parent.

Replacement father syndrome When a new husband or lover engages in abusive and life-threatening actions against the children of the wife's previous mate.

Serial killer A person who commits murders on repeated occasions.

Terrorism Violence or threat of violence in which civilians are the targets.

Tsunami A series of extremely long waves generated by earthquake, landslide, or underwater volcanic eruption. Previously known erroneously as "tidal waves."

■ ON FURTHER THOUGHT . . .

Learn more about the effects of mass violence on children:

Nancy Boyd Webb (Ed.), (2003*). Mass trauma and violence: Helping children cope.* New York: Guilford Press.

Learn more about the eruption of suicide terrorism:

Pape, R. A. (2005). *Dying to win.* New York: Random House.

Genocide, Up Close:

Does genocide still feel like something distant and abstract? It is difficult to realize the raw reality of genocide if we have not been victim or witness, or *perpetrator*. For an intense, illuminating account from interviews with people who massacred their neighbors in Rwanda:

Hatzfeld, J. (2005). *Machete season*. New York: Farrar, Straus and Giroux.

For another informed perspective, read the harrowing report from the commanding officer of the U.S. assistance mission to Rwanda:

Dallaire, R. (2005). *Shake hands with the devil*. New York: Carrol & Graf.

Useful Online Resources:

Assassination Archives and Resource Center
  http://aarclibrary.org/
Murder Victims.com
  www.murdervictims.com
National Hazard Center
  http://www.colorado.edu/hazards/
National Organization for Victims Assistance
  www.try-nova.org
The History Place
  http://www.historyplace.com/

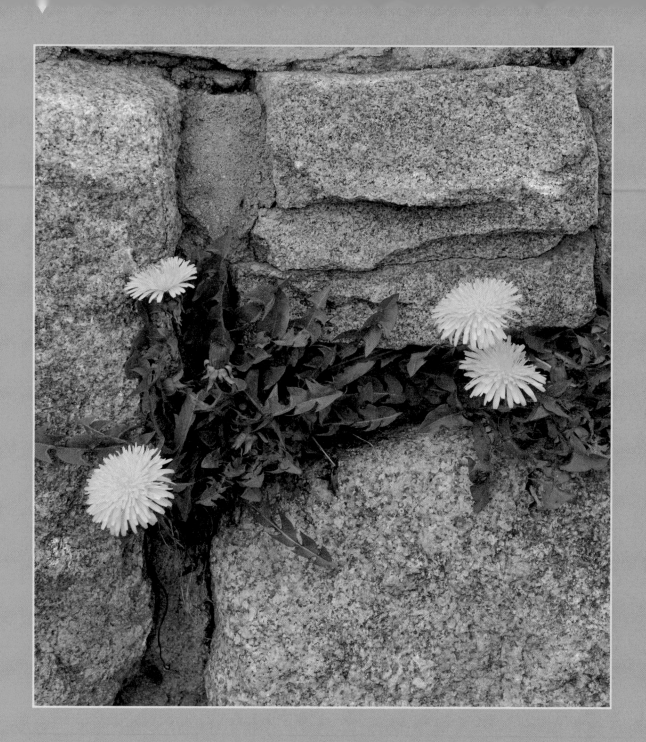

9

Euthanasia, Assisted Death, Abortion, and the Right to Die

There's a grim, rarely-talked-about twist to all that medical know-how doctors learn to save lives: it makes them especially good at ending their own . . . a suicide rate higher than in the general population.

—Associated Press (May 9, 2008)

Loss of autonomy and fear of losing dignity were reasons most often given by terminally ill cancer patients who made use of the recently-enacted right-to-die law in Washington.

—Yardley (2010)

A rare form of cancer left Chantel Sebire blind, in agony, and deprived of smell and taste. She suffered with these effects for years before asking help in ending her life.

—Associated Press (2008)

Theresa suffered a cardiac arrest. During the several minutes it took for paramedics to arrive, Theresa [Schiavo] experienced loss of oxygen to the brain, or anoxia, for a period sufficiently long to cause permanent loss of brain function. Despite heroic efforts to resuscitate, Theresa remained unconscious and slipped into a coma. She was intubated, ventilated and trached, meaning that she was given life saving medical technological interventions, without which she surely would have died that day.

—Wolfson (2003, p. 4).

We heard screaming coming from another crater a bit away. . . . He kept begging us to shoot him. But we couldn't shoot him. Who could shoot him? We stayed with him, watching him go down in the mud. And he died. He wasn't the only one. There must have been thousands up there who died in the mud. Or almost worse, suffered in it, wounded.

—Quoted by Winston Groom (2002, p. 215)

I swear by Apollo the physician, and Aesculapius, Hygeia and Panacea and all the gods and goddesses, that, according to my ability and judgment, I will keep this oath and this covenant. I will give no deadly medicine to anyone if asked, nor suggest any such counsel, and in like manner I will not give to a woman an abortive remedy. With purity and with holiness I will pass my life and practice my Art.

—The Hippocratic Oath (fifth century, B.C.)

DEATH COUNSELING IS SOMEONE IN YOUR FAMILY TERMINALLY ILL?
Does he or she wish to die—and with dignity?
Call Physician Consultant [Telephone No.]

—Classified newspaper advertisement (June 1987)

The woman said the baby's naked body, spotted alongside a road in a small town in Hunan province, was still warm—she had been dumped and had just died. Many passers-by on their way to work ignored the child . . . while some stopped to look, then walked on, until an elderly man eventually put the tiny body into a box and carried it away.

—CNS News (2001)

Euthanasia is still one of the important things we do.

—Veterinarian Nick Trout (2008a)

You could find Nature in the South Bronx if you legged your way to a park where they kept grass and trees, and even squirrels. But you could also find Nature on the very sidewalks of New York as a single blade of grass reached for the sun between cracks in the pavement. Nature is famously insistent about filling earth, water, and sky with life forms, and these life forms are famously insistent about staying alive. Humans are an especially puzzling life form. Sometimes we are vigorous and resourceful about staying alive. Sometimes, though, we terminate life by suicide (Chapter 7) or violence against others (Chapter 8).

In this chapter, we look at *euthanasia,* assisted suicide, and abortion. These endings differ in significant ways, but all involve decision making under stressful conditions. Here is a brief sampling of situations:

- It is the physician who is called on to enable an assisted death. What has been overlooked, however, is that physicians themselves remain exceptionally vulnerable to suicide. "The American Medical Association has called physician suicide 'an endemic catastrophe,'" and pledged two years ago to work to prevent the problem. But the suicides have persisted. (AP, p.1) Why has more attention not been given to the interaction between suicidality in physician and patient?

- If you were approaching the end-stage of a terminal illness, would you have the option of asking your physician for an assisted death? Not if you live in Alaska, Florida, Michigan, South Carolina, or Texas. Or any other state—with the exception of Oregon, Washington, and, problematically, Montana. The right-to-die movement has stirred controversy, and resulted in significant developments, such as the informed consent policy and advance directives (Chapter 6). Active *euthanasia*, also known as assisted suicide or assisted death, has met with far more resistance. Now, however, we have two ongoing programs from which we might learn.

- The lives of Chantel Sebire and Theresa Schiavo were devastated by personal catastrophes that became the core of national controversy. Schiavo remained on life support for 15 years, never regaining consciousness. Sebire was acutely aware of her disfiguring facial tumor, loss of function, and intense pain. Schiavo's situation came to general attention only when her husband requested removal of the feeding tube. Similar requests are not unusual when brain death (Chapter 2) is involved. However, in this instance it led to a controversy in which political power plays crowned the fire of a medical, legal, ethical, and religious controversy. Sebire's ordeal quickly had an impact on French law, medical practice, and public opinion. There was enormous compassion for the former school teacher, but French law, although permitting withdrawal of treatment, did not countenance active euthanasia. Sebire was found dead in her home a few days after a court had rejected her doctor's request to provide euthanasia. Her death was ruled "not natural," but the legal system declined to prosecute. Every case in which the question of euthanasia arises has its unique aspects, and the local attitude and practice can also differ.

- "Mercy death" is probably the earliest and purest form of euthanasia. A dying person or animal is spared further suffering by a blow or shot that ends its life quickly. This kind of action has been known and respected on battlefields and accident sites for longer than anybody can remember. War memoirs are filled with instances in which a soldier provided

mercy death for either a fallen comrade or enemy. In the example given above, the British infantryman was one of many soldiers on both sides of the war who would be slowly pulled into the muddy, quicksand-like depths of a bomb crater. His comrades had tried hard to save him, but there was no way. As horrifying as it was to watch him slowly sink into the mud, none of the young men could bring themselves to shoot him. That same day—and the next day for years to come—British, French, German, and other soldiers would be slowly dying in the "no-man's land." The fatally wounded called out for relief while they still had breath. A comrade who responded to these pleas would most likely be cut to pieces by machine gun fire or blasted apart by a mortar round. Mercy death was almost a luxury in the trench warfare that relentlessly claimed the lives of the young men of Europe and, near the end, of the United States. Euthanasia, however, is not always such a straightforward proposition, as we will continue to see.

- The *Hippocratic Oath* is based on the writings of a physician who practiced on the Greek island of Cos 2,500 years ago (Edelstein, 1943). This ancient document has resonated through the centuries. Can a physician violate the injunction to give no deadly medicine and still be a physician? Dr. Jack Kevorkian is not the only physician who intentionally contributed to the death of his patients, but his example had a powerful influence on the right-to-die controversy. Furthermore, people who know their twentieth century history have understandable concerns about any movement that would encourage the taking of a life under the name of euthanasia.

- Seeing the dead and discarded baby alongside a road must have been profoundly painful to the passersby who could not bring themselves to deal with it. Babies and children are considered precious in Chinese culture. Nevertheless, the people of China have been confronted with a combination of forced abortion and infanticide ever since the regime decided upon a drastic policy of population control. Abortion issues, like euthanasia, take many forms. Seeing the more familiar form of the abortion controversy within a larger perspective could be helpful.

• Many of us have been faced with a euthanasia decision close to home and heart—an animal companion who is a distinctive part of the family. Veterinarian Nick Trout was providing an update on the improved care and longevity of animal companions ("Age 15 is the new 11 for dogs!") when the issue of euthanasia came up. His thoughtful observations (Trout, 2008a; 2008b) are worth consulting when and if the situation arises in our own lives.

In this chapter, we consider the related topics of euthanasia, physician-assisted suicide, abortion, and the right to die. The Black Stork (Pernick, 1996) phenomenon reminds us of the connection between eugenics, euthanasia, and assisted death. We have prepared ourselves for this challenge by studying end-of-life decisions (Chapter 6), suicide (Chapter 7), and killing (Chapter 8). We begin here with the Hippocratic Oath, then acquaint ourselves with key terms and concepts. This is followed by attention to public attitudes toward the set of right-to-die issues, and a review of some of the major cases that have influenced the right-to-die controversy. We will then be ready to look at the assisted death issue in some detail, with particular attention to Oregon and Washington, the only states in which assisted termination is legal. The emotionally and politically divisive issue of abortion will conclude our exploration. Can we keep open minds through it all?

"I SWEAR BY APOLLO THE PHYSICIAN": WHAT HAPPENED TO THE HIPPOCRATIC OATH?

Kevorkian's classified advertisement was a signal that "death with dignity" was becoming more than a rallying cry. Here was a physician who offered to perform a service that most of his colleagues did not even want to talk about. It was a service specifically banned by the Hippocratic Oath.

It is often assumed that (a) all physicians have sworn allegiance to this oath and that (b) this covenant does, in fact, represent the core belief system for physicians from antiquity forward. Neither assumption is correct. Many physicians graduate from medical school without being asked to take the Hippocratic Oath. Kevorkian (1991)

characterizes the oath as irrelevant. Furthermore, the Hippocratic Oath has encountered opposition since its inception. Many in the ancient world considered it reasonable and even honorable to seek release from the rigors, pains, and disappointments of life. The prohibition against giving "deadly medicine" probably had become a widespread practice. The concurrent prohibition against abortion was also contested, with Aristotle as one of the leading dissenters.

Today some physicians continue to rely on the Hippocratic Oath, but many have never entered into this covenant, and all are confronted with new and complex problems that Hippocrates never had to deal with. Even physicians who accept the Hippocratic Oath must find a way to reconcile these precepts with the decisions they make day by day. Physicians in the United States generally work within the system. They must find ways to help their terminally ill patients without violating either their own moral code or the law of the land. Whatever one's position on physician-assisted death, though, one cannot simply invoke the Hippocratic Oath as the unquestionable authority. We must work things out for ourselves.

KEY TERMS AND CONCEPTS

Controversies about life-and-death issues often involve the following key terms and concepts.

A literal translation of the term *euthanasia* would be good or happy (*eu*) death (*thanasia*). It would be more accurate to understand this original usage as "dying without pain and suffering." At first, euthanasia referred to the individual's state of being (e.g., "She died peacefully"). Later, euthanasia came to signify actions performed to hasten death. Today, the term euthanasia retains something of its original meaning: a peaceful, painless exit from life. But it has taken on another meaning as well: the intentional foreshortening of a person's life to spare that person from further suffering.

Many people distinguish sharply between a life that is foreshortened by doing something and a life that is foreshortened by deciding not to do something. Active euthanasia refers to actions that intended to end the life of a person or animal that is suffering greatly and has no chance of recovery.

A lethal injection would be a clear example of active euthanasia. Passive euthanasia is the intentional withholding of treatment that might have prolonged life. Deciding not to place a person with massive brain trauma on a life-support system would be an example of passive euthanasia, as would the decision not to treat pneumonia or an opportunistic infection in an immobilized and cognitively impaired long-term patient.

The legal system and society in general have been more tolerant of the "letting go" approach. Few are inclined to make trouble when health care providers and family members agree that it would be pointless to introduce further procedures that would only prolong suffering or a vegetative state. An *advance directive* (Chapter 6) is a legal request to control end-of-life management. The patient's specification, "Do not resuscitate" (DNR) is, at least theoretically, a choice that is a type of passive euthanasia. Active euthanasia, however, is still opposed by many physicians who object to placing their services at the disposal of death. Furthermore, a person who engages in active euthanasia could be accused of manslaughter or homicide.

We will still hear about active and passive euthanasia because these were the original terms of the controversy. Today, however, most physicians and bioethicists speak instead of withdrawing or withholding life supports. Instead of dealing with the somewhat abstract concept of euthanasia, focus is directed to whether certain practical actions should be introduced, continued, done, or discontinued.

A challenging question continues to be asked: How much does it really matter whether the life is terminated by passive or active means? The outcome is the same, but discontinuing life support and administering a lethal injection seem very different. What do you think—and why? Perhaps considering the ventilator and the slippery slope argument (which follow) will help.

There is also a fairly new term to consider: *terminal sedation*. This alternative is selected by physicians who are committed to relieving a dying patient's distress without resorting to active euthanasia (Rietjens, et al., 2004). Medications keep the patient in deep sedation or coma until death. What family and caregivers see is a person who appears to be sleeping peacefully but never wakes up. Terminal sedation is used most often when the patient is suffering severe pain, agitation, or dyspnea. Physicians conversing among themselves sometimes refer to this practice as "slow euthanasia." This is an apt term because the terminal sedation regimen is understood as an unobtrusive way of hastening death. Do you see terminal sedation as significantly different from traditional medical management at the end of life? As significantly different from the more recognized forms of passive and active euthanasia?

Three other concepts are keys to our understanding of the controversies that swirl around euthanasia, assisted death, and the right to die. The foundation is built on a principle that goes by several names: liberty, privacy, autonomy, and self-determination. The *liberty principle* affirms that individuals are free to make their own decisions and exercise their own rights except in ways that have been specifically reserved for the state. We can do anything that has not been forbidden by law. The state reserves for itself the right to protect public security and safety, and this obligation can take precedence over individual choice. The balance between the liberty principle and the rights of the state pervades all spheres of society and has shifted back and forth over time. It is only in recent years, however, that the liberty principle has become salient in health care decisions. A series of court rulings held that "the State's interest in preserving an individual's life was not sufficient by itself to outweigh the individual's interest in the exercise of free choice" (Veatch, 1998, pp. 155–156).

These judicial rulings helped to pave the way for the eventual legalization of advance directives (Chapter 6). Nevertheless, the courts were also aware that not all individuals are in a position to exercise a right-to-die decision. This is where the other two concepts become important. What does it take to be in a position to choose death over life? It takes *informed consent*, and it takes *competence*. Medical authorities must give full disclosure to patients before proceeding with treatments. What risks as well as benefits might occur? Only when armed with adequate information would a person be in a position to make an informed decision. This right to informed consent became federal law as a result of scandals involving medical experimentation with patients who did not realize they were participating in a research project that could have critical effects on their health and survival. The most notorious of these studies had been conducted by the government itself when the U.S. Public Health Service:

> examined the effects of untreated syphilis among rural black men in Tuskegee, Alabama. Thousands of men were kept in total ignorance of the experiment, their infection, and the seriousness of syphilis. They were consistently steered away from receiving effective treatment so the United States government could monitor how the disease progressed, its many serious side effects, and its rate of fatality (Lens, 2002, p. 475).

Physicians are now required to explain the procedures, benefits, and risks in such a way that patients clearly understand what is involved. That brings us to the other key concept: "competence" to understand the information, make a rational decision, and express that decision cannot be assumed. The person might be profoundly mentally retarded, suffering from severe brain damage, or unable to communicate in speech or writing. I have known instances in which competence depended on the interaction between physician and patient, as when they lacked a shared language with which to communicate effectively.

We have already noted (Chapter 10) that children tend to be excluded from participation in decision making about their own care. The child is not considered competent to give or withhold informed consent for medical procedures in general. Does this mean that every possible treatment must be given (imposed) on a child? And who should decide? Guidelines for pediatric decision making are nonexistent or vague at present and can contribute to making a difficult situation even more difficult (Plotz et al., 2008).

In this chapter, we will see how difficult it can be when patients cannot participate fully in decision making and when, therefore, it is not clear what choices they would have made if given the opportunities.

Nazi "Euthanasia"

There is another really hard question to consider: *Can we—and should we—detach ourselves from the memory of horrors that have been perpetrated in the name of euthanasia?* There are still many people who remember how the political, medical, economic, and military forces of a modern nation all collaborated in the murder of millions of people. The holocaust that

eventually claimed millions of lives was preceded by Hitler's policy of *Vernichtun lebensunwerten Lebens*. Nazi doctors participated in the "extermination of valueless life." The victims were fellow German citizens, non-Jewish, invalids, infirm, unable to care for themselves—a large proportion of the institutionalized population (Lifton, 1986). Killing these helpless people required the cooperation of physicians and other people who had been entrusted with their care.

German society might have rejected this brutal program had it been exposed for what it was. However, the murders were disguised as euthanasia. The Nazi leadership declared that these people were being put out of their misery for their own good. And, yes, it would also save the cost of feeding and housing them. Enough physicians believed (or pretended to believe) this explanation in order to make the program a success.

What the Nazis did to their helpless citizens had nothing at all to do with euthanasia. These people were not terminally ill. They were not suffering intractable pain. They did not ask to be killed. They were simply murdered, one by one, through a process that had a bureaucrat at one end and a physician at the other. Discovering that he could induce physicians, lawyers, and other responsible people to engage in "mercy killing," Hitler moved on to his genocidal assaults against Jews and Gypsies (Friedlander, 1995).

Are we supposed to forget this? Can "euthanasia" ever be completely cleansed of this abuse?

The Black Stork

An almost forgotten episode in U.S. history brings the euthanasia issue even closer to us. A keen interest in both *eugenics* and euthanasia developed early in the twentieth century. Preventive medicine was starting to reduce mortality rates and increase life expectancies. Why not go all the way? Why not keep "defective" people out of the population in the first place? Eugenicists proposed sterilization of people thought to have defective genes. And why not also let defective newborn infants die? And, while we are at it, why not end the lives of patients as soon as it is clear that they are incurable? A crusade was born! A prominent Chicago surgeon by the name of Harry J. Haiselden combined eugenics with euthanasia. He boasted of having allowed the deaths of at least six "defective" infants. Then he urged other physicians to

An influential movement in the United States urged death for babies with birth defects and for others who were considered to be burdens on society. The Black Stork was a symbol used by critics of this movement.

help him weed out those unfit for the new and improved version of society.

Physicians who saved defective infants came under attack by eugenicists (Pernick, 1996). At first the public was divided in its response to the eugenics and euthanasia movements. By the 1920s the public had pretty much rejected the euthanasia component—but not before it had attracted the enthusiasm of some German physicians and political thinkers:

> By the 1930s racial hygiene, eugenics, and eutha-
> nasia played a complex but central role in the evo-
> lution of Nazi ideology and in the legitimization
> of Nazi genocide. Depicting their intended vic-
> tims as carriers of racial "diseases" constituted a
> key feature of Nazi propaganda. . . . Programs for
> killing incurably ill institutional patients, such
> as the operation code-named "T-4" that secretly
> gassed over 100,000 disabled Germans, pioneered
> the machinery and trained the medical personnel
> who were then transferred to run the death camps
> for the "racially diseased" (Pernick, p. 164).

Can there be any wonder that the terms *euthanasia* and *mercy killing* still trigger suspicion, and anger? The Native American woman who told me of the forced sterilization of many women in her tribe was not being paranoid: she was simply reporting facts.

The Ventilator and the Slippery Slope

The *ventilator* (Iserson, 2002) is a familiar piece of equipment in the intensive care unit. It is frequently used for short-term situations; for example, when a patient who is likely to recover from illness or trauma needs respiratory assistance. It is also used in potentially long-term life-support situations. Suppose that a patient has been attached to a ventilator for weeks or even months. At some point, families and hospital staff might agree there is no chance for recovery and that the patient is receiving no quality-of-life benefit from the life-support system. Somebody pulls the plug. The patient dies (or sometimes does not). This would be an example of withdrawing treatment. But suppose instead that a person has just been brought to the hospital after a massive stroke or with severe brain trauma from an accident. It is obvious to the medical team that the higher brain centers have been destroyed. Death will soon occur unless the unresponsive body is hooked up to a life-support system. The decision is made against using a ventilator. The patient is soon certified as dead.

The patient dies in both of these scenarios. The "instrument" of death in both scenarios is the ventilator. How much importance should we attach to the difference between withdrawing and withholding treatment? Are both methods equally moral and acceptable (or equally immoral and unacceptable? And what if it were up to you? Would pulling the plug be no more difficult than deciding not to connect the plug in the first place? Whatever

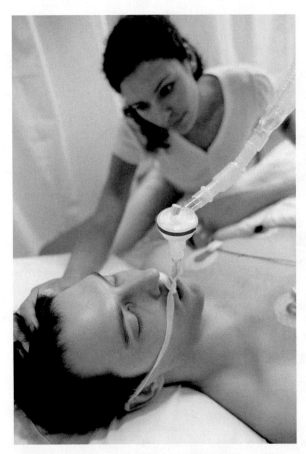

The iron lung came into widespread use during polio epidemics in the 1920s. It has been replaced by improved mechanical devices and, currently, sophisticated electronic models. Ventilators are used as part of extended life support systems, but also in short-term situations, such as recovery from surgical procedures.

your judgment and your decision, you are sure to find some experts agreeing and others disagreeing.

Euthanasia, assisted suicide, physician-assisted death, medicide, and other such terms all differ from suicide by involving the actions of another person. Suicidal people carry out their own intentions. Assisted death, by definition, requires another person to contribute actively to the outcome.

We use the *slippery slope argument* when we oppose a particular instance of assisted death because it might contribute to widespread abuse in other instances. "I can understand and sympathize with a person's request to be put out of his or her suffering," we might say. "But if society consents to 'mercy killing' in this instance, then tomorrow we will be asked to consent in a case where the right to die is not quite so clear. And so it will go, until we slide all the way down the slope." The ordeal of Chantal Sebire is an example.

Perhaps too many people would give up too soon when confronted not only with a terminal illness but with other life crises as well. Perhaps death would become too easy a way out. Perhaps euthanasia would even become the normative way of ending our lives. And perhaps that option would be seized on by the bean counters as a nifty way to control the costs of health care in a graying society. Depending on our anxieties and imagination, we could visualize a very slippery slope indeed. There are sharp disagreements today regarding the applicability of the slippery slope argument to a particular life-and-death decision.

It is important to keep in mind that the *living will* and other advance directives do not include provisions for assisted death. Many people who support the living will as an expression of the individual's preferences do not support assisted death. However, one sentence in the standard living will does walk the boundary: "I do, however, ask that medication be mercifully administered to me to alleviate suffering even though this may shorten my remaining life."

Suppose that you are a physician. The patient to whom you are attending has entrusted you with a signed and witnessed copy of her living will. She is dying in physical and emotional distress. "I want to die," she tells you. It had been your intention to control her pain with morphine. A heavier dose would not only relieve her pain but also hasten an easy death. Would you feel justified in prescribing a lethal dose because it is consistent with the advance directive (". . . even though this may shorten my remaining life")? Or would you feel that you were dishonoring your profession or even committing murder? Many physicians have faced this dilemma.

OUR CHANGING ATTITUDES TOWARD A RIGHT TO DIE

In recent years, the public has had more opportunity to learn about right-to-die issues. As we have already seen (Chapter 6), the doctrine of informed consent has made a difference, and the public soon proved supportive of natural death acts that support advance directives such as the living will. A national survey was conducted while open discussion of right to die issues was still in its early phases (Times Mirror, 1983). Most Americans already believed that there were circumstances in which a person should be allowed to die and that terminally ill people do have the right to accept or reject treatment options. Most people also said they would ask their doctors to stop treatment if they were in great physical pain and unable to function in daily activities because of an incurable disease. Yet there was also a consensus that medical personnel were not paying much attention to the patients' wishes (i.e., trying to resuscitate patients who had asked that this procedure not be done). Most respondents had heard about the living will and thought it a good idea, but few had actually completed such a document for themselves.

But what about the possible next step—euthanasia or assisted death? Perhaps surprisingly, 7 of 10 people felt it was justified to terminate a life if a person was suffering terrible pain from a terminal disease. The survey question was specific to married couples: if the pain was severe and could not be relieved, would it be an act of mercy to end the life of one's dying spouse (with the consent of the spouse, of course)? At this point, the role of the physician as terminator was not yet salient. The attitudinal picture was not as clear-cut as it might seem from the findings already mentioned. Do people have the moral right to end their own lives if afflicted with incurable disease? The public was divided on this question. There was a slight edge for those who agreed there is a moral right to suicide under this circumstance—but firm disapproval for ending one's life simply because it has become burdensome either to one's self or family. Americans were also about equally divided on whether they would want to have everything done to save their lives or choose comfort management instead.

Subsequent national polls have been summarized by the Death with Dignity National Center (2002) and the Pew Research Center (2006). The public has become much more aware of advance directives. There is also a marked increase in willingness of family members to discuss end-of-life medical care issues with each other. Most respondents believe that people should be able to exercise the right to make their own decisions in seeking or rejecting medical procedures, or choosing the hospice action. The public remains divided, though, about physician-assisted suicide. Withholding or withdrawing medical treatment is often regarded as an acceptable choice, but taking direct action to end a life is most often regarded as an immoral or criminal intervention. And the public remains about equally divided between their own end-of-life preferences. The next person you talk to is about as likely to say, "I want them to do everything they can to keep me going," as "I don't want to linger in pain and dependency. When the time comes, I want to go peacefully."

A useful study of changes in attitudes toward death in the United States has been reported by Bert Hayslip, Jr., and Cynthia A. Peveto (2005). Findings of their own recent study were compared with the pioneering research of Richard A. Kalish and David K. Reynolds (1976). Respondents now believe that physicians should tell terminally ill patients the truth about their conditions and that funerals and memorial services should reflect the personalities and values of the deceased individuals and their families. The public has become more active in participating in their own end-of-life decisions. Interestingly, there was also a higher priority given to spending time with loved ones and remaining in the interpersonal flow, as compared with the earlier tendency to withdraw when terminally ill.

Professional organizations such as the American College of Physicians have continued to oppose assisted death. According to physicians Timothy E. Quill and Christine K. Cassel (2003) these organizations:

rightly emphasize that palliative care should be the standard of care for the dying, and that the

inadequacies that exist in its delivery should be remedied. But such position statements generally understate the limitations of palliative care to alleviate some end-of-life suffering, and they do not provide adequate guidance about how physicians should approach patients with intractable suffering who are prepared to die (p. 208).

Individual physicians and nurses have their own opinions on this difficult and controversial subject. There continue to be situations in which responsible and well-informed health care providers might disagree on what should—and should not—be done.

THE RIGHT-TO-DIE DILEMMA: CASE EXAMPLES

We have examined some of the key concepts and learned how the public views them. Now we consider some of the specific human experiences that have influenced the present status of the right-to-die issue and that will also play a role in future developments. The most discussed and consequential cases have been those of Karen Ann Quinlan, "Debbie" (a pseudonym), Nancy Cruzan, and Terri Schiavo. All women. All young. All white. A coincidence?

The Ethics of Withdrawing Treatment: The Landmark Quinlan Case

Karen Ann Quinlan became the center of national attention when she lapsed into a coma after a party on the night of April 14, 1975. One friend applied mouth-to-mouth resuscitation while another called the police, who also attempted resuscitation and took her to a hospital. She started to breathe again, but did not return to consciousness. Traces of valium and quinine were found in her blood. Drug-induced coma was the preliminary diagnosis. Later this diagnosis was disputed, and it has never been fully clarified. Whatever the cause, Quinlan suffered severe and irreversible brain damage as a result of oxygen deprivation.

Weeks and then months passed. Quinlan remained in the hospital. Her vegetative functions were maintained on a ventilator, with intravenous tubes providing fluids and nutrition. Her body gradually wasted away. After a few months, the once vital and attractive young woman had become a 60-pound shriveled form, curled into a fetal position. Talk of recovery and a miraculous return to life became less frequent as time went by. The hospital expenses continued to mount day by day.

Karen Ann was the adopted child of deeply religious parents. Joseph Quinlan maintained hope for nearly half a year. Finally his priest persuaded him that morality does not require that extraordinary means be used to prolong life. The Quinlans asked two physicians to turn off the ventilator. They declined to do so. The physicians were not sure of the moral implications of such an action. Their professional training had not prepared them for this kind of situation. They were also concerned about the possibility of facing malpractice or even felony charges. For those physicians at that time, the request to "pull the plug" was almost equivalent to the first astronauts' walk in space.

What were the Quinlans to do? They pursued their request through the courts. This time-consuming legal process provided the opportunity for many to air opinions in the media and in professional circles as well as in the courts. Confusion was also generated. For example, there was a tendency to speak of Karen Ann as though she were already dead, even though *EEG tracings* still showed weak electrical activity in the brain. A neurologist described her condition as a "persistent vegetative state." This phrase would be repeated many times about many other nonresponsive persons in the years to come. An attorney for New Jersey described a brief visit to her room:

> *Her face is all distorted and she is sweating. Her eyes are open and blinking about twice a minute. She's sort of gasping. I've never seen anything like that. . . . I was there for seven minutes and it seemed like seven hours (Kron, 1975, p. 22).*

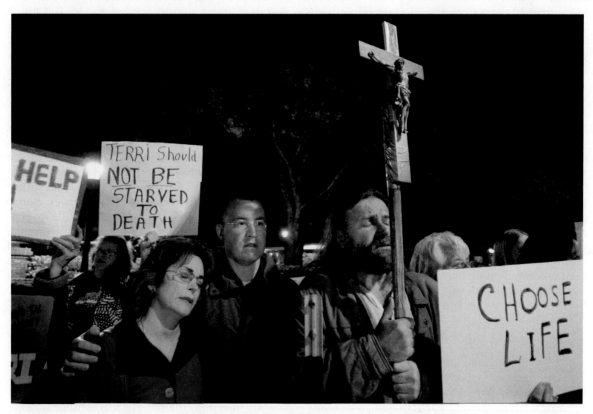

Court and medical findings were challenged by demonstrations against the decision to remove Terri Schiavo's feeding tube.

Medical testimony was given that Karen Ann would die within a short time if removed from the ventilator.

The judge rejected the argument that religious freedom should be the basis for approving the removal of the life-support system. This decision was appealed to the New Jersey Supreme Court. Here, for the first time, a court ruled that a ventilator could be turned off. However, the court imposed a condition: Physicians must first agree that Karen Ann had no reasonable chance of regaining consciousness. The New Jersey attorney general decided not to challenge this decision. The United States Supreme Court's turn would come later in the Nancy Cruzan case.

Finally, 14 months after she had lapsed into a nonresponsive state, Karen Ann was disconnected from the ventilator. She was expected to die quickly. However, her persistent vegetative state proved persistent indeed. Karen Ann remained alive (in some sense of the word) for more than 10 years until she succumbed to pneumonia in 1985.

There has been a long and winding road from the Karen Ann Quinlan dilemma to the present day. It has been estimated that 10,000 to 35,000 Americans exist in a persistent vegetative state and as many as another 150,000 have minimal consciousness syndrome (Maitland, 2005). Nobody knows for sure how many people are in such a condition. Some could remain unresponsive and "brain dead" (Chapter 2) yet alive for years. Families and caregivers must deal with this difficult situation day after day. Court decisions have sometimes clouded and sometimes clarified our understanding. Meanwhile, physicians and other health care providers responded in various ways to their new challenges. One of these responses became the subject of a continuing controversy. The principals in this drama were a young physician and a young woman who became known as Debbie.

"It's Over, Debbie": Compassion or Murder?

The Quinlan case was characterized by a long period of consultations, discussions, and legal proceedings. Many people participated, and many facts were brought forward for public, as well as family and professional, scrutiny. A very different case was reported in a leading medical journal. No author's name was attributed to "It's Over, Debbie," when this brief report was published in the *Journal of the American Medical Association* (Anonymous, 1988). The article was offered as a personal experience and consisted of only three paragraphs. This is the story:

A presumably young physician, a resident in gynecology, was called in the middle of the night by a nurse on the gynecologic–oncology (cancer) unit. This was not the physician's usual duty station. The doctor "trudged along, bumping sleepily against walls and corners and not believing I was up again." He picked up the patient's chart and was given some "hurried details" by the nurse. A 20-year-old patient was dying of ovarian cancer. An attempt had been made to sedate her by using an alcohol drip, but this had led her to vomit "unrelentingly."

Entering the patient's room, the resident saw that the patient was emaciated and looked much older than her actual age. "She was receiving nasal oxygen, had an IV, and was sitting in bed suffering from what was obviously severe air hunger," the physician reported. Another woman in the room stood by the bed, holding the patient's hand. The physician observed that "The room seemed filled with the patient's desperate effort to survive." The physician also observed that the patient was breathing with great difficulty. The article adds that the patient had not eaten or slept in two days nor had she responded to chemotherapy. Presumably this information had been gleaned from the doctor's quick glance through the patient's chart.

The resident felt that it was a "gallows scene, a cruel mockery of her youth and unfulfilled potential. Her only words to me were, 'Let's get this over with.'" The physician returned to the nurses' station to think things over. There the physician decided that he would "give her rest." The nurse was asked to draw morphine sulfate into a syringe. "'Enough,' I thought, 'to do the job.'" The physician returned to the patient's room and told the two women that he was going to give Debbie "something that would let her rest and say good-bye." Within seconds of the intravenous injection, the patient's breathing slowed, her eyes closed, and her distress seemed to be at an end. The other woman stroked Debbie's hair as she slept.

The doctor "waited for the inevitable next effect of depressing the respiratory drive." Four minutes later, the breathing slowed further, sputtered, and came to an end. The dark-haired woman stood erect and seemed relieved. "It's all over, Debbie," (p. 272).

This brief report raised a furor among the readers of this widely read and respected medical journal. The media picked it up, and the public was immediately drawn into the controversy as well. The response was divided, but critical reactions dominated.

What really had happened, and why? Here are what I see as the most salient questions and concerns:

- The physician had no prior acquaintance with the patient or her companion. This means that a stranger made the life-and-death decision. Should a physician assist the death of a patient with whom he or she has no previous relationship and knowledge?
- The decision was made very quickly and without consultation. Did the decision have to be made that quickly? Do physicians have the responsibility to get a second opinion before taking a life? The physician was fatigued. Should physicians be able to take their own states of mind and body into account when on the verge of making important decisions?
- The physician's anxiety was heightened by the fact that the patient was also young. It was difficult to establish a protective sense of emotional distance: This terrible thing could also happen to the physician.
- The physician seems to have projected his or her own thoughts and feelings on the patient. The "gallows" and "cruel mockery" images emerged from the physician's own mind and might or might not have resonated with Debbie's own thoughts. Should physicians be required to demonstrate competency in dealing with their own emotions before being entrusted with other people's lives?
- The nurse was ordered to prepare a lethal injection. Is it morally defensible to order another person to participate in an assisted death? Should the nurse have been given the opportunity to express her feelings and philosophy?

Did the nurse have the responsibility to refuse this order and inform the physician that she is reporting this incident immediately?
- The physician ordered a lethal dose of medication instead of a dose that might have provided relief without ending the patient's life. This alternative does not seem to have been considered. Does a physician have the right to end a life before attempting to relieve pain and other symptoms by nonlethal means? Was the physician adequately trained in symptom alleviation?
- The patient's distress had been intensified by a procedure (the alcohol drip) that had produced new symptoms without alleviating the existing symptoms. Why not dispense with the alcohol drip and see what improvement that might have made? Did this hospital routinely fail to provide adequate pain relief because of ignorance, indifference, or the fear of making an addict out of a terminally ill patient? Was it the failure of the hospital's overall symptom relief program that placed both the young resident and the young woman in this extremely stressful situation?
- Debbie spoke only one sentence to the doctor. Did the doctor try to converse with her or her companion? Did the physician hold her hand, establish eye contact, and attempt to have more guidance from her before making the decision to end her life? Should doctors be required to demonstrate communication competence in critical care situations before being entrusted with other people's lives?
- The doctor told the two women that he was giving Debbie (a) something that "would let her rest" and (b) and say good-bye. What actually happened, according to the report, was that Debbie closed her eyes and died shortly thereafter without having the chance to say good-bye or anything else. Was the physician actually concerned with enabling leave-taking communication between Debbie and her companion? Did the physician really believe that death and "rest" are identical outcomes? Or did the physician misrepresent what he or she was actually doing in order to reduce his or her own anxiety level? What responsibility to truth and open communication should be expected of the physician in critical care situations?

An Arrow Through the Physician's Armor

One of the painful lessons in this episode involves the physician's own physical, mental, and spiritual state and the nature of the health care system. A tired and probably overworked physician found himself in a stressful situation that neither medical training nor personal experience had equipped him to master. His own insulation from dying and death was pierced momentarily by seeing another young person in such a painful and vulnerable condition. The physician felt an urgent need to relieve Debbie's anguish as well as his own sense of personal vulnerability and inability to restore her health.

The physician had several options. These included taking other measures to relieve the patient's distress and discontinuing those that were adding to her distress. The physician could have consulted with others—the nurses who had been caring for Debbie as well as more experienced physicians. The physician could have made more effort to learn who Debbie was and what she wanted. It is not unusual for people to wish themselves dead when experiencing acute distress—but to be grateful later that another alternative had been found.

All these options required time and patience—and time was not what this tired, poorly prepared, overmatched, and anxious physician could afford. The decision to end Debbie's life was influenced by the physician's urgent need to terminate a situation in which he or she felt powerless, vulnerable, and depressed.

Much of the critical response called attention to the physician's disregard of standards and due procedure. Other doctors were aware that their own images and reputations were endangered by such episodes. The ease with which one young physician disposed of Debbie's problems by disposing of Debbie in the middle of the night seems to be a prime example of how slippery the slope can be.

Anxiety within the health care system can also lead to the opposite outcome: bodies being maintained on life-support systems despite the obvious futility of this procedure and despite the family's and patient's own expressed wishes. Decisions hastily made in the middle of the night by doctors who are poorly trained in self-monitoring and interpersonal communication afford few if any safeguards.

A Supreme Court Ruling: The Nancy Cruzan Case

The Supreme Court of the United States issued its first direct ruling on the subject 15 years after the Quinlan case brought the right-to-die issue to public attention. Nancy Cruzan, 26, had been critically injured in an automobile accident on January 11, 1983. When discovered by paramedics, Cruzan was lying face down in a ditch—no respiration, no heartbeat. The paramedics were able to revive her respiration and cardiac functions, but the young woman remained unresponsive. Physicians judged that she had suffered trauma to the brain and oxygen deprivation.

Three weeks later she could grimace, display motor reflexes, and take a little nourishment by mouth. There may have been slight responsivity to pain and sound. Nevertheless, Nancy Cruzan did not respond to conversation, express thoughts and needs, or engage in either verbal or nonverbal communication. Surgeons implanted a feeding tube with the permission of her husband. It was not necessary to use a ventilator because she continued to breathe on her own. Rehabilitation efforts failed. No improvement was noted or expected, but she remained alive and the state of Missouri continued to pay for her care. Nancy Cruzan's parents asked hospital personnel to discontinue the tube feeding and hydration. It was understood by everybody involved that this action would result in the young woman's death. The hospital declined to do so without court authorization. This request would go all the way to the U. S. Supreme Court (1989). This is a summary of what happened:

1. The trial court ruled that Nancy Cruzan had a fundamental right to refuse or accept the withdrawal of what it termed "death-prolonging procedures."
2. It was also ruled that she had expressed her general intent in a conversation with a close friend a year previously. Nancy had told her friend that if very ill or seriously injured she would not want to continue her life unless she could live "at least halfway normally."
3. The Missouri attorney general appealed this ruling to his state's supreme court. By a four-to-three margin, the lower court's ruling was overturned. The life-support procedures

would have to be continued. A key point in this decision was the fact that Nancy had not prepared a living will or any other document that established her intent beyond a reasonable doubt.

4. The U.S. Supreme Court recognized the principle that "a competent person has a constitutionally protected . . . interest in refusing unwanted medical treatment" (p. 183). Nevertheless, by a five-to-four margin, the nation's highest court refused to overturn the decision. Nancy Cruzan had the right to refuse "death-prolongation" procedures, but the state of Missouri had the right to require what it considered to be clear and convincing evidence that this would really have been Ms. Cruzan's intentions if she could now express herself.

5. The Supreme Court, however, had created a way out of the dilemma. The state itself could reconsider the evidence and approve withdrawal of life-support activities. And that is just what happened. Nancy Cruzan's physician had opposed withdrawal of life support. But now, after six years, he had seen enough. A court-appointed guardian asked the physician if he still thought it was within the patient's interest to continue the tube feeding and hydration. "No, sir. I think it would be personally a living hell!" A Jasper County judge ruled that the parents' request could be honored. There were no further legal challenges this time, although a throng of protesters (people who had not known Nancy Cruzan personally) voiced their disapproval. The young woman died quietly 12 days after the tubes were removed.

What was learned from this ordeal? The U.S. Supreme Court did affirm the principle that a competent person has the right to refuse treatment that would only prolong suffering, and that local jurisdictions could require due process. The *Cruzan vs. Missouri* decision, however, did not address all the issues that can arise in right-to-die cases; it did not even address all the salient issues in the Cruzan case.

What lessons can we draw? We can see it would be useful to establish our wishes in the form of a written advance directive. Nancy Cruzan's situation would have been resolved sooner and with less

stress for everybody concerned had she executed a living will—but how many 23-year-olds (or 46-year-olds, for that matter) do you know who have actually done this? We can also see that the decision to withdraw life support is a difficult one when respiratory, cardiac function, and motor reflexes persist without external aids. The Missouri State Supreme Court emphasized that "Nancy is diagnosed as in a persistent vegetative state. She is not dead. She is not terminally ill. Medical experts testified that she could live another thirty years" (1989, p.180). We need to be well informed and secure in our understanding about what it means to be alive and a person.

Finally, we are left with the question of perceived social value. Both Karen Ann Quinlan and Nancy Cruzan were young people who seemed to have full lives ahead of them. What about elderly people who find themselves in similar predicaments? Hemlock Society author Donald W. Cox (1993) notes:

> On November 30, two weeks prior to Judge Teel's order to remove Nancy's feeding tube from her stomach, the Court of Common Pleas in Lackawanna County (Scranton), Pennsylvania, held that a sixty-four-year-old incompetent woman in a persistent vegetative state was entitled to have a naso-gastric tube withdrawn. The hospital removed the tube and the woman died peacefully and quietly, in sharp contrast to the front-page publicity that enveloped Cruzan's death a few weeks later (p. 86).

Many elderly men and women have died in this manner. Others have died when health care personnel have decided against starting life-support procedures. As a nation, we seem to place less value on the lives of older adults. We assume that old people are supposed to be depressed and therefore seldom intervene. When older people seem ready to die—well, that's what they're supposed to do, right?

TERRI SCHIAVO: WHO DECIDES?

There is a sequence of events to be considered before we come to the "Schiavo case" as it emerged in the media spotlight. Jay Wolfson's (2003) official report to Florida Governor Jeb Bush is a balanced, detailed, and humane account of a complex situation, as is the succinct report Daniel Eisenberg published in *Time* (2005). Other sources are cited as appropriate.

The Ordeal Begins

The Theresa (Terri) Schiavo known to her family and friends vanished in the early morning of February 25, 1990, when she was felled by a heart attack, apparently linked to her eating disorder, and possibly to a fertility program. A decade later she remained on life support in a skilled nursing facility, unknown to the general public. She received physical, occupational, recreational, and speech therapies, but showed only reflexive movements, random eye opening, and no communication ability (Wolfson, 2003). At first, husband Michael and the Schindlers [Terri's parents] had worked together closely in hoping to rehabilitate Terri. However, Terri's husband and parents eventually came to different opinions about her possibility for recovery. Furthermore, a court judgment had found a fertility clinic guilty of malpractice in overseeing Terri's attempts to become pregnant. The award was in the million-dollar range. Money started to matter.

Following this court judgment, the Schindlers petitioned the court to remove Michael as guardian, alleging that he was not caring for Terri. The court ruled against this petition, noting that Michael had taken a forceful role in assuring that Terri consistently received the best care possible and had managed the award fund meticulously.

In 1994, Terri contracted a urinary tract infection. Michael Schiavo and the physician agreed there was no longer even a remote chance for her recovery and decided not to treat the infection. Additionally, a DNR order was posted so that no resuscitation would be attempted if she should have another cardiac arrest. After waiting another three years, Michael petitioned to discontinue life support. Clinical review confirmed that Terri's condition was that of "a diagnosed persistent vegetative state with no chance of improvement." Mrs. Schindler stated that Terri displayed special responses, mostly to her, but these were not observed or documented by others.

The Schindlers continued their efforts to revoke the decision to remove Terri's feeding tube. There were repeated court considerations of this request, in which the Schindlers were given opportunity to produce testimony and offer evidence. The court gave credibility to testimony that when still in good health Terri had mentioned that she would never want to be put on life support if something happened to her. The decision once again approved the request to discontinue life support. Much more was yet to happen, but it will be useful to pause for comment before describing the next phase.

Comments I

The situation that enveloped Terri Schiavo, her husband, parents, and caregivers had many significant elements.

When it started: Paramedics, emergency rooms, and life-supporting technology are fairly recent additions to the health care system. There was a 911 telephone number for Michael to call, and skilled personnel to respond, although in this case it was not possible to prevent the anoxia.

All that would follow—the years of persistent vegetative functioning, the family disputes, the national controversy—would not have happened in an earlier generation, when fewer emergency options were available. These efforts added Terri to the lengthening list of people existing on the life/death borderline.

Who decides? The ordeal of the Schiavo and Schindler families occurred at a time when the living will and the right to exercise informed consent had been affirmed. Much had been discussed and learned from earlier cases, particularly those of Quinlan, Debbie, and Cruzan. An advance directive in which Terri expressed the wish to have resuscitation and life-support efforts withheld would very likely have been respected. However, it was unusual at that time for a young person to make a living will, and it is still uncommon today. The courts sifted through reports of conversations in which Terri might or might not have clearly communicated her views. Unfortunately, Terri was in no condition to express her wishes once she had become incapacitated. She might have designated a person to speak in her behalf if such a situation should arise, a health care proxy. However, this would also have been an unusual action for a young person. From this lack of definitive knowledge of Terri's own wishes there developed a long, complex, and adversarial process to determine who should make the decision about Terri's fate and on what basis.

Michele Mathis (2005) explains that:

when a patient is no longer able to make medical treatment decisions for herself, care providers and those who know the patient well should try to effectuate the treatment choices she would have made. This is the substituted judgment *standard of surrogate decision-making. Substituted judgment is a way of carrying the value of patient self-determination forward into a time when the patient is incapable of autonomy. This is now referred to as the best interests standard for medical decision-making, and is relied upon when there is no information about what the patient might have wanted (p. 3).*

But whose judgment should be substituted for the incapacitated Terri Schiavo's?

Whose fault? Relationships among the people close to Terri were also strained by uncertainty regarding the cause of her collapse. Had the fertility clinic failed to safeguard her health? Had Terri seriously harmed her body by her weight-loss program? The lack of closure kept uncertainty and anxiety at a high pitch. (Later the Schindlers would charge that Michael had physically abused Terri, a claim that earned little support and was dismissed after the autopsy.)

These uncertainties were augmented by distrust of medical judgment by the Schindlers and, later, by some politicians and media professionals. Terri was seen by numerous physicians, and her records were reviewed by outside experts, including those who were court-appointed. The same finding kept coming up: persistence (or permanent) vegetative state. Nevertheless, the Schindlers insisted that Terri continued to have thoughts and experiences and might yet recover.

The Public Controversy

The Schiavo case moved into public awareness when Michael petitioned a court for removal of Terri's feeding tube. The court stayed the order to give the Schindlers time to appeal. The Florida Supreme Court denied the appeal and the U.S. Supreme Court refused to consider a further appeal. The Schindlers continued to pursue other courses of action in the legal system. Judges gave both sides ample opportunity to present evidence and arguments. A medical panel was appointed with five doctors, one chosen by the court, and two by each side in the controversy. These proceedings carried forward into 2002, when the judge ruled that there was no substantial possibility that Terri's condition could be improved. For the second time, an order was issued to withdraw the feeding tube, and for the second time, postponed to give the Schindlers opportunity for further appeal. Florida governor Jeb Bush filed a brief on their behalf, and Terri Schiavo's 13-year ordeal was now in the national spotlight.

The next medical procedure was followed by an unprecedented political action. The feeding tube was disconnected, but Governor Bush asked the state legislature to pass "Terri's Law," which, quickly enacted, provided the opportunity to have the tube reinserted. President George W. Bush praised this action, thereby further rallying pro-life support. Politics now towered over the medical and legal systems.

Headlines and talk shows blazed with opinions and expert (and not so expert) commentary. Federal and state government had chosen to oppose medical opinion and the judgment of several courts. The courts did not give in. A Florida judge ruled that Terri's Law was unconstitutional, and the Florida Supreme Court agreed. The U.S. Supreme Court was again petitioned to hear the case, and again declined. As Mathes (2005) notes, Terri Schiavo had become the central figure in one of the most adjudicated cases in the nation's history. There was still more to come (Eisenberg, 2005). The Florida legislature came up with a new law to prevent removal of the feeding tube, but this one was also rejected in court. Just a few weeks later, it was the U.S. House and Senate that agreed on a federal bill to counter the court ruling to take Terri off life support.

These fast-moving proceedings were unprecedented in American history—the executive and legislative branches of the government putting other issues aside (e.g., post 9/11 terrorism) to overturn the judicial branch and the medical opinion on which it had relied. The bill was quickly passed and signed by the president, but not before the feeding tube was disconnected. The courts were firm in their judgment that Terri Schiavo was in a persistent vegetative state and had no hope of recovery.

Terri Schiavo died of dehydration after seven years of heated public controversy surrounding her condition. The Schindlers had never given up their efforts to keep her alive. According to medical experts, Terri had been unconscious since the loss of oxygen to her brain 15 years earlier. Repeated assessments had never discovered any electrical activity in her brain. Autopsy found that her brain had shrunk to half its size and suffered severe and irreversible damage. The medical examiner concluded that "no amount of therapy or treatment would have regenerated the massive loss of neurons" (Stacy, 2005).

Surveys made it clear that the public disapproved of Congress's attempt to intervene, and thought that the opposition to removal of life support had more to do with politics than ethical principles and values (Eisenberg, 2005). There was particular scorn for Senate Majority Leader Bill Frist, a heart surgeon. He had stated that Terri Schiavo was "not somebody in persistent vegetative state," although he had not examined her nor reviewed her case. His later denial of that statement undermined his credibility, and might have contributed to his loss of the Senate leadership position (Babington, 2005).

Comments II

Consider considering: The anguish and tensions experienced by Terri's husband and parents might have been intensified by the way our judicial system works. The system is basically adversarial. By contrast, a system with the purpose of coming to the best possible outcome would encourage examination of perspectives, sharing, and mediation. Family courts have had some success in offering a less confrontational approach. Ethics committees have also resolved right-to-die issues without a pressurized court situation. Perhaps more opportunity should be provided for respectful consideration of values and viewpoints instead of giving in to the impulse to make a federal case out of a deeply emotional situation.

The knowledge gap: A brief videotape of Terri Schiavo was shown repeatedly on television. I saw what you saw. She was alive and moving! Perhaps there was purpose! Perhaps she was responding to a relationship! It was not difficult to suppose that the diagnosis of persistent vegetative state was too extreme. Nevertheless, I trust the medical experts on this one. The diagnosis of severe brain impairment has gone well beyond guesswork. The medical experts who examined Terri Schiavo and analyzed the findings knew what they were doing, as court after court agreed. For the most part, however, the media did not come up to that level. The videotape was routinely presented without reference to the date it had been recorded and without competent discussion of what we were seeing. Furthermore, it was later revealed that the videotape reviewed by lawmakers had been edited to make the best possible case for Schiavo's status. A continuing problem is the gap between general public conceptions of brain damage and the specialized knowledge that is continuing to develop in clinical practice and neuroscience. Finding a way to reduce that gap would make for fewer misunderstandings and unnecessary confrontations. It might also avoid the distress we feel when we assume that thirst and hunger can be experienced when a person is locked into a persistent vegetative state.

Prime people: A disturbing headline flashed across the newspaper page in my hands two months after Terri Schiavo's death: "MISSING: News Coverage on the Disappearance of Anyone Who's Not an Attractive, White Female" (Texeira, 2005). The article focused not on Terri, but on what was at that time the latest example of an attractive white female (Natalee Holloway) whose disappearance was a top story. The author points out that most of the missing adults tracked by the FBI are men, and that many of those abducted or kidnapped are black. News editors believe, however, that the public is more interested in "prime people," especially attractive white females. This bias certainly exists in the right-to-die realm. The most reported, studied, and influential cases have had the same demographics as the prime people who have gone missing. I am not suggesting that we should have ignored the disappearance of Natalee Holloway or the ordeal of Terri Schiavo. I wonder, though, about the spectacular lack of attention to the many people in life-challenged conditions who are aged or otherwise not perceived as valuable or "interesting" enough. The death system takes its priorities from the values and caprices of society at large.

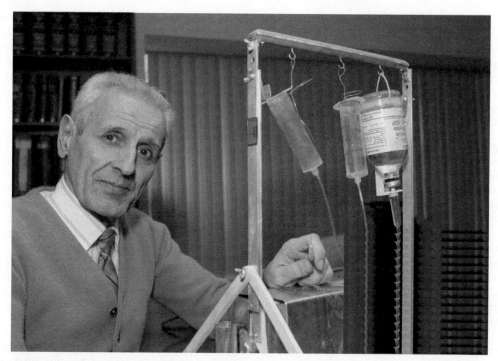

Jack Kevorkian (1923-2011) with his suicide machine. Kevorkian was "present" at the deaths of more than a hundred people before being found guilty, imprisoned, and eventually released on his promise not to resume this practice.

DR. KEVORKIAN AND THE ASSISTED-SUICIDE MOVEMENT

The assisted suicide controversy in the United States is closely associated with Dr. Jack Kevorkian, a retired pathologist. His activities dominated the media spotlight until the television program *60 Minutes* featured a video that showed him giving a lethal injection to Thomas Youk. Kevorkian challenged prosecutors to try him for murder. Kevorkian was then convicted of second-degree murder and imprisoned in a Michigan penal facility. He served eight years of his sentence and, at the age of 79, was released from prison with his promise to refrain from any further assisted death activities.

Kevorkian often described his services as assisted suicide. This term locks in a particular interpretation (suicide), with which not all proponents of assisted death agree. We will use the more neutral term, *assisted death*, which provides maneuvering room for a variety of interpretations. The most common term now in use is physician-assisted death. Family members and friends have also been known to assist in bringing about death, but it is medical participation that has been at the center of controversy.

Assisted Death in the Kevorkian Manner

The mainstream medical establishment had been firmly opposed to any form of assisted death when Kevorkian entered the scene. The case against assisted death was based on the following considerations:

- Taking a life is inconsistent with the responsibilities and values of a physician, a healer.
- Some physicians could not even begin to consider the possibility of assisting death because of their deeply held religious convictions.

- The life might be "mis-taken." Nature often surprises even the most adroit physician. The impulse to relieve suffering might therefore result in ending a life that had potential for recovery.
- Serious legal consequences might befall any physician who engaged in assisted death.

When Kevorkian started his campaign in 1990, he had practically no support from either medical organizations or court rulings. He hoped to arouse the public and thereby force the medical profession to change its position. This plan required Kevorkian to reveal rather than conceal his actions. He was eminently successful in arousing public opinion, both pro and con.

People who have known Kevorkian over the years characterized him as a very intelligent man with a keen grasp of medical history (Nicol & Wylie, 2006). Families who have sought his services often described him as a compassionate and understanding person. On the other hand, critics resented Kevorkian's verbal attacks on those who do not agree with him, his delight in publicity, and his "lone wolf" approach. Not just what Kevorkian did, but how he did it has had a continuing influence on attitudes toward assisted death.

Kevorkian's Agenda

Kevorkian's agenda included the establishment of centers in communities across the nation in which people could not only have assisted deaths upon their request, but also in which biomedical research could be done on dying and death. These *orbitoria* would go much further than previously has been possible to investigate the nature of death. We should not be squeamish about pursuing research across the borders from dying to death. Kevorkian was also a strong advocate for organ donation and attempted to establish a program through which condemned prisoners could donate their body parts. He was angered and disappointed when prisoners as well as officials declined this opportunity.

Kevorkian's Method

People turned to Kevorkian when there did not seem to be either hope for improvement or relief from suffering. He would discuss the situation with the patient and family members. Some of these sessions were recorded on videotape, others are excerpted in a biography co-authored by two of his close friends (Nicol & Wylie, 2006). Kevorkian repeatedly emphasized that he did not pressure patients to make the final decision quickly or in the direction of assisted death. Carol Loving (1995/1996) describes the final scene in which her son Nick was to be terminated by Kevorkian:

> Dr. Kevorkian kept telling him, "If you don't want to go through with this, you don't have to. You don't have to worry about hurting our feelings. If you want to postpone for a week, a month, a year, don't even hesitate." My son kept saying, "No, No, let's do it. I want to go. I want to go. So I helped him with his mask to get it all adjusted. . . . Dr. Kevorkian told him, "Now anytime you feel comfortable and ready you just go ahead and pull it. The gas will start." (p. 175).

The death of Nick Loving was accomplished through an apparatus constructed by Kevorkian that he sometimes referred to as the "Merciton" but became better known as "the suicide machine." Whether Kevorkian used this or some other procedure for a particular patient, it was intended to be the patient who took the decisive action. Kevorkian therefore could speak of having "assisted" at a death. The fact that Kevorkian did not himself take the final action also was intended as protection against possible charges of murder. He forfeited this protection when he gave Thomas Youk a lethal injection on national television.

Evaluating Kevorkian's Approach

Physician-assisted death as advocated and practiced by Kevorkian has been criticized on the grounds that only God can give and only God should take life. There is also the objection, linked to the Hippocratic Oath, that the physician must always be on the side of life.

Additional problems demand attention when we look at the data for the deaths that Kevorkian has acknowledged facilitating. A detailed presentation of these data has been provided in two articles written by Kalman J. Kaplan et al. (2000a; 2000b). The most important data come from medical examiners who personally investigated the cases. Information of this kind was available for 93 cases.

1. *Most of the people whose deaths have been assisted by Kevorkian were not terminally ill.* Only 28.3 percent were terminally ill. Since the majority (69.9 percent) were not terminally ill, (a) How adequate was Kevorkian's medical assessment of the patients? (b) How valid is his claim for relieving the suffering of dying people if most were not dying? and (c) Do these data confirm the fears of a very slippery slope? In other words, did the availability of "death on demand" lead to premature death?

2. *The gender bias in Kevorkian's clientele suggests that his practice encouraged increased suicidality among women.* All of Kevorkian's assisted deaths had been women before the Michigan law against assisted suicide was signed by the governor. During the period in which Kevorkian was dealing with legal proceedings against him, he participated in the deaths of 11 men and 9 women. Acquitted on charges of assisted suicide, Kevorkian returned to the original pattern, in which by far the greater number of assisted suicides were women. In the general population, women are much less likely than men to commit suicide. The reverse is true among Kevorkian's assisted-death patients.

3. *Those assisted to death by Kevorkian fit the general profile of suicide attempters rather than terminally ill people.* They had a high incidence of depression and dependency and a low incidence of the conditions that are the most common causes of death in the United States. The implication is that Kevorkian either stimulated or was the receptive target for unhappy people who might otherwise have either attempted nonfatal suicide attempts or found other ways to deal with their situations.

4. *Another disturbing element was Kevorkian's failure to diagnose or treat their depression.* Many people with depressive episodes or tendencies are effectively treated every day. Some of these people do express the desire to end their lives in order to end their miseries. Competent medical help has often contributed to a restoration of their spirits—but competent medical help with their lives is not what they receive from Kevorkian.

5. *Kevorkian functioned without adequate medical information and consultation.* He seldom asked for a second opinion—and did so less and less as he continued his practice. This was especially unfortunate because Kevorkian did not have expertise in psychiatric evaluation or palliative care. Part of the problem came from the unwillingness of other physicians to cooperate with him. He could have done much more, however, to make sure his patients had the advantage of medical and psychiatric expertise before assisting them to death.

6. *Death is much too extreme a solution to the relief of suffering.* For those people who are in severe pain (most of his patients were not) there were alternatives. It is interesting to take an international example here. There was a sharp negative response after an eminent Japanese physician administered a lethal drug to his patient. Philosopher Histake Kato reflected on a friend who was in excruciating pain during an attack of pancreatitis. The first doctor he saw did not take painkilling measures. His friend switched to another hospital where the pain was removed. "In other words, both doctors who have the best know-how about eliminating pain and doctors who have no know-how at all exist side by side in the Japanese medical system." Kevorkian did not establish his credentials for the up-to-date and effective relief of pain, and he has shown little familiarity or interest in the hospice movement. He did not offer an alternative other than death.

7. *Despite his disclaimers, Kevorkian rushed some people into assisted death without adequate safeguards and consideration.* His very first case, Janet Adkins, was in good health, was suffering no pain, and, in fact, had been playing tennis with her teenage son. Kevorkian seemed to have been influenced by the promptings of her husband. She was still playing tennis at the time her husband sent for Kevorian. I don't think we really have to add this. There are other cases in which Kevorkian seems to have strayed from his own criteria (see Box 9-1). Data show that as time went on, Kevorkian moved more rapidly from first meeting with the patient to the death. He increasingly violated the criteria he had himself

BOX 9-1

KEVORKIAN'S STANDARDS AND KEVORKIAN'S ACTIONS

Kevorkian's Standards	Kevorkian's Actions
Call for psychiatric consultation	Rarely called for consultation
Call for pain specialist consultation	Rarely called for pain specialist
24-hour waiting period after final request	Many deaths in less than one day
Extensive patient counseling	Brief conversations; no professional counseling
Stop the process if any sign that patient is ambivalent	Some patients were clearly ambivalent but assisted death was carried out

insisted upon in his public statements. Kaplan reported on one of these cases (1998):

> Gale, a 72-year-old former merchant marine, was suffering from emphysema. There is no question that he asked to die, but there is evidence that Gale had a great deal of ambivalence after the gas mask was put on his face, asking twice that it be removed. Kevorkian's original record of the incident . . . found in a garbage bag outside his assistant's house, indicated that Kevorkian removed the mask in response to Gale's first request, but did not remove it in response to the second (p. 173).

8. *Kevorkian used "silencing" techniques to defend his actions.* This pattern is clear in his book and in many of his presentations through the media. It is only the physician who should assist deaths. It is only the physician who understands. This attitude dismisses the experiences, values, knowledge, and feelings of a great many other people, including clergy, nurses, social workers, attorneys, sociologists, anthropologists, and philosophers. Kevorkian is open to the charge of excessively medicalizing dying and death.

Oakland County (Michigan) Judge Jessica Cooper offered her own evaluation of Kevorkian's activities in sentencing him to a term of 10 to 25 years when he was found guilty of second-degree murder: Kevorkian had been convicted of second-degree murder after he invited CBS's *60 Minutes* program to show a videotape in which

he administered a lethal injection (a departure from only "assisting" in a death).

> This trial was not about the political or moral correctness of euthanasia. It was all about you, sir. It was about lawlessness. It was about disrespect for a society that exists and flourishes because of the strength of the legal system. No one, sir, is above the law. No one. You were on bond to another judge when you committed this offense; you were not licensed to practice medicine when you committed this offense, and you hadn't been licensed for eight years. And you had the audacity to go on national television, show the world what you did and dare the legal system to stop you. Well, sir, consider yourself stopped.

But that was not the end of the story. Three years after his release from prison, Kevorkian became the subject of a well-received HBO movie, *You Don't Know Jack.* Al Pacino plays Kevorkian in a thoughtful representation of his quest and experiences.

The Netherlands: A Social Experiment Watched Closely by the World

When Kevorkian first advertised his services, he was aware that physician-assisted death had already gained a foothold in the Netherlands, the first nation to accept the option of assisted death. Belgium followed suit in 2002 (Gastmans,

Van Neste, & Schotsmans, 2004). Dutch courts had sanctioned cases of medically assisted death brought before them during the 1980s (Gomez, 1991). These decisions drew a mixed reaction from legal experts, health care professionals, and the general public. Euthanasia was not officially made legal, but a new law passed in 1993 spared doctors from prosecution if they followed an established set of rules. This was followed in 2000 by a law that more clearly decriminalized assistance in dying. It was opposed strenuously by several religious groups, but passed by a large margin (Religious Tolerance, 2008). Since that time, public opinion in the Netherlands has been strongly favorable to this policy, though with occasional expressions of concern about the way it has been carried out by some physicians. You will notice in Box 9-2 that there is a provision that goes beyond the more limited conception of euthanasia as acceptable only for terminally ill people.

The issue is not so easily resolved, however. Some Dutch health care providers remain opposed to assisted death for personal and/or moral reasons. Others are worried about the adequacy of the decision-making process: Do the people involved always communicate adequately with each other and have full knowledge of the available options? Still others accepted the legalization of assisted death in its present form but harbored concerns about the possibility of their nation taking more dangerous steps down that slippery slope. This fear was intensified on April 29, 1995, when an infant born in terrible pain with a spinal column defect was injected with a muscular relaxant that stopped her breathing. The baby girl's parents had authorized the procedure. The Dutch Ministry of Justice prosecuted the physician on the charge of premeditated murder. The physician was found guilty but not convicted. The trial was intended not to punish this physician but to establish new guidelines for assisted death (or, as some still prefer, euthanasia) for newborns with severe disabilities.

This case was important not only because it involved a newborn, but also because (a) the decision was in the form of substituted judgment and (b) despite the infant's serious physical defect and pain, she was not terminally ill. The little girl could not speak for herself. Is it reasonable and moral for anybody, even her parents, to make the decision to end her life? Or is the acceptance of this act of assisted death a dangerous slide further down the slippery slope that could result in widespread killing of newborns and perhaps others who do not meet somebody's criteria for being an acceptable person? Opponents were concerned that the slope had now become much too slippery. Euthanasia had become involuntary, and therefore verged on homicide. However, proponents pointed out that the parents had loved their baby and accepted her disabilities. What they could not bear was the fact that the baby was suffering pain and that the pain could not be relieved. From this perspective, the parents and the sanctioning government were approving a compassionate end to a life that would have been dominated by suffering.

Unexpected situations continue to arise and unexpected conclusions sometimes follow.

BOX 9-2

RULES FOR ASSISTED DYING IN THE NETHERLANDS

- The patient must be suffering unbearably. However, they need not be terminally ill.
- The patient must make a request on a voluntary, well-considered, and sustained basis.
- The doctor and patient must have had a long-term relationship.

- There must be no reasonable alternative to relieve the patient's suffering.
- The doctor must consult at least one other independent physician.
- Due medical care must be followed.

For example, an institutionalized Dutch woman requested assisted death. The request was denied, but she was told that the institution could not force her to eat. She took no food and only a little water for several days and continued to express her wish to die. The institution then respected her decision and stopped offering her food. Well, they did give her some apple juice.

To the surprise of those who attended to her needs, her physical situation had not really deteriorated after three weeks. It was discovered that the contents of apple juice can keep people alive well over a hundred days and that, if she kept drinking apple juice, she would probably not die from starvation. A week later the nurses happened to serve the residents a hot meal with French fried chicken. At the smell of this dish, the woman all of a sudden asked whether she could have some, too. Ever since she has been eating her meals again and for many months afterward she happily participated in all different kinds of activities the nursing home had to offer (Meijburg, 1995/1996, p. 192).

Gradually the woman's physical condition deteriorated, and "she died a natural death." This is one of many vignettes suggesting that there may be a lot of unknowns and a good deal of ambiguity in the interaction between a person requesting assisted death and those who must respond to this request in some way. Perhaps it is not surprising that physician-assisted death remains a deeply divisive issue in the nation that has been most receptive to the idea.

Criticisms of euthanasia practice in the Netherlands continue to accumulate. There are charges that the lives of newborns who are regarded as severely and incurably impaired are terminated much more often than reported—but that the same practice almost certainly occurs quietly in other countries (Johnson, 2005). Substantial research reports indicate that consultations with patients and families are sometimes bypassed and that other safe practice guidelines are also frequently disregarded (Cohen-Almagor, 2003, 2004). Daniel Callahan (2008), a leading bioethicist, observes that there is still an unresolved history of probable unreported physician-assisted deaths in which patient's consent seems to have been bypassed. He does, however, praise the Netherlands' strong effort to require physicians to explain and document every assisted death decision.

The Netherlands' experience suggests that any movement toward legalization of assisted death or other forms of euthanasia should be accompanied by thorough discussion, clarification, and enforceable regulations.

ASSISTED DEATH IN THE UNITED STATES

Many people in the right-to-die movement were opposed to Kevorkian's approach. They did not want to rely on the judgment of one physician operating outside the legal and medical system. There was particular concern that some of the people whose lives were being terminated by Kevorkian might have found another way to cope with their situations, given adequate counseling and support. The nation as a whole was moving toward the enactment of natural death acts (successors to the living will) that affirmed the right of individuals to control their end-of-life care through informed consent and advance directives. However, performing an action with the intent of terminating a life remained beyond the emerging consensus that people have the right to have treatment withheld or withdrawn.

The Oregon Death with Dignity Act

The voters of Oregon were the first to take that one long step further by supporting a measure legalizing assisted death in 1994 and reaffirming it in 1997. The act applies only to terminally ill adults in Oregon. Eligibility for assisted death in Oregon requires that the person be older than 18 years and have an incurable and irreversible disease that will probably produce death within six months ("tired of living" or depressed do not qualify). Furthermore, the regulations rule out people who have progressively deteriorating conditions but are not at a high risk for death at the present time. An important example is multiple sclerosis (MS). Kevorkian would later state that he had participated in 133 assisted deaths. The known number was 93 at the time. It was found that at least 20 of these people were afflicted with MS and not currently at high risk for death.

Oregon's requirements are more comprehensive and detailed than those of the Netherlands.

BOX 9-3

OREGON DEATH WITH DIGNITY REQUIREMENTS

Basic Provisions

- The DWDA allows terminally ill Oregon residents to obtain and use prescriptions from their physicians for self-administered, lethal medications.
- Ending one's life in accordance with the law does not constitute suicide.
- The DWDA specifically prohibits euthanasia, where a physician or other person directly administers a medication to end another's life.

Eligibility

- 18 years of age or older
- A resident of Oregon
- Capable of making and communicating health care decisions
- Diagnosed with a terminal illness that will lead to death within six months

Procedure

- Patient must make two oral requests to his or her physician, separated by at least 15 days.
- Patient must provide a written request to his or her physician, signed in the presence of two witnesses.
- The prescribing physician and a consulting physician must confirm the diagnosis and prognosis.
- The prescribing physician and a consulting physician must determine whether the patient is competent to make and communicate the decision.
- If either physician believes the patient's judgment is impaired by a psychiatric or psychological disorder, the patient must be referred for a psychological examination.
- The prescribing physician must inform the patient of feasible alternatives to DWDA, including comfort care, hospice care, and pain control.
- The prescribing physician must request, but may not require, the patient to notify his or her next-of-kin of the prescription request.

Additional Physician Responsibilities

- Physicians must report to the Department of Human services all prescriptions for lethal medications. Reporting is not required if patients begin the request process but never receive a prescription.
- Pharmacists must be informed of the prescribed medication's intended use.

Protections from Criminal Prosecution

- Physicians and patients who adhere to the requirements of the Act are protected from criminal prosecution.
- The choice of DWDA cannot affect the status of a patient's health or insurance policies.
- Physicians, pharmacists, and health care systems are under no obligation to participate in the DWDA.
- Action taken in accordance with the DWDA does not constitute suicide, mercy killing or homicide under the law.

Adapted from Oregon Revised Statutes as found at http://oregon.gov/DHS/ph/pas/ors.shtml.

There is an especially significant difference: the lethal medications are to be self-administered. A physician supplies the medication, but the patient is the one who ends his or her own life. Euthanasia as such is specifically prohibited.

The requirements of the Death with Dignity Act (DVDA) are presented in Box 9-3. These provisions were worked out after several years of consultation among health care providers, legal experts, and bioethics specialists.

What has happened since the DVDA became operative in 1998? About 30,000 people die in Oregon each year. People who self-terminated under DVDA rules were a small fraction of this total. In 2009, 59 terminally ill people received took lethal medication as part of the program. Over an 11-year period (1998–2009), 244 men and 216 women self-terminated. A total of 341 patients have self-terminated through the decade. The DWDA has been responsible for about 16 deaths out of 10,000 (http://oregon.gov/DHS/ph/pas/index.shtml). Older adults made the most use of this provision: about four out of five terminations were by people age 75 or above. Most often the underlying illness was some form of cancer. Hospice was the choice or end of life care by more than 9 out of 10 who eventually chose termination. None of these deaths were rushed: there was usually about a six-week interval between the patient's request and the termination.

The practicing physicians who participated had an average of 20 years of experience and worked mostly in the specialties of internal medicine, oncology, and family medicine. The prescribing physician or other health care providers were present at the time of all the deaths. Most of the patients were in their late 60s, and cancer was by far the most common primary illness.

Why did these terminally ill people express the wish for assisted death? Most frequent was the fear of continuing to lose autonomy, having less ability to participate in actions that make life enjoyable, losing control of body functions, and the feeling of a progressive loss of dignity. None of the self-terminating patients called for emergency intervention after ingesting the final medication.

Unbearable pain was not among the most frequently mentioned reasons. Although it might seem surprising that pain is not necessarily the most common reason for requesting assisted death, this finding has also been observed in other studies (e.g., Arnold, 2004).

There have been interesting side effects of the Oregon program. More (90 percent) of the patients died at home and, as mentioned, were enrolled in hospice care. Physicians report that they have been improving their knowledge of pain medications for the terminally ill as well as their skill in recognizing depression; they were also referring patients to hospice more frequently (Ganzini et al., 2001). The effect of this program on physicians has been perhaps stronger than anticipated (Dobscha, Heintz, Press, & Ganzini, 2004):

Requests for assisted suicide had a powerful impact on physicians and their practices. Physicians often felt unprepared, and experienced apprehension and discomfort before and after receiving requests. Prominent sources of discomfort included concerns about adequately managing symptoms and suffering, not wanting to abandon patients, and incomplete understanding of patients' preferences, especially when physicians did not know patients well. . . . Regardless of whether they prescribed or not, physicians did not express major regrets about their decisions. Requests often facilitated discussion of important issues, and many physicians felt that the process increased their confidence (p. 451).

Nurses have reported that they try to explore what patients really mean when they ask to have their lives terminated (Schwarz, 2005). As one hospice nurse observed: "Things are often not as they seem. It takes detective work to find out what they mean by 'help me die,'" (p. A8). When nurses listened actively to the wishes of dying patients, they often discovered that the patients had specific needs in mind, for example, reassurance that they would not be connected to machines or that they would be given adequate pain relief medication. In many instances, the nurses could help arrange the situation so the patients did not feel desperate and overwhelmed—and the wish for assisted suicide was withdrawn.

The apprehension that the DWDA would lead to an explosion of deaths-on-demand has not materialized. Two other fears—that women would be exceptionally vulnerable to this option, and that palliative care would be ignored—have also failed to occur. It seems clear that Kevorkian's idiosyncratic approach to assisted death has influenced many people to resist even the markedly different approach established in Oregon.

The Oregon DWDA has faced repeated challenges from its beginnings to the present time. The Catholic Church has been a consistent and often effective adversary. This opposition has much to do with the fact that Oregon remains the only state with such an act on the books. Dowbiggen (2005) observes that disagreements among the several right-to-die groups advocating such legislation have created additional difficulties. The U.S. Department of Justice has repeatedly challenged the law, but was rejected by a federal appeals court. The majority of the Ninth Circuit Court ruled that then Attorney General John Ashcroft had overstepped his authority. Judge Richard C. Tallman wrote that:

> *The attorney general's unilateral attempt to regulate general medical practices historically entrusted to state lawmakers interferes with the Democratic debate about physician-assisted suicide and far exceeds the scope of his authority under federal law (Liptak, 2004, p. 1).*

The State of Washington Death with Dignity Act

Initiatives for Death with Dignity Acts were introduced in several other states, but Oregon remained the only place in the U.S. with such a law in effect. It was not until 2009 that the assisted death option became legal in another state. Washington's approach is closely modeled on Oregon's, including the same regulations and safeguards. After its first year of operation, who and how many people chose self-termination? The official report tells us that:

Medication was dispensed to 63 individuals, the prescriptions written by 53 different physicians and dispensed by 29 different pharmacies. Forty-seven of these people died (7 without having ingested the medication). As in Oregon, the patients were most middle aged or older adults with cancer as the most common underlying condition. Again as in Oregon, none of the individuals requested emergency intervention after ingestion. Most died at home. Almost all were white and non-Hispanic. Three of five were college educated. The parallels with Oregon continue: all were concerned about loss of autonomy and many also spoke of the loss of dignity and losing the ability to do things that made life enjoyable (Washington State Department of Health, 2010).

The availability of a legal assisted-death process in both states did not result in a rush for termination, but does seem to have encouraged both professional and public sensitivity and education. Will other states join Oregon and Washington? Should they? The Montana Supreme Court [Byock, 2010] has ruled that physicians can legally prescribe medications for terminally ill people to use

in ending their lives. This was a divided decision, however, and has since been challenged. Both advocates and opponents of legalized assisted death also assert that the current ruling does not adequately resolve the issue

INDUCED ABORTION

Assisted death involves medical, legal, ethical, and political dimensions that make it difficult to form a clear and coherent picture. Abortion also confronts us with a complex challenge, but with a major difference. A competent adult can decline medical treatment and a limited precedent has been set for requesting assisted death. Courts, legislators, and ethics committees have tried to make sure that the decision represents the individual's own intentions, not the guesses, beliefs, or wishes of others.

The fetus, however, cannot participate in the decision-making process. Who, then, has the right to decide? The woman? Her partner? A doctor? A judge? A religious establishment? Society at large? Everybody? Nobody? The debate about whose decision should stand often brings the rights of the individual and the rights of societal institutions into sharp conflict. The tension crackles among institutions as well. For example, which interpretation of which set of religious teachings should be taken as the will of God? The abortion controversy has its rational arguments pro and con, but powerful emotions often dominate and can lead to actions as extreme as the murder of physicians. It makes sense, then, to begin with some basic facts about abortion.

Basic Facts About Induced Abortion

Some pregnancies do not result in the birth of a live and viable infant. These spontaneous abortions are usually classified as miscarriages, although statisticians sometimes use the term fetal loss. Unintended abortions are not unusual. It is estimated that in the U.S., about one pregnancy in five ends in abortion. "Strictly defined, abortion is the expulsion or removal of an embryo or fetus from the uterus before it has developed sufficiently to survive outside the mother (before viability)" (DeFrain, 2002, p. 1). We will focus here on induced abortion, an intentioned action.

Abortions usually are performed in the first 12 weeks of pregnancy. The earlier the abortion, the simpler the procedure, and the less risk to the woman. In recent years, a combination of two drugs (mifepristone and misoprostol) has become frequently used to halt development and expel the embryo. Few serious medical complications have been reported with this procedure. About 9 out of 10 abortions in the United States occur in the first trimester and therefore require the less invasive procedures.

Most radical and controversial are late-term abortions, conducted four or five months into the pregnancy. Now also known as a partial-birth abortion, this procedure destroys the brain of the infant and delivers the body. This type of abortion has been banned by laws in many states. An exception is usually made for late-term abortions that are considered necessary to save the woman's life. This type of regulation has been contested intensely by many physicians as well as women rights activists. It is argued that there is a right to protect one's health, and that this should be based on the judgment of a physician involved with the case, not a remote and prohibitive law. For example, Dr. Nada Stotland (2007), president of the American Psychiatric Association, is one of the many who have pointed out that federal legislation on this issue was based on lack of attention to research findings: induced abortion does not result in the mental and physical trauma claimed by its opponents and now enshrined in law.

Abortion Becomes a Major Issue

Abortion was neither a crime nor a major issue in the United States until newspapers started to advertise abortion-inducing preparations. Moralists quickly rallied against abortion as a way of concealing extramarital affairs and thereby corrupting the nation's values. Antiabortion measures were signed into law throughout most of the nation by the early 1900s. Women had no enfranchised voice in this development, as almost all politicians were men, and women had not yet been given the constitutional right to vote. It is unknown how many potential abortions were prevented by the criminalization of abortion. However, it soon became clear that abortions were still taking place but under more unsanitary and dangerous conditions, too often at the hands of careless or unskilled

practitioners. The rules changed again in 1973 in the historic *Roe vs. Wade* case, in which the U.S. Supreme Court concluded that states did not have the right to regulate early term abortions: that decision must be left to the woman and her physician. This did not really settle the issue, however,

The continuing opposition to abortion expresses itself in campaigns to overturn the *Roe vs. Wade* decision. Meanwhile, public opinion has tended toward a "permit-but-discourage" attitude, favoring the continued legality and availability of abortion but suggesting that more efforts be made to reduce the number of abortions (Alan Guttmacher Institute, 1999a; 1999b, and website: http://www.guttmacher.org/).

Public attitudes toward abortion have been changing, according to the latest Pew Research Center Survey (2009), with fewer Americans expressing support but also that:

> The abortion debate has receded in importance, especially among liberals. At the same time, opposition to abortion has grown more firm among conservatives, who have become less supportive of finding a middle ground on the issue and more certain of the correctness of their own views on abortion (p. 1).

It remains to be seen if this will be a continuing pattern, or is mostly a reflection of current political issues.

Difficult Issues and Questions

Many thoughtful people are tormented by abortion-related issues. People on both sides of the issue would prefer that the situation never arises in which a woman feels unable or unwilling to see a pregnancy through. The same person can feel compassion for a woman in a stressful, even overwhelming situation, but also pain for the child who never will be. Unfortunately, mutual respect and effective communication have sometimes been blocked by the strong feelings that are understandably associated with the abortion controversy.

Here are three of the issues that remain challenges to our hearts and minds:

1. *State policy vs. individual and family needs.* International human rights organizations have severely criticized the Chinese government for its policy of limiting married couples to one

child and one child only. The policy started with the good intentions of controlling population growth and, therefore, extricating China from its long-standing cycle of poverty and making it a more technologically advanced nation. China has made significant strides toward both goals. The government claims it has prevented 250 million births. But the stress and pain suffered by the Chinese people, especially in the vast rural regions, has been enormous. The pleasures and supports of family life have been denied to many people—children have been growing up without brothers and sisters. More to the point—the systematic abortion and infanticide of girls has become a national horror and disgrace. An estimated 500,000 to 750,000 female fetuses are aborted every year after (illegal) ultrasound screening (CNSNews, 2001). That number does not include the many other babies who are delivered live but are then killed or abandoned out of parental desperation. In Chinese tradition, boys have been crucial for supporting the parents in their later years and keeping the family going. The punishment for disobeying the law is harsh, and many abortions are forced upon women who desperately want to have the child (Livingstone, 2005). The government has been trying to make its policy more humane, but reports of oppression, reprisal, and forced abortion are still being heard. How far can or should a government go to regulate birth and pressure for the death of the unborn? What rule or guide would you establish?

2. *General principle or particular situation?* The Catholic Church's rejection of abortion is a prominent example of applying a general rule to individual situations. The opposite extreme would be the position that a woman has the right to do whatever she chooses with her body, including its contents. Other positions could also be identified or imagined. But are any two circumstances identical? Should the realities of a particular situation be considered with an open mind, or is it best to deal with all cases on the basis of a firm and simple rule? (This is not a new dilemma for the Catholic Church: For centuries, "case books" have been prepared to help priests bridge the gap between general rules and the many unique situations they are likely to encounter.)

How would you have it? One rule for all situations, reliance on good judgment in particular situations, or some way of integrating both approaches?

3. *When do life and personhood begin?* The question of when or under what circumstances life ends (Chapter 3) has its counterpart here. A moment's reflection teaches us that the beginning of a life and the beginning of a human life are not necessarily the same. Sperm and ova are life forms even if they never meet. The embryo is a different proposition from either sperm or ova. The developing fetus has significant new attributes. It would be difficult to deny the existence of life before birth. But when does this become a human life, a person? We can choose to approach this question by reading theological discourses on when in the course of development the soul is created, implanted, or transformed. Instead we might prefer to rely upon developmental psychobiology and judge on the basis of the functions available to a fetus or infant. Then again, we might feel that the anthropologists hold the key to this question as they describe the ways in which a society either bestows or denies personhood even to adults. It has not been all that unusual for one group of people to consider other groups less than human and, therefore, not equal, not deserving, not exempt from enslavement and killing. What is the most realistic, sensible, and humane way to regard the life and personhood of the unborn?

■ SUMMARY

There was a time when few people discussed the right to die from a theoretical perspective. Today many people are intensely involved on a personal level. Should terminally ill people have the right to ask a physician to end their suffering by ending their lives? This question has become complicated by factors such as: (1) memories of the abuse of eugenics and so-called euthanasia through the last century; (2) differing interpretations of the power of the Hippocratic Oath; (3) concerns about the adequacy of care that physicians offer to terminally ill people; but also (4) concerns about the failure to take advantage of the palliative care (hospice) options that now are available; (5) the attempt to broaden physician-assisted suicide to include any person who wants to die, terminally ill or not; and (6) the gap between theory and practice in carrying out physician-assisted death. Moral and religious considerations play a significant role in all these issues. While defining our key terms, we explored the unsavory side of some past euthanasia programs, then looked at current attitudes toward a right to die. We next acquainted ourselves with some of the most important individual cases that brought the right-to-die issue to national attention and led to the first round of rulings and decision making. Although each case was unique, all revealed the complexities and ambiguities that often confront us in life-and-death situations. Particular attention was given to the ordeal of Terri Schiavo and her family. It eventually became a national issue in which federal and state governments, the judicial and medical system, and many private individuals became deeply involved. Possible lessons to be learned from this experience are offered.

We then devoted sustained attention to physician-assisted suicide, starting with brief looks at developments in the Netherlands and then focusing on the approach taken by Jack Kevorkian, M.D. We learned that there are many troubling questions about the practice of physician-assisted death as carried out by Kevorkian. Next, we looked at continuing developments concerning the Death with Dignity Act in Oregon and Washington, the only states in which assisted death has legal status, and in Montana where a ruling is still under appeal. Finally, we explored the key issues surrounding the abortion controversy.

■ REFERENCES

Alan Guttmacher Institute. (1999a). *Induced abortion worldwide.* New York: Alan Guttmacher Institute.

Alan Guttmacher Institute. (1999b). *Sharing responsibility: Women, society, and abortion worldwide.* New York: Alan Guttmacher Institute.

Alan Guttmacher Institute. (2000). *Fulfilling the promise: Public policy and U. S. family planning clinics.* New York: AGI.

Anonymous. (1988). It's over, Debbie. *Journal of the American Medical Association,* 259–272.

Arnold, E. M. (2004). Factors that influence hastening death among people with life-threatening illness. *Health and Social Work, 29,* 27–35.

Associated Press. (2008, March 20). French woman who sought euthanasia dies. http://www.msnbc. msn.com/id/23715513/ns/health-health_care/t/ patient-who-sought-euthanasia-found-dead/.

Associated Press. (2009, May 9). Doctor-suicide rate believed higher than the general population http:// www.foxnews.com/story/0,2933,354676,00.html

Babington, C. (2005, June 17). Frist defends Schiavo case remarks. *Arizona Republic,* p. A21.

BBCNews (2008, March 19). French euthanasia-row woman dies. http://news.bbc.co.uk>/2/ hi/7305970.stm

Byock, I. (2010). Dying with dignity. *Hastings Center Report, 40,* 3.

Callahan, D. (2008) Organized obfuscation: Advocacy for physician-assisted suicide, *Hastings Center Report, 38,* 30–32.

CNSNews.com. (2001, February 15). China uses abortion as female genocide. http://archive.newsmax.com/ archives/articles/2001/2/14/202119.shtml.

Cohen, R. (2000). Feelings about assisted suicide— survey of people with multiple sclerosis. http:// findarticles.com/p/articles/mi_m0850/is_1_18/ ai_59448731/.

Cohen-Almagor, R. (2003). Non-voluntary and voluntary euthanasia in the Netherlands: Dutch perspectives. http://www.ncbi.nlm.nih.gov/ pubmed/12693180.

Cohen-Almagor, R. (2004). *Euthanasia in the Netherlands: The policy and practice of mercy killing.* Boston: Kluwer.

Cox, D. W. (1993). *Hemlock's cup.* Buffalo, NY: Prometheus.

Death with Dignity Center. (2002). www.deathwith dignity.org.

DeFrain, J. (2002). Abortion. In R. Kastenbaum (Ed.), *Macmillan encyclopedia of death and dying* (Vol. 1, pp. 1–5). New York: Macmillan.

Dobscha, S. K., Heintz, R., Press., N., & Gazini, L. (2004). Oregon physicians' responses to requests for assisted suicide: a qualitative study. *Journal of Palliative Medicine, 7,* 451–462.

Dowbiggin, I (2005). *A concise history of euthanasia. Life, death, god, and medicine.* Lanham, MD: Bowman & Littlefield.

Edelstein, L. (1943). *The Hippocratic Oath: Text, translation, and interpretation.* Baltimore: Johns Hopkins University Press.

Eisenberg, D. (2005, April 4). Lessons of the Schiavo battle. *Time,* pp. 24–30.

Friedlander, H. (1995). *The origins of Nazi genocide.* Chapel Hill: The University of North Carolina Press.

Gastmans, C., Van Neste, F., & Schotsmans, P. (2004). Facing requests for Euthanasia: A clinical practice guideline. *Journal of Medical Ethics, 30,* 212–217.

Gazini, L., Nelson, H. D., Schmidt, T. A., Kraemer, D. F., Delorit, M. A., & Lee, M. A. (2001). Physicians' experiences with the Oregon Death with Dignity Act. *New England Journal of Medicine, 342,* 557–563.

Gomez, C. R. (1991). *Regulating death.* New York: Free Press.

Groom, W. (2002). *A storm in Flanders. Tragedy and triumph on the western front.* New York: Atlantic Monthly Press.

Hayslip, B., Jr., & Peveto, C. A. (2005). *Cultural changes in attitudes toward death, dying, and bereavement.* New York: Springer.

Hoffman, K. B. (2007, May 26). Kevorkian's cause founders as he's freed. http://groups.able2know.org/nurse-forum/topic/26636-1.

Iserson, K. V. (2002). Persistent vegetative state. In R. Kastenbaum (Ed.), *Macmillan encyclopedia of death and dying* (Vol. 2, pp. 668–669). New York: Macmillan.

Johnson, L. A. (2005, March 9). Study: Newborn euthanasia often goes unreported in Netherlands—and probably other countries. http://tech.groups.yahoo.com/group/Bioethics/message/9235.

Kaldjian, L. C., Jekel, J. F., Bernene, J. L., Rosenthal, G. E., Vaughan-Sarrazin, M., & Duffy, T. P. (2004). Internists' attitudes toward terminal sedation in end of life care. *Journal of Medical Ethics, 30,* 499–503.

Kalish, R. A., & Reynolds, D. K. (1976). *Death and ethnicity: A psychocultural study.* Los Angeles, CA: University of Southern California Press.

Kaplan, K. J. (1998). The case of Dr. Kevorkian and Mr. Gale: A brief historical note. *Omega, Journal of Death and Dying, 36,* 169–176.

Kaplan, K. J., Lachenmeier, F., Harrow, M., O'Dell, J. C., Uziel, O., Schneiderhan, M., & Cheyfitz, K. (2000a). Psychosocial versus biomedical risk factors in Kevorkian's first 47 physician-assisted deaths. *Omega, Journal of Death and Dying, 40,* 109–164.

Kaplan, K. J., O'Dell, J., Dragovic, L. J., McKeon, C., Bentley, E., & Telmet, K. J. (2000b). An update on Kevorkian-Reding 93 physician-assisted deaths in Michigan: Is Kevorkian a savior, serial-killer or suicidal martyr? *Omega, Journal of Death and Dying, 40,* 209–230.

Kastenbaum, R. (1994/1995). Ralph Mero: An Omega interview. *Omega, Journal of Death and Dying, 29,* 1–16.

Kato, H. (1995/1996, June 25). Doctors need re-educating. Sankei Shimbun.

Kevorkian, J. (1991). *Prescription: Medicide.* Buffalo, NY: Prometheus.

Kron, J. (1975, October 6). The girl in the coma. *New York Magazine,* pp. 17–24.

Lens, V. (2002). Informed consent. In R. Kastenbaum (Ed.), *Macmillan encyclopedia of death* (Vol. 1, pp. 473–476). New York: Macmillan.

Lifton, R. J. (1986). *The Nazi doctors.* New York: Basic Books.

Liptak, A. (2004, May 17). Ruling upholds Oregon law authorizing assisted suicide. *The New York Times.* http://www.nties.com/2004/05/27/national/27SUIC.html7h

Livingstone, J. (2005, November 29). Forced Abortions: First Minister's Chinese Guest Oversaw Horrendous Abuses. *The Daily Mail, London.*

Loving, C. (1995/1996). Nick Loving and Dr. Jack Kevorkian: An Omega Interview with Carol Loving. *Omega, Journal of Death and Dying, 32,* 165–178.

Maitland, L. (2005, April 8). Talk of the Nation Science Friday [radio broadcast]. *National Public Radio.*

Mathis, M. (2005, June 1). Terri Schiavo and end-of-life decisions: Can law help us out? *Medical and Surgical Nursing,* 1–4.

Meijburg, H. H. V. D. K. (1995/1996). How health care institutions in the Netherlands approach physician-assisted death. *Omega, Journal of Death and Dying, 32,* 179–196.

Nicol, N., & Wylie, H. (2006). *Between the dying and the dead. Dr. Jack Kevorkian's life and the battle to legalize euthanasia.* Madison: University of Wisconsin Press.

Nitschke, P. (2000). "Desiring death, dispensing death" by Annette Street and David Kissane: A commentary. *Omega, Journal of Death and Dying, 40,* 249–254.

Pernick, M. S. (1996). *The black stork.* New York: Oxford University Press.

Pew Center Report (2009). Support for abortion slips. http://people-press.org/2009/10/01/support-for-abortion-slips/.

Plotz, F. R., van Heerde, M., Kneyber, C. J., & Markhurst, D. G. (2008) End-of-life decision in a paediatric intensive care unit: decision making in light of the parents' religious beliefs. *Archives of Internal Medicine, 34,* 1355-364.

Quill, T. E., & Cassel, C. K. (2003). Professional organizations' position statements on physician-assisted suicide: A case for studied neutrality. *Annals of Internal Medicine, 138,* 208–211.

Rietjens, J. A. C., van de Heide, A., Vrakking, A.M. Onwuteaka-Phillipsen, B. D., Van der Maas, P. J., & van der Wal, G. (2004). Physician reports of terminal sedation without hydration or nutrition for patients nearing death in the Netherlands. *Annals of Internal Medicine, 141*, 178–185.

Schwarz, J. (2005, April 1). Before the storm, there was Terri. *East Valley Tribune*, p. A8.

Stacy, M. (2005, June 16). Schiavo autopsy backs husband. *East Valley Tribune*, pp. 1, 11.

Stotland, N. (2007, July 20). The myth of abortion trauma syndrome: Update, 2007. *Psychiatric News, 42,* 28.

Street, A., & Kissane, D. (2000). Desiring death, dispensing death. *Omega, Journal of Death and Dying, 40,* 231–248.

Texeira, E. (2005, June 16). Missing: News coverage on the disappearance of anyone who's not an attractive, white female. *East Valley Tribune*, p. 10.

Times Mirror Center for the People and the Press. (1983). *Reflections of the times: The right to die.* Washington, DC: Times Mirror Center for the People and the Press.

Trout, N. (2008a). Animal medicine from a vet's-eye view. National Public Radio: Fresh Air, March 22, 2008.

Trout, N. (2008b). *Tell me where it hurts.* New York: Broadway Books.

United States Supreme Court. (1989). *Missouri vs. Cruzan.* In R. M. Baird & S. E. Rosenbaum (Eds.), *Euthanasia. The moral issues* (pp. 179–212) Buffalo, New York: Prometheus.

Veatch, R. M. (1998). The ethics of death and dying, In A. R. Jonsen, R. M. Veatch, & L. Walters (Eds.), *Source book in bioethics* (pp. 113–252). Washington DC: Georgetown University Press.

Vedantam, S., & Weiss, R. (2005, March 22). Schiavo: Always "unconscious." *Arizona Republic*, p. A9.

Washington State Department of Health. (2010). Washington State Department of Health Death with Dignity Act Report.

Wolfson, J. (2003). *A report to Governor Jeb Bush and the 6th Judicial Circuit in the Matter of Theresa Marie Schiavo.* http://jb-williams.com/ts-report-12-03.htm.

Worthen, L. T., & Yeatts, D. E. (2000–2001). Assisted suicide: Factors affecting public attitudes. *Omega, Journal of Death and Dying, 42,* 115–136.

Yardley, W. (2010, March 5). Report finds 36 died under assisted suicide law. *The New York Times*, p. 17A

■ GLOSSARY

Advance directive A document that specifies the type of health care individuals wish to receive should they not be in a position to express their wishes in a critical situation.

Assisted death An action taken by one person to end the life of another person, at that other person's request.

Competence The mental ability to make a rational decision about important matters in one's life (a concept of law).

Double effect A decision that has its intended but also an unintended effect. Example: Increasing opiate dosage may have the intended effect of alleviating pain but also the unintended effect of hastening death.

EEG tracings Electrical activity of the brain as displayed on a moving scroll or computer monitor, using an electroencephalogram.

Euthanasia Originally, an easy death, one without suffering. Later applied also to actions taken to end a life. "Active" euthanasia involves an action that ends the life; "passive" euthanasia refers to withdrawal or withholding of actions that might prolong life.

Hippocratic Oath A code offering ethical principles for the practice of medicine, attributed to a Greek physician of the fifth century B.C.

Informed consent The principle that patients should be provided with sufficient information to make decisions for or against accepting a treatment.

Liberty principle Individuals are free to make their own decisions and exercise their own rights except in ways that have been specifically reserved for the state.

Mercy killing At one time, the more common term for what is now referred to as assisted death.

Orbitoria Clinics or centers at which assisted death would be provided at patients' request and in which biomedical studies would be conducted.

Slippery slope argument Holds that accepting assisted death for any person will increase the demand and approval of death for many other people.

Terminal sedation Administering drugs to dying patients with severe pain or other stressful symptoms with the purpose of keeping them in a deep sedative or comatose state until death. Also known informally as "slow euthanasia."

Ventilator A machine that provides respiration for people who are unable to breathe adequately on their own.

■ ON FURTHER THOUGHT . . .

The Double Effect

Many people experience mixed feelings when euthanasia or assisted death situations arise. One strong impulse is to approve a course of action that will prevent or relieve suffering. Another strong impulse is to refrain from actions that are likely to foreshorten a person's life. The principle of *double effect* is sometimes seen as a way of resolving this conflict. A distinction is made between intent and consequence. One intends to relieve suffering: this justifies the action. If the patient's death is hastened by this action, it is an unfortunate, but not an ethically negligent consequence. Suppose you find yourself as part of the decision-making process. Would you accept the double-effect principle? Why or why not? Is this a sound, logical, and ethical way of making the decision or an unconvincing way to cope with an uncomfortable situation? If you reject the double-effect principle, what alternative would you choose, and why?

Useful online resources:

http://www.growthhouse.org/. There's also an email address: Info@growthhouse.org

www.access2eolcare.org
American Society for Bioethics and Humanities
www.asbh.org
American Society of Law, Medicine, and Ethics
www.aslme.org
Center for Death Education and Bioethics
http://www.uwlax.edu/sociology/CDEB/index.html
Hastings Center
www.thehastingscenter.org
National Institutes of Health Bioethics on the Web
www.nih.gov/sigs/bioethics/
University of Miami Ethics Program
www.ethics.miami.edu

Learn more about euthanasia and ethics:

Battin, M. B. (1994). *Least worth death. Essays in bioethics on the end of life.* New York: Oxford University Press.

Dowbiggin, I. (2003). *A merciful end. The euthanasia movement in modern America.* New York: Oxford University Press.

Smith, W. J. (1997). *Forced exit. The slippery slope from assisted suicide to legalized murder.* New York: Random House.

Learn more about the quest to live long without exactly growing old:

Boia, L. (2004). *Forever young: A cultural history of longevity.* London: Reaktion.

Gruman, G. J. (2003). *A history of ideas about the prolongation of life.* New York: Springer.

Kastenbaum, R. (1995). *Dorian, Graying: Is youth the only thing worth having?* Amityville, New York: Baywood.

"It's dark. I'm alone. Really bad things could happen."
These fears are often experienced even before there is
a firm conception of death.

Death in the World of Childhood

The little boy was too scared to talk. I could see why he was sent to me. I told him I was really scared sometimes but it helped to talk about it. A cliché, I know, but it's true and it worked . . . It was the white rabbit that had him so scared.

—Nancy Durkee, school psychologist, sharing an experience

You might be afraid to go into your grandfather's house again. Or you may suddenly be scared that your dog will get lost, Mostly you are afraid that your mom or dad will die, as your grandparent did. You might even be worried that you will die.

—Victoria Ryan & R. W. Alley (2002)

Children aged birth to five years are exposed to a disproportionately increased amount of potentially traumatic events compared to older children.

—Anne T. Chu & Alicia F. Lieberman (2010, p. 167).

I was dead. Then I wasn't. In my dream I was dead, then I knew it was a dream, and that's how I knew I wasn't dead, only dreaming that I was. And then I woke up. [Okay. You said you had a question] I do. I was sleeping and I dreamed I was dead. Do dead people—sometimes—dream they are sleeping and not really dead? [That's a great question. I don't know the answer.]

—8 year-old boy, conversing with author

My father doesn't feel good. He doesn't actually say anything, but you can see it in his eyes. (Girl, age 8)

I think that he was very sad and upset. He didn't say it directly, but in the way he talked. He was so stressed and he shouted. (Girl, age 9)

I think that he is sad, but he's good at hiding it. He's strong, he helps mother a lot. (Girl, age 13)

—Quoted by Mikael Thastum et al. (2008)

Carlos asked whether hearts stop beating and then start again, and what happens to your heart when you die. "Does it go on vacation then?" he asked.

—Elizabeth Rider (2004, p. 328)

It was proof that his father had died on Sept. 11, 2001. But for Brendan, who is five, the news that a piece of Thomas Fitzpatrick's humerus had been re-covered was vexing. "Can we get all the pieces and put them together?" he recently asked his mother at their home in Tuckahoe, N.Y. "So he could be alive."

—Andrea Elliott (2004, www.nytimes.com/2004/09/11/ nyregion/11kids.html)

The mother died in the hospital, where the children were not allowed to see her. I came to the funeral with the children, where they saw their mother's body in the open casket. The two older children seemed satisfied with just touching their mother and giving her a kiss, but the youngest one wanted to do more. He was about three years old, and he wanted to see if he could wake her up.

—Margarita M. Saurez & Susan J. McFeaters (2000, p. 58)

One night, after visiting the cemetery, Coleen asked her father how deep her mother was buried. She seemed relieved when Joseph explained that it was very deep—six feet. Coleen was consoled because she had stepped on the mound and was worried that she had stepped on her mother.

—Grace Hyslop Christ (2000, p. 103)

How was the frog? The frog was dead, dead, dead. What else could it be? We buried it a whole summer ago!

—Three-year-old Cynthia's report after she and her older brothers checked out the place where they had held the funeral and burial for a frog briefly known the previous summer

Children are more observant than many adults have supposed. Observant of life. Observant of death. The ability to enter the child's world of life and death can be immensely valuable in responding to the needs of children as illness, death, and grief enter their minds and lives.

RESPECTING THE CHILD'S CONCERN AND CURIOSITY

What does it mean to be dead? Why does a person get dead, and what can we do about it? Who else might get dead? These are among the questions that arise as children experience absence, loss, separation, and change. The second grad-er's baby sister had died. Everybody was sad. Nobody said anything. He had to ask. What happened? The answer that he heard: "the white rabbit." He had since become a "behavior prob-lem," and that's what had him sent to the psy-chologist. A white rabbit might pop up any time, any place, and he would "get dead" like his baby sister and then nobody would even talk about him, either.

The authors of *When Your Grandparent Dies* enter into the thoughts and feelings of a sad, con-fused, and anxious young child who has lost an important person to death. It guides the child from the final illness through to the funeral and memory-making, and articulates, respects, and comforts the child's concerns. This is one of many books intended for children and parents to read and discuss together in death-related situations, books inspired by advances in death education and grief counseling. For a useful annotated list of such books, see Corr (2010).

Each of the children mentioned in the intro-ductory quotations was attempting to compre-hend something important about death—and life. The eight-year-old was testing out the distinction between sleep and death, dream and reality. The three girls were keen observers of what they were not supposed to notice: their fathers' struggles with terminal cancer. These and other children de-scribed here represent many others who, as Chu & Lieberman (2010) document, have early exposure to loss and trauma.

It was his yearly checkup. Carlos, "a quiet seven-year-old with light brown tousled hair and big brown eyes, sat on the examination table, swinging his legs back and forth" (Rider, 2004, p. 1). His question about hearts that stop beating did not seem related to any recent deaths or other losses. The doctor explained that "It's a natural curiosity. Children are curious about death at all ages. Younger children see death as transient, yet around Carlos's age they begin to understand . . . that death is permanent." Carlos still wanted his question answered. "When do people die?" The answer: they usually do not die until they are very old with white hair and wrinkles. Carlos consid-ered this deeply, then said that he could make his hair white and paint wrinkles on his face. "Would I die then?" "No," the doctor replied, "You would

still be seven years old." Carlos relaxed. The doc-tor was right: It does not take a death in their own lives to prompt children to wonder about mortal-ity. Curiosity about life almost certainly leads to curiosity about death. Carlos was attempting to assimilate death into his comprehension of the world (e.g., the heart going on vacation). Fortu-nately, his mother had not dismissed his concern and the doctor had said something reassuring. That Carlos leaned back and relaxed suggests that he, like many other normal children, can experi-ence the physical discomfort associated with death anxiety—but also that adults have the ability to al-leviate this distress.

Brendan's father was a victim of the 9/11 ter-rorist attacks on the World Trade Center. The an-guish of many bereaved adults was intensified by the absence of an intact body that could be hon-ored in funeral and memorial services. How, then, could a five-year-old comprehend what had hap-pened? Brendan's wish to assemble the remains and return his father to life might be dismissed as naïve and magical thinking. The longing for renewal and resurrection, though, has been a re-silient theme for untold centuries. The boy was urgently seeking some way to return his world to the way it should be. The death of a loved one in childhood can be a spur to creative and critical thinking, with the underlying intention of making things right again and escaping further loss. But as unresolved grief can also haunt a person through-out the adult life course.

The youngest of the three children at the fu-neral wanted to see if he could awaken his mother.

> *I let him try, and he did it as little ones do. First he tried to open her eyelids, and then he touched her face. Finally he called her name. After sev-eral attempts he turned to me and said, "I can-not wake her up." He wanted to try again, and I let him try one more time, because through my own Latina cultural filters, there was nothing wrong or disrespectful in touching a dead body* (Saurez & McFeaters, 2000, p. 58).

This three-year-old had the courage to put his hands on this strangely unresponsive form. And what about the courage and perspective shown by the adult companion who permitted him to try, even though it would be painful to watch?

The young child's conception of death and the dead is not the same as the adult's. Coleen did not yet fully comprehend the difference between alive and dead. She knew that her mother was buried, but she might be disturbed if somebody stepped on the grave. This attribution of life qualities to the dead was associated with Coleen's level of mental development, limited experience with death situations, and the cultural milieu from which she was drawing her language, concepts, and attitudes. We will be looking at these factors in more detail later.

Cynthia and her older brothers had taken an experimental approach to the same issue: What is the difference between alive and dead? Many conduct their own little experiments, often without their parents' knowledge. Burying the frog (please note that it was dead at the time!) was also a way of acquiring a sense of partial control over the mysterious disappearance from vibrant life to unresponsive object. Perhaps—just perhaps—the frog might recover and hop back to its nearby pond. Already sensitive to the fragility of life, the young experimentalists were vicariously burying and attempting to restore a little of themselves through the fate of the bog dweller. Cynthia seized the spokesperson role, proudly announcing their discovery that dead is dead. Had she comprehended the permanence of death at such an early age? Yes, and no. This seeming contradiction will be addressed later in the research section.

It is understandable that adults would want to protect children from the anxiety and sorrow associated with the death of a loved person and from intimations of their own mortality. However, no child is spared the possibility of losing loved ones. No child is exempt from life-threatening risks. No child grows up without noticing that sometimes what is here today is gone tomorrow. Whether we are ready to accept it or not, death is a part of the child's world.

Our exploration begins with the adult's conception of the child's conception of death. Next we explore the child's understanding of death as observed in both research and natural settings. This is followed by learning how children cope with the death of others, and how we can be helpful to them in their grief experiences. Some children also must cope with their own life-threatening conditions. We then examine our society's tradition of excluding children from participating in life-and-death decisions that are of personal concern to them. The chapter concludes with an exploration of bedtime rituals as practices for death, and guidelines for sharing and responding to the child's death concerns.

ADULT ASSUMPTIONS ABOUT CHILDREN AND DEATH

How was the subject of death treated in your home when you were a child? This is the first of several questions that are raised in Box 10-1: Exploring Your Experiences with Death in Childhood. Please turn to these questions now. They will help you bring your childhood experiences forward into the present moment. The activity of writing down your memories will also help you compare your experiences with those of other people and to think about how these experiences may have influenced your life.

Here are examples of some of the most frequent responses to the first question:

- They sat in dark rooms and became quiet.
- Very hushed and away from us as children. There were two deaths and three near deaths, from when I was 7 to when I was 10. I felt like I was left out of all of them. No one ever explained anything to me.
- I don't remember any conversations about death with my parents. My mom went back East for my uncle's funeral and my grandparents' funerals, but I did not go.
- Death was not something that was discussed with children. When my grandfather died, though, it was chaotic. The adults talked to each other about how the death took place. Everyone offered opinions of how the wake and funeral should be carried out. There were arguments and disagreements. All of us kids were completely left out.
- Since I come from a Christian home, death was addressed often as a concept and limited to an afterlife. When someone actually did die, it was put into perspective with God at the center. "He or she is in a better place . . . ." At times I found this very comforting; at other moments I felt put off by their rehearsed responses.

BOX 10-1

Exploring Your Experiences with Death in Childhood

Write your answers on a separate sheet of paper.

1. How was the subject of death treated in your home when you were a child? What questions did you ask of your parents? What answers did you receive?
2. What most interested or puzzled you about death when you were a young child?
3. Do you remember the death of a pet or other animal at some time in your childhood? What were the circumstances? How did you feel about it? How did other people respond to your feelings?
4. Do you remember the death of a person at some time in your childhood? What were the circumstances? How did you feel about it? How did other people respond to your feelings?
5. Can you identify any ways in which childhood experiences with death may have influenced you to this day?
6. What do you now think is the best thing a parent could say to or do with a child in a death situation and why?
7. What do you now think is the worst thing a person could say or do with a child in a death situation and why?

• After the cat died, we were told about death in that the life is gone. No more movement, no more breath, etc. It seemed to make sense.

Some people remember being given straightforward, naturalistic information. Most often, however, families followed a family rule of silence (Book, 1996). Why do adults often have such difficulty in communicating with children about death? The answer has much to do with the adults' own fears, doubts, and conflicts. Perhaps Sigmund Freud (1914) was on the mark when he suggested that, having lost our own childhood innocence, we want very much to believe that our children live in a fairy-tale world, safe from the stings of reality.

CHILDREN DO THINK ABOUT DEATH

Children, even young children, do think about death. Evidence comes from many sources.

Early Experiences with Death in Childhood

One of America's first distinguished psychologists, G. Stanley Hall (1922) and his student, Colin Scott, asked adults to recall their earliest experiences

with death. These childhood experiences were recalled in vivid detail:

The child's exquisite temperature sense feels a chill where it formerly felt heat. Then comes the immobility of face and body where it used to find prompt movements of response. There is no answering kiss, pat, or smile . . . . Often the half-opened eyes are noticed with awe. The silence and tearfulness of friends are also impressive to the child, who often weeps reflexly or sympathetically (p. 440).

Funeral and burial scenes often were the very earliest of all memories. This remains true for many people today. For example, an Italian-American butcher shared his earliest memory with me:

I was still in the old country. We all lived in a big old house, me, my family and all kinds of relatives. It was just a few days after my fourth birthday, and there was grandmother laid out on a table in the front room. The room was full of women crying their eyes out. Hey, I didn't want any part of it, but somebody said grandmother was just sleeping. I doubted that very much. Grandmother never slept on a table in the front room with everybody crying their eyes out before. But what I really remember most is what I want to forget most. "Kiss your grandmother!" Yeah, that's right. They made me walk right up and kiss grandmother. I can still see her face. And I can still feel her face. Is that crazy? I mean, after all these years, I can still feel her cold dead face and my lips against it.

Although this man was owner and chief butcher of a specialty meat shop, he experienced panic when he was in the presence of a human corpse. His early childhood experience with death had become part of his adult personality. Another compelling example was reported by a college student to another researcher who was inquiring into earliest memories:

As a young child, I would receive ducks and chickens as an Easter present. One of these chicks was able to survive the playing and was able to grow into a nice white hen. She was my pride and joy, following me and coming when I called. The hen stayed at my Grandmother's. One Sunday dinner the main course was "fried chicken." It took me several minutes to realize just what had happened. To say the least, I was devastated and do not eat chicken to this day (Dickinson, 1992, p. 83).

In a follow-up study, Dickinson (1992) found that college students still had intense memories of their early childhood experiences with death. It was startling to learn how anger, "outright hatred at times," continued to be felt toward "a parent who had killed the (pet) animal, whether it was a parent who had accidentally run over the animal or the vet who 'put the animal to sleep'" (p. 172). These students often felt that the explanations their parents gave them in childhood were unsatisfactory. Most often the children had been told that a deceased person had gone to heaven. Some had been reassured because heaven was said to be a happy place. One four-year-old girl, however, became upset when her father told her that her kitten "went to heaven to be with God." She responded: "Why does God want a dead kitten?" A three-year-old also became angry when told her grandmother had gone to heaven: "I don't want her in heaven. I want her here!" Not only are young children affected by death-related events, but they may recall these experiences with intense emotions many years later.

Fortunately, pet loss has become increasingly recognized as a significant and consequential event in a child's life. Toray (2010) calls particular attention to the child's need to be somehow included in the process when an animal companion is to be euthanized, and McMahon (2010) offers practical suggestions for reducing threats and worry.

The childhood loss and death theme was evident again in early memory research interviews several students and I conducted with residents of Arizona retirement communities. The respondents went back at least 60 years and sometimes more than 80 for their memories. Many incidents were pleasant to recall; others were odd and hard to explain. However, more than one person in three reported an earliest memory that conveyed some encounter with death, loss, or separation:

- "The green chair nobody sat in any more. I remember going into the room and out of the room and back into the room time after time. Maybe Grandfather would be sitting in his chair the next time I entered the room. I know I was four because I just had a birthday with four candles on the cake."
- "There were lots of people in the street, and there had been some kind of accident. I wanted to see what. A horse was on the ground and there was a twisted up, tipped over cart behind it. Somebody, a man, was saying they ought to shoot it. I got one look and then somebody pushed me away or led me away. I don't know what I thought about it at the time, but I can still see that horse."

Some previous readers of this book have taken their early memories as the starting point for their personal research. One young woman, for example, recalled having felt alone and frightened, "and there was something about the ocean and the beach in it." No other details came to mind from this memory that seemed to have taken place just before her kindergarten days. She decided to ask her parents what had actually happened. They were reluctant, but:

then we had one of our best talks ever! Mom had had a miscarriage and the doctor had said she couldn't have any more babies or she might die herself. It never occurred to them to say any of this to a little kid like me. But while we were talking I suddenly remembered them getting rid of baby things, a crib and all, giving them away, and my mother looking real strange and distant. And that was when they sent me to live with a family I didn't like much so they could also get away a few days, together, and try to feel normal again. I can understand that perfectly now. But then, it was like they were going to get rid of me, too! And in my little kid's mind, the beach and the ocean were part of it all. Maybe they were going to leave me all by myself on the beach, or maybe a big wave was going to come and get me!

This student had developed a pattern of avoiding beaches and large bodies of water, although she was also attracted to these places. The frank conversation with her family not only helped her understand the unpleasant and unaccountable early memory but also dissipated her anxieties about going to the beach. Other students have also found that it was possible to gain a better understanding of their own quirks and fears by recalling early memories of loss. It would be going much too far to say that a particular childhood experience "causes" us to behave or feel in a particular way in adult life. Nevertheless, childhood experiences tinged with death, loss, or separation can become significant influences on the way we see life and cope with death.

Death in the Songs and Games of Childhood

The "innocent" songs and games of childhood through the centuries have often been performances of death themes. The familiar "Ring Around the Rosie" song and round dance achieved popularity during the peak years of the *plague* in fourteenth-century Europe. The "rosies" referred both to a symptom of the disease and the flower petals that people hoped would protect them; the "all fall down" is self-explanatory. The children who enacted this little drama knew their danger. We can imagine the security they sought by joining hands. The ritual impersonated the trauma and separation death. Helpless passivity and fear were transformed into a group effort to master the threat. The children who had fallen to the earth would leap to their feet with joyful shouts after completing the ring-around-the-rosie dance. For the moment, at least, they were still very much alive.

The death theme is explicit in many hide-and-seek and tag games, such as "Dead Man Arise!" This type of game has many names and local variations. In Sicily, for example, children played *A Morsi Sanzuni* (Opie & Opie, 1969).

One child lay down pretending to be dead while his companions sang a dirge, occasionally going up to the body and lifting an arm or a leg to make sure the player was dead, and nearly stifling the child with parting kisses. Suddenly he would jump up, chase his mourners, and try to mount the back of one of them . . . . In Czechoslovakia . . . the recumbent player was covered with leaves, or had her frock held over her face. The players then made a circle and counted the chimes of the clock, but each time replied, "I must still sleep." This continued until the clock struck twelve when, as in some other European games, the sleeping player sprung to life, and tried to catch someone (p. 107).

In tag games, the person who is "It" must not peek or move while the other players conceal themselves. The scary thrill is experienced both by the victim and the monstrous "It" who has discovered the hiding place. Every participant gets to be both slayer and slain. Even the slightest touch has grave significance: The victim instantly is transformed from lively participant to death personified ("It"). Further resemblances to death are suggested in those variations in which the victim must freeze until rescued by one who is still free (alive).

Lethal violence has been a common theme in children's play through the centuries. As a child in the streets of New York, my friends and I played cops and robbers, sporting wooden guns armed with rubber bands. Medieval children brandished their stick swords as they replayed Crusader–Saracen battles. Today high-tech computer games feature multiple killings that allow players to rack up an imposing score. There is no personal relationship between killer and slain and, of course, no remorse. It is thought that the practice of violence in the games children play might have a disturbing effect on their cognitive and emotional development (Wass, 2002; see also "killing begets killing" Chapter 8). It is also possible that children's attitudes toward death can be distorted by an emphasis on the act rather than the consequences of killing.

Research and Clinical Evidence

Formal research indicates that there is a consistent developmental pattern: A very young child does not, cannot, comprehend the essential facts of death. However, sometimes they do! These discoveries occur not when scheduled by research but when child and situation come together. We offer first three examples of spontaneous discoveries, followed by a review of formal research findings:

- A boy, aged 16 months, was enjoying one of his regular visits to a public garden, accompanied by his father, an eminent biomedical scientist. The boy's attention was captured by a fuzzy caterpillar creeping along the sidewalk. Suddenly, large adult feet came into view, and the caterpillar was crushed (unwittingly). Immediately the boy showed an alarmed expression. He then bent over the remains, studying them intently. After a long moment, he stood up and informed his father, in a sad and resigned voice, "No more!" "No more!" Can there be a more direct and concise comment? From that moment, the boy became reluctant to stay in the garden. He looked with distress at fallen blossoms that he had not previously seemed to notice. It took several comforting attempts from his father before he would again visit this place of beauty and, now, of death.
- An 18-month-old discovered a dead bird as he and his father walked through the woods. The boy crouched over the bird, his face taking on the expression of the classic Greek mask of tragedy. "Bird!" he said. "Yes," his father replied, "A bird; a dead bird." For the next several days the boy insisted on visiting the dead bird, looking at it very carefully but not saying anything. One day there was a crisp autumn breeze, and leaves floated down from the trees. The boy picked up a leaf and handed it to his father—insisting that his father place the leaf back on the tree. The father said this could not be done, but, with the boy's insistence, he tried. The leaf would not stay put. The father tried again and again. The boy then looked sad and turned away. He never asked again to have a leaf restored to its tree nor did he look again at the dead bird.

There was no doubt in the minds of these very young children that death was something special.

Older children explored ways of expressing and overcoming the sorrow of loss:

- An eight-year-old boy was improvising loudly at the piano. He was in a mood of deep contemplation, not just idly banging away. "What are you playing?" his father asked. "A funeral song for Lovey" (the family cat, recently killed on the highway). As the boy continued his improvisations, he explained the meaning of each passage, "This is Lovey sharpening her claws on a tree . . . This is Lovey when she has just heard the can opener . . . This is Lovey curled up and purring . . . ."

The toddler's "No more!" in his encounter with the crushed caterpillar is a flash of insight into mortality that is occasionally heard even from very young children. How, then, can researchers conclude that young children do not comprehend death? There is a reason: the flash of insight usually disappears, replaced by more age-appropriate ways of thinking. I suggest that this is a hurried retreat from an alarming discovery, facilitated by the lack of a mature system of thought in which the mortality insight can be integrated. As adults, we are often situational in our responses—perhaps operating mostly on logic in one situation, emotion in another. Children are even more inclined to respond according to the feeling of a particular situation. Children's comprehension of death seem to vary from situation to situation, and mood to mood, although this phenomenon has seldom been studied.

RESEARCH CASE HISTORIES

Three brief case histories drawn from my research will provide a glimpse of individual and family patterns. A general review of research findings will follow. This section presents narrative data from structured interviews with the mothers of schoolchildren.

Teresa

Teresa is a seven-year-old described by her mother as a quiet girl who enjoys her own company: "She's just a very nice girl, not afraid to express any emotions at all." Teresa is especially interested in plants and how they grow and is much involved in her family.

INTERVIEWER: Has death come into Teresa's life?

MOTHER: My mother died, her grandmother, in January of this year. . . . We all knew she was dying. I told Teresa and I told June [her sister] that she was dying. They wanted to know, "What is dying, where is she going to go, why is she going, why is she leaving me? She's my Grandma! I don't want her to die!" . . . And she was just very curious about the whole business of the wake and the funeral and "Why do we have to do this, why do we have to do that." The big thing was, "I don't want to see other people sad, because it makes me sad."

INTERVIEWER: How did Teresa respond to the death when it actually came?

MOTHER: She comforted me. She would cry when I cried. She would put her arms around me and she would say, "Please don't cry; everything will be all right. Grandma isn't suffering anymore. Grandma is happy now."

INTERVIEWER: What did Teresa understand about Grandma's death?

MOTHER: She understands that she was put in the ground in that cold outer casket, but Teresa realizes that she is not there. She's in spirit, beside her, watching and loving her always. And Teresa sees a bird—my mother was a bird freak—and she said, "I wonder if Grandma can see that bird?"

INTERVIEWER: What did Teresa not understand about this death?

MOTHER: She still doesn't understand why. You know, why take her from us now, she wasn't old; Grandma was a young woman [age 54]. Why was she so sick, you know. Did she do something bad?

INTERVIEWER: Does Teresa have any death concerns or fears?

MOTHER: I think she'd be very much afraid of losing me at this point because since my mother has died she's becoming extremely touchy with me; she gets a little bit upset when I have to go out, you know. "Please come back soon!"

INTERVIEWER: How have you answered her questions about death?

MOTHER: I don't want to get into hell and heaven and that, because I don't want them to get hung up on it. . . . I really don't think we discussed it, you know, before it actually hit us; we never really discussed it with the children. . . .

INTERVIEWER: Has it been difficult to discuss death with Teresa?

MOTHER: Not with Teresa, not at all. With June, yes, but not with Teresa.

INTERVIEWER: How do you feel in general about the way Teresa thinks about death?

MOTHER: I think she's got her head pretty well together. She's really probably done better than I have. . . . Two or three months after my mother died, I was sitting by myself, having my crying jag and getting it all out, and Teresa got up out of bed. You know, I was sitting in the dark. I just knew it was coming. I had put them to bed. So she got up, and she came beside me and she said, "Mama, I know why you're crying." And I said, "Why, Teresa?" And she said, "Because you miss your mother." And I said, "You're right." And Teresa said, "But you always have to remember, how good she was to us, remember she used to take us uptown and buy us ice cream and she used to sing us songs and remember when she bought me this bracelet." And within a matter of, say three minutes, I felt so relieved, like, you know, tons had been lifted off me; from this seven-year-old child, you know, really laying it on me and telling me, come on, you know, you got to go on living. . . . And the oldest one [June] will not discuss it at all. You know, it's too bad.

INTERVIEWER: Do you have any questions of your own about what to do with a child in things related to death?

MOTHER: There are things I don't know, and so I wouldn't know how to explain it to them. I don't know how to make it easier for them. Everybody dies— why do you grieve then? Why is there a wake, why is there a funeral? There are things I don't understand, so I'm sure they don't understand, you know, why the pain?

INTERVIEWER: Should parents and children discuss death together?

MOTHER: It's so very important! I can remember my own first experience with death and how frightened I was of it. When we were children; we saw grieving after death—and my children will grieve over death.

INTERVIEWER: What is the worst thing a parent could say or do with a child in a death situation?

MOTHER: I would hate to stifle emotions. I would hate to say, "Stop all that crying!" Or, the other thing is, "He's gone away for a vacation. He's left us, but he'll come back." That's a bunch of lies, and children see through these things.

INTERVIEWER: What is the best thing a parent could say or do with a child in a death situation?

MOTHER: Let the children see what goes on. Let them be totally involved with the family, to be able to express with the family their own emotions and to be totally included in what goes on instead of shifted off to a friend's house.

INTERVIEWER: How curious about death were you when you were Teresa's age?

MOTHER: I wasn't at all . . . until I was about 10 years old. . . . I lost my cat, and, I remember, I cried all day upstairs in my room because I thought: This is death. I'm going to lose my mother. And I cried and cried, and I was so scared and I had nightmares.

INTERVIEWER: How was death handled in your home when you were growing up?

MOTHER: It wasn't. I said to my mother once, "I'm so afraid that you were going to die." And she just said, "I'm not going to die." And . . . she died. [These words were spoken very softly and sadly.]

INTERVIEWER: Was that the way she should have handled it, or what do you think she should have done instead?

MOTHER: I think that she should have drawn more out of me and really given me time that I needed . . . just be able to sit down and discuss it . . . .

INTERVIEWER: What are your thoughts and feelings about death now?

MOTHER: Since my first death was my mother, I think it was very hard. . . . I just accept the fact that she is dead and I will no longer see her, but I just hang on to the thought that she's not suffering and that she knew she was dying even though nobody told her. . . . She said more with her eyes, more than anything else in the world. I feel peace within myself.

INTERVIEWER: Did she tell you her thoughts or feelings at all?

MOTHER: No, she was aphasic . . . and paralyzed. She couldn't talk. The only thing she could do was move one arm and one hand and the night before she died . . . she just kept pointing up to heaven. She knew she was dying and she just . . . made us feel at ease. Because I was glad she knew, and she knew that I knew, so we wouldn't have to play the game.

INTERVIEWER: Is there anything you would like to add?

MOTHER: I think we should teach children about death in schools. I don't mean we shouldn't teach them at home, but in school, too. Should start early because it's like sex education, you know, you almost don't talk about it until it happens, until there is a problem.

Stanley

Stanley is another seven-year-old who is described by his mother as "just the nicest boy a mother could ever want. Does what you tell him to—most of the time. . . . His life is pretty much centered around the family and his dog."

INTERVIEWER: What does Stanley understand about death?

MOTHER: That whoever would die they're not going to see again and that's about all. I would say he would be too little to think much about it.

INTERVIEWER: What does Stanley not understand about death?

MOTHER: What the purpose of death is. Why we were put on the earth for a reason and why we're going to die. Stanley is definitely too little to understand why somebody's laying in a casket. Especially if it is somebody young. You try to explain to him that God put him on this earth but He called him back. He wanted him back. I don't think he can comprehend that at all.

INTERVIEWER: How have you answered Stanley's questions about death?

MOTHER: Sometimes I tell him that the person was very old and very sick. If it was a little boy, that the little boy was very sick and God wanted him back. . . . God put us here but He isn't going to let us stay here. We're all here temporarily and even though you boys are little doesn't mean you couldn't die tomorrow. Even Stanley, I told him, you could die tomorrow. I could die tomorrow. We don't know when. God doesn't tell us. It doesn't mean that just sick people die. Anybody can die—people get hit by cars.

INTERVIEWER: What is the worst thing a parent could say or do with a child in a death situation?

MOTHER: To hide it from them. If you want to cry, cry. That's the best thing. Make him experience it with you. Why not? They've got to be exposed to it the way it is.

INTERVIEWER: How was death handled in your home when you were growing up?

MOTHER: My parents shielded us from all of that. . . . We never got the answers we really wanted, so we stopped asking. That was about anything. But death can bring people together, it's just that in our family it didn't. Would have been nice if our parents had let us join in, instead of getting our relatives to babysit us while they went and did it all . . . going to the funerals

and all of that. . . . I would have liked to have been at their side.

INTERVIEWER: What are your thoughts and feelings about death now?

MOTHER: I'm very conscious about death now. It panics me, truthfully, it really panics me. I know we can't live forever. If I knew I was dying, I just wouldn't want to wake up in the morning. I'm not too happy about other people dying either. . . . Dead people are supposed to be with God. We're supposed to be happy but we still can't. Part of us says we are—part of us says we're not!

Brian

Brian is eight years old and "a bright boy with lots of curiosity. He's especially interested in rocks and minerals, gems, animals, underwater stories. He reads about them all the time, and talks about anything. But not death."

INTERVIEWER: What does Brian understand about death?

MOTHER: Oh, he understands it . . . I think. But he doesn't really like to talk about it. He doesn't like the idea that any of us will die. Like he said to me, "You'll never, never die, Mom." I tried to explain to him, well, that's not true, that I will die and so will Daddy, and when that time comes he must accept it because that's part of living. He understands what I'm saying. You can see that from the look in his eyes. But it makes him very, very sad, and he'll go, "I don't want to talk about that, I'd rather not—please, Mom!"

INTERVIEWER: What does Brian not understand about death?

MOTHER: Only one thing I can think of. His Daddy likes to hunt. He goes deer hunting and he killed, you know, a young deer. Brian couldn't quite understand that. He thought the deer was so beautiful and to kill him. . . . Well, we had to tell him why he killed the deer, and the deer hurt, and if he wasn't killed, if so many deer weren't killed a year, the balance of nature would be off.

INTERVIEWER: Does Brian have any death concerns or fears?

MOTHER: Losing one of us that he loves. He's very, very close to Cris [his sister] so, of course, he doesn't want her to leave the house. If she doesn't come home when she said she's supposed to come home he'll call me and say, "I'm awfully worried because she's out in the car, if she has an accident and gets killed, Mom, I don't know what I'll do." And I mean upset. I've seen him cry and tears going down his face and he'll say, "I would just die if my Crissy dies."

INTERVIEWER: What is the worst thing a parent could say or do with a child in a death situation?

MOTHER: Well, I'm going to say this from experience. I think the worst thing to do is not let the child grieve. To tell them they can't cry . . . bottling up these emotions does something to that person and carries on into their adult life. It does irreparable damage if you ask me, and I guess you did.

INTERVIEWER: How was death handled in your home when you were growing up?

MOTHER: Nobody prepared me for it, nobody answered my questions, nobody told me one thing or the other. "I don't want to talk about it," would be the answer, or "I don't know why you ask me such foolish questions."

INTERVIEWER: What are your thoughts and feelings about death now?

MOTHER: Now, it's much different. I feel the more I think of it, the more at peace I feel with the fact that death is going to come. When I was younger I was hoping, oh, I'd never die, and now I know that I am, and the time comes I don't think I'll be afraid to die. . . . I think it comes with time. Even so, having children makes death more important in a way, too, your responsibility to them.

Reflections and Questions

Young as they are, Teresa, Stanley, and Brian already differ in their experiences and concerns. Following are a few reflections and questions on their research case history excerpts:

1. It is often the death of particular people or animals that arouses the child's concern: Grandma for Teresa, Crissy and the deer for Brian. The possibility (Crissy) as well as the actuality (Grandma) of death can stimulate thought and feeling. Stanley is confronted with specific death concerns by his mother ("you could die tomorrow. I could die tomorrow"). Children do not have to comprehend death in its most abstract aspects to recognize that it threatens their relationships with the people who are important to them.

2. Experiences, attitudes, and ways of coping with death are part of the intimate flow of life between children and their parents. The influence operates in both directions. Brian's questions about the slain deer, for example, and his intense fear for Crissy's well-being present challenges for the parents' own attitudes toward death.

3. People within the same household can have different orientations toward death. Teresa and June, for example, differ in their openness to discussion of death. The same death also may have varying effects on the children, depending upon their developmental phase, personality, and position in the family. It is useful to become well acquainted with the entire family constellation if we want to understand the implications of one particular child's view of death. From other data, it was clear that Brian, as the only boy in the family, wanted very much to be like his father—but does this mean he, too, will have to go deer hunting?

4. Teresa's mother favors an open communication process and reflects thoughtfully on her own behavior as well as her children's. She has unresolved questions in some areas, such as the value of funerals and the grief process. Despite these unresolved concerns, Teresa's mother shows flexibility and the ability to learn from experience. By contrast, Stanley's mother does not seem to have sorted out her own assumptions about life and death. When Stanley notices a death-related incident, she

BOX 10-2

Lessons from the Research Case Histories

- It is the death of particular people or animals that enlists the child's concern.
- Death-related related experiences, attitudes, and behaviors are part of the intimate flow of life between children and their parents.
- There may be several different orientations toward death within the same household.

- Parents whose own discomfort interferes with their response to their children's death-related curiosity are likely to perpetuate these anxieties for another generation.
- There is now a transitional generation of parents who are trying to communicate in an open manner with their children, although their own experience was of family silence about death.

passes along a received dogma that has been familiar to her since her own childhood—but that she has never much thought about. The abstraction level and tone of her explanation was of doubtful help to Stanley. Parents who are not able to cope with a child's death-related curiosity on a simple, naturalistic level because of their own discomfort may be perpetuating the anxieties for still another generation. Imagine Stanley's thoughts after his mother's explanation: "God does not want healthy people? Is it wrong to want people to live? Is God the enemy who takes my friends away? Do I have to get very sick and die to be loved by God?" I have, in fact, heard reflections of this type from children whose curiosity about death was answered by verbose patter that placed the blame on a loving but inscrutable God.

5. Although Teresa's mother had a warm and loving childhood, her parents had glossed over the topic of death. This made it more difficult to cope both with the death of her mother—who had promised she was not going to die—and the feelings of her own daughters. Brian's and Stanley's mothers also grew up in homes where death was not to be discussed with the children. This background of death avoidance in the childhood home was typical for the mothers in our study. Today's young mothers seem to be more aware of the value of discussing death with their children as part of their general preparation for life. However, most often they have not benefited from such good examples in their

own homes while growing up. We now have a transitional generation of parents who are trying to relate to their children in an area that was off-limits when they themselves were young. This leads to second guessing of their own responses: "Did I say the right thing?" Eventually, however, the new openness should make death a less divisive topic between parent and child in generations to come.

It is not by accident that the research case histories sampled here are based on the mothers' reports. The fathers declined to discuss this subject. Family death education seems to be viewed as something for "the women" to handle (Box 10-2).

CONCEPTS AND FEARS: DEVELOPING THROUGH EXPERIENCE

It is clear that death has a place in the thoughts of children. But just what do children make of death? How do their ideas develop from early childhood onward? And what is the relationship between how children think about death and their fears? Early studies emphasized maturation. Children's understanding of death was found to improve along with the general development of their mental abilities. Later studies indicated that life experiences also play a significant role. A 13-year-old, for example, generally will show an understanding of death that is more accurate and complete than that of a four-year-old. Is this because the older child has developed more advanced cognitive structures? Or is it simply because the older child has had another nine years of life experience from which to learn? The evidence suggests that the child's understanding of death is influenced by both maturation level and life experience, although much remains to be learned about the interaction of these factors.

"Auntie Death's" Pioneering Study

Our understanding of the way children think about death has been greatly influenced by a pioneering study that is worth reviewing in detail. Hungarian psychologist Maria Nagy (1948/1969) invited 378 children, ranging in age from 3 to 10 years, to express their death-related thoughts and feelings. The children came from a variety of social and religious backgrounds. The older children were asked to draw pictures and to "write down everything that comes to your mind about death." Children of all ages were engaged in conversation. As Nagy reviewed the children's words and pictures, she found that three age-related stages could be established (Table 10-1).

Stage 1 Stage 1 includes the youngest children, from about the third until the fifth year. The dead are simply less alive. They cannot see and hear—well, maybe they can, but not very well. They are

TABLE 10-1 *Stages of Death Comprehension in Childhood (Nagy)*

Stage	Age Range	Interpretation of Death
1	3–5	Death is separation.
		The dead are less alive.
		Very curious about death.
2	5–9	Death is final—but one might escape it!
		Death is seen as a person.
3	9–adult	Death is personal, universal, final, and inevitable.

not as hungry as the living. They don't do much. Being dead and being asleep are pretty much the same, but not exactly. The youngest children also thought of death as temporary. The dead might return, just as the sleeping might awaken. Uppermost in the minds of many children was the theme of death as departure and separation. What has actually become of the dead person is a matter of guesswork, imagination, and wishful thinking. However, it is the absence of that person that is most obvious and most compelling.

Nagy's preschoolers were full of questions about details of the funeral, the coffin, the cemetery, and so on. The child's active engagement with the challenge of comprehending death was also observed by Sylvia Anthony (1940/1972) with young British children. Respondents in both studies believed that death was not much fun, having to lie around in a coffin all day, and all night, too. The dead might be scared and lonely, too, away from all their friends. Even very young children knew what it was like to feel scared or lonely, so these states of mind could readily be attributed to the dead.

The combination of what the young child knows and does not know about death can arouse anxiety. "He would like to come out, but the coffin is nailed down," one five-year-old told "Auntie Death," the name bestowed on the psychologist by the children. People are being cruel by nailing down the coffin. There are many possibilities for misinterpretations based on the young child's limited conception of death, especially if adults fail to understand how the child is likely to interpret death-related phenomena.

Stage 2 The next stage begins at age five or six and lasts until about age nine. The child now recognizes that death is final. The older the child within this age range, the more firm the conclusion. The dead do not return. Another new theme also emerged during this stage. Many of the children represented death as a person. Interestingly, *personification* is one of humankind's most ancient modes of expressing the relationship with death. One nine-year-old confided:

> *Death is very dangerous. You never know what minute he is going to carry you off with him. Death is invisible, something nobody has ever seen in all the world. But at night he comes to everybody and carries them off with him. Death is like a skeleton. All the parts are made of bone. But then when it begins to be light, when it's morning, there's not a trace of him. It's that dangerous, death (p. 11).*

*This child's under-the-bed monster
knows how how to make itself useful".*
Source: www.CartoonStock.com

The association of death with darkness is an ancient habit of mind, expressed by people in the earliest civilizations that have left us record. It is not unusual for the child's conception of death to include elements that once were the common property of adults.

The personification of death as a skeleton was fairly common in Nagy's sample of five- to nine-year-olds. These personifications often were frightening. "Kill the death-man so we will not die" was a frequent comment. Some children also depicted death as a circus clown—supposedly the embodiment of mirth. Other children saw dead people as representing death, while still others personified death in the form of angels. Even angelic death, however, did not remove the sting of fear. "The death angels are great enemies of people," declared a seven-year-old. "Death is the king of the angels. The angels work for death."

There is one more significant characteristic of Nagy's Stage 2. *The realization of death's finality is accompanied by the belief that this fate might still be eluded.* The clever or fortunate person might not be caught by the "death-man." Children in this age range tend to see death as an outside force or personified agent. "It's that dangerous, death." However, the saving grace is that we do not absolutely have to die. Death is not yet recognized as universal and personal.

Stage 3 The final stage begins at about age 9 or 10 and is assumed to continue thereafter. The child now understands that *death is personal, universal, and inevitable as well as final.* All that live must die, including oneself.

Discussion of death at this age has an adult quality: "Death is the termination of life. Death is destiny. We finish our earthly life. Death is the end of life on earth," declared one nine-year-old boy. A 10-year-old girl added a moral and poetic dimension: "It means the passing of the body. Death is a great squaring of accounts in our lives. It is a thing from which our bodies cannot be resurrected. It is like the withering of flowers."

This new awareness is compatible with belief in afterlife, as with the nine-year-old boy who said, "Everyone has to die once, but the soul lives on." Perhaps the child does not really have a grasp of afterlife concepts until death itself is appreciated as final and inevitable.

What Has Been Learned Since "Auntie Death"?

Nagy's findings remain useful today, although the tendency to personify death between ages five and nine seems to have diminished greatly, according to most follow-up studies. Perhaps this is a change wrought by the new childhood with its exposure

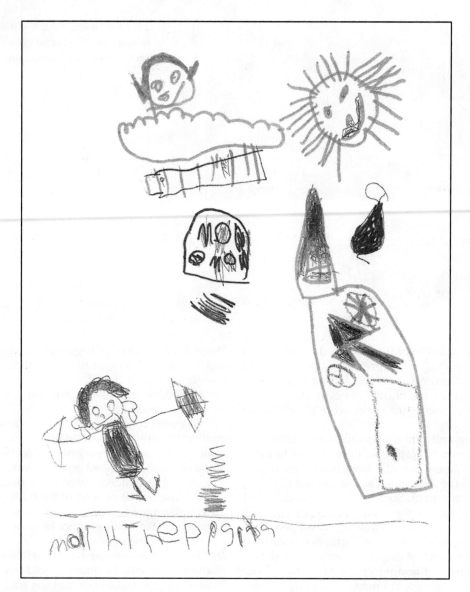

FIGURE 10-1

Michael's God Machine. Reprinted with permission from D. W. Adams & E. J. Deveau (Eds.), Beyond the Innocence of Childhood, *Vol. 1: "Perceptions of Death Through the Eyes of Children and Adolescents. Amityville, NY: Baywood, 1995.*

to mass media and high technology. There also seems to be a tendency for children in America today to move through the stages at an earlier age than what was found by Nagy.

Five-year-old Michael gives us an example of the way some young children today are integrating technological developments into their dawning

conceptions of dying and death. Researcher E. J. Deveau (1995) comments on Michael's drawing (Figure 10-1):

> Michael . . . is concerned with burial, fantasy, and the world beyond. He integrates modern technology into his account of how God converts

Run and hide! "It" has been a proxy for death in many versions of this childhood game.

Children can not only feel a parent's sorrow but also offer the comfort that was once given to them.

the dead into angels after hauling them up to heaven. His description of how people die is very concrete and practical, in keeping with what might be expected at this age (p. 86).

In the picture, according to Michael, "God uses a machine that turns them into an angel." People die "when they eat bad food, the bad food sticks to their heart and the blood can't get in the heart and then you have a heart attack . . . or something like that."

It is also probable, as Deveau has suggested, that the stages are not absolute and fixed, but, rather, represent temporary "resting places" in the child's continuing attempt to come to terms with death both cognitively and emotionally.

There is general agreement that basic understanding of death is usually achieved by about age 9 or 10. Nagy had identified the basic components as inevitability, nonreversibility, universality, and personal inclusion ("I will die, too"). Later studies added cessation and causation: Children come to understand that in death the body no longer can perform its functions (cessation), and that it is this loss of function that results in death (causation). Studies reviewed by Kenyon (2001) find that children with superior intellectual and verbal skills demonstrate more advanced concepts of death than other children of the same age. Boys are more likely than girls to depict violent causes of death.

Developing a mature comprehension of death is but part of the child's project to understand what the whole world is about. There are many stimulating contributions to the study of children as fledgling philosophers and scientists (e.g., Rosenberg, Johnson, & Harris, 2000). Of particular interest here

are those studies finding that preschool children already have the knack of distinguishing between living creatures (e.g., a starfish) and nonliving objects (e.g., a robodog). Many three- and most four-year-olds realize that living creatures eat, grow, and die, while toys and stuffed animals do not (Jepson & Gelman, 2007). [This does not mean that these very young children have firmly grasped the more abstract meanings of death.] It is possible to confuse children—and adults—if presented with sophisticated robotic devices that are designed to simulate speech, memory, and conversational characteristics. Nevertheless, children seem to get off to a fast start in distinguishing between alive and not alive. "Dead" would have little or no meaning if one did not recognize the basic alive/not-alive distinction.

Preschool children are also working on their ability to distinguish sleep from death. This remains a fuzzy issue throughout adult life because "sleeping" and "resting" are often used as euphemisms for "dead." Cross-cultural research indicates that many children are able to make this distinction by age four (Barrett & Behne, 2004). Studies also find that children often rely on what they hear from adults, as well as on their own observations (Harris & Koenig, 2006). This is not always a good thing. Adult language sometimes baffles children ("Argggh! The battery's dead!").

Does Anxiety Influence Children's Thoughts About Death?

Children with more mature levels of understanding have lower levels of death anxiety (Slaughter & Griffiths, 2007). Awareness of the biological basis of death seems to reduce uncertainty and climate the more fantastic type of fears. The researchers encourage adults to discuss death and dying with children in biological terms. Fears are most common in the nighttime, by younger children, and by girls, though very common for both gender (Gordon, King, Gullone, Muris, & Ollendick, 2007). The fears are often vague. What they have in common is anxiety about personal safety. Most of the children had found somebody with whom to share their fears. The researchers note that death-related fears show up early in childhood and continue thereafter. Their explanation: survival is an urgent issue right from the beginning of life, so one should be ever vigilant.

Does *death anxiety* take on different characteristics from early to later childhood? Lonetto (1980) found that younger children expressed more *separation anxiety*, while older children expressed more sadness about death itself. "The happy smiles of the dead depicted by the younger children have all but faded away in the representations given by ten-year-olds, who show the dead with closed mouths and eyes" (p. 146). The older children were more likely to depict death as scary and horrible, and they also focus more on their own possible death as compared with others.

By age 11, there was more use of abstract symbols in the drawings, indicating a new way of coping with death. At this age children could hint at death and represent its meanings (e.g., a valentine with tears pouring down its face) without having to draw all the unpleasant details. The use of black as the only color became dominant among the older children. Jenny put it into words:

> Death is blackness . . . like when you close your
> eyes. It's cold and when you die your body
> is cold. Frightening, I don't want to die . . .
> I wonder then, how I'm going to die . . . I feel
> scared and I try to forget it (p. 154).

Children's response to traumatic events takes a form related to their general level of cognitive and emotional development. In the wake of a natural disaster, preschool and elementary-school children expressed fear openly, while older children and adolescents more often showed withdrawal, and antisocial behavior (Baggerly & Salloum, 2010). The trauma stress response for both younger and older children usually included other signs of distress in addition to fear. It was useful to look for a larger pattern of behavior and mood change.

A parent's reassurance presence helps the child not feel alone, confused, and frightened in her grief.

Cultural Influences on Children's Concepts of Death

Children's thoughts about death are influenced by cultural belief systems and patterns of communication. In the United States, adults have often tried to avoid death talk with children, a situation that has been moderating in recent years. Chinese children in Taiwan perhaps have more to deal with in constructing their own views (Yang & Chen, 2007). They are exposed to a lively mix of religious traditions that have varying interpretations of dying, death, mourning, and afterlife. There is, however, a prevailingly negative climate of feeling regarding death—even more intense for those who have abandoned all religions. As compared with the United States, Taiwanese children are more likely to have been influenced by the belief that death is death: if anything happens thereafter it is strange and hardly worth thinking about. Many children try to discuss death with their parents, who turn out to be even more avoidant than their American counterparts. Like American children, the Taiwanese draw images from the media with its emphasis on violent deaths. Unlike American children, they also have ghosts to deal with, an enduring part of the Chinese legacy.

Japanese culture presents similar challenges to the child's development of death concepts and attitudes.

> The negative view of death is so deeply embedded in Japanese society that even professionally trained personnel think that the mention of death could hurt and shock children . . . a taboo almost unavoidable in Japanese culture. . . . Children symbolize hope and the future, and as such, are to be kept as far as possible from death. Consequently, very little is known about Japanese children's perceptions of death (Sagara-Rosemeyer & Davies, 2007, p. 204.)

Japanese children today are exposed not only to the death communication taboo, but also to the sharp edges of a fragmenting traditional culture. Violent crimes by youth and suicide rates are among the signs and alarms of this accelerating shift from "the old ways" to whatever new situation will emerge. Sagara-Rosemeyer & Davies sampled children's responses through interviews, drawings, and discussion of the drawings. The children conceived of life, death, and afterlife as a totality, a flow that begins with God's gift of *Inochi* (life) to the embryo. This differs from the attitude most often observed in the United States and other Western nations, namely, that life and death should keep their places in separate categories. Japanese children tend to view the course of life and death within the frame of a larger picture. Nevertheless, like the Chinese children, they also encounter the challenge of integrating Eastern religious tradition with Christianity and its images of heaven and hell.

Exposure to violence becomes an issue wherever children's death concepts are studied. For example, children in Sweden and the United States had similar concepts of death at the same age. However, U.S. children more often depicted violent causes of death, while Swedish children more often depicted chapels in cemeteries, tombstones, crosses on church steeples, caskets, and other cultural symbols of loss and grief. It is possible that the much greater frequency of violence and death on U.S. television as compared with Swedish television may have a strong bearing on these differences in children's representations of death (Wass, 2002). There is growing evidence that witnessing sudden and violent death can have a powerfully disturbing effect on children, including severe post-traumatic stress syndrome (Eksi et al. (2007). Such a traumatic experience, especially if not ameliorated by supportive interventions, can have an enduring effect on the individual's basic conception of life, death, and self.

The role of religious beliefs and expectations is suggested by a study of Muslim girls, ages 6 through 10, in South Africa (Anthony & Bhana, 1988/1989). The realization that death is universal and inevitable seemed to be grasped at an earlier age by Muslim children—but this did not mean that they also accepted the irreversibility of death. "They believe that the dead come alive again under certain circumstances, such as when angels question them in the grave. It can, thus, be seen that the responses of the children are characteristic of their cultural and religious environments" (p. 225). The Muslim children were also more likely to believe in the importance of praying for the dead. No doubt there are many other variations in children's thinking about death as they respond to their culture's belief systems and expectations. It has become all too common to see newsreel footage of children playing at being soldiers in cities where many continue to die of actual violence.

Children born before and after the conquest of fatal childhood diseases and the introduction of television differ in their experiences. Children who view Disney movies could come across more than 20 death scenes. They will notice that all the justified deaths are those of "the bad guys" (Cox, Garrett, & Graham, 2004/2005). This suggests:

> the trend in Disney films to vilify the antagonists to a point where they are seen as deserving their death . . . . All unjustified deaths were those of protagonists, showing that good characters never deserve to die (p. 278).

Parents seem to have their work cut out for them in helping children interpret deaths seen in movies or television, or inflicted through computer games. Before movies and television took hold, children were more likely to learn about death from real life events. My father would occasionally speak of his brothers who died of diphtheria in childhood. Many other long-lived adults have memories of family members dying from contagions and infections that are seldom encountered today. On the other hand, school shootings that have traumatized many children were practically unknown in past generations. Every new generation of children brings distinctive experiences to its understanding of death-related issues. It would be questionable to assume that tomorrow's children, growing up in tomorrow's world, will have precisely the same ways of thinking and feeling about death as the children of today and yesterday,

Do Imaginary Friends Die?

Some children have very good friends who live only in their imagination. These imaginary friends (IFs) can play many roles in a child's life and most often occur within a normal course of development. Many and varied *imaginary companions* has been well described (Gleason, 2004). Although known in the literature as "companions," almost all our respondents preferred to speak of them as "friends," so both terms will be used here. Could these IFs help us learn more about the child's understanding of loss, change,

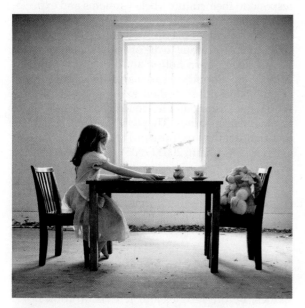

Imaginary companions often become part of a preschool child's family, but depart when replaced by the excitement of new friends and situations. What becomes of the make-believe friends?

and death? Taylor (1999) shares of the few reports in the literature of an imaginary friend's death. A four-year-old boy had played regularly with Tippy, an imaginary girl, and Tompy, an imaginary boy, both a year older than himself. A few months later, though, his great friends were no longer part of his life.

ADULT: Do you have a pretend friend named Tompy?

CHILD: Oh, Tompy, Tompy. They were dead. They got dead today. Oh . . . the day before the day. They just got dead.

ADULT: So how old is Tompy?

CHILD: Well, he's 7,200 years old. . . . But Tompy's real defective. He has a sore knee. . . . We're really good friends (nodding). The other one's a girl.

ADULT: They're good friends?

CHILD: Yeah, they were.

ADULT: They were? So, are they still alive?

CHILD: Oh, they're still alive but . . . (makes sound effect and falls back as though hit). . . .

ADULT: Do you play with Tompy sometimes?

CHILD: (In critical tone of voice) Did you forget what I told you? (pp. 123–124).

This interaction was more complicated than the summary given above. In the middle of the discussion, the child was distracted by Gadget—his latest imaginary friend, a small and frisky mouse. The child capriciously shifted Tompy back and forth between alive and dead. Furthermore:

The child's words and his tone of voice suggested that Tompy was remembered with some fondness, but no profound sense of loss. Gadget had clearly taken over (p. 124).

Dr. Lynn Fox, one of my nonimaginary friends, and I decided to explore this facet of the child's world. Retrospective interviews were conducted with university students and staff (Kastenbaum & Fox, 2007). Two children who were still acquainted with their IFs also were scooped into the study. The general findings were consistent with previous studies. Most of the IFs had entered their lives during the preschool years and exited around the time they entered kindergarten; a few stayed in the picture much longer. The IF usually looked like anybody else, although only visible to the lucky child. Most were obedient and adoring companions. Some were a more daring version of one's own self. The IFs were most often regarded as being as real as "regular" people. However, there was also a floating quality: the IF could be more or less real, depending on circumstances (at its "most real-ist" when nobody else was around).

So—did imaginary friends die? Yes, but that was not the most common outcome. The relationship usually ended with the IF fading away as school days began with a host of new friends and activities. These partings were uneventful and unmourned. It had been time for the IF to go. However, about one IF in five did perish. Their deaths were the result of accident, error, disaster, or bad luck—but sometimes because of something the child either did or failed to do. In most cases, the children had believed their IF would never—and should never—die. "She was *mine*, and should always be there when I wanted her!"

The circumstances of death offer illuminating glimpses of the young child's developing and rather experimental worldview. An IF could be killed in an event that the child actually experienced. For example:

> I was wearing my green coat that I wore all the
> time. I was naughty, I climbed the credenza.
> It fell on us both. And that's how he died. . . .
> I remember it was 2 p.m. and sunny outside.
> I looked at the wallpaper as the light shone on
> it, and saw the gold flecks, and said, "Oh, that
> looks pretty." Then the shelves fell over us. . . .
> I didn't talk to him. I just knew he was gone. No
> tears, No sadness.

Another type of death involved the impulsive use of word magic. IF Todd was so well accepted by the (real) family that the boy's father asked what kind of pizza he would like when they went out that night. The boy replied:

> "Todd's not coming. He got run over. By a fire
> engine. Run over dead. He just ran out into the
> street to see what was happening and the fire
> engine got him." I don't know why I said that.
> It just came into my head and that's the way
> it was. . . . I don't know if I felt sad at all. Just
> something that happened.

There was more context for the unexpected death of IF Barneybus. The girl's mother had been pregnant but "lost" the baby: a disturbing and mystifying event. When a neighbor girl demanded a turn at playing with Barneybus,

> I told her that he had gone to the hospital
> because he was dead. That wasn't true, but that's
> what popped out of me. But after I said that, that
> seemed to be it. He must have been dead because
> that's what I said!"

If words could kill, so loving, even desperate, attention could keep either an IF or a "regular" person alive:

> If I think hard about people, they won't die. I
> was worried about the school work and if the
> kids would like me, I noticed [IF] Emmy wasn't
> there any more. She just stopped breathing, dead.
> I had stopped thinking about that much
> about her, so that's what happened.

Mother, having made a batch of her delicious ice cream, told IF Bobby there was not enough for him to have a share this time:

> He died. Bobby was very upset that he could not
> be part of the family any more, and he died. That
> was the end of Bobby.

Many of the children were not ready to accept the adult insistence on a firm distinction between categories. An IF did not have to be always either alive or dead. There was an easygoing fluidity in the children's way of thinking. For example, Graham had not said much about the imaginary friend he had wanted to keep to himself. He surprised his family one day by saying that Jeff Green was dead: no further information forthcoming. Come Halloween, though, and Jeff Green was brought back to life "this one more time, so he could go trick and treating." Jeff would replace Graham for this occasion. The next day, Jeff was dead again, which did not disturb Graham. "Jeff was like me, only more cool. We thought he should have a good time." Nevertheless, Graham was adamant that alive and dead were absolutely different conditions—and that Fred Green, alive or dead, would be with him for the rest of his life.

The overall picture is of lively young minds that move between fantasy and reality without the constraints that are expected of adults. Ideas of life and death flow and float as part of this sea of adventuring. Identity is also subject to whatever transformations the child can come up with.

For example, the essence of an IF can be shape-shifted to a frisky little mouse, and friends can be created, multiplied, and dismissed as need or whim dictates.

Deaths of imaginary friends are recognized as significant but do not appear to have a deep and enduring impact. This could be a way of developing a sense of mastery over loss, change, and death. One can experience a kind of real loss and yet also a kind of not real loss, and so build up confidence. Furthermore, the older child and adult often report a sense of having survived their imaginary friends, even if those friends have just faded away into the mists of time rather than died. The creation and loss of imaginary childhood friends could be regarded as a rite of passage to the adult world, with its harsh separation of reality and fantasy.

> I love the juice, but the sun goes up; I see the
> stars and
> the moonstar goes up,
> And there always goes today. And the sun
> Loves people. But one always dies.
> Dogs will die very sooner
> Than mummies and daddies and sisters
> and
> brothers because
> They'll not die til a hundred and
> Because I love them dearly
> —Hilary-Anne Farley, age 5
> (in Lewis, 1966, p. 143)

Hilary-Anne Farley, a Canadian girl only five years of age at the time, was bursting with love but also acutely aware that time and loss are inevitable: "there always goes today"; "but one always dies." Does this sound like a child who has no clue about the reality and universality of death? She even recognizes differential longevity and the ambiguity of time. Here is time as the enemy that takes people away, but here also is time as insulation between now and death ("They'll not die til a hundred"). Young Ms. Farley calls upon the force of her love and need to protect her family from death. They will live til a hundred "Because I love them dearly." Wish fulfillment? Of course. But the poem as a whole resolutely faces the reality of death and loss. Children who relinquish their IFs one way or another are also testing and practicing for the more profound losses that time and circumstance will bring.

HOW DO CHILDREN COPE WITH BEREAVEMENT?

For some children, death has already become a reality. They have lost a person who had been very important in their lives. We look now at the effects of *bereavement* on children and the ways in which they attempt to cope. An increasing number of American children may be at risk for prolonged and disturbing grief reactions as a result of a traumatic bereavement.

A Death in the Family: Effects on the Child

A death in the family can draw attention away from the needs of the children. When a parent dies, for example, the surviving parent's grief can interfere temporarily with the ability to care for the emotional, or even the physical, needs of the children. Sometimes it is a sibling who dies. The parents may have become so involved in the plight of the dying child that other children are neglected. The surviving children may feel isolated if the adults fail to recognize their distress signals. Sensitive adults take into account both the child's developmental level and the role that the deceased person had played in the child's life. What does this child understand about separation and death? Does the child understand that death is final and universal? Was the deceased person an older sibling whom the child had looked up to? Was the deceased a younger sibling whom the child had resented as a competitor for parental competition? Does the surviving child believe that she could join the lost sibling if she managed to get himself killed? Some children grieve silently for their lost sibling, but develop sleep, eating, and self-esteem problems (Davies & Limbo, 2010). Yet the surviving sibling sometimes "grows up" sooner and stronger, in part as a way of honoring the one whose life had ended. Children, like adults, have the potential to develop positive motivations, skills, and self-concept after bereavement.

Attention should be given to the quality of the child's personal and family situation prior to the bereavement. Had this been a tightly knit family in which the child enjoyed a strong sense of love and security? Was it a broken or bent family characterized by anxiety and insecurity? The impact of bereavement is influenced by the child's developmental level, the specific loss that has been experienced, and the previous pattern of family security and affection.

Bereaved children may express their distress in ways that do not seem closely associated with the loss. For example, serious problems in school may appear for the first time. Children may turn on playmates with sudden anger. Fear of the dark or of being alone may reappear. The child's behavior pattern can show the effect of bereavement without an obvious show of sorrow. They may be further inhibited from direct expression if commanded by the surviving parent to be "brave." Tears are then stigmatized as signs of weakness and disobedience.

Young children often express their memories of a lost parent through activities that had linked them together. An adult can preserve a valued relationship by replaying memories in private or sharing them with others. But a two-year-old boy who loses his father is more likely to express his longing and sadness through actions:

> For weeks he spent much of his time repeating the daily play activities that had constituted the essence of his relationship with his father. He also insisted, over and over, on taking the walks he had taken with his father, stopping at the stores where his father had shopped and recalled specific items (Furman, 1974, p. 55).

The toddler's need added to the mother's emotional pain, but she recognized that it was the best way he had to adjust to the loss. Young children are likely to focus on a few strong memory images, in contrast to the bereaved spouse who has many recollections from all the years of marriage, and more skill in verbalization. The young child carries much of the remembrance of the lost parent in the form of scenes and activities shared with the lost person. Many years later, there might be an episode of unexpected overwhelming sadness when a situation touches off a precious memory. The mental image of the lost parent often remains with children long after the death. The silent sadness of the bereaved child can be painful for the adult to acknowledge. But how are we to support and comfort unless we can accept the reality of the child's suffering?

It can be even more difficult to accept the child's response when it includes anger. The surviving parent may be horrified to hear criticisms of the deceased parent coming from the children. This can happen precisely at the time that the widowed spouse is at the peak of idealizing the lost husband or wife. Yet the expression of anger may be a necessary part of the child's adaptation to the loss. Some adults find it very painful to accept the child's expression of mixed feelings toward the deceased because these feelings are within them as well.

Several consistent differences have been found in the behavior of children who have suffered parental bereavement as compared with children who have both parents living.

Children with parental bereavement:

- Tend to be more submissive, dependent, and introverted;
- Show a higher frequency of maladjustment and emotional disturbance, including suicidality (Chapter 8);
- Show a higher frequency of delinquent and criminal behavior;
- Perform less adequately in school and on tests of cognitive functioning;
- Experience more physical symptoms;
- Become more concerned that the family will fall apart.

Coleen, the girl who was afraid she had hurt her mother by stepping on her grave, experienced several of these difficulties. Within a month of the death, she reported headaches and stomachaches and became extremely worried about her father's increased drinking and grouchiness. To make it even worse, her father and her sister were giving each other a hard time. "Mother used to make it better and stop them, but she isn't here anymore" (Christ, 2000, p. 103). It is useful to note that (1) many of Coleen's concerns were linked with specific situations and (2) she was already trying to deal with these problems. For example, she would soon be a junior bridesmaid for her cousin, even though Mom wouldn't be there with her, "but I'll pretend she is watching me from heaven." Pretend! She had the mental flexibility to find comfort in the idea of her mother watching her from heaven while not necessarily taking this to be an objective fact. Coleen was also anxious about the way her friends would treat her when she returned to school—would they be asking a lot of uncomfortable questions, or what?

As it turned out, the friends were supportive and understanding, sending her condolence and encouragement cards even before she came back to school. And it was that much better when she was chosen to dance in a show at school. Coleen was fortunate in having a supportive family and the opportunity to meet with a school counselor, but she also demonstrated her own resourcefulness in coping with her situation. We see bereaved children's realistic concerns and strenuous efforts to deal with them repeatedly in case histories such as those described by Grace Hyslop Christ (2000). Although children may have incomplete conceptions of death, their ability to recognize and deal with the realities should not be underestimated. The more fully we can enter into the child's private world of hurt and fear, the better position we are in to provide understanding and comfort.

Useful guidelines are offered for parents and teachers for helping bereaved children (Webb, 2010). Specific approaches such as bereavement groups and camps (Ruffin & Zimmerman, 2010) and storytelling (O'Toole) are accompanied by discussion of often-encountered issues.

Post-Traumatic Stress Disorder (PTSD) Following a Violent Death

Sudden, unexpected death has a more severe impact on the survivors, whether children or adults (see Chapter 11). This impact can be further intensified by threatening features of the death—for example, a drive-by shooting, a suicide, or mutilation of the corpse in an accident.

There is now more professional and public awareness of the syndrome known as *post-traumatic stress disorder* (PTSD). This condition was officially recognized as a diagnostic entity in 1980. It became salient during the Vietnam War, and again with people serving in Afghanistan or Iraq. A person comes through extremely stressful situations and at a later time suffers "flashbacks" of the experience. During these episodes, the individual behaves in seemingly irrational, bizarre, and perhaps dangerous ways—not at all in keeping with his or her previous personality. These episodes often are frightening to family, friends, and the individual experiencing them.

Recognition of PTSD in children who have experienced traumatic bereavements or other encounters with death is now starting to receive some of the attention it deserves (e.g., Doka, 2000). Some teachers and school systems have already developed programs and techniques for reaching out to children who have been exposed to traumatic death.

Children with PTSD are more likely than others to have difficulty paying attention, concentrating, and making and keeping friends. Such a dysfunctional pattern is especially harmful in childhood, when so many basic personal and interpersonal skills are being developed (Weaver & Festa, 2003). The child with PTSD is also likely to be frightened, as shown by the following excerpt from a psychotherapy session with Nancy Boyd Webb (2002) in which Susan, age nine, shares her reaction to the automobile death of a school mate.

SUSAN: I'm having bad dreams that wake me up every night. Then in the morning I don't want to get up. I'm tired all the time, even when I go to bed at 8 o'clock.

WEBB: That sounds pretty bad! Can you tell me what the dreams are like?

SUSAN: I dream that there is a gorilla in my closet and that he is going to sneak up to my bed and grab me and then take me away and roast me on a barbecue.

WEBB: That must be pretty scary! Does the dream wake you up?

SUSAN: Yes, and then I run into my mom's bed (p. 196).

Children can be helped to overcome PTSD, but first we must be observant enough to recognize their distress and its possible connection to a disturbing death-related experience. In recent years, it has become evident that children are vulnerable to PTSD as a result of terrorist attacks. Children who had lost a friend or acquaintance in the 1995 Oklahoma City bombing of a federal office building had PTSD symptoms and also watched more television coverage of the disaster. Even children who did not know any of the victims experienced distress and disturbance, though not to the same extent (Pfefferbaum et al., 2000).

The 9/11 attacks on the World Trade Center affected many children in the New York City area. Nearly one child in five suffered a severe or very severe reaction (Fairbrother et al., 2003). Parental bereavement through terrorist attack has been found to have physiological as well as psychological effects that persist for years afterward (Pfeffer et al., 2006). Their severe stress reaction includes dysfunction of the endocrine system, which undermines influence personality balance and coping skills. Anxiety and depression continue in body as well as mind. Family counseling and therapy has proven useful.

Long-Term Effects of Childhood Bereavement

The effects of childhood bereavement are not limited to childhood. Major physical and mental illnesses occur more often in the adult lives of those who were bereaved as children. For example, some children take on the identity of their dead sibling. This is most likely to happen when the family had given preference to the child who is now deceased and then responds with approval to the impersonation. The borrowed identity can generate significant problems in adult life.

Nevertheless, people bereaved in childhood often demonstrate resilience. For example, mothers whose own mothers had died in childhood showed symptoms of depression, worried about their own deaths, were overprotective, and perfectionists (Zall, 1994, p. 225). Despite these problems, however, many proved to be effective mothers themselves. They responded to the challenge of their own parental role by completing their unfinished grieving over the deaths of their mothers.

> *For many years I didn't want children. I decided to take the risk, with my husband's encouragement, and the experience of motherhood has been the most challenging and even more delightful than I ever dreamed. Because of my early loss and fear of dying and leaving my children, I have been extremely conscientious about teaching the children to separate from me very early in their lives. I tend to spend a great deal of time with them.*

Parental bereavement can be found in the childhood of many people who made exceptional achievements in adulthood. Consider, for example, the great naturalist, Charles Darwin. All through his life Darwin retained the memory of his mother's deathbed, her black velvet gown, and the work table. Curiously, though, he remembered hardly anything of her appearance or his conversations with her. He remembered being sent for, going into her room, being greeted by his father, and crying afterward. Even stranger, Darwin had much more detailed recollections of the funeral of a soldier that he attended a few weeks later.

Biographer Ralph Colp, Jr. (1975) was struck by Darwin's apparent repression of many of his memories of his mother and her death while details of the soldier's death remained fresh in his mind. Colp finds that death-related themes were closely interwoven with Darwin's work throughout his life. These themes showed up even in the notes he made in the margins of books, as well as in his dreams. One of the major themes disclosed was a "keen instinct against death." Colp and others believe there is a connection between Darwin's ardent advocacy of life and his fascination with the evolution of new life forms. Darwin's growing awareness of a process of natural selection in which entire species die off resonated with the feelings he still carried from the time of his mother's death. In his middle adult years, Darwin expressed fear of sudden death and regarded his theory as an indirect form of continued personal survival.

Near the end of his life, Darwin returned to the first creatures that interested him as a young boy—worms. He had enjoyed fishing and had mixed feelings about sacrificing worms to this cause. As an elderly and ailing man, Darwin studied worms. In Colp's words, "Thus, the old man, who as a boy had killed worms, now, night after night, observed how he would soon be eaten by worms" (1975, p. 200). Scientist Darwin respected worms as coinhabitants of planet Earth, who have a key role in maintaining the living ecology by literally passing the earth through themselves. That he, too, Charles Darwin, would become part of the worm and part of the earth again was not a horror story but an acceptable aspect of our natural history.

Ten thousand examples would provide ten thousand different stories of the direct and indirect ways in which childhood bereavement influences the entire life course. How each story turns out years later is likely to depend much on the kind of attention and support the child receives. We look now at some approaches that have proved useful.

Helping Children Cope with Bereavement

1. *Develop and maintain an open communication pattern with children*. It is unrealistic to wait until a crisis situation develops. The child who is shunted aside whenever there are "important things" to discuss is deprived of opportunity to learn communication skills that would prove useful in difficult situations.

2. *Give children the opportunity to decide about attending the funeral.* Adults often assume that children would either not understand funerals or be harmed by the experience. However, many children appreciate the opportunity to make their own decisions. It can be helpful to describe what the funeral will be like in words the child can understand, and answer questions that might arise at that time. Books suggested by Corr (2010) can be useful for this purpose. Some families also encourage children to make suggestions about details of the funeral. By being included in the family drama, children felt acknowledged and supported by their families. They could feel close to their parent for one last time, and for being part of the family in doing this. Nevertheless, Silverman (2000) and other experts suggest that the child who has decided against attending the funeral should not be forced to do so against his or her wishes.

3. *Check out what the child is thinking and feeling— do not assume that we know what the death means to him or her.* Griffith (2003) observes that the youngest are many times the unseen, unknown, and invisible grievers (p. 217). Children as young as three years of age have been helped with the expression of their grief through art therapy (Wood & Near, 2010) but first we must be willing to enter their worlds of experience rather than make assumptions:

   > With children never interpret a head nod when you are explaining something to them as you would with an adult. They have learned the gesture from adults, but frequently it is for the child simply the easiest way to get the "helping" adult to leave them alone. . . . Always gently ask the child to tell you what they have just heard and to explain it to you in their own words (Hersh, 1995, p. 91).

4. *Encourage the expression of feelings.* This point was made by many of the mothers in our case history study. Mental health professionals agree. Young children can express themselves through play and drawings, often enhanced by storytelling. Feelings can also be expressed through vigorous games that allow the discharge of tension and anger. An especially valuable way for children to express their feelings is to help comfort others. For example, a child attending a funeral later reported that

"At the end while I was crying, my little cousin came up to me and gave me a hug and said it was okay. She was only three" (Silverman & Worden, 1992, p. 329). Comforting and altruistic behavior can begin early in life.

5. *Provide convincing assurance that there will always be somebody to love and look after the child.* The death of a parent arouses fears that the surviving parent and other important people may also abandon the child. Verbal assurances are not always sufficient. Bereaved children may become anxious when the surviving parent is out of sight or has not come home at the expected time. Sending the children away for a while often intensifies the feeling of abandonment. Adult relatives and friends who spend time with the children after their bereavement are helping the surviving parent to provide reassurance that there will always be somebody there for them.

6. *Professional counseling deserves consideration if the bereaved children are at special risk.* The death of both parents, for example, constitutes a special risk, as does a death for which the children might feel that they are somehow at blame. There is one special risk that each year arises for thousands of children:

   > Mom told us to sit down and she said, "Girls, your Dad died." We both cried right away. We went down to the garage where everybody was. People began holding us and trying to make us feel better. No one knew what to say. We felt like everyone was just staring at us. It was like a big, bad dream. And to make matters worse, we found out from our Mom that Dad had killed himself . . . . It still is hard for us to understand. We were only five and nine years old (Carolyn and Kristin as quoted in Dahlke, 1994, pp. 116–117).

   The two girls had to contend—suddenly—both with the death of their father and the puzzle and possible stigma of his suicide. Their consuming question was: "If Daddy loved me, why did he leave me?" This became the title of a short book that the girls wrote together over a period of time with the encouragement of a professional counselor, David Dahlke. Every page of the girls' book reflects their personal growth experience as they explored their thoughts, feelings, values, and choices with the counselor's assistance. We learn, for example, that the children became afraid that if mother married again her new husband would also commit suicide. Carolyn reported, "I felt Dad threatened suicide a lot. I asked him, 'What if you kill yourself?' and he said, 'I won't do that!' . . . But he did. He lied to us. . . . Dad was mixed up" (p. 117).

Carolyn and Kristin showed insight and resilience as they dealt with their loss and the questions it raised. Other children who suffer parental bereavement under traumatic and stressful conditions can also receive valuable assistance from qualified counselors.

7. *Consider the option of a therapeutic group experience to help bereaved children start to work through their grief and fear.* There are a variety of group settings, including camps, that have proven helpful to some bereaved children (Ruffin & Zimmerman, 2010; Schuurman & DeCristofare, 2010).

THE DYING CHILD

Children sometimes think about death, loss, and separation even when there has been no obvious event to arouse their concern. Writing about his own childhood, Spalding Gray (1986) recalls:

the time when I woke up in the middle of the night and saw my brother Rocky standing on his bed, blue in the face and gasping for air, crying out that he was dying. My mother and father were standing beside the bed trying to quiet him, and Mom said, "Calm down, dear, it's all in your mind." And after he calmed down, my father went back to bed, and my mother turned out the light and sat on the edge of Rocky's bed in the dark. . . . We were all there, very quiet, in the dark, and then Rocky would start in, "Mom, when I die, is it forever?" And she said, "Yes, dear." And then Rocky said, "Mom, when I die, is it forever, and ever, and ever?" and she said, "Uh-huh, dear." And he said, "Mom, when I die is it forever and ever and ever . . . ?" I just went right off to this (p. 14).

It should not be surprising, then, to learn that children who actually are afflicted with life-threatening illnesses are keenly aware of their predicaments. Shira Putter, who died at the age of nine from a rare form of diabetes, left a diary that includes this sadly perceptive entry: "Daddy doesn't care about me. I know he comes to visit me practically every day, but once he comes he always seems so far away. It's like he can't wait to leave again" (Grollman, 1988, p. 12). She was reluctant to share this concern with her mother because "I didn't want her to get upset." But she did tell her mother, who then explained "that Daddy does love me and that was part of the problem. He loves me so much that it hurts him to see me sick and in pain. She asked me to please try to understand." This little episode put everybody more at ease, including Daddy, and restored the usual family pattern of warm and caring interactions.

Dying children may hesitate to share their concerns because of the fear that this would make their parents feel even worse. On other occasions, Shira did remain silent when she could see that her parents were upset by new complications in her condition. Far from being unaware of the perils they face, children may take a kind of parental role themselves and try to protect adults from anxiety and sorrow.

Each day can bring some new threat or challenge. Shira, for example, had to cope with the fact that her favorite doctor took himself off her case because he was so upset by her continued physical decline. The fear of abandonment by the most important people in their lives is often a major concern of the dying child—and too often based upon the way that some adults do distance themselves from the child. [The adult's personal anxiety in other type of response. Neonatologists with intense personal fear of dying were more likely to approve of hastening the death of terminally ill infants by sedation or withdrawal of treatment (Barr, 2007).]

Shira and her family were able to maintain mutual support until the very end. In one of her last diary entries Shira describes their Passover celebration that became a loving farewell. It was time for her to go, and she was no longer afraid of dying.

Anthropologist Myra Bluebond-Langner (1977, 1988) spent many hours listening to hospitalized children and observing their interactions with parents and staff. The children were keenly aware of their situations. One morning, for example, Jeffrey asked Bluebond-Langner to read to him from the classic children's book, *Charlotte's Web* (White, 1952)—"the part where Charlotte dies." This chapter, "Last Day," offers a combination of humor, drama, and consolation. "Nothing can harm you now" is one of its thoughts. Another is: "No one was with her when she died." When Bluebond-Langner completed her reading of the chapter, Jeffrey dozed off. He died that afternoon.

Many of the terminally ill children that Bluebond-Langner observed passed through five stages in the acquisition of information:

1. I have a serious illness.
2. I know what drugs I am receiving and what they are supposed to do.
3. I know the relationship between my symptoms and the kind of treatment I am getting.
4. I realize now that I am going through a cycle of feeling worse, getting better, then getting worse again. The medicines don't work all the time.
5. I know that this won't go on forever. There's an end to the remissions and the relapses and to the kind of medicine they have for me. When the drugs stop working, I will die pretty soon.

The children soon became sophisticated about hospital routines. They learned the names of all their drugs and how to tell one kind of staff member from another. Little escaped them. Staff members would have been astonished had they realized how much the children picked up. Most of all, perhaps, the children learned from each other. They would notice that they were now on the last drug that another child had received before his or her death or that people were now starting to treat them differently, meaning that something important had changed in their conditions. Seriously ill children work hard at understanding what is happening to them. The adult who assumes that a sick child is too young to understand anything is probably making a serious mistake. Consider this sequence reported by Sourkes (1996):

A three-year-old boy played the same game with a stuffed duck and a toy ambulance each time he was hospitalized. The duck would be sick and need to go to the hospital by ambulance. The boy would move the ambulance, making siren noises.

THERAPIST:　How is the duck?
CHILD:　　　Sick.

THERAPIST:　Where is he going?
CHILD:　　　To the hospital.
THERAPIST:　What are they going to do?
CHILD:　　　Make him better . . .

During what turned out to be the boy's terminal admission, he played the same game with the duck. However, the outcome of the ritual changed dramatically:

THERAPIST:　How is the duck?
CHILD:　　　Sick
THERAPIST:　Is he going to get better?
CHILD:　　　(Shaking his head slowly) Ducky not get better. Ducky die (pp. 157–158).

Two days later, the boy drew a picture of "a vibrant firefly, smiling broadly as it emerges from the blackness into the . . . light." He explained: "Fireflies glow in the dark and show others the way" (p. 158). He died that evening.

Care of the Dying Child

Along with emotional support and sensitive communication, dying children need medical, nursing, and other support services. In recent years, the hospice approach to terminal care has been extended to include children. The basic philosophy is the same as with hospice care in general: to help the dying person experience the highest quality of life possible under the circumstances. This is accomplished by skillfully controlling pain and other symptoms and by working with the family to support their own caregiving efforts.

Although a hospital stay is sometimes necessary, the focus is usually on home care. Children as well as adults often feel most secure within their own homes. Because there can be situations in which neither the hospital nor the home seems to be the best place to care for the dying child, some hospice organizations have also established respite care facilities. These are usually small, home-like centers in which the child can receive care for a few days or weeks while the family copes with other problems. Levetown (2002) points out that the children's own views of their situations are more likely to be understood and respected if the care team includes a child psychologist or child life therapist.

Whether the children are at home, in a respite care center, or in a hospital-based hospice service, the overall philosophy remains the same: give comfort, relieve distress, and help the patients and family preserve their most basic values of life during this difficult time. A growing number of pediatric caregivers are applying hospice principles and techniques. Up-to-date information can be obtained from Children's Hospice International (http://www.chionline.org). Another useful source of information is the Initiative for Pediatric Palliative Care (http://www.ippcweb.org). There are encouraging trends. Recent reports demonstrate advances both in compassionate (Mellix, 2007) and technologically sophisticated care (Hooke et al., 2007).

Care of dying children has much in common with the situation of bereaved children:

1. The opportunity to express their concerns through conversation, play, drawing, writing, shared reading—whatever modality is most effective and natural for the particular child. Modeling clay figures or drawing pictures of the family may help transform inner feelings into a tangible communication that can be shared with others. Resentment and anger may be expressed on occasion in the children's play or art; this is usually a natural response to overwhelming circumstances, and the opportunity to "get it out" often proves valuable.

2. Confirmation that they are still normal and valuable people, despite the impairments and limitations imposed by illness. Sensitive parents and other caregivers will find ways to affirm and strengthen children's basic sense of self. They will not allow "dyingness" to overshadow every interaction, every plan, every project. Instead, opportunities will be found for children to do things that are still within their sphere of competence and to stay involved with roles and activities that have brought pleasure. One 10-year-old boy, for example, taught his younger siblings how to play chess while he was dying of *leukemia*; a girl, also 10, kept the statistics and figured the batting averages for her softball team after she herself could no longer play.

3. Assurance that family members and other important people will not abandon *them*, no matter what happens. Nonverbal behavior is a vital component of interaction that can either affirm or undermine the family's words of reassurance. As illustrated by Shira's diary, children are aware of discomfort, tension, and conflict on the part of the adults in their lives. By their everyday actions as well as their words, parents and other caregivers must continue to convey their dedication to being with—to staying with—dying children, come what may.

4. Reassurance that they will not be forgotten. Often dying children fear they will not be a part of what will happen in the family when they are no longer there. They may also fear that they will be replaced in the family constellation by another child, instead of remembered and valued for their uniqueness. In some situations, it may be useful to use mental imagery exercises to help children prepare for impending separation and to participate in the future through imagination. Children may also come up with their own ways of feeling a part of the future, requiring of the adults only their sympathetic attention and cooperation. For example, a child may wish to give some favorite toys to a sibling or friend, or to make a video that can be watched on birthdays or other special occasions.

In addition to these common needs and themes, each child with a life-threatening illness is almost certain to have distinctive ideas, hopes, and apprehensions. What special wish or secret fear is on the mind of this particular child? There is no substitute for careful listening and observation and for respecting the individuality of each child.

Siblings of the Dying Child

He's been sick a lot this year. . . . But I kind of get used to him being sick. . . . I really want to know what it's like to stay home and watch and take care of my brother for a whole day when he's sick. And I know what to do. Every night you (a person with cystic fibrosis) have to get on this machine. And it's because you get all this mucus in your lungs and it's hard to breathe. And when you get sick, you really get sick . . . . And sometimes you die at an early age. But I don't think that will happen to Jason, because he's in pretty good shape. That's about it (Bluebond-Langner, 1996, pp. 78–79).

Eleven-year-old Regan and her family lived every day with nine-year-old Jason's illness and with the prospect of his early death. She adjusted to this situation as did everybody else in the family: Life has to go on, and people have to do what they have to do. She was well informed about her brother's condition and had personal knowledge of somebody who had died young of the same medical condition, cystic fibrosis. But nobody in her family had died—yet. Nobody was dying—yet. Nevertheless, Regan's own childhood experiences were shadowed by the possibility of her brother's death and by the family's daily efforts to carry on "normally" despite their burden of anxiety.

Anxiety and sorrow about the dying child can lead to neglect of other family needs. Parents may not give adequate attention to their own health, for example. The continuing stress can lead to a narrowing of attention, a concentration on "just what most needs to be done," and increased irritability and distraction even on the part of the most devoted parents. And, as recent findings suggest, the brothers and sisters of dying children may be at particular risk during this difficult period.

Bluebond-Langner observes that "The well siblings of terminally ill children live in houses of chronic sorrow. The signs of sorrow, illness, and death are everywhere, whether or not they are spoken of. The signs are written on parents' faces: 'My mother always looks tired now,' and 'Even my Dad's crying a lot.' The signs are there in hushed conversations: 'You learn everything by listening in on the (phone) extension . . .'" (1988, p. 9).

The following problems were observed in well siblings in the course of Bluebond-Langner's pioneering research (1977; 1988):

1. Confusion about what role they are supposed to play in the family. Should they try to be like the sick child? Should they try to become "assistant parents"? Or should they become invisible, "just blend into the woodwork and get out of the way"?
2. A feeling of being deceived or rejected by their parents: "They don't tell me the truth . . . . Nobody really cares about me anymore. . . ."
3. Uncertainty about the future. "What's to become of all of us? . . . Does it do any good to have plans anymore?"
4. Changes in the relationships among the siblings. For example, the illness and hospitalization of the sick child deprives the others of a companion:

   For example, while Jake lay dying, complaining of his back hurting him and not being able to

breathe, his brothers offered to rub his back. He pushed them away saying, "No, no, not you. Only Mommy now." (Bluebond-Langner, 1988, p. 13).

5. Feelings of guilt and ambivalence. The well siblings are distressed by the suffering of the sick child, but may also feel relieved—and feel guilty about feeling relieved—that they are not the ones who are dying.
6. Frustration in not being able to express their feelings and fears to their parents, who are so preoccupied with the dying child and with their own feelings.

Not all well siblings had all these reactions, nor did these feelings occur all the time. In some families, few obvious problems developed until the sick child had become extremely frail and disabled. Until that time, the parents had managed to find some time and energy for the other children and keep a semblance of normal family life going. But the well siblings themselves often took account of changes in the sick child's condition and needs. They recognized that the sick child now required a great deal of attention from the parents and they were less likely to feel rejected or in competition.

Compassionate relatives, friends, neighbors, and teachers can lighten the burden by giving attention to the well siblings during and after the terminal process and by unobtrusively helping the parents in coping with the responsibilities of everyday life. The family with a dying child certainly needs and deserves sensitive, understanding, and mature companionship from all the community.

The Stress of Working with Dying Children

"I can't make good things happen or prevent bad things from happening, no matter how hard I work, no matter what I try. So I just can't keep doing this, I just can't!" "Burnout" has become a familiar term in the workplace. It is used most often in reference to a sense of exhaustion, frustration, and futility. All who provide care for dying children are vulnerable to anxiety and sorrow—sometimes a sense of guilt as well because they are unable to save the child. Papadatou (2006; 2009) has identified a condition she calls "the wounded healer." Her research has found that many nurses and physicians become grief-stricken while working with terminally ill children. This is a form of disenfranchised grief (Doka, 2002): Professional caregivers are not supposed to experience and express their patient-related sorrows and anxieties. Unfortunately, health care professionals are not always well prepared for this challenging kind of work. Papadatou believes that the medical profession's traditional emphasis on diagnosis and treatment of the disease has contributed to neglect of the dying child as a person—and neglect as well of the feelings of those who work closely with the dying child.

She describes an innovative educational program for pediatric nurses at Children's Hospital (Athens, Greece). Pediatric nurses are provided with close and supportive supervision as they work with dying children and their families. They are given the opportunity to discuss their cases with a psychologist and work with a supportive professional team. A sensitivity group experience is also included and group members keep a journal of their experiences, providing another outlet for personal reflection. Papadatou (2009) observes that sensitivity and cooperation within a team of helping professionals can be decisive value in caring for the terminally child. She offers constructive suggestions for preventing and resolving dysfunctional interaction patterns among pediatric caregivers.

SHARING THE CHILD'S DEATH CONCERNS: A FEW GUIDELINES

It is in children's own interests to identify threats to their well-being, even within the harbor of a loving family. Our children will encounter death in many forms—close and distant, imaginary and realistic. Many parents today received little guidance in death-related matters when they were young. And so may face inner struggles when called upon to respond to a child's questions.

This is not a "how-to" book, but there are several guidelines that have proven helpful.

1. *Be a good observer.* Notice how the child is behaving. Listen to what he or she is really saying. Do not rush in with explanations, reassurances, or diversions unless there is some overriding necessity to do so. You will be more helpful to the child if you are relaxed, patient, and attentive enough to learn what needs the

child actually is expressing rather than those you might assume to be there. For example, the child who suddenly asks a parent, "Are you going to be dead?" might have been thinking about something Grandmother said last week or any number of other happenings that aroused this concern. Taking a moment to learn how this question arose in the child's mind could also help to provide an appropriate response.

2. *Do not wait or plan for "one big tell-all."* Maintain a continuing dialogue with the children in your life as occasions present themselves. The death of pets, scenes in movies, newspaper articles, or television programs—whatever brushes with mortality the children have—all can offer the opportunity for discussion. This does not mean, of course, that parents should remain poised to jump on a death dialogue opportunity. But it is more natural and effective to include death as one of the many topics that adults and children can discuss together. And we are more likely to be helpful when we are not ourselves caught up in the midst of a death situation. Combine a child who has been kept ignorant about death with an adult who is grief stricken or uptight and will have something less than the most desirable situation.

3. *Do not expect all of the child's responses to be obvious and immediate.* When a death has occurred or is impending, the child's total response is likely to unfold over time and to express itself in many ways. Changes in sleeping habits, mood, relationships with other children, and demands on adults may reflect part of the child's reaction to the death, even though the connection may not be obvious. Be patient; be available.

4. *Help the child remain secure as part of the family.* Sometimes adults have the panicked impulse to remove children from the scene when death has come too close (e.g., sending them off to a relative or neighbor). Examine such impulses before acting on them. Consider what the children might learn from the opportunity to participate in the family's response and what lingering questions, misinterpretations, and fears might remain if they are excluded.

5. *Use simple and direct language.* Too often what adults say to children becomes a sermon,

peppered with words and concepts that mean little to them. Provide children with accurate information. See if they understand what you have said (e.g., by having them explain it back to you) and make sure that you have responded to what they really wanted to know in the first place. At the same time, do not overwhelm the child with a barrage of information that could confuse rather than instruct.

6. *Be accessible.* The child's sense of comfort will be strengthened by the very fact that you are available to talk about death when the need arises. Your expression of feelings that are natural to the situation (worry, sorrow, perhaps even anger) are not likely to harm the child but rather will provide a basis for sorting out and expressing his or her own feelings.

7. *Be aware of all the children in the family.* It is natural to concentrate the family's resources and attentions on the seriously ill child. Other children in the family continue to need love and reassurance, however, and need to participate somehow in the total process.

8. *Keep the relationship going.* How a life-threatened child responds at a particular moment might be disturbing to parents and other adults. We do not want to see or hear certain responses. Losing the closeness and support of important adults is a great danger to the child. This, in fact, is one of the reasons why children may not share their thoughts and feelings with us. We do not have to approve or agree with everything the child tells us about death, but we do have to maintain a supportive relationship.

THE "RIGHT" TO DECIDE: SHOULD THE CHILD'S VOICE BE HEARD?

The controversial "right to die" issue (Chapter 9) usually focuses on adults but also can arise with children. Consider Marie, for example. Marie was a patient for most of her young life. She had little opportunity to experience a normal childhood because of severe kidney disease and the effects of treatment.

> During Marie's short life, she experienced numerous hospitalizations and separations from her family, who eventually abandoned her. Massive nosebleeds . . . terrified her mother and led to

> seven emergency hospitalizations and transfusions. Marie's lonely, monotonous hospital days were interrupted only by traumatic episodes which affected her both physically and emotionally (Meagher & Leff, 1989/1990, p. 178).

Marie was especially fearful of the kidney dialysis sessions. She was put in restraints for this procedure, producing long periods of unrelenting stress. "Marie's mother would not be waiting for her after the ordeal had ended. Sedatives would not be used to ease the passage of time" (p. 179). Marie did not receive medication for her pain whether in or out of dialysis. A dialysis nurse stated that giving her sedatives would only "spoil" Marie—she must learn to cope with pain. When Marie cried out for relief from pain, her pediatricians went through an elaborate placebo procedure, attempting to deceive the girl rather than offering actual medications. The placebo stunt did not relieve Marie's pain, and no other relief was offered. Marie's agony, her anger, and her fear all intensified until she became comatose and died.

How could this little girl have been allowed to suffer so long and so greatly? Did this pattern of "care" represent a violation of her rights? Do children have the right to participate in decisions regarding the quality of their own lives and the prospect of their own deaths? Meagher and Leff are firm in their own opinion: "Marie has the absolute right to expect that any procedure or course of treatment be in her best interest" (p. 283). She has the right to be spared the pain and stress of undergoing procedures that offer no reasonable probability of extending her life for a sustained period. She would seem to have the right "at least to participate in the decision to refuse treatment or to withhold further interventions" (p. 185). However, as Meagher and Leff are quick to point out, the law does not necessarily agree with this conclusion. A person must be competent in the eyes of the law in order to make decisions, and "competent" is invariably part of the phrase, "competent adult." The competency of adults is determined on a case-by-case basis: Some adults are competent, others are not, and this status may change with time and circumstance. By contrast, children are considered not competent as a class. The legal decision maker is either a parent or a person who has been entrusted with the responsibility of acting in place of the parent (*loco parentis*, in legal parlance).

Marie's predicament is part of a larger pattern described by Klugman (2005):

> Many people are reluctant to write a document that suggests withholding or withdrawing life-sustaining treatment from a child . . . . Parents often feel responsible for their child's illness and have difficulty dealing with their emotions. Such turmoil does not create an environment for well-informed, well-reasoned decision-making (p. 230).

Klugman urges that children capable of understanding their situation be allowed the opportunity to participate in the decision-making process by expressing their own preferences. A child's assent to the withholding or withdrawal of medical interventions still does not have legal standing, but deserves careful consideration.

There is a growing movement toward giving children more of a say in the management of their conditions. The American Academy of Pediatrics has recommended that children be included in medical decision making and the National Commission for Protection of Human Subjects of Biomedical and Behavioral Research has proposed that by age seven, a child should be given the opportunity to accept or reject participation in a research project (Hinds, Bradshaw, Oakes, & Pritchard, 2002).

■ SUMMARY

Adults often believe—or want to believe—that children do not understand death and should be protected from all death-related situations. The facts are quite different. Children are naturally curious about loss, disappearance, and death. Furthermore, no child is too young to experience the anxiety associated with separation experiences. Most studies indicate that children do not have a firm grasp of death's finality, irreversibility, and universality until about age ten. Nevertheless, even very young children can have moments of sudden discovery (e.g., the frog was "dead, dead, dead. What else could it be?"), and the mystery of death is very much in their minds throughout their developmental process. Many of today's parents grew up in homes in which death was never to be discussed, especially in the presence of children. This increases their difficulties in communicating about death with their own children. We learned something about the interaction between parents and children on the subject of death through a sampling of research case histories. It was clear that experiences, attitudes, and ways of coping with death are part of the intimate flow of life between children and their parents, and it is also clear that it is the death of particular people or animals that evoke children's concern.

Studies indicate that young children's experiences of death and loss often become life long memories that last through adulthood. Psychologist Maria Nagy ("Auntie Death") found three stages of progressive understanding of death in her pioneering research. The youngest children thought of death as a continuation of life in a diminished form. The realization that death is final occurs in the next stage, about age five, but there is still hope that one can be smart or lucky enough to elude death. By age 10 (Stage 3), most children understand that death is personal, universal, and inevitable as well as final. More recent studies emphasize the relationship between *separation anxiety* and children's thoughts of death. For children as well as adults, our thoughts about death are often, if not always, tinged with anxiety. There are basic similarities in death conceptions among children in various cultures, but also some culture-specific characteristics, as exemplified in Japan and Taiwan.

The study of imaginary friends in childhood has added another perspective. Floating conceptions of "living" and "dead," and "real" and "pretend" contribute to a creative exploration of life's mysteries. The deaths of imaginary friends generally are educational rather than devastating.

The death of a parent or other family member is highly stressful to children. We have seen that children's responses to this stress may be deeper and more intense than what appears on the surface. Posttraumatic stress disorder (PTSD) is a particularly disturbing response to a death that has occurred in a sudden and violent manner, as in terrorist attacks. PTSD has not often been recognized in children, but research and clinical experience has been directing more attention to this problem. Suggestions are made for helping children cope with bereavement.

Dying children often understand more about their conditions than adults realize—but also often have little voice in how their conditions are managed, as we discovered in Marie's situation. Nurses and others who work closely with dying children also experience high levels of stress. Fortunately, there is now some attention being given to helping nurses prepare themselves for serving the needs of dying children while reducing their own stress.

The family with open and supportive communication patterns can offer much to children as they discover death and loss in its many forms. Many of us, though, must first overcome our own reluctance to accept the fact that death does touch children and that children are very much attuned to loss and separation experiences.

■ REFERENCES

Anewalt, P. H. (2010). Violent, traumatic death in schools and community response. In N. B. Webb (Ed)., *Helping bereaved children* (pp. 190–214). New York: Guilford.

Anthony, S. (1972). *The discovery of death in childhood and after.* New York: Basic Books, Inc. (Revision of *The child's discovery of death.* New York: Harcourt Brace and World, 1940).

Anthony, Z., & Bhana, K. (1988/1989). An exploratory study of Muslim girls' understanding of death. *Omega, Journal of Death and Dying, 19,* 215–228.

Baggerly, J. & Salloum, A. (2010). Deaths connected to natural disasters. In N. B. Webb (Ed.), *Helping bereaved children* (pp. 249–262). New York: Guilford.

Barr, P. (2007). Relationship of neonatologists' end-of-life decisions to their personal fear of death. *Archives of Disease in Childhood, 2,* 104–107.

Barrett, H. C., & Behme, T. (2004). Children's understanding of death as the cessation of agency: A test using sleep versus death. *Cognition, 96(2),* http://www.sciencedirect.com/science/article/pii/S0010027704001453.

Bertoia, J. (1993). *Drawings from a dying child: Insights into death from a Jungian perspective.* London: Routledge.

Bluebond-Langner, M. (1977). Meanings of death to children. In H. Feifel (Ed.), *New meanings of death* (pp. 47–66). New York: McGraw-Hill.

Bluebond-Langner, M. (1988). Worlds of dying children and their well siblings. *Death Studies, 13,* 1–16.

Bluebond-Langner, M. (1993). Children, dying. In R. Kastenbaum & B. Kastenbaum (Eds.), *Encyclopedia of death* (pp. 46–48). New York: Avon.

Bluebond-Langner, M. (1996). *In the shadow of illness.* Princeton, NJ: Princeton University Press.

Book, P. (1996). How does the family narrative influence the individual's ability to communicate about death? *Omega, Journal of Death and Dying, 33,* 323–342.

Christ, G. H. (2000). *Healing children's grief.* New York: Oxford University Press.

Chu, A. T., & Lieberman, A. F. (2010). Clinical implications of traumatic stress from birth to age five. In *Advances in clinical psychology* (pp. 469–494). Palo Alto: Annual Reviews.

Colp, R. J. (1975). The evolution of Charles Darwin's thoughts about death. *Journal of Thanatology, 3,* 191–206.

Corr. C. A. (Guest Ed.). (2003–2004). Special issue: Death-related literature for children. *Omega, Journal of Death and Dying, 48* (p. 4), whole issue.

Corr, C. A., & Corr, D. M. (Eds.). (1996). *Handbook of childhood death and bereavement.* New York: Springer.

Corr, C. A., & Corr, D. M. (2002). Children. In R. Kastenbaum (Ed.), *Macmillan encyclopedia of death and dying* (Vol. 1, pp. 123–130). New York: Macmillan.

Corr, C. A. (2010). Appendix: Selected books to be read by or with children. In C. A. Corr & D. E. Balk (Eds.), *Children's encounters with death, bereavement, and coping* (pp. 455–476). New York: Springer.

Cox, M., Garrett, E., & Graham, J. A. (2004/2005). Death in Disney films: Implications for children's understanding of death. *Omega, Journal of Death and Dying, 50,* 267–280.

Dahlke, D. (1994). Therapy-assisted growth after parental suicide: From a personal and professional perspective. *Omega, Journal of Death and Dying, 23,* 113–152.

Davies, B., & Limbo, R. (2010). The grief of siblings. In N. W. Webb (Ed.), *Helping bereaved children* (pp. 69–90). New York: Guilford.

Deveau, E. J. (1995). Perceptions of death through the eyes of children and adolescents. In D. W. Adams & E. J. Deveau (Eds.), *Beyond the innocence of childhood* (Vol. 1, pp. 55–92). New York: Baywood.

Dickinson, G. (1992). First childhood death experiences. *Omega, Journal of Death and Dying, 25,* 169–182.

Doka, K. J. (2000). Using ritual with children and adolescents. In K. J. Doka (Ed.), *Living with grief. Children, adolescents, and loss* (pp. 153–160). New York: Brunner/Mazell.

Doka, K. J. (2002). Disenfranchised grief. In R. Kastenbaum (Ed.), *Macmillan encyclopedia of death and dying* (Vol. 1, pp. 359–362). New York: Macmillan.

Eksi, A., Braun, K. L., Ertem-Vehid, H., Peykerli, G., Saydam, R., Topariak, D., & Alyanak, B (2007). Risk factors for the development of PTSD and depression among child and adolescent victims following a 7.4 magnitude earthquake. *International Journal of Psychiatry in Clinical Practice, 11,* 190–199.

Elliott, A. (2004, September 11). Growing up grieving, with constant reminders of 9/11. http://www.nytimes.com/2004/09/11/nyregion/11kids.html.

Fairbrother, G., Stuber, J., Galea, S., Fleischman, A. R., & Pfefferbaum, B. (2003). Posttraumatic stress reactions in New York City children after the September 11, 2001 terrorist attacks. *Ambulatory Pediatrics, 6,* 304–311.

Farley, H-A. (1966). Sun goes up. In R. Lewis (Ed.*),* *Miracles.* New York: Simon & Schuster.

Freud, S. (1914). On narcissism: An introduction. In *Collective Works* (Vol. 4, pp. 30–59). London: Hogart.

Furman, E. F. (1974). *A child's parent dies: Studies in childhood bereavement.* New Haven, CT: Yale University Press.

Gleason, T. R. (2004). Imaginary companions and peer acceptance. *International Journal of Behavioral Development, 28,* 1–6.

Gleason, T. R., Jarudi, R. N., Cheek, J. M. (2003). Imagination, personality, and imaginary companions. *Social Behavior and Personality, 31,* 721–738.

Gordon, J., King, N., Gullone, E., Muris, P., & Ollendick, T. H. (2007). Nighttime fears of children and adolescents: Frequency, content, severity, harm expectations, disclosure, and coping behaviors. *Behaviour Research and Therapy, 45,* 2464–2472.

Gray, S. (1986). *Sex and death to the age of 14.* New York: Vintage Books.

Griffith, T. (2003). Assisting with the "big hurts, little tears" of the youngest grievers: Working with three-, four-, and five-year-olds who have experienced loss and grief because of death. *Illness, Crisis & Loss, 11,* 217–225.

Grollman, S. Shira. (1988). *A legacy of courage.* New York: Doubleday & Co.

Hall, G. S. (1992). *Senescense: The last half of life.* New York: Appleton.

Harris, P. L., & Koenig, M. A. (2006). Trust in testimony: How children learn about science and religion. *Child Development, 77,* 505–524.

Hersh, S. P. (1995). How can we help? In K. J. Doka (Ed.), *Children mourning; mourning children* (pp. 93–96). Washington, DC: Hospice Foundation of America.

Hinds, P. S., Bradshaw, G., Oakes, L. L., & Pritchard, M. (2002). Children and their rights in life and death situations. In R. Kastenbaum (Ed.), *Macmillan encyclopedia of death and dying* (Vol. 1, pp. 139–147). New York: Macmillan.

Hooke, M. C., Grund, E., Quammen, H., Miller, B., Mc-Cormick, P., Bostrom, B. (2007). Propofol use in pediatric patients with severe cancer pain at the end of life. *Journal of Pediatric Oncology Nursing, 1,* 29–34.

Jipson, J. L., & Gelman, S. A. (2007). Robots and rodents: Children's inferences about living and nonliving kinds. *Child Development, 78,* 1675–1678.

Kastenbaum, R. (2000). *The psychology of death* (3rd ed.). New York: Springer.

Kastenbaum, R. (2004). *On our way: The final passage through life and death.* Berkeley: University of California Press.

Kastenbaum, R., & Fox, L. (2007). Do imaginary companions die? *Omega, Journal of Death and Dying, 56,* 123–152.

Kenyon, B. L. (2001). Current research in children's conceptions of death: A critical review. *Omega, Journal of Death and Dying, 43,* 63–91.

Klugman, C. M. (2005). A life cut short: When children die. In K. J. Doka, B. Jennings & C. A. Corr (Eds.), *Ethical dilemmas at the end of life.* Washington, DC: Hospice Foundation of America.

LeBaron, S., & Zeltner, L. K. (1985). The role of imagery in the treatment of dying children and adolescents. *Journal of Developmental Behavioral Pediatrics, 5,* 252–258.

Lee, P. W. H., Lieh-Mak, F., Hung, B. K. M., & Luk, S. L. (1983/1984). Death anxiety in leukemic Chinese children. *International Journal of Psychiatry in Medicine, 13,* 281–290.

Levetown, M. (2002). Children, caring for when life-threatened or dying. In R. Kastenbaum (Ed.), *Macmillan encyclopedia of death and dying* (Vol. 1, pp. 147–154). New York: Macmillan.

Lonetto, R. (1980). *Children's conceptions of death.* New York: Springer.

McMahon, S. M. (2010). The loss and death of a pet.

Meagher, D. K., & Leff, P. T. (1989/1990). In Marie's memory: The rights of the child with life-threatening or terminal illness. *Omega, Journal of Death and Dying, 20,* 177–191.

Mellichamp, P. (2007). End-of-life care for infants. *Home Healthcare Nurse, 1,* 41–44.

Nagy, M. H. (1969). The child's theories concerning death. In H. Feifel (Ed.), *The meaning of death.* New York: McGraw-Hill. (Reprinted from *Journal of Genetic Psychology,* 1948, 73, 3–27).

Opie, I., & Opie, R. (1969). *Children's games in street and playground.* London: Oxford University Press.

Papadatou, D. (2006). Care provider responses to the death of a child. In *Oxford textbook on pediatric palliative care.* New York: Oxford University Press.

Papadatou, D. (2009). *In the face of death.* New York: Springer.

Pfeffer, C. R., Altemus, M., Heo, M., & Jiang, H. (2007). Salivary cortisol and psychopathology in children bereaved by the September 11, 2001 attacks. *Biological Psychiatry, 61,* 957–965.

Pfefferbaum, B., Gurwitch, R. H., McDonald, N. B., Leftwich, M. J. T., Sconzo, G. M., Messenbaugh, A. K., & Schultz, R. A. (2000). Posttraumatic stress among young children after the death of a friend or acquaintance in a terrorist bombing. *Psychiatric Services, 51*, 386–389.

Rider, E. (2004). Does your heart go on vacation? *BMJ Public Health Journals.* http://www.ncbi.nlm.nih.gov/pmc/articles/PMC387489/pdf/bmj32800890.pdf.

Rosenberg, K. S., Johnson, C. N., & Harris, P. L. (Eds.) (2000). *Imagining the impossible. Magical, scientific, and religious thinking in children.* Cambridge, UK: Cambridge University Press.

Ruffin, P. A., & Zimmerman, S. Al. (2010). Bereavement groups and camps for children. In N. B. Webb (Ed.), *Helping bereaved children* (pp. 296–317). New York: Guilford.

Ryan, V., & Alley, R. W. (2002). *When your grandparent dies.* St. Meinran, IND: Abbey Press.

Sagara-Rosemeyer, M., & Davies, B. (2007). The integration of religious traditions in Japanese children's views of death and afterlife. *Death Studies, 31,* 223–247.

Saurez, M. M., & McFeaters, S. J. (2000). Culture and class: The different worlds of children and adolescents. In K. J. Doka (Ed.), *Living with grief: Children, adolescents, and loss* (pp. 55–70). New York: Brunner/Mazal.

Schuurman, D. L., & DeCristofaro, K. J. (2010). Principles and practices of peer support groups and camp-based interventions for grieving children. In C. A. Corr & D. E. Balk (Eds), *Children's encounters with death, bereavement, and coping* (pp. 359–372). New York: Springer.

Silverman, P. R. (2000). When parents die. In K. J. Doka (Ed.), *Living with grief. Children, adolescents, and loss* (pp. 215–228). New York: Brunner/Mazal.

Silverman, P. R., & Worden, J. W. (1992). Children's understanding of funeral ritual. *Omega, Journal of Death and Dying, 25,* 319–332.

Slaughter, V., & Griffiths, M. (2007). Death understanding and fear of death in young children. *Clinical Child Psychology and Psychiatry, 12,* 524–535.

Sourkes, B. M. (1996). *Armfuls of time. The psychological experience of the child with a life-threatening disease.* Pittsburgh: University of Pittsburgh Press.

Stuber, J., Fairbrother, G., Galea, S., Pfefferbaum, B., Wilson-Genderson, M., & Vlahov, D. (2002). Determinants of counseling for children in Manhattan after the September 11 attacks. *Psychiatric Services, 53,* 815–822.

Taylor, M. (1999). *Imaginary companions and the children who create them.* New York: Oxford Press.

Taylor, M., Carlson, S. M., Maring, B. L., Gerow, L. G., & Charley, C. M. (2004). The characteristics and correlates of fantasy in school-age children: Imaginary companions, impersonation, and social understanding. *Developmental Psychology, 40,* 1173–1187.

Thastrum, M., Johansen, M. B., Gubba, L., Oleson, L. B., & Romer, G. (2008). Coping, social relations, and communication,: A qualitative exploratory study of children of parents with cancer. *Clinical Child Psychology and Psychiatry, 13,* 123–138.

Toray, T. (2010). Children's bereavement over the death of pets. In C. A. Corr, D. E. Balk (Eds.), *Children's encounters with death, bereavement, and coping* (pp. 237–256). New York: Springer.

Wass, H. (2002). Children and media violence. In R. Kastenbaum (Ed.), *Macmillan encyclopedia of death and dying* (Vol. 1, pp. 133–139). New York: Macmillan.

Weaver, R., & Festa, D. K. (2003). Developmental effects on children suffering disruption from paternal loss in infancy. *Illness, Crisis & Loss, 11,* 271–281.

Webb, N. B. (2010). Guidelines to help parents and teachers. In N. B. Webb (Ed.), *Helping bereaved children* (pp. 374–384). New York: Guilford.

Webb, N. B. (2002). Traumatic death of friend/peers: Case of Suan, age 9. In N. B. Webb (Ed.), *Helping bereaved children* (2nd ed., pp. 189–211). New York: Guilford.

White, E. B. (1952). *Charlotte's web.* New York: Harper & Row.

Wood, D. D., & Near, R. L. (2010). Using expressive arts when counseling bereaved children. In C. A. Corr & D. E. Balk (Eds.). *Children's encounters with death, bereavement, and counseling* (pp. 373–394). New York: Springer.

Yang, S. C., & Chen, S-F (2007). Content analysis of free-responses to personal meanings of death among Chinese children and adolescents. *Death Studies, 30,* 217–241.

Zall, D. S. (1994). The long term effects of childhood bereavement: Impact on roles as mothers. *Omega, Journal of Death and Dying, 29,* 219–230.

Zelizer, V. A. (1994). *Pricing the priceless child.* Princeton, NJ: Princeton University Press.

■ GLOSSARY

Bereavement The loss of a loved one through death.

Cystic fibrosis A hereditary disorder in which lungs and other organ systems are blocked by abnormal mucous secretions. A life-threatening condition.

Death anxiety Emotional distress and insecurity aroused by encounters with dead bodies, grieving people, or other reminders of mortality, including one's own thoughts.

Imaginary companion A "pretend friend" that is real to the child but does not exist in objective reality.

Inochi (Japanese) Life, as a gift from God to the embryo.

Leukemia A progressive disease that produces distorted and dysfunctional white blood cells, increasing susceptibility to infection, bleeding, and anemia. Sometimes a life-threatening condition.

Neonatologists Health care professional who works with newborn infants.

Personification Representing an idea or feeling as a human or humanlike form.

Plague A virulent contagion that resulted in the deaths of at least one fourth of the population in the late fourteenth century and that is generally considered to have been bubonic disease, carried by rats and fleas as well as stricken humans. Also known as "The Black Death."

Post-traumatic stress disorder A delayed response to a death that has occurred under highly stressful conditions. The traumatic event is reexperienced repeatedly, and other disturbances of feeling, thought, and behavior are also likely to occur.

Separation anxiety Emotional distress and insecurity aroused by loss of contact with a valued and protective person (also observed in animal behavior).

■ ON FURTHER THOUGHT . . .

Useful online resources:

Candlelighters Childhood Cancer Foundation
    www.candlelighters.org
Child Trauma Academy
    www.childtrauma.org
Child Trauma Institute
    www.childtrauma.com
Children's Hospice International
    http://www.chionline.org/

Dougy Center for Grieving Children
    www.grievingchild.org
National Alliance for Children with Life-Threatening Conditions
    http://www.chionline.org
National Institute for Trauma and Loss in Children
    http://www.starrtraining.org/tlc

Books for children or adults, or for children and adults to read together:

Many deal with loss of animals and include sad moments but have been praised for helping children to understand and express grief.

Coburn, J. B. (1964). *Anne and the Sand Dobbies: A story about death for children and their parents*. New York: Seabury.

Gipson, F. (1990). *Old Yeller*. New York: HarperTrophy.

Goldman, L. (2005). *Children also grieve: Talking about death and healing*. London: Jessica Kingsley.

Hurd, E. T. (1980). *The black dog who went into the woods*. New York: Harper & Row.

Krasny, L., & Brown, M. (1998). *When dinosaurs die: A guide to understanding death*. New York: Little Brown.

Lewis, P. G., & Lippman, J. (2004). *Helping children cope with the death of a parent: A guide for the first year*. New York: Praeger.

O'Toole, D. (2010). Storytelling with bereaved children. In N. B. Webb (ed.), Helping bereaved children, pp. 318–344. New York: Guilford Press.

Ruffin, P. A., & Zimmerman, S. A. (2010). Bereavement groups and camps for children: An interdisciplinary approach. In N. B. Webb (ed.), Helping bereaved children, pp. 296–317. New York: Guilford Press.

Stoll, E. G. (1964). *My turtle died today*. New York: Holt, Rinehart & Winston.

Viorst, J. (1971). *The tenth good thing about Barney*. New York: Atheneum.

White, E. B. (1952). *Charlotte's web*. New York: Harper.

Books to help adults help children understand death and grief:

Dougy Center. (1997). *Helping children cope with death*. Portland, OR: The Dougy Center.

Nadeau, J. (1998). *Families making sense of death*. Thousand Oaks, CA: Sage.

Silverman, P. R. (2000). *Never too young to know: Death in children's lives*. New York: Oxford University Press.

Webb, N. B. (ed.) (2010). Helping bereaved children. Third edition New York: Guilford Press.

Worden, J. W. (1996). *Children and grief: When a parent dies*. New York: Guilford.

Bereavement, Grief, and Mourning

The neighbor who bought our land leveled our farmhouse, chopped down our trees, and turned the entire 160 acres into farmland. He even straightened the creek. I often drive by now without even recognizing it. The first four feet of our dirt driveway is all that remains of my childhood. The dance hall remains, and the old speakeasy, but both are shuttered. In a few years, they'll probably be gone, too.

—Myron & Witter (2008, p. 56)

She had it all mapped out and we were at that house cleaning out closets, you know, doing this… getting rid of old stuff, anything that had to go back to the . . . you know, the insurance people . . . like she was, like, [snap, snap], very focused and it went through, like, there was not a sign of my dad within a week.

—Excerpt, research interview: Miriam Moss & Robert L. Rubenstein (2010)

Our forefathers have enacted that, in the case of women, a year should be the limit for mourning; not that they needed to mourn for so long, but that they should mourn no longer. In the case of men, no rules are laid down, because to mourn at all is not regarded as honorable.

—Seneca, first century C.E., quoted by Darja Sterbene Erker (2009, p. 136).

Though a stranger to you I cannot remain silent when so terrible a calamity has fallen upon you and your country. . . . No one can better appreciate than I can, who am myself utterly brokenhearted by the loss of my own beloved Husband, who was the Light of my Life,—my Stay—my All,—What your sufferings must be; and I earnestly pray that you may be supported by Him to whom alone the sorely stricken can look for comfort, in this hour of heavy affliction.

—A widow, quoted by Susan Stamberg (2008, p. 3)

The first time I met a close colleague after the death of my child he was sitting right across the table but turned away from me and conversed intensely with the guy next to him. Then he left the room without even saying goodbye to me—that had never happened before.

—Kai Dyregrov (2003/2004, p. 31)

I've seen my father, literally seen him standing in the lane with his hand out to me. I talk to him all the time. I talk to my mother. I saw my son standing by the road waiting to be picked up a couple of times. And then it wouldn't be anybody there, or it would be a post, or it would be somebody who looked like him.

—Terkel (2001, p. 273)

A fleet of unlicensed vehicles would close off a street, heavily armed men in plainclothes would storm an apartment or house, terrify the family, break in and pillage possessions, then assault and kidnap one or more family members, usually a young adult. The victims would be brutally tortured for hours to days to months before being killed.

—Thornton (2000, p. 281)

It may make us uncomfortable, or even anger us, but we must realize that it's never our place to force someone to grieve in a way we find acceptable. When someone dies, the bereaved family members must be forgiven if they are pleased to be getting their lives back, even if they can't say it out loud.

—Jennifer Elison (2008, P. 18)

Many of us can remember the moment that we learned a treasured life had been taken away from us. Perhaps it was a telephone call or a knock on the door. Perhaps we had witnessed the passing for ourselves. Some of us continue to live within that moment years later. And almost all of us discover that the loss has remained an ongoing part of our lives even when the moment of separation has long passed. We are the bereaved. We are the grieving. We are the mourning. And, as will be seen, we are also the vulnerable. This chapter examines one of most profound links with the whole procession of the human race: the capacity to suffer deeply and yet to renew our commitment to life when separated by death from a beloved person.

SOME RESPONSES TO LOSS

We have stepped briefly into the lives of people who responded to a death in their distinctive ways. However, we started with a woman whose loss was her cherished past: the old farmhouse and land. Now the companions of her youth were also vanishing:

Forty years after the closing of the Moneta School, the annual reunion still drew a thousand people a year back to the field where we used to hold those baseball games and end-of-the-year parties. Now the reunion is down to a hundred or so. The school has been closed fifty years; there aren't that many graduates left. Soon the sign on Highway 18 will be the last thing standing, still pointing two miles down the lonely road to Moneta (p. 56).

Myron's biography of *Dewey*, the inimitable library cat, was set in a town that had once provided stability and support to its citizens. Now it was experiencing a change in fortunes that has also been affecting many other communities. There is a palpable sense of loss when memories and sense of identity no longer are affirmed by the world around us. When we experience the loss of a person significant to us, this grief can add to the feeling that much of what we have known and loved has vanished. It is almost as though we had never had that past life at all.

Much different is the widow who efficiently removed all remembrances of her husband within a few days after his death. She also had little use for the funeral and memorial activities. "It was kind of like she killed him," one of her sons reported with a laugh. "He's in the wall," she said. "Let's move on". This is not the basic textbook response to spousal bereavement. How might this woman's response be understood? She had not lost the home they had shared for more than 40 years and she was supported by a thriving multigenerational family that represented their parents' achievements and brought the memories forward. The answer will have something to do with the fact that she was essentially her husband's 24/7 caregiver for the previous decade, her own needs mostly set aside. In effect, she had paid her grief in advance with her service, day after night. Her caregiving efforts were not compensated by a loving relationship. Four decades of marriage had been pretty much four decades of barking at each other. Enough was enough: it was time for her to renew something of her own personal life! This is not the more familiar phenomenon of *anticipatory grief* that will be discussed later. It is a less-researched pattern in which the surviving spouse has exhausted her feelings after a long period of restriction and servitude (actual or perceived).

Real men do not weep and mourn, and women should not do too much of that either, so say the forefathers. There are two reasons to take notice of this attitude. It was part of the imperial Roman credo that has been so influential on subsequent cultures, and the sharp gender differential in approved mourning behavior was closely related to how the nature and worth of men and women was conceived in general. The prime-time Romans did not engage in excessive displays of mourning.

In fact, mourning behavior was calibrated to meet social and political expectations. Mourning was essentially a ritualistic activity, often carried out by professionals in the trade. Furthermore, in condemning tears, the Romans had turned away from the Greek tradition that mentored their development. Follinger (2009) notes that Greek heroes of legend and myth gave way to tears when in despair—and also when bursting with desperation or rage. The heroes were praised rather than criticized when they engaged in copious weeping and dramatic acts of mourning at the death of a beloved companion.

What has our society today selected from the gender/mourning attitudes of foundational cultures? Is the direct expression of sorrow "a womanly weakness," or a natural human response to a painful bereavement?

The widow who wrote that compassionate letter based on her own loss was Queen Victoria. The widow who received the letter was Mary Todd Lincoln. Today many people continue to feel that solace and understanding is best conveyed by a person who has experienced a similar devastating loss. The grieving mother abandoned by her colleagues was one of many people who shared such experiences with sociologist Kari Dyregrov. People would cross the street or just look away—and probably thought that this avoidance behavior wasn't noticed! Studies often find that our society does not offer effective support for the bereaved. Why do we withdraw when a person most needs support, and what kind of support is experienced as most helpful?

Folk singer Rosalie Sorrels had known many deaths during her long life, starting with her childhood on a farm. "You know, I never thought of death as unfriendly" (Terkel, 2001, p. 266). Furthermore, she did not find it alarming that she still met some of her favorite dead people from time to time. In her interview with Studs Terkel, the distinguished oral historian, Sorrels described a continuing bond with the dead. Is this unusual? Is it "pathological," or "healthy"?

Death squads terrorized the citizens of Argentina during an oppressive military regime. This was terrorism carried out as government policy. People were afraid to protest or even ask questions. *Los Madres de la Plaza de Mayo* was an improbable response to this intolerable situation. One by one, women whose children had been kidnapped by the regime reached out to each other for support. The slow process of healing could not begin while the fate of their children remained unknown. That the women should bond together to protest against the terrorist regime was almost unbelievable. Women were supposed to restrict themselves to their duties at home and not meddle in public affairs, even when these affairs touched them deeply (Thornton, 2000).

> *When ordered to move on by the police, they …*
> *started* la ronda, *the walk around and around*
> *the Plaza, which was to become a trademark*
> *of their peaceful protest. . . . The women were*
> *threatened with weapons and dogs, sometimes*
> *had cocked guns put to their heads, and sprayed*
> *with water cannons or tear gas . . . (p. 282).*

Despite intimidation, ridicule, and some "disappearances" within their ranks, the mothers persevered. Hebe de Bonafini, mother of two missing sons, explains why:

> *If they cannot be here, then I have had to take*
> *their place, to shout for them. . . . I feel them*
> *present in my banners, in my unending fatigue,*
> *in my mind and body, in everything I do I think*
> *that their absence has left me pregnant forever*
> *(de Bonafini, 1991, p. 287).*

The Mothers of the *Plaza de Mayo* experienced an inner transformation through which they realized that they were rebelling not only against the constricted role of women in their society but also against a militaristic regime in which force and violence were systematically employed against the public at large. The public eventually responded to their example, contributing to the downfall of the militaristic government. Their grief had been transformed into action for the good of all (Thornton, 2000, p. 283).

In this chapter, we will look carefully at the grief and recovery process. The term "recovery" does not necessarily mean that life goes on just as it was before the bereavement (Balk (2004). "Recovery" as used here refers to the ability to continue with a life that is meaningful to the individual and to cope with obligations and challenges. We consider parents who have lost children and children who have lost parents, husbands who have lost wives and wives who have lost husbands, and siblings who have lost siblings. Sometimes, though we do not seem to have the right to grieve—we were not family, yet the pain is there. Accordingly, we will also look at hidden or *disenfranchised grief.*

There are also circumstances in which none of us are "supposed" to grieve because the person who died was not considered to be really a person in the full sense of the word (for example, developmentally disabled children, Milo, 1997). We also consider the concepts of "normal" and "complicated" grief and evaluate the effectiveness of counseling.

We begin by clarifying basic concepts and becoming acquainted with major theories of grief. How people actually cope with loss will then be examined in some detail. This will include attention to the impact of grief on the survival of the survivors: Is grief hazardous to our health? Although we will discover common patterns and themes, we will also become aware of great individual differences and of the role played by sociocultural expectations. Finally, we will build upon these observations to improve our ability to recognize and respond helpfully to the grief experience, whether in ourselves or others.

DEFINING OUR TERMS: BEREAVEMENT, GRIEF, MOURNING

Bereavement, grief, mourning—these words cannot convey the impact a death can bring upon the survivors. However, a clear understanding of these words will help us to find our way through these challenging experiences.

Bereavement: An Objective Fact

Bereavement is an objective fact. We are bereaved when a person close to us dies. There is no hard and fast rule about how far this term should be extended. The death of a coworker, for example, might or might not be considered a bereavement, depending on the relationship that had existed. Bereavement conveys the idea of a tearing apart, a forcible separation that results in the loss of something we once had. That "something" is a vital and perhaps sustaining relationship.

Bereavement is a change in status. A child becomes an orphan, a wife a widow, a husband a widower. It is an objective fact that serves as a clue to psychological, social, and physical distress.

Bereavement is an outcome of large-scale social phenomena. Widowhood and orphanhood are consequences of epidemics, natural disaster, terrorism, and war. Thousands of families had their lives shattered by deaths in the terrorist attacks of September 11, 2001. The lethal events were swift; the consequences will be enduring. Perhaps we can spare a thought for the millions who were bereaved by the killing fields and trenches of World War I ("The War to End All Wars"). Thousands of men died each day (Groom, 2002). World War I slaughter and bereavement had profound and far-reaching effects. As the acid smoke of battle started to clear, millions died worldwide from a savage variety of influenza that was especially lethal for youth and left family survivors in shock and grief. Large-scale bereavement can also occur less conspicuously. Although more people now live longer, there are also more widows than ever. Social isolation and loneliness have become recognized as a major source of stress and vulnerability. Although bereavement by itself is only a bare objective fact, it is also a fact that tends to generate increased vulnerability and stress.

Grief: A Painful Response

Grief is a response to bereavement; it is how the survivor feels. It is also how the survivor thinks, eats, sleeps, and makes it through the day. The term itself does not explain anything. Grief requires careful understanding on a person-by-person basis; it is not a word that can be taken as a simple explanation of what is being experienced and why.

Furthermore, grief is not the only possible response to bereavement. There may be anger or indifference, for example. Some individuals show what psychiatrists term a *dissociative flight* from the impact of death—a pattern of extreme, even psychotic denial. Other people recognize their loss but delay their emotional response, as when a person has critical responsibilities to perform and temporarily places personal feelings aside. Nevertheless, the grief response is so frequent and distressing that it is of primary importance for those who wish to understand and comfort the bereaved.

A useful distinction is often made between the grief experienced at the first recognition of the loss and the grief that continues long afterward. Here is the classic description of acute grief (Lindemann, 1944):

> The picture shown by people in acute grief is remarkably uniform. Common to all is the following syndrome: sensations of somatic distress

> occurring in waves lasting from 20 minutes to an hour at a time, a feeling of tightness in the throat, choking with shortness of breath, need for sighing, an empty feeling in the abdomen, lack of muscular power, and an intensive subjective distress described as tension or pain (p. 145).

Other symptoms commonly seen are insomnia, failures of memory, absentmindedness, problems in concentrating, and the tendency to do the same things over and over again.

Erich Lindemann was working with people who had been stunned by the sudden death of loved ones in the Cocoanut Grove fire (Boston, 1942), in which 400 people perished in less than 15 minutes and others died later of burns and smoke inhalation. It has since been learned that the total symptom picture seen by Lindemann may not be expressed by every person who has an acute grief reaction. Nevertheless, Lindemann's description still conveys a vivid sense of what it is like to be overwhelmed by grief.

Grief affects all spheres of life. The grieving person's body doesn't work very well. George Engel (1963) was among the first to suggest that an intense and prolonged grief reaction can precipitate a life-threatening serious condition in bereaved people with underlying physical problems. Current theory and research continues to provide support for considering grief to be a physical disorder as well as a personal crisis. It is the whole person who grieves, and this person is part of a network of interpersonal relationships. Grieving, then, takes place both within and between people and shows its effects in all spheres. Consider, for example, a few of the major changes in the way our bodies function and how the way in which we grieve can influence our thoughts and relationships.

Grief is not an illness, although it can increase vulnerability to illness. Grief is both a distressing response to a significant loss, and part of the adaptive process.

Neuroendocrine Changes in Grief

The grief experience operates as a stressor. The particular type of somatic reaction often depends on whatever physical weaknesses preexisted in the bereaved person (Hall & Irwin, 2001). Individual differences in cognitive, behavioral, and relational responses also influence the neuroendocrine system's response to the stress of grief. The response to loss can itself contribute to further distress. For example, if we become withdrawn and inactive, we also increase our vulnerability to opportunistic infections because of lowered body tone. Furthermore, new problems continue to arise as the survivor attempts to adjust to an altered life situation. The homeostatic mechanisms of the body try to moderate the stress as the first shock of the loss is followed by a period of active grieving. Unfortunately this adaptation to chronic stress itself can be a source of further problems. Some grief responses become increasingly difficult to "get over" because our central nervous system has dedicated itself so effectively to moderating the effect of the stress. In other words, we may have to deal with our physiological response to stress, as well as the stress itself.

Studies indicate that the stress of grief intensifies wear and tear on the body, along with increased risk of cardiovascular, infectious, and inflammatory disorders. Stress-related hormones become more active. Hall and Irwin (2001) report that the higher levels of cortisol, epinephrine, and norephrine are signs that grieving people are undergoing a destabilization of their physiological systems that place their health and survival at higher risk.

The immune system, our primary defense against pathogens, appears to be especially vulnerable to the stress of grief (Genevo, 2003). The "killer cells" that destroy threatening invaders have been shown to become fewer and less active in women who have either experienced a death or are living with the anxious expectation of a death. Unfortunately, there are also some indications that this heightened vulnerability may persist over an extended period of time.

Infant monkeys show significant immunological and other physiological changes when they are separated from their mothers for even a short time (Laudenslager et al., 1993). The infant monkeys who were most agitated, slouching, and withdrawn were also those whose immune systems were most affected by the stress of separation. However, when the mother and infant are reunited, the young monkey's immune system returns to normal. (It would be interesting to know what is happening to the mother's immune system during this time as well!) Behavioral and physiological stress was reduced during maternal separation when the monkeys were kept in a familiar environment and could see their peers.

Familiar surroundings seem to have some value in buffering the effects of the loss experience. Monkeys as well as humans experience both behavioral and physiological stress when separated from their "significant others"—and monkeys as well as humans can cope with this stress more successfully when provided with social support before and during the grief process. Physical aspects of distress can be intensified by how we respond to the loss. Going without proper nutrition and rest and neglecting self-care is a dysfunctional pattern—and alcohol and indiscriminate use of medications and it gets worse.

Promising new research is exploring the relationship between neuroendocrine changes, individual adaptation skills, and social context. For example, Charuvastra and Cloitre (2008) find that the hurt response to stress is more severe when it has been caused by human error or malice, e.g., a death that did not have to have happened. The stress response to death of a loved one can also include fear arousal, thereby complicating response and adaptation (Rodriguez et al., 2009). Furthermore, sensitivity to loss varies considerably from one person to another. Learning more about how the individual's biosystem operates within society's death system might help us to understand and help more effectively.

Personal and Interpersonal Responses to the Stress of Grief

The mind of the grieving person might not work as well as usual. Problems with attention, concentration, and memory increase the risk to self and others. A person who usually is alert and responsible becomes an inattentive driver, a parent who fails to notice household hazards, or a worker who is careless on the job. It is the emotional side of grief that often besets the survivor with the greatest distress, however. Glick, Weiss, and Parkes (1974) report examples such as the following from their pioneering study of spousal bereavement:

> When I got home from the morgue, I was just out for the rest of the day. I just couldn't help myself. I thought I would have a nervous breakdown, and my heart was going so fast. The man at the morgue said, "Well, if you don't stop crying, you're going to have a nervous breakdown." But all I could do was cry. That's all I could do.

And I told him, "If I don't cry, God, my heart will burst." I had to cry, because he wasn't going to be back no more (p. 17).

This woman had just found herself transformed from wife to widow. She first experienced shock and could not feel or think at all. Then she could not stop herself from overwhelming feelings. People in acute grief sometimes feel that they are "going crazy," that they will keep "getting worse and worse and then just fall all apart." Those who have made it through such intense grief themselves can be very helpful to those who are in the midst of such experiences. Distress does not end with the first wave of shock and grief. It is not enough to realize that a loved one is dead. One now faces the further realization that life is supposed to go on. There may be further waves of confusion, anxiety, rage, and other painful inner states. The sense of numbness can also return, sometimes to linger as though it would never go away.

That grief can return in wave after wave of distress was discovered in an important study of nineteenth-century American diaries. Paul C. Rosenblatt (1983) found that recurring experiences of grief were common. People who felt they had recovered completely from the pangs of grief might be engulfed in a wave of distress months or years later. Some of the diary entries expressed a more profound sense of grief years after the loss than they had at the time of the death. Many occasions can renew the sense of grief: "I think of Henry every time I sit at table and see his place is vacant. [Sitting again] in our old pew, I could not help thinking of my dear parents and before I could stop myself was crying bitterly . . ." (p. 27).

Anniversaries, places that rekindle a memory, and people who remind us of the lost person have the power to start a new wave of grief long after the death. Grief may return again and again, long after the bereavement. The vulnerability often remains, although subsequent episodes are likely to be much briefer—an image, a sudden pang, a catch of the breath, a readiness to weep . . . and then, after a pause, a going on with life.

Mourning: A Signal of Distress

Mourning is the culturally patterned expression of the bereaved person's thoughts and feelings. Bereavement is a universal experience. No society has been spared

the loss of people it valued, loved, and depended on. How people express their loss is not universal, however. These expressions vary from culture to culture and also change over time. Dennis Klass (2002) observes that even the basic concepts of grief and mourning differ appreciably across cultures:

> *Grief as a real subjective state grows from a culture that prizes and cultivates individual experience. There is no equivalent to the term grief in some other languages; indeed, in some cultures the concept of emotions that are only in the individual seems foreign (p. 373).*

But since most of us do live within a society that emphasizes individual experience, the distinction between mourning and grief remains helpful. For example, people who have no close friends available sometimes keep their grief to themselves rather than burden acquaintances with whom there has been no prior history of mutual sharing. Other people may continue mourning rituals for years even when grief has long dissipated.

There are signs of mourning that are recognized throughout much of the world. It is believed that the first influential example of a flag being displayed at half-mast occurred in 1612 when *Heart's Ease*, a ship returning from a discovery expedition, came into view (Prothero, 1997). A member of the crew had been killed during an altercation with Eskimos. Two possible symbolic reasons have been suggested for the half-masting: (1) the sea-going equivalent to bereaved people neglecting their appearance as a signal of their distress; and (2) the lowered flag leaves a space above for the to-be-imagined emblem of Death. Half-masting became an established maritime practice, and then came ashore with the observance of a recent death by lowering the flag at public places. When war ships took to the air, a related practice developed: the missing man formation.

Too Many Deaths to Mourn?

Geoffrey Gorer (1977) observed striking changes in mourning behavior within a few years in England. His father died aboard the Lusitania, capsized by a torpedo in 1915, and his mother became "a tragic, almost a frightening figure in the full panoply of widow's weeds and unrelieved black, a crepe veil

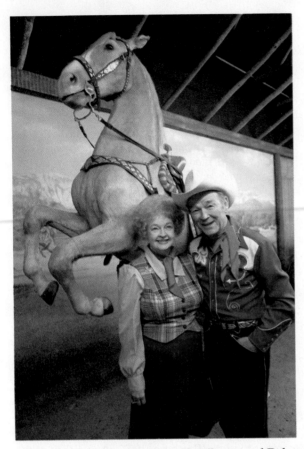

Trigger was dear to cowboy stars Roy Rogers and Dale Evans and their many fans. The hoof beats of memory receive a boost from the taxidermist's art.

shrouding her . . . so that she was visibly withdrawn from the world." But within a few months, there had been so many deaths from World War I that "Widows in mourning became increasingly frequent in the streets, so that Mother no longer stood out in the crowd." Too many people were being touched too closely by death. The functioning of society as a whole would have been impaired had every bereaved person pursued every step of the traditional mourning ritual.

The gold star in the window of many a home in the United States during World War II indicated that a unique life had been lost. Each gold star mother experienced her personal bereavement, but collectively they signified a loss felt by the entire nation. This communal support did not develop for families grieving for loved ones killed in Vietnam, a war that divided rather than unified the country. It would take the long-delayed creation of the Vietnam Memorial Wall (Chapter 12) to link individual with public loss.

The first Gulf War produced still a different type of public mourning response. Death was notably absent from news about the Gulf War that reached viewers and readers in the United States (Umberson & Henderson, 1992). Smart bombs "serviced" their targets, while not-so-smart bombs resulted in "collateral damage." The attempt to eliminate images of death from Gulf War reports may have contributed to the public's difficulty in mourning those who died on all sides of the conflict. The Oklahoma City bombing aroused sorrow and anger throughout the general public. By contrast, the community and its leadership worked together in a sense of sustained purpose that not only resulted in an innovative memorial (see Chapter 12) for the victims but also made it evident that healing was everybody's endeavor.

Mourning for the September 11, 2001, victims had even larger dimensions. There were numerous memorial services, some informal and limited to the people most closely concerned, and some replete with prominent officials, celebrities, and national television coverage. Strenuous efforts were made to identify and recover remains so that family mourning could begin. Two other responses also stand out: (1) the individuality of each victim was recognized at every opportunity (e.g., reading of the names, displaying their photographs), and (2) New York City itself was treated as victim (e.g., sorrow for loss of the WTC towers, and, indirectly, for the blow to the image and stature of a city that had been the first destination of many immigrants and the long time symbol of American power). Some catastrophes strike so severely at the core of a people that intensive mourning seems to be essential for recovery even to begin.

The ongoing military actions in Afghanistan and Iraq have generated discordant types of public response. The government restricted viewings of the flag-draped coffins, fearing that they might increase criticism of the war effort. Local news programs, however, reported casualties, honored their service, and voiced support for family. Some websites also report and discuss individual deaths, while the Internet offers a public arena for consolation and protest. Where there is acknowledgment of the deaths, it is with compassion untainted by the stigma that haunted those who served in the Vietnam War.

CULTURAL VARIATIONS IN MOURNING

Within the United States there are varied patterns of mourning—compare those of Americans who are of African, Chinese, Korean, Japanese, Italian, or Central European–Jewish heritage, for example. Furthermore, mourning traditions are subject to change. Many people have been uprooted from their native lands or have chosen to move elsewhere in search of opportunities for an improved quality of life. Their practices can encounter difficulties in their new surroundings. Consider, for example, the challenges faced by the Hmong when relocated to the United States.

Hmong Mourning Practices in Laos and in the United States

The Hmong people have been known to history for almost 5,000 years. Those who selected Laos as their home became victims of that nation's violent political upheavals during the 1960s. Many fled in fear for their lives in the mid-1970s, and of these refugees about 120,000 relocated in the United States.

Mourning in Hmong Homelands

Hmong mourning practices are closely related to their religious beliefs. A spiritual world coexists with the physical. The newborn infant is under the care of spirit-parents before its birth and must be inducted into the world of the living through an appropriate ritual. Ancestor-spirits interact with the world of living people. These spirits can either help or harm the living, so it is important to show them all possible respect.

Bliatout (1993) has identified the following types of helpers who must be available for the mourning rituals to provide safe conduct for the dead and comfort for the survivors:

- *Guide to the spirit world:* This person will recite the *Qhuab Ke* verses from memory, with mention of every place in which the deceased lived. Unless this recitation is offered, the deceased will neither know that he or she has died nor find his or her way back to the place of birth. It is crucial to return to one's birth place because the placenta has been buried there and is needed if the soul is to make its return to the spirit world.
- *Reed pipe player and drummer:* Their music provides safe passage for the soul of the deceased. The performance makes great demands on the stamina of the musicians, and the instruments themselves are sacred. Mourning cannot start without this music.
- *Counselor to the family:* An elder is selected to sing comforting traditional songs to the family on the evening before the funeral.
- *Counselor to the dead:* Only deceased elders receive this special attention in which texts are recited to guide the soul on its journey between the world of the living and the world of ancestral spirits.

Hmong funerals include complex rituals for the passage of the deceased person to the next life and the safety of the family. Here the body is being checked for metal or other foreign objects that might leave a curse on the family.

- *Shoemaker:* "These special shoes turn up at the toe; without them, the souls will be unable to cross the big river, walk the treacherous paths, step over valleys of snakes . . . and arrive at the spirit world" (p. 87).
- *Stretcher-maker:* This person creates a symbolic horse from bamboo thatch and two long wooden poles. The deceased will lie on this pallet for several days until the burial.
- *Geomancer* (a kind of shaman): This person determines the best time for the burial.
- *Food server:* This person is specially trained to communicate with the souls of the deceased.
- *Warrior:* This person shoots arrows or fires his gun in the air and engages in other rituals to help protect the deceased on his or her journey.
- *Coffin makers:* This individual must also locate just the right tree to cut down and use. There must be no metal in the coffin.
- *Sacrificial ox slayers:* They must choose the right ox or oxen for this purpose. A whole day may be devoted to rituals associated with the sacrifices.

The funeral and mourning processes blend into each other all along the way. For example, the 13th Day End ritual must be performed after that amount of time has passed since the burial. It is on this occasion that the soul is finally released from its body and is free to journey to the spirit world. In the meantime, nobody works at their normal tasks other than preparation of food and other basic life-support activities.

Hmong Mourning in the United States

What happens when Hmong relocate to the United States? Here is a sampling of the problems that Bliatout (1993) has identified:

- *The American medical system requires autopsies in some cases.* "This is considered one of the most horrible things that can happen to a Hmong person, as it is believed that the person will be born mutilated in the next life" (p. 96).
- *Often there is no opportunity for the Hmong to wash, dress, lay out the body themselves, or provide the symbolic (stretcher) horse.* This can interfere significantly with the grieving and mourning process.
- *The reed pipes and funeral drum may not be allowed because they might disturb the neighbors!* Again, mourners may fear that they are

jeopardizing the safety of the deceased soul as well as their own lives because of this failure to honor and protect their dead. The sacrifice of oxen, the firing of guns, and other traditional rituals are also likely to be banned or to become impractical in their new environment.

- *Some Hmongs convert to Christianity and adopt lifestyles associated with our industrial–technical, mass media culture.* This can lead to a rift within and between Hmong families which, in turn, is likely to interfere with their established patterns of communal mourning.

The Hmong story—still in the process of transition—has many other parallels in our pluralistic society. Long-established traditions of mourning are not immune from challenge, whether by culture conflicts or catastrophic events, as the following examples illustrate.

Appreciating Universality and Diversity in the Response to Bereavement: Three Examples

People living within one culture sometimes misinterpret the bereavement responses of people within another culture. The mistaken assumption that life is cheap in Asia, for example, has been fostered by outsider ignorance of culturally expressed modes of mourning. Even within the "same" culture, there can be a lack of understanding about what the bereaved person goes through.

Racism and Grief: Dying Was His Specialty

Pulitzer Prize–winning poet and novelist Alice Walker describes personal experiences that illuminate both what is universal and what is distinctive about a particular culture's response to grief. In a book written primarily for children—*To Hell with Dying* (1988)—Walker tells of her love for an old man by the name of Mr. Sweet. He was not the usual type of elderly person who is found in a children's story: "Mr. Sweet was a diabetic and an alcoholic and a guitar player and lived down the road from us on a neglected cotton farm" (p. 1). Nevertheless, he was a continual source of delight and instruction for Walker and her older brothers and sisters. Dying was one of Mr. Sweet's specialties. He seemed very close to death on several occasions but was rescued by the Walker children who, on a signal from their father, would:

> Come crowding around the bed and throw themselves on the covers, and whoever was the smallest at the time would kiss him all over his wrinkled brown face and begin to tickle him so that he would laugh all down in his stomach, and his mustache, which was long and sort of straggly, would shake like Spanish moss and was also that color (p. 3).

Mr. Sweet had long ago discovered that the careers he wanted for himself—doctor, lawyer, or sailor—were out of reach for a poor black boy. He might have lived in grief all his life, having lost his childhood vision of an exciting and rewarding career. Instead, he excelled in bringing joy to the children in his rural neighborhood. Alice Walker, belonging to a new generation, achieved the college education that contributed to her brilliant writing career. Using these skills, she has given us a portrait of love and grief during a period of time in American history when many people of African heritage were denied equal access to opportunity.

The smiles and tears of *To Hell with Dying* have universal resonance—but the particulars reflect the unique patterns of life in a rural black community during a recent period of our own society. An outsider, for example, would have no way of knowing that the old guitar in a young black woman's hands was a tangible expression of both loss and continuity, grief and love.

Yoruba Compassion

How do Africans cope with grief and mourning in their homelands? There are as many answers as there are varied heritages, but an instructive example comes from the Yoruba of Western Nigeria (Adamolekun, 1999). There is a strong tradition of support for people in mourning. Every person in mourning is greeted daily by other members of the community with expressions of concern, support, and encouragement. These expressions are specific to the kind of bereavement that was experienced (e.g., a spouse, parent, or child); how the death occurred (e.g., long illness or sudden accident); and to the age, gender, and situation of the mourning person. This careful differentiation of message makes it clear that the society is aware of the distinctive loss.

All of the salutations acknowledge the pain of the loss and many congratulate the mourner for having the courage to bear up to this sorrow. The bereaved person is reminded to take good care of one's self in order to meet obligations for the family.

The Yoruba response clearly shows that the community is aware of the grieving person's loss, recognizes the sorrow and stress, and encourages the person to go on with life. This supportive, community-wide support is less evident in the United States and other urbanized, technologically driven nations where there is little patience with the mourning process.

AIDS, Multiple Deaths, and Grief

Somebody dies. Family and friends grieve. The community comes forward with practical and symbolic support in accord with its traditions. The long process of healing begins.

What happens, though, when there are just too many deaths within too short a time? When all the community survivors are in grief and many in jeopardy of losing their own lives? Traditional ways of grieving and mourning can be overwhelmed, leading to catastrophic individual and societal consequences (Kastenbaum, 2004a; 2004b). In our own times, the AIDS pandemic continues to be responsible for such stressful situations, although less pervasive in the news media. Jennifer Hunt (2004, p. 285) observes that:

> Multiple deaths in one extended family over a short time have become the norm in many parts of sub-Saharan Africa. In Zimbabwe, deaths due to AIDS are common, and the traditional grief models do not account for the ability of families to survive in the face of consecutive and concurrent deaths.

The traditional Zimbabwe way of life is difficult to sustain in this situation, and such is also the case with the traditional way of coping with death. Many people are practicing Christians, yet with continuing influence from earlier folk and religious traditions. The mourning rituals differ in many details from those of the Hmong but are comparable in the intensity, time, and effort required. Our usual ideas about grief and mourning do not seem adequate to comprehend the challenge of respecting the dead and moving ahead with life in such challenging circumstances.

A grieving person in one society probably has much in common with grieving people in other societies. However, tradition and ongoing circumstances can exercise powerful influence over the nature and effectiveness of the mourning process.

WHAT KIND OF GRIEF?

It is clear that the grieving process is not identical for all people in all circumstances. There is an ongoing effort by clinicians and researchers to make useful distinctions among types of grief. We will look at terms that have been proposed to describe different forms of grief: *normal, pathological, complicated, traumatic, resolved, unresolved,* and *anticipatory,* and the most recent addition, *prolonged grief disorder.*

Normal and Complicated Grief

Mental health experts now agree with the poets that grief is a human, not necessarily a weak or pathological response to loss. This departs from the once-common opinion that people should promptly get on with their lives without making a fuss. Nevertheless, there are situations in which grief is so extreme, so debilitating, and so enduring that the individual seems heading for catastrophe. The difference between a "normal" and a potentially endangering grief response has therefore become a focus of interest.

I don't much care for the term "normal" because the grieving person often feels anything but that. Instead, let's accept the suggestion of distinguished researcher Margaret S. Stroebe (2001), who proposes that *grief is normal when it stays within the bounds of a particular cultural tradition.* What, then, of grief that escapes these bounds? Stroebe rejects the terms "abnormal" and "pathological" grief because they neglect the interpersonal side of the situation and unnecessarily stigmatize the distraught person. Stroebe prefers the emotionally neutral, *complicated grief.* The grief response can be complicated in various ways. The common feature is that the bereaved person does not move from the shock and pain of loss toward a substantial return to an active and fulfilling life.

Recently, the concept of prolonged grief disorder (PGD) has emerged (Prigerson et al., 2009). It will be included in the next edition of the diagnostic guide that is used regularly by mental health professionals, and therefore can be expected to have considerable influence. The case in favor of PGD is that it can be distinguished from other types of grief and then treated effectively. It builds on studies that identified disabling symptoms for six months after a bereavement. The case against PGD is that it might transform grief into a mental disorder (Silverman, 2009).

Traumatic grief (Range, 2002) is a severe and disabling response to sudden, unexpected, and, often violent death. Family and friends of terrorist attack victims are especially vulnerable to traumatic grief. The survivor's whole world seems to have collapsed, and it is difficult to restore a sense of meaning and purpose. Helping people who are experiencing the traumatic form of grief can benefit from professional counseling or therapy and special attention to the circumstances surrounding the death. The reestablishment of belief systems, rituals, and dependable relationship patterns would seem to be a major priority.

Anticipatory Grief

Grieving sometimes begins before a death occurs. Some counselors believed that anticipatory grief has become increasingly common in recent years as people live longer with life-threatening conditions (Beder, 2002). There is more time to worry, and experience stress, but also more time to make decisions, clarify values, and strengthen relationships. The concept of anticipatory grief has directed attention to the state of mind of people prior to bereavement. It has often been assumed that people who have the opportunity to prepare themselves for the loss will experience less distress when it does occur. Pioneering thanatologist Robert Fulton (2003) does not find the evidence persuasive. Joan Beder (2003) notes that anticipatory grief does not seem beneficial in situations such as Alzheimer's disease where death is expected, but not imminent. The possible benefits of anticipatory grief might best be regarded as a working hypothesis in need of further study. Nevertheless, we would do well to improve our understanding of the individual and the situation prior to an expected death.

Resolved and Unresolved Grief

There are competing points of view on recovery from grief. Some experts believe that grief can and should be resolved within a reasonable (but not standard and fixed) period of time. Others believe that the loss of a crucial relationship is never completely resolved: We move on with our lives, but we will never again be the same. The term "recovery" therefore might not really be appropriate. This controversy is significant because it can influence the way we respond to grieving people. What should we expect? I doubt that it's useful to push people toward resolution on any imposed time schedule, and I also share the doubt that the effects of a profound bereavement will dissolve simply with the passage of time. From the practical standpoint, though, we can be helpful by attending to signs of movement or lack of movement toward recovery from the most debilitating effects of grief. Resolved and unresolved grief can be useful concepts, but only when linked to careful observations and not subject to arbitrary expectations.

Hidden and Disenfranchised Grief

Grief may be intensified and its resolution delayed when the bereaved are denied the opportunity to express their feelings. This is the concern with hidden or *disenfranchised grief*. A person's grief is hidden when it is not recognized by others because the individual has not expressed feelings about the loss. For example, Gail, a school teacher, did not believe she had the right to express her grief in the presence of her students (Rowling, 1995):

> I knew I was heading towards a class in an hour's time. I knew that even within an hour I would not have myself pulled together enough to face the class. I mean, if you went and sat in front of a class and cried for forty minutes they would riot, because they haven't got the rapport with what is happening with you at the moment (p. 323).

Grief may be hidden because the individual is not considered "entitled" to these feelings. In such a case, it can be said that the grief is also disenfranchised.

I observed many examples of hidden and *disenfranchised grief* among nurses and other caregivers. For example, staff members of a long-term-care facility often become attached to the people in their care. An aged woman with no living relatives would be "adopted" by a nurse who had lost her own grandparents. The caregiver would then experience grief when this resident died. However, our society often does not acknowledge the right

of a caregiver to grieve and mourn. The health care system has had a history of being intolerant of professionals who become "too involved" with their patients and "too upset" at their deaths. Staff members in a geriatric facility who had been emotionally close to recently deceased patients were more likely to be involved in single-car accidents and to experience a variety of illnesses requiring sick days. These negative outcomes were sharply reduced after the staff organized peer support groups and gave each other permission to love and mourn their patients.

AIDS continues to bring many additional examples of *disenfranchised grief*, even though symptom control has improved. The lover–companion of a person with AIDS may not be considered "family" and therefore denied the right to mourn. In fact, lovers in general have often been excluded from supportive interactions because their relationships to the deceased were not that of spouses, parents, children, or siblings. There is now increasing recognition that lovers and life companions have both the need and the right to mourn.

Parents of stillborn babies often have been forced to keep their grief to themselves. We have seen (Chapter 3) how difficult it was to persuade the health care system to regard the loss of a stillborn infant as the real death of a real person, and, therefore, "acceptable" for grieving. Validating the reality of a death is an essential first step in providing support to women experiencing stillbirth (Cacciatore, 2007). The sorrow of losing a companion animal has often also been excluded from serious consideration by society, though many families know better. Grief counselor Michelle Linn-Gust (2007) and veterinarian Nick Trout (2008) are among the experts who recognize how much animal companions can mean to a family and how much their deaths can be mourned.

Lavin (1989) brings another neglected kind of hidden grief to our attention in discussing the bereaved person who is developmentally disabled:

> If they have been sheltered all their lives, they may face the death of a loved one unprepared. Often parents shield their normal children from death and are reluctant to include them in the rites of mourning, keeping them away from wakes and funerals. There is a greater tendency for the parents of the developmentally disabled to continue the shielding process longer. Thus the disabled . . . may be denied access to mourning rituals . . . and

therefore are not exposed to role models who show them how to cope effectively with loss (p. 231).

Similarly, experiences have been reported by foster parents who look after children with severe disabilities and are therefore at higher risk for death (Schormans, 2004). The foster parents feel grief comparable with the loss of a birth child: "We don't feel like foster parents . . . Mom and Dad, we consider ourselves as mother and father" (p. 357).

THEORIES OF GRIEF

Here we consider several approaches to understand the meaning of grief in human experience. We will see that a key issue is at dispute: is it better to detach ourselves from strong attachment to the deceased loved one, or somehow to integrate this lost relationship into our ongoing life?

The Grief-Work Theory

Sigmund Freud (1919/1959) introduced the first influential theory following World War I. He was shaken to discover that supposedly civilized nations could behave so brutally toward each other. Freud offered the following propositions from his personal sorrows as well as his observation of widespread grief and mourning:

1. *Grief is an adaptive response to loss.* It is not just an expression of emotional pain. Grief is also a kind of work that must be performed. Our "pay" for this work is the restoration of our peace of mind and social competence.
2. *The work of grief is difficult and time consuming.* It goes on day after day, night after night. We increase the stress and make grief work more difficult if we demand that the bereaved person quickly snap back to "normal."
3. *The purpose of grief work is to accept the reality of the death and thereby become liberated from the strong attachment one had to the "lost object."* We must recover the *cathexis*—the emotional investment—we made in the deceased person—so that we can reinvest it in other relationships. The detachment (*decathexis*) process requires accepting the fact that the loved one is really and truly lost to us. This acceptance must occur on a deep emotional level; it is not

The pioneering psychoanalyst Sigmund Freud developed an influential theory of grief as he experienced his own sorrows and recognized the losses experienced by many other people in World War I.

enough to have only an intellectual acknowledgment of the loss.

4. *Grief work is carried out through a long series of confrontations with the reality of the loss.* Survivors must deal with all the feelings and memories that bring to mind their attachment to the deceased person. Often one must confront the same point of attachment over and over again. For example, the survivor might have to listen repeatedly to a particular song that was a favorite of the deceased person before this song loses its power to overwhelm one with anxiety and sorrow.
5. *The process is complicated by our resistance to letting go of the attachment.* We want to stay in touch with the "lost object" in any way we

can. This need can sabotage our efforts to accept the loss and return to normal life.

6. *The failure of grief work results in continued misery and dysfunction.* Time itself does not heal. In fact, we do not reenter the mainstream of time until we have liberated ourselves from attachment to the deceased person. Survivors who remain intensely attached to the deceased person over a prolonged period of time are considered to be suffering from pathological grief. (We would now call it complicated or prolonged grief and not expect resolution neatly within the first year of bereavement.)

Despite its limitations, grief-work theory deserves much credit for acknowledging grief as a core aspect of the human experience and encouraging sensitive attention to the bereaved person.

From Grief-Work to Attachment

Freud's original theory emphasized the *intrapsychic* response to loss: how we attempt to deal with our own thoughts and feelings. Later contributors have called more attention to the interpersonal context of grief work: how a loss affects our relationships. The current interest in *attachment behavior* and bonding owes much to British psychiatrist John Bowlby's investigations. Bowlby (1969, 1973, 1980) connects the biological need for survival with grief and mourning. The vulnerable young of many species exhibit distress and attempt to draw their absent mother to their sides by whatever sounds and other communication signals they have in their repertoire. The mothers also seek their missing young by calling or signaling to them. Neither the young nor the mothers can relax until they have rejoined each other. Adults also show the need for attachment when there is danger afoot. For example, citing a study of baboons, Bowlby (1969) notes that

> Not only infants but adults also when under stress are strongly disposed to cling to a companion. Thus an adult female, when alarmed, clings to the back of her husband or is embraced by him. Conversely, when he is under stress during a fight, a male is likely to embrace one of his wives (p. 42).

Adult grief resonates with our early experiences of separation. Every dog has been a frightened puppy, every cat a stressed kitten, and every adult human an anxious baby. We have all had the anxiety of separation experiences, even if these were but fleeting episodes. The depressive state of a bereaved spouse has its precedent in the infant who felt himself or herself to be abandoned and vulnerable. The feeling that "I can't live without you" may have its roots in the sense of vulnerability that also accompanies separation between parent and young and between mates in many other species.

Why, then, is grief work so difficult? The goal of attachment behavior is to maintain the security provided by a significant interpersonal relationship. Any situation that threatens this bond will call forth:

> action designed to preserve it; and the greater the danger of loss appears to be, the more intense and varied are the actions elicited to prevent it. In such circumstances all the most powerful forms of attachment behavior become activated—clinging, crying and perhaps angry coercion. This is the phase of protest and one of acute physiological stress and emotional distress. When these actions are successful the bond is restored, the activities cease, and the states of stress and distress are alleviated (Bowlby, 1980, p. 42).

Here Bowlby provides a valuable insight for understanding the intensity and persistence of grief responses. We respond effectively to a threatened loss of relationship by communicating our concern and putting ourselves on full alert. This response does not work, though, when it is death that separates us from a loved person. We can whisper, shout, and ready ourselves for heroic efforts, and yet the other person does not return. This persistent absence may be accompanied by persistent stress. What is the survivor to do when efforts to restore the relationship by yearning, remembering, crying, praying, and raging have failed? The survivor may keep trying and trying (Bowlby, 1980):

> This means that the person's attachment behavior is remaining constantly primed. . . . The condition of the organism is then one of chronic stress and . . . distress. At intervals, moreover, both stress and distress are likely again to become acute (p. 42).

Bowlby's description is consistent with ongoing research into the physiological stress of bereavement. Our response to the stress of loss can itself become the source of continuing stress: we can't get what we want and we can't stop trying and, in the meantime, not much else gets done. Grief work is so difficult because it must overcome our desperate yearning to restore the lost love object through fantasies and emotions.

Another British researcher, Colin M. Parkes, studied the *psychosocial transitions.* How do people attempt to get on with their lives after bereavement? Under what conditions does grief work fail, leaving the survivor in a state of prolonged social and personal dysfunction? Parkes (2001; 2006) identified three basic components of grief work:

- *Preoccupation with thoughts of the deceased person.* This represents a continuing search process, reminding us of the attachment-seeking signals and behaviors Bowlby describes in many species.
- *Repeatedly going over the loss experience in one's mind.* This is a painful process in which the survivor seems to be testing out the reality of the loss (Did this terrible thing really happen?).
- *Attempts to explain the loss.* It is somewhat easier to accept the reality of a death if the loss makes sense, had a reason behind it. During this part of the grief-work process, the survivor is asking self and others "Why, why, why?"

How Useful is Grief-Work Theory?

Our understanding of grief has been enriched by the contributions of Freud, Bowlby, Parkes, and others who cultivated the grief-work approach. Nevertheless, this theory has its limits. Margaret Stroebe (2001) is among those who have suggested that grief-work theory was accepted before sufficient research had been done. Her own findings indicate that some bereaved persons had not devoted themselves to grief work yet were functioning well and free of depression—while some who were hard at grief work were making only a limited recovery. These outcomes do not support the proposition that we must detach ourselves through a long, difficult, and painful process. Nevertheless, the absence of grief work was related to adjustment problems for some individuals—mostly on the part of widowers who attempted to distract themselves from the loss. In light of these findings, it would be useful to give more attention to individual differences in personality and coping styles.

Although Freud was fascinated by cultural differences, he did not take them into account in his grief-work theory. Many thanatologists today recognize the importance of cultural influences on the ways people cope with grief. For example, bereaved persons in Bali are expected to distract themselves and participate in cheerful interactions, whereas those in Egypt are encouraged to share their pain and sorrow with others. Quite possibly there is more than one way to cope effectively with the loss and stress of bereavement, with both personality style and sociocultural expectations having their influences.

From Attachment to Continuing Bonds

Attachment theory soon bonded itself to the original grief-work formulation. There was a logical next development and it was advanced by Dennis Klass, Phyllis R. Silverman, and Steven L. Nickman, along with other contributors to *Continuing bonds* (1996, p. 3). Examples from many cultures and situations indicated that the lost loved one somehow was kept alive to the survivor over the years. The authors challenged "the idea that the purpose of grief is to sever the bonds with the deceased in order to free the survivor to make new attachments. We offer an alternative model based on the mourner's continuing bonds with the deceased." It is no longer to be considered pathological if a person keeps an attachment with the deceased over a long period of time. Counselors therefore are advised to cease attacking the bereaved person's attachment to the person who was somehow present as well as absent.

Advocates of continuing bond theory point out that the bereaved person does not necessarily become trapped in time, condemned to repeating and recycling the lost relationship. Silverman (2003, p. 187), for example, observes that:

> *A continuing bond does not mean that people live in the past. . . . The way the bereaved relate to the deceased changes as they develop over the life cycle, whether they be young or old mourners. People need to stop thinking of grief as being entirely present or absent. People rarely just "get over it," nor do they ever really find closure.*

But are continuing bonds always or even usually helpful? This question is proving rather difficult to study, e.g., how accurately can "continuing bonds" be disentangled from "grief" (Schut et al., 2006)? A review of the research literature (Field, 2006) offers two conclusions: (1) continuing bonds are often an adaptive part of adjustment to loss, but (2) can also contribute to difficulties in adjustment in certain circumstances. Researchers and counselors are now attempting to identify the situations in which continuing bonds are most likely to have positive or negative effects on the grieving person's adaptation. In the meantime, we might refrain from drawing hasty conclusions about whether a bereaved person "should" or "should not" maintain a strong emotional attachment to the deceased. Compassionate support serves well whether one is more attached to grief-work or continuing bonds theory.

Other Theoretical Approaches to Understand Grief

There are now other alternatives or supplements to grief-work theory. Each offers something useful to think about.

Stage Theory

The Kübler-Ross (1969) stage theory of dying has also been applied to grieving. Stage theorists usually specify that the first response to bereavement is shock, numbness, and disbelief. The final phase is the reestablishment of physical and mental balance. Descriptions of the middle phases of the grief process and the total number of phases are points that differ from one stage theorist to another. Many grieving people do experience some of the feelings, and attempt some of the coping strategies, that are listed in the various stage theories. Nevertheless, the available evidence does not support the proposition that everybody in fact does go through these stages. Many writers, counselors, and educators did not seem troubled by the continued absence of research confirmation, or by clinical reports that also raised questions about the validity of this model. Now there are findings from a substantial study. Maciejewsi et al. (2007, p. 716) drew their data from the Yale Bereavement Study that followed more than two hundred people for

three years following their loss. It was found that "Counter to stage theory, disbelief was not the initial, dominant grief indicator. Acceptance was the most commonly endorsed item."

In a follow-up article, Maciejewski et al. (2007, p. 297) caution that:

> The stage theory of grief has captured the imagination of clinicians and the public. Despite its recognized limitations (e.g., that it will not predict exactly how every bereaved person will grieve), it remains taught in medical schools, posted on authoritative Web sites (e.g., National Cancer Institute), and continues to guide thinking about bereavement for many clinicians, educators, and researchers.

A Meaning-Making Perspective

A major study by Jason Holland and Robert Neimeyer (2010) does more than evaluate stage theory. It also acknowledges the desire to find a meaning in life and death. People bereaved by either a violent or natural death were followed over the next two years and interviewed at several time periods. People who had been bereaved through a natural death were more adept at making sense of what had happened. This contributed to their acceptance of the loss and often took place soon afterward, not requiring a long period of stage-like progression. Those bereaved by a violent death found it more difficult to make sense of the loss and also experienced more symptoms of distress. Their anger and depression seemed to interfere with coming to terms with the loss and starting to move on with their lives. However, most participants proved resilient over time even if the death had been traumatic. This did not mean that "time heals all wounds." There were individual patterns of grief episodes over time, suggesting that personality, coping skills, and the availability of social support network can help many people move forward in their lives. *Overall, the ability to find meaning in what happened was the best predictor of how people dealt with their grief: time and stages were less useful.*

Holland and Neimeyer (2010) reflect on the continuing popularity of stage theory although not well supported by research. One answer might be that "human beings are inveterate seekers of patterns to organize the flux of experience in a fashion that enhances their sense of prediction and control." Furthermore, we have a tendency to organize our thought into narratives that include a beginning, a middle, and an end. We work hard to "discover" patterns that might or might not have occurred in the events in order to "tell a good story" to ourselves and others (Neimeyer et al., 2009).

And then—something really to think about: Stage theory suggests a narrative structure to grieving, one in which the protagonist is thrust into what Joseph Campbell (1949) described as the hero's journey, an archetypal narrative discernible across widely varying cultures in which the hero is called forth from the normal world to face and overcome a series of great trials, ultimately to return triumphant with special knowledge or a special gift to bestow on others... The seemingly magnetic draw of a stage-like depiction of grieving that begins with a disorienting separation from the "normal," pre-bereavement world, and that progresses heroically through a series of clearly marked emotional trials before eventuating in a triumphant stage of acceptance, recovery, or symbolic return, may owe more to its compelling coherence with a universal narrative structure than to its objective accuracy (Holland & Neimeyer, op. cit.):

> In this view, stages of grief offer a welcome and persuasive story that imposes meaning and purpose that might not actually be inherent in the events and experiences.

The Dual-Process Model

Stroebe and Schut (2001) were impressed by the marked differences in grief responses that found in years of research. The dual-process model acknowledges this variability and suggests that a "normal" response can take many different forms. Key to this model are two processes: (1) emotional working through of grief and (2) adapting to new roles and situations in the altered world. A bereaved person might deal effectively with one of these processes while experiencing significant problems with the other. Recovery is in trouble if a person focuses on only one of these areas of concern. In robust recovery, a bereaved person tends to oscillate between emotional recovery and coping with the external realities of life. The person who is quickly back at work might seem to be making a strong recovery, but it is at the expense of avoiding the emotional issues. It is often thought that men and women grieve differently. The facts, however, suggest that there are two general styles of grieving, and both of these can be found in each gender. Masculine-style grieving puts the emphasis on keeping busy and getting things done. Feminine-style grieving gives more attention to emotions, but the person who is immersed in thoughts and feelings might drift away from obligations and interactions.

The dual-process model is particularly useful for those interested in exploring both grief-work and continued bonding approaches. It also invites attention to individual differences and suggests caution in generalizing about "the normal" course of grief (Archer, 2009).

Cultural traditions and pressures tend to lead bereaved people toward either the internal or the external mode of coping with grief. Hunt (2004) uses the dual-process model in her enlightening case example of "what it means to be a grieving black Zimbabwean woman today" (p. 288). The dual-process model can be recommended for consideration by both counselors and researchers.

An Evolutionary Biology Model of Grief

Is grief adaptive? Does this distressing condition actually have a positive function? Yes, according to the evolutionary biology model proposed by John Archer (2001). He suggests that grief is not only a human universal but that a grief-like reaction also occurs in social birds and mammals when they lose a significant other either through death or separation. This conclusion had already been reached by John Bowlby and, before that, by Charles Darwin (1872). Archer has refined this principle: The grief expressed by birds and mammals is similar to that of young children rather than to that of adult humans. Their distress is acute but less complicated.

Archer's (2001) second conclusion is that grief is maladaptive: It has detrimental effects on the survival of the bereaved animal or person. This is a puzzle from the evolutionary perspective: Why would humans and other animals have such a strong response pattern that jeopardizes survival?

Archer answers this question in a fascinating way. The grief itself is not adaptive—but social bonds are very much advantageous for survival. Grief is an unavoidable byproduct of a bird, mammal, or human determination to build and maintain strong emotional bonds with others. A journey to the evolutionary biology realm, then, offers a renewed appreciation for the significance of intimate relationships. The pain of separation is a risk that comes with attachment to another person (or dog, cat, horse, or macaw). By implication, when we decide against having any close relationships, we may be reducing the sorrow and anxiety of bereavement but also the benefits of social support.

HOW DO PEOPLE RECOVER FROM GRIEF?

We have already seen that there are more ways than one to cope with bereavement. In this section, we explore these patterns in more detail. First we consider what has been learned about the death of a spouse. This will include a harrowing visit with Third World widows. Next we will turn to responses to the death of children, to the grief and death of elderly adults, and then to survivors of traumatic or stigmatized death. Finally, we will complete our examination of the impact of grief by looking at the most extreme outcome: death of the bereaved person.

When a Husband or Wife Dies

"Until death us do part." This traditional phrase in marriage vows continues to be meaningful. Death as the event that ends a marriage occurs ever more frequently in the later adult years. Consider the situation at age 65 and older: The U. S. Census Bureau estimates that about 45 percent of women and 14 percent of men who had been married were now widows or widowers. At age 85 and older, spousal bereavement rises to 80 percent for women and 43 percent for men (2003). These numbers would be even higher were it not for the increase in divorces. Coping with the loss of a marital partner and somehow going on with life are challenges that many people will be facing at some point. Fortunately, spousal bereavement has been the subject of many careful studies that have included interviews as well as background information. We will draw upon findings from major studies by Glick, Weiss, & Parkes, (1974;) Parkes, (2001); Parkes & Weiss, (1983), and Stroebe, Abakoumkin, & Stroebe (2010).

The Immediate Impact of Spousal Bereavement

Most of the women had been experiencing anticipatory grief. However, the impact of the actual death was still felt deeply. But those who found themselves suddenly transformed into widows suffered even more intensely. They felt overwhelmed, anguished, as though there were no limits to the catastrophe that had befallen them. The suddenly bereaved woman might feel so numb that she feared she would never again move, act, or think, or she might cry as though she would never be able to stop.

The husband who became a widower usually responded to the impact of the death very much as the widow did. The men differed, however, in how they interpreted their feelings. Although the women often emphasized a sense of abandonment, the men reported feeling a sort of dismemberment. The women would speak of being left alone, deprived of a comforting and protecting person. The men were more likely to feel "like both my arms were being cut off." These differences seemed related to what marriage had meant for widow and widower. Marriage had sustained the man's capacity to work. For the woman, marriage had provided a sphere of interpersonal engagement.

Emotional and Physical Reactions Soon After Bereavement

Bewilderment and despair often continued beyond the first impact of loss. There were still periods of weeping, especially for the women. Physical symptoms appeared and sometimes lingered for weeks or months. Many women reported aches and pains, poor appetite, sleep disturbances, loss of stamina, headaches, dizziness, and menstrual irregularities. Often a widow would wake up in the middle of the night and remain tormented by grief and the reality of her partner's absence. Some women tried to wear themselves out by working hard and staying up late. Others turned to sleeping medications. The dread and emptiness of facing the night alone were relieved for some of the bereaved by having close friends or relatives who kept them company until sleep finally took over. Each woman had to find her own balance between the desire to receive help and the fear of becoming dependent on others.

The typical widower attempted to maintain control over his feelings because he considered it unmanly to let go. Such statements as "it's not fair!" were seldom made by men. Although less troubled by anger than the widow, the widower did have difficulty with guilt. He was more likely to blame himself. "I wasn't sensitive enough to her." "I should have made things easier." The widower's guilt reaction tended to subside fairly soon, although the need for rational control over all responses to the death persisted.

Leave-Taking Ceremonies

Leave-taking ceremonies went well for most of the bereaved in Parke and colleagues pioneering study. It was helpful to hear from others that they had done their part to ensure a proper farewell. This bolstered their sense of confidence in managing difficult affairs despite their shock and suffering. The widow was seen by all as the final authority on what should be done, regardless of different wishes that, for example, the husband's family might have. In this way, the widow began to gain public acceptance as the new head of the family.

The funeral directors usually were seen as supportive and caring persons. Nevertheless, there were painful moments. Some widows suddenly felt the full pangs of their husband's death at the last viewing of the body. Most widows seemed to be operating on very limited emotional energy. They neither sought out nor took in what the clergy might have had to say. Understandably, the widows tended to be absorbed in their own feelings. Many of the widows were religious, however, and seemed to find some comfort in clergy's repetitions of traditional beliefs about the continuation of soul or spirit after death.

The leave-taking ceremonies did not seem to be quite as important to most of the widowers in this study. They gave less attention to the details and did not express as much gratitude toward the funeral directors. They were also more likely to feel that the cost of the funeral was too high. The funeral and all that it involved was something that they had to "get through" rather than the milestone it represented for many widows.

Grief and Recovery: The First Year

The long months after the funeral often were the most difficult for both widow and widower. For a short time, there had been concentrated attention upon the needs of the bereaved. But the deceased spouse remains dead and the bereaved person's emotional and pragmatic problems continue day after day. The widows realized that they had to reorganize their lives, but often felt that they should not burden others with their sorrow.

Sorrow and anxiety remained intense even though the widows now seldom spoke of their grief. Many engaged in obsessional reviews. Events surrounding the husband's death were relived over and over. The obsessional reviews often were concerned with what might have happened instead of what actually did happen. How could the accident have been avoided? How might it all have turned out differently? The widows frequently searched for meaning through these reviews. It was not the name of the disease or the technical reason for the accident that concerned the widow so much as the need to make sense of the death. These questions often lost some of their intensity over time, but the search for meaning continued to linger. Convincing answers proved hard to find. As we have seen, meaning-making as a dominating theme in bereavement has become a more salient concept during the years following this study.

Although it remained painful to review the events leading up to the death, memories of the husband generally were positive. This was especially true in the early weeks and months. A tendency to idealize the lost spouse was observed. The deceased husband was the best man who ever lived, a wonderful husband, a marvelous father—he had no faults whatsoever. Later a more balanced view usually emerged. The widow would still think about him frequently and positively, but now some of his quirks and imperfections gained recognition as well. The widow might also find herself suddenly angry at the husband for leaving her with the children to raise by herself. These episodes of negative feelings seemed to be part of the long process of developing a realistic attitude that the widow could live with through the years.

Often the widow's feelings about her husband went beyond vivid memories. She might have a strong sense that he was still there with her. This impression would make itself felt soon after the death and remain with her off and on for a long time. The sense of presence was especially persistent for women who had experienced the sudden loss of their spouses. More extensive haunting experiences were reported by women who had had no opportunity to prepare themselves for their losses. Even when the sense of presence was vivid, the widows knew that their husbands were really dead. It was neither unusual nor crazy for widows to feel this sense of presence.

Widows with children at home usually recognized their responsibilities clearly and felt that the need to provide parental care helped to keep them from becoming lost in their own grief. Often there was a new resolve to be a better mother. The widows felt the need to be straightforward and realistic with the children yet also to shelter and protect them and keep their spirits up. The widows were in a difficult position in trying to provide answers to their children while still searching for answers themselves.

The Widowers' Response

Although the bereaved man was almost as likely to feel the presence of his wife soon after the bereavement, as time went by this phenomenon became much less common. The men also tended to cut off the obsessional review after just a few weeks. The widower pushed himself right back to immediate realities, although, like the widow, he too felt a desire to replay the circumstances of the death. The widowers were also less likely to speak openly about their feelings.

The typical widower gave no outward sign of his grief. Yet a close look at the quality of the widower's personal life, including the occupational sphere, indicated a decrease in energy, competence, and satisfaction. The widower usually made a more rapid social recovery but a slower emotional recovery than the widow. A year after his wife's death, the widower was much more likely than the widow to feel lonely and depressed.

Other studies have found that for both women and men, the lost spouse might occasionally return as a dream–visitor over many years—perhaps even throughout the survivor's lifetime. These dream visitations do not proceed through stages or tasks. Instead, many different themes are expressed in the dreams (Belicki, Gulko, Ruzycki, & Aristotle, 2003), including:

- Dreamer and deceased encounter one another, greeting each other enthusiastically.
- Dream of romantic or sexual encounter with deceased.

- Deceased appears to dreamer's surprise. Often the apparent death is seen as a mistake.
- Dreamer is physically separated from the deceased, for example, by some physical barrier (pp. 100–101).

Dreams of the deceased spouse often linger in the waking memory and become a part of the mental and emotional fabric of ongoing life.

Types of Recovery from the Impact of Marital Bereavement

The response to early bereavement provides useful clues as to how the individual will respond as the months go by. Those who were most disturbed a few weeks after the death usually were the ones who continued to be disturbed a year later. The person who had strong feelings that the death was unreal and who tried to behave as though the spouse were still alive also was likely to have more difficulty than others over an extended time.

The quality of the marital relationship influences the grief and recovery process. When the partners had very mixed feelings toward each other, the experiences associated with bereavement often were more disturbing. Similarly, it was harder for the survivor to adjust if the relationship had been based on a clinging dependence. If soon after bereavement the surviving spouse felt cast adrift, empty, and helpless, then difficulties in adjustment were likely to be more prolonged. More recent studies also indicate that the kind of attachment bond that existed between the couple has a strong relationship to the way in which grief and recovery occur (Waskowic & Chartier, 2003).

Relationship quality before the death also proved to be influential on the course of grief in the other major follow-up study of spousal bereavement (Stroebe et al., 2010). Here it was *yearning* that emerged as a characteristic of bereaved people who had a troubled relationship with their deceased spouse. In fact, yearning for the lost spouse was the characteristic that most distinguished bereavement from other critical life events. Furthermore, social support did not seem to have much effect on yearning and the related feeling of loneliness and isolation. Social support did help to alleviate depression, but could not heal the loss of their vital, though troubled, attachment to the deceased spouse.

The dual process theory is called on by Stroebe and her colleagues in distinguishing two types of response to bereavement: the loss-oriented, and the recovery-oriented. A strong ambivalent marital relationship appears linked to a loss-oriented response.

Unresolved Grief

All of the newly bereaved people studied had to face the question of who they were now, having lost part of their identities with the loss of their spouses. Two years later, some had made substantial recoveries from grief. Those still in despair had not formed a coherent and acceptable conception of the death, nor were they able to modify their self-images in preparation for new lives without a spouse. These were the type of bereaved people that would later be described by Stroebe et al. as loss-oriented. Furthermore, they were more likely to use tranquilizers, drink and/or smoke heavily, and to wonder whether anything in life was worthwhile. Three types of concepts of unresolved grief were observed.

- *The unexpected grief syndrome* occurs in some people when the spouse dies without warning. Disbelief and intense anxiety often became not only the first but also the continued responses.
- *The conflicted grief syndrome* occurs when death ends a troubled relationship. Some of the marriages in the study had been to alcoholic men whose behavior had created a climate of fear and disorder. The unresolved grief experienced by survivors of troubled marriages appears in a sense to be continuations of the frustrations and disappointments that had characterized the relationships while the spouses were alive.
- *The chronic grief syndrome* is marked by the survivors' strong feelings of dependency. The survivors have unusually powerful dependence on the deceased spouses and do not feel personally capable of taking on the responsibilities of life with their partners gone.

The Psychosocial Transition

Parkes (2001) calls attention to the *psychosocial transition*, the change from who we were to who we are now after a death has altered our lives:

> All of us, from the moment of our birth, have been building inside ourselves a model of the world, a set of assumptions on the basis of which we recognize

> the world that we meet and plan our behaviour accordingly. . . . Not only does a major psychosocial transition require us to revise a great number of assumptions about the world, but most of these assumptions have become habits of thought and behavior that are now virtually automatic. A widow will come down for breakfast in the morning and find that she has laid the table for two when there is now only one person to eat it (p. 91).

This could be regarded as an example of what anthropologists have described as *rites of passage* (Gennep, 1960; Turner, 1969, 1992). Whether through physical or symbolic space, a person might need to move from "here" to "there" and in so doing shed an existing status for a new one. It happens, for example, when a youth is initiated into adulthood through traditional rituals or two single people go through a wedding ceremony. People are most vulnerable when they are between "here" and "there." This is what is meant by being in limbo, a period during which one is not quite who one used to be and not yet who one will become. That is clearly the situation for a person in the midst of psychosocial transition after bereavement—and it suggests that appropriate social rituals could be helpful in guiding and protecting the individual during this precarious time.

The Family That Has Lost a Child

Losing a child to death is one of the most painful of all human experiences. Anguish is immediate and can also be long lasting, though seldom obvious to outsiders.

Shadow Grief: Perinatal Death The sorrow of a child's death often seems to follow a family like a shadow. After observing the reactions of mothers who had lost a baby before or soon after birth, Peppers and Knapp (1980) introduced the term, shadow grief. Years after the death, many of the mothers were still feeling the anguish. In a later study, Knapp (1986) found the same phenomenon among parents who had lost older children to death. They were no longer completely dominated by grief, but the shadow or cloud followed them as they moved through life:

> On the surface most observers would say that the "grief work" has been accomplished. But this is not the case. Shadow grief reveals itself more in the

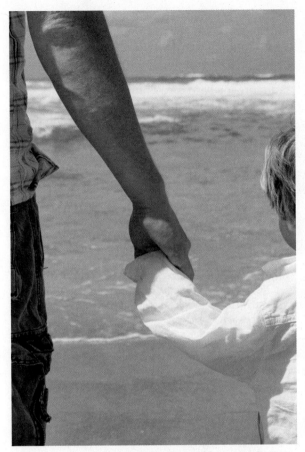

Parents who are themselves grieving sometimes become emotionally unavailable to their children—who very need their comforting hand.

form of an emotional "dullness," where the person is unable to respond fully and completely to outer stimulation and where normal activity is moderately inhibited. . . . Under certain circumstances and on certain occasions, comes bubbling to the surface, sometimes in the form of tears, sometimes not, but always accompanied by a feeling of sadness and a mild sense of anxiety . . . (pp. 40–41).

Parents who have lost a child often feel that their own lives also changed at that moment. Furthermore, they may not want to relinquish the grief. The pain is part of the memory—and the memory is precious.

The death of so young a child has often been given relatively little attention by society. The lack of communal recognition and support tends to isolate the parents in their grief. Some newspapers have even prohibited publication of newborn death notices, and it is difficult to find sympathy cards on the market for perinatal death. This term refers to infants who die at any point from the twentieth week after conception through the first month after birth. Premature birth is still the most common cause of perinatal death, although advances in medical and nursing techniques have saved some neonates who otherwise would have died. Deaths also occur for a variety of other reasons (e.g., a genetic defect or a prenatal infection) and sometimes for reasons that are never clearly determined. We cannot exclude socioeconomic causes, either. Even in the United States, many pregnant women still do not have access to perinatal health services.

Complications of Perinatal Grief Grief over a perinatal death is similar in many respects to grief over any loss. There are some special circumstances, however. For example, the mother may still be sedated or exhausted at the time she learns of her child's death. She is also ready to mother her baby, both physically and emotionally. This total readiness, including lactation to provide breast milk, now has no opportunity to express itself. Parents may have to listen to such unhelpful comments as "Well, you still have other children," and they may also find it difficult to explain the loss and provide comfort to the other children while they are troubled by their own grief. The family that has experienced perinatal death often feels misunderstood and abandoned by others:

> Most bereaved parents tell us that the support they received from others at the time of the baby's death did not continue very long. They think that others do not continue to "live" their grief as they do. Others expect them to recover within a few short weeks (Cordell & Thomas, 1997, p. 299).

The health care system is becoming more responsive to the emotional needs of family members. In some hospital settings, the family is encouraged to interact with the newborn in a natural and loving way. Photographs may be taken of parents holding the baby, and memorabilia (such as the child's first footprints or a lock of hair) may be given to them. Reynolds (2003/2004) suggests that parents be informed of the option to see and hold their stillborn infant but that they not be pressured to do so; whether or not this practice is helpful is a matter of controversy at present. "Bereavement protocols" that help prepare hospital staff to provide emotional support for family members are becoming more common, and group counseling has also proved helpful (Cordell & Thomas, 1997). Cacciatore (2007) made a breakthrough contribution toward expression of grief and mourning by persuading officials to issue birth certificates for stillborn infants.

Effects of a Child's Death on the Parents' Worldview The loss and sorrow that follows the death of the child may be intensified by a crisis of belief or faith. This response is especially strong when the child's life was taken by murder (Mathews & Marwit, 2003/2004) and is also thought to occur in other sudden and traumatic types of death. The parents may feel that the world no longer makes sense, that one can count upon neither upon God nor community.

There is some evidence that preserving an emotional connection with the deceased child helps to prevent the destruction of the parents' worldview. Klass (1992/1993) found that the "inner representation" of the dead child continues to be experienced by the parents for many years, if not throughout all their lives. He defines inner representations "as characterizations or thematic memories of the deceased, and the emotional states connected with these characterizations and memories" (p. 383).

Staying in contact with the inner representation of the dead child makes it easier for the survivors to keep their worldviews intact. The sorrow and sense of loss are still there, but the feeling that something of the child still lives with or within them seems to reduce doubts about their worldviews. Symbolic interactions with the deceased are not signs of pathology—for example, it is not "crazy" to sense the child's presence or even to catch fleeting glimpses of the child.

Talbot (1998/1999) has found that the hardiness of some mothers:

> seems to have been forged in the fire of agonizing grief—grief which has been consciously confronted and transformed into the gift of compassion and personal growth. By understanding what has been learned from loss and grief, it is possible to reach out and help make the world a better place for self and others (p. 184).

The Future of the Marital Relationship After the Death of a Child The loss of a child creates stress and strain for the family unit as a whole (Rubin & Malkinson, 2001). For example, sexual intimacy can diminish, even though many couples report an increased need for physical contact and comfort. The parents often report feeling more irritable and more likely to direct anger at each other. This can become particularly destructive when one parent blames the other either for the death or for past actions related to the lost child. Furthermore, communication tends to break down for bereaved couples. The parents may withdraw into their own grief and therefore away from each other. Nevertheless, most couples do not divorce or even seriously consider this possibility after the death of a child. Recent studies indicate that most parents achieve what Barrera et al. (2007, p. 152) call *integrated grief*.

> This is a difficult process that does not overcome the sense of devastation and loss, but enables the parents to experience a sense of control over their expression of grief and a relatively effective style of navigating life without the deceased child. . . . They also expressed a positive outlook on life and described having learned from their experience.

The Grief of Grandparents Grandparents and parents experience many of the same feelings of loss. In addition, grandparents also are likely to experience vicarious grief for the parents (Kastenbaum, 1987; Rando, 2002) as well as their own direct grief over the death of the child. It hurts them to realize how much their adult children are sorrowing for the death of the grandchild. Furthermore, it is even more unexpected for people to outlive their grandchildren. Such an unexpected and "untimely" death can generate a worldview crisis just as in the case of the parents.

White (1999) has found that the death of a grandchild causes extreme anguish, regardless of the child's age. Most of the bereaved grandparents had a strong need to talk about their grandchildren. This need could be frustrated if the family has responded with withdrawal and silence or if communication patterns between the grandparents and their adult children had previously been inadequate. Some grandparents felt helpless because they could not protect their adult children from the pain of loss—similar perhaps to the frequent desire of parents to shield their young children from awareness of death and dying. Nevertheless, grandparents often did provide valuable support to the bereaved parents just by being there with them, as well as by helping with chores and expenses. The overall message is clear: Grandparents often are much affected by the death of a child and have a significant role to play in the family's response.

Today, grandparents often remain overlooked when counseling and other forms of social support are provided. Nehari, Grebler, and Toren (2007) found that many grandparents were struggling with their perceived "right to grief" and for a sense of isolation from their bereaved children: "They won't talk with us about the pain." The researchers set up meetings between parents and grandparents of the deceased child. The sessions were highly emotional and intense, resulting in improved communication among all the grieving family members.

BEREAVEMENT IN LATER LIFE

We are vulnerable to bereavement at any age. In the later adult years, there is an increased vulnerability, but loss is often met with a vitality and resilience that exceeds what one might have expected.

Sorrow upon Sorrow, Loss upon Loss

Life satisfaction does not necessarily decline with age. Gerontologists have discredited the assumption that usefulness and the enjoyment of life end at a certain age. Nevertheless, it is also true that the longer a person lives and forms loving attachments, the more there is to lose. Loss may follow upon loss, taxing the individual's ability to cope. This is the concept of bereavement overload (Kastenbaum, 2009a). Long-lived people usually have survived many people to whom they were deeply attached. We accumulate these losses just by staying alive over an extended period of time. Reactivated grief from previous losses can reduce the emotional energy available to respond fully to the most recent death. Survivors of the Holocaust and other disasters have often been burdened in this way. An upsurge in fear of personal death is also not unusual, especially when it is a sibling who has died. Therapists have found it useful to bolster the individual's sense of competence and autonomy, as well as to encourage sharing of the concern.

What changes would be expected in people of any age who have been forced to cope with too many losses in too short a period of time? They

Sorrow shared is easier to bear.

might try to reconstitute their personal world by replacing the losses, or lose themselves in work or other engrossing activities. These alternatives, however, are often closed to elders. What now? One might become increasingly preoccupied with bodily functions and experience less free energy to invest in new activities or relationships. Furthermore, the experience of multiple losses may lead to a sense of extreme caution. "I had better not care about anybody or anything else. I just cannot bear to lose and mourn again."

The whole constellation of "old behaviors," then, can develop from multiple, unbearable bereavement. Suicidal thoughts and attempts also can arise. The individual may give up when stricken by a relatively minor ailment and allow the condition to worsen or reduce his or her activities so drastically that both body and mind are in poor tone to respond to any kind of stress.

The older person is vulnerable to deaths of many kinds. Most common is the death of siblings (Moss, Moss, & Hansson, 2001). But elderly adults also lose a spouse, adult children, grandchildren, and even parents. I have stood at the side of a 74-year-old man as tears ran down his cheeks because his 97-year-old father was dead. The outsider might rush to the conclusion that the death of a very old parent should not mean so much to a child also advanced in years. Consider, however, how long this relationship had to develop and flourish and what a blow it now was to go on without the father he had known for three-quarters of a century.

It is not only the death of a human member of the family that can prove devastating. On several occasions, an elderly patient with whom I was working had withdrawn into a depressed, no-point-in-living state following the death of an animal companion. What might seem to be "the depression that comes with age" can turn out to be a grief reaction to the death of an animal companion as well as to the death of a human companion.

However, the overall picture is more positive than it has usually been assumed. Older widowed persons often have effective coping abilities that help them to get on with their lives, even though they regard the death of their spouses as having been the most stressful event they have ever experienced. For example, the elderly widows studied by Bennett and Bennett (2000/2001) experienced the feelings described by stage theories but not in any particular order (no fixed sequence > no stages!). They also explained that life goes on for them but that it is not really the same life. As one widow put it:

> There's always this great hole inside that hurts, and . . . I was building a pattern, a life round it. I couldn't—you can't ever fill it, but you build a life round (p. 244).

Studies continue to find that elderly people often maintain their physical health and remaining interpersonal relationships after the death of a loved one (D'Epinay, Cavalli, & Spini 2003). They sorrow for the loss and are more likely to experience loneliness but still find meaning and satisfaction in life. As a woman a week shy of her 100th birthday told me, "There is life, dear, and there is death. What else can anyone expect?"

Elderly bereaved people often have a wealth of experience and skills that not only can be applied to reintegrating their own lives but also to enriching the lives of others.

ARE BEREAVED PEOPLE AT HIGHER RISK FOR DEATH?

Yes, in general the risk of illness and death does increase following the loss of a person who has been very important to us. "A broken heart" is not just a picturesque phrase. Research supports folk knowledge here. We should not underestimate the physical effects of sorrow and anxiety.

Differential Mortality Risk: The Statistical Pattern

Almost all studies have found excessive mortality rates for bereaved persons. This pattern holds true in Europe and Japan as well as in North America and has been consistent throughout the twentieth century. Large-scale prospective studies (Lillberg et al., 2003; Kaprio et al., 1987) found convincing evidence for greater risk of illness and death among bereaved as compared with nonbereaved people. Most subsequent studies have also found this differential, and go on to explore specific risk factors (e.g., cardiovascular stress and failure, Buckley et al., 2009). We should remember, however, that most bereaved people come through the stress of grief and continue or regain their resiliency.

Who is Most at Risk?

Some people are more at risk than others. Widows and widowers are at higher risk than married men and women. This risk is even greater for widowers. The mortality rate is higher for men than women at every adult age level, and bereavement further increases the differential.

The relationship with age is not what one might have expected. Younger adults have a relatively higher excessive mortality rate after bereavement. The death of a spouse is followed by a sudden rise in the mortality risk of bereaved young adults. Most at risk is the young man whose wife has recently died. This risk is further intensified if the death was sudden and unexpected. Bereavement-related deaths most often occur within the first six months. These findings suggest that more attention should be given to the vulnerability of bereaved young men in the period of time immediately following the death. Lichtenberg (1990) remembers having felt "out of control: one moment I was torn apart, and the next moment I was calm. It was frightening to hurt, to be numb, to feel panic, and I worried that I would collapse . . ." (p. 86). We never want to forget that there is always a human story behind the statistics. Still uncertain: the mortality risk for parents when a child has died. The available results are limited and mixed (Hendrickson, 2009).

What are the Leading Causes of Death Among the Bereaved?

Heart disease and cancer are the leading causes of death among bereaved people, just as they are for the population in general. However, there is another type of death that increases greatly after bereavement—violent deaths, especially suicide. Stroebe & Stroebe (1993b) report that within the first week after bereavement, the suicide rate for men was 66 times greater than would have been expected. The suicide rate for women was more than nine times greater than expected. Suicide shows the greatest increase among all causes of death, although heart disease accounts for most of the fatalities. This heightened risk of suicide soon after the death of a spouse has not yet received the attention it deserves.

As noted earlier, the body's ability to resist infection through the immune system can also be impaired during the turmoil of grief, as it is in other types of stressful situations (Goodkin et al., 2001).

We do not have to be medical experts to offer companionship and support to bereaved people—and by so doing, perhaps to reduce stress levels, protect immune functioning, and even save a life.

HOW WELL DO WE SUPPORT THE BEREAVED?

The widower is reducing his colleagues' anxieties when he goes right back to work and gives no indication that he expects special concern. "I am okay," he is saying, in effect, "I am not mourning." The widow releases others from obligation by refraining from displays of mourning. "She's a strong woman," her friends say with admiration. Many other cultures have expected and respected a sometimes extended period of mourning—not so with our rather impatient mainstream society today. The absence of culturally endorsed mourning behaviors too easily gives the illusion that the person is "over" the loss. This is one of the reasons why some bereaved people have fears of going crazy. All of the anxiety and confusion, all the depths of feeling, seem to be on the inside, while the rest of the world continues to move along without missing a beat. The bereaved therefore can be made to feel as though their sorrow and stress are signs of pathology or weakness.

American Society's Discomfort with Grief and Mourning

How well a culture's death system is functioning can be estimated by examining the support it provides for the bereaved. Mourning gets in the way of a society that is oriented toward time and efficiency. It does not seem to serve any real purpose. Pressures have been increasing against the expression of personal loss, with the exception of unusual circumstances such as the 9/11 terrorist attacks. There are still places in the United States where people will pause in respectful silence when a funeral procession goes by, whether or not they know the identity of the deceased. But the funeral procession has become a target of efficiency practitioners in most urban areas: "Traffic is bad enough as it is!" Similarly, there are pressures against the use of land for cemeteries. Why should the dead stand in the way of progress?

Memorialization of the dead and support for the bereaved have fallen relatively low on the list of priorities of the mainstream American death system. People still gather around for the funeral—often with reluctance—and for a short period of ritual and visiting. After that, however, the bereaved is frequently left alone. How long do colleagues sympathize with somebody who has suffered a significant loss? How long are relatives and neighbors prepared to be sensitive and supportive? I have noticed an increasing impatience with grief. It was not surprising to come across a doctoral dissertation (DiMeo, 1978) featuring a "prescribed degriefing intervention method (DIM)" that requires but a single treatment session! DIM, indeed! Quicker is cheaper, better, more cost-effective. But are we really prepared to line up for "degriefing" when overcome by profound sorrow and loss? There are still powerful local customs in which the living do offer their companionship unstintingly to the dead and the grieving. James K. Crissman (1994) describes such practices in *Living and Dying in Central Appalachia*. Perhaps our impatience with grief is one of the reasons why so much attention is given to the question of how long grief is supposed to endure. It is one of the questions most frequently raised by the public and bruited about by professionals. What would be your answer?

American society's withdrawal of support from the bereaved represents a break from most historical traditions. In some religious and ethnic groups, there remains a sense of closeness, of reconfirming bonds with each other. This may include a legitimized relationship with the dead (as in the Hmong). The survivors may have prayers to say, offerings to make, vigils to keep. There is time and opportunity for personal grief to find expression in a socially approved form. Some cultures, such as the Chinese continue the tradition of employing professional mourners to express the collective grief (e.g., Ning, 2010). The newly dead can remain as an important person during a critical period of psychological adjustment to the loss. The bereaved need not pretend that the funeral marks the end of the relationship with the parent, spouse, sibling, child, or friend. It is possible to have thoughts and feelings about the deceased, even to sense the presence vividly, without violating social norms.

The need to feel connected with those who have passed from our lives might, however, seems to be finding new avenues of expression. "Expressions of Grief on the World Wide Web" (De Vries & Roberts, 2004) documents the increasing use of online communication as an innovative means of mourning. Deaths are even finding their way into Second Life and similar Internet programs. Not long ago, mental health experts and researchers Klass, Silverman, and Nickman, (1996) urged that we give ourselves permission to establish continuing bonds with the dead, rather than trying to free ourselves of all attachments to the "lost object." This reconsideration now seems to be in progress.

MEANINGFUL HELP FOR BEREAVED PEOPLE

Society is coming to realize that we can help each other through our times of grief. Phyllis Silverman (Kastenbaum, 1993/1994), founder of the Widow-to-Widow Program, reviews the issues that had to be resolved in establishing this pioneering peer-support program.

Widow-to-Widow: The Phyllis Silverman Interview

There were no peer-support programs to deal with bereavement, grief, and mourning when Silverman was completing her doctoral studies at Harvard. It was thought that grief was a kind of illness that had to run its course. Silverman rejected this medical model.

> *When we talk of grief as illness, we make it sound like a foreign or alien object that has invaded our bodies and which we must in some way expunge, as, for example, a wound that heals after the scab falls off, or a cold that must run its course. With the "proper treatment" we can make it go away. With this model we maintain a sense of ourselves as machines. . . . We get no sense of context, of the complexity of an experience, and of its fullness (p. 251).*

Silverman observed grief as central fact of human existence, not simply an illness from which we hope to recover.

People, living or dead, are part of who and what we are. . . . We don't "get over" people. We live in a web of relationships. We are still connected to the dead. . . . Because my father died, I haven't stopped being his daughter. The self we knew with that other person is gone. We need to re-organize, find a place for this relationship, and develop other selves (p. 252).

One of her first research findings was that grief did not simply fade away after a brief period of crisis. Public health specialists at the time were endorsing a crisis theory of mental health and illness. With skillful professional intervention, the crisis should be resolved within about two weeks.

When I first offered this view to widowed women—they laughed at me! They said that if you had your act together in two years—so that your head felt screwed on, so you could look ahead—you were lucky! The more I talked with the widowed, the more I realized that our models of grief were not correct (p. 253).

Silverman came up with a different model and a different approach to helping bereaved people. This model includes the following principles:

- *Grief does not have a final outcome.* Bereavement leads to a series of changes over many years. "People grow, gain new perspective on who they are, and learn how to deal more resourcefully with their own feelings and with other people."
- *Grief can most usefully be regarded as a life transition.* Although bereavement does produce a crisis and does have significant physiological aspects, it is basically a human experience that alters one's relationship to self and others. Life does go on, but it goes on somewhat differently.
- *People can help each other.* One does not necessarily have to turn to professional assistance, although this may be indicated in some circumstances. Peer support—such as widows comforting each other—can be effective. Furthermore, when people with similar problems help each other, they do not thereby become "patients" who are dependent on the medical system.

Silverman introduced the Widow-to-Widow Program at a time when neither professional grief counselors nor other peer-support groups had yet appeared. The program was very successful and soon became replicated throughout much of the nation. Many other peer-support groups have since emerged (e.g., The Compassionate Friends, who help parents who have lost a child through death). Silverman thinks of peer support as "the first line of defense. Most of us get through major crises in our lives with help from our friends."

Although many people have found comfort in peer-support groups of various types, there are hazards here as well. Julie Wambach (1983) conducted a series of participant–observer contacts with self-help bereavement groups. She reported an inflexible philosophy that assumed widows should go through a sequence of stages of mourning in a prescribed time period. This rigid timetable and the concept of stages had no basis in fact. Many widows felt pressured by the timetable and rigid expectations. Discrimination against the older widows was also observed. As Wambach also notes, there are probably many important differences among self-help bereavement groups, so that a reasonable degree of caution is recommended. Even the best of ideas can go wrong.

Helpful and Unhelpful Responses to the Bereaved Person

Not everything that we communicate to bereaved people is helpful. Range, Walston, and Polles (1992) obtained ratings for a number of statements that are often made to bereaved people. The statements rated most and least helpful are shown in Table 11-1.

As we can see from Table 11-1, the most appreciated statements were those that expressed the individual's commitment to being there for the bereaved. The first two statements were by far the most favorably rated. Asking specific questions or reminding them of specific sources of distress (e.g., "It was so sudden!") were not felt to be helpful comments. This study implies that we should raise and answer a question of our own: "Is my intention to comfort the bereaved person or control my own anxiety?"

"No response" can be at least as painful as saying something unhelpful. The participants in

TABLE 11-1 *Five Most and Least Helpful Statements to Bereaved People*

Most Helpful	Least Helpful
"I'm here if you need somebody to talk to."	"Didn't the funeral home do a good job?"
"If there is anything I can do, please let me know."	"Did you know this was going to happen?"
"Put your faith in God."	"Was he/she in much pain?"
"Tell me how you are feeling."	"It's okay to be angry at God."
"He/she will always be in your memories."	"It was so sudden!

Source: Range et al. (1992).

Dyregrove's study (2003/2004) often felt abandoned when family, friends, and colleagues did not offer the support the bereaved had expected:

> According to the survivors, it hurt even more when network members tried to excuse their absence by claiming to have been "so busy," "having to work so much lately," etc. . . . Survivors gave a lot of examples in which network members had avoided talking about anything associated with death, or did not refer to the deceased by name. . . . Some frenetically talked about anything but what had happened and the situation of the survivor (pp. 31–32).

Emotional honesty would seem to be the basic requirement for helpful interactions with the bereaved.

Professional Help: When Is It Needed?

"Grief counseling" as such was almost unknown until recent years. It has now become an accepted mental health service when practiced by people with adequate training and experience (Wolfe, 2002). There have been many reports that counseling can be very helpful when grief is overwhelming and the bereaved person is unable to cope. However, there is controversy about the usefulness of counseling for all people who have recently experienced a bereavement.

There are advocates for providing grief counseling for most if not all bereaved people. The benefits of this service should not be restricted to traumatic or complicated grief situations. The distress and dysfunction associated with "normal" grief should not really be considered "normal"—it would be better to help people move more swiftly and securely through this ordeal. Others take a more cautious attitude. They note that most people do cope with their grief and move on with their lives without professional intervention.

The controversy became heated as overzealous counselors were charged with being "grief police." Simplistic interpretations of Kübler-Ross's (1969) presentations had led to ill-advised attempts at hustling people through "the five stages of dying." Critics of grief counseling feared that the same thing may be happening again. Fortunately, this issue does not have to be contested solely on the basis of enthusiasms and suspicions. There have been studies of bereavement interventions, so perhaps some facts would help.

The Project on Death in America sponsored an intensive analysis of all recent research on bereavement interventions. This work was carried out by the Center for the Advancement of Health, which recruited a scientific advisory committee to review and evaluate the studies (Genevo, 2003). The report (Genevo, 2003) concludes:

- There is no one "normal" way of experiencing and responding to grief. Instead, there are such tremendous individual differences that it would not be wise to apply a judgmental attitude or insist that every bereaved person should follow a "standard" procedure.
- Normal grief does not usually lead to long-term problems, and the ways in which people come to terms with loss can be positive for emotional health.
- Health problems often result from prolonged and intense grief.
- Counseling and medical interventions can be helpful for people who are overwhelmed by what is currently called "complicated" grief.

Research findings and clinical experience suggest that many bereaved people do not need professional counseling: they get by with the help of their friends. But is counseling likely to do harm to a grieving person? Recently there has been a short but lively controversy. Neimeyer (2000) contended that grief therapy is usually ineffective and perhaps even harmful for persons experiencing a normal bereavement. This statement was widely reported in the media as though an established fact. Larson and Hoyt (2007) point out that this conclusion was based on a dissertation (Fortner, 1999) that used a flawed methodology and had not received peer review or publication. Stroebe (2009) finds that the evidence supports the value of counseling when grief is overwhelming and persistent and the intervention is made by a qualified professional. There is much still to learn about the effectiveness of grief counseling in a variety of situations, but it is also clear there is no clear reason for dismissing its value.

WIDOWS IN THIRD WORLD NATIONS

We have been considering bereavement, grief, and mourning with some attention to world cultures, but mostly to our own experiences in the United States and other developed countries. There are cultures, though, in which both life and death are harder for most people. This brings us to the plight of widows in Third World nations. Stresses and challenges that are encountered even when the widow has significant support from the community. Imagine what it would be like if she had to deal not only with what most widows have to deal with but also faced the absolute devastation of her life from that point forward. This is the fate even today of many widows in Third World countries.

It has been shown that widows in Third World countries often are deprived of the most basic human rights. Margaret Owen (1996; 2002) reports that spousal bereavement is a kind of death for the woman as well, a social death. Widowhood deprives them almost completely of status (Owen, 2002):

and consigns them to the very margins of society where they suffer the most extreme forms of discrimination and stigma. Widows in these regions are generally the poorest of the poor and

least protected by the law because their lives are likely to be determined by local, patriarchal interpretations of tradition, custom, and religion. Unmarried women are the property and under the control of their fathers; married women belong to their husbands. Women are in limbo and no longer have any protector. The misery inflected upon third world widows is not a matter of chance or particular circumstance: It is rooted in cultural values and practices, and not restricted to just a few countries. Across cultures they become outcasts and are often vulnerable to physical, sexual, and mental abuse. It as if they are in some way responsible for their husband's death and must be made to suffer for this calamity for the remainder of their lives (p. 947).

The AIDS pandemic continues to create more widows who themselves are at increased risk for this disease as they become sexually vulnerable to male relatives of the deceased husband and to other men as they become impoverished and unprotected. In Nigeria and some other places, there is even the expectation that widows will submit to "ritual cleansing by sex" through taking on strangers or other men designated by her husband's family. Far from "cleansing," of course, this practice further increases the risk of contracting a sexually transmitted disease. Many other women have also been widowed and subject to rape as a consequence of violence in such nations as Afghanistan, Angola, Cambodia, Rwanda, Sierra Leone, and Uganda.

Fortunately, this large-scale abuse of widows has started to attract international attention. An organization known as Empowering Widows in Development (EWD) has been established as an umbrella group for more than 50 grass-roots organizations of widows in East Asia, South Asia, Africa, and Eastern Europe as well, where similar same conditions have been observed. Operating with limited funds and not much cooperation from some world governments, advocates are hoping to educate the public about this mostly neglected tragedy and encourage corrective efforts. There is a long way to go if widows in third world countries are to receive acceptance and support. Remigius Nwabueze (2010) reports that widows in Sub-Saharan Africa continue to be mistreated in almost every way. He notes that widows often are even denied her right to control the time, place, and manner of her husband's burial—and therefore deprived of this sociospiritual connection as well as any other rights. The grief of a widowed African woman is seldom tempered by the prospect of a hopeful life ahead.

ON THE FUTURE OF GRIEVING AND MOURNING

How we grieve and mourn are processes rooted in whatever might be universal in human nature, but also in society's currents and cross currents. Here we call attention to several significant changes that could become more pervasive in the years ahead.

- *Who will mourn for the mourners?* A death has occurred among people who preserve a way of life that has spanned many centuries. There is an intense and moving response in, for example, a Bulgarian mountain village and an Israeli desert settlement (Gamliel, 2007). Central to the ritual is a passionate lament expressed by

an elderly woman. She explains, sorrows, and rages for the whole community. Less and less is this traditional event taking place. There are few if any to replace the woman who it might be said conveys the soul of the people at the time of parting. Soon there may be nobody to mourn in the old way, and in this silence something of the people's tradition might be forever.

- *Growing up dead? The grief of orphans and other lost peoples.* Campaigns of terror have continued into the twenty-first century, often accompanied by a breakdown in economy, education, and social support. Survivors of childhood trauma and deprivation are at risk for chronic, unresolved grief that is likely to impair their own lives and those around them.

- *Imitating the dead? Dazing through oblivion.* It turns out that heroin addiction often originates in grief (Allen, 2007). People already stressed and depressed in their deprived urban surroundings are particularly vulnerable to a drugged escape from the pain of life after a traumatic bereavement. Deaths that occur to the wrong person— say, a child—or the wrong way—violence or

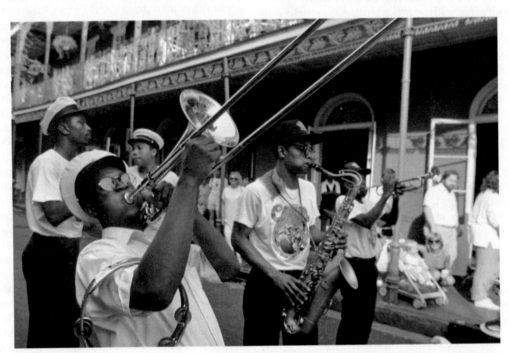

A New Orleans tradition: the band plays a solemn procession on the way to the funeral, then celebrates life on the way back with the boisterous, "When the Saints Go Marching In!"

unrelieved suffering—can be overwhelming, especially if social support is lacking.

- *A sorrow management theory?* It is becoming clearer that sorrow and anxiety are closely related (Horwitz, & Wakefield, 2007; Straube, 2009). More attention can be expected to be paid to the development of a sorrow management theory comparable in some ways to terror management theory in its integration of individual and societal dynamics (Kastenbaum, 2009b; Kastenbaum & Heflick, 2010–2011). This could provide a more coherent approach to the mix of thoughts and feelings that we experience in bereavement situations, while also evaluating and improving societal response.

■ SUMMARY

A person important to us dies. This loss is known as bereavement. We experience a shifting mix of feelings including anxiety, anger, and confusion. This condition is known as grief. We express our bereavement and loss to others in ways that are culturally patterned. This is known as mourning. We have seen that grief does not necessarily run its course in a year or any other fixed period of time. Instead, each individual and family has its own pattern of response and recovery that depends much on the nature of the death and the survivor's own general patterns of coping with stress and loss. Grief is more than an emotional state: It also is accompanied by the body's response to stress, especially in the neuroendocrine system. The health and even the survival of the survivors can be endangered by a severe or prolonged stress reaction.

There are marked cultural differences in the way people have learned to respond to a death, and these differences are represented within the diverse U.S. population as well as in other societies, as we have seen through numerous examples. Freud's influential grief-work theory emphasizes that it is a long and arduous process to accept the reality of the death and liberate one's self from the emotional pull of the deceased. Many counselors and researchers now believe that it is not necessary to cast off the lost loved one; instead one can reconstruct the relationship and cherish the continuing bonds in a revised and more adaptive way.

We have also seen that people differ considerably in how they recover—or fail to recover—from bereavement. Gender differences and the way in which the person died (e.g., suddenly or with time to prepare for the loss) are among the important influencing factors, but so is the nature of the relationship between the deceased person and the survivor. Particular attention was given to grief and recovery when the deceased person is a child or spouse, as well as bereavement among grandparents and other elderly people. The limited support given to bereaved people in the United States remains a subject of concern, and suggestions were offered for providing support to the bereaved people in our own lives. There is now evidence that counseling can be effective for people with intense and prolonged grief responses but that it is seldom useful and can even be harmful for people experiencing normal grief who are coping with loss in their own distinctive ways. There is now a growing consensus that counseling is most effective when requested by the grieving person.

■ REFERENCES

Adamolekun, K. (1999) Bereavement salutations among the Yorubas of Western Nigeria. *Omega, Journal of Death and Dying, 39*, 277–286.

Allen, C. (2007). The poverty of death: Social class, urban deprivation, and the criminological consequences of sequestration of death. *Mortality, 12*, 80–94.

Archer, J. (2001). Grief from an evolutionary perspective. In M. S. Stroebe, R. O. Hansson, W. Stroebe, & H. Schut (Eds.), *Handbook of bereavement research* (pp. 263–284). Washington, DC: American Psychological Association.

Archer, J. (2009). Theories of grief: Past, present, and future perspectives. In M. S. Stroebe, R. O. Hansson, H. Schut, & W. Stroebe (Eds.), *Handbook of bereavement research and practice* (pp. 45–66). Washington, DC: American Psychological Association.

Balk, D. (2004). Recovery following bereavement: An examination of the concept. *Death Studies, 28*, 361–374.

Barrera, M., D'Augustino, N. M., Schneiderman, G., Tallett, S., Spencer, L., & Jovcevska, V. (2007). Patterns of parental bereavement following the loss of a child and related factors. *Omega, Journal of Death and Dying, 55*, 145–167.

Becvar, D. S. (2001). *In the Presence of Grief: Helping Family Members Resolve Death*. New York: Guilford Press.

Beder, J. (2002). Grief: Anticipatory. In R. Kastenbaum (Ed.), *Macmillan encyclopedia of death and dying* (Vol. 1, pp. 353–355). New York: Macmillan.

Beder, J. (2004). *Voices of Bereavement. A Casebook for Grief Counselors*. New York: Brunner-Routledge.

Belicki, K., Gulko, N., Ruzycki, K., & Aristotle, J. (2003). Sixteen years of dreams following spousal bereavement. *Omega, Journal of Death and Dying, 47*, 93–106.

Bennett, K. M., Bennett, G. (2000/2001). "And there's always this great hole inside that hurts": An empirical study of bereavement in later life. *Omega, Journal of Death and Dying, 42*, 237–252.

Bliatout, B. T. (1993). Hmong death customs: Traditional and acculturated. In D. P. Irish, K. F. Lundquist, & V. J. Nelsen (Eds.), *Ethnic variations in dying, death, and grief* (pp. 79–100). Washington, DC: Taylor & Francis.

Bowlby, J. (1969). *Attachment*. New York: Basic Books.

Bowlby, J. (1973). *Separation*. New York: Basic Books.

Bowlby, J. (1980). *Loss*. New York: Basic Books.

Bozeman, J. C. (1999). A journey through grief: An analysis of an adult child's grief in the loss of a mother. *Illness, Crisis, and Loss, 7*, 91–99.

Buckley, T., McKinley, S., Toffler, G., & Bartrop, R. (2009). Cardiovascular risk in early bereavement: A literature review and proposed mechanisms. *International Journal of Nursing Studies. 47*, 229–238.

Cacciatore, J. (2007). Effects of support groups on post traumatic stress responses in women experiencing stillbirth. *Omega, Journal of Death and Dying, 55*, 71–90.

Campbell, J. (1949). *The hero with a thousand faces*. Princeton: NJ: Princeton University Press.

Charuvastra, A., & Cloitre, M. (2008). Social bonds and posttraumatic stress disorder. *The annual review of psychology*. http://www.annualreviews.org/doi/abs/10.1146/annurev.psych.58.110405.085650.

Chethik, N. (2001). *Father Loss. How sons of all ages come to terms with the deaths of their dads*. New York: Hyperion.

Clark, C. A. (2009). Tears in Lucretius. In T. Fogen (Ed.), *Tears in the Graeco-Roman world* (pp. 161–178). Berlin: de Gruyer.

Colp, R., Jr. (1975). The evolution of Charles Darwin's thoughts about death. *Journal of Thanatology, 3*, 191–206.

Conner, P. (1996). *Letting go: The grief experience*. Carrolton, GA: AUM Productions.

Cordell, A. S., & Thomas, N. (1997). Perinatal loss: Intensity and duration of emotional recovery. *Omega, Journal of Death and Dying, 35*, 297–308.

Crissmann, J. K. (1994). *Death and Dying in Central Appalachia*. Urbana, IL: University of Illinois Press.

Darwin, C. (1872). *The expression of the emotions in man and animals*. London: Murrey.

De Bonafini (1991). Life Stories. In S. Castro-Klarén, S. Molloy, and B. Sarlo (Eds.), *Women's writing in Latin America: An anthology*, (pp. 280–284). Boulder, CO: Westview.

De Frain, J., Martens, L., Stork, J., & Stork, W. (1990/1991). The psychological effects of a stillbirth on surviving family members. *Omega, Journal of Death and Dying, 22*, 81–108.

D'Epinay, C. J. L., Cavalli, S., & Spini, D. (2003). The death of a loved one: Impact on health and relationships in very old age. *Omega, Journal of Death and Dying, 47*, 265–284.

De Vries, B., & Roberts, P. (Eds.). (2004). Expressions of Grief on the World Wide Web. Special issue of *Omega, Journal of Death and Dying, 49*, 1.

DiMeo, V. V. (1978). *Mourning and melancholia: A prescribed degriefiing intervention method (DIM) for the reduction of depression and/or belated grief*. Unpublished doctoral dissertation. United States International University, San Diego.

Dyregrov, K. (2003/2004). Micro-sociological analysis of social support following traumatic bereavement: Unhelpful and avoidant responses from the community. *Omega, Journal of Death and Dying, 48*, 23–44.

Engel, G. L. (1963). A unified theory of health and disease. In D. Ingele (Ed.), *Life and disease* (pp. 7–24). New York: Basic Books.

Erker, D. S. (2009). Women's tears in ancient Roman ritual. In T. Fogen (Ed.), *Tears in the Graeco-Roman world* (pp. 135–160). Berlin: de Gruyter.

Field, N. P. (2006). Continuing bonds in adaptation to bereavement. Introduction. *Death Studies, 30*, 709–714.

Follinger, S. (2009). Tears and crying in archaic Greek poetry. In T. Fogen (Ed.), *Tears in the Graeco-Roman world* (pp. 17–36). Berlin: de Gruyter.

Freed, P. J., & Mann, J. J. (2007). Sadness and loss: Toward a neurobiopsychosocial model. *American Journal of Psychiatry, 164*, 28–34.

Freud, S. (1959). Mourning and melancholia. *Collected papers* (Vol. 4). New York: Basic Books. (Original work published 1919.)

Fulton, R. (2003). Anticipatory mourning: A critique of the concept. *Mortality, 8*, 342–351.

Furman, E. F. (1974). *A child's parent dies.* New Haven: Yale University Press.

Gamliel, T. (2007). "Wailing lore" in a Yeminite-Israeli community: Bereavement, expertise, and therapy. *Social Science & Medicine, 65,* 1501–1511.

Gennep, A. V. (1960). *The rites of passage.* Chicago: University of Chicago Press. (Original work published 1909.).

Glick, L. O., Weiss, R. S., & Parkes, C. M. (1974). *The first year of bereavement.* New York: Wiley.

Goodkin, K., Baldewitz, T. T., Blaney, N. T., Asthana, D., Kumar, M., & Zheng, W. L. (2001). Physiological effects of bereavement and bereavement support group interventions. In M. S. Stroebe, R. O. Hansson, W. Stroebe, and H. Schut (Eds.), *Handbook of bereavement research* (pp. 671–704). Washington, DC: American Psychological Association.

Gorer, G. D. (1977). *Grief and mourning.* New York: Arno Press.

Groom, W. (2002). *A storm in Flanders. Tragedy and triumph on the Western front.* New York: Atlantic Monthly Press.

Guyer, B., Martin, J. A., MacDorman, M. F., Anderson, R. N., & Strobino, D. M. (1997). Annual summary of vital statistics—1996. *Pediatrics, 100,* 905–918.

Hall, M., & Irwin, M. (2001). Physiological indices of functioning in bereavement. In M. S. Stroebe, R. O. Hansson, W. Stroebe, & H. Schut (Eds.), *Handbook of bereavement research* (pp. 473–492). Washington, DC: American Psychological Association.

Hendrickson, K. C. (2009). Morbidity, mortality, and parental grief: A review of the literature on the relationship between death of a child and health of parents. *Palliative Support Care, 7,* 109–119.

Hogan, N. S., Worden, J. W., & Schmidt, L. A. (2003/2004). *Omega, Journal of Death and Dying, 48,* 263–278.

Horwitz, A. V., Wakefield, J. C. (2007). *The loss of sadness: How psychiatry transformed normal sorrow into depressive disorder.* New York: Oxford University Press.

Hunt, J. (2004). Sole survivor: A case study to evaluate the dual-process model of grief in multiple loss. *Illness, Crisis, & Loss, 12,* 284–298.

Ingram, K. M., Jones, D. A, & Smith, N. G. (2001). Adjustment among people who have experienced AIDS-related multiple loss: The role of unsupportive social interactions, social support, and coping. *Omega, Journal of Death and Dying, 43,* 287–310.

Jacobs, S. (1999). *Traumatic grief.* New York: Brunner/Mazel.

Kappas, A. (2009). Mysterious tears: The phenomenon of crying from the perspective of social neuroscience. In T. Fogen (Ed.), *Tears in the Graeco-Roman world* (pp. 419-438). Berlin: de Gruyter.

Kaprio, J., Koskenvuo, M., & Rita, H. (1987). Mortality after bereavement: A prospective study of 95,647 widowed persons. *American Journal of Public Health, 77,* 283–287.

Kastenbaum, R. (2011). Bereavement. In M. T. Abou-Saleh, C.L.E. Catona & A. Kumar (eds.), *Principles and practice of Geriatric Psychiatry,* (3rd ed., pp. 555–559). New York: Wiley Blackwell.

Kastenbaum, R. (1987). Vicarious grief: An intergenerational phenomenon? *Death Studies, 11,* 447–454.

Kastenbaum, R. (1993/1994). Phyllis R. Silverman: An Omega interview. *Omega, Journal of Death and Dying, 28,* 251–260.

Kastenbaum, R. (2004a). *On our way. The final passage through life and death.* Berkeley: University of California Press.

Kastenbaum, R. (2004b) Death writ large. *Death Studies, 28,* 375–392.

Kastenbaum, R. (2009a). Grieving in contemporary society. M. S. Stroebe, R. O. Hansson, H. Schut & W. Stroebe (Eds.), *Handbook of bereavement research and practice. A twenty first century perspective* (pp. 67–85). Washington, DC: American Psychological Association.

Kastenbaum, R. (2009b). Should we manage terror—if we could? *Omega, Journal of Death and Dying, 59,* 271–304.

Kastenbaum, R., & Heyflick, N. (2010–2011). Sad to say: Is it time for sorrow management theory? *Omega, Journal of Death and Dying, 62,* 305–327.

Kauffman, J. (2005). *Guidebook on helping persons with mental retardation mourn.* Amityville, NY: Baywood.

Kim, K., & Jacobs, S. (1993). Neuroendocrine changes following bereavement. In M. S. Stroebe, W. Stroebe, & R. O. Hansson (Eds), *Handbook of bereavement* (pp. 143–159). London & New York: Cambridge University Press.

Klass, D. (1988). *Parental grief: Solace and resolution.* New York: Springer.

Klass, D. (1992/1993). The inner representation of the dead child and the worldviews of bereaved parents. *Omega, Journal of Death and Dying, 26,* 255–273.

Klass, D. (2002). Grief and mourning in cross-cultural perspective. In R. Kastenbaum (Ed.), *Macmillan encyclopedia of death and dying* (Vol. 1, pp. 382–389). New York: Macmillan.

Klass, D., Silverman, P. R., & Nickman, S. L. (Eds.). (1996). *Continuing bonds: New understandings of grief.* Bristol, PA: Taylor & Francis.

Knapp, R. J. (1986). *Beyond endurance.* New York: Schocken Books.

Kübler-Ross, E. (1969). *On death and dying.* New York: Prentice-Hall.

Larson, D. G. & Hoyt, W. T. (2007). What has become of grief counseling? An evaluation of the empirical foundation of the new pessimism. *Professional Psychology: Research and Practice, 38,* 347–355.

Laudenslager, M. K. (1988). The psychology of loss: Lessons from humans and nonhuman primates. *Journal of Social Issues, 44,* 19–36.

Laudenslager, M. K., Boccia M. L., and Reitre, M. L. (1993). Consequences of loss in nonhuman primates, individual differences. In M. S. Stroebe, W. Stroebe, and R. G. Hansson (Eds.), *Handbook of bereavement* (pp. 129–142). Cambridge, UK: Cambridge University Press.

Lavin, C. (1989). Disenfranchised grief and the developmentally disabled. In K. J. Doka (Ed.), *Disenfranchised grief* (pp. 229–238). Lexington, MA: Lexington Books.

Levy, L. H., Derby, J. F., & Martinowski, K. S. (1992). The question of who participates in bereavement research and the Bereavement Risk Index. *Omega, Journal of Death and Dying, 25,* 225–238.

Lee, K. (2010). Hmong funeral: A guidebook for teachers to better understand the process their Hmong students experience in a time of family loss. http://hdl.handle.net/10211.4/179.

Lichtenberg, P. A. (1990). Remembering Becky. *Omega, Journal of Death and Dying, 21,* 83–89.

Lillberg, K., Verkasalo, P. K., Kaprio, J., Teppo, L., Helenius, H., & Kosekenvuo, M. (2003). Stressful life events and risk of breast cancer in 10,808 women: A cohort study. *American Journal of Epidemiology, 157,* 415–423.

Lindemann, E. (1944). The symptomatology and management of acute grief. *American Journal of Psychiatry, 101,* 141–148.

Lindstrom, T. C. (1995). Experiencing the presence of the dead: Discrepancies in "the sensing experiences" and their psychological concomitants. *Omega, Journal of Death and Dying, 31,* 11–22.

Linn-Gust, M. (April, 2007). From the backyard to the pet bed: The changing role of animals in society.

The Forum (Association for Death Education and Counseling), *33,* 1, 3.

Maciejewski, P. K., Zhang, B., Block, S. D., & Prigerson, H. G. (2007). An empirical examination of the stage theory of grief. *Journal of the American Medical Association, 297,* 716–723.

Maciejewski, P. K., Zhang, B., Block, S. D., & Prigerson, H. G. (2007). The stage theory of grief—reply. *Journal of the American Medical Association, 297,* 761–765.

Mathews, L. T., & Marwit, S. J. (2003/2004). Examining the assumptive world views of parents bereaved by accident, murder, and illness. *Omega, Journal of Death and Dying, 48,* 115–136.

McCrae, R. R., & Costa, P. T., Jr. (1993). Psychological resilience among widowed men and women: A 10-year follow-up of a national sample. In M. S. Stroebe, W. Stroebe, & R. O. Hansson (Eds.), *Handbook of bereavement,* (pp. 196–207). Cambridge, UK: Cambridge University Press.

Milo, E. M. (1997). Maternal responses to the life and death of a child with a developmental disability. *Death Studies, 21,* 443–476.

Moos, N. L. (1995). An integrative model of grief. *Death Studies, 19,* 337–364.

Moss, M., & Rubenstein, R. L. (2010). National Institute of Aging Grant 1R01Ago318096-ARRA: *The meaning of the death of the first elderly parent: A family perspective.*

Moss, M. S., Moss, S. Z., & Hansson, R. O. (2001). Bereavement and old age. In M. S. Stroebe, R. O. Hansson, W. Stroebe, & H. Schut (Eds.), *Handbook of bereavement research* (pp. 241–260). Washington, DC: American Psychological Association.

Myron, V., & Witter, B. (2008). *Dewey.* NY: Grand Central.

Nehari, M., Grebler, D., & Toren, A. (2007). A voice unheard: Grandparents' grief over children who died of cancer. *Mortality, 12,* 71–80.

Neimeyer, R., van Dyke, J. G., & Pennebaker, J. W. (2009). Narrative medicine: Writing through bereavement. In H. Chochinov & W. Breitbart (Eds.), *Handbook of psychiatry in palliative medicine* (pp. 454–459). New York: Oxford.

Ning, C. (2010, July 23). Performing at funerals: Professional mourners in Chonking and Chengdu. *Danwei.* www.danwei.org.

Nwabjueze, R. M. (2010). Securing widows' sepulchral rights through the Nigerian constitution. *Harvard Human Rights, 23,* 141–150.

Owen, M. (1996). *A world of widows*. London: ZED Books.

Owen, M. (2002). Widows in third world nations. In R. Kastenbaum (Ed.), *Macmillan encyclopedia of death* (Vol. 2, pp. 947–952). New York: Macmillan.

Parkes, C. M. (2006*). Love & loss: The roots of grief and its complications*. New York: Taylor &: Francis.

Parkes, C. M. (2001). *Bereavement* (3rd ed.). New York: International Universities Press.

Parkes, C. M., & Weiss, R. S. (1983). *Recovery from bereavement*. New York: Basic Books.

Peppers, L. G., & Knapp, R. J. (1980). *Motherhood and mourning. Perinatal death*. New York: Praeger.

Prigerson, H. G., Horowitz, M. J., Jacobs, S. C., Parkes, C. M., Aslan, M., et al. (2009) Prolonged grief disorder: Psychometric validation of criteria proposed for *DSM-V* and *ICD-11*. PLoS Med 6: e1000121. doi:10.1371/journal.pmed.1000121.

Prothero, D. (1997) Origin of the term "half mast" or half staff. http://flagspot.net/flags/xf-half.html#origin.

Rando, T. A. (1992/1993). The increasing prevalence of complicated mourning: the onslaught is just beginning. *Omega, Journal of Death and Dying, 26*, 43–60.

Rando, T. A. (2002). Bereavement, vicarious. In R. Kastenbaum (Ed.), *Macmillan encyclopedia of death and dying* (Vol. 1, pp. 59–60). New York: Macmillan.

Range, L. (2002). Grief: Traumatic. In R. Kastenbaum (Ed.), *Macmillan encyclopedia of death and dying* (Vol. 1, pp. 379–382). New York: Macmillan.

Range, L. M., Walston, A., & Polles, P. M. (1992). Helpful and unhelpful comments after suicide, homicide, accident, or natural death. *Omega, Journal of Death and Dying, 25*, 25–32.

Reynolds, J. J. (2003/2004). Stillbirth: To hold or not to hold. *Omega, Journal of Death and Dying, 48*, 85–88.

Rodrigues, S. M., LeDoux, J. F., & Sapolsky, R. M. (2009). The influence of stress hormones on fear circuitry. *Annual review of neural science, 32*, 289–313, http://www.annualreviews.org/doi/abs/10.1146/annurev.neuro.051508.135620?journalCode=neuro.

Rosen, E. J. (1998) *Families facing death*. San Francisco: Jossey-Bass.

Rosenblatt, P. C. (1983). *Bitter, bitter tears*. Minneapolis: University of Minnesota Press.

Rowling, L. (1995). The disenfranchising grief of teachers. *Omega, Journal of Death and Dying, 31*, 317–330.

Rubin, S. S., & Malkinson, R. (2001). Parental response to child loss across the life cycle. In M. S. Stroebe, W. Stroebe, and R. O. Hansson (Eds.), *Handbook of bereavement research* (pp. 219–240). Cambridge, UK: Cambridge University Press.

Schormans, A. F. (2004). Experiences following the deaths of disabled foster children: "We don't feel like 'foster' parents." *Omega, Journal of Death and Dying, 49*, 347–370.

Schut, H. A. W., Stroebe, M. S., Boelen, P. A., & Zijerveld, A. M. (2006). Continuing relationships with the deceased: Disentangling bonds and grief. *Death Studies, 30, 757–766*.

Schwab, R. (2002). Grief: Family. In R. Kastenbaum (Ed.), *Macmillan encyclopedia of death and dying* (Vol. 1, pp. 362–366). New York: Macmillan.

Selder, F., Kachoyeanos, M., Baisch, M. J., Gissler, M., Santos, S. R. (Eds.). (1997). *Enduring grief: True stories of personal loss*. Philadelphia: The Charles Press.

Silverman, P. (2003). Continuing bonds. In R. Kastenbaum (Ed.), *Macmillan encyclopedia of death and dying* (Vol. 1, pp. 184–188). New York: Macmillan.

Silverman, P. (2009). Raising grieving children. www.psychologytoday.com/blog/raising-grievimg-children/200907/medeicalizing-grief.

Sprang, G., & McNeil, J. (1995). *The many faces of bereavement*. New York: Brunner/Maazel.

Stamberg, S. (2008, April 18). "Dear first lady": Letters offer glimpse of history. http://www.npr.org/templates/story.php?storyId=89723829.

Stroebe, M. S. (2001). Introduction: Concerns and issues in contemporary research on bereavement. In M. S. Stroebe, W. Stroebe, R. O. Hansson, and H. Schut (Eds.), *Handbook of bereavement research* (pp. 3–22). Cambridge, UK: Cambridge University Press.

Stroebe, M. S. (2009). *Beyond the broken heart: Mental and physical health consequences of losing a loved one*. Utrecht, Netherlands: Utrecht University.

Stroebe, M. S., & Schut, H. (2001). Models of coping with bereavement: A review. In M. Stroebe, W. Stroebe, & R. O Hansson (Eds.), *Handbook of bereavement research* (pp. 375–404). Cambridge UK: Cambridge University Press.

Stroebe, M. S., & Stroebe, W. (1993). The mentality of bereavement: a review. In M. S. Stroebe, W Stroebe, and R O. Hansson (Eds.), *Handbook of bereavement research* (pp. 175–195). Cambridge, UK: Cambridge University Press.

Stroebe, M. S., & Stroebe, W. (2001). The mortality of bereavement: A review. In M. S. Stroebe, W. Stroebe, & R. O. Hansson (Eds.), *Handbook of bereavement research* (pp. 175–195). Cambridge, UK: Cambridge University Press.

Stroebe, W., Abakoumkin, G., & Stroebe, M. S. (2010). Beyond depression: Yearning for the loss of a loved one. *Omega, Journal of Death and Dying, 61*, 85–101.

Talbot, K. (1998/1999). Mothers now childless: Personal transformation after the death of an only child. *Omega, Journal of Death and Dying, 38*, 167–186.

Terkel, S. (2001). Will the circle be unbroken? *Reflections on death, rebirth, and human hunger for a faith.* New York: New Press.

Thornton, S. W. (2000). Grief transformed: The mothers of Plaza de Mayo. *Omega, Journal of Death and Dying, 41*, 279–290.

Trout, N. (2008). *A day of humor, healing, and hope in my life as an animal surgeon.* New York: Broadway.

Turner, V. (1969). The ritual process: Structure and anti-structure. Chicago: Aldine.

Turner, V. (1992). Death and the dead in the pilgrimage process. In E. Turner (Ed.), *Blazing the trail. Way marks in the exploration of symbols.* Tucson: University of Arizona Press.

Umberson, D., & Henderson, K. (1992). The social construction of death in the Gulf War. *Oms. (April 18, 2008). Omega, Journal of Death and Dying, 25*, 1–16.

Walker, A. (1988). *To hell with dying.* San Diego: Harcourt Brace Jovanovich.

Wambach, J. A. (1983). *Timetables for grief and mourning with and without support groups.* Unpublished doctoral dissertation, Arizona State University, Tempe.

Waskowic, T. D., & Chartier, B. M. (2003). Attachment and the experience of grief following the loss of a spouse. *Omega, Journal of Death and Dying, 47*, 77–91.

Weinfield, I. I. (1990). An expanded perinatal bereavement support committee. *Death Studies, 4*, 241–252.

Weisman, A. D. (1990/1991). Bereavement and companion animals. *Omega, Journal of Death and Dying, 22*, 241–248.

White, D. L. (1999). Grandparent participation in times of family bereavement. In B. de Vries (Ed.), *End of life issues* (pp. 145–166). New York: Springer.

Wolfe, B. (2002). Grief counseling and therapy. In R. Kastenbaum (Ed.), *Macmillan encyclopedia of death and dying* (Vol. 1, pp. 389–393). New York: Macmillan.

Worden, W. (1991). *Grief counseling and grief therapy: A handbook for the mental health practitioner.* (Rev. ed.). New York: Springer.

Wortman, C. B., & Silver, R. C. (1989). The myths of coping with loss. *Journal of Counseling and Clinical Psychology, 57*, 349–357.

Wortman, C. B., & Silver, R. C. (1992). Reconsidering assumptions about coping with loss: An overview of current research. In S. H. Filipp, L. Montada, & M. Lerner (Eds.), *Life crises and experiences of loss in adulthood* (pp. 341–365). London: Cambridge University Press.

Wortman, C. B., & Silver, R. C. (2001). The myths of coping with loss revisited. In M. S. Stroebe, R. O. Hansson, W. Stroebe, & H. Schut (Eds.), *Handbook of bereavement research* (pp. 405–430). Cambridge, UK: Cambridge University Press.

■ GLOSSARY

Anticipatory grief Anxiety and sorrow experienced prior to an expected death.

Attachment behavior Originally, the communications and actions by which a mother and her young seek to preserve their proximity and security. Now, the same in relation to any individuals.

Bereavement The status of having lost a family member, friend, colleague, or other significant person through death.

Continuing bonds A meaningful relationship with a deceased loved one that enhances rather than interferes with ongoing life.

Disenfranchised grief A response to a death in which the individual is not regarded as having the right to grieve and must keep the sorrow hidden.

Dissociative flight An extreme avoidant or denial response to a death.

Grief The complex emotional, mental, social, and physical response to the death of a loved one.

Grief-work theory The process of gradually accepting the reality of the loss and liberating oneself from attachment to the deceased (Freud).

Intrapsychic Within the mind.

Mourning The expression of the sorrow of loss and grief in a manner understood and approved by the culture.

Spontaneous memorialization Voluntary public response to the death of a person by violence; characterized by expression of personal feelings and bringing mementos to the site of the death.

Traumatic grief The intense response to a death that has occurred in a sudden and violent manner.

■ ON FURTHER THOUGHT . . .

What is the future of grieving and mourning?

Consider what has already happened. Once infants and children were at greatest risk for death. Families grieved intensely, but there was also a powerful theme of fatalism: so many children die; that's the way it is. Today in fortunate nations many people reach or exceed the Biblical allotment of three-score-and-ten. If their deaths to be grieved and their lives celebrated, it will seldom be by their parents. Who will be grieving and mourning and how when long lives fade into death?

Throughout much of human history people lived patterned lives: a continuity of kin, places, activities, beliefs. The United States and many other societies are now much more mobile, with discontinuities and fragmentation of life patterns partially disguised by mass media illusions of unity and belonging. What is becoming of grieving and mourning as people less often die from a coherent, patterned way of life that will mean what to whom? And what of the challenge to faith, justice, and meaning in a world where many become victims to devastation and violence? How—and again, who—will grieve and mourn?

It is now your turn to observe and reflect. What is the future of grief and mourning, and how would we prefer to see it take shape?

Useful online resources:

Bereaved Parents of the USA
    www.bereavedparentsusa.org
The Compassionate Friends
    www.compassionatefriends.org
Concerns of Police Survivors (COPS)
    www.nationalcops.org
Dougy Center for Grieving Children
    www.grievingchild.org
GriefNet
    www.rivendell.org
    info@griefshare.org
Mothers Against Drunk Driving (MADD)
    www.madd.org
National Organization of Parents of Murdered Children
    www.pomc.com
Pet Grief Support Page
    www.petloss.com
SHARE: Pregnancy and Infant Loss Support
    http://www.nationalshare.org/
SIDS Alliance
    www.SIDSalliance.org
Society of Military Widows
    www.militarywidows.org
WidowNet
    www.widownet.org

Many nations honor one of their unknown soldiers. This monument in Philadelphia pairs a soldier who fell on this site during the Revolutionary War with General George Washington. Nobody knows for sure whether this soldier fought for or against the revolution.

The Funeral Process

I didn't expect him to pull a gun on me. But suddenly it was in his hand and pointed my way. "That's a surprise," I said, lamely. "I don't like surprises. That's why I carry." The oldest respondent in my little community survey explained that he could not afford to be a victim: nobody else would do what he had to do.
—A cloudy morning in McKeesport, Pennsylvania

Cremation diamonds made from ashes are available in brilliant and beautiful yellows, blues, greens, and now, red. Like a sunset captured in time of a wave upon the ocean, each cremation diamond will have its own individual hue within the color family you select.
—Commercial website (2010)

Win a pre-paid cremation. Complete all of the reply slip information and you will be eligible for a drawing each month.
—Advertisement received by author (2008)

In America, the First World War remains a largely forgotten conflict. It has no national monument on the Washington Mall, no blockbuster film, no image equivalent to soldiers' raising the flag on Iwo Jima.
—Tony Dokouph (February 18, 2007, p. 50)

No person shall picket or engage in other protest activities, nor shall any association or corporation cause picketing or other protest activities to occur, within three hundred feet of any funeral process.
—Quoted from Ohio statutes by Nieri Mathis Rutledge (2008)

To look at a skeleton as the missing relative of a person I might pass on the street was dangerous: it would challenge my stamina for the work we had to do. . . . The bones were almost shouting at me, and it was the stress-based fatigue I was working under that made this shouting so painful.
—Clea Koff (2004, p. 154)

"Our Father, who art in heaven," the 17 year-old said, shackled to four other teen-age inmates, "hallowed be thy name. Thy kingdom come. Thy will be done."

—Judi Villa (2004)

The wind blew the head down one night in 1685. A sentry secreted it beneath his cloak and took it home. Then began its long wandering, passing from hand to hand and indignity to indignity before obtaining a decent burial almost two centuries later.

—Edwin Murphy (1995, p. 20)

The parent who brought her child to see a body followed a passed-on narrative tradition for the African American community. Another explained that he planned to bring his children back to the funeral home to let them understand "you're not too young to die."

—Karla FC Holloway (2002, p. 136)

Religious definitions of individuality have become less prominent in the twentieth and twenty-first centuries. . . . Crucifixes and crosses no longer constitute the marker's centre or apex. Instead it has become customary to put the name and/or portrait of the deceased much more central. The references to the particular identity of the deceased push the other-worldly references to the margins. The [memory of the] deceased is moved into the centre of the social rites of remembrance. . . . Individualisation goes at the cost of religious frames of meaning, but the possibility of an individual definition of individuality is made possible within and by society.

—Raf Vanderstraeten (2009, p. 3)

. . . approximately two thousand men, armed with rocket-propelled grenades, explosives, and shovels, demolished the cemetery built around the shrine of a local saint in Aden. Not only was his sanctuary destroyed along with some elaborate wood décor, but many graves were exhumed and their remains burnt. A bulldozer had even been brought along to level the graves.

—Ondrez Beranek & Pavel Tupek (2009, p. 4)

There are powerful reasons for respecting the dead and their physical remains. The most powerful reason might be the most personal, as upon the death of a person we have loved. However, there are also reasons that extend beyond our personal relationships.

I respect the dead because:

- This also shows respect to the people who were close to them;
- It would violate social expectations if I did not show respect;

- It is difficult go on with our individual and communal lives until feelings and issues aroused by the death have been settled amicably;
- I am troubled by death, so this is a way to do something positive;
- The dead have moved into a spirit realm whose god or gods I must respect;
- The spirits of the dead might take revenge on me if I did not show respect;
- I hope that my physical remains will be treated with respect when the time comes.

You might not agree with all of these statements, but you probably don't disagree with all of them, either. Furthermore, as a decent person you probably don't have to think twice about treating the dead and their remains with respect.

It's all the more striking, then, that there have been so many exceptions. And, as usual, we can learn from the exceptions as well as the more common practices. We will also see that the dead are often caught up in societal change and conflict.

A SAMPLER OF RESPONSES TO THE DEAD

The man with the gun explained: He had lived in the same neighborhood all his life, but it stopped being the same neighborhood years ago. Now it was mostly warehouses and closed-down factories. His mother and father were still there, along with most all of family and friends. Somebody had to tend the graves at the nearly forgotten *cemetery*. That was his obligation, his connection, his satisfaction. These days, people were getting mugged for the loose change in their pockets. Somebody thinks he can't take care of himself, they'd be dead wrong.

"Ashes to ashes!" How about ashes to diamonds? We have a choice of Web-based vendors who are eager to compact and shape our most cherished love ones into a brilliant gem. The funeral process has always been about transition and transformation. Is ash-diamonding an example of commercialism going off the deep end, or is it just one way to ease the pain of loss?

Pre-prepared funeral tributes. Solve funeral eulogy problems for ONLY $15. These funeral tributes come in sets of three, all of which are about one minute long. They are especially written to

enable you to mix and match them. . . . Send us your credit card details. (A commercial website)

I was dead in the sights of two funeral enterprises when one invited me to participate in a drawing for a pre-paid cremation, and another (above) to purchase a pre-paid funeral tribute. Perhaps this was treating "Occupant's" future corpse with respect. Who wouldn't want to "solve funeral *eulogy* problems," and "mix and match" the wonderful things that will be said about us? Or perhaps these solicitations are simply making it clear that death, not long ago taboo in U. S. culture, has now been embraced as a source of marketing opportunities?

Remember and Respect

Respect for the dead requires remembering the dead. Sometimes, though, society seems in the grip of collective amnesia. Dokouph (2007, p. 50) observes that

WWI was the last war fought without modern methods of bearing witness. There are virtually no film reels, few battle photographs, only a smattering of reliable frontline news reports, and much of what exists was either produced under suffocating censorship or made as propaganda . . . Nobody filmed a single battle.

The American Civil War, fought half a century before, has not been forgotten. It resonates in photography, diaries, military records, histories, novels, films and re-enactments. The nation is perceived as having nearly forgotten its men and women who lost their lives in "The Great War." The call for appropriate memorialization is intended to recognize family survivors as well as the fallen, and to close a gap in national consciousness (Bertman, 2000).

The African Burial Ground in Manhattan was among the many historical sites that were overtaken by rapid urban expansion. New construction often included new destruction, often without a thought for what would be lost. Perhaps ironically, it was during another new construction project in 1991 that the burial ground was rediscovered with more than 400 sets of remains. In this case, the public was ready to remember and respect. The site was quickly designated as a national historic landmark, and then as a national monument.

The dead and their mourners are not always safe from ongoing societal conflict. Funeral services have been attacked and mourners massacred as part of Middle East violence. In the United States, there have been disturbances of the funeral process that convinced most states to enact laws that criminalize such behavior (Ohio is one example among many). Rutledge (2008) notes that:

> Funeral picketing has resulted in a frenzy of legislation in a short period of time. The group responsible Westboro Baptist Church, has targeted soldiers killed in Iraq and Afghanistan, homosexuals, political figures, and even children. Some may want to dismiss Westboro as a fringe group that should not be taken seriously, but they have been taken seriously by at least twenty-seven states, the federal government, and mourners who have been eyewitnesses to the group's tactics.

Funeral picketing continues to be an ethical and legal issue with additional court cases pending (Sherman, 2010). Is consecration of the body a sacred ritual that should be respected, or does the First Amendment guarantee the right to protest, no matter how distressing to the mourners?

Repeat: the dead are not always safe from ongoing social conflict. Add: religious disputation. The episode of grave destruction in Yemen in 1994 was not an isolated event. For example, the grave of Khadija, the first Prophet's wife, was destroyed a few years later. Muslims who adhere to the fundamentalist Salafis interpretation of scriptures and tradition regard visiting graves as a potentially idolatrous practice that should be dealt with by destroying the remains of saints as well as entire cemeteries. A greeting to the dead as one passes by is acceptable—the Prophet Mohammad is said to have done so (Beranek & Tupek)—but that could lead to praying to the dead and seeking their help, even to the extreme of touching a grave memorial. It should be noted that other Islamic religious authorities and several governments have strongly condemned these actions.

The Bones Start Screaming

Forensic anthropologist? This could be a person who studies prehistoric skeletons in a university museum, perhaps living her own good life in Berkeley, California. Clea Koff, however, was still in her early 20s when the bones started screaming at her. Koff was part of an international team trying to identify the thousands of Rwanda genocide victims. One mass grave held almost 500 men, women, and children who had been brutally massacred. She did her best to keep her objective attitude in place. There were detailed observations to record, skull after skull. One day, though, it was too much for her. While inspecting the skeletal remains of a teenager, Koff:

> lost an element of self-control. I felt so awful, so full of hurt and emotion, and mixed in with that was a knee-buckling sense of privilege that I was touching the bones of someone whose family was out there and wanted more than anything to have him back, no matter what condition he was in, and yet I was the only one holding him. I felt sorry for him and for everyone in the world (Koff, 2004, pp. 153–154).

Koff's older colleagues recognized her distress as well. They had been through that flood of grief themselves. Soon she was back at her work: there were so many more bodies and so many more relatives waiting for closure, waiting to memorialize their loved ones, waiting to start the painful process of getting on with their own lives. Identifying and respecting the dead could not come close to making up the loss, but it could restore an intangible sense of rightness to the bereaved families and communities. Koff became known as "the bone woman" and, along with her colleagues, helped a devastated nation move toward rebuilding itself.

"These People Got Nobody"

Compassion and respect were also foremost when a chain gang of juvenile criminals completed another of its assignments at the White Tanks Cemetery for indigents in the Phoenix, Arizona, area. The bodies lowered into earth were not victims of genocide, although some had been murdered or shot while committing crimes. Most had lived and died alone. All seemed to be without family or friends to acknowledge the deaths and accompany them to the grave. The young convicts surprised themselves by feeling sorrow for the people they had never met. They also could see themselves unloved and abandoned at the end of their lives. "God be with you," one of the teenagers prayed, as he scooped up a handful of dirt and tossed it on the casket. "These people got nobody," another said. Another reflected: "Some of them probably took our paths. This is where I could end up. Not only dead but in this place. You're never going to forget" (Villa, 2004).

Postmortem Abuse

The toppled head in question had suffered six axe wounds on the neck because the executioner was having a bad day. Perhaps he was nervous. Oliver Cromwell had been until recently The Lord Protector of England. He was the most formidable person in the kingdom until his adversaries gained the upper hand and impaled his head on a spike so that all could see what becomes of traitors (Murphy, 1995). This postmortem abuse was a political action to intimidate anybody else who might be of a mind to threaten the Crown. Preventing dignified burial is a way of disrespecting both the dead and their mourners. Tatanka Yotanka was such a victim. The leader (better known as Sitting Bull) of the Hunkpapa Teton Sioux was assassinated in 1890 while in federal custody. The government refused to release his body for traditional Sioux funeral rituals, rejecting family requests, religious protests, and court proceedings. It was not until 1953 that a raiding party comprising his descendants and the town mortician succeeded in "kidnapping" the remains and providing a burial on Sioux land.

Funerals have often been deeply significant events in African American life (Holloway, 2002). African Americans had to live with and sometimes die from the consequences of racial discrimination. It was therefore not realistic to bring up children as though life would always be safe and sweet. Funerals were occasions to educate the young and to express the strong emotions of the adults within a positive and supportive framework. Cromwell and Tatanka Yotanka had exceptional lives but were flagrantly disrespected in death by mainstream society. Many African Americans have had to cope with disrespect from mainstream society from cradle to grave.

Individualism in the Graveyard

Funeral and burial practices are perhaps the most tradition-oriented of cultural rituals Nevertheless, they are subject to change. Sharp-eyed observer Raf Vanderstraeten (2009) is among those who have documented cemetery-related changes that represent larger trends in society. He finds that Western culture with increasing average life expectancy, "celebrates joyful life in the here and now; its cult of health, fitness and youth has become omnipresent . . . It is no longer seen as the mere earthly frame of an immaterial spirit or soul." Examples of this attitude shift include the inclusion of healthy person photographs on the gravemarker—first in black and white, but increasingly in color. At the same time, the deaths of infants and children have become less frequent and therefore even more disturbing when they do occur. Children's gardens within cemeteries are no longer unusual.

Funeral director Thomas Lynch (1997) adds his perspective to the relationship between changes in the American way of life and funeral practices:

> There were households in which, just as babies were being birthed, grandparents were aging upstairs with chicken soup and doctors' home visits until, alas, they died and were taken downstairs to the same room the babies were christened in to get what was then called "laid out." Between the births and deaths were the courtships—sparkings and spoonings between boys and girls just barely out of their teens, overseen by a maiden aunt. . . . The smitten young people would sit on a "love seat"—large enough to look into each other's eyes and hold hands, small enough to prevent them getting horizontal (p. 35).

As time went on, though, more of life's activities took place outside the home, although the professional establishment became known as funeral home. Death in the United States became increasingly removed from intimate family life, although there are signs of a reversal, as we will see in the home and green funeral movements.

Today there are more options than ever about our own participation in funeral and memorial observances, and each decision either affirms or weakens our sense of meaningful involvement. It would be useful, then, to reflect on our understanding of the funeral process (Gross, 2007).

WHAT DO FUNERALS MEAN TO US?

Why go to a funeral? In fact, why have funerals at all? Perhaps we should replace the expensive and inconvenient funeral service with the click-click of the computer keyboard as we visit the departed at their cyberspace addresses. But perhaps there is something so fundamental in the human response to death that we need the physicality, the companionship of the funeral.

I believe the funeral is part of a deeper and more complex process in which we both separate ourselves from the dead and try to establish a new relationship with the dead and with each other. This chapter, therefore, examines not only the funeral but the total process through which society responds to the death of one of its members. We will look both at what is happening today as well as the cultural traditions from which our own needs, beliefs, and practices have emerged.

In the *Old Testament* we learn that:

> David went and took the bones of Saul and the bones of his son Jonathan from the men of Jabesh-gilead, who had stolen them from the public square of Beth-shan. . . . And they buried the bones of Saul and his son Jonathan in the land of Benjamin in Zela, in the tomb of Kish his father (Old Testament, Sam. 21:12, 14).

King David's enemies valued these remains as negotiable symbols. Those who possessed these bones also possessed power. A great many other people, before and after King David, have also felt that a proper funeral and secure disposition of the body are essential for the family's peace of mind. The powerful need to possess and respect the physical remains of the dead asserted itself immediately after the terrorist attacks of September 11, 2001. Emphasis at first was on rescue efforts and hope. Later the emphasis shifted to recovery and identification of the remains. A respectful funeral would not heal the grief, but it would help to begin the process of healing.

Nevertheless, there is also resistance to the funeral process as it has been commonly practiced in mainstream society. It has been variously criticized as too costly, time-consuming, depressing, and artificial. As a teenager, I was appalled by the perfunctory funeral services held for a neighbor, "the old man who lived around the corner." It was a standard issue performance by a major funeral service corporation, with the "master of ceremonies" showing no knowledge or interest in the person who had died. I still get angry thinking about this! It is not difficult to understand why people who have had alienating experiences at a funeral

service would have some reservations about the whole process.

What are *your* thoughts and feelings about the funeral process? Please answer the questions presented for your consideration in Box 12-1.

Respondents to these questions tend to sort themselves out into two major types: *rationalist* and *romantic*. A thoroughgoing rationalist would agree that funerals are an expensive waste of time that make people too emotional. Cemeteries should be phased out so the land can be used more productively. By contrast, a romanticist would observe that funerals are a comfort to the next of kin and not all that expensive when one considers their meaning. Funerals are decisive and memorable events. Furthermore, people should show more, not less, emotion at funerals, and not begrudge the dead a peaceful place to rest their bones. Do you recognize yourself as a rationalist, or a romantic?

Not all the questions bear on the rationalist–romantic attitude split, however. We will return to these questions after we have surveyed the funeral process.

FROM DEAD BODY TO LIVING MEMORY: A PROCESS APPROACH

How do we transform our relationship to a living person into our acknowledgment of this person's death and a lasting memory integrated into our ongoing lives? This process has many dimensions, ranging from the legal, technical, and financial to the personal and the symbolic. Sometimes the survivors succeed in converting what has become a dead body into a living memory. Sometimes the process fails, and the survivors must shoulder a burden of unresolved feelings and unanswered questions.

Common Elements of the Funeral Process

We have already reflected on the passage from life to death (Chapters 2, 4, and 6). It is a biological process, societal rite of passage, and, perhaps most of all, a mystery. The funeral process has a significant role in the symbolic transformation of a person into a corpse and the corpse into—what?

BOX 12-1

THE FUNERAL PROCESS: A SELF-EXAMINATION OF ATTITUDES, FEELINGS, AND KNOWLEDGE

1. Funerals are a waste of time.
   Agree _____ Tend to agree _____
   Tend to disagree _____ Disagree _____

2. Bodies should be donated for scientific use.
   Agree _____ Tend to agree _____
   Tend to disagree _____ Disagree _____

3. Funerals are a comfort to the next of kin.
   Agree _____ Tend to agree _____
   Tend to disagree _____ Disagree _____

4. People often are too emotional at funerals.
   Agree _____ Tend to agree _____
   Tend to disagree _____ Disagree _____

5. The death of a family member should be published in the newspaper.
   Agree _____ Tend to agree _____
   Tend to disagree _____ Disagree _____

6. All things considered, most funerals are not excessively costly.
   Agree _____ Tend to agree _____
   Tend to disagree _____ Disagree _____

7. People often do not show enough emotion at funerals.
   Agree _____ Tend to agree _____
   Tend to disagree _____ Disagree _____

8. The size, length, and expense of a funeral should depend on the importance of the deceased person.
   Agree _____ Tend to agree _____
   Tend to disagree _____ Disagree _____

9. Allowing for some exceptions, cemeteries waste valuable space and should be diverted to other uses.
   Agree _____ Tend to agree _____
   Tend to disagree _____ Disagree _____

10. It would be preferable to be cremated.
    Agree _____ Tend to agree _____
    Tend to disagree _____ Disagree _____

11. It would be preferable to be buried in a cemetery.
    Agree _____ Tend to agree _____
    Tend to disagree _____ Disagree _____

12. A funeral director should be required to give a summary of laws stating what is and what is not required before the bereaved purchase a funeral.
    Agree _____ Tend to agree _____
    Tend to disagree _____ Disagree _____

13. The average cost of a funeral in the United States is between $_____ and $_____.

14. Embalming the body is required:
    Always _____
    Under certain specified circumstances _____
    Never _____

15. An open-casket funeral can be held after body organs are donated:
    Always _____
    Seldom _____

16. My idea of the perfect funeral process is the following:
    _____
    _____
    _____

17. For me, the best or most useful aspects of a funeral are:
    _____
    _____
    _____

18. For me, the worst or most distressing aspects of a funeral are:
    _____
    _____
    _____

Cultures differ in their beliefs about the new status taken on by the dead, and these differences show up in funeral and mourning practices. Nevertheless, certain basic elements often can be found.

Premortem Preparations U.S. law recognizes that actions taken in contemplation of death are unique. Gifts made under the shadow of death often are taxed more severely. Transfers of property and obligations between the dead and the living are of concern to all societies and usually are regulated by formal or common law (Miller, Rosenfeld, & McNamee, 2003). The community demands assurance that debts will be paid and its rules of inheritance enforced.

Either the dying person or a family member takes the initiative, giving instructions for cremation or burial and disposal of personal property. Colleagues might have to prepare for replacing the coworker who will not be coming back to the job. The physician may be interested in obtaining permission to remove an organ for transplantation or conduct an *autopsy* to determine the precise cause of death. A funeral director may have already made preliminary arrangements to see that the wishes of the family are respected. Often there is considerable anticipatory activity so that the right things are done when the death does occur. An unexpected death creates quite a different and more disturbing situation because there has been no opportunity for emotional or organizational preparation.

Immediate Postdeath Activities The death becomes official when it is certified by a physician. The revised U.S. standard *death certificate* is shown in Figure 12-1. One immediate postdeath activity, then, is to convert the person into a statistic and complete

The long and loving marriage of Paris industrialist N. Pigeon and his wife is commemorated in the Cimetiere de Montparnasse.

TYPE/PRINT
IN
PERMANENT
BLACK INK
FOR
INSTRUCTIONS
SEE OTHER SIDE
AND HANDBOOK

U.S. STANDARD
CERTIFICATE OF DEATH

LOCAL FILE NUMBER   STATE FILE NUMBER

DECEDENT

1. DECEDENT'S NAME *(First, Middle, Last)* | 2. SEX | 3. DATE OF DEATH *(Month, Day, Year)*

4. SOCIAL SECURITY NUMBER | 5a. AGE—Last Birthday *(Years)* | 5b. UNDER 1 YEAR (Months / Days) | 5c. UNDER 1 DAY (Hours / Minutes) | 6. DATE OF BIRTH *(Month, Day, Year)* | 7. BIRTHPLACE *(City and State or Foreign Country)*

8. WAS DECEDENT EVER IN U.S. ARMED FORCES? *(Yes or no)* | 9a. PLACE OF DEATH *(Check only one; see instructions on other side)*
HOSPITAL: ☐ Inpatient ☐ ER/Outpatient ☐ DOA   OTHER: ☐ Nursing Home ☐ Residence ☐ Other *(Specify)*

9b. FACILITY NAME *(If not institution, give street and number)* | 9c. CITY, TOWN, OR LOCATION OF DEATH | 9d. COUNTY OF DEATH

10. MARITAL STATUS — Married, Never Married, Widowed, Divorced *(Specify)* | 11. SURVIVING SPOUSE *(If wife, give maiden name)* | 12a. DECEDENT'S USUAL OCCUPATION *(Give kind of work done during most of working life. Do not use retired.)* | 12b. KIND OF BUSINESS/INDUSTRY

13a. RESIDENCE — STATE | 13b. COUNTY | 13c. CITY, TOWN, OR LOCATION | 13d. STREET AND NUMBER

13e. INSIDE CITY LIMITS? *(Yes or no)* | 13f. ZIP CODE | 14. WAS DECEDENT OF HISPANIC ORIGIN? *(Specify No or Yes—If yes, specify Cuban, Mexican, Puerto Rican, etc.)* ☐ No ☐ Yes Specify: | 15. RACE—American Indian, Black, White, etc. *(Specify)* | 16. DECEDENT'S EDUCATION *(Specify only highest grade completed)* Elementary/Secondary (0-12) | College (1-4 or 5+)

PARENTS

17. FATHER'S NAME *(First, Middle, Last)* | 18. MOTHER'S NAME *(First, Middle, Maiden Surname)*

INFORMANT

19a. INFORMANT'S NAME *(Type/Print)* | 19b. MAILING ADDRESS *(Street and Number or Rural Route Number, City or Town, State, Zip Code)*

DISPOSITION

20a. METHOD OF DISPOSITION ☐ Burial ☐ Cremation ☐ Removal from State ☐ Donation ☐ Other *(Specify)* _____ | 20b. PLACE OF DISPOSITION *(Name of cemetery, crematory, or other place)* | 20c. LOCATION—City or Town, State

21a. SIGNATURE OF FUNERAL SERVICE LICENSEE OR PERSON ACTING AS SUCH | 21b. LICENSE NUMBER *(of Licensee)* | 22. NAME AND ADDRESS OF FACILITY

PRONOUNCING PHYSICIAN ONLY

ITEMS 24-26 MUST BE COMPLETED BY PERSON WHO PRONOUNCES DEATH

Complete items 23a-c only when certifying physician is not available at time of death to certify cause of death. | 23a. To the best of my knowledge, death occurred at the time, date, and place stated. *Signature and Title* ▶ | 23b. LICENSE NUMBER | 23c. DATE SIGNED *(Month, Day, Year)*

24. TIME OF DEATH ___ M | 25. DATE PRONOUNCED DEAD *(Month, Day, Year)* | 26. WAS CASE REFERRED TO MEDICAL EXAMINER/CORONER? *(Yes or no)*

CAUSE OF DEATH

27. PART I. Enter the diseases, injuries, or complications that caused the death. Do not enter the mode of dying, such as cardiac or respiratory arrest, shock, or heart failure. List only one cause on each line. | Approximate Interval Between Onset and Death

IMMEDIATE CAUSE (Final disease or condition resulting in death) ➔ a. _____
DUE TO (OR AS A CONSEQUENCE OF):

Sequentially list conditions, if any, leading to immediate cause. Enter UNDERLYING CAUSE (Disease or injury that initiated events resulting in death) LAST b. _____
DUE TO (OR AS A CONSEQUENCE OF):

c. _____
DUE TO (OR AS A CONSEQUENCE OF):

d.

PART II. Other significant conditions contributing to death but not resulting in the underlying cause given in Part I. | 28a. WAS AN AUTOPSY PERFORMED? *(Yes or no)* | 28b. WERE AUTOPSY FINDINGS AVAILABLE PRIOR TO COMPLETION OF CAUSE OF DEATH? *(Yes or no)*

29. MANNER OF DEATH ☐ Natural ☐ Accident ☐ Suicide ☐ Homicide ☐ Pending Investigation ☐ Could not be Determined | 30a. DATE OF INJURY *(Month, Day, Year)* | 30b. TIME OF INJURY ___ M | 30c. INJURY AT WORK? *(Yes or no)* | 30d. DESCRIBE HOW INJURY OCCURRED

30e. PLACE OF INJURY—At home, farm, street, factory, office building, etc. *(Specify)* | 30f. LOCATION *(Street and Number or Rural Route Number, City or Town, State)*

CERTIFIER

31a. CERTIFIER *(Check only one)*
☐ CERTIFYING PHYSICIAN *(Physician certifying cause of death when another physician has pronounced death and completed Item 23)*
To the best of my knowledge, death occurred due to the cause(s) and manner as stated.
☐ PRONOUNCING AND CERTIFYING PHYSICIAN *(Physician both pronouncing death and certifying to cause of death)*
To the best of my knowledge, death occurred at the time, date, and place, and due to the cause(s) and manner as stated.
☐ MEDICAL EXAMINER/CORONER
On the basis of examination and/or investigation, in my opinion, death occurred at the time, date, and place, and due to the cause(s) and manner as stated.

31b. SIGNATURE AND TITLE OF CERTIFIER | 31c. LICENSE NUMBER | 31d. DATE SIGNED *(Month, Day, Year)*

32. NAME AND ADDRESS OF PERSON WHO COMPLETED CAUSE OF DEATH (ITEM 27) *(Type/Print)*

REGISTRAR

33. REGISTRAR'S SIGNATURE | 34. DATE FILED *(Month, Day, Year)*

PHS-T-003

Left margin: NAME OF DECEDENT: For use by physician or institution — SEE INSTRUCTIONS ON OTHER SIDE — SEE DEFINITION ON OTHER SIDE — SEE INSTRUCTIONS ON OTHER SIDE — SEE DEFINITION ON OTHER SIDE

Far left vertical: DEPARTMENT OF HEALTH AND HUMAN SERVICES — PUBLIC HEALTH SERVICE — NATIONAL CENTER FOR HEALTH STATISTICS — 1989 REVISION

Figure 12-1

the record keeping that started with the certificate of birth. Another immediate action is to contact next of kin, should they not already be on the scene. It is common these days for the body to be cleaned and wrapped in a plastic sheet. If the death occurred in a hospital, the body will either be kept in the same room or transferred to an available nearby room pending the arrival of the next of kin. If a hospital is pressed for space, the body may be removed to the morgue after a short time.

Preparations for Burial or Cremation Often there are both practical and symbolic reasons for placing a space of time between death and final disposition. One of the most common is to allow time for distant friends and relatives to gather for the funeral. Disposition of the body may also have to await financial arrangements. Did the deceased have an insurance policy with funeral benefits? Precisely who is prepared to spend how much on the funeral? Problems arise in less bureaucratic societies as well. Was there sorcery at work in this death? And, if so, was it a personal enemy within the tribe who must confess and make amends, or was it caused by another tribe; therefore, demanding lethal retribution?

Some deaths also raise questions that require action in the public interest. Was this death caused by negligence, suicide, or murder? Was the deceased the victim of a disease that poses a hazard to the general population? It is usually the medical examiner (or coroner) who must decide if a full investigation is needed. Relatives may want to prove that a death that appears to be self-inflected actually is homicide because at stake is a considerable inheritance from an insurance contract that prohibits suicide. Insurance investigators may suspect fraud. Bereaved family members may feel that they cannot get on again with their lives until they are convinced the cause and circumstances have been firmly established.

Send for the Medical Examiner A medical examiner may order an autopsy when there is the possibility of a danger to public health. This happened when swine flu and Legionnaire's disease became threats in the 1970s, and, more recently, with West Nile virus and avian flu. *Death's Acre* (Bass & Jefferson, 2003) offers an inside view of forensic laboratory work at "the body farm." Medical examiners are also called upon when murder or criminal negligence are possible causes of death. *CSI (Crime Scene Investigation)*, the popular television series, dramatizes the work of field and laboratory specialists who augment the traditional work of the medical examiner. Other television programs also regularly feature *postmortem* detective work, invariably featuring an eccentric but endearing pathologist. (Who's your favorite?) Public appetite for slab scenes does not yet seem to have reached its satiation point—a startling turnabout from the former denial-driven attitude of see no, hear no, speak no death that prevailed not so long ago.

The examination itself can vary. It may be sufficient to look for one or two telltale signs (e.g., the trace of certain substances in the lungs or intestines, the presence or absence of cerebral hemorrhage). However, dissection and examination of the body also may be considered necessary, along with bacteriological and toxicological laboratory tests. Removing a corpse from its burial site requires careful thought and good judgment. Courts may order *exhumation* to obtain bullets, hair fragments, or other physical evidence that could bear on the cause of death in criminal cases, including malpractice. Corpses are also sometimes exhumed by accident, as when a graveyard is disturbed by flood or construction activities.

Survivors' Responsibilities After a Death

The interval between death and funeral also allows symbolic and psychological needs to be met. Among some ethnic and religious groups, the survivors have specific tasks to perform. These tasks help survivors express their affection for the deceased and support each other during the period of acute grief. Carrying out these responsibilities is also an act of piety. Society and its gods expect selected individuals to prepare special foods or create special objects to be placed in the grave. The symbolic meaning is often more important than the length of the interval. The Cheyenne, for example, buried their dead quickly so that the ghosts would swiftly take their departure. By contrast, societies as distant as Egypt and Greenland (Hansen, Meldgaard-Jorgen, & Nordgris, 1991) mummified their dead as a way of keeping them part of the community, calling upon their symbolic powers, or enhancing their chances for a brilliant afterlife.

The recently deceased person occupies a transitional status in many cultures: no longer a live member of the community but not yet all the way dead. There is still the need to complete a rite of passage from the world of the living to the realm of the dead

(Kastenbaum, 2004a, 2004b). The spirit is vulnerable while detained between both worlds and this makes it a dangerous time for the community. Death and the newly dead are polluting influences that the living must avoid in cultures as disparate as the Old Testament Hebrews, Navaho, and Japanese—all of whose traditions still carry forward stringent precautions against contact with the physical remains of the newly dead (Stone & Walter, 2008).

Embalming is far from universal and was seldom practiced in the United States until thousands of soldiers died far from home during the American Civil War. Embalming does not confer lasting protection. The funeral industry quickly withdrew its claims that embalming preserved bodies permanently as lawsuits were filed and penalties

assessed for deceptive advertising (Roach, 2003). Embalming is not required by law unless the body is to be transported out of state or for some other clearly specified reason. Embalming can serve emotional and symbolic needs. For example, each year Arizona ships more than 3,000 bodies back to the hometowns of those people who had left to spend their retirement in Arizona. "Postmortem emigration" also occurs in other Sun Belt states so that a body may be brought to a family plot in the hometown cemetery.

In some societies, considerable effort, expense, and artistic skill have been devoted to the embellishment as well as preservation of the body. The ancient Egyptians' creation of mummies (see Box 12-2) is the most famous example, but not

Embalming first became widely practiced during the American Civil War in order to return bodies in the best possible condition to families for burial in their own hometowns.

the only one. Some rich and powerful people in Western nations have also received extensive post-mortem treatment before burial. The wife of Louis XVI's minister "ordered her body to be preserved in alcohol, like an embryo" so that her widowed spouse could spend the rest of his life gazing at her beautiful face (Aries, 1981, p. 386). Less is known about the circumstances that led to mummifications (known as "the Bog People") in northern Europe about 2000 years ago, although ritualized killing is suspected for at least some of the cases. Societies around the world, including the Incas and Aztecs, have pursued methods for achieving some form of preserving remains.

Modern embalming was prompted by the ritual of placing royal corpses on public display. They had to look good. Pioneering anatomists in the fifteenth century discovered how to inject preservatives, a big step forward (Trompeter & Lemonnier, 2009). The English in the eighteenth century flocked to displays of embalmed corpses, the latest curiosity (Zigrovich, 2009). By the nineteenth century, embalming had moved beyond its primary medical research origins and became one of commercial significance—competing methods were as hotly contested as rival computer systems today.

Plastination: The Dead as Instructors

And now we have plastination. This is a process that converts material—like you and me—into durable objects. Water is removed, tissue dissected, acetone applied to further dehydrate, and a silicone bath is provided under vacuum conditions. This process usually takes about a month; The product can be passed around a classroom and placed on a shelf or display. Plastination is a breakthrough in medical education and a significant draw for enterprising museums.

The art and science of mummification took many years to develop before reaching its pinnacle in ancient Egypt.

BOX 12-2

THE SACRED ART OF MUMMIFICATION: HOW AND WHY?

How were mummies made in ancient Egypt?

- The family selects the grade and price level of mummification, choosing from several wooden models. Royal mummification is, of course, the highest quality, whatever the expense. It is a first-class mummification that is described here.

- The internal organs are removed—the brain first, caught on an iron hook and fished out through the (slit) nostrils. The abdominal organs are then removed through an incision.

- In royal mummifications, the heart is replaced by the carved replica of a *scarab* (a dung beetle), symbolizing the perpetual cycle of life into death and death into life. The internal organs are transferred to canopic jars (stone vessels).

- The body cavity is thoroughly rinsed with palm wine.

- The face and body may be reshaped to restore blemishes and disfigurations that occurred during the final illness or the mummification procedure. This could include reshaping the breasts to provide a more natural appearance for a woman.

- Spices and many other aromatic substances are placed inside the body, which is then sewn up.

- The body is then covered by "divine salts" to foster drying and preservation. The standard period of time for the drying phase is 40 days, followed by another 30 days for final preparations.

- The salted and dried body is washed and wrapped in linen strips that are undercoated with gum. Features such as eyes and eyebrows are drawn in ink on the linen to recreate the face.

- The mummy of a powerful person is placed in a tapered coffin, and the coffin is lodged within a sarcophagus (stone chamber), which itself is sealed into a tomb.

- It should be emphasized that this is mummification on the grand scale. The procedure was simplified and less expensive measures were used for people who lacked regal or other high-power status.

But why?

- The practical aim was to preserve the body by emptying it of its fluids and the parts most subject to rapid decay, producing a dehydrated but otherwise faithful—almost lifelike—version of the deceased person. When conducted by skillful embalmers and not desecrated by tomb robbers, the results could be very impressive. There are pharaohs who look as though they are ready to reclaim their thrones more than 3,000 years after they drew their last breath. The high art of mummification was itself achieved only after many years of trial and error, with frequent failures.

- The more crucial aim was to guide a spirit that departed from the body at death—the *ba*—back to its former physical home where its companion spirit—the *ka*—awaited its nightly visits. The preserved body made it easier for the winged *ba* to locate its companion spirit, *ka*. Some archaeologists believe that the great pyramids were constructed not only to honor the sacred dead and protect their bodies but also as a sort of astral communications center that provided a stronger signal for the communion of the spirits.

Principle sources: Ikram and Dodson (1998), Harris (1973).

Plastination is currently used to prepare anatomical specimen for biomedical education. It has also taken a spectacular form with the human action figures created by Dr. Gunther von Hagens (Chapter 2), which have been widely exhibited throughout the world. Not surprisingly, Dr. Hagen has also been both widely praised and criticized for confronting us with possibly more than some of us want to see.

Settling into Earth

So familiar is the practice of embalming a deceased person, placing that person horizontally in a coffin, and the coffin in a cemetery gravesite, that we might consider this to be a natural and universal tradition. Not so. For example, many tribal societies have believed that one's afterlife is critically affected by the precise way in which that person's corpse is managed. One common practice has been to place the body in a fetal position. The body is then wrapped or bound so that it will maintain this position and then placed on its side. The fetal position might be seen as an attempt to return the deceased to the womb of earth, possibly to be reborn. There have also been societies in which people have been buried in a seated position, or even upside down. Occasionally members of a tribal society have shared their reasons, as when Solomon Islanders around the turn of the twentieth century reported that they bound their dead in seated positions so they wouldn't come back to annoy them. Cynical observers in Western societies have claimed that gravestones are intended to accomplish the same purpose.

Up in Flames: The Cremation Alternative

Cremation is an ancient practice whose beginnings are lost in the mist of prehistory (Davies & Mates, 2006). Some of the earliest writings refer to cremation (e.g., the works attributed to Homer, Ovid, and Virgil, as well as Buddhist, Hindu, and Jewish scriptures). Historians believe that most ancient peoples (Egyptians excepted) chose cremation (Prothero, 2001). Some cultures use flames to purify and free the soul for its new form of existence. The Vikings, for example, would build a spectacular long boat to set afire with the corpse of their chief aboard. The flaming vessel crossed to the spirit domain, taking along not only their chief but his sacrificial companions.

Practical considerations influenced a society's method. Cremation was not a realistic option for people who lived where trees were scarce. Some cultures had multiple ways of dealing with the dead. In former days, for example, Adaman Islanders would bury those who died very young or very old in a shallow hole, but those who perished in their prime received the prestigious treatment of having their bodies placed on a tree platform. Dead strangers would be cut into pieces and consumed by fire without ceremony because their ghosts immediately left for their homeland and therefore posed no local danger.

Cremation was generally opposed by Christianity from the later Middle Ages until the Reformation. Martin Luther shifted attention away from the body to spiritual salvation. Cremation gradually became seen as less of a threat to one's fate in the afterlife. Several events prepared Europe to give more consideration to the cremation alternative. One of the most influential was the death of English poet Percy Bysshe Shelley in 1822. He died when he was overtaken by a storm while boating on a Swiss lake. Shelley's body was cremated on a pyre by his fellow poet and friend, Lord Byron—who then reached into the flames to rescue Shelley's heart. (Years later Shelley's heart was buried with his widow, Mary Wollstonecraft Shelley, who, still in her teens, had written a novel called *Frankenstein*.) By the middle of the nineteenth century, medical experts were criticizing burial as a breeding ground for disease and recommending its replacement with cremation. Not long after, Queen Victoria's personal physician wrote a pro-cremation work that started a spark in the United States (Prothero, 2001). Concern for public health has remained a significant theme in the advocacy of cremation.

But—times change! There is now rising concern about gases produced during the combustion process. In England this has already "resulted in the introduction of increasingly stringent laws governing the output of gases from cremator chimneys" (Davies, 2003, p. 768). The cost of preventing the release of mercury and other toxic products is also of concern. We cannot help but think again of the folk societies that for centuries have feared assault from spirits of the dead. In the twenty-first century, public health officials are troubled about breathing in the toxic fumes of crematory ovens. We have probably not heard the last of cremation-related health concerns.

Despite a number of problems associated with the cremation process, this form of body disposal has become increasingly utilized even in strongly traditional societies. South Korea is an instructive example (Chang-Won, 2010). For centuries it was expected that people would end their lives at home and receive a burial in concordance with tradition. Now, however, more lives end in hospitals and more cremations are performed. There is much to be learned about the connection between how and where people die and how arrangements are made for body disposal.

Cremation in the United States There were two "first" cremations of Euro-Americans. The "official" first cremation occurred on December 6, 1876, in Washington, Pennsylvania. Baron Joseph Henry Louis Charles De Palm's cremation was hailed by some as a significant achievement in transforming society from sentimentality to science, and denounced by others as Satanic blasphemy. The debate was on—and has continued to this day. The actual first cremation had occurred much earlier. Henry Laurens, a former president of the Continental Congress, was given the open-air cremation he desired, though over the misgivings of practically everybody else. Why did he make so unusual and so unpopular a choice? Because he was afraid of being buried alive (see also Chapter 1). And why was he afraid of that? Because his daughter, pronounced dead of smallpox, was close to being placed in the grave when she revived just in time. But even Laurens's cremation was not the first to have taken place in North America. Cremation had been practiced by some Native American peoples (such as the Tolkotin of Oregon) before the first Europeans came ashore.

Today in the United States, cremation is selected by about 1 person in 4, as compared with about only 1 in 14 in the 1970s. There are significant differences by state. Cremations are still uncommon (10 percent or less) in Alabama, Kentucky, Louisiana, Mississippi, Tennessee, and West Virginia. By contrast, upwards of 60 percent of the dead are cremated in Alaska, Arizona, Colorado, Florida, Idaho, Kansas, Montana, Nevada, New Hampshire, New Jersey, New Mexico, Oregon, and Washington. Estimates of cremation rates in other nations place Japan clearly at the top (95 percent). Cremation has also become the most common practice throughout Europe in general (63 percent), as well as Australia/New Zealand, Britain, China, and India. Cremation is uncommon however, in sub-Saharan Africa, Islamic countries, and Israel. Kearl (2004) links the increase in cremations to the decrease in attachment to a particular place in nations with mobile populations.

The Funeral Service

Both whole-body burial and cremation offer the possibility of a funeral service. Two major purposes of the funeral service include final placement of the remains, and society's public recognition that one of its members has made the transition from life to death. Perhaps the most familiar form is the church funeral service, in which respects are paid to the deceased in a church or funeral home; then mourners gather in the cemetery to hear eulogies and witness the casket being placed in the grave. Most often the arrangements are carried out by the funeral director—ordering flowers, providing the hearse and possibly other vehicles, and so on. A member of the clergy usually presides over the commemorative services. In "small town America" the clergyperson often knew the family well.

Some rural areas still continue a family- and neighbor-oriented process in which the funeral director has a less significant role. James Crissman (1994) describes a traditional approach that is being affected by changing times in *Death and Dying in Central Appalachia*. He speaks of "the code of the mountains," under which independence and loyalty help people to survive hard times. Outsiders are not that welcome. The funeral service can become unsettled. An elaborate funeral might attract so much attention to itself that it is difficult to keep a focus on the deceased. A lack of consensus among the mourners can also heighten the tension. For example, there might be disagreement about an open or closed casket. These two options are of equal popularity—almost a guarantee that some participants will be displeased with whatever choice is made. Even those who prefer an open casket may disagree on the way it is handled. Should Louise's visage be restored into a semblance of the robust person she was most of her life or be shown with the lines of exhaustion that developed during her last illness? Should Harry be displayed in his favorite old sloppy clothes or an elegant dark suit that he would literally never have been caught dead in? Nevertheless, the underlying purposes remain: to make a final disposition of the body and to use this occasion as a way of acknowledging that a valued life has passed from among us.

Memorializing the Deceased

Most societies attempt to fix the deceased in memory. In the United States, a death notice is often (but not always) published in a local newspaper. An *obituary* may also appear, especially if requested by the family. Today many newspapers require a fee to print an obituary unless the individual is considered especially "newsworthy." Furthermore, metropolitan newspapers have been reducing the number of obituaries published because of space and economical pressures. Is this trend weakening the ability of our death system to meet the need of survivors? Do people feel alienated because the deaths of their loved ones are not acknowledged in the state's major newspaper? We do not yet know the answers to these questions, but traditional acknowledgments and responses to death are vulnerable to general social trends.

Traditional burial is almost always accompanied by a grave marker, whether simple or elaborate. Survivors often experience severe stress when war, terrorist attack, or natural catastrophe make it impossible to know precisely which grave is that of a relative or dear friend. Tens of thousands of unidentified soldiers lie buried in foreign lands, their graves usually marked by simple crosses. Many American families visited World War I burial grounds such as Flanders Field so they could be close to the place where their loved ones had fallen. In our own time, there are families who have experienced emotional pain for years because a member is still listed as "missing in action" in Vietnam. The despair of people who have lost family members in the tsunami disaster is often intensified by the lack of identified remains. The increasing use of DNA testing may assist in the identification of people who have died in war or catastrophe and thereby ease some of the survivors' grief. There was some success in identifying the victims of the September 11, 2001, terrorist attacks. Whether it takes the form of lighting a candle on the deceased's birthday, saying prayers, or making sacrifices or gifts in the name of the deceased, memorialization appears to be one of humankind's deepest needs when separated from a loved one by death.

Getting on with Life

The "life must go on" motif has often taken the form of a festive occasion. Family, neighbors, and best friends gather to eat, drink, and share lively conversation. In former generations, the abundant food was usually prepared by family members. There might be dancing and, as the feasting proceeded, even some romancing. Death had been given its due, now it was time for life to show what it was all about.

This type of festivity started to give way as society became more impersonal, mobile, and technologically oriented, and as efforts were made to banish death from public awareness. A cup of coffee with a few family members and friends has often replaced the elaborate proceedings of earlier generations. Although the size and splendor of the postfuneral gathering might change, the underlying function is usually the same—to help people redirect their attention to the continuation and renewal of life. This is why conversation may seem unnaturally lively and why people may seem to eat, drink, and laugh too much. If you happen to walk in while a risqué story is being told, it is easy to be offended and think that insensitivity and disrespect are afoot. However, lively and lusty behaviors after a funeral can represent a partial release from tension and the compelling need to show each other that life can and should go on—"Harry (or Louise) would have wanted it that way!"

MAKING DEATH "LEGAL"

Society's claim on the individual is demonstrated clearly at the points of entry and exit. Births and deaths have been recorded at the neighborhood church since medieval times. Demands of the faith required that each soul be entered into the books. A written notice was also required as the soul was released to join its maker—proof that clergy was tending over the flock. These records would be consulted if questions arose about kinship rights and obligations. Now, centuries later, the surviving records continue to be valuable. Historians seeking to understand the effects of a harsh winter in rural England in the seventeenth century or migration patterns in northern Italy 100 years later will consult entries preserved at the local parish.

Certificates of death (Figure 12-1) and birth continue to serve similar functions in today's more secular society. The newborn and the deceased are affirmed as citizens beginning or ending their active roles in society. Church records now provide supplementary rather than official documentation. Despite all the changes that have occurred through the years, governing authorities still insist on "keeping the book" on the individual. Society presumes that none of us belong entirely to ourselves but are subject to "legalizations" both coming and going.

We now examine in more detail some of the major features of making death legal as part of the contemporary funeral process.

Establishing the Facts of Death

A death is real but not official until certified. It is the responsibility of the physician to establish the principal facts of the death and initiate an investigation if questions arise. Cause of death often requires the physician to identify several contributing factors. The following are examples:

- "Cardiovascular accident, secondary to hypertension"
- "Pneumonia, secondary to lung cancer"
- "Hemorrhage, secondary to cancer of the larynx"
- "Septicemia, secondary to extensive third-degree burns"

The actual situation may be more complicated than a death certificate can express. A woman in her 80s suffers from heart and urinary tract disorders in addition to a loss of bone mass and resiliency (osteoporosis). One day while she is simply ascending a staircase, the brittle bones give way. She falls. Both hips are broken. Her already impaired cardiovascular system is subjected to further stress. Internal bleeding proves difficult to control. Confined to bed and fitted with a catheter, she develops an infection that further saps her strength. Medical and nursing management becomes very difficult because treatments that might improve one condition can worsen another. Her lungs fill with fluid, and she dies. But what is the cause? Or what is the precise relationship among the many interacting factors that lead to death? The physician may or may not be able to give a definite answer but often can specify the major contributing causes.

The death certificate has its limits as a source of research data. Even so, it provides useful information. For example, the information about this elderly woman's death adds to a growing body of data that emphasizes the need for better understanding and clinical and environmental management to prevent falls. Relatively few death certificates specify the underlying cause. Many death certificates also omit other information that would be needed to understand the circumstances of the individual's death. It is hard to escape the inference that some physicians are not giving much priority to completing thorough and accurate death certificates (Iserson, 2003).

The cause of death is often the most salient item of information required on the certificate, but the other entries are also of potential significance. Who is the next of kin? Was the death related to occupational hazard or stress? Has there been an unusually high rate of death from the same cause in this geographical area in the past few years? Questions such as these can have many implications for the well-being of surviving individuals.

WHAT DOES THE FUNERAL PROCESS ACCOMPLISH?

The funeral process would not have become so important to so many societies unless it served significant needs and values. In this section we gain additional perspective by observing how society responds to the death of its most powerful members. We might believe that every life and therefore every death should be considered of equal importance. In practice, however, societies consider some people more important than others.

When Great People Die

The loss of a great person often triggers a massive response. What is it that society feels it must accomplish through the funeral and memorialization process? Here are a few examples that will illustrate the dynamics and principles involved.

The Silent Army of Ch'in Shih-huang-ti Ch'in Shih-huang-ti was one of the most powerful of monarchs. He unified the peoples of an enormous and diversified region into nationhood and stimulated the development of a distinctive culture. It was Ch'in, as the first emperor of China, who built the Great Wall more than two centuries before the birth of Christ.

Ch'in's tomb was discovered in 1974. It had been concealed within a large mound whose location was selected through the art of *feng-shui*, intended to deter evil spirits. To call the site a tomb is understatement—it answers better to the name of palace. Ch'in's tomb was built near the graves of earlier rulers and designed to surpass them all. Several of the huge underground chambers have been excavated. Pit number one, for example, is a rectangle approximately 700 by 200 feet. It is divided into 11 parallel corridors, with the entire structure skillfully constructed by a combination of rammed earth, bricks, and timber crossbeams.

In this pit, excavators found an entire army! Arthur Cotterell (1981) describes the scene:

> The chambers are arranged in the battle order of an infantry regiment . . . 3,210 terracotta foot soldiers. They do not wear helmets; only Ch'in officers have these. But most of the infantry soldiers wear armour. These armoured men are divided into forty files; they stand four abreast in the nine wide corridors, and form two files in each of the narrow ones. The head of the regiment in the eastern gallery comprises a vanguard of nearly 200 sharpshooters, the ancient equivalent of artillery. They would have fired their arrows from a distance, once contact was made with the enemy. Between these sharpshooters and the armored infantry are six chariots and three unarmored infantry squads. Each chariot is pulled by four terracotta horses and manned by a charioteer and one or two soldiers. The guards would have wielded long flexible lances, measuring as much as six metres (20 feet), in order to stop enemy soldiers from cutting off the heads of the horses (pp. 22–23).

The funeral for a Viking chief involved an elaborate ritual that was consummated when the long boat constructed for this purpose was set afire as it moved toward its destination with the gods. Valued goods accompanied the deceased chief, and, at times, so did a consort of women who were sacrificed to the gods as the journey began.

The artistic craftsmanship devoted to the creation of this subterranean army and the enormous economic resources poured into the enterprise are truly staggering. But why? What purpose was served by such a vast expenditure of labor and resources?

Ch'in's motivation probably included the following components:

- To support his claims as the greatest of all monarchs.
- To impress the deities and ensure his place among the immortals.
- To confound his enemies and secure continuation of his royal succession.

Ch'in made history, but also enemies. His military adventures strained the economy. He was also not the most tolerant of men. Scholars who displeased him were buried alive. The impressive tomb served to display his ability to defend his regime even from the grave, but it had another purpose as well. Like many another ruler, the first emperor of China craved immortality. Just as he literally required his subjects to sing his praises throughout his life, so he established a mute army to protect his afterlife from both earthly and spiritual foe. The plan didn't work, though. A fierce peasant revolution soon toppled the regime, and it is only in our own time that China has been able to recover detailed knowledge about its first emperor.

Death Makes a Hero Dynamics of a very different sort produced one of the most elaborate funeral processes of the nineteenth century. England's Prince Consort died unexpectedly. Prince Albert of Saxe Coburg-Gotha, had been married to the illustrious Queen Victoria. The public had disliked Albert because he was not an Englishman. Unexpectedly, after his death, a national cult developed around the late Prince Consort.

Examine the monuments and portraits throughout the British Isles—Balmoral, Aberdeen, Edinburgh, Nottinghamshire, South Kensington, Whippingham, Frogmore, Manchester, and so on. Among the physical tributes in London alone there is a memorial chapel in Windsor Castle and the Albert Memorial, which itself is only part of the impressive Victoria and Albert Museum. Parks were renamed in Albert's memory. Small statues of the dashing prince were sold as memorabilia. One could purchase Prince Albert belt clasps,

lamps, pencil cases, and stationery. Eventually his handsome likeness would be put on packages and cans of tobacco (my father's favorite brand three generations later). Alfred Lord Tennyson wrote one of his most famous poems to honor him ("Idylls of the King"). Upon his death, the late Prince Consort became the most popular image and also something of an industry.

The widowed Queen of England demonstrated a worshipful attitude toward her late husband and would not allow people to speak of him in the past tense. His private rooms at three favorite residences were preserved just as they had been during his life. A visiting nobleman observed (Darby & Smith, 1983):

Queen Victoria of England gave her name to an entire age. She remained in mourning long after the death of her beloved husband, Prince Albert, and maintained his rooms as though he were about to return any day. One of her most comforting companions also is seen here: Sharp, who had a natural gift for looking mournful.

She . . . referred to the sayings and doings of the Prince as if he was in the next room. It was difficult to believe that he was not, but in his own room where she received me everything was set out on his table and the pen and his blotting-book, his handkerchief on the sofa, his watch going, fresh flowers in the glass . . . as if he might come in at any moment (p. 4).

The observant Lord Clarendon noted a subtle contradiction in the arrangements. On the one hand, there were the fresh clothes, jug of hot water, and clean towels laid out for the use of the Prince, yet a tinted photograph of his corpse hung by the side of his bed. Obviously, the Queen was having difficulty in reconciling her conflicting needs to acknowledge reality and to preserve the illusion that her beloved was still with her.

What purposes did the funeral and memorialization process for Prince Albert achieve? I suggest the following:

1. The elaborate memorialization process symbolically incorporated Albert into the British Empire. He became an Englishman after his death. This was both a gesture of support for the queen and a way of grafting Albert's attributes onto the national self-image. His noble figure would always stand at alert attention or gracefully sit astride a beautiful horse.
2. Albert's death provided an excellent opportunity to express current sentiment and belief. Victorian England had developed increasingly elaborate mourning practices. There was even competition to see who could express bereavement most impressively through dark clothing ("widow's weeds"), withdrawal from customary social activities and responsibilities, and idealization of the deceased. Cemetery architecture prospered, impressive statuary art aggrandized the departed and, therefore, the affluent mourners as well. These customs affirmed the prevailing belief in the certainty and blessings of immortal life, although there were critics of such ostentatious mourning. It was the Victorian age, after all, that provided Sigmund Freud with the raw material for his exploration of hidden motives and thwarted impulses (Gay, 1984). Albert's death, then, provided an opportunity to soothe personal fears and doubts through displays of confidence in divine justice and mercy.

The postmortem cult of the Prince Consort became an ideal representation of the virtues his generation cherished. He had been just the way they wished they could be. Further, once the man was dead, his memory could be polished and fixed for posterity without the danger of competition from his ongoing life. It is easier to admire dead heroes. They are less likely to turn around and do something that would disappoint us.

A common feature of elaborate funeral processes is the slow, stately tempo favored for the procession itself. This provides more time for the realization of the death and its meanings to sink in. In contrast, the final arrangements for a person without fame or influence is likely to be simple, routine, and brisk. At Vienna's Central Cemetery, for example, most funeral services are run by the clock, with every element determined by the status of the deceased and family. How many shiny medals would you like to have displayed on how lengthy a carpet? How much money are you prepared to spend? The disassembly line I witnessed one cloudy day was more efficient than many a factory assembly line and so ever more depressing.

Great Britain was a nation swathed in tradition and ornamented by the trappings and figures of royalty. What would happen when a new regime has taken hold—forcibly—in a not especially unified nation, and then loses its founder? Consider, the public afterlife of Vladimir Ilyich Ulyanov.

From Revolutionary to Relic There's Lenin. The man himself. Let's stand beside him and have a look.

Can it be true he died ten years ago? I really feel like I'm looking at a man sleeping. You find yourself walking on tiptoe so as not to wake him. In preserving the body of its historic leader the USSR has achieved the seemingly impossible. The embalming of Lenin is the most perfect example I've ever seen of the art—better even than the mummies of ancient Egypt. Don't the Russian scientists say Vladimir Ilyich's body may be preserved for all eternity, without ever suffering the ravages of time? (An American visitor, quoted by Zbarsky & Hutchinson, 1997, p. 91)

Lenin led a failed revolution in czarist Russia in 1905 and fled the country. In 1917, Russia was at war and in crisis at home. Czar Nicholas II was overthrown, and the provisional government was more than shaky. At this moment in history, a mysterious sealed train entered Russia from neutral Switzerland. Lenin was its most important passenger. His ruthless leadership soon brought the Bolshevik Party to power. Germany, Russia's adversary, had financed this venture to knock Russia out of the war. Lenin became the founding father of a new nation, and the Communist experiment was up and running.

Seven years later, Lenin was dead. Wounded and then partially debilitated by strokes, Lenin became more of symbol than active leader during the last year of his life. Few shed tears. Lenin was an ice-cold person, obsessed by his plans and merciless in their execution. Presumably a liberator of the people, he showed little compassion or even interest in them. His death sparked a national crisis; those hoping to take his place engaged in savage infighting. The genocidal Josef Stalin came out the winner, and millions of Russian people were thereby doomed to suffering and death.

The newly formed Soviet Union could not afford to lose its father figure. What if Lenin's corpse could be preserved indefinitely in a lifelike condition? And what if this corpse were installed within a grand mausoleum that would dominate Red Square, the spiritual heart of the nation? The people would see for themselves that their founding father was still with them!

The irony here was obvious to all who dared take notice. Lenin's Soviet Union had no use for religion, the grandeur of the abolished czarist regime, or "the cult of personality." Nevertheless, a shrine was created for Lenin so he could be revered as a *de facto* patron saint. However, the task of preserving Lenin's body for the ages had been bungled. The first efforts were primitive, leading to serious deterioration of the body (Zbarsky, 1997). The face and hands still looked presentable and were regularly touched up with ointment to prevent drying and cracking. Burial would have been a national scandal, the admission that Soviet science had failed. Zbarsky and his colleagues had to come up with innovative techniques to preserve the already deteriorated body. The restoration process included cosmetic repair of the face and substitution of false for real eyes to prevent the sockets from further shrinking.

How has Lenin fared as a relic? Well, and not so well. Millions of people have visited his tomb, which became one of the most visible symbols both of Russia and of communism. But statues of Lenin were pulled down in countries that had been subservient to Moscow soon after the Soviet Union ceased to exist. The Russian people have increasingly expressed themselves in favor of burying Lenin's body. Now, years later, few are still passionately concerned about the fate of Lenin's remains.

Strange, strange, strange—but then, not so strange after all. Many societies have not only venerated but used their powerful dead. The skulls of past chiefs are consulted for advice, and the shrines of saints visited in hope of miraculous healing. Lenin's public afterlife is an instructive reminder that a core of ancient belief and feeling can retain its potency into modern times. This emotional core was strong enough to entice a materialistic antireligious regime to devote itself to enshrining a corpse with more desperate determination than craftsmanship.

Balancing the Claims of the Living and the Dead

Another major function of the funeral process is to achieve a balance between the competing claims of the living and the dead. This may sound like a strange idea. We often hear it said that funerals are for the living. However, the need to honor the claims of the dead is also well-entrenched in most death systems. Some of these traditions have been eroded by changing social conditions. Nevertheless, even today the need to balance the claims of the dead and the living can still be discovered if we look beneath the surface. First consider how this process expresses itself in three traditional contexts: rural Greece, the Kotas of Southern India, and Orthodox Judaism.

In the Shadow of Mount Olympus

Potamia is a village in northern Greece not far from Mount Olympus. The 600 people who live there remain in close physical and symbolic contact with the dead. The small cemetery is crowded with 20 or more grave markers that memorialize villagers who have died in the past few years. Anthropologist Alexander Tsiarias (1982) entered a building in the corner of the cemetery:

Although I knew what I would find inside, I was still not fully prepared for the sight that confronted me when I opened the door. Beyond a small floor space a ladder led down to a dark, musty-smelling area filled with the bones of many generations of villagers. Near the top of the huge pile the remains of each person were bound up separately in a white cloth. Toward the bottom of the pile the bones—skulls, pelvises, ribs, the long bones of countless arms, and legs—lay in tangled disarray, having lost all trace of belonging to distinct individuals with the disintegration of the cloth wrappings. Stacked in one corner of the building were metal boxes and small suitcases with names, dates, and photographs identifying the people whose bones lay securely within (pp. 10–11).

Bodies remain in the graveyard for five years and then are removed to the bone house. During this temporary burial, the survivors have ample time to visit their lost loved ones. The survivors' feelings often become expressed with great intensity as the time nears to exhume and transfer the body. Tsiarias recorded a mother's lament:

Eleni, Eleni, you died far from home with no one near you. I've shouted and cried for five years, Eleni, my unlucky one, but you haven't heard me. I don't have the courage to shout any more. Eleni, Eleni, my lost soul. You were a young plant, but they didn't let you blossom. You've been here for five years. Soon you'll leave. Then where will I go? What will I do? Five years ago I put a beautiful bird into the ground, a beautiful partridge. But now what will I take out? What will I find? (p. 15)

The small graveyard in Potamia is often filled with mourners, usually women. They come not only to express their sorrows through song, speech, and prayer but also to tend the graves. Candles are kept burning at the foot of each grave, and the grounds are tended with scrupulous care. Then they sit and talk to their dead and to each other. The village's communal life is strengthened through their role as survivors of the dead. For the women especially, the graveyard provides an opportunity to express their *ponos* (the pain of grief). The men find a variety of outlets, but the women are usually expected to be at home and to keep their feelings to themselves. "A woman performs the necessary rites of passage and cares for the graves of the dead 'in order to get everything out of her system'" (p. 144).

Through their graveside laments and rituals, the women try for a balance between the dead and the living. The custom of temporary burial is helpful in this process. The recently deceased is still treated as an individual and as a member of the community. In effect, there is a second and final death when the physical remains are deposited among the bones of the anonymous dead. It is easier to cope with the symbolic claims of the dead when a definite time limit has been set—in this case, five years. The memory of the deceased will continue to be honored, but removal of the remains to the bone house releases the survivors to devote themselves to their own life-oriented needs.

As Tsiarias points out, this process involves a symbolic interaction and continuation between the living and the dead. The dead have the right to expect it, just as those who are now among the living can expect their survivors to honor their postmortem rights when the time comes. In Potamia and in some other communities where traditional value systems remain in place, the obligations of the living to the dead are clear, specific, and well known.

Kotas and Orthodox Jews

Peoples as different as the Kotas of Southern India and Orthodox Jews dispersed throughout the world perpetuate extensive rituals to ensure that both the dead and the living receive their due. Their observations differ greatly in detail. The Kotas, who cremate their dead (Goldberg, 1981/1982):

believe that death is contaminating and all who come into contact with death are defiled. Through the rituals of two funerals, the Green Funeral and the Dry Funeral, the spirit of the deceased is assisted in departing to the "Motherland" and the survivors are thereby cleansed so that they might resume their normal life within the society. Since the concept of an afterlife is not clear to most Kotas, the adherence to ritual is seen more as a cleansing process for the survivors, than for the attainment of existence in another world for the deceased (p. 119).

Orthodox Jews obey strict laws that reject embalming and cremation and require simple funeral arrangements no matter what the family's financial status. The interval between death and burial is regarded as quite apart from everyday time and custom. This period is known as *Aninut*—a time in which time stands still (Schindler, 1996). During *Aninut*, the grieving survivors are exempted from all social and religious obligations, other than arranging for the funeral. Aninut therefore helps the survivors to begin the long process of recovery from grief by providing a little time to focus on the death in their own private ways without other distractions. The *Kaddish* prayer affirms faith in God; Shiva, the seven days of mourning, unites the family in grief.

The ritual action of washing hands before sitting at Shiva has its parallel in the more elaborate purification rites of the Kotas. The Kota, the Orthodox Jew, the rural Greek villager, and many others with long ethnic traditions must fulfill obligations to the dead. When these obligations have been faithfully performed, it is time to again turn their full attention to life.

MEMORIES OF OUR PEOPLE: CEMETERIES IN THE UNITED STATES

At first a nation of farmers and small town artisans, the United States soon became a coast-to-coast industrial power with humming factories, crowded cities, opportunistic ventures, and a large and mobile population. The history of cemeteries has moved in step with our changing ways of life. In colonial times, most of the dead were buried in a church graveyard. This practice continued into the early years of the republic. As the population increased, the dead as well as the living were becoming crowded.

The New Haven Burying Ground is a surviving example of the response to this emerging need. The city had established a cemetery in 1639 in what is now the center of New Haven (Plunkett, 1999). Graves were dug by friends and relatives, who placed, marked, and tended the graves as they saw fit. Just 20 years later, there was already concern that the burial ground had become too crowded, but nothing was done about it. The poorly tended and helter-skelter burial ground was otherwise becoming an eyesore in the growing community. The closely packed grave sites did not affirm dignity and respect. Moreover, the seasonal death toll from diseases such as malaria and tuberculosis further strained the resources of the graveyard. Some

people worried that the burial ground itself might be a source of infection.

The community finally responded in 1796 with the establishment of the New Haven Burying Ground (also known as the Grove Street Cemetery). Care was taken to select land that was accessible and yet would not block further community development. Furthermore, each grave lot became the property of a purchasing family—here was one of the first cemeteries in which "the family plot" became established. Unfortunately, many grave sites were neglected. Animals and vandals invaded at night, the former digging up graves, the latter desecrating memorial stones and littering. The people of New Haven again rallied to protect their cemetery. This basic story has been repeated in many cemeteries as communities try to cope with urban change and years of neglect. The challenges and efforts continue.

Memorial Parks

Major changes in cemeteries occurred throughout the nineteenth century. One of the most important was the introduction of "memorial parks," also known as "garden parks" and "landscapes of memory" (Linden-Ward, 1989; Morris, 2002). The first of these was Mount Auburn Cemetery (Cambridge, Massachusetts), whose spacious and inviting grounds became the inspiration for similar developments throughout the nation. The other major development was the establishment of national cemeteries to honor those who had fallen in war. Lincoln's Gettysburg Address on November 11, 1863, dedicated the first national cemetery. By the end of the American Civil War, there were 14 national cemeteries for both Union and Confederate dead. The National Cemetery System today tends to the graves of more than 2 million veterans in more than 100 sites throughout the country. In history's odd way of doing things, the United States became that much more of a nation when the dead of the Blue and the dead of the Gray were placed to rest in the same meadows.

Ethnic Cemeteries in the United States

The shores of the United States have attracted millions of people who sought to make new lives for themselves and their children. Others were brought here involuntarily, wrenched from their homelands and sold into slavery. Still other people lived freely in forests and on the plains until they encountered the aggressive newcomers who would eventually transform a wilderness into a powerful industrial nation. Memories of this incredible variety of people remain with us in many forms. One of the most painful memories has lingered for more than a century by a creek in South Dakota. There, the 7th Cavalry Regiment slaughtered upwards of 150 men, women, and children of the Lakota Sioux people in 1890. Wounded Knee became a National Historic Landmark, but no less an accusation.

The land also remembers. Ethnic cemeteries affirm that "our people" contributed to the nation's history. Here are a few examples of cemeteries whose responsibility it is to preserve not only physical remains but memories and symbols of those who have gone before us.

1. *African American section,* the Common Burying Ground, Newport, Rhode Island. This colonial cemetery dates from 1650. More than 8,000 people were buried here until it became an historical site. Ann Tashjian and her husband, Dickran Tashjian (1989), photographed the gravestones and researched the history. Many of the grave markers described the deceased as "servant," a New England euphemism for "slave." Some of the gravestones are elaborate in design and execution, suggesting that the deceased had been held in high regard by the white families they served.

Do the gravestones or burial sites show any trace of the cultures and belief systems that the African Americans brought with them to the American colonies? *Not a trace.* The dominant white American culture of the time prevailed. Make your way to the northern edge and you will see African American grave markers that have survived the vicissitudes of time. You will see that they are similar to the other grave markers of the same time periods. Cherubs, for example, were popular adornments, and these appear alike on white and African American grave markers. In death as in life, their own culture was denied expression. Death would bring freedom from servitude, but in public memory

the African American would still be under the control of the dominant society.

2. *Navajo and Mormon companions, Ramah Cemetery, Ramah, New Mexico.* Members of the Church of the Latter-day Saints (often referred to as Mormons) started a community in Ramah, New Mexico, in 1876. The Ramah people of the Navajo Nation already lived there. The same graveyard serves families of both cultures, although their beliefs and practices differ markedly. There are no large memorial statues, and the ground is covered by native grasses and weeds.

The Navajo section includes 71 graves that could be positively identified. Most are undecorated. Cunningham (1984) noted:

> There is no indication of any attempt to bury family members side by side or close together. All the graves are approximately the same distance apart and are laid out in what is basically a straight line. The headstone or other marker and the grave are placed so that the main side of the marker and the head of the deceased point toward the West, and the deceased would face East if sitting or standing (p. 204).

Navajo culture expresses itself through valued objects placed with the dead. In burying turquoise jewelry with the deceased, the family speeds the deceased's spirit on its journey to the afterlife and confuses and thwarts any *ch'iidii* (evil ghosts) that might covet these powerful objects.

The Mormon section (209 graves) has numerous markers, some of them homemade by family members. These markers display a large variety of style and materials, in contrast with the simple metal markers that identify the Navajo graves. The Mormon markers include examples of folk art revival (e.g., in red sandstone carvings) and such others as "an actual picture of the deceased as a part of their design and contemporary sand-blasted stones which allow very intricate and exact representations of floral motifs and even recognizable representations of Mormon temples at Mesa, Arizona, and Salt Lake City, Utah" (Cunningham, 1989, p. 204). The LDS graves further differ from those of the Navajo in spatial arrangement: They are usually grouped according to family relationships, including some joint stones for husband and wife. The memorial stones also provide more information about the deceased.

The Navajo and Mormon dead in New Mexico appear to be more companionable than the African Americans and colonial whites in Newport. The New Mexico cemetery itself blends easily into its surroundings, the "landscaping" for both Navajo and Mormon being left up to nature. The family-oriented Mormons preserved this orientation in the arrangement of graves and markers but did not impose their beliefs and practices on their Native American neighbors nor object to the jewelry burials. For their part, some Navajos have chosen to become Mormon—or "semi-Mormon"—and have expressed the thought that the worst of the evil spirits have departed from the burial grounds because of the Mormons' presence.

3. *Mexican Americans in San Antonio's San Fernando Cemetery.* Many urban cemeteries look like many other urban cemeteries. Lynn Gosnell and Suzanne Gott (1989) describe the activity at a cemetery that has retained its special character:

> *Throughout the year, but especially during religious and secular holidays, including Halloween, All Souls' Day, Christmas, Valentine's Day, Easter, Mother's Day, and Father's Day, the visitor to San Fernando takes part in an energetic practice of grave decoration and visual display. During these days, cars and trucks jam the narrow traffic lanes which provide access to each block of this ninety-three acre cemetery. Relatives crowd the burial grounds, bringing with them gardening tools, flowers, and other decorative materials. . . . Some people busily tend to a gravesite, while others take time to chat and remark on a particularly well-decorated grave site. Still others stand quietly, singly or in groups, near the grave of a loved one. Grave decorating days within San Fernando Cemetery are therefore marked by a lively social interaction between the living and a heightened interaction between families and their deceased loved ones (p. 218).*

Each family could remember and honor its own dead privately. But having a cemetery to share with other people who hold similar beliefs and values enhances the memorial process. Furthermore, at the gravesite, there are things to do for the loved ones, reminiscent of what living family members do for each other.

No less important is the vista: "We are not the only people to have lost a loved one. It is the human condition. We are, all of us, together in our respect for the dead and our celebration of life." Finally, after the trip, the decorating, the interaction, the family returns home and is able to separate, for a while, from the dead. Some outsiders might be puzzled or even annoyed by all this activity at a cemetery: Have they never felt isolated by a loss, and never carried a death around with them, unable to set it down even for a moment?

These are but three examples of the ethnic cemetery in the United States today. What examples are in your own area? And what stories do they tell?

THE PLACE OF THE DEAD IN SOCIETY: YESTERDAY AND TODAY

Society today places a strong emphasis on curing illness and preventing death. By contrast, most death systems in the past emphasized relationships with the dead. Here is a brief comparison of the place of the dead in the past that will prepare us to consider the meaning and impact of the Vietnam Veterans Memorial, the World War II Veterans Memorial, and the World Trade Center Memorial that is—still!—yet to come.

When Are the Dead Important to the Living?

1. *The dead are more secure in past-oriented societies.* They maintain a role in the symbolic continuity of people with shared language and cultural values who have lived in the same place for many generations, perhaps for centuries. For example, the Penang Gang people of central Borneo give new names or titles to their family members when they die. This practice conveys their continuing affection for deceased people they loved and also provides them with powerful words (the death-names) that can be called upon in vows and curses (Brosius, 1995/1996).

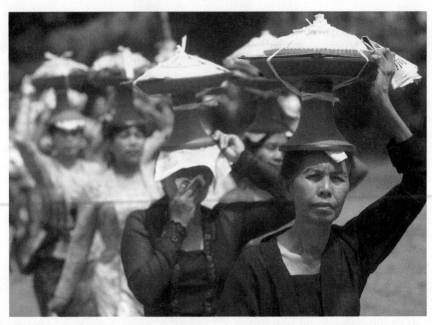

This funeral procession is traditional among the Balinese, but the occasion bears the mark of contemporary worldwide violence. Nearly 200 people were killed in a terrorist attack on a nightclub in Bali, Indonesia on Oct. 22, 2002.

2. *Separation from the dead is more likely to cause distress to the living in past-oriented societies.* Vietnamese families who were relocated by the American military during "pacification" efforts experienced great anguish in having to depart from the land inhabited by the spirits of their ancestors. The world today includes many other people from traditional backgrounds who were forced to leave their homeland and, therefore, their ancestors. Perhaps when we have all become ancestors, there will be less concern for the dead because fewer people will have formed deep, long-term attachments to particular places (Scheidt, 1993).

3. *The dead will be remembered and "used" more often in societies in which children are highly valued as continuing the family soul over the gap created by death.* The only available study (Kastenbaum, 1974) suggested that young couples did not regard children as important for generational continuity. It is every generation, every family for itself. Should one generation feel responsibility for projecting the "family soul" across the death line to the next generation?

4. *Longer life expectancy and low vested power of the elderly make the dead less important.* In earlier times, most people died at an age we would now consider premature. The unfinished lives were likely to be carried forth in memory, an example of psychology's well-known Zeigarnik (1927) effect. Today more people live to an advanced age, and the survivors are less likely to experience a sense of incompleteness that needs to be compensated for by memorialization. Furthermore, in today's youth-oriented world, the older person does not as often control property and wealth and is therefore less likely to command obedience. And now there are so many long-lived people around that we have lost the status reserved for rarities. Are we no longer as close to the gods and ancestral spirits? (On the other hand, there are those senior discounts.)

5. *A society lacking unifying and transcending themes will assimilate the funeral and memorialization process into its utilitarian motives.* Without unifying beliefs, societies are more apt to doubt and quibble about funerals. The time and cost of the funeral may become most salient. If the dead are not very important, then

why spend a lot of time and money on their disposal? (Even in the slower-paced, rural South, I have heard mourners complain that a funeral "dragged on too long. One flower girl wasn't enough! They had to have three, and all of them took their own sweet time!") For the dead to be useful they will have to be considered functional, just like everybody else, and continue to earn their place.

6. *Societies that live close to nature need the assistance of the dead to assure fertility and regeneration.* The Merina of Madagascar, for example, made sure that the female element (the body) had thoroughly decomposed so that the male element (the bleached bones) would emerge purified so that both the people and their harvests are fertile (Bloch, 1982). As in many other traditional cultures, the decomposition process is considered both dangerous and vital. It is from decay that the miracle of regeneration is wrought. Bloch sees one of the major functions of the Merina funeral process as transforming death into life. The dead are crucial to the cycle of life because it is literally from their breath and bones that the species regenerates itself. We might remind ourselves that "Hail to thee, dung beetle!" was a celebration of this phenomenon among the dynastic Egyptians. Furthermore, the ambivalence toward our neighborhood vampire (Chapter 3) reveals our fascination as well as our revulsion about the mysterious transactions between the living and the dead.

American Memory and the Casualties of War and Terrorism

With the rise of technology and industrialization, the dead have been losing status. There are signs, however, that many people are longing to reintegrate the dead into their lives.

Vietnam Veterans Memorial What would persuade a nation so often described as death denying to be so moved by a memorial to a war that that we had wanted to forget as quickly as possible? And why would so many people not only make a pilgrimage to the memorial but also bring objects of personal and symbolic meaning to leave by the wall?

Kristin Ann Hass (1998) recounts the fierce objections to Maya Lin's design. It was too abstract, too intellectual. The black stone suggested mourning rather than heroism. The response to the design

clearly revealed the nation's divided response to the war itself: Had we won a noble victory, or had the war been a human disaster, a senseless killing field? One of the decisive factors in the go-ahead was the support given by many veterans of the conflict who felt that making war should be not celebrated but that the names of their buddies deserved to be honored and remembered.

The innovative design of the memorial wall proved to be ideally suited for its purpose. Everything about the wall invites reflection and personal involvement. The reflection is literal as well as symbolic: Visitors see themselves mirrored by the wall at the same time that they read the names. We all become part of the wall and its memories, if only for the moment. Furthermore, how the names are *not* arranged makes its own point. It was decided not to present the names in alphabetical order. Rank, military unit, and home state were also ignored. Instead, with unassailable logic, the names are placed in the order of their deaths. This was a compelling way to make it clear that men and women died as individuals and should be remembered as such.

That so many people continue to bring something of their own to leave at the wall also suggests that this memorial still has much work to do.

The things left at the wall make a lot of noise. They constitute a remarkable conversation. It is a conversation about the shape of the nation, the status of the citizen, and the problem of patriotism. It is a conversation about the impossibility of loss, the deaths of sons, and the births of granddaughters. . . . It is impassioned and unfinished, and it gives us a tremendous opportunity to witness the process of ordinary Americans struggling to make meanings of, to make sense of, the Vietnam War and all of its difficult and complicated legacies.

child's painting	red panties	Zippo
lighter eagle feather	cornhusk	cookie
stuffed dog	poem	key chain
tissue with lipstick	(Hass, 1998, pp. 123–124).

World War I Memorial Despite its scope, horror, casualties (116,000 American deaths) and enduring consequences, World War I has received little memorial attention. There is a valuable museum in Kansas City (info@theworldwar.org), and a secluded memorial on the National Mall in Washington D.C. for residents of that city who died in the war. Neglected and in extreme disrepair for many years, it was

The Vietnam Memorial Wall initially faced a wall of criticism, but since has been recognized as a compelling remembrance of the men and women who did not return from the war.

re-dedicated as a national monument, but funds are still being sought for its restoration. Named for the last survivor of World War I, the Frank Buckles World War I Memorial Act (S.2097) is still awaiting congressional action.

World War II Memorial More than half a century passed before a national memorial was created to honor those who served and those who died (about 400,000) while in the armed forces in World War II. It took years of advocacy and private fundraising. Many of the veterans felt that the war had been almost forgotten—and with this neglect, the neglect of comrades who did not return. Creation of the Vietnam Veterans Memorial led to recognition that World War II veterans and their families were also deserving of this recognition.

The World War II memorial was dedicated on May 29, 2004, with an estimated 150,000 people in attendance. It can be visited 24/7 in Washington, D.C., flanked by the memorials to Washington and Lincoln.

World Trade Center Memorial While the smoke was still rising from Ground Zero, there were already calls for a memorial to the World Trade Center victims. Attention was focused on this largest site of death and destruction, although memorialization would later be created for the Pentagon and rural Pennsylvania sites as well. Many plans were offered, and many critics had their say. The nation itself had not yet decided how best to fix the disaster in its collective memory. What should the memorial express and accomplish? Should it be designed primarily to honor the dead? To comfort the bereaved? To restore a sense of national security? To tell the world that American business is still in business? To discourage other possible terrorists? To demonstrate the skill and creativity of the memorial planners? To become a prime tourist attraction? The project was soon entangled in competing emotional, political, and economic interests. It remains to be seen how the nation and the world will respond to the restoration of Ground Zero and its memorial tribute, a process now underway. The sense of national unity immediately following the disaster did not endure long enough to inspire a memorial consensus.

Oklahoma City Memorial Another city that was victimized by a domestic terrorist attack developed an innovative memorial that has been very well received. The lives of 168 were lost when the Murrah Building, a federal facility, was destroyed on April 19, 1995. The people of Oklahoma City realized that clearing away the debris was not enough: A memorial should be erected on the site. They invited designs from around the world, but the decision was made by a committee that included family members, survivors, and rescuers as well as design professionals. The result was the Oklahoma City National Memorial and Memorial Center Museum. The Museum includes an institute for the prevention of terrorism as well as an education and outreach service.

A compelling feature is a room-to-room procession that illuminates the course of events, from the chaos of the explosion, through the rescue and recovery efforts, and culminating in a tribute to hope in the form of a "water wall" that flows over a dark stone background. For many visitors, the most moving experience occurs in the "Gallery of Honor." Here there is a photograph or other image of each person who was killed in the bombing. The images are accompanied by a personal object that was selected by a family member. This memorial demonstrates the individuality of the victims and the caring response of family and community. The human tragedy is not distanced by a monumental and impersonal structure. By practically all accounts, this memorial and the process that created it was ideal for the people of Oklahoma City.

Who "Owns" Human Remains?

Rival claims for "ownership" of human remains are more frequent than we might have supposed, and tell us something about varying perspectives and motives in society. A significant example is the custody and treatment of human remains and artifacts found in Native American grave sites.

Indigenous people throughout the world have protested the desecration of their grave sites by individuals eager to sell or possess remains and artifacts. Scientists and museum curators have also been criticized for studying and displaying ancestral objects that should be with their own people. There is a long and painful history behind this protest movement: Looting Native American graves started with the Pilgrims. It was readily agreed that grave looting was unethical, although difficult to prevent. More difficult to resolve was the scientist's and historian's claim for the right to correct and advance knowledge. It is to the credit of all parties involved that an accord was reached after many years of controversy and frustration. The agreement was achieved through an international conference in Vermillion, South Dakota, with face-to-face discussions between representatives of native peoples and those involved in studying or displaying human remains and artifacts.

The document generated by this conference is known as the *Vermillion Accord* (the meetings having been held in Vermillion, South Dakota). Its main points are as follows (Davidson, 1990):

- Universal respect shall be given to the mortal remains of the dead.
- Disposition of human remains will be made in accordance with the wishes of the dead

themselves whenever this is known or can be reasonably inferred.
- The wishes of the local community will be respected "whenever possible, reasonable, and lawful."
- The scientific value of studying human remains will be respected whenever such value can be demonstrated to exist.
- Negotiations with an attitude of mutual respect shall be conducted to accommodate both the legitimate concerns of communities for the proper disposition of their ancestors and the legitimate concerns of science and education (p. 641).

The Native American Graves Protection and Repatriation Act (NAGPRA) has since established criminal penalties for the sale, purchase, or transport of Native American human remains or cultural artifacts without an established legal right of possession. Notification and consent procedures were introduced to affirm the rights of Native American organizations to participate in all relevant decisions. In recent years, there has been a significant transfer of human remains and cultural artifacts from schools and museums to tribal organizations. Scientists and Native American organizations have been learning how to work together in mutual respect.

Does the availability of new technologies justify "disturbing" human remains to satisfy curiosity, make an interesting documentary, advance careers, or test the claim that a particular set of famous bones are in residence in a particular location? Or is it also in the interests of the dead to learn more about them and dispel assumptions that have clouded their reputation? For example, the powerful Medici family of sixteenth-century Florence has been absolved of infamous murders by a team of forensic experts (Lorenzi, 2005).

"You Were the Best Dog Ever": The Pet Cemetery

I have turned over the rocky ground of Massachusetts and the dry sands of Arizona to bury several very important cats. When the first dog of the family died quietly in his basket bed, none of us could regard Toby's body as only the corpse of an animal. The same was true when Honey, the second dog, asked to go outside and moved with a purpose and stride we no longer expected in her enfeebled condition. A few minutes later, she was still beautiful, but dead. Millions of other people have had close attachments to their pets—or to animals they have worked with: the horse who drew the milkman's wagon, the dog who guided its visually impaired owner, and the elephant who hauled lumber. Attachment does not end at the moment of death, whether the loss be that of another human or of an animal companion.

The modern version of the pet cemetery seems to have started in France at about the turn of the twentieth century. Not only dogs and cats, but also horses, monkeys, rabbits, birds (and a lioness) have been buried there. Perhaps the most famous is Rin-Tin-Tin, once the reigning animal star of Hollywood. However, the impulse to honor the memory of an animal companion through a funeral and burial process has been expressed throughout history. There are examples among the ancient Greeks and in the early years of our own nation. It is estimated that there are about 400 pet cemeteries in the United States.

Pet cemeteries express some of the same mixed and changing attitudes toward death that characterize society in general. For example, ritual has long played a significant role in Japanese culture. In recent years, memorial services have been developed for animal companions; their services are simplified versions of those performed for the passing of humans. They may be held at a pet cemetery or on family property. Smaller animals are returned to their elements, for example, a pet fish to the sea (but never flushed down a toilet, which would be regarded as desecration) (Kenney, 2004). Owners often continue their relationship with the animal companion through postmortem rituals and visitations. Beloved dogs and cats were "family" and are honored and mourned as such.

For an example in the United States, consider Pet Rest Memorial Mortuary and Cemetery. Once located just up the road from Arizona State University (Tempe), Pet Rest provided the opportunity for a study by Vivian Spiegelman and me (1990). At the time of our visits, Pet Rest resembled many another small cemetery—a fenced-in, park-like space with grave markers designed to individual specifications. Some markers displayed a photographic or sculptured representation of the deceased. Ceramic cats played inside a white picket fence. However, some monuments had already toppled into the weedy grass, and there was a general impression of neglect.

Pet Rest had already become a "dead cemetery"—that is, no more burials were allowed, nor had anybody accepted responsibility for maintenance. The continuing influx of people into Arizona, the change from an agricultural to a residential community, the transformation of a small college into one of the nation's largest universities—these are among the factors that contributed to the decline and eventual destruction of Pet Rest. The land had become too valuable, and officials were uncomfortable with having death on display while attempting to upscale commercial properties. The "final resting place" had proven vulnerable to the economic pressure and social change that also affect many "people cemeteries" across the nation. And now, Pet Rest no longer exists, its "eternal memory" replaced by a nationally franchised restaurant.

Some people choose to conduct their own memorial services and to satisfy themselves with photographs or personal videos. Few people can commission a taxidermist to preserve their horse in three glorious dimensions, and not everybody is prepared to purchase a box turtle–shaped pendant containing the ashes of their own, well, box turtle. A trip to the local animal shelter would be more likely. This will not erase memories of the lost animal companion, but bring a new and lively life into the home. (We came home with Angel, the Incredible Leaping Dog and now dutiful servant to the resident cats.)

Pet cemeteries have invited parody and mockery. Nevertheless, those who understand and value the bonds of affection that can form between one creature and another may judge that giving "too much" love is not the worst thing that might be said of a person.

THE FUNERAL DIRECTOR'S PERSPECTIVE

Funeral and memorialization practices are very much part of the world of the living and, therefore, subject to change. An interview with funeral director Tom Carrick proved helpful in identifying some of the major challenges and developments.

- *The impact of AIDS?*
  "Everybody in the funeral industry overreacted at first. Now we realize that we can do our part in dealing with AIDS and cannot behave in a discriminatory manner. We do give more attention to personal safety. Precautions

are used in handling all cases now because one can never be certain about AIDS. For example, we wear gloves every time we touch a cadaver. Instead of smocks, we now use rubber aprons and complete protective clothing, including eye wear. All 'sharps' go into specified and controlled waste containers. Funeral personnel are doing the same things that health care providers are doing—being more careful."

* *Are there changes in the way that funeral directors do business?*

"Enormous changes. Laws have changed and regulations have increased. For example, we are now mandated to provide full price disclosures to the public. Written consents are required for embalming. Employees must be given time off for continuing education sessions. Fair employment practices have increased access by women who are entering this field in larger numbers than ever before. These changes provide benefits to the public."

* *Have these regulations affected your cost of operations?*

"Yes, considerably so. Every funeral home has had to remodel to provide access for handicapped individuals and to meet other health and safety standards. Chemicals must be stored in sealed compartments with security locks, so that people do not become exposed to any risk from them. Most of these changes are worthwhile, but they are costly."

* *You mentioned that more women have become funeral directors in recent years. How has this change been received?*

"The public has had a favorable response. Many client families feel more comfortable in dealing with women. Frequently it is a widow who is making the arrangements. She may perceive a woman funeral director as more understanding and sympathetic. In the past, there was a reluctance to hire women and only a few women were qualified. Part of this reluctance came from the enormous amount of lifting that is involved. But now women work in construction; women drive trucks; women work successfully in many occupations that were thought to be for men only. It's not that the conditions of work have changed so much, it's the attitudes that have changed about what women can and should do. Funeral directing is a very conservative business that tends to be slow in adapting to change."

* *What does a person have to know to become a funeral director?*

"A person needs to become proficient in anatomy, chemistry, restorative art, pathology, business, accounting, and some law. These subjects are included in the licensure exams. Once a person is licensed, it is important to keep up with new developments through continued education; for example, handling a situation that may involve a contagious disease. Unfortunately, there has been a tendency for continued education sessions to be oriented toward sales rather than consumer services."

* *Can you take us through a typical funeral?*

"The funeral itself will typically begin with a musical prelude, followed by an opening prayer. About half the people we deal with are 'churched.' This leaves the other half in need of a presiding clergyperson, so we frequently recommend one. Some families give a high priority to the choice of a particular clergyperson. Others say, 'I don't care who you get for my Mom's funeral. I want it brief!' This illustrates the larger differences in how families approach funeral planning. Some are concerned about every detail; some could care less.

"After the opening prayer, there are often introductory remarks by a person who represents the family. In recent years, there has been more participation by family and friends. In particular, more teens are stepping up to contribute to the memorialization. Any number of family and friends may give scripture readings, recite poetry, eulogize the deceased, or play music, either live or recorded. Words of comfort are usually offered by the clergyperson, but others may also express themselves in their own words."

* *What is the usual length of a funeral these days?*

"The typical funeral lasts between 20 and 40 minutes. The public seems to prefer brief services. I don't really know why this is the case."

* *And what about the question of open or closed casket?*

"Most people still prefer the casket open for a portion of the time. Today it is most common for the deceased to wear their own clothing. It is usually a suit, shirt, and tie for a man, a dress for a woman. There are regional differences, however. Yesterday we had a funeral in which the man wore a western shirt and jeans. This might seem unusual in New York City, but not here

Arizona or in Aspen. If people never wore a suit or necktie, why should they be forced to change their habits now? If a woman was always seen in a pink dress, they're probably going to bury her in a pink dress, and get pink flowers. . . ."

- *How much is the typical funeral likely to cost?*
"The national average is between $6,000 and $8,000 for a complete, traditional funeral. This includes both mortuary and cemetery expenses, such as the burial plot, flowers, clergy, musicians, and limousine. The cost differs somewhat from one place to another. It tends to be higher in the eastern than in the western states."

- *There are different opinions about the appropriateness of including children in the funeral process. How do you see this?*
"I'm all for it. Death is part of life. Children should be exposed to it as often as it occurs. Parents may be poorly prepared to educate our kids about death and dying, but the best way to do that is to attend funerals when opportunity presents itself. We shouldn't be running and hiding from death. The ideal funeral should be an uplifting experience, reinforcing all the values this person stood for and why we loved this person and why we are here today."

- *What is your worst-case scenario about what might go wrong in performing a funeral?*
"I worry most about breakdown of equipment. What if the hearse breaks down or the air conditioning fails in the summer months either in the building or the limousine?

"In some 30,000 funerals only one stands out as a total embarrassment to me personally. I call it 'The Funeral from Hell.' Every conceivable thing went wrong—from equipment failures right down to the cemetery digging the wrong grave! The mother's name was even on the headstone, but they dug 25 feet away on a 115-degree day. To make it even worse, the death was a sudden and tragic one. Oh, yes, and the sound system at the church picked that day to quit working; actually, it exploded! A key family member was late, one limo didn't show up, another broke down. There was a mix-up with the flowers as well. Fortunately, this was the memorable exception, and I don't feel the need to have another funeral memorable in this way, ever!"

- *Looking back over more than 30 years as a funeral director, what stands out as most important to you personally?*

"I've walked in the shoes they're walking in, and I think people appreciate that. I identify with their loss, so it is natural for me to offer all the time they need and all the understanding I can bring to the situation. I remind myself each time that I am a total stranger who has been invited into a family's life at a time of loss and sorrow. My challenge is to put them at ease. This is not easy: 'How can I relax—my mother just died!' I derive my satisfaction from helping people through these stressful situations.

We, as a society in general, need to understand how much death is part of life. As parents and teachers, we don't do a particularly good job of it. We are still a death-denying society. We don't talk about funerals unless we have just came from one!"

For more about funeral planning and expenses, please see Chapter 6, End-of-Life Issues and Decisions.

IMPROVING THE FUNERAL PROCESS

Turn the calendar back to the middle of the twentieth century and we find the physician and the funeral director bearing the major responsibility for society's confrontations with death. Few families felt prepared to take end-of-life decisions into their own hands: It was less anxiety-provoking to depend on the experts. A more independent-minded and participatory orientation has since been evident as, for example, in the vigorous development of hospice and palliative care programs and the swirling controversies about the right to die and physician-assisted death. Funeral practices have not escaped criticism in this reevaluation of tradition. There is a fairly broad consensus that a standard funeral "taken off the shelf" is not necessarily the most appropriate choice for all families. It is time, then, to consider some of the emerging options.

Alternative Funerals

Some families and funeral directors have stayed within the traditional approach, but with a flexibility that makes it more personal and comforting. There are also alternatives that are starting to become traditions of their own. Our examples here are the memorial society and natural (home and green) funeral options, along with a proposal from the funeral industry that is not for the squeamish. We also explore virtual memorials, though these do not encompass the physical remains.

The Memorial Society Option

Funerals can be simple, inexpensive, and responsive to the needs and values of particular individuals and families. This is the essence of the memorial society option. First coming to general attention in the early years of the twentieth century, this type of funeral arrangement has become favored by an increasing number of people who dislike what they consider the ostentation and outworn rhetoric of traditional funerals. It has also been appreciated as a cost-saving measure and as a way of avoiding the sales tactics of some commercial funeral services. Local nonprofit memorial societies were first created by farm grange organizations and churches. Each of these organizations defined its own mission but shared the purpose of helping families retain control and make their own choices rather than turning all the details over to a commercial funeral service (Bergonzi, 2004).

A new level of coordination and influence was achieved with the establishment of the Funeral and Memorial Societies of America (operating in Canada as well as the United States). This coalition was responsible for a major improvement in consumer rights. In 1984, the Federal Trade Commission (kind of reluctantly) affirmed the right of consumers to receive information about the cost of specific funeral services and supplies, as well as their right to be informed of the applicable state regulations. Consumers are now in a better position to evaluate and compare services and costs. There are now also more funeral directors who welcome the opportunity to arrange funerals that are in keeping with the family's wishes. The coalition has since changed its title to Funeral Consumers Alliance (FCA) to distinguish itself from numerous other organizations that have since described themselves as "societies." A useful website is the Funeral Ethics Organization (www.funeralethics.org).

I remember a wintry New England morning during which no music was performed, no prayers voiced, no ceremonies enacted. The coffined body of a neighbor's friend was lowered into the earth. Heads did bow and a few moments elapsed in spontaneous silence. There was not much to see, hear, or think about—except death. Then people started to breathe again, and walk back to their cars.

Natural Funerals: The Home Funeral and Green Burial Never mind the dressing up, the slow procession of vehicles to a place nobody really wants to go, the expectations and rituals that somebody else came up with. Instead: why not a home funereal?

Never mind embalming. Never mind solid coffins. Sooner or later, earth will claim the remains of humans as well as other land-based creatures. Why not a natural processes? Why not plan a green funeral? In fact, why not choose a home funeral and green burial?

More people seem to have agreed with these propositions in recent years. Although closely related in spirit, home funerals and green burials do not necessarily occur together. Practical circumstances can favor one rather than the other.

No longer uncommon in Great Britain, the green funeral movement is now also active in the United States. Burials take place in woodlands or meadows, with the intention of allowing the remains to return to earth in a natural form. The bodies are wrapped or placed in containers (such as willow) that do not resist biodegrading. One advocate writes that this process produces

> Wildlife habitats and forests from green burial sites, where native trees, wildflowers and protected animals are encouraged and meadow brown butterfly colonies, grasshoppers, insects, bats, voles, and owls multiply . . . where the mechanical mower does not prey on a regular basis and a self-supporting ecosystem can evolve (Holmes, n.d.).

Joe Sehee, director of the Green Burial Council describes green burial as:

> . . . essentially the way most of humanity has cared for its dead for thousands of years. Returning to earth simply, without a metal casket, without a concrete burial vault, without formaldehyde-based embalming. It's just ashes-to-ashes, dust-to-dust burial (Henzi, 2009, p.1).

In the United States, the green burial movement seems to be planning land trusts or park service agencies where the facility can receive continuing protection. There are now a few cemeteries that are also participating in this plan, such as Prairie Home Cemetery in Waukesha,

Wisconsin. A useful information resource is www.prairiehomecemetery.com/

The green funeral can also serve as protest against cultural traditions that are perceived as outworn, impersonal, and oppressive:

> Mum chose a wonderful spot in a private area overlooking the hills and under a large, shady oak tree. . . .There was no rent-a-frock religious representative spouting unfelt platitudes and thinly veiled threats to those who might not sign up to his particular big truth. . . . The speeches were made by the birds and the wind in the trees. Strong words were spoken by the people who knew and cared for my mum and what she believed in (Ross-Bains, n.d.).

Some environmentalists advocate green funerals for their potential to conserve resources and reduce pollution. For example, it has been estimated that more than 800,000 gallons of embalming fluid and 30 million feet of increasingly scarce hardwood are buried in the United States each year (Smith, 2003).

Not everybody agrees with this rejection of tradition. There may also be inherent limitations. Two that come readily to mind: (a) situations in which embalming could be a necessity for public health reasons, and (b) availability of appropriate natural spaces.

Home funerals have several features that are welcomed by many people: a familiar setting, a tempo and schedule that can be arranged to meet the participants' needs, opportunities for personal expression without having to deal with standard protocol. Some home settings can seem ideal as when Nathaniel Rose, 92, died at his eighteenth-century farm house. The family:

> . . . washed Mr. Roe's body, dressed him in his favorite Harrods tweed jacket and red Brooks Brothers tie, and laid him on a bed so family members could privately say their last goodbyes (Zezima, 2009, p.1).

The next day, he was placed in a pine coffin made by his son, along with a tuft of wool from the sheep he once kept.

Problems? Not all families have a home setting that would be appropriate. Not all members of the family might be comfortable with the idea. Not all neighbors would be considerate. Furthermore—and unsurprisingly—some elements of the funeral industry are attempting to restrict the right to carry out a home funeral.

Flushing the Dead: Alkaline Hydrolysis Through the centuries, the dead have been buried or cremated. Norma Love (2008) introduces us to a possible new option:

> Dissolving bodies in lye and flushing the brownish, syrupy residue down the drain. The process, called alkaline hydrolysis, was developed in this country 16 years ago to get rid of animal carcasses. It uses lye, 300-degree heat and 60 pounds of pressure per square inch to destroy bodies in stainless-steel cylinders that are similar to pressure cookers.

Love quotes a funeral industry newsletter as enthusing that "It's not often that a truly game-changing technology comes along in the funeral service, but we might have gotten a hold of one." This "game-changing" technology has been quickly opposed by clergy, and, although legal in two states (Minnesota and New Hampshire), it has not yet received regulatory approval anywhere in the United States.

Advocates claim environmental advantages for alkaline hydrolysis. Most of the body is dissolved into a coffee-colored liquid "with the consistency of motor oil and a strong ammonia smell. If all goes well, it can be poured safely down the drain. The reduced solid remains take the form of a dry bone residue that resemble cremains, but without having produced crematorium emissions that can include mercury from silver dental fillings. The remains can be buried (taking up less of the limited cemetery space) or preserved in an urn. Presumably, funeral and memorial services could be arranged to suit family values, even though the process of body disposition is not traditional.

Dissolving corpses is not such a new idea, although technology seems to have become more efficient. Criminals have been known to dispose of awkward evidence in that manner, and communities faced with the threat of epidemics have done the same with possibly contagious corpses. Furthermore, it is estimated that about 50 facilities currently produce liquid medical waste from humans, animals, or both. An industrial waste manager observes that the public might be more troubled if it knew how much blood and embalming fluid already flow into sewage plants.

Are we today radically different from those who have had to deal with the physicality of death in the past without the mediation of advanced technology? Or are just as squeamish when faced with this raw side of nature? No need to answer that question—let's move on quickly to a more comfortable realm.

Virtual Memorials Stone has long been a valued material for marking grave sites. It seems so solid, so enduring. It presides over a particular location and stands as a beacon to draw visitors near. An Internet memorial occupies no fixed space. It is everywhere and nowhere. We cannot touch it or observe the changes that time and weather have wrought. The Internet is opening new possibilities for honoring the dead and sharing our personal thoughts and feelings. Bereaved persons have their choice of creating a new memorial Web page or placing a memorial in one of the existing Web cemeteries. The Virtual Memorial Garden (www .virtualmemorialgarden.net/), it seems to have morphed into something a lot more commercial, and Worldwide Cemetery (www.cemetery.org) were among the first Web cemeteries to be established and all three offer free services. Establishing a personal Web page requires computer expertise and upkeep effort that not all bereaved people can manage. "Web rings" make it possible for virtual visitors to explore a broad spectrum of memorials.

Virtual memorials devoted to deceased children seem to be the most common. Many of these websites present the story of the child's life and death, photographs and other images, and a guestbook or e-mail link for visitors. Older adults make less use of the Internet and therefore seem less likely to be constructing and visiting memorial websites. It is likely that as more computer-savvy people grow older, they will make more use of the potentials of bereavement support and memorial sites. An exploratory study (DeVries & Rutherford, 2004) has found that missing the deceased is the most common theme in virtual cemetery memorials. Seldom was either the cause of death mentioned and, perhaps surprisingly, there were relatively few references to God or religion. Most online memorials were written in the form of a communication to the deceased rather than as a statement about the deceased.

Roberts (2004) identifies several distinctive advantages:

> Web memorialization provides unique, supplemental postdeath rituals for the bereaved. Web memorials, unlike most postdeath rituals, can be created at one's pace . . . and can be created by friends and others who were not included in standard mourning rituals. . . . Memorials can be changed and updated . . . and visited at any time and from any location. . . . The opportunity to visit a web memorial may be especially valuable to elders with limited mobility, for whom visiting an interment site is difficult. . . . Many of our survey respondents report sitting in front of the computer screen with others, visiting the memorial together (p. 43).

At present, Web-based memorials seem to be supplementing rather than replacing traditional practices. It remains to be seen whether distinctive websites created by individuals and families will continue to flourish or give way to sites sponsored by mortuaries and other organizations.

SPONTANEOUS MEMORIALIZATION IN RESPONSE TO VIOLENT DEATH

Spontaneous memorialization has been defined as a public response to violent and unexpected deaths (Haney, Leimer, & Lowery, 1997). It provides the opportunity for members of the community to express their personal sorrow and compassion. Not all violent deaths elicit this response: The public must feel a sense of connection or identification with the victims and bereaved family. The widespread public response to the attacks of September 11, 2001, included many examples of spontaneous memorialization.

Spontaneous memorialization usually takes place at the site of the death or some other place that is associated with the deceased. It differs in this respect from traditional services that take place at a funeral home, church, or cemetery. Mementoes are left at the site of the death. These may include a wide variety of objects—flowers, teddy bears, bibles, even beer cans. (Some of the objects that have been left at the Vietnam Memorial Wall have already been mentioned.) These objects usually have meaning to the individual mourners and have some connection to the victim's life. The mourners often raise funds to assist survivors of the victim and may also become advocates for improved public safety measures.

People who did not know the deceased person may be touched by the death and decide to participate. As Haney et al. (1997) stated: "Spontaneous memorialization extends the boundaries of who is allowed or expected to participate in the mourning process." There is no formal organization of the response to the death, at least at first. People respond out of their shock, sorrow, or anger, and find a way of expressing their feelings. Haney, Leimer, and Lowery also found that there are no set time limits: Spontaneous memorialization ebbs and flows as individual mourners make their pilgrimages and contribute their offerings either immediately after the death, or during the weeks or months that follow (p. 162).

Not everybody favors spontaneous memorialization. There have been protests based on concerns as varied as the public expression of religious beliefs and the possible depressing influence of witnessing so many reminders that life can end so quickly. Collins and Rhine (2003), among the first to identify the resistance to spontaneous memorialization, ask: "Which is the greater right; to grieve and mourn, or to be spared reminders of our mortality?" (p. 241).

INTEGRITY AND ABUSE IN THE FUNERAL AND MEMORIAL PROCESS

The corpse reminds us of the life that was and the life that is no more. It occupies a symbolic space between presence and absence, and between the mundane and the sacred. A society that neglects or abuses its dead has been driven to the edge of destruction by catastrophe (Kastenbaum, 2004b). Doing right by the dead remains a core value for most societies today. We have seen the strength of this motivation in the survivors of the tsunami and the September 11, 2001 terror attacks, but it can also be observed in the smaller circle of a family-oriented memorial society or green funeral. The funeral industry realizes that it is expected to provide its services not only with professional competence, but also with sensitivity to the feelings and beliefs of the survivors. It is all the more disturbing, then, when the public trust is betrayed. Sometimes it is not the funeral industry but other organizations that violate society's expectations for respectful treatment of human remains. There are appalling historical examples of neglecting and abusing corpses (e.g., Richardson, 1987). Unfortunately, there are also enough examples in our own time to warrant concern.

These examples include:

- Tri-State Crematory of northwest Georgia was discovered to have dumped corpses in a shed and scattered others throughout its property. Eventually 334 bodies were discovered, many in advanced stages of decomposition. Relatives were given "ashes of the loved ones" that were actually cement dust. Ray Brent Marsh pleaded guilty to theft, corpse abuse, burial service fraud, and making false statements, and received a 12-year prison sentence (Poovey, 2004). He offered no explanation for his abuse and fraud. From time to time there have been allegations that other crematories or funeral homes have not properly conducted their operations or failed to return remains to the right families.

- Tulane University's School of Medicine admitted to having sold its oversupply of donated bodies to the Army—which then blew up the bodies while conducting experiments to reduce land mine fatalities (Yerton, 2004a).

- UCLA medical school admitted having sold cadaver body parts to a broker who in turn sold them to commercial biomedical corporations. The brokers involved in these medical school cases denied they had done anything wrong in arranging the deals. However, Yerton (2004b) confirmed that "Donor's families grieve all over again."

- Cadavers have also been used in some impact studies to test and develop improved vehicle safety (Roach, 2003). Crash dummies, despite their starring role in television commercials, provide less information than actual bodies.

- A series of investigative articles (Flatten, 2004a, b, c, d) found evidence that "Harvesting bodies and tissues is big business in Arizona—but families often are left out of the process" (2004b, A1). Brokers were also active in these arrangements. There is reason to believe that body harvesting for profit occurs on a national and international as well as local level, sometimes legally, sometimes illegally, and sometimes in that gray area in between.

- The burial insurance industry has been found guilty of overcharging and otherwise defrauding black Americans (Donn, 2004). Black families have been the target of persistent marketing for purchase of burial insurance and then sometimes have been denied payment of

"The mystery of Stonehenge has apparently been solved. The mysterious circle of large stones in southern England was primarily a burial ground for almost five centuries, and the site probably holds the remains of a family that long ruled the area, new research concludes" (Kaufman, 2008).

the benefit after having paid inflated premiums for many years.

There are larger issues to consider as well. Have major social institutions (e.g., armed forces, universities) distanced themselves from the cultural values inherent in respect for the dead? Have religious and spiritual beliefs become so marginalized that turning a profit can so easily take precedence? Is our society strengthened or weakened when special interests commandeer the dead? It should be noted that the universities and various organizations in the funeral and insurance fields have condemned the abuses mentioned here, but these questions are far from being resolved.

■ SUMMARY

The funeral is part of a complex process in which we both separate ourselves from the dead and try to establish a new relationship with them that we can carry forward in our lives. We have examined the meaning of the funeral process in many places and times, including our own. How a society cares for its dead tells us much about the beliefs and lifestyles of that society in general. We noticed that society sometimes does forget even those dead who would seem deserving of special respect (e.g., World War I casualties, African American pioneers in colonial New York). You were invited to reflect on your own attitudes, feelings, and knowledge about the funeral process, and consider whether you are more the rationalist or more the romantic. Attention was given to the process of transforming a dead body to a living memory.

We identified basic elements of the funeral process, such as establishing the facts of death, the autopsy, the *death investigator*, legal issues, *organ donation*, *premortem* preparations, immediate post-death activities, preparations for burial or cremation, the funeral service itself, and the longer process of memorializing the deceased. We gave particular attention to the sacred art of mummification, brought to a high level by the ancient Egyptians. We gained further insight through the case histories of three influential people whose deaths were the occasion for extraordinary memorialization: Ch'in shih-huang-ti, the first emperor of China; Prince Albert, husband of Queen Victoria; and Lenin, founder of the Soviet Union. Another major function of the funeral and memorialization process is to achieve a balance between the competing claims of the living and the dead. We learned how the dead have been regarded within three traditional contexts: rural Greece, the Kotas of Southern India, and Orthodox Judaism. Next, we came back home to see how cemeteries in the United States have been shaping memories from colonial times to the present, and how the nature and upkeep of these cemeteries have been closely related to powerful events such as the Civil War and sociotechnological change such as population pressures.

We also visited several ethnic cemeteries to see how the challenges of diverse people living together are reflected in the way their deaths are memorialized. We wondered under what circumstances the dead are most important to the living and learned that the dead are more secure in past-oriented societies (and under several other conditions that were identified). How public tributes to those casualties of war and victims of catastrophe can contribute to national healing was illustrated through the memorials to World War II and Vietnam veterans and to the victims of the Oklahoma City and September 11, 2001, terrorist attacks. We also noted progress in respecting the human remains and artifacts taken from the graves of Native American ancestors and returned to their people whenever possible.

Memorialization of our animal companions was also considered through a visit to Pest Rest Memorial Mortuary and Cemetery (itself a recent casualty of urban development). Our curiosity about the current status of funeral practice led us to an interview with a funeral director who provided frank and engaging answers to many of our questions. We then reminded ourselves that there are a variety of alternative funeral and memorialization possibilities, including the ever more common phenomenon of public spontaneous response to a particularly disturbing death or deaths. Virtual memorials are now offering a new way for the bereaved to honor and remember those they have lost. Results from early studies of Web-based memorials are reported. The memorial society movement developed around the theme of simple, inexpensive, and participatory funerals. Green funerals take this approach further and could become increasingly favored in the United States. The funeral industry's own new proposal for disposal by liquidification was also taken into account. We concluded with a brief inquiry into deceptive and abusive practices that can threaten the integrity of the funeral and memorial practice and do emotional harm to the bereaved.

■ REFERENCES

Aries, P. (1981). *The hour of our death*. New York: Knopf.

Bagchi, I. (2005, February 9). Grave error? Singapore erases history for future. www.taphophilia.com/modules.php?name—News&file5article&sid51976.

Bass, B., & Jefferson, J. (2003). *Death's Acre. Inside the legendary forensic lab*. New York: Putnam.

Beranek O., & Tupek, P. (2009) *From visiting graves to their destruction: The question of Ziyara through the eyes of Salafis*. Waltham, MA: Crown Center for Middle East Studies, Brandeis University.

Bergonzi, J. A. (2004). The memorial society option. *Generations, 28*, 57–58.

Bertman, S. (2000). *Cultural amnesia: American future and the crisis of memory*. New York: Praeger.

Benet, S. V. (1942). American Names. In *Poetry of Stephen Vincent Benet* (pp. 367–368). New York: Farrar & Rinehart.

Bloch, M. (1982). Death, women, and power. In M. Bloch & J. Parry (Eds.), *Death and the regeneration of life* (pp. 1–44). Cambridge, UK: Cambridge University Press.

Carlson, L. (1987). *Caring for the dead*. Hinesburg, VT: Upper Access.

Chang-Won, P. (2010). Funerary transformations in contemporary South Korea. *Mortality, 15*, 18–37.

Collins, C. O., & Rhine, C. D. (2003). Roadside memorials. *Omega, Journal of Death and Dying, 47*, 221–244.

Cotterell, A. (1981). *The first emperor of China*. New York: Holt, Rinehart & Winston.

Crissman, J. K. (1994). *Death and dying in central Appalachia*. Urbana: University of Illinois Press.

Cunningham, K. (1989). Navajo, Mormon, Zuni graves: Navajo, Mormon, Zuni ways. In R. E. Meyer (Ed.), *Cemeteries and gravemarkers* (pp. 197–216). Ann Arbor: University of Michigan Research Press.

Darby, E., & Smith, N. (1983). *The cult of the Prince Consort*. New Haven: Yale University Press.

Davidson, G. W. (1990). Human remains: Contemporary issues. *Death Studies, 14*, 491–502.

Davies, D. J. (2003) Cremation. In C. Bryant (Ed.), *Handbook of death and dying* (Vol. 1, pp. 767–774). Thousand Oaks: Sage.

Davies, D. J., & Mates, L. H. (2006). *Encyclopedia of cremation*. London: Ashgate.

Day, M. H. (1990). The Vermillion Accord. *Death Studies, 14,* 641.

DeVries, B., & Rutherford, J. (2004). Memorializing loved ones on the World Wide Web. *Omega, Journal of Death and Dying, 49,* 5–26.

Dokouph, T. (2008, February 18). The war we forgot. *Newsweek,* p. 50.

Donn, J. (2004, October 11). No insurance against bias. Industry held to account for burial policies. *East Valley Tribune,* D1, D5.

Flatten, M. (2004a, July 11). Brokering for the dead. *East Valley Tribune,* A5–8.

Flatten, M. (2004b, July 12). Missing persons. *East Valley Tribune,* A5–7.

Flatten, M. (2004c, July 13). Immunity widespread: Current tissue donation laws offer families little protection. *East Valley Tribune,* A1, A6.

Flatten, M. (2004d, July 14). Lawmakers step in. *East Valley Tribune,* A1, A7.

Gay, P. (1984). *Education of the senses.* New York: Oxford University Press.

Glover, R. (2001). Plastination laboratory. www.med.umich.edu/anatomy/plastinate.

Goldberg, H. S. (1981/1982). Funeral and bereavement rituals of Kota Indians and Orthodox Jews. *Omega, Journal of Death & Dying, 12,* 117–128.

Gosnell, L., & Gott, S. (1989). San Fernando Cemetery: Decorations of loss in a Mexican-American community. In R. E. Meyer (Ed.), *Cemeteries and gravemarkers* (pp. 217–236). Ann Arbor: University of Michigan Research Press.

Green Burial Council (2010). Natural burial in the U.S.A. http://naturalburial.coop/USA/green-burial-council/.

Gross, S. (October 5, 2007). African burial ground in Manhattan opens to public after dedication ceremony. *Associated Press.* http://www.msnbc.msn.com/id/21150548/ns/technology_and_science-science/t/african-burial-ground-opens-manhattan/.

Haney, C. A., Leimer, C., & Lowery, J. (1997). Spontaneous memorialization: Violent death and emerging mourning ritual. *Omega, Journal of Death and Dying, 35,* 159–172.

Hansen, J. P., Meldgaard-Jorgen, J. & Nordqvis, J. (1991). *The Greenland mummies.* Washington, DC: Smithsonian Institution Press.

Harris, J. E. (1973). *X-raying the pharaohs.* New York: Scribner.

Hass, K. A. (1998). *Carried to the wall.* Berkeley: University of California Press.

Henzi, A-E. (2009). Remaining eco-friendly, even after death. WUMM Milwaukee Public Radio. http://www.wuwm.com/programs/news/view_news.php?articleid=4444.

Holloway, K. F. C. (2002). *Passed on: African American mourning stories.* Durham, NC: Duke University Press.

Holmes, A. (n.d.). Willow coffins. http://druidnetwork.org/ethical/death/willowcoffins.

Ikram, S., & Dodson, A. (1998). *The mummy in ancient Egypt.* London: Thames & Hudson.

Iserson, K. (2003). Death certificate. In R. Kastenbaum (Ed.), *Macmillan encyclopedia of death and dying* (Vol. 1, pp. 211–213). New York: Macmillan.

Kastenbaum, R. (1974). Fertility and the fear of death. *Journal of Social Issues, 30,* 63–78.

Kastenbaum, R. (1994). R. C. W. Ettinger: An Omega interview. *Omega, Journal of Death and Dying, 30,* 159–172.

Kastenbaum, R. (2004a). Why funerals? *Generations, 28,* 5–10.

Kastenbaum, R. (2004b). *On our way. The final passage through life and death.* Berkeley: University of California Press.

Kearl, M. (2004). Cremation: desecration, purification, or convenience? *Generations, 28,* 15–20.

Kenney, E. (2004). Pet funerals and animal graves in Japan. *Mortality, 9,* 42–60.

Koff, C. (2004). *The bone woman.* New York: Random House.

Linden-Ward, B. (1989) *Silent city on a hill: Landscapes of memory and Boston's Mount Auburn Cemetery.* Columbus: Ohio State University Press.

Lorenzi, R. (2005, February 9). Medici family murders debunked in Italy. http://www.freerepublic.com/focus/f-news/1244428/posts.

Love, N. (May 9, 2008). Funeral industry explores use of lye to dissolve bodies. *Arizona Republic,* p. A14.

Lynch, T. (1997). *The undertaking. Life studies from the dismal trade.* New York: Penguin.

Miller, R. K., Jr., Rosenfeld, J. P., & McNamee, S. J. (2003). The disposition of property: Transfers between the dead and the living. In C. Bryant (Ed.), *Handbook of death and dying* (Vol. 1, pp. 917–925). Thousand Oaks: Sage.

Morris, R. (2002). Lawn garden cemeteries. In R. Kastenbaum (Ed.), *Macmillan encyclopedia of death and dying* (Vol. 2, pp. 518–520). New York: Macmillan.

Murphy, E. (1995). *After the funeral. The posthumous adventures of famous corpses.* New York: Barnes & Noble.

Plunkett, T. (1999). The New Haven burying ground. A brief history and discussion of the Grove Street Cemetery. http://www.smithie.com/nhcemetery.html.

Poovey, B. (1994, January 21). Ex-crematory operator gets 12 years in prison. *East Valley Tribune,* p. B1.

Prothero, S. (2001). *Purified by fire. A history of cremation in America.* Berkeley: University of California Press.

Redden, E. (2007, August 13). Rooted in tradition on very hallowed ground. *Washington Post,* p. C01.

Richardson, R. (1987). *Death, dissection, and the destitute.* London: Routledge & Kegan Paul.

Roach, M. (2003). *Stiff. The curious lives of human cadavers.* New York: Norton.

Roberts, P. (2004). Here today and cyberspace tomorrow: Memorials and bereavement support on the Web. *Generations, 28,* 41–46.

Rodman, G. B. (1996). *Elvis After Elvis.* Florence, KY: Routledge.

Ross-Bains, I. (n.d.). Perception of a green funeral. http://www.globalideasbank.org/site/bank/idea.php?ideaId=3425.

Rowles, G. (1984). Private communication.

Rutledge, N. M. (2008). A time to mourn: Balancing the right of free speech against the right of privacy in funeral picketing. *Maryland Law Review, 67,* 295–311.

Scheidt, R. J. (1993). Place and personality in adult development. In R. Kastenbaum (Ed.), *The encyclopedia of adult development* (pp. 370–376.) Phoenix: The Oryx Press.

Schindler, R. (1996). Mourning and bereavement among Jewish religious families: A time for reflection and recovery. *Omega, Journal of Death and Dying, 33,* 121–130.

Sherman M. (2010, October 7). Justices face a quandary. Empathy for dead GI's family vs. free-speech rights at issue. *The Arizona Republic,* p. A5.

Smith, N. (2003). Green burials and home funerals. *Mother Earth News,* April–May, 26–32.

Spiegelman, V., & Kastenbaum, R. (1990). Pet Rest Cemetery: Is eternity running out of time? *Omega, Journal of Death and Dying, 21,* 1–13.

Stone, J. L., & Walter, M.N.(2009). *Death and the afterlife in Japanese Buddhism.* Honolulu: University of Hawai'i Press.

Tashjian, A., & Tashjian, D. (1989). The Afro-American section of Newport, Rhode Island's common burying ground. In R. E. Meyer (Ed.), *Cemeteries and gravemarkers* (pp. 163–196). Ann Arbor: University of Michigan Research Press.

Trompeter, P., & Lemonnier, M. (2009). Funeral embalming: The transformation of a medical innovation *Science Studies, 22,* 9–30.

Tsiarias, A. (1982). *The death rituals of rural Greece.* Princeton, NJ: Princeton University Press.

Vanderstraeten, R. (2009) Modes of individualization at funerals. *Sociological Research Online, 14*(4), 10.

Villa, Judi. (2004, April 23). Burial chain gang gets to juveniles. *Arizona Republic,* p. B6.

Yerton, S. (2004a, March 10). Donated bodies blown up by Army. *The Times-Picayune.* http://www.tbrnews.org/Archives/a856.htm.

Yerton, S. (2004b, March 12). Donors' families grieve all over again. Use of bodies by Army prompts sadness, anger. *The Times-Picayune.* www.nola.com/news/t-p/frontpage/index.ssf?/base/news-1/107907 860840.xml.

Zbarsky, I., & Hutchinson, S. (1997). *Lenin's embalmers.* London: The Harvill Press.

Zeigarnik, B. (1927). Untersuchungen zur Handlungs und Affektpsycholigie. Das Behalten erlediger und underlediger Handlungen. *Psychologisches Forschung, 9,* 1–85.

Zezima, K. (2009, July 20). Home burials offer an intimate alternative. http://www.nytimes.com/2009/07/21/us/21funeral.html.

Zigarovich, J. (2009). Preserved remains: Embalming practices in 18th-century England. *Eighteenth-Century Life, 33,* 65–104.

■ GLOSSARY

Aninut The interval between death and burial in which "time stands still" and family members are given the opportunity to grieve in private (Orthodox Jewish).

Autopsy Medical examination performed on a corpse.

Ba In ancient Egypt, a spirit that departs from the body at death.

Cemetery A place set aside for burial of the dead.

Ch'iidii Evil ghosts who rob graves (Navajo).

Cremation Reduction of a corpse to ashes in a burning chamber.

Cryonic suspension Preserving a (certified dead) person at a near-freezing temperature with the intention of subsequent revival, treatment, and restoration to healthy life.

Death certificate Required legal form that is completed or verified by a physician, including basic information on the deceased person and cause(s) of death.

Death investigator Physician who examines autopsy findings and other evidence when there are questions about circumstances and cause of death. (Also known as a medical examiner.)

Embalming A procedure that retards physical deterioration of a corpse by use of a preservative fluid.

Eulogy Words said or written to honor a deceased person.

Exhumation Also known as disinterment, this is the removal of a corpse from its place of burial.

Funeral The rituals, observances, and procedures that accompany the burial or other disposition of the body of a deceased person.

Green funeral Burial without embalmment in a forest or field with the intention of returning remains to nature simply and directly.

Kaddish Prayer on behalf of a deceased person (Jewish).

Obituary A (usually brief) published report that provides information on a person's life after his or her death.

Organ donation Providing a heart, kidney, cornea, or other tissues available for the benefit of another person. Some types of organ donations can be made by living donors; others are available only from people who have been certified as dead.

Ponos The pain of grief (Greek).

Postmortem After death.

Premortem Before death.

Scarab A stone carved in the shape of a dung beetle; used to replace the heart in mummification (ancient Egypt).

Spontaneous memorialization Voluntary public response to the death of a person by violence; characterized by expression of personal feelings and bringing mementos to the site of the death.

Vermillion Accord A position statement on the ethical principles that should govern our treatment of human remains (based on a conference held in Vermillion, South Dakota).

■ ON FURTHER THOUGHT . . .

Useful online resources:

Cremation Society of North America
    www.cremationassociation.org
Death Rituals & Funeral Customs
Funeral Consumers Alliance
    National Funeral Directors Association
6530 gconnic1@maine.rr.com
    www.abfse.Org
Funeral & Memorial Socs of America
    www.funerals.org
Funeral and Memorial Societies of America:
    www.ubiweb.champlain.edu/famsa.directory.htm
International Association of Pet Cemeteries
    www.iaopc.com
Internet Cremation Society
    www.cremation.org
National Funeral Directors and Morticians Association
    www.nfdma.com
World Wide Cemetery

You Have a Decision to Make

They are three of your best friends. One is a contractor who finally has the opportunity to build an upscale residential development on choice land that has recently become available. Another is that brainiac who, to nobody's surprise, has become a rising star in science. The other person has the most interesting background, a Native American who has introduced you to a world you would not have otherwise known. What's the problem, then? The burial ground. The building project came to a halt. Lawyers now are the only people able to do anything. The developer wants to dig and build. The scientist wants to patiently excavate all the remains and artifacts as a contribution to knowledge. The Native American wants the remains to be respected and undisturbed. It happens that you are the person in the position to make the call. What do you decide—and on what basis? How can the rival claims be fairly evaluated? What is the best, and what is the worst, possible outcome? That's it! Have a nice day!

Do We Survive Death?

It started with what Reader lovingly referred to as his Cell Factory. In Bethesda, Maryland, in the middle of a wide-open warehouse that was once a Fritos factory, he built a glass-enclosed room that housed a rotating conveyor belt with hundreds of test-tube holders built into it.

—Rebecca Skloot (2010, p. 1910)

Now, what does this hell look like? Demons lay out rope and nets and prod everyone "Cross, cross." If one can't cross, one sinks into the pool, though one's hair stays aloft like floating weeds. Insects with black, metallic long snouts cover one's whole body to pierce the skin and eat the flesh.

—Quoted by Hank Glassman (2008, p. 226)

I once asked a young Hezbollah fighter how he knew there was a life after death. "I can prove it to you," he replied. "Do you believe that justice exists? Yes? Well, since there is no justice in this life, it must mean there is justice in the next life—so there is life after death."

—Robert Fisk (2005, p. 1)

I looked over Jordan and what did I see,
Comin' for to carry me home!
A band of angels comin' after me,
Comin' for to carry me home!
Swing low, sweet chariot,
Comin' for to carry me home!

—Traditional American spiritual (arranged by
Harry Thacker Burleigh)

Tasty vegetables of every kind
Grow in heaven's garden:
Good asparagus, beans . . .
Whole dishfuls are ready for us.

Good apples, pears and grapes;
The gardeners let us have anything.
—Traditional Austrian-German folk lyric
(musical setting by Gustav Mahler)

As Lord Krishna said to his disciple:
Who thinks that he can be a slayer,
Who thinks that he is slain,
Both these lack knowledge:
He slays not, is not slain.
Never is he born nor dies; Unborn, eternal, everlasting be . . .
—Kramer (1988, p. 32)

Chinese police have arrested three men for killing two young women and
selling their corpses as "ghost brides" for dead, single men.
—Jan Brea (2007)

Behold, I show you a mystery; We shall not all sleep, but we shall all be
changed, In a moment, in the twinkling of an eye . . . for the trumpet shall
sound, and the dead shall be raised incorruptible, and we shall be changed. . . .
O death, where is thy sting? O grave, where is thy victory?
—I Corinthians, 15

The skeleton he will cause to be put together in such a manner that the whole
figure may be seated in a chair usually occupied by me when living, in the
attitude in which I am sitting when engaged in thought.
—Jeremy Bentham (1832)

"I'd like backup copies of myself," one told me at a transhumanist conference,
"something more durable than a carbon-based system."
—Brian Alexander (2003, p. 51)

Who will go to heaven and who to hell? The four men had different opinions,
all lubricated by a night of drinking before they settled around a trailer park
table. One of the men knew how to decide the argument. He loaded a shotgun
and opened his mouth wide.
—Reuters (2008)

Henrietta Lacks died of cancer in 1951. She was a hard-working Virginia tobacco farmer and mother of five whose ancestors were emancipated from slavery by Lincoln. But HeLa—cells extracted and cultured from her body—is alive today and an integral part of medical research. The use and abuse of her cells has been done without personal or family permission, as reported in Rebecca Skloot's revelatory biography. But what are we to make of this unusual form of biological

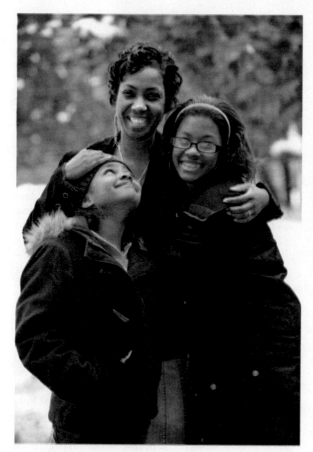

This family enjoys a life richer in opportunity than what was experienced by their semi-immortal greatgrandmother, Henrietta Lack.

survival of death and its bid for immortality? It is not what we usually have in mind when contemplating an afterlife.

The Blood Pool Hell is also not the first vision of the afterlife that comes to mind for most of us. The excerpt quoted here is not even the most nightmarish in the lengthy description from a Japanese Soto Zen Buddhist source. It has much in common with visions of hell in other religions, but is actually customized to accommodate women and children who died in childbirth. The Blood Pool experience purifies, one way or another. What are we to make of designer hells for particular kinds of people? And how did this prospect affect the mental health of women of child-bearing age?

Before examining the present scene, we will sample some of the ways in which other people have tried to come to terms with the certainty of death and the uncertainty of what happens next. We begin with an historical perspective, and then consider the question of whether survival is something that needs to be proved.

CONCEPT OF SURVIVAL IN HISTORICAL PERSPECTIVE

The opening quotations immediately remind us that survival of death has taken on a wide variety of meanings and associations. Let's revisit them:

1. The soldiers in a sandbagged bunker during the Iran–Iraq war ranged in age from 14 to 21. Several had already been killed in combat, and all expected their turn would come soon. The young leader:

   It is impossible for you in the West to understand. Martyrdom brings us closer to God. We do not seek death—but we regard death as a journey from one form of life to another. . . . Our first duty is to kill the enemy forces so that God's order will be everywhere (Fisk, p. 2).

2. "Swing Low, Sweet Chariot" is one of many spirituals that originated during the long years of slavery and the troubled aftermath of emancipation. Death would liberate the oppressed people from their sorrows. But there was also a hidden message: how to escape from their slavemasters. For example, the popular spiritual "Wade in the Water" also conveyed useful advice: Walk through streams so the hounds of pursuit would have a more difficult time finding you.

3. Heaven was food in abundance! The musical setting of these verses in the finale of Mahler's Fourth Symphony is all charm and innocence—but ironically so. "Tasty vegetables of every kind . . ." is a starving child's vision of heaven. In real life through the centuries, many children did starve. "Give me some bread, or I'll die," pleads the boy in another of Mahler's songs. That boy does not get his bread, and he dies. We must have an afterlife because there's no justice on earth, or there's

no freedom, or there is not even enough to eat. The young soldier, the American slave, and the Austrian child rely upon the next life for what is so painfully missing in this life.

But what of death itself? Consider several of the most influential religious perspectives:

1. Hindu tradition regards birth and death as illusions. The spirit or soul is always in process. *There is no death that one must survive.* It is in our nature to be "everlasting," even though we may not have a conscious memory of who we were in previous incarnations. Similarly, in Buddhist tradition we are always dying and undergoing rebirth through the course of our lives. What survives is the pattern of consciousness that has been shaped through many previous births, lives, and deaths.

2. China and Taiwan are impressively modernizing realms. Nevertheless, there are hardy survivals of ancient superstitions. These include the belief that the unmarried dead can invade the dreams of the living and make them thoroughly miserable. A constructive solution is to find a spouse to accompany the unmarried young to the grave. Ordinarily, the ghost bride would be a person recently deceased of natural cause. Murdering young women with the purpose of selling them as ghost brides was threatening to become an attractive money-making scheme when corpses started to fetch a high price. Although ghost brides may seem to be far out, they are still part of a society's death system. A major social dynamic here is China's one-child policy, which has resulted in an acute shortage of women and an oversupply of bachelors (Chen, 2007). Digging up a bride or murdering a woman unsuitable for marriage in order to market her corpse trades under the banner of supply and demand.

3. The passage from I Corinthians has been subjected to several interpretations over the years. For example: Does this transformation occur for all or only some people? Does it occur on a person-by-person basis or for all eligible humans in one ultimate "twinkling?" There is a striking difference between the New Testament vision and those associated with the Hindu and Buddhist traditions. Death

had been the enemy, the relentless adversary against which no human strength or strategy could prevail. Now it is death that has been defeated, its sting made harmless, and consigned to its own grave ("swallowed up in victory"). This electrifying message from the early years of Christianity did much to attract disciples and disseminate the faith throughout much of the world.

4. The academic skeleton in the closet was an attempt to devise a nonspiritual form of survival. Jeremy Bentham was as cool, collected, and sober as always when he drew up his last will and testament in London. Eminent during his life, he also has had a lasting influence on social philosophy with his utilitarian theory that advocated the greatest amount of happiness to the largest number of people. As for Bentham's post-death agenda, he intended to look like himself as much as possible, keep his trusty walking stick, and attend occasional faculty meetings. (There are unverified reports that Benthams have multiplied, attending faculty meetings in many universities with glazed eyes and mummified heads. Sorry, no list available.)

5. Technological substitutions for spiritual survival have come a long way since Bentham—at least, in theory. The quest to add years to life was already a prime motivating force during the era of myths and legends and became a spur to the development of science and technology, ever accompanied by superstition and humbug. The man who demanded a "backup copy" of himself has now arrived on the scene. Should his desire to overcome the limits of a "carbon-based life form" be fulfilled? Would we feel the need for heaven, if we could stay right here for a long, long, really long time?

6. Inquiring minds want to know. There have been countless arguments about heaven and hell through the centuries, but on a July evening in Godley, Texas, two young men concluded their discussion by putting the matter to a test. Clayton Frank Stoker swallowed as much of the shotgun as he could to discover whether he would go to heaven or hell. Johnny Joslin snatched the gun out of his friend's mouth, saying, "If you have to shoot somebody, shoot me." The shotgun fired

British philosopher Jeremy Bentham decided that the afterlife should include occasional appearances at faculty meetings, complete with a sturdy walking stick to maintain discipline.

(circumstances unclear), and it was Joslin who would be first to discover whether he was going to heaven or hell. (Yes, both had been drinking some that night.)

The gentlemen of Godley have made their inquiry into heaven and hell. It is our turn now.

We begin with a self-quiz that provides an opportunity to express our personal views of some survival-of-death issues. It's okay to respond to all the questions whether or not you firmly believe in an afterlife (e.g., a person can have an image of heaven or hell even if not convinced of their existence).

Key Points

We will see how other people of our own time respond to survival of death questions. Several key points are worth emphasis at this time, however:

- *People differ in their interpretations of the afterlife as either literal or metaphorical.* For example, Pope John Paul II explained to a Vatican audience that:

  > rather than a place, hell indicates the state of those who freely and definitely separate themselves from God (Sheler, 2000).

  By contrast, many other Christians believe in an actual hell with actual flames and torments. Islamic paradise is also interpreted variously as an actual garden of comfort and pleasure and as a state of being that can only be hinted at by poetical descriptions (Wasilewska, 2002).
- *A dualistic philosophy is associated with most afterlife beliefs.* Body and soul are temporary companions with different purposes and fates. This idea has been influential from earliest known history to the present time.
- *What we might call the conservation theme has often been a powerful influence on survival beliefs.* People mighty in life also should be mighty in the afterlife. Status and privilege should be preserved. This theme was already salient with the dynastic Egyptians. The democracy of the dead eventually made significant inroads, although never completely overcoming the conservation impulse.
- *The final exam theme is common but not universal.* Death brings us to the moment of judgment: salvation or damnation? The final exam theme is salient in Christianity and Islam, though muted in early Judaism, where all souls enter the same pit (*sheol*).

We are ready now to look at the afterlife from the perspective of several belief systems. The journey of the dead is a good place to start, and then on to the destinations themselves.

The Journey of the Dead

Souls undertake a perilous journey after death. That has been the belief of many world cultures. "Undertake" is the right word here, because there are dark passages under the earth and dangerous arrivals. Most societies perform rituals to reduce the hazards in transitioning between the worlds of the living and the dead. On arrival, often one must pass through trials and judgments. Mythology tells us of a few living people who made voluntary journeys to the Land of the Dead. Their experiences are instructive.

Consider first Gilgamesh, the mythical king who ruled the Mesopotamian city-state of Uruki perhaps 5,000 years ago (Westwood, 2002). He is desired by Ishtar, but rejects her advances, knowing that her ex-lovers had very short lives. The spurned goddess of love sends her "hit man," the Bull of Heaven, but he is slain by Gilgamesh and his best friend, Enkidu. Offended, the gods kill Enkidu. Here is where it gets interesting: Gilgamesh starts to reflect on his own mortality. Even though his parents are gods, the young king faces the same fate as other mortals. Gilgamesh risks a journey to the underworld in hope of persuading the one immortal man to grant him immortality as well. Adventures and misadventures ensue. At the end, Gilgamesh fails in his quest. He will not be an immortal. No human will ever escape death. This hard lesson has been passed on for thousands of years: If the great Gilgamesh with his god connections could not escape death, who can? We mortals had best adjust our attitudes and expectations.

Orpheus grieves for his beloved wife, Eurydice. She was murdered by the gods who commanded a serpent to bite her. Like Gilgamesh, Orpheus has a connection in high places as son of a divine muse and a mortal king. He boldly ventures into the underworld, where his music charms even Cerberus, the vicious three-headed watchdog. Orpheus persuades the gods of Hades to allow Eurydice to return with him. There is a condition, however: He must not look back at her until they cross the border. Orpheus cannot restrain himself quite that long, though—and Eurydice is gone forever. Cultural history again decrees that the dead must remain so.

The journey to the land of the dead has taken many forms. In Greek mythology, a cranky fellow by the name of Charon ferried the dead across the river Styx to Hades. The poet Virgil suggested that the entrance to this realm can be found near the volcanic Mount Vesuvius, where vapors and weird sounds issue from the mysterious realm below.

Young lovers who died before they could experience the fulfillment of their union might find themselves in the Elysian Fields for an eternity of pleasure, or so a Roman poet suggested.

The Hades welcoming committee was not especially encouraging: The souls of the dead moaned horribly and displayed their disfiguring wounds. The worst of the new arrivals were assigned to the most hellish regions for their crimes. The fate of Tantalus has given us the word tantalize. He was suspended from a tree, condemned to perpetual hunger while fruit remained just beyond his reach. Mortals who had not offered the gods by making a stew from their own children were abandoned to the ordinary miseries of Hades.

Arriving in the underworld was only the opening act. Fearsome demons would need to be convinced that the soul had not stolen, uttered evil words, judged others too quickly, killed a person—or fouled water. This was the preliminary test. The final exam involved weighing the deceased's heart against a feather that represented truth, order, and justice. If the heart was heavier (with wrongdoings), it would be fed to The Devourer, and the spirit would be cast into the darkness (Kastenbaum, 2004).

The vision of a dark passage to a dangerous or dreary place contrasts with another type of journey that is reserved for the elite, heroic, or especially lovable. These fortunates travel over great waters to a land of perpetual sunshine where fruit ripens for the picking, pure water flows, and every day is a vacation. Taylor (2000) notes that the blest isles were almost always in the far west or far east, depending on the location of the nearest great body of water. The Aztecs, living between two oceans, had two islands of the blest, one in either direction. The Blest Isles were considered to be real, though distant, places on earth. Centuries later, travel brochures and Hollywood movies would tout tropical island paradises that were prefigured by the happy lands reserved for the few most-deserving Aztecs, Scandinavians, Greeks, Celtics, and others.

The Roman poet Tibullus described a paradise garden where lovers enjoy each other's company forevermore. Tibullus asserted that in times gone by (the so-called Golden Age), people enjoyed free and uninhibited lovemaking. Alas, this pleasure was no longer available in the modern world of the first century B.C. Paradise Island, though, still awaited young lovers who had been taken by death before consummating their desires (McDannell & Lang, 1988).

The Buddhist journey as detailed in *The Tibetan Book of the Dead* (Evans-Wenz, 2000; Agha, 2003) differs from both a dread underground passage and a cruise to everlasting delights. In effect, we are birds of passage. To death we bring the selves we have been and the level of spiritual enlightenment we have achieved—and then we go on from there. A glimpse of this process was given in the description of Buddhist stages of dying (Chapter 4); Blood Pool Hell is a somewhat less enlightened version. Like the other great world religions, Buddhism has been interpreted in many ways, ranging from the literal to the abstract.

HEAVENS AND HELLS

Most people in most societies took survival as a fact. Sometimes the dead were buried with tools and other objects useful in the next life. The dead continued their interest in the living, either as guides and guardian angels or as vengeful spirits. Ideas about the afterlife eventually became elaborated and woven into theology, philosophy, poetry, song, and drama. Although belief was the norm, the words of a few dissenters have survived. Titus Lucretius Carus (54 B.C.) made the argument that "nothing can be produced from nothing," and, further, that "A thing . . . never returns to nothing, but all things after disruption go back into the first bodies of matter" (p. 3). Nature continually shapes, destroys, and reshapes her basic materials. Although there is no complete annihilation, there is also no imperishable soul that is immune from the general principle of transformation.

Love, death, and the brevity of life have been the doleful obsession of poets since ancient times:

> All who come into being as flesh
> > Pass on—and all men rest in the grave.
> So, seize the day! Hold holiday!
> > Be unwearied, unceasingly alive,
> You and your own true love.

This excerpt is from a poem written more than 3,000 years ago somewhere in Mesopotamia (Washburn & Majors, 1998, p. 22). The poet is not comforting us with a vision of paradise: Here is life today—enjoy the moment with those we love,

for all who have become before us have passed on, and the same will be true of us.

THE DESERT RELIGIONS AND THEIR ONE GOD

In time, the deserts of Mesopotamia gave the world three enduring religions. All agreed that there is one supreme being. *Zoroastrianism* (Boyce, 1979; Mehr, 2003) anticipated some of the doctrines and images of Judaism, Christianity, and Islam, but lost its Persian homeland and has fewer followers today. Within each faith, there are believers in a literal heaven and hell and others who take these descriptions as allusions to peaceful and stressful states of being.

Jewish Survival Belief in the Ancient World

The Christian message emerged from competing sets of beliefs within Judaism. McDannell and Lang (1988) have identified three currents within Jewish survival belief:

1. Yahweh *is the God of life—and this life is all that we have.* We should therefore live for this one life in this one world that God has given to us. The Sadducee sect contended that the holy scriptures offer no promise of an afterlife. One can experience the presence of God in everyday life, so there is no need to ask for more.
2. *The faithful among the dead will arise to participate in a new and improved society.* This concept, associated with the Pharisees, shared the Sadducee's primary interest in life on earth. Bad things happen to good people, especially when under oppressive foreign rule. This dilemma will be resolved when "the dry bones of a conquered Israel rise up and claim their place on a renewed earth" (p. 21). Only the right kind of person will live again, however, and the main point of this return is to create a more perfect society on earth.
3. *There is a spiritual rather than a physical afterlife, in which the individual soul contemplates God.* This concept, associated with the Essenes, shifted the emphasis from materialistic life on earth to a purified existence on another plane. The Essene

The message of Christianity's victory over death was enhanced by reports that Jesus had brought a dead man back to life, as depicted in Rembrandt's (1630) The Raising of Lazarus.

conception was the last to emerge within the Judaic tradition and had moved closer to what would become the Christian interpretation.

Heaven and Hell for Christians

The boundary between the dead and the living can be crossed from either side. Ghosts do it, and so do *necromancers* who interrogate the dead. Jesus became part of this tradition when he raised Lazarus. He added an astonishing new dimension through his own resurrection. Jesus was hailed as a mortal who had died and resurrected for everybody's

salvation, a proposition endorsed by St. Augustine, a founding father of Christian theology. The Israelites longed to be masters of their own nation on earth. The new cult turned eyes toward heaven. Earthly life paled by comparison. Nevertheless, it was difficult to imagine heaven's realm of glory. The challenge of "picturing heaven" (Zaleski, 2003) remains with us. It seems easier to imagine the absence of fear and suffering than the bliss of heaven.

Hell was more vivid. The wicked suffered terribly. Fire in the darkness, the stench of sulfur, chains, cages, impalement—the torments seemed all too palpable. Agonies awaited those "who had rejected the gospel, spurned baptism, or for other reasons remained independent of the new revelation" (Bernstein, 1993, p. 340). Hell did change over the centuries. The baroque era, for example, reveled in flash and festivity. "Good, old-fashioned hell" became an entertainment for an increasingly literate and worldly population. The Jesuits acted decisively to re-empower the horrors of hell for a new kind of Christian (Turner, 1993):

> They eliminated all tortures except fire, and all monsters except possibly "the worm that never sleepeth." What they added was unnervingly apt for the times—urban squalor. The Jesuit Hell was unbearably, suffocatingly, repulsively crowded. . . . In a dank claustrophobic amalgam of dungeon and cesspool, dainty aristocrats and prosperous merchants jostled . . . with coarse, foul-smelling, verminous peasants, lepers, and slum dwellers. . . . The infernal stench was disgusting and everlasting and composed of filth and feces and pestilence and running sores and bad breath . . . (p. 173).

Hell was no longer a cartoon, an amusement for sophisticates. All that the rising tide of individualism cherished would evaporate in everlasting flames and unbearable stench. The Jesuit version was influential, and some Protestant sects also adopted the "sulfur and brimstone" approach.

Islamic Paradise and Jahannam

Islam emerged as a religious movement in seventh-century Arabia, inspired by the prophet Muhammad. The word *Islam* is often translated as *submission* but could also be known as *conversion* (Segal, 2004). Abraham and Jesus were both regarded as prophets who had preceded Muhammad. A person who accepted The One God was tolerated even if the worship took Jewish or Christian form. Islam soon divided itself into rival power bases when none of the founder's sons survived into adulthood. It remains a less centralized religion than Christianity, the followers united by scripture and belief rather than organizational hierarchy.

In Islam, life is regarded as a spiritual struggle between good and evil. *Jihad* refers to the constant struggle between one's own lower and higher impulses, as well as to conflict with enemies of the faith. Muslims are expected to resist temptations and devote themselves to a moral life. Death and the Day of Judgment are brought to mind repeatedly through prayer, practice, and instruction. One should live in preparation for the "appointed hour" (Hanson, 2003). In this respect, Islamic doctrine has much in common with the European *Ars moriendi* tradition that was most dominant in the fifteenth century.

The Day of Judgment can come at any time. All souls will then meet their Creator. There will be paradise for the virtuous, *Jahannam* for the failed. A Book of Deeds is kept for every person. There is an inherent ambiguity in specifying a "day" of judgment or, as often described, the "hour" in which the judged mortals begin their spiritual existence. The day could be 50,000 years or a fleeting instant because Allah is not constrained by human notions of time.

At the end of time, there will be a final triumph of Islam. The heavens will storm, the mountains vanish, and the earth shaken (Qur'an 52: 9–10). There is more than a passing similarity here to Native American religions that also predict that all the world, not excepting the apparently everlasting mountains, will become as nothing.

Death itself is described by the Qur'an as a deep, dreaming sleep that Allah concludes either by making it permanent or sending the person back for another go at life (Wasilewska, 2002). (There is an obvious similarity to many contemporary near-death experience reports, as will be discussed here.) The faithful Muslim will be ready to face the Creator at any time. Forget about erasing a life of indolence and immorality by a deathbed conversion or a special favor from God. Repentance cannot wait until the last minute, but must be demonstrated in a change in the course of life.

The Muslim version of heaven is a garden with rivers of pure water, milk, wine, fruit, and honey. The garden of paradise offers much to please. (Although alcoholic beverages are forbidden by the Qur'an, the wine of paradise does not intoxicate and can be enjoyed with no sin attached.)

The Qur'an does not support the type of paradise reportedly imagined by the September 11th terrorists. The male fantasy of 72 virgins seems to have originated in folk tales that were devised by numerologists. There is, in fact, no specific number of "virgins" mentioned in the Qur'an, nor is it described as an arrangement for male use of females. In the Qur'an (13:23; 36:56), women and children are equally eligible for paradise if they have shined in the Book of Deeds. Both men and women enjoy the companionship of "those modest in gaze, having beautiful eyes, carefully protected, pure and beautiful ones . . . reclining on green cushions and beautiful carpets." The women dwelling in paradise are pure of character, carrying forward the Islamic emphasis on female virtue in earthly life. Paradise is a garden of delights for people who have reached an advanced level of spiritual development and who have the potential to continue their advancement in this favored setting.

Furthermore, it is by no means required that one become a martyr to win admission to paradise. People with blood on their hands and lust in their hearts are better candidates for Jahannam, the Muslim version of hell. Molten brass, boiling water, and infernal flames are featured here, as they were in the earlier hells conceived by Zoroastrians and Christians. The fiery torments have a therapeutic as well as punitive purpose: The fallen eventually might be purified of their sinful inclinations.

It is not clear, however, what benefits they might derive from encounters with:

> Scorpions and snakes as big as camels and stinking rivers fully of slimy creatures who cause them to vomit . . . The dwellers in Jahannam will wish to die but continue to exist in torment (Taylor, p. 199).

Consigned to hell are not only the obvious sinners but also those who refuse to help the needy, cheat in commerce, abandon themselves to luxuries, or commit adultery. The most severe punishments await those who worship idols or multiple deities instead of accepting the oneness of God—or those who deny Allah's resurrection and judgment of the dead.

You can express your beliefs in a self-quiz (Box 13-1). The American people have also been asked to share their views on survival on several occasions. What have they been saying?

BOX 13-1

SURVIVAL OF DEATH?
A SELF-QUIZ

Part I. Beliefs

1. I believe in some form of life after death.

   Yes _____ No _____ Uncertain _____

2. I believe that a spirit or soul is separable from the body.

   Yes _____ No _____ Uncertain _____

3. I think of Heaven as a

   _____ Place in a divine sphere of being
   _____ A joyful state of mind or spirit, not an actual place

4. I think of Hell as

   _____ An actual place of torment and punishment
   _____ An anguished state of mind or spirit

5. Heaven is for people who

   _____ Believe in a particular religious faith, but not others

   _____ Believe in any religious faith
   _____ Perform exceptional and heroic acts
   _____ Live virtuous lives
   _____ End their lives with rituals and blessings
   _____ Are judged worthy by God

6. It is possible for living and dead people to communicate with each other.

   Agree _____   Disagree _____

7. We are reincarnated in a cycle of births, deaths, and rebirths.

   Agree _____   Disagree _____

8. It will be possible to overcome death someday by medical and technological advances.

   Agree _____   Disagree _____

9. It is morally acceptable to seek alternative forms of survival such as cloning, cryonics, and digital transformations.

   Agree _____   Disagree _____

(Continued)

BOX 13-1 (Continued)

10. My dog and cat will go to heaven if they are very, very good.

    Agree _____   Disagree _____

Part II: Persuasion and Imagination

11. Suppose that you really wanted to persuade somebody that there is not life after death. What evidence, experiences, or line of reasoning would you use? Be as specific as possible and put your heart into it, as though you wanted very much to convince a person that there is no afterlife and had to call upon the strongest objections to this belief.

12. Suppose now that you wanted to persuade somebody that there is life after death. What evidence, experiences, or line of reasoning would you use? Again, be specific and put your best efforts into it.

13. You have already stated your own ideas and beliefs. What kind of experience, evidence, or logic could persuade you to change your mind? It does not matter if you consider the contrary evidence or experience to be very unlikely. What might lead you to change your mind if it did happen or were true?

14. Suppose that you actually have changed your mind. You have discovered that your present belief is mistaken. What difference would it make in your life? In what ways and to what extent would your life be different if you had to accept the opposite of your present belief about life after death?

15. What influence has your actual belief or disbelief had upon the way you live? What decisions has it influenced and in what way?

16. What do you think would be the best thing about life after death (whether or not you are a believer)?

17. What could be the worst thing about life after death?

18. How did you come to your present belief or disbelief about life after death?

19. What would you tell a child who asks what happens when a person dies?

WHAT OTHER PEOPLE BELIEVE TODAY

Every now and then the public is asked to express its views about death and afterlife. A fairly consistent pattern has emerged, but it should be kept in mind that the surveys ask different questions of different population samples at somewhat times. That being said, the findings are well worth our attention.

Baby Boomers Scan the Afterlife

The girls and boys born January 1, 1946, became involuntary pioneers of the baby boomer generation. That each generation has its own general profile had not been a secret to social scientists, but the boomers were the first to be named famously and analyzed endlessly. Our focus here is on how boomers think of last things as they observe more wrinkles in the mirror, fill more prescriptions, and attend more funerals.

A study conducted by AARP (Newcott, 2008) harvested the thoughts of people 50 and over. Most (about 7 of 10) believed in an afterlife, the women more so (8 of 10). The boomers' afterlife belief was prevailingly optimistic: there is a Heaven (capitalization preferred by the respondents), and they will be there. However, the boomers judge that a great many other people will not make it. About 4 of 10 respondents believed there is a literal Hell awaiting future consignments of sinners.

Although citizens of the information age and explorers of cyberspace, many boomers find a place for the occult. Ghosts are real to most of the boomers. Many have had something that felt like an experience with a disembodied spirit. Reincarnation belief had been rarely reported in the United States in the past, perhaps 1 person in 100, as estimated by Russell (1998). It is not an uncommon belief among boomers (23 percent). Nevertheless, a substantial number of boomers (about one in four) believe that death is the end-all—but continue to cherish their religion and attempt to live up to its moral code. Some, like Tom, operate with a conditional premise:

> You just gotta make up your own mind about things. I go to Mass. I live my life like there's life after death. But I don't believe there is. If it's true, well, hey, it's a plus. But if it ain't, I didn't lose anything (p. 2).

Unfortunately, these findings cannot tell us how much of the boomers' views have been shaped by their distinctive childhoods (e.g., the first generation to grow up on television) and by their experiences as they continue to move through the life course.

United States: A Nation of Believers?

Belief in life after death has been increasing in the United States since the 1980s, according to most studies (Gallup Poll, 1999; Greeley & Hout, 1999; Hayslip & Peveto, 2005; Lester, et al., 2000/2001; Morin, 2000). There are more believers than non-believers in all the major studies, usually by a decisive margin. This finding encompasses both genders and all the ethnic and racial groups that have been surveyed.

Morin notes that even people who say they have no religious preference are more likely (63 percent) to believe in an afterlife, as compared with 44 percent who believed in an afterlife in the 1970s. Most respondents expect the afterlife to be comforting, and many believe it includes reunion with family and friends. There was also consensus that any physical problems they have in this life would not be carried over to the next. Most (71 percent) respondents to the Morin's Fox News Survey were sure that hell is a real place—but even more (88 percent) said the same of heaven. Nevertheless, there was a sense of risk and foreboding as well. For example, most Gallup Poll (1999) respondents believed that there will be a day of judgment to determine who belongs among the blessed, but they were about evenly divided on whether a good person can go to heaven without a belief in God.

There was consensus that we need faith in God and *immortality* to make it through the tribulations of life. Beliefs were formed early in childhood, according to almost all respondents, but the nonbelievers were more likely to have reconsidered this topic in recent years. What to tell a child proved to be most difficult for those who were not very sure of their positions on survival, whether believers or nonbelievers. Nonbelievers more frequently expressed some conflict or uncertainty in what to say, but wavering believers also had their difficulties.

The apparent increase in afterlife belief could be a little misleading. A major survey (Pew Research Center, 2008) finds that more than a quarter of the American people have left the faith in which they were raised "in favor of another religion—or no religion at all" (p. 2). The percentage of people who how consider themselves unaffiliated has risen sharply, and is even higher among younger adults, where one in four reports no current association. Many Americans seem to be shopping around for a religious affiliation that meets their needs. This raises questions about the certainty with which core beliefs—such as the afterlife—are held. The Pew survey makes a contribution toward answering this question: most of the immigrants moving into the United States bring a strong religious faith with them, including a belief in an afterlife. Overall, the Pew survey depicts a diversity and fluidity of religious belief in the United States.

Another look at consistency and change is provided by a study that compares death attitudes at four decade points from the 1970s to the 2000s (Brabant et al., 2009). More than twice as many year 2000 respondents stated that they believe in an afterlife than did in the 1970s. It was always a small minority of respondents who declared they would prefer there to be no afterlife; this percentage has further diminished since the 1970s.

Alan F. Segal (2009) places contemporary attitudes in a broad perspective that finds U.S. residents more taken up with religion and afterlife than is true of most other nations. He notes that belief and disbelief are in constant play. We seem to care a lot about the prospect of afterlife even if our ideas and feelings are all over the place:

> Asking about the afterlife still defines a crucial and highly conflicted battlefield in American life . . . that runs through our political as well as religious convictions . . . It runs to the very quick of what we Americans think is important in life (pp. 79–80).

A Southern Perspective

Residents of 13 Southern states are most likely to participate in evangelical forms of Christianity (Miller, 2001). Charles Reagan Wilson, director of the University of Mississippi's Center for the Southern Culture, explains that

> Southerners have a very literal understanding of heaven and hell. Death is not abstract. . . . It's something you think about. Ministers talk about it, preach about it. "Are you ready to meet the Lord?" You drive down the road in the rural South, you see these signs, "Get right with the Lord" (Miller, p. 1).

The abiding role of religion in Southern life is expressed in the respondents' concerns about dying. "Not having a chance to say goodbye to someone" is the most frequently stated concern and one that is shared by many other people throughout the nation. The next two most common concerns, though, seem to be more salient in the South than in the nation in general: "Dying when out of touch with God or a higher power;" "Not being forgiven by God."

Belief in resurrection of the body has slowed the acceptance of cremation, which has been becoming a more frequent choice in other regions. In Alabama, for example, cremation is selected in only 1 of 20 funerals, the lowest percentage in the nation.

Southerners, especially in rural areas, seem to be carrying forward religious and social support traditions that once were more widespread. These include laying out deceased loved ones at home for visitations, and preparing tables full of dumplings, ham, deviled eggs, and many other dishes for friends and family after the funeral.

What Do Belief-Oriented People Believe About the Afterlife?

Some people give more attention to belief issues than others. These include the membership of Beliefnet, a major Internet site. What views do they hold? Beliefnet conducted a survey of 10,567 members. The respondents included self-described wiccans, agnostics, atheists, and "spiritual not religious" as well as those within a major traditional religion at www.beliefnet.com/Faiths/2006/. A briefer report on "Who's Going to Hell?" can be accessed at http://www.beliefnet.com/Faiths/2006/. . ./Whos-Going-to-Hell.aspx. Most respondents (four out of five) believed in an afterlife and, of those (three out of four) also believed in hell. About half the sample knew somebody who was hell-bound; considerably fewer expected that to be their own fate. Born-again Christians were by far the most likely to answer that there was not a chance of hell in their destiny.

Ask a few questions of the data and we learn that:

- Christians are the most likely to believe that at death the soul or spirit moves on to an eternal afterlife, and that the souls of the dead protect the living as angels or spirit guides and can hear our prayers.
- Muslims are most likely to believe there is an in-between stage between death and the afterlife.

- As expected, Buddhists, Hindus, and Wiccans were the most likely to believe in *reincarnation*—but, less expectedly, more than half of respondents within these faith categories did *not* affirm reincarnation. Why? We don't know.
- Wiccans have most often dreamed about and felt the presence of a dead person. Many in the sample as a whole reported dream visitations from a dead person.
- Jews and atheist/agnostics are most likely to say "I don't know what happens after death."
- Some respondents in all the belief categories (including agnostics) report that they have had an experience with the dead—and this experience has almost always been positive.

The Afterlife: A Mirror of Society?

Observers with a sociological perspective have been puzzled by the hardiness of afterlife belief in the United States. Zuckerman (2004), for example, notes that religiosity and belief in an afterlife have been declining sharply in Europe for many years. Americans are much more likely to report belief in God and afterlife than citizens of Belgium, France, Iceland, Italy, Germany, the Scandinavian countries, the United Kingdom, and so on. One possible explanation is that the vigor of fundamentalist religious traditions provides a sense of community and social support that is difficult to find elsewhere in a mass, technological society.

Segal (2004) offers an in-depth review of afterlife beliefs throughout history. He concludes that

> the afterlife is not a single eternal truth that is an unchanging reward of the righteous or faithful. It is, instead, a mirror of the values of the society that produced it. Watching the afterlife change is watching a society's hopes and fears change. . . . Heaven is the best we can think of for ourselves at any historical time and hell is the worst we can imagine (p. 698).

One of the few questions not examined by Segal proved of interest to many of us: the best-selling book *Do All Pets Go to Heaven?* (Wohlberg, 2002). Wohlberg does not claim to have a definitive answer, but raises the possibility that a merciful god might decide to open the gates of heaven to Angel, Nova, Pumpkin, Serena, Snowflake, and your animal companions as well. (I hope they all will get along.) Also worth consideration is the possibility that our societal mirror of the afterlife is taking the form of a computer monitor with its invisible connects to everywhere and nowhere.

DOES SURVIVAL HAVE TO BE PROVED—AND, IF SO, HOW?

Some form of afterlife has been assumed by most, perhaps all, societies. Nevertheless, there has also been doubt along the way. The ancient civilizations of Mesopotamia, for example, were painfully aware of the sands of time that erased rulers, dynasties, and the memory of great events and achievements. A few royal souls might be immortal, but the common person's prospects were grim. The Christian victory over death was a source of jubilation in the faith's early years, but that great day failed to arrive, and miseries and loss continued as before. Belief in afterlife would eventually face daunting challenges from science.

Today not everybody agrees that survival needs to be proved or that science is equipped to answer the question. However, even confident believers often seek affirmation and support, if not from science, then from custom and personal experience. In this section, we consider some of the major ways in which people have been persuaded—or not—that there is life after death. We begin where the human mind did: with the dead and their ghosts. Next stop is the attempt to find evidence for the durable ancient belief in reincarnation. It will then be time to dim the lights but keep our eyes open as curiosity, hope, greed, and powerful cultural forces collide around the possibility of spirit visitors. Next, we consider the continuing interest in reports of *near-death experiences (NDEs)* as possible evidence for survival, and then venture into symbolic immortality.

Ghosts

It is not easy to take ghosts seriously today. Ghosts have been for so long the stuff of campfire stories, parodies, and late-night movies that they might seem to be the least-promising source of evidence for survival. But ghosts deserve better than that. For one thing, ghosts have had a firm social reality in many cultures. A partial list of societies with strong traditions of interaction with the dead would include the Asian Indian, Celtic, Chinese, Japanese, Mexican, Scottish, and Welsh (Bryant, 2003; Freed & Freed, 1993). For example, villagers in the Delhi region of India must be cautious in their dealing with each other, because an aggrieved neighbor could become a troublesome ghost. Ghost Month in China (including Taiwan) encourages families to express their love and respect for those who have passed on (Emmons, 1982). By the end of the festivities, the spirits are ready to return to the other side, now with a fresh supply of ghost money to pay for special favors.

For some unfortunate people, ghosts still are nightmare stuff. Cambodians by the thousands were murdered during the brutal regime of Pol Pot. One common method of execution was to place a bag over the head. People forced to witness these executions often developed breath anxiety. Some Cambodian refugees found sanctuary in the United States, but not within their troubled dreams. They experience sleep paralysis during which a shadowy figure is felt to be approaching them—the mournful ghost of a murdered person they had known well. Traumatized sleepers report, "The ghost pushes you down" (Hinton et al., 2005). This anxiety-provoking experience is interpreted as a flashback intensified by survivor guilt.

How did the belief in ghosts arise, and what keeps it going? Nobody truly knows the answers. Anthropologists report the widespread belief that a spirit version of one's self wanders off from the sleeper during dreams and perhaps on other occasions. It follows that the spirit would also exit from the dead, and perhaps mingle with the living. Ghosts would be among the usual suspects when something strange or alarming happens. A ghost might be visible, but we could also infer its presence by the mischief it produces. What keeps ghosts in circulation might well be exposure to stories from childhood, the power of suggestion, and their functionality in customs and rituals. Furthermore, one can never be quite sure that there is not a ghost around, even if one chooses not to believe in them. Catherine Crowe's collection, *Night Side of Nature or Ghosts and Ghost Seers* (1848/2008) created widespread excitement and strengthened many people's belief in spirit survival. This book has been raided fiercely by other writers ever since,

and some of the tales have been taken as proof of survival, despite the author's cautions.

In our own society, everyday people still report encountering everyday-type ghosts. These are not the stereotypes associated with haunted houses and scary music. They are an entire family downstairs in the rented house, making their breakfast, the aroma of freshly brewed coffee rising to the visitor's bedroom. The ghost is an old man who sits quietly reading a newspaper at the same hour each early evening. The ghost is a cat who visits so often that he is considered a part of the family (even by the dog) and whose habits have become as familiar to them as their own. The woman who told me about the ghost cat had not at first thought it was even worth mentioning because "it was just part of our life; it was just there when it wanted to be."

Myers (1903/1975) was more impressed with such innocuous ghosts than with the reports he collected of exotic apparitions with their mysterious purposes and profound messages. Who would have invented such useless ghosts, and why would they have bothered? Apparitions (visible ghosts) that did not fit into cultural belief systems and did not seem to have any particular agenda or message seemed more credible to Myers than those featured in ghost stories.

Nevertheless, it is the consequential spirit who has attracted the most attention and who has most often been taken as proof of survival. Perhaps most common is the ghost who visits to provide comfort during a time of crisis:

> *My mother died in June. One Sunday morning early, we had a terrible thunderstorm. My husband was working away at the time, and as I have always been very nervous of storms, I went downstairs, taking the baby with me, and my eldest daughter also came down with me. She could see how I was shaking with fright. Suddenly I felt a very slight pressure on my shoulders, and heard my Mother's voice say, "don't be afraid Winnie dear, nothing will harm you." I immediately stopped shaking, and felt quite calm, and my daughter noticed the change in me, and said, "What's happened, Mum, you don't look frightened any more"* (Green & McCreery, 1989, p. 201).

Another popular ghost figure is the one who warns us of danger: There is a problem with the electrical system in the new house; the bridge is unsafe to cross, and so on. How should a person

The Lakota Sioux (shown here in 1892) and other Native American tribes performed exhausting rituals to invoke their ancestors to rescue them from the invaders who had taken over their lands and threatened their survival.

respond to episodes in which one seems to have been comforted or warned by a ghost? Most of the people who have related such experiences to me were not sure just what had happened. Still another type of ghost is reported to seek us out when it is the one in danger. We will meet the *crisis apparition* when we visit prime-time spiritism.

The Ghost Dance: A Peaceful Vision Becomes a Tragedy

A belief in ghosts and survival contributed to one of the most shameful pages in U.S. history. By the 1880s, life had changed radically for the Native American peoples. The whites were in control almost everywhere. Meanwhile, Jack Wilson, a Paiute orphan, was being raised by a white family. He was chopping wood one day when he heard a great noise and fainted. Wilson awakened with a spiritual vision. Wovoka (the new name he had taken) had been to heaven, met his mother and other deceased people, and conversed with God (Hittman, 1990). He now dedicated himself to

teaching his people that they must not drink whiskey or fight. Instead, they must love one another and live in peace with the whites.

Wovoka encouraged his followers to renew their traditional circle dance while singing religious songs. There was nothing warlike about this ceremony, but nervous settlers were disturbed by a ritual they did not understand. Eventually, a militant spirit did arise around some campfires (Mooney, 1996). An earlier prophecy about the destruction of the whites and the raising of the dead became associated with the new movement. Some of the tribes recently defeated in combat with the U.S. Army believed that the dead could protect them. The ghost dance was created in the depths of their desperation.

Dancing to the point of exhaustion brought the warriors into contact with the powerful spirits of the dead who were also longing for liberation. From these rituals came the idea of a sacred article of clothing that could protect them from the white man's bullets. They would be safe in their ghost shirts. Accordingly, they did not give much attention to defensive precaution, and were in no position to defend themselves when attacked in their encampment at Wounded Knee—an attack that was more slaughter than military operation. Belief in ghosts and their powers had contributed to the massacre, though the savagery of the attack upon women and children became the shame of the army.

Deathbed Escorts: Safe Conduct to the Other World

Mythology and folklore provide many examples of a guide who escorts the living across the border to death. (If the guide is an angel or other spirit deity, it is sometimes referred to as a *psychopomp*.) The guide often resembles the "gentle comforter" personification of death that was discussed in Chapter 2. A famous example from the nineteenth century features a "gray lady" who appeared to dying patients in a London hospital. When a modern physician decided to examine this legend, he discovered that some dying patients still insisted that the gray lady visited them often and even filled their water jugs. The reports were always of a gray uniform; the staff nurses actually wore blue. These patients had not known that gray was the color of the nurses' uniforms in the earlier years of the hospital. For other examples, see Sir William Barrett's interesting, if perhaps not entirely reliable, *Deathbed Visions* (1926/1986).

The most substantial study was conducted by Karlis Osis and his colleagues (Osis, 1961; Osis & Haraldsson, 1977), who collected observations from more than 2,000 physicians and nurses in India and the United States. What did they find?

1. Patients at times were observed interacting with a visitor that others could not see. These patients were clear of mind, and not drugged, confused, or delusional.
2. The visitations usually came to people who were known to be dying, but there were also instances in which the escort appeared to a person who was not thought to be gravely ill—and that person did pass away soon afterward.
3. The visitations were not always welcome. Sometimes the escort had to convince the patient that the time was near.
4. The escorts were varied: a parent, an angel, a messenger of God.

5. On rare occasions, something happened that physicians or nurses could witness:

There was a staircase leading to the second floor. Suddenly he exclaimed "See, the angels are coming down the stairs. The glass has fallen and broken." All of us in the room looked toward the staircase where a drinking glass had been placed on one of the steps. As we looked, we saw the glass break into a thousand pieces. It did not fall; it simply exploded. The angels, of course, we did not see. A happy and peaceful expression came over the patient's face and the next moment he expired. Even after his death the serene, peaceful expression remained on his face (p. 42).

The deathbed visions had similar features in the United States and India. The visions could be distinguished easily from ordinary hallucinations, and many experiencing them had received no sedation.

Do these reports provide evidence for survival? The data were retrospective, therefore, memory dependent. It is possible that the visitors were wish-fulfilling fantasies, perhaps released by physiological changes such as decreased oxygen uptake in the brain. The escorts might have been created by the dying person's own unconscious and projected into the outer world, where it would then be experienced as "real." One part of the dying person's self might have communicated with another part through the hallucination.

I have witnessed perhaps a dozen incidents in which a person near death seemed to be interacting with a companion that we could not see, and I have been told of others, but most people near death do not show evidence of having such experiences. Perhaps deathbed escorts are highly selective in their visitations, or perhaps they reside exclusively in the mind of the dying person.

Reincarnation

The ancient belief in reincarnation has itself come back to life in recent years in Europe, Australia, and North America, having remained influential in Asia and Africa through the centuries. Although Hindu and Buddhist versions of the reincarnation doctrine are the most widely known, other religions have also featured this idea. Judeo-Christian religious authorities generally have opposed reincarnation beliefs, but with only partial success. The idea of living more than one life seems to thrive even when it does not fit well into a particular religious dogma. Many in the United States today who believe in reincarnation were raised in the Christian tradition. The popularity of this belief was stimulated by so-called past life regressions (as with Bridey Murphy, discussed later) and by heightened interest in survival of death as near-death experience reports made the rounds.

Believers in reincarnation have more than one interpretation of precisely what happens after physical death (Dillon, 2003). Some think the soul is born (or reborn) until its desires draw it toward the next incarnation. Others view the state between death and rebirth as a deep, restful sleep. A striking feature of most reincarnation beliefs is that the state of consciousness at the moment of death persists into the next station of the journey.

Is there persuasive evidence for reincarnation? One researcher stands out for his many years of careful investigation. Ian Stevenson's *Twenty Cases Suggestive of Reincarnation* (1974) did much to establish the credibility of reincarnation research and was followed by many subsequent contributions. His detailed case histories are models of their kind.

A typical case "suggestive of reincarnation" starts early in childhood, usually between ages two and four:

> *The child often begins talking about this previous life as soon as he gains any ability to speak, and sometimes before his capacity for verbal expression matches his need to communicate. Some children make only three or four different statements about a previous life, but others may be credited with 60 or 70 separate items pertaining to different details in the life remembered. . . . In most cases the volume and clarity of the child's statements increase until at the age of between five and six he usually starts to forget the memories. Or he talks about them less. Unexpected behavior . . . nearly always accompanies the statements the child makes about the previous life he claims to remember. . . . This behavior is unusual for a child of the subject's family, but concordant with what he says concerning the previous life, and in most instances it is found to correspond with what other informants say concerning the behavior of the deceased person about whom the subject has been talking, if such a person is traced (p. 324).*

I asked Stevenson about the difficulties involved in his research (Kastenbaum, 1993b).

> *The effort to exclude the normal transmission of information exists even in cases in which the two families are completely unknown to each other and perhaps live many miles apart. I have often had to content myself with saying that normal communication was improbable; only rarely can I say it was impossible (p. 169).*

Stevenson investigated cases from Burma, India, Sri Lanka, Turkey, Lebanon, and in Native Americans. Smaller sets of cases have come from Brazil, Nigeria, Finland, Thailand, the United Kingdom, and the United States. Cases come to attention more readily in cultures that favor belief in reincarnation. Whether belief generates the experiences or whether the experiences simply are easier to share within a sympathetic cultural milieu is difficult to determine. The specific elements in each case would have to be explained in any event.

Stevenson (1997a) crowned his long research career with a mammoth collection of case studies that are accompanied by medical records and photographs bearing on the validity of children's statements about a past life. He selected cases that had all the following characteristics:

1. The child described the way he or she died in a past life.
2. The child had a birthmark or birth defect that is consistent with that form of death (e.g., two bullet wounds in the chest or a knife wound on the neck).
3. A deceased person whose life and death matches the past life story given by the child is identified.
4. Medical records documenting the specific cause of death and condition of the body are obtained.
5. There is a very close match between the fatal wounds suffered by the deceased person and the marks or defects found on the child at birth.

Stevenson offers these physical evidence matchups as the best evidence available that is "suggestive of reincarnation." Readers who wish to examine these cases in depth can consult his *Reincarnation and Biology* (1997a), a two-volume set of more than 2,000 pages with many photographs. Stevenson presents a summary and discussion of these findings in *Where Reincarnation and Biology Intersect* (1997b). (The response from the bioscience establishment? Silence.)

Stevenson's cases raise two questions: First, why were so many of the reported past lives ended by sudden and violent death? The number of murders and other violent deaths in Stevenson's sample goes well beyond expectations. Secondly, how could anybody be reincarnated unless everybody is reincarnated? What do you think?

There is an even more radical possibility I cannot resist sharing with you: Perhaps death is not the same for everybody. The possibility of *pluralistic death* would challenge our basic assumptions about the nature of life and the universe. There is survival of death, or there is not survival—or so it is generally believed. Either of these alternatives seems more rational than the possibility that death might be different at different times to different people in different situations. Nevertheless, as I have suggested elsewhere, this bizarre-seeming idea appears consistent with some basic precepts of the philosophy of science (Kastenbaum, 1993). The idea that death might be relative to life and its variable context opens the possibility that there might be both survival and nonsurvival! But who is ready for this kind of thinking?

WHEN SPIRITISM WAS IN FLOWER

Like to be part of history? The year is 1848. With other neighbors in this upstate New York village we crowd into the home of the Fox family. Young daughters Margaret and Katie put on a show for us. They ask questions of an invisible spirit who replies with knocks ("yes") or silence ("no"). The raps seem to come from deep within the walls. We learn that Mr. Splitfoot (as the girls have named him) was murdered and his killer never brought to justice. This is hot stuff on a chilly evening long before, radio, television, and the Internet!

We want more. So do thousands—make that millions—of people across the nation, and then across the Atlantic. Spirit communication becomes an international fascination. The Fox sisters are now celebrities, but cannot begin to meet the demand. We then do what so many others are doing. We gather around a table and invite spirits of the departed to satisfy our curiosity about the other side of death. Sometimes it seems to work, often it doesn't, but maybe next time. New methods are devised. Everybody hold hands. No, everybody

place your hands on the table; it will tip when a spirit visits. Even better: use a planchette, a pencil held by a heart-shaped piece of wood on small wheels. Spirit energy will guide the pencil to write notes from the beyond. Wait—forget the planchette. We can buy a Ouija board from Sears.

But why, exactly, are we doing this? For some people it is cheap entertainment, a social occasion, and the thrill of playing at the fringes of mystery. For others though, it is a desperate enterprise. There are grieving widows who need a word of comfort, sons and daughters who long to be forgiven, and people of deep religious sensitivity tormented by doubts about survival of death. Enough people are hopeful enough to keep spirit communication flourishing, skeptics notwithstanding. Nevertheless, there is a limit to what we

World-famous illusionist Harry Houdini also relentlessly exposed fraudulent mediums who preyed on the grief of bereaved people.

can learn from yes/no responses. We have not yet discovered much about the lives of the dead and their secrets.

Four developments soon transform our innocent efforts to contact family members and friends on the other side of the grave:

- The American Civil War claims more than 600,000 lives—equivalent to 6,000,000 in today's United States population. Grief is widespread and profound. The emotional need for comfort and closure is intense. Furthermore, raging epidemics (e.g., cholera and typhoid) fill graveyards throughout much of the world, adding every day to the ranks of the anguished bereaved.
- We are now seeking out those who seem especially gifted in spirit communication. We call these people *mediums* (a later generation would be renamed *channelers*). Control of the situation shifts to the medium, away from the participants. Obliging spirits visit with a trance-state medium who then passes the message along in her own or the spirit's voice. The *séance* (literally, sitting) in a darkened room is now a favored setting for a session with the spirits. The elite of society as well as the most humble members become devoted to the séance. There is money to be made.
- Deceit, fraud, and greed invade and conquer. Bogus mediums seize the opportunity to cadge money from emotionally needy seekers of spirit communication. They conduct rigged séances, and introduce other devices and techniques to convey messages from the beyond. For example, a blank slate is mysteriously written upon by a spirit hand, or one actually sees a ghostly shape flit across the dimly lit room. These procedures are routinely exposed as fakery by sharp-eyed investigators. Nevertheless, spirit communication continues to flourish and attract easy money.
- The dubious proceedings in dimly lit séance rooms are now becoming matters of concern for two powerful societal forces: church and science. This practice is not countenanced by church dogma. It is regarded as a threat to the religious establishment. The perceived threat becomes more urgent in 1859 when Charles Darwin finally gets around to publishing *On the Origin of Species*. Darwin himself is not motivated to contest church teachings; he has

simply followed his data where they lead. Nevertheless, the war is on. Science and its technological advances have already made significant inroads on religious explanations of how the world works. Many individuals do merge scientific acumen with religious faith. Extremists on both sides, however, are choosing Darwin's thesis as the prime battleground to determine whether religion or science should hold sway.

And so we come down to this question: are humans no more than animals who perish as do all mortal creatures, or are we favored by God with an immortal soul? Fail to prove survival, and who are we then, really, and with what prospects? Now begins a long, bitter, and complex struggle in which hard-nosed scientists will not admit that the survival question even deserves to be studied, while equally resolute religionists try to hold their ground without calling on support from fraud-ridden spiritism.

A Frustrating Quest

A few exceptionally able scholars attempted to study the survival question with open minds. Deborah Blum's *Ghost Hunters* (2006) offers a masterful account of this unique enterprise and its quirky participants. Societies for the study of psychical research were established first in England, then in the United States and other nations. Much of their limited resources were spent on the investigation of mediums. Some investigators were fooled a few times, but generally they excelled in exposing the cheats. It was satisfying to establish the credibility of their project in this way, but also discouraging because they did hope to find and validate the real thing.

Occasional medium sessions produced such remarkable results that the investigator was left shaken. "How could she have known these obscure details of my childhood, and that secret I have been carrying all these years? Perhaps she *is* in contact with my father." Perhaps the medium picked up the information from the mind of another living person. Yet even this speculative explanation was itself in need of verification. All in all, by no reasonable standard of evidence could mediums be said to have demonstrated proof of survival.

What, then, about "spirit photography"? These productions were also quickly discredited by professional photographers who demonstrated how easy it was to concoct pictures of deceased people and disembodied forms. "Photoshopping" is not really that new and seeing was not necessarily believing, after all.

The investigators sought other lines of inquiry, such as automatic writing. This phenomenon occurred in a dissociative state of consciousness. The individual would not be aware of what she was writing, or, often, that she was writing at all. This technique soon was appropriated by bogus mediums, but was also practiced under control conditions by respectable people. Again, there were episodes that suggested the participation of a deceased spirit, but that conclusion could not be drawn as a certainty.

Eventually, automatic writing would morph into the most intricate of investigative techniques. F. W. H. Myers (1903/1975) had come as close as anybody to making sense of previous findings in his monumental two-volume work, *Human Personality and Its Survival of Bodily Death.* Did Myers invent a new method of inquiry after his own death? Some people think so. Messages started coming through to several people who did not know each other. When compared, the enigmatic—almost teasing—messages made excellent sense and were anchored in obscure literary passages well known to Myers but to few others. These cross-correspondences continued for several years, and included other deceased contributors. Was this all an elaborate hoax? A construction of pattern and meaning from random bits and pieces? Or was Myers actually proving survival of death by his own efforts from the other side? Material of this kind satisfied some people, and drew ridicule from others. Is it too late now to analyze the cross-correspondences with high-tech procedures and also take into account the cultural milieu in which they occurred?

Why not turn to the public for evidence? Did ordinary people have experiences that are suggestive of survival? Two surveys were conducted. The researchers culled through thousands of responses and conducted follow-ups on the most promising cases. The researchers did not claim they had proven survival, but hoped they had provided enough material to encourage others to develop more refined scientific methods to study the problem. The scientific establishment, though, still considered the subject to be unworthy of attention and heaped scorn on those who did take up the quest.

Is there anything in these nearly forgotten reports that might still deserve attention? The *crisis apparition* might be the best candidate. In the midst of daily life, a person unexpectedly sees somebody known to him or her who shouldn't be there. There is also something curious about how the person looks or is behaving. The encounter is fleeting, odd, just one of those things. Later it is learned that the person whose image was perceived had at that moment died in another part of the world and often in a manner consistent with the fleeting image. The scholars who investigated the most impressive of these reports could not draw a firm conclusion either. A level-headed explanation would be that these reports were made up or distorted—and were unreliable. Skeptics can certainly insist on this explanation, but that becomes increasingly difficult if one follows the investigation closely. The most radical conclusion would be that crisis apparitions demonstrate survival of death. That, however, would be going beyond what the reports can offer.

Past Life Regression and the Channelers

Every now and then claims are brought forward that spirit communication has been proven through the reported experiences of a channeler. Most famous is the story of Bridey Murphy. Under hypnosis, Ruth Simmons, a twentieth-century American woman, recounted her experiences as "Bridey Murphy," who was said to have been born in Ireland in 1768 and to have died there in 1864. The book reporting this account (Bernstein, 1965) became a best seller and stimulated interest in so-called past life regression. Unfortunately, this good story was later found to be a compendium of experiences from Simmons's own everyday life but which had emerged during the hypnotic sessions as hidden memories. Authentic-sounding memories of Ireland had slipped into her mind from a childhood visit to the World's Fair in St. Louis, where an Irish village had been recreated. There have been other reports of past lives since Bridey Murphy came and went, and the same doubts and limitations remain. "My past life" seems to function as an enabling metaphor that opens the door to memory fragments that come together as though reports of an actual set of meaningful experiences.

The elite quest for scientific proof of survival faded away with the generation of scholars who had devoted themselves to this project. The enterprise had failed by its own success: bogus mediums had been discredited; solid evidence had not been found. Perhaps the investigators shouldn't be taken seriously either. A more fundamental issue was—and continues to be—the lack of a persuasive explanation for findings that do hint at survival. Those who believe can take comfort in the fact that science has already surprised itself on many occasions. Those who hold that survival has already received adequate scientific evidence and explanation have a difficult case to make.

An Apple on a String

This exploration of prime-time spiritism started with the Fox sisters in 1848. Fast forward now to October 21, 1888. Our scene is the glittering Academy of Music, one of the largest auditoriums in New York City, and on this evening crowded to capacity. The attraction is Margaret Fox Kane. She is hardly less the celebrity 40 years after introducing the world to Mr. Splitfoot, though seldom seen in public. Here is the gist of her message (Kane, 1888/1987) as recorded by a newspaper reporter:

> I was the first in the field and I have the right to expose it. My sister Kate and I were very young children when this horrible deception began. . . . We were very mischievous children and wanted to terrify our dear mother, who was a good woman and easily frightened. At night, when we went to bed, we used to tie an apple to a string and move the string up and down, causing the apple to bump on the floor. . . Mother listened to this for a time. She could not understand it and did not suspect us of being capable of a trick because we were so young (p. 226).

The girls refined their art when neighbors came by and apple-dropping no longer would do the job. They then made the "wonderful discovery" that they could produce resounding raps by snapping their toes and fingers, a skill they possessed to an astounding degree. From that point on, the girls were trapped in their own success: enjoying the attention, but shamed by their deception and fearful of admitting it. The now-elder Margaret offered more detail on production of the raps, and she even took off her shoes and strolled down the aisle, rapping as loudly as a wall full of Mr. Splitfoots. To make matters perfectly clear, she stated that she

had never believed in spirits and the like: it was all childish fun that had gotten out of hand.

The audience response to these revelations? Almost all those present continued to believe in Mr. Splitfoot and other spirit manifestations despite Margaret's disavowal and dramatic demonstration. Why spoil an appealing belief just because the facts are against it?

There is a postscript, the very sort of uncomfortable incident that has kept some skeptics from closing the book completely. It is now 10 years after both Fox sisters have died. Children are playing in the cellar of the abandoned house where the spirit fraud introduced itself to the world. All right, you know what they found, don't you! The skeleton and tin cup of a murdered peddler whose body had finally been exposed behind a crumbling wall (Blum, 2006). And that means—what?

NEAR-DEATH EXPERIENCES: EVIDENCE FOR SURVIVAL?

The survival question had been in the doldrums for a while, but snapped back to renewed attention with the publication of *Life After Life* in 1975. Raymond A. Moody, Jr. listened to the experiences of people who had recovered after coming close to death, then added his own thoughts. Many additional near death experience reports (NDERs) soon came forth from people who had been reluctant to share them until Moody's book brought the phenomenon into the open.

Here is a typical case from Moody's collection:

> I was hospitalized for a severe kidney condition, and I was in a coma for approximately a week. . . . During this period when I was unconscious, I felt as though I were lifted right up, just as though I didn't have a physical body at all. A brilliant white light appeared to me. The light was so bright that I could not see through it, but going into its presence was so calming and so wonderful. There is just no experience on earth like it. In the presence of the light, the thoughts or words came into my mind: "Do you want to die?" And I replied that I didn't know since I knew nothing about death. Then the white light said, "Come over this line and you will learn." I felt that I knew where the line was in front of

*me, although I could not actually see it. As I
went across the line, the most wonderful feelings
came over me—feelings of peace, tranquility, a
vanishing of all worries" (p. 56).*

This report illustrates major features of the primary near-death experience (NDE). Instead of panic
or despair, there is a sense of serenity and well-being.
The sensation of being "lifted right up" is also one of
the most striking characteristics. Known popularly
as the "out-of-body experience," it is also known as
the *autoscopic experience*. There is frequently a sense
of journey, a going toward something. A "brilliant
white light" may be discovered as the journey continues. There might also be a turning-point encounter that guides the person back to life.

The big question now arose: Does the NDER
constitute proof for survival of death? Moody later
stated that neither NDERs "or any sort of conven-
tionally established methodological procedures
will be able to get evidence of life after death"
(Kastenbaum, 1995a, p. 95). Moody's disavowal of
NDEs as proof of survival, however, did not discourage others from drawing this conclusion and
his own subsequent words were ambiguous.

Evidence Favoring the NDE as Proof of Survival

The experience seems to have a powerful effect on
many survivors, as Ring (1980, 1992) and subsequent researchers have found. Survivors of a close
brush with death often have a renewed sense of
purpose in life. Daily life also becomes more precious. Many survivors report that they have become
less concerned about dying and death; their close
encounter had been comforting. Some respondents
were convinced they had been dead; therefore, their
recovery proved the existence of an afterlife. These
personal reports were convincing to the experienc-
ers and to many of the people who learned of them.
However, scientists and more cautious members of
the public required evidence more convincing than
subjective reports of an altered states of consciousness.

Biomedical Attempts to Verify NDE Phenomena

Cardiologist Michael B. Sabom (1982) and his colleagues wondered if a person could make accurate
observations while trapped within a horizontal,
impaired, and endangered body. Most patients

undergoing life-threatening surgery had no memories to report, but six survivors seemed to remember details of their experiences that could not have
been obtained through guesswork or prior knowledge of cardiopulmonary resuscitation.

Sabom did not claim that his findings proved
survival of death. Instead, he suggested that perhaps during this altered state a person can make accurate observations of immediate reality as well as
enter into the mystical state of being often reported
for NDEs. He also came up with an interesting finding that has been mostly confirmed by later studies:
NDERs had no demonstrable relationship to age,
gender, socioeconomic status, or the cause of the crisis (e.g., cardiac arrest, motor vehicle accident).

Sabom's first study had relied upon retrospective accounts. Now he would observe a patient
who was "clinically dead" (the terminology in use
at the time). A woman was placed in a state of minimal functioning in preparation for brain surgery.
The electrical activity of her brain was suspended,
accompanied by intentional cardiac arrest, and
reduction of body temperature. Upon recovering,
she claimed to have been highly alert and was able
to make accurate reports of things she had seen
and heard (Sabom, 1998).

This was an impressive experience, but did
it prove survival after death? The patient's recollections were tested against actual events that occurred in the operating room. However, there is no
such direct way to test a person's account of having
met a spiritual being of light, and the other subjective phenomena included in NDERs. Furthermore,
the patient had an intact body to host and support
her recovery. This is a luxury not available to people who have been dead and buried or cremated.
As Sabom himself noted, it would be a long stretch
to conclude that the results had proved survival.

A team of cardiologists in the Netherlands later
made a determined effort. They identified 344 consecutive patients who had been resuscitated after
cardiac arrest. All these patients had lost consciousness because of insufficient blood supply and/
or circulation within the brain. The patients were
interviewed shortly after their resuscitation, and
those who were still alive and willing to participate
were interviewed again two years and eight years
later. Pim von Lommel and his colleagues (2001)
found that NDERs were uncommon (18 percent).

*If purely physiological factors resulting from ce-
rebral anoxia caused NDE, most of our patients*

should have had this experience. Patients' medication was also unrelated to frequency of NDE. Psychological factors are unlikely to be important as fear was not associated with NDE (p. 2043).

The NDEs they did find were similar to those reported by Moody, Ring, and other researchers. They also came up with additional support for previous findings that people often feel their attitude toward life has been positively transformed by their NDE. There was also an interesting new finding made possible by the repeated interviews: Positive changes such as becoming more intuitive and having no fear of death actually became more evident years after the event. The authors suggest that the profound impact of the NDE might take years to become fully integrated in the individual's personality.

A similar study is reported by British researchers Sam Parnia and Peter Fenwick (2001, p. 10). They also found that "memories are rare after resuscitation from cardiac arrest." The relatively few memories (11 percent of the sample) did have some features of an NDE and were usually pleasant. There was a hint in the findings that NDEs were more common among patients who had more oxygenation and therefore better brain function during the resuscitation. These researchers tried to determine if the patients with NDEs had seen events from an out-of-body floating perspective, but, as in the Netherlands study, there were insufficient data to draw a conclusion.

How does the matter stand now? More than a decade has passed without a new controlled biomedical study to test the NDE/survival hypothesis. In her recent literature review, Janice Miner Holden (2009) found many sources for anecdotal reports of accurate memory by people assumed to have been in a nonresponsive brain state. However, she came up with only five direct hospital-based studies, including one of her own. Holden notes how difficult it is to conduct well-controlled research within the tense drama of a major medical procedure. Things happen, and recovery takes precedence over research. Reluctantly, but with the rigor of a true scientist, Holden concludes that there is not yet a conclusion—that is, no well-controlled cases that clearly support the thesis that NDEs provide evidence for survival of death. She calls for more research—and perhaps a little more luck in the quest.

Michael N. Marsh (2010), both a biomedical research physician and a Christian theologian, delves even more intensively into the details of the available cases. His criticism of Sabom's best case needs to be considered in any further discussions. He provides an incisive analysis of the biomedical facets of NDEs that I have ever read. Marsh also offers a broad historical perspective on out-of-body experiences, religiosity, and the survival question. He concludes that the NDE enterprise has not contributed much either to religion or science, though the many reported subjective experiences have inherent interest.

Eliminating Other Explanations

Skeptics soon developed alternative hypotheses to explain or explain away NDERs. Glen Gabbard and Stuart Twemlow (1984) dismissed several of these alternatives by noting that:

1. NDEs are not caused by nor are they necessarily symptoms of mental illness.
2. NDEs are not related to level of education.
3. There is no evidence that NDEs occur mostly among people who previously had been fascinated by mystic or other unusual phenomena.
4. The NDE does not have much similarity to dreams. It is a different kind of mental state.

These findings suggest that NDEs cannot be easily explained away as a dream state or as a function of education or mental illness. However, there are other alternative hypotheses still to consider, as well as some problems with the data and logic of the survival interpretation.

The Case Against the NDE as Proof of Survival

There are logical as well as empirical objections to interpreting NDEs as evidence for survival:

1. Many people who return from a close encounter with death recall nothing at all or only vague and dreamlike fragments.
2. Some survivors return with nightmarish experiences. Atwater (1992) reports that these cases are more frequent than previously thought, and can be compared with visions of hell. I have collected both positive and negative reports myself (see Box 13-2).
3. NDEs occur sometimes in situations in which the individual is not in physical peril. For example, the out-of-the-body component of the NDE has also been reported frequently in parapsychological experiments in which there is no

BOX 13-2

Some Frightening Near-Death Experiences*

- There were so many pews on each side, and each pew was filled with people wearing black robes with hoods. I couldn't see their faces but if I turned my eyes I could see the inside of the hoods were lined with red. . . . I stood there wondering where I was and what I was doing there, when a door opened to the right of the altar and out came the devil. . . . I saw that what he was pouring from the jug was fire, and I screamed, dropped the goblet, and started to run . . . (Irwin & Bramwell, 1988, p. 42).

- I was thrilled to meet this person—or was it an angel—and then all at once I saw that she or it was truly horrible. Where the eyes were supposed to be were slits, and kind of blue-green flames flickered through them, through the eye places. I can still see this demon, this whatever-it-was. With my eyes wide open, I can still see it.

- She told me to go back. I didn't want to. I said I was so happy being where I was, not that I knew where I was. I thought she was being mean to make me go back into that bloody wrecked body. I could feel myself shaking and crying. I didn't feel good any more.

*Told to the author by survivors of motor vehicle accidents, except where indicated otherwise.

life-threatening situation. Gabbard and Twemlow (1991) conclude that "the state of mind of the near-death subject is far more important than the state of the body" (p. 46). NDEs may be triggered by the belief that one is close to death or some other impending catastrophe.

4. Medical records reveal that many people who report NDEs actually had not come close to death. Only about half of the NDE reporters had survived a life-threatening illness or injury. Nevertheless, some patients had decided for themselves that they had been "dead" or "clinically dead." Others misinterpreted what they had been told by doctors or nurses. The researchers comment that "having had the NDE itself may have led some people to believe retrospectively that their condition must have been worse than it otherwise seemed" (Stevenson, Cook, & McClean-Rice, 1989/1990, p. 52).

5. People who had been in severe pain were more likely than others to experience a sense of distance from their bodies. Gabbard and Twemlow (1984) note that, in hypnotic pain experiments, it is a common suggestion to dissociate the painful part from the body so that it is treated as "not self." Furthermore, patients who had been under anesthesia were especially

likely to see brilliant lights and hear unusual sounds. These effects occur with many people who have been anesthetized, whether or not their conditions were life threatening.

6. We hear NDERs only from the survivors. There is no evidence that what happens when a person really dies "and stays dead" has any relationship to the experiences reported by those who have recovered from a life-threatening episode. There is always an observing self that categorizes the observed self as inert or dead. This split consciousness may result in the opinion that "I was dead," but there was always another "I" lively and perceptive enough to make that judgment.

Mystical, Depersonalization, and Hyperalertness Responses to Crisis

What else do people experience in crisis situations? Psychiatrist Russell Noyes, Jr. and his colleagues interviewed people who survived a variety of life-threatening crises. Three dimensions were often found: mysticism, depersonalization, and hyperalertness.

The *mystical* dimension of experiences close to death includes the feeling of great understanding; sharp and vivid images; revival of memories; the sense of harmony, unity, joy, and revelation. There may also be visions and strange bodily sensations. The *depersonalization* dimension includes loss of emotion, the sense of the self being detached both from the body and the world, an altered sense of time, objects appearing small and far away, strange sounds, and the body having been altered in some weird way. The *hyperalertness* dimension includes the feeling that vision and hearing have become sharper, and thoughts either more vivid or more dull and speeded up or blurred. One has an overall feeling of being mechanical in both thoughts and movements.

Hyperalertness and depersonalization help us through dangerous circumstances. Hyperalertness sharpens our ability to detect dangers and routes of escape. Depersonalization dampens the excessive emotionality that could disorganize us. We deal with a crisis more resourcefully when hyperalertness and depersonalization set us up in a cool, calm, and objective response mode.

When Do People *Not* Have NDEs? An Alternative Explanation

Ask the other side of the question—when do people in a crisis *not* have NDEs—and we discover something interesting (Kastenbaum, 1995b). Consider the individual's role in the crisis situation. A driver faced with an impending collision is more likely to make an emergency maneuver than to split off into an autoscopic experience. We engage in instrumental actions—we do something—when the circumstances permit. This is a survival mechanism: action to avoid catastrophe. I have learned from conversations with crisis survivors that the NDE is much more likely to occur when the jeopardized person had no instrumental action available. In a situation of perceived helplessness, the NDE serves a quieting, energy-conserving function. The resulting sense of serenity implies the activation of self-produced brain opiates (*endorphins*). This altered state enables body functions to continue with minimum expenditure of energy and is represented at the psychic level by comforting imagery. The imagery becomes more coherent as the individual recovers, although in retrospect it is attributed to an earlier phase of the crisis. If we can do something in a crisis situation—we do it (or at least make the effort). If there is nothing we can do to escape the danger physically, we do so by switching to a transcending state of being, with major assistance from our neural and spiritual imaging resources.

NDEs as Exercises in Religious Imagination?

Perhaps you have noticed similarities between religious conceptions of the journey of the dead and contemporary NDERs. Others would agree with you.

In *Otherworld Journeys* (1987), Carol Zaleski offers the following example:

> Four days ago, I died and was taken by two angels to the height of heaven. And it was just as though I rose above not only this squalid earth, but even the sun and moon, the clouds and stars. Then I went through a gate that was brighter than normal daylight, into a place where the entire floor shone like gold and silver. The light was indescribable, and I can't tell you how vast it was (p. 58).

Salvius had been left for dead one evening on a funeral bier. He was said to have revived and, inspired by his vision, became a bishop. Zaleski concludes that there is "a fundamental kinship" between these visions (or NDEs) and the imaginative powers that we use in everyday life:

> We are all, in a sense, otherworld travelers. Otherworld visions are products of the same imaginative power that is active in our ordinary ways of visualizing death; our tendency to portray ideas in concrete, embodied, and dramatic forms; the capacity of our inner states to transfigure our perception of outer landscapes; our need to internalize the cultural map of the physical universe, and our drive to experience that universe as a moral and spiritual cosmos in which we belong and have a purpose. . . . Near-death testimony is one way in which the religious imagination mediates the search for ultimate truth (p. 205).

A reading of *The Tibetan Book of the Dead* (Evans-Wentz, 2000) would provide us with further examples.

The G-LOC Problem

Still another possible explanation remains in the wind. A loss of consciousness occurs with acceleration during fighter aircraft operation or centrifuge simulation (Whinnery, 1997) The *G-LOC* problem, as it is known, continues to challenge fighter aviation medicine. Pilots who black out under acceleration stress are in danger for their lives. Whinnery concludes that:

The major characteristics of G-LOC experiences that are shared in common with NDEs include tunnel vision and bright lights, floating sensations, automatic movement, autoscopy, out-of-body experiences, not wanting to be disturbed, paralysis, vivid dreamlets of beautiful places, pleasurable sensations, psychological alterations of euphoria and dissociation, inclusion of friends and family, inclusion of prior memories and thoughts, the experience being very memorable (when it can be remembered), confabulation, and a strong urge to understand the experience (p. 245).

There is much in common between typical NDE reports and the reports given by pilots who have undergone G-LOC. These similarities do not prove anything, but certainly encourage further exploration of experiential states and the neurophysiological conditions that influence them so strongly.

SHOULD WE SURVIVE DEATH?

Should we survive death? This is a question that perhaps should be asked more often. Let's begin with responses from college students to item 3 ("I think of Heaven as") in the self-quiz earlier in this chapter.

- "I really can't answer that question. That's funny, isn't it? Here I am, a good Christian and I believe in heaven and all that, but I can't get what it's all about clear in my mind. I think my problem is in the idea of a literal heaven, a Sunday school fairytale. I can't really accept that any more, but I don't have anything to replace it."

- "You tell me! I imagine eternity as a state of perfection. No more worries, no more problems. Best of all, no more deadlines and exams! But then what? All I can imagine is God and all the rest of us posing forever for our portrait with this transcendental smile on our faces. I'd go crazy! I need to worry and rush around or I'm not really myself. More beautiful and peaceful than anything we can know on earth. Maybe the closest would be a long and relaxed Sunday afternoon. What makes a Sunday afternoon so great, though, is that it comes after one hectic week and before another. I don't know how I would do if there was only Sunday afternoon. This is probably a dumb way to think about heaven, but it's the best I can do."

These respondents were hesitant about survival of death because the "what do we do after we get there?" image was unclear. Easier to grasp is the afterlife that has been envisioned by many tribal peoples: Afterlife is much like the familiar here-and-now life, with such familiar activities as hunting, fishing, feasting, outsmarting adversaries, demonstrating valor, and so forth. Such conceptions of the afterlife involve not only continuing activity but also change, risk, and danger. Afterlife is life going on with perhaps more similarities than differences.

Survival: Not Good for Us?

A more radical orientation can also be taken toward the desirability of survival. There are two propositions here: (1) we do not deserve survival, and (2) the prospect of survival encourages the worst side of human nature.

The first proposition would be supported by the cruelty, stupidity, greed, and pettiness that abound in the lives of individuals and societies through the centuries. Make your own list. How many examples of genocide will you include? How many examples of fortunes being made by inflicting suffering on others? How many corporate executives deceiving the public and exploiting their own employees' retirement funds? How many examples of wanton destruction, royal whim, or bureaucratic arrogance? How much use and abuse of other people for personal satisfaction? Perhaps *Homo sapiens* have not earned the right for survival beyond the grave. We might also count against ourselves the ways in which we often waste time and therefore life. Should eternal life be granted to those who snooze or booze through earthly life? If our discretionary time is merely filled or killed, what claim dare we make on immortality? (Time devoted to reading this book is, of course, exempt from such criticism.)

The second argument also shines a harsh light on the human race. The prospect of eternal life has been used repeatedly in the service of power, greed, and fanaticism. We cannot help but think about the September 11, 2001, terrorists who believed that they were earning admission to paradise (a dubious assumption according to scholarly interpretations of the Qur'an). The promise of immortal blessing for those who die while slaughtering designated enemies has contributed to some of history's most ferocious episodes of violence. The moral case against survival, then, is that we might become better people and learn to make more constructive use of our time on earth if we did not have the prospect of an afterlife as either an all-dominating or fail-safe goal.

Eastern thought and practice adds still other dimensions. The way of the Buddha, for example, differs greatly from Christian conceptions of life, death, and afterlife (Bonney, 2002). "Death," in effect, disappears for those who can attain a heightened spiritual development in which birth and beginnings, cravings and ambitions all dissolve. The character of the Buddhist survival doctrine is also distinctive in its implications for individual and social action. Militant violence against others, for example, does not flow readily from this tradition.

BUT WHAT KIND OF SURVIVAL?

Suppose that there is survival after death. Suppose, further, we are in a roomful of people who agree with this statement—but each in their own ways. Here is what they might tell us:

- "Survival? Yes—as a burst of pure energy at the last moment of life. There is a discharge of electromagnetic radiation (or something like that). Does this death encode and preserve the individual's identity? Perhaps, perhaps not. It's not out the realm of possibility that this burst of electromagnetic radiation could be documented. This might be a long way from immortality, but a burst of glory—isn't that something?"

- "Have you seen a ghost? Most apparitions seem rather lost and slow-witted, not like the real people they once were, more like shadows or representations. What sometimes happens after death is that a temporary trace of the person remains in the locale. This 'person-shaped force field' is real but transient. It is not the survived person, merely his or her energy traces, and these will soon fade. Like the death flash, the ghost is a kind of survival, but not much to write home about."

- "When we die, we move from light to the realm of darkness. There is sad survival here, a slow fading away to poor, lost, empty souls in a dank necroscape. The Greeks called them shades, and were none too happy about it."

- "These quaint ideas miss the real point. There is true immortality—but not for everybody. Like much else in life, survival of death is *conditional*. What is it conditional on? Some wise people

have believed that those who develop great spiritual strength will not perish along with their bodies. The soul is not endowed with immortality: That has to be earned. Perhaps the rest of us are recycled as buttons, as Ibsen's Peer Gynt was informed after a life of self-seeking escapades."

- "Survival? How can you avoid it? We are born but to die, and die but to be reborn. Not only those of us who are at the moment human beings, but all living things (and perhaps 'inanimate' things as well) go through cycles of existence. There are many beginnings and ends: but, for most of us, no Beginning and no End."

- "We live. We die. We are judged. We are damned, or we are granted salvation. The righteous dwell forever with the Lord; those who live in ignorance or defiance will know the fires of hell. Are you listening?"

- "Human life is—or should be—a progression toward spiritual development. This does not have much to do with the external forms of religion but rather with each person's journey from ignorance to understanding, from concern with individuality and materiality to becoming part of a universal consciousness."

- "Leaving this life produces an altered state of consciousness. Somebody survives, but not the somebody we have been all along. There are many examples of altered states as part of our life experiences, so death may be simply the most impressive of these changes."

- "A person dies, of course. This always happens. And then that person just goes on with his life or with her life. This always happens, too. The next life is much like this one. Pleasures. Troubles. Dangers. Say the wrong thing or annoy the wrong person and you can get yourself killed again. What else are we to do in the next life but be who we are and do what we do?"

All the views paraphrased above have been expressed at various times. The concept of the next life as continuation of the present life has been held by many tribal peoples over the centuries. By contrast, the death flash theory is based upon inconclusive experiments on electromagnetic radiation in living tissues (Slawinski, 1987), and the force-field theory was first suggested by Myers (1903/1975). Conditional immortality was proposed by one of the few twentieth-century philosophers who took the question of survival as a serious intellectual issue (Hocking, 1957). And a specialist in the study of altered states suggests that death results in—what else?—an altered state (Tart, 1990).

It is not likely that any one person would find all of these versions equally plausible or appealing. Nevertheless, we have reminded ourselves that more than one possibility has been envisioned in the ongoing scrimmage between the evident fact of death and the vast reaches of imagination and desire.

ASSISTED AND SYMBOLIC SURVIVAL

Two other types of possible survival are so different from those already identified that we need to give them separate attention here. Symbolic immortality is the more familiar and better established of these concepts. The other type is still emerging—let's call it assisted survival.

Symbolic Immortality

Somebody—actually, several somebodies—had carved their initials into the old desk where I did a lot of my daydreaming in Public School 35, the Bronx. Third graders before me had made at least these marks in the world. The impulse to leave an enduring mark on the world begins early in life. Times of danger intensify this need. "Kilroy was here!" became a famous phrase during World War II, scrawled on everything that could be scrawled upon, mostly by young men and women in the armed forces who were assigned to unfamiliar places in hazardous conditions. "Kilroy" represented those who might never return—but they had been here, meaning they had been alive, had existed, had done something.

The concept of symbolic immortality became salient through the writings of Robert Jay Lifton (1979) as he reflected upon the psychological effects of World War II. Death had become increasingly difficult to deny, and not all mourners were consoled by belief in a traditional afterlife. There was a subtle shift from talk of "soul" to "self." What was to become of the self when the body was finished? Perhaps it could live on in the memories of others. This was not a new idea. Many world cultures remembered their dead through sacred keepsakes and ritual. In our own society, fundraisers persuaded wealthy people to pay for buildings that would bear their names forever.

The upsurge of interest in symbolic immortality was, in part, a consequence of twentieth-century mass brutality. Holocaust survivors saw themselves as witnesses with the responsibility to bear testimony: "We saw these things happen. We knew and loved these good people who were tormented and killed!" It was essential to pass the memories of the victims and the atrocities on to the next generation.

Engrossment in symbolic immortality can also be motivated by the desire to remain influential, after death, even if we are secure in our faith in an afterlife. Symbolic immortality might also confirm our reputations of people of exceptional merit. Sometimes this postmortem reputation, set in stone, is in fact well deserved. Late in my seemingly endless graduate student days, I happened to meet an elfin and spry old man with a flowing white beard and a merry demeanor. He could have come straight from the Black Forest and any number of folktales. Rufus von Kleinschmidt lives in my memory as an extraordinary person—and I suppose I am mentioning this brief encounter because I would like to continue his symbolic immortality through you. But the former chancellor of the University of Southern California now is officially immortal through a large building that carries his name. Beautiful building, but I miss the man. There are many people who achieve symbolic immortality without seeking or realizing it. Teachers, for example, can become role models who influence their former students throughout their lives. A mentor can survive not only in memory but also as an inner representation that influences a person's life in many ways (Marwit & Lessor, 2000).

The desire for symbolic immortality can be just one part of a person's motivational repertoire, or a driving and distorting force. It is natural, for example, to hope that something of oneself might live on in our children and grandchildren—but "control freak" is seldom a term of endearment. Transmitting the family genes remains the most direct method, but so can passing some good (or fascinatingly bad) family stories that can be retold to later generations. Home videos are increasingly becoming part of that package.

The "immortality" in symbolic immortality is vulnerable to time and circumstance. The remembering people themselves die. Once-famous events and achievements become obscure. Buildings are destroyed, memorials worn down or defaced. Every generation contributes by its selective remembering and forgetting.

Assisted Immortality

Technology is opening new possibilities for symbolic immortality. Recorded images and sounds, so familiar to us now, were an historic breakthrough. The past could now be part of the present, and the present part of the future. Furthermore, some of the most brilliant inventors labored on devices that might prove or assure survival of death. Marconi made radio possible, and Edison helped to bring electricity into everyday life—yet both considered themselves failures because they couldn't come up with a working immortality machine. Perhaps technologically assisted survival is an especially attractive proposition for people who do not have a strong faith in a religion that promises an afterlife.

The following are some modes of speculative assisted survival (Cryonic resuscitation is in something of a class by itself and was considered in Chapter 6.)

Clone thyself. Make a perfect digital copy of a document or compact disk? We do that all the time now. Why not duplicate ourselves? Wouldn't that be the way to go? Or, actually, not to go! Cloning is also known as "twinning," in reference to the naturally occurring process that results in identical twins. The identical twins come from genetic contributions by both parents. Experimental cloning works differently to achieve the same result. The most famous sheep since Mary's Little Lamb was created through nuclear transfer: The nucleus of a cell was removed from an adult ewe, implanted in an egg, developed into an embryo, and then placed within a surrogate ewe who became Dolly's birth, though not her biological, mother (Wilmut, Schnieke, McWhir, Kind, & Campbell, 2001). This was neither the first nor the last laboratory production of a cloned animal.

J. B. Gurdon and his colleagues had spawned swimming tadpoles by nuclear transfers (2001), and soon there were also cloned monkeys scrambling about. Research has been directed primarily toward improving crops or developing genetic fixes for life-threatening conditions. What mostly concerns us here is cloning as a possible form of assisted survival. Presumably, additional clones could be grown as the need arose and the funding held up. Such familiar concepts as "resuscitation" and "reincarnation" would need to be looked at in a different light, and clone vs. clone would be an attractive plot for your favorite TV series.

Successful cloning is difficult, and would be even more so if attempted with humans. There were many failures in the attempts to produce viable tadpoles and sheep. The painful issue of dealing with genetically defective infants would expand if human cloning were to be attempted.

The fundamental question, though, is whether the clone will actually be the original in all its significant respects. Yes, Clone looks like Original, and perhaps walks and talks like Original. But— hold on! Does Clone have the same life history as the Original? Did Clone grow up during the same sociohistorical period? And hold on again—has Original's consciousness been installed in Clone? Can science replicate our inner sense of self? The most perfect Clone will not be the Original if it does not experience itself and the world through the unique consciousness of the Original. If a person's consciousness does not survive, that person will not even be aware of his or her "survival." Is that a good thing?

Become a smart chip. Perhaps bodies are overhyped. Perhaps we would be better off without them. William Gibson's futuristic novel

---

BOX 13-3

We'll never forget what's his name: part 1

Please fill in the blanks—

_____'s great poem _____ describes a classic example of the way in which time can cancel the symbolic immortality of a once-mighty person.

BOX 13-4

We'll Never Forget What's His Name: Part 2

Percy Bysshe Shelley's great poem, "Ozymandias," describes a classic example of the way in which time can cancel the symbolic immortality of a once-mighty person. Is this—or any—poet still remembered, or have those who reflected on symbolic immortality lost theirs as well?

Neuromancer (1994) dismissed bodies as "meat," useless burdens that we should abandon to enjoy the infinite delights of "the matrix." Margaret Wertheim (1999) cited stories in which people downloaded themselves into computers. Joslyn, Turchin, & Heylighen (1997) suggest that computer and biological systems might blend into a single system when used together continuously. The person could be said to have survived as part of the merged system.

Uploading oneself as a smart chip is still a work in progress. However, many people already enjoy sporting about in simulated cyberspace communities, e.g., avatars in Second Life. *Avatar* is the Sanskrit word for a Hindu god who is incarnated in human form. In computer-speak, avatars are fantasy figures who are shaped by players to represent them in a digitalized proxy world. Is the customized avatar a fail-safe digital replacement for the immortal soul? Or is the avatar an expendable self that one can triumphantly survive? Death in Second Life is an unsettled process at this point, still feeling its way.

Mail ourselves to the future. Time capsules have been around for a while. Selected objects are placed in a container to be opened by a future generation. Could this become a form of assisted survival? A commercial organization known as Highway Products, Inc. assures us that an Infinity Time Capsule is not only "the best gift you can give to your future generation" but also "your chance at immortality." The technological assist in this case is through argon, a dry, inert gas that is intended to prevent deterioration of objects by acid, oxidation, or ultraviolet light. "Each Infinity Time Capsule is then punched with a serial number that we record and keep as a record.

Your valuable contents are now safe and secured from the elements until your ancestors open your Infinity Time Capsule" (p. 2).

I would definitely be intrigued if a time capsule came my way from ancestors little known to me. But would this make them immortal in any meaningful sense of the term? We come back once again to a question for each of us to consider: What would be a meaningful or essential form of survival—and would I make use of a technological assist, if available?

THE SUICIDE–SURVIVAL CONNECTION

When Christianity was a new sect struggling for its survival, many tried to emulate Jesus through martyrdom at the hands of the Roman authorities. A thousand years later, both Islamic and Christian warriors sought deaths that would earn them entry into their respective realms of eternal bliss. A thousand years after that—four hijacked jets headed toward a suicide mission. The idea that people who die a heroic death will find an eternal reward has been a motif in many cultures. See a production of Wagner's music drama *Der Valkyrie* and you will be treated to an imaginative reenactment of an ancient Norse legend in which fallen heroes are scooped up from the field of battle and escorted to Valhalla, a Viking warrior's version of heaven.

What about those who believe that there simply is no death? This is by far the most common response of people who identify themselves with the "New Age" movement. As one respondent put it, death "is just changing clothes." What remains to be learned is whether or not suicide will be seen as an action that is unimportant, therefore not to be prevented or mourned.

We have known for some time what Hamlet thinks. In that most famous of monologues (Act III, Scene 1) he begins with the question: "To be or not to be?" For a moment it looks as though "Not!" will be his answer:

> and by a sleep to say we end
> The heart-ache and the thousand natural shocks
> That flesh is heir to, 'tis a consummation
> Devoutly to be wish'd. To die, to sleep. . .

But is death really a consummation? If he copes differently with his ordeal, Hamlet and Ophelia might yet have each other—now there would be a consummation! The imagery of sexual fulfillment is substituted for the reality of death, making it easier to edge his way toward the grave. He continues to blur the reality of death by reassuring himself: "To die, to sleep." That's all death is—sleep—and who's afraid of sleep? So, he's going to pack it in then, right? Not so fast!

> To sleep: perchance to dream: ay, there's the rub;
> For in that sleep of death what dreams may come
> When we have shuffled off this mortal coil,
> Must give us pause. . . .

There is that one troubling reason to stay his hand from seizing his "bare bodkin" and putting an end to it all:

> . . . the dread of something after death,
> the undiscover'd country from whose bourn
> No traveller returns, puzzles the will
> And makes us rather bear those ills we have
> Than fly to others that we know not of.

Every day there are people who confront their own "to be or not to be" dilemmas. Each person, each dilemma is unique. Nevertheless, all involve assumptions about life, death, and afterlife. Perhaps we can be wiser companions in these situations if we have explored our own undiscovered countries deeply enough to offer them a life-giving pause.

■ SUMMARY

Most people in most societies throughout the centuries have believed in some form of survival. Several of these belief systems were described, with particular attention to Judaic, Christian, Islamic, and Buddhist traditions. Terrorists who believe that becoming martyrs will earn them honor and pleasure in paradise are operating on fantasies that are at variance with the Qur'an. The journey of the dead as well as the heavens and hells imagined by various religious faiths are explored. Recent surveys indicate that afterlife belief remains strong in the United States, although it is declining in Europe. The baby boomer generation reports an abundance of belief: in heaven, in encounters with spirits of the dead, and, to an increasing extent, in reincarnation. Nevertheless, doubt and questioning have also continued since the emergence of science, with its revisionary views of life and the universe. Much of this chapter, therefore, was concerned with attempts to strengthen afterlife belief with evidence. You were asked to put your own ideas and beliefs on the line in a self-quiz. We examined near-death experience reports (NDERs) in some detail because many have often taken these reports as proof of survival. Many who have had this kind of experience report that their lives had changed—for the better—as a result. This outcome does not in itself prove survival, however. The NDE material offered as proof of survival was reviewed and critiqued. It is difficult to make an evidence-based case for the NDE/survival thesis. We also considered several theories that attempt to explain the NDE. These included the spiritual/survival explanation but also alternatives that interpret the NDE as (a) a split-off psychological reaction to stress; (b) a quieting, energy-conserving function when we can do nothing to extricate ourselves from a life-threatening situation; (c) an hallucination produced by psychophysiological changes; (d) an exercise in religious imagination; (e) a healing and illuminating metaphor, and, most recently; (f) a stress response that parallels the G-LOC experience of pilots subjected to extreme acceleration pressure. Next we examined another source of possible evidence for survival: the dead themselves, or their spirit representatives. This discussion included folktales, deathbed escorts, contacts made through mediums and channelers, and my personal favorite, ghosts. The tragic consequences of belief in the reality and power of ghosts was illustrated by the Ghost Dance: some Native American peoples hoped to invoke the protection of their ancestors and raise them from the dead through this dance, but instead exposed themselves to massacre. Reincarnation, although usually associated with Asian and African belief systems, has gained a large following in the United States and other Western nations in recent years. Ian Stevenson's careful and prolific research into "evidence suggestive of reincarnation" was the center of our attention. Before concluding, we forced ourselves to consider the question, should we survive death? This was followed by perhaps an even more unsettling question: what kind of survival? After considering several traditional concepts of how we survive death, attention was given to symbolic immortality, cloning, and becoming a kind of "smart chip" that enters into the cosmic matrix.

■ REFERENCES

Agha, A. (2003). Tibetan book of the dead. In R. Kastenbaum (Ed.), *Macmillan encyclopedia of death and dying* (Vol. 1, pp. 896–898). New York: Macmillan.

Alexander, B. (2003). *Rapture. A raucous tour of cloning, transhumanism, and the new era of immortality.* New York: Basic Books.

Atwater, P. M. H. (1992). Is there a Hell? Surprising observations about the near-death experience. *Journal of Near-Death Studies, 10,* 149–160.

Barrett, W. (1986). *Death-bed visions.* Northampton: The Aquarian Press. (Original work published 1926).

Bentham, J. (1832). *Last will and testament,* Westminster, UK. http://www.utilitarian.net/bentham/ .

Bernstein, W. (1965). *The search for Bridey Murphy.* Garden City, NY: Doubleday.

Bernstein, A. E. (1993). *The formation of Hell.* Ithaca, NY: Cornell University Press.

Blackmore, S. (2004). *Consciousness.* Oxford: Oxford University Press.

Bonney, R. (2002). Buddhism. In R. Kastenbaum (Ed.), *Macmillan encyclopedia of death and dying* (Vol. 1, pp. 74–80). New York: Macmillan.

Boyce, M. (1979). *Zoroastrians: Their religious beliefs and practices.* London: Routledge & Kegan Paul.

Brabant, S., Kalch, D., & Breaux, B. D. (2008–2009). The *Psychology Today* "You and Death" questionnaire revisited. *Omega, Journal of Death and Dying, 58,* 193–212.

Brea, J. (January 26, 2007). "Ghost bride" returns to haunt Chinese trio. hhttp://www.scotsman.com/news/international/ghost_bride_returns_to_haunt_chinese_trio_1_679558.

Bryant, C. (2003). Ghosts: The dead among us. In C. Bryant (Ed.), *Handbook of death and dying* (Vol. 1, pp. 87–95). Thousand Oaks, CA: Sage.

Chen, S-C. J. (2007). In China: A macabre trade in ghost brides. Forbes.com.

Crowe, C. (2008) *Night side of nature or ghosts and ghost seers.* (Original work published 1846). Whitefish, MT: Kessinger.

Darwin, C. (1859). *On the origin of species.* London: John Murray.

Dillon, J. (2003). Reincarnation: The technology of death. In C. D. Bryant (Ed.), *Handbook of death and dying* (Vol. 1, pp. 65–76). Thousand Oaks, CA: Sage.

Emmons, C. F. (1982). *Chinese ghosts and ESP: A study of paranormal beliefs and experiences.* Metuchen, NJ: Scarecrow.

Evans-Wentz, W. Y. (Ed.). (2000). *The Tibetan book of the dead, or the afterdeath experiences on the Bardo plane.* Oxford: Oxford University Press.

Fisk, R. (2005). In the Middle East, those who are about to die believe profoundly in the afterlife. http://www.independent.co.uk/opinion/commentators/fisk/in-the-middle-east-those-who-are-about-to-die-believe-profoundly-in-the-afterlife-6151400.html.

Flew, A. (1967). Mind-body problem. In P. Edwards (Ed.), *The encyclopedia of philosophy* (Vol. 5, pp. 336–353). New York: Macmillan.

Freed, R. S., & Freed, S. A. (1993). Ghosts: Life and death in North India (Anthropological Papers, No. 72). New York: American Museum of Natural History.

Gabbard, G. O., & Twemlow, S. W. (1984). *With the eyes of the mind.* New York: Praeger.

Gabbard, G. O., & Twemlow, S. W. (1991). Do "near-death experiences" occur only near-death? *Journal of Near-Death Studies, 10,* 41–48.

Gallup Poll Survey No. GO 129321. (1999, December). CNN/USA Today.

Gibson, W. (1994). *Neuromancer.* New York: Ace Books.

Glassman, H (20098) At the crossroads of birth and death: The Blood Pool Hello and postmortem fetal extraction. In J. L. Stone & M. N. Walter (Eds.), *Death and the afterlife in Japanese Buddhism* (pp. 175–206). Honolulu: University of Hawai'i Press.

Greeley, A. M., & Hout, M. (1999). Belief in life after death increasing in the United States. *American Sociological Review, 64,* 813–836.

Green, C., & McCreery, C. (1989). *Apparitions.* Oxford, UK: Institute of Psychophysical Research.

Gurdon, J. B. (2001). The birth of cloning. In M. Ruse & A. Sheppard (Eds.), *Cloning* (pp. 39–48). Amherst, NY: Prometheus.

Hanson, H. Y. (2003). Islam. In R. Kastenbaum (Ed.), *Macmillan encyclopedia of death and dying* (Vol. 1, pp. 484–489). New York: Macmillan.

Harris, S. (2004). *The end of faith.* New York: W. W. Norton.

Hayslip, B., & Peveto. C. (2005). *Historical shifts in attitudes toward death, dying, and bereavement.* Amityville, NY: Baywood.

Hinton, D. E., Pich, V., Chean, D., & Pollack, M. H. (2005). "The ghost pushes you down": Sleep paralysis-type panic attacks in a Khmer refugee population. *Transcultural Psychiatry, 42,* 46–77.

Hittman, M. (1990). *Wovoka and the ghost dance.* Lincoln: University of Nebraska Press.

Hocking, W. E. (1957). *The meaning of immortality in human experience.* New York: Harper.

Holden, J. M. (2009) Veridical perceptions in near-death experiences. In J. M. Holden, B. Grayson, & D. James (Eds.), *The handbook of near-death experiences: Thirty years of investigation* (pp. 185–212). Santa Barbara, CA: Praeger.

Irwin, H. J., & Bramwell, A. B. (1988). The devil in heaven: A near-death experience with both positive and negative facets. *Journal of Near-Death Experiences, 7,* 38–43.

Joslyn, C., Turchin, V., & Heylighen, F. (1997). Cybernetic immortality. Principia Cybernetica Web. http://pespmc1.vub.ac.be/CYBIMM.html.

Kane, M. F. (1888). Spiritualism exposed. In P. Kurtz (Ed.) *A skeptic's handbook of parapsychology.* Buffalo, NY: Prometheus.

Kastenbaum, R. (1993). Ian Stevenson: An Omega interview. *Omega, Journal of Death and Dying, 28,* 165–182.

Kastenbaum, R. (1995a). Raymond A. Moody, Jr.: An Omega interview. *Omega, Journal of Death and Dying, 31,* 87–98.

Kastenbaum, R. (1995b). *Is there life after death?* London: Prion.

Kastenbaum, R. (1996). Near-death reports: Evidence for survival of death? In L. W. Bailey & J. Yates (Eds.), *The near-death experience reader* (pp. 245–264). NY: Routledge.

Kastenbaum, R. (1998b). Temporarily dead. *Readings, 13,* 16–21.

Kastenbaum, R. (2004). *On our way: The final passage through life and death.* Berkeley: University of California Press.

Kearl, M. C. (2002). Immortality, symbolic. In R. Kastenbaum (Ed.), *Macmillan encyclopedia of death and dying* (Vol. 2, pp. 461–464). New York: Macmillan.

Kelly, E. W., Greyston, B., & Stevenson, I. (1999/2000). Can experiences near death furnish evidence of life after death? *Omega, Journal of Death and Dying, 40,* 513–520.

Klugman, C. M. (2006). Dead men talking: Evidence of post death contact and continuing bonds. *Omega, Journal of Death and Dying, 53,* 249–262.

Lester, D., Aldridge, M., Aspenberg, C., Boyle, K., Radsniak, P., & Waldron, C. (2001/2002). What is the afterlife like? Undergraduate beliefs about the afterlife. *Omega, Journal of Death and Dying, 44,* 113–126.

Lifton, R. J. (1979). *The broken connection. On death and the continuity of life.* New York: Simon & Schuster.

Lommel, P. V., Wees, R. V., Meyers, V., & Elfferich, I. (2001). Near-death experience in survivors of cardiac arrest: A prospective study in the Netherlands. *Lancet, 358,* 2039–2045.

Lucretius (Titus Lucretius Carus). *On the nature of things.* (Original work published 54 B.C.) In R. M. Hutchins (Ed.), *Great books of the Western world* (Vol. 12, pp. 1–97). Chicago: Chicago University Press.

Marsh, M. N. (2010). Out-of-body and near-death experiences. New York: Oxford.

McDannell, C., & Lang, B. (1988). *Heaven. A history.* New Haven, CT: Yale University Press.

Marwit, S. J., & Lessor, C. (2000). Role of deceased mentors in the ongoing lives of proteges. *Omega, Journal of Death and Dying, 41,* 125–138.

Mehr, F. (2003). Zoroastrianism. In R. Kastenbaum (Ed.), *Macmillan encyclopedia of death and dying* (Vol. 2, pp. 956–960). New York: Macmillan.

Miller, J. Y. (2001, August 5). AJC Southern Poll: Southerners' thoughts about death and dying are set apart by traditions and religious beliefs. *The Atlanta Journal and Constitution* online.

Moody, R. A., Jr. (1975). *Life after life.* Atlanta: Mockingbird Books.

Mooney, J. (1996). *The ghost dance.* North Dighton, MA: JG Press, Inc.

Morin, R. (2000). Do Americans believe in God? http://www.washingtonpost.com/wp-srv/politics/polls/wat/archive/wat042400.htm.

Myers, F. W. H. (1975). *Human personality and its survival of bodily death* (Vols. 1–2). New York: Arno Press. (Original work published 1903.)

Newcott, B. (2007). Life after death. http://www.aarpmagazine.org/people/life_after_death.html

Noyes, R., Jr. (1979). Near-death experiences: Their interpretation. In R. Kastenbaum (Ed.), *Between life and death* (pp. 73–88). New York: Springer.

Osis, K. (1961). *Deathbed observations by physicians and nurses.* New York: Parapsychology foundation.

Osis, K., & Haraldsson, E. (1977). *At the hour of death.* New York: Avon.

Parnia, S., & Fenwick, P. (2002). Near death experiences in cardiac arrest: Visions of a dying brain or visions of a new science of consciousness. *Resuscitation, 52,* 5–11.

Pew Research Center (2008, February 25). The U.S. religious landscape survey reveals a fluid and diverse pattern of faith. http://pewresearch.org/pubs/743/united-states-religion.

Reuters (2002). Man shot dead over heaven and hell argument. http://news.excite.com/odd/article/id/255902%7Coddlyenough%7C07-30-2002::10:00%7Creuters.html.

Ring, K. (1980). *Life at death.* New York: Coward, McCann & Geoghegan.

Ring, K. (1992). *The Omega project.* New York: William Morrow.

Robinson, R. (2003). *Famous last words, fond farewells, death diatribes, and exclamations upon expiration.* NY: Workman

Sabom, M. B. (1982). *Recollections of death.* New York: Simon & Schuster.

Sabom, M. B. (1998). *Light and death: One doctor's fascinating account of near-death experiences.* Grand Rapids, MI: Zondervan.

Sheler, J. L. (2000, January 31). Hell hath no fury. *U. S. News & World Report* online.

Segal, A. F. (2009). The afterlife in modern America. In M. K. Bartolos (Ed.), *Speaking of death. America's new sense of mortality* (pp. 78–101). Westport, CT: Praeger

Siegel, R. K. (1980). The psychology of life after death. *American Psychologist, 35,* 911–931.

Skloot, R. (2010). *The immortal life of Henrietta Lacks.* New York: Crown.

Slawinski, J. (1987). Electrometic radiation and the afterlife. *Journal of Near-Death Studies, 6,* 79–94.

Stevenson, I. (1974). *Twenty cases suggestive of reincarnation* (Rev. ed.). Charlottesville: University Press of Virginia.

Stevenson, I. (1997a). *Reincarnation and biology. A contribution to the etiology of birthmarks and birth defects* (Vols. 1–2). Westport, CT: Praeger.

Stevenson, I. (1997b). *Where reincarnation and biology intersect.* Westport, CT: Praeger.

Stevenson, I., Cook, C. W., & McClean-Rice, N. (1989/1990). Are persons reporting "near-death experiences" really near death? A study of medical records. *Omega, Journal of Death and Dying, 20,* 45–54.

Stevenson, I., & Greyson, B. (1996). Near-death experiences: Relevance to the question of survival after death. In L. W. Bailey & J. Yates (Eds.), *The near-death experience reader* (pp. 199–206). New Haven: Yale University Press.

Tart, C. (1990). Who survives? Implications of modern consciousness research. In G. Doore (Ed.), *What survives?* (pp. 138–152). Los Angeles: Jeremy P. Tarchers.

Taylor, R. P. (2000). (Ed.). *Death and the afterlife.* Santa Barbara: ABC-CLIO.

Turner, A. K. (1993). *The history of Hell.* New York: Harcourt Brace.

Wallis, J. (2001). Continuing bonds: Relationships between the living and the dead within contemporary spiritualism. *Mortality, 6,* 127–145.

Washburn, K., & Majors, J. S. (1998). *World poetry: An anthology of verses from antiquity to our time.* New York: Norton.

Wasilewska, E. (2002). So the soul can rest—Death and afterlife in the Qur'an: Part 2. http://www.highbeam.com/doc/1G1-98780135.html.

Wertheim, M. (1999). *The pearly gates of cyberspace.* New York: Norton.

Westwood, J. (2002). Gilgamesh. In R. Kastenbaum (Ed.), *Macmillan encyclopedia of death and dying* (Vol. 1, pp. 331–334). New York: Macmillan.

Whinnery, J. E. (1997). Psychophysiologic correlates of unconsciousness and near-death experiences. *Journal of Near-Death Studies, 15,* 231–258.

Wilmut, I., Schnieke, A. E., McWhir, A., Kind, A. F., & Campbell, K. H. S. (2001). Viable offspring derived from fetal and adult mammalian cells. In M. Ruse & A. Sheppard (Eds.), *Cloning* (pp. 31–38). New York: Prometheus.

Wohlberg, S. (2002). *Do all pets go to heaven?* Enuclaw, WA: Winepress Publishing.

Zaleski, C. (1987). *Otherworld journeys.* New York: Oxford University Press.

Zaleski, C. (2003, April 5). When I get to heaven: Picturing paradise. The Christian Century online.

Zuckerman, P. (2004, March 1). Securalization: Europe—yes, United States—no: why has securalization occurred in Western Europe but not in the United States? *Skeptical Inquirer* online (SICOP.org).

■ GLOSSARY

Autoscopic experience Perceiving one's own body as though from above, a facet of the out-of-the-body experience.

Avatar A Hindu god who is incarnated in human form. This ancient Sanskrit word has been appropriated by computer gamers, usually to refer to a cybenetic version of one's self.

Channeler A person with the reputed power to communicate with the past lives of oneself or others.

Depersonalization A sense of emotional distance from one's own body and self.

Endorphins Substances the brain produces that effect mood and awareness.

G-LOC An altered state of consciousness produced by the stress of extreme acceleration in fighter planes or ground simulations.

Hezbollah An Islamic resistance movement. Literally, "the Party of God."

Hyperalertness A state of heightened attention, usually to danger signals.

Immortality The persistence of spirit, soul, or personality after death. Not all afterlife beliefs hold that people survive death on a permanent basis, therefore, not all survival has immortal status.

Jahannam Islamic concept of hell.

Jihad It refers to the constant struggle between one's own lower and higher impulses, as well as to conflict with enemies of the faith.

Medium A person with the reputed power of receiving messages from the dead (earlier term for channeler).

Mystical experiences Often include vivid imagery and a sense of secrets and wonders revealed and accompanied by a joyous harmony.

Near-death experience (NDE) Images, perceptions, and feelings that are recalled by some people after a life-threatening episode.

Necromancer A person who evokes the dead through secret spells and rituals.

Pluralistic death Concept that death and possible afterlife might not be the same for all living creatures under all conditions.

Psychopomp A spirit being or messenger from God who escorts a dying person to the next life.

Reincarnation The return of the spirit or soul in another physical form after death.

Séance Literally, a sitting. The name given to sessions with a medium.

Yahweh A name given to God in the Old Testament.

Zoroastrianism An ancient religion centered in Persia that had significant influence on the later Judaic, Christian, and Islamic belief systems.

■ ON FURTHER THOUGHT . . .

Your Heaven:

History—right up to the present time—suggests that people have found it easier to imagine Hell. Detailed ideas about an enjoyable afterlife are found mostly in societies that conceive of the next life as being mostly similar to the life one is leaving. In the United States, most people express a belief in survival of death, but most also are vague about Heaven and what one does there all day. Perhaps Heaven is simply beyond imagining. Give it a try, though!

1. What is your best idea of what Heaven really is? Go for accuracy. What makes Heaven Heaven? Be as absolutely clear and detailed as you can.
2. What would Heaven be if you could design your own and have it come true? Again, challenge yourself to be as clear and detailed as you can. Do your friends and family have similar, or perhaps quite different, visions of Heaven? If you can get them to talk about them, proceed to the next questions.
3. What Heaven can you, your family, and friends construct together? What might this exercise tell you about what you are looking for in your life right here and now?

Where's all that fascinating and frustrating old stuff?

Books and journal articles written during the heyday of spiritism and survival research have been almost ghostlike in their appearances and disappearances. Arno Press issued a sizable set of reprint books in 1975, but these have been out of print for some time. *Phantasms of the Living*, an 1886 report of the first British Society for Psychic Research survey, is half-available at the moment through Amazon.com. *The Census of Hallucinations* (Sidgwick et al., 1889) is more or less available through reprinted excerpts from journal articles. Kessinger Publishing (www.kessinger. net, also available through Amazon.com) is at present the most promising source for rediscovering writings that were influential in the controversy. I do recommend becoming better acquainted with the field in a general way through Blum's (2006) book, already mentioned; Alfred Douglas's *Extrasensory Powers* (1976), Woodstock, NY: The Overlook Press, and my book, *Is There Life After Death?* (1995, revised edition), London: Prion. Whoops! That's out of print, too!

We turn to each other as well as to professional
caregivers when our lives are threatened.

▼

14

How Can We Help?

Caregiving and Death Education

You just never know how this is going to happen. It's like the birth of a baby. You never know how long it is gonna take. You never know how the labor's gonna go. It's just gonna go the way it's gonna go.
 — Family caregiver quote by Phillips & Reed (2009, p. 84)

How could I help them? They spoke mostly Polish. I didn't know only a few words I picked up from their children, and they were the same with English. But a really nice family. You could see they meant everything to each other. Then when the mother got sick and wasn't going to get better. . . sick rooms make me sick, and there was me not speaking their language. How could I help them?
 — A memory from the old neighborhood (South Bronx)

And he was young and energetic and full of life going into it. And the pain . . . there was just this horrible pain. The next day, it made him unable to talk, and we were sitting there watching the death and there was nothing we could do.
 — Quoted by Sharon R. Kaufman (2005)

I have done just about everything from long-term care to hospitals. They are all the same. It is always give more, more, more. I reached a point about a year ago where I began having anxiety attacks. . . . Working conditions are terrible. There are too many patients with critical needs and not enough help to do the things that need to be done. I felt like such a failure. . . . I felt that every day I worked the floor as a nurse I was putting my license on the line.
 — Anonymous (2005, p. 9)

I have been a nurse for ten years. I started as an LPN and thought I would be treated better if I became an RN. Big mistake. Treated just as badly, but now

I'm responsible for everything and everybody. You are blamed for everything and thanked for nothing. You may work like a dog for years, never take breaks, give it your heart, your soul, your blood, sweat and tears, and ruin your back. . . . You'll end up a bitter old person with a bad back.

—Val Salva (2005, p. 1)

I picked him up, ran out here, and laid him on the counter and called 911. And of course screamed hysterically into the phone. "Help me!" And they said they called the paramedics and they were on the way, and they want you to do CPR. And I had been trained in CPR (crying). I probably didn't do it the way I should have. I'm sure I didn't. They did stay on the line with me. I think a woman answered first, and I think they put a man on the phone. He kind of talked me through the CPR.

—Gail (as quoted by Paul C. Rosenblatt, 2000, p. 34)

In the weeks that followed Josh's [19 months old] sudden death, Toby [2½ years old] began to imitate all Joshua's mannerisms, including his baby talk. It was as though, in a desperate attempt to make everything better for the grown-ups, he had decided to "be" his dead brother, a notion I find particularly heart-wrenching.

—R. W. Weinbach (as quoted in Iserson, 1999, p. 136)

With little peeks over his shoulder as his mother was rolled out the door, Tristen told me when he becomes president, he's going to make a law that no one's mother will have to be carried out in a plastic bag. I told him it was a good law to make.

—Laura R. Smith (1996, p. 16)

Before he got sick, the most physical contact we would have was a warm handshake. A real blessing during that last month in the hospital was that we both felt more free to display affection. . . . I would kiss him on the forehead. I massaged his feet with lotion. I could tell he liked it. So did I.

—A man reflecting on caring for his dying father (as quoted in Chethik, 2001)

People needing help. People in a position to offer help. Many of us will be in both roles at some point in our lives. In this chapter, we focus on the support that can be provided in death-relevant situations by people with professional training, but also by friends, families, and the community at large.

The family caregiver quoted by Phillips and Reed experienced:

a sense of unpredictability and unreality. . .On the one hand, from day to day, little changed . . . on the other hand, at any second, a crisis could occur. . . Even when death was imminent, the experience was unpredictable. . . "The whole house was crying and then, ta da, he wants a milk shake (laughs)" (pp. 84–85).

Professional caregivers sometimes also have difficulty in "reading" the status of a life-limited patient, but they generally bring more experience and less intense personal involvement to end-of-life care. The family caregivers in Phillips and Reed's study felt unremitting responsibility and vulnerability to criticism—there seemed to be no rules, no right answers, and no do-overs.

The neighbor who didn't know how to help suddenly came up with a way—simple, natural, and most welcome. She brought them food they would appreciate, first from her kitchen, and then from theirs. Her preparation of food was itself a comforting and life-affirming event, for herself as well as the stressed and soon-to-be bereaved family. In our multicultural society, language barriers can interfere with the impulse to help, but often good neighbors can find a way. In this instance, it was preparing homemade food, an act of benevolence that is appreciated almost everywhere (Holloway, 2008; Walters, 2008).

The nurse at the bedside of the dying young man was suffering along with him. There would be no medical miracles to save his life. But what about his terrible pain? "At this point, he hadn't had anything, no pain medicine whatsoever. The doctor on call didn't know him, and he wasn't thinking about the long night this human being was going to have" (Kaufman, p. 44). The nurse intervened. She persuaded the doctor to shift his attention from the patient's blood pressure to his suffering. Pain medication was given. The young man relaxed, and his final hours were much less an ordeal. Care providers often find themselves in situations in which the treatment options are limited, and comfort decisions can go one way or another—or simply be ignored. This nurse is one of many experienced health care providers who have learned how to make a difference in desperate situations, but the stress continues for nurses and physicians patrolling the borderline between life and death. Many physicians as well as nurses describe themselves as so emotionally exhausted and frustrated that they would not recommend professions in the health care field to their own children (Manion, 2005). Caregiver *burnout* also places patients at a heightened risk.

The parents of young Toby and even younger Josh recognized that the surviving child's reversion to baby talk was a meaningful action. Somebody else might have dismissed Toby's behavior as silly and not have connected it with Josh's death, or might even have punished the boy for being so childish. Fortunately, Toby's parents took a different approach:

> *It was very important then to let Toby know that we loved him for being himself, and that he did not have to "become" Josh to gain our approval. So we never admonished him for taking the role of Josh, but we did remind him often that we loved him very much (Iserson, 1999, p. 136).*

It was a certified death educator and counselor in Oregon who helped 10-year-old Tristen and his 8-year-old brother Clayton through the end phase of their young mother's terminal illness. During their sixth visit together in the hospital room, she started to discuss with the brothers the various times in people's lives when they have to say good-bye to places, things, and each other.

> *Tristen crawled up right in front of me and looked me in the eyes. "In case you didn't notice. I don't want to talk about this." His look was steady. I was so proud of him for speaking up. "Thank you, Tristen. I'm really glad you told me and I respect your need not to talk about this right now." I patted his shoulder and we went on to play with something else (Smith, 1996, pp. 13–14).*

"I cried all the way home and into the night," Smith reports, but she also felt the sense of love that the dying woman, her fiancé, and her children had shared with each other (p. 16). She knew the road ahead for the children, though very difficult, had been made that much easier by loving memories.

It was not a death educator but an adult son who spent many hours by his father's bedside as the older man died of kidney failure. The son experienced a sense of closeness and closure. Journalist Neil Chethik (2001) interviewed men to learn how they dealt with the deaths of their fathers. In general, he found that sons who spent time caring for the fathers before their deaths or talking with them directly about death reported that such actions helped them in their grieving process afterward. Communication and sharing did much both to comfort the dying fathers and to help the sons go on with their lives.

Professional caregivers and community volunteers who choose to work with hospice programs try to comprehend the whole person, rather than just the terminal illness. They also usually have less need to protect themselves from the impact of dying and death (Turnipseed, 1987).

We found (Kastenbaum & Schneider, 1991) that most hospice staff and volunteers call upon personal prayer—a communication just between themselves and God—to give them the strength to go on. One volunteer was speaking for many others when she told us, "I feel it is a privilege to be with a person at this vulnerable and sacred time of their lives." No respondents described themselves as discovering prayer or becoming religious as a result of their experiences with dying persons: It was the other way around. People who had already discovered prayer as a source of strength continued to do so as they encountered the challenges of hospice work. They did not ask for divine intervention or miracles in their prayers, nor did they impose these prayers on patients and families. Praying was a way of staying in touch with themselves and their deepest beliefs. Although the term was not mentioned, the volunteers seemed to have found prayer an effective means of preventing or reducing burnout.

"COMPASSIONATE FATIGUE": BURNOUT AND THE HEALTH CARE PROVIDER

Anxiety and depression have shadowed the human condition through the centuries. What is special about burnout? Maslach and Leiter (2000) provide a crisp explanation:

> Burnout is a prolonged response to chronic emotional and interpersonal stressors on the job. It is defined by the three dimensions of exhaustion, cynicism, and inefficacy. . . . Burnout clearly places the individual stress experience within a larger organizational context of people's relation to their work (p. 358).

Burnout is more likely to develop when people feel trapped in an intolerable situation over which they have little or no control. Lack of social support is one of these conditions, as identified by nurse Salva ("You are blamed for everything and

thanked for nothing"). Nurse Anonymous feels like a failure because she cannot continue to meet the demands for "more, more, and more." After a while, even the most resolute person might experience exhaustion, cynicism, and reduced efficiency.

People in the helping professions, such as teachers, counselors, firefighters, and police officers, are among those at particular risk. Nurses are often more vulnerable than physicians because they have less structural power in the situation. An alternative term, *compassion fatigue* (Figley, 1995), expresses the dilemma of health care workers who work with many chronically ill and life-threatened patients. Many health care providers have chosen their professions with the expectation of providing the best possible care to people in their times of suffering and vulnerability. Compassion fatigue develops after repeated experiences of frustration and disappointment in which circumstances have interfered with providing the needed level of care. This differs from post-traumatic stress disorder (Chapter 11), which often results from a single devastating experience (being witness to an act of violence, for example). The health care provider who once looked forward to the day's challenges now, worn down by pressure-filled and frustrating situations, feels tense and apprehensive, and has to make a special effort just to show up for work. A traumatic experience, such as the sudden death of a student or colleague, can lead to the burnout syndrome that has been held barely in check up to that point (Tebrani, 2004).

Typical signs of burnout are listed in Table 14-1.

The burnout syndrome includes physiological, behavioral, and social elements (Lundberg, 2000). Some victims of burnout have brought their pre-existing anxiety and depression into the situation. For example, hospice nurses whose own lives were stressed by trauma experiences, excessive obligations, and a painfully high degree of empathy have been found to be at greater risk for compassion fatigue (Abendroth & Flannery, 2006). Widowed nurses with limited social support also are higher risk for compassion fatigue (Ifeagwazi, 2005–2006). There is also reason for concern about the limited training in working with life-threatened patients that is made available to health care providers do not receive adequate training in working with life-threatened patients, thereby increasing their risk for burnout and compassion fatigue (Al-Sabwah & Abdel-Khalek, 2005–2006).

TABLE 14-1 *Signs of Burnout*

Most obvious signs

- Exhaustion, lack of energy, feeling rundown
- Tension headaches
- Sleep disturbances
- Appetite and digestive disturbances
- Increased errors at work
- Becoming irritable and negative
- Anger flare-ups
- Self-criticism
- Feeling helpless
- Feeling depersonalized and distant in relationships

Less obvious signs

- Reduced immune function
- Increased secretion of stress hormones
- Elevated blood pressure
- metabolic dysfunctions

Caregivers in Death-Salient Situations

Health care providers face even higher risk when they are responsible for the care of life-threatened or dying patients. The cultural taboo against discussing death and the philosophy of distancing and avoiding avoidance passed on from one generation of physicians to the next condemned many health care providers as well as their patients to isolation and denial (Kastenbaum, 2004). I saw plenty of this. The compassionate nurse who had a single car accident after one of her long-term geriatric patients died: "We were not supposed to get involved in the first place." The surgery resident who had "lost" another patient, although "I did everything right, and then she had to go off and die on me." He wasn't sure that he wanted to continue his medical career. "I'm mad at everybody," he admitted, "God, too! I must be hell to live with!" These were but two of the many health care professionals who were not prepared or supported by the system when they encountered limits, loss, stress, in the course of their work.

Research has consistently found burnout or compassionate fatigue among health care providers to life-threatened and dying patients. In her pioneering study, Mary L. S. Vachon (1987) interviewed about 600 professional caregivers from hospitals, palliative care facilities, chronic care institutions, and voluntary agencies. What was the basic source of stress for physicians, nurses, and others who care for dying patients? And how did they cope with this stress?

Her answer might surprise those who have not worked in a health care setting. The findings are crisply expressed in one of her chapter titles: "Dying Patients Are Not the Real Problem." The caregivers reported they were most stressed by their work environment and occupational roles, not by their contact with dying patients and their families. Their stresses included poor communication within the health care facility, conflicts between one unit and another, and lack of continuity as staff come and go.

Vachon's findings continue to ring true. Tense, anxious, frustrated, and exhausted caregivers have difficulty bringing their best selves to dying patients and their families. We do not have to assume that a nurse who withdraws from a dying person is motivated by her own excessive death anxieties. She might instead be caught in a role conflict between being technical expert and a humane caregiver. It is also probable that she is trapped in a time bind created by understaffing, mixed priorities, and poor communication patterns.

A major study of hospices in the United Kingdom (Addington-Hall & Karlsen, 2005) finds that about half the staff was considering leaving because of a perceived lack of respect from colleagues in other disciplines and a lack of support from management. These findings are of particular concern because hospice programs give high priority to teamwork and mutual support. Reviewing a number of studies, physician Kernan Manion (2005) concludes that:

> Many doctors throughout the country are finding themselves so worn down by the overwhelming array of issues continuously confronting them in health care as to be approaching frank burnout (p. 1).

Tension increases when a new health crisis emerges. Toronto was threatened with a possible catastrophic epidemic in 2003, when cases of severe acute respiratory syndrome (SARS) were identified. There could have been widespread contagion, with many deaths in Toronto and then rapidly spreading elsewhere. The tensions already experienced by hospital staff in their everyday work were sharply increased. Nurses were the most severely affected because the peer support they relied on had been overwhelmed by the emergency response effort, and they also felt less informed and less empowered to participate in decision making (Tolomiczenko et al., 2005). As Maslach and Leiter (2000) have noted, the sense of "inefficacy"—the lack of opportunity to influence the course of events—is a major component of burnout.

Caregivers for terminally ill children are perhaps the most vulnerable to severe burnout experiences. Danai Papadatou (2006) interviewed many distressed pediatric care providers with experiences such as the following:

> *I think I age quickly, both biologically and psychologically, as a result of this work. Now I experience a pressure upon my heart, a constant weight that does not allow me to breathe. Now, I don't want to be close to any dying child or family. I cannot handle their suffering or my pain any more. I cannot even sit by their side, the silence seems very heavy. I have nothing to offer. Words don't come out. I cannot even give this special and tender look I once gave to my patients. If ever I give it, it's filled with despair* (p. 311).

Staff Burnout: What Effects on Patients?

Does caregiver stress have negative consequences for the patients? Studies suggest that pressured work conditions are associated with increased patient risk. The term "vicious cycle" seems to apply. The shortage of registered nurses has been linked to stressful work conditions. Experiencing burnout, a substantial number of nurses leave hospital service, and this career option has become less attractive to new waves of students. Unfortunately, the nurses who are on duty are expected to do "more, more, and more" under increasing pressure. Larger case loads and longer shifts result in more errors on the job (Rogers et al., 2004). The exhausting schedules not only lead to more errors but also to less opportunity to attend to life-threatened patients. There is also less "down time" for nurses to reflect on and recover from stressful experiences.

Does this mean that more people die because of staff shortages and overwork? The answer is yes, according to a major study reported by the Joint Commission on Accreditation of Healthcare Organizations (Aiken, 2002). Key findings were:

- The risk of death increases by 7 percent for surgical patients for each additional patient over four in a nurse's workload.
- The risk of death increases by 31 percent in hospitals where nurses have a caseload of eight as compared with four patients each.
- Increased patient caseload also increased burnout, with more than two out of five nurses intending to leave their position within the next 12 months—an action that could again increase caseload and patient risk.

These explosive findings created ripples of reflection, controversy, and calls for action. It cannot be said, however, that the overwork/burnout problem has been resolved. Economic and other large-scale problems in the health care system continue to require attention. What, if anything, can individuals do to prevent or alleviate burnout?

How Can We Protect Ourselves from Burnout?

The caregiver quoted by Papadatou (2006) "never gave herself the time to process her experiences and did not seek support." Education and training programs could do more to prepare health care professionals for the challenges they will encounter. A crucial step would be to acknowledge burnout as a serious threat to the health care system at large, responsible for patient and family stress, high staff stress and turnover, and other added expenses.

An organizational solution to the organizational problems would be a logical course of action. Tahiti or the Bahamas? When the president of the United States sends you a text-message, offering a choice of ambassadorships, reply that you would rather be director of the Health Care and Finance Administration. Devote yourself to establishing a policy for health care education and practice that takes the well-being of professional staff seriously, and makes it one of the crucial factors to consider. Enforce this policy immediately and find effective people who will make sure that prevention of burnout is accepted as an essential for all health care organizations. Now you can choose one of those ambassadorships!

Until your friend is elected, however, there are other useful things that can be done:

- Develop a peer network in which staff discontents and rivalries give way to whole-hearted support for all care providers. Caregivers such as the person interviewed by Papadatou would not have to be alone and isolated in their stress. Take a cue from "the voices of nursing home staff" that find ways of supporting each other behind the scenes even when the institution is not keen about facing end-of-life situations (Oliver, Porock, & Oliver, 2006). The staff's "backstage interactions" (i.e., having a closer relationship with dying residents than expected or countenanced by the administration) not only provide comfort to people who otherwise would have been isolated during their last days of life, but also fulfill the staff's need to be truly helpful.
- Develop consensus for shared decision making. Staff with various specialties could do more listening to each other and less pulling of rank. "Empowering" achieved the status of a buzzword a few years ago but has vital meaning for caregivers; nurses, physicians, and other care providers who feel empowered to use their own knowledge, skills, and compassion are much less likely to experience burnout.
- Learn basic relaxation techniques that are useful within and beyond the work situation. Most of these techniques are simple and can be done without special equipment. They are also mostly pleasant to perform. There are many other exercises and techniques available for exploration, including "mindfulness" instruction that has already been shown to be helpful to caregivers (Bromley, 2005).

Whose Problem? Whose Need?

Care providers sometimes contribute mightily to their own stress and frustration. This situation is most likely to develop when one's own feelings are confused with those of the client. For example, a young psychologist is stewing in his own anxiety because he cannot make his aged client any younger or healthier, not even provide him with an environment more congenial than a grim state institution. The psychologist naturally assumes that the patient is even more anxious and depressed because it is his life that is becoming ever more distressful. In this state of mind, the psychologist is not useful to the patient or himself. Fortunately, though, the light goes on before it is too late. I realize the old man has made peace with his situation. Just listening, I learn how he had made it through a hard life that he would not exchange with any other. "Even my bruises have bruises, but they're all mine." Now he does not expect anything but the inevitable. That's not quite true, though. The nurses were doing too much tippy-toeing around him. Nobody teased him anymore. And they wouldn't give him any real food to eat, if you could call that cafeteria stuff real food. Basically, he wanted to be treated as himself and alive while still he was. This could actually be made to happen! The nurses, like the psychologist, started to feel a little more normal around the patient. Bustling, teasing, and "real" food returned.

As a psychologist, I was familiar with the concepts of *transference* and *countertransference*. Clients in psychotherapy are inclined to project their own characteristics or characteristics of important people in their lives upon their therapists, who therefore find themselves intensely loved, hated, or both. That's transference, in the psychoanalytic sense of the term. But therapists are somewhat human also, and can project their moods and motives on the clients. That's countertransference. Psychotherapists are expected to recognize both transference and countertransference and act accordingly.

I had to learn on the job that transference and countertransference also are likely to develop during interactions with life-threatened and terminally ill people. For example, a patient might remind us—not quite consciously—of somebody in our own lives with whom we have had a strong emotional attachment. Our own hidden anxieties about death might also force themselves into our caregiving activities. The result can be unfortunate, as Kelly and Varghese (2006, p. 44) illustrate:

> In the case of a gravely ill or difficult patient, the clinician may experience intense feelings of frustration, helplessness, and anger toward the patient. As much as we may hate to admit to these feelings, they are not uncommon and may in fact, be unconsciously detected by the patient as a wish that he or she would die. . .

Unexamined projective identification can shape the helping professional's clinical actions and responses.

Empathy is one thing. Confusing another person's moods and needs with our own is another and more problematic thing.

DEATH EDUCATORS AND COUNSELORS: THE "BORDER PATROL"

Most people who serve as death educators and counselors draw upon personal experiences as well as academic and professional education. They realize that the boundary between the land of the living and the land of the dead is as subtle as the next breath we take.

Some people still have difficulty in understanding how death can be studied or taught. Others are fearful that strangers under the guise of educators and counselors might invade the sanctity of their innermost beliefs. Research questions are also raised. Is there a solid basis for this field, or does death education purvey only untested assumptions and fancies? What do people derive from death education and counseling? And what should people derive?

We begin our exploration with a brief historical introduction, then examine the current scene in death education and counseling, and conclude with some observations about future prospects and challenges.

Death Education in Historical Perspective

The term death education itself and the field to which it refers did not become a recognizable part of our society until the 1960s, as noted in Chapter 4. In the broader sense, however, we have never been without some form of instruction and guidance.

From Ancient Times Ancient documents from Tibet and dynastic Egypt offer detailed accounts of what becomes of the soul after death and what preparations should be made for a safe passage. These documents have become known in the Western world as "books of the dead." It helps if one knows the names of the underworld demons and deities and the challenges they will put to the spirits of the deceased. In dynastic Egypt, 42 gods sit in judgment as the newly dead person confesses a lifetime's worth of faults and misdeeds. One's soul is then measured against a feather: paradise is ahead if the scale balances perfectly. What happens if the soul fails to pass? All the horrors the imagination can devise, and then some! Ancient death education had much to do with how one should prepare for the ordeal of judgment after taking that last breath. In contrast, death education today often focuses on people attempting to cope with death in the midst of life (e.g., the hospice nurse, the grieving family member, the individual who has just been informed of a life-threatening disease).

Through the centuries, many images and ideas have been offered about our relationship to death. One of the most common themes has been the fleeting nature of life. Job (13:12) laments: "Man that is born of a woman is of few days, and full of trouble. He cometh forth like a flower, and is cut down: he fleeth also as a shadow, and continueth not." The *Old Testament* compares human life with the grass that withers and is blown away by the whirlwind. The evanescence of life is linked with the limits of human knowledge and power. Do we suppose ourselves to be lordly beings? Proverbs (27:1) quickly deflates us: "Boast not thyself of tomorrow; for thou knowest not what a day may bring forth."

It is not only the Judeo-Christian tradition that brings mortality to the fore. The collection of stories known as *The Arabian Nights* is best known for its celebration of sensuality. But death is also given eloquent attention. The following passage demonstrates how awareness of our mortality might provide the basis for a mature philosophy of life:

O sons of men,
Turn quickly and you will see death
Behind your shoulder.
Adam saw him,
Nimrod saw him
Who wound his horn in the forest,
The masters of Persia saw him.
Alexander, who wrestled with the world
And threw the world,
Turned quickly and saw death
Behind his shoulder. . . .
O sons of men,

When you give yourselves to the sweet trap of life
Leave one limb free for God.
The fear of death is the beginning of wisdom
And the fair things you do
Shall blow and smell like flowers
On the red and fiery day.
(Mathers, 1972, pp. 300–301)

Both the *Old Testament* and *The Arabian Nights* contrast the power of God with the powerlessness of the mortal person, but not with the same emotional tone. The troubled, fleeting shadow portrayed in the *Old Testament* finds neither pleasure nor solace. By contrast, the readers of Scheherazade's tales of 1,001 nights are expected to give themselves to "the sweet trap of life." What are we to do, then? Should we spend our lives lamenting and "eating worms" before the worms eat us? Or should we enjoy the sweet trap while we can, knowing full well that our pleasures and triumphs will not endure because we will not endure?

The *New Testament* introduced a radically different perspective: "Whoso eateth my flesh, and drinketh my blood, hath eternal life; and I will raise him up at the last day" (John 6:54). "And this is the promise that he hath promised us, even eternal life" (John 3:15). "And the sea gave up the dead which were in it; and death and hell delivered up the dead which were in them: and they were judged every man according to their works" (Revelations 20: 13–14).

In centuries to come, Christians would differ among themselves on many issues (e.g., is it faith, good works, or predestination that will ensure the triumph over death?). From the start, however, at the core of Christianity was its bold contention that man had been redeemed from death through Jesus. The early Christian death education lesson advised us not to sorrow our way through life, nor surrender to the "sweet trap" with the bittersweet knowledge that it will soon snap shut upon us. Instead, we should feel joyful about the life to come after this brief sojourn on earth is completed. This rousing lesson did not escape change through time, however. Other themes became salient as Christianity expanded and became more diverse. Three related themes remain influential today:

1. Death is *punishment* for Adam and Eve's disobedience (original sin doctrine).
2. Death is a *test* that separates the worthy from the unworthy: the most final of all exams.

3. Death is blessed *release* from the illusions and miseries of life.

Not all Christians subscribe to all these views. However, they have the cumulative weight of centuries behind them. Consider for example the born-again minister who paid an unexpected visit to a woman hospitalized with a terminal illness. He burst into her room with these words: "God knows what a sinner you are! Prepare yourself for the moment of judgment!" The astonished woman quietly replied, "God and I have never given each other any trouble." Undeterred, he made repeated attempts to bully the exhausted woman into confessing sins and placing her life into his hands. Upon learning of this incident, the official hospital chaplain was even more distressed than the woman who had fallen victim to this brutal intervention. Responsible death educators and counselors hold a variety of religious beliefs themselves, but they also are aware and respectful of the traditions that influence their students and clients.

The Medieval Heritage Traditional ways of communicating about death developed in societies that differed from ours in many ways. In medieval times, for example, most people lived in small, agrarian communities. They had little formal education and little contact with people outside their own circle. The concepts of having "inalienable" human rights, holding one's own political and religious opinions, and being free to pursue unlimited personal interests and ambitions were unknown. These low-technology societies were fairly stable from generation to generation and that offered little protection against the forces of nature and the disasters encountered in everyday life. When darkness fell at night, few would venture out of doors, where both real and fantasy terrors lurked.

Little faith could be placed in the medical treatments of the time that frequently caused as much suffering as the diseases themselves. Many newborn babies failed to survive into adulthood. Infections associated with childbirth, wounds, and injuries often proved fatal to adults, and epidemics periodically decimated the population. Exposure to corpses, human and animal, was commonplace. In short, death was part of almost every person's experience from childhood onward, not hidden away from view.

Death, coming so early and often, became a pervasive character in the medieval and renaissance imagination. That even the high-born and powerful could not escape Death's claim was a realization that encouraged movements for more social equality.

Medieval society's raw encounters with dying and death produced striking themes and images. The dance of death, for example, was a compelling image that was introduced by poets, artists, and performers in the thirteenth century, if not earlier. The living and the dead are portrayed as companions in a slow and solemn dance. The *danse macabre* theme often depicted death as a skeletal figure who laid claim to all mortal souls, whether low or high born (Kastenbaum, 2002). "We all look the same to Death: kings, bishops or peasants, we are all mortal beings" was part of the core message. And a powerful message this was—bearing in mind that society was highly stratified at the time, with a few "high and mighty" people lording over the masses. The colossal idea that people are created equal was nurtured by the common person's awareness that all souls are harvested by death.

Another significant tradition arose in the fifteenth century: the use of Christian guidebooks to help people in their last days and hours of life. This has become known to historians as the *Ars moriendi* tradition—literally, the art of dying well. Most of the guidebooks were brief descriptions of rituals that should be performed as part of the deathbed scene. The earliest guidebooks featured cartoonish illustrations of the dying person under assault by Satan's legions while being encouraged by guardian angels to withstand temptations. Later guidebooks were more subtle. The passage from life to death was presented as the critical test of the soul's worthiness for salvation. People were never more at risk than at the moment of death.

The priest tried to help the dying person resist the assaults and temptations of demons who hoped to consign the soul to the flames of hell.

The *Ars moriendi* guidebooks expressed some beliefs and concerns that can be observed in our own death awareness movement. These include: (a) the view that how a person dies is a significant matter; therefore, (b) some deaths are better than others; so (c) a "good death" is a real achievement, and (d) flows more readily from a life that has been lived in the recognition of mortality, with (e) the support of caring people who have also prepared themselves properly for the encounter with death.

The capstone of the *Ars moriendi* tradition was reached in 1651 with the publication of Jeremy Taylor's *Rules and Exercises of Holy Dying*. Reverend Taylor, chaplain to ruling monarch Charles II, urged a daily "refresher course" on life and death. Today we might describe this as a life review. Taylor, however, would not have us wait until we are well up in years and reluctantly aware that this final act of life is not long in coming:

> *For, if we make but one general account, and never reckon till we die . . . we shall only reckon by great sums, and remember nothing but clamorous and crying sins, and never consider concerning particulars, or forget very many. . . . But if we observe all the little passages of our life . . . see everyday sins increase so fast, and virtues grow up so slow . . . we may see our evil and amend it. . . . As therefore every night we*

*must make our bed the memorial of our grave, so
let our evening thoughts be an image of the day
of judgment (pp. 48–49).*

Death education and counseling had to begin
anew after centuries of avoidance. What is the nature of death education and counseling today? We
begin with death education.

DEATH EDUCATION AND COUNSELING: THE CURRENT SCENE

We can gain a quick view of the changed scene by
becoming familiar with an organization known as
the Association for Death Education and Counseling (ADEC). This nonprofit organization was incorporated in 1976 to improve the quality of death
education and death-related counseling (Wass,
2002). ADEC offers national training workshops
and certification procedures for death educators
and counselors. If you attend one of ADEC's national conferences, you will probably be impressed
with the combination of maturity and dedication. What you will probably not see is the person
who has read one book, attended a workshop,
and is therefore eager to impose his or her ignorance upon the world. The "pop death" people
who hatched in the 1970s have mostly drifted off
to other enthusiasms. Today there are more human service providers who bring substantial experience and a disciplined mind to the challenges.
ADEC members usually are aware of their own
death-related feelings and have experience in areas
of real life concern (e.g., supporting families after
the death of a child, counseling people who have
tested positive for the AIDS virus, training hospice
volunteers).

　　Some people still do put themselves forward
as death educators or counselors without pos-
sessing either the personal or experiential quali-
fications. The minister who burst into the dying
woman's hospital room was motivated by a personal agenda, not by the expressed needs of a
person he had never met. The teacher who never
opens the pages of peer-reviewed scholarly journals such as *Omega; Death Studies; Illness, Crisis, and
Loss;* and *Mortality* will be lecturing from untested
assumptions and limited personal observations.

　　People come to this topic with a variety of needs
and expectations. Students hope to add to their

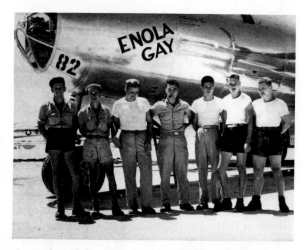

*A member of the ground crew on Tinian Island heard
rumors that this B-29 carried a new kind of bomb; they
called it "Little Boy." After* Enola Gay *dropped the
atomic bomb on Hiroshima, the young man reflected
on death and on how little we talked about it. This
experience led Herman Feifel to become a psychologist
and a pioneering thanatologist.*

competencies as nurses, paramedics, social workers,
counselors, or psychologists. Others have had personal experiences that give the topic special urgency.
Still others are keenly interested in working with the
dying or the bereaved; others have become curious
about some particular facet of death (e.g., funerals
or near-death experiences). Clinical skills are probably developed best in clinical situations. Classroom
examples can be helpful, but case experience and
supervision is also needed. "Deep learning"—an
experience that is emotional as well as intellectual—
often requires a series of in-depth and personal
discussions that are not always possible within the
classroom. It is useful, then, for all participants to
recognize what can and should be accomplished in
a particular course, conference, or workshop and
what must be achieved in other settings.

　　Richard A. Kalish (1980/1981) observed that
the death educator came along at a time when
two of society's most important traditional roles
have undergone significant change. The priest
was once the dominant person who mediated our
relationship to death. The physician gained increasing prestige, however, as society shifted its
orientation from hopes of a better life after death
to a longer and healthier life on earth. The death
educator entered the scene, then, when society

was no longer as enthusiastic about accepting an afterlife as substitute for a long and fulfilling life on earth—but also at a time when society had judged that the physician did not have the "magic" either. Death educators can come into conflicts with priests and physicians when perceived as venturing into their turfs. They can also seem to be promising too much and thereby set themselves up for failure: "Death educators and counselors are treading sacred ground, and must be expected to be attacked for their errors, their vanities, any signs of greed or lust or need of power" (Kalish, 1980/1981, p. 83). Kalish's point that death educators and counselors should be aware of their role relationships with other professionals is well taken, as is the caution that they should refrain from creating unrealistic expectations on the part of students or clients.

Effective death educators come from a variety of established fields, such as psychology, psychiatry, medical ethics, nursing, sociology, and the ministry. It is valuable to have a solid grounding in one or more substantive fields as well as particular competency in death-related topics. Death education takes a variety of forms. Corr and Corr (2003) remind us that informal death education can occur when we learn from life experiences, as well as within family homes and church or other religious groups. They also call particular attention to teachable moments—"unplanned life events from which important lessons can be drawn" (p. 294). (Examples of teachable moments in childhood are given in Chapter 10.) Formal death education has been introduced into the curriculum of middle schools, high schools, colleges, and universities.

Adult education in death-related issues is becoming more common. Corr and Corr (2003) point out that these programs take such forms as continuing education courses, workshops, and professional conferences; clinical pastoral education; hospice training sessions; and special programs to help people cope with disasters or traumatic loss. The Widow-to-Widow Program and AARP's Widowed Persons Service are among the community-based resources for bereavement guidance and counseling.

It would be simplistic to maintain that death education courses have the basic function of reducing death anxiety. As we have seen (Chapter 1), there is little solid information available on what constitutes the "right" level of death anxiety. Most people express only a moderate level of death anxiety most of the time. Furthermore, anxiety can serve as a signal of possible danger, part of our survival repertoire. Skilled death educators can help people distinguish between anxiety as a vigilant alarm and as a dysfunctional response that can actually obstruct effective response.

Person-to-person contact is at the core of death education, but sometimes one can recruit a little help from an instructor who has had no actual birth but has been subjected to many deaths. Meet SimMan.

SimMan: An Interview with Beatrice Kastenbaum, MSN

Beatrice Kastenbaum, a pioneer in the hospice movement, is a faculty member of Arizona State University's College of Nursing and Health Care Innovation, and a special friend of SimMan.

INTERVIEWER: Who is SimMan?

KASTENBAUM: SimMan is a human patient simulator. Examine him and you will discover his physiologically correct carotid, femoral, brachial, and radial pulses. Check his blood pressure. Listen to his heart, lung, bowel, and vocal sounds—he speaks and moans, and could sing, whistle, or yodel if need be.

INTERVIEWER: He breathes, too?

KASTENBAUM: He can realistically simulate all relevant airway management and patient care situations. SimMan also comes equipped with over 2,500 cardiac rhythm variants that can be monitored.

INTERVIEWER: Is he healthy?

KASTENBAUM: Healthy or end-stage dying, or anything in between. For example, sometimes he has wounds and skin lesions that need management. You can practice your skills in administering peripheral intravenous therapy in his IV training arm. If SimMan needs to have a chest tube insertion, you can help him out in that way, too. You can apply a defibrillator if he has a cardiac emergency.

INTERVIEWER: Is he always a he?

KASTENBAUM: Not when he's being a she. There are realistic male/female genitalia for practice of urologic procedures.

INTERVIEWER: How does SimMan do what he does?

KASTENBAUM: He is integrated into a system with a patient monitor that can be operated through a PC or handheld remote controls.

INTERVIEWER: How does he decide what to say?

KASTENBAUM: His vocal responses can be prerecorded or produced spontaneously via operator microphone. In other words, SimMan can talk. He answers questions. He describes his pain.

INTERVIEWER: How does SimMan contribute to nurse education?

KASTENBAUM: SimMan offers the students experiences that real patients can't. He is very patient with them. Students can be slow and practice things over again and again. He can help them make comparisons, for instance, between different breath sounds: Is it a crackle or a wheeze? He allows students to stop midpractice to ask questions. The student can do something terribly wrong, but SimMan will come back to life and try again. SimMan is a novel experience for most students. This attracts their attention. Our students want to know, "What else can he do?" Students who are comfortable with computers and game playing learn further by creating their own scenarios and programming his responses.

INTERVIEWER: One more question: How can SimMan contribute to nursing care of life-threatened and dying patients?

KASTENBAUM: Nursing students worry about having patients die. They worry about whether they will be responsible for the death. They worry about what they will feel when the death occurs. Will they be able to stay calm and do what they should be doing? We believe that practicing the "code" situation in a simulation scenario helps to decrease some of the unknowns about what is going on and how to act. In addition, if the scenario feels real to the student, they may come to understand their own potential responses to a death. When scenarios and actual experiences are paired with self-reflection, students may be able to cope better with the stressful death-related situations they will face in the future. At least, that is my hope.

INTERVIEWER: Thank you very much. Actually I do have one more question; why is SimMan wearing my second-best pair of brown shoes?

KASTENBAUM: Because they fit him perfectly, and thank you!

COUNSELING AND THE COUNSELORS

Counseling, like education, can occur under informal circumstances or as part of a systematic program. The boundary between counseling and education can also be crossed easily from either side. A classroom discussion, for example, may become transformed into an advice-sharing session to help a student decide whether or not to continue his or her practice of avoiding funerals. Similarly, a priest who is counseling the spouse of a dying person may be able to reduce anxiety by providing specific information about church beliefs and practices. In exploring counseling and the counselors, then, we are not entirely forgetting death education.

Characteristics of Professionals in the Death System

It is an article of faith that people who would help others must also be aware of their own personalities and in control of their own conflicts. Several early studies looked into this situation. Professionals representing five different fields were neither more nor less anxious than a comparison population (Morrison, et al., 1981/1982). Neimeyer et al. (1983) found that the medical residents who personally felt most strongly threatened by death were also those who most often used avoidance strategies when caring for a dying patient. These were the young physicians who busied themselves in reviewing charts and finding other things to do instead of meeting their patients' needs for personal contact, information, guidance, and emotional support.

Fortunately, it is possible to improve our skills and thereby also reduce our anxieties in communicating with people in difficult situations. Attention can be given to body language as well as verbal communication. People preparing for careers in nursing, medicine, social work, and other human service fields have often found it useful to take courses and workshops to improve their communication skills.

Thanatologists are the scholars, researchers, and clinicians who study death-related issues. How do they deal with death in their own lives? Feifel and Strack (2001) analyzed questionnaire responses from a sample of early (1970s) thanatologists. The authors note that these pioneering thanatologists:

> reported real apprehensions and concerns about their own death and the consequences of death. At the same time, gazing steadily at death over long periods of time does not seem to cause morbid preoccupation or increase one's fear of mortality. Indeed, across the 15-year time interval of this survey, many participants reported a lessening fear of death, greater acceptance of death, and/or an increased appreciation of life accompanying their continued exposure to thanatology (p. 208).

The self-reported death anxiety of thanatologists was pretty much the same as the population in general. Furthermore, their lessening fear and increased acceptance over a 15-year period is also consistent with the attitudinal shift that seems to occur with many other people as they move deeper into the adult years. Many students after completing a course in death education have told me that they are still concerned about death but feel more competent and comfortable in dealing with death-related issues—and, above everything, their appreciation of life has been enhanced.

Collective Ideals or Creation Myths? The professional caregiving organizations that offer death education, end-of-life care, and grief support are relatively young. They do not have long traditions to draw upon. Papadatou (2009) points out that professional caregiving organizations have their own collective ideals—or creation myths depending on how they are perceived. Individual caregivers are influenced by these "creation myths," although they might not have examined them carefully.

One of the examples is the popular but unverified story that a wealthy couple donated their entire estate to establish a pediatric hospital in memory of their son who bled to death after an automobile accident. "The myth that prevailed in this organization was one of medical expertise and omnipotence over any life-threatening disease or critical health condition" (p 196).

Palliative and bereavement care organizations often develop a storyline based on death-related experiences of their founders. Cicely Saunders's relationship with terminally ill patient David Tasma (Chapter 5) "served as the trigger for humanitarian actions and a profound social contribution." Unfortunately, these missions can be deflected or even overwhelmed by the realities of the all-pervasive economic and regulatory system. Furthermore, those imbued with the collective ideals can themselves go astray, for example, "setting as a task the achievement of a 'perfect' death transforms the dying person . . . into a personal institutional success story. Similarly, striving for a 'perfect' bereavement through the open expression of feelings, management of unfinished business, and maintenance of a bond with the deceased may not always reflect the needs and desires of dying or bereaved individuals, to the dismay of health care providers" (p. 199).

Points well taken?

Counseling and Psychotherapy People do not necessarily need counseling or psychotherapy when death enters their lives (see also Chapter 11). Sometimes the needed strength can be drawn from love, friendship, a familiar environment, and one's own beliefs, values, and coping resources. Financial security and competent nursing and medical care are also likely help to see the person through. Before considering counseling or therapy, then, it is usually wise to assess the total situation. Perhaps what this man needs is a more effective pain management regimen; perhaps what this woman needs is the opportunity to spend some time with the sister or brother she has not seen for years. Counseling and therapy are options that may be worth considering but not to the neglect of the many other factors that could provide comfort and peace of mind.

Many counselors believe that one of the most important goals is to help their clients draw on their own inner strengths. A sense of helplessness can reduce an individual's ability to cope with illness, not only physically but also psychologically. The counselor can help to restore self-confidence, relaxation, and a renewed sense of still being a valuable and lovable person. This more positive psychological state can have a favorable effect on bodily response (e.g., through improved cardiovascular circulation or more vigorous functioning of the immune system). Therapeutic touch, music therapy, guided imagery, and storytelling are among the techniques that have been used effectively (e.g., Winslade, 2001). Hedtke (2002) suggests that "Reconstructing the language of grief" focuses on the way our habits of thought and speech influence the response to death and dying. For example, well-meaning friends:

> often say "I am sorry" to someone whose loved one is dead. However, . . . these words bind the grievers to an unspoken agreement about how they will proceed with their grief. This process is both produced and sanctioned to not take too long, not be too messy, not dwell on our loved one's memory, and not include public displays of extreme emotion. (pp. 287–288).

Becoming more aware of such language-mediated "rules" can help to improve communication and relieve grieving people of unrealistic and burdensome expectations.

The success of any approach depends as much upon the caregiver's personality as his or her "technique." It is difficult to imagine a nervous, time-conscious, and hard-driving person achieving the same results as a firm but patient and gentle individual. Those who would provide counseling or psychotherapy in death-related situations would be wise to select an approach that is in harmony with their own personalities as well as one that is well-grounded in the knowledge of human nature.

There is no definitive list of counseling and therapeutic approaches that can be effective in death-related situations, nor is there compelling evidence to demonstrate that one approach is generally superior to another. Furthermore, there is no reason to suppose that all dying people require such interventions. Counseling and therapy does have a place, however, in the total spectrum of services that should be available when appropriate.

HOW WE ALL CAN HELP

We all can help by realizing that *prosocial* action is well within our capabilities. Even though we live in a world where self-interest and competition are salient, we are also a species that has repeatedly demonstrated concern and compassion for others. As a matter of fact, some of our other fellow creatures have also shown this ability.

I am thinking, for example, of that alarming moment when a three-year-old fell into the outdoor gorilla exhibit at the Brookfield Zoo in Illinois. The boy landed 18 feet down in the rock-studded pit, injured, unable to move, and probably unconscious. A gorilla, Binti Jua, rushed over to the injured boy, with Koola, her own 16-month-old daughter, clinging to her back. The gorilla gently took the boy in her arms and brought him to a gate where he could be rescued easily. The boy survived his injuries. It turns out that Binti had been raised by humans, but it is possible that, as a good mother, she would have saved the little boy's life anyway.

Binti Jua's prosocial action is a useful reminder that murder, suicide, loss, and indifference do not tell the entire story. An aging Sigmund Freud came to the conclusion that our journey through life spins around our relationship to opposing instincts: Eros, the drive toward experience, stimulation, and love; and Thanatos, the drive toward self-destruction and death. According to Freud, the only hope for survival of the human race as well as a rewarding life for individuals is to moderate the force of Thanatos with the caring and joy of Eros (Freud, 1915, 1917). Later, Abraham Maslow (1954, 1968) would make the cogent counterargument that we do not always have to transform instinctual dangers and conflicts into positive feelings but that the healthy and creative side of our personalities comes directly from healthy and creative experiences. Either way, there is a caring and loving side to human nature that can be called upon when we face peril and loss—as well as in our everyday interactions. Developing our own caring impulses should be a major priority for the individual and society. And, when we need a refresher course, perhaps we can call upon that outstanding death educator and counselor: Binti Jua!

One way in which we can help, then, is to recognize our potential for helping and, therefore, not feel obliged to leave everything to "experts." The experts will usually tell you that there is no substitute for the comforting presence of a family member or intimate friend. Another way in which we can help is to become more competent in communicating with each other about sudden, unexpected deaths. Communication is especially difficult because nobody really wants to break the bad news and nobody wants to hear it. There is no magic way to convert a tragic into a positive situation. Some approaches are better than other, though, in helping people start the long and difficult process of acknowledging and coping with the unexpected loss. An excellent resource is Kenneth Iserson's book, *Grave Words: Notifying Survivors about Sudden, Unexpected Deaths* (1999). Iserson provides guidelines for telephone notifications as well as direct conversations in a variety of circumstances. Iserson emphasizes the importance of clear and accurate communication to avoid adding confusion to grief:

> *Although to some it may seem cruel and to others obvious, notifiers must use one of the "D" words when informing survivors about a death. "D" words include: "Died," "Death," and "Dead." For many reasons, including their own discomfort, many notifiers prefer to use euphemisms instead. The more common ones use such phrases as "passed away," "passed on," "left us," "checked out," "fatally injured," "gone," "deceased," or "expired." But it is better if you use a "D" word (Iserson, 1999, p. 43).*

Another way we can help is to improve our awareness of the total family response to death. We respond to dying, grief, and loss as individuals but also as members of family constellations that often have their own styles of coping with stress. Elliott J. Rosen's *Families Facing Death* (1998) focuses on not the sudden death but the sometimes lengthy

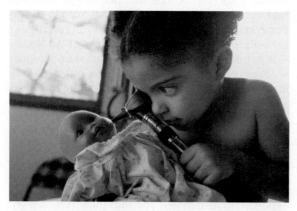

"Hmmm! Dolly needs expert medical attention. Good thing that I'm here!" Many people who choose a career of helping others first discovered this impulse in childhood.

period in which family life is under stress in the anticipation of death. His observations include some facts that have not been generally appreciated, for example, the early onset of family stress:

> *A family actually begins to address the prospect of loss with the very first symptoms of disease. As incredible as this may seem, when any member of a family is stricken with illness, even the mildest of physical ailment, the family automatically begins a process of adaptation to preserved threatened homeostasis. . . . If little Mary Smith gets the sniffles, her parents may become overly solicitous, aware of every twitch of the youngster's nose. Mary may want to crawl into Mommy's lap, a behavior she had more or less abandoned, and Mommy will readily comply . . . (Rosen, 1998, p. 76).*

Families sense the threat quickly and do what they can—for as long as they can—to keep things seeming and feeling "normal." The more aware we are of such family dynamics, the more likely we are to provide intelligent and effective support.

These are but a few of the ways in which we—all of us—can help each other.

■ SUMMARY

Often we experience a feeling of helplessness when people close to us are dying or grieving. Perhaps we should just stand back and leave it all to the experts. This chapter proposes that there is much all of us can do, whether as professional care providers, family members, friends, colleagues, or neighbors. Learning how to communicate effectively—both verbally and nonverbally—is a key.

We saw that death education and counseling have their roots in ancient times. In the past, the emphasis often was on guiding people safely from one life to the next. Much of the emphasis today is on the individual and family facing death or living with grief. Common to both past and current philosophies is the belief that death is a central fact of life and deserves our most serious and enlightened attention. We cannot simply repeat the approaches taken in the past, however, because conditions of life in ancient and medieval times differ so much from our own. Nevertheless, attention to the Arabian perspective on mortality, and the Christian *Ars moriendi* guidebooks reminds us that we are not the first to face life-and-death issues.

The modern death awareness movement in the United States established itself during the 1970s with such developments as the beginnings of the Association for Death Education and Counseling. Effective death educators come from a variety of fields, including anthropology, psychology, psychiatry, medical ethics, nursing, social work, sociology, and the ministry. The scope of death education continues to expand, now reaching more people who are preparing for professional caregiving careers. Nevertheless, many human service providers (teachers, in particular) still complete their studies without preparation for helping the dying, grieving, or suicidal people they will encounter from time to time.

Professional caregivers often experience intense stress as they struggle not only to communicate with patients and families but also to cope with difficult work environments. Burnout and compassion fatigue have become major problems among nurses and physicians, increasing staff turnover and interfering with quality care. It has become clear that improved communication among caregivers is needed to reduce their frustration and anxiety. Caregivers also face the challenge of distinguishing their own needs, stresses, and impulses from those of their patients. Organizational solutions, strengthened peer support, and individual relaxation techniques can help to prevent or reduce burnout. People do not necessarily need counseling or psychotherapy when death enters their lives. Often the needed strength can be drawn from love, friendship, a familiar environment, and one's own beliefs, values, and coping resources. Financial security and competent nursing and medical care are also important.

We all can help each other when faced with death-related stress and loss. Specific examples were given about communicating in unexpected, sudden death situations and understanding family responses to life-threatening illness. Expert care providers often play a significant role, but there is no substitute for compassion and companionship shared between one person and another.

■ REFERENCES

Abenroth, M., & Flannery, J. (2006). Predicting the risk of compassion fatigue: A study of hospice nurses. *Journal of Hospice & Palliative Nursing, 8*, 346–356.

Addington-Hall, J. M., & Saffron, K. (2005). A national survey of health professionals and volunteers working in voluntary hospices in the UK: Staff and volunteers' experiences of working in hospices. *Palliative Medicine, 19*, 49–57.

Aiken, L. H., Clarke, S. P., Sloane, D. M., Sochalski, J., & Silber, J. H. (2002). Hospital nurse staffing and patient mortality, nurse burnout, and job dissatisfaction. *Journal of the American Medical Association, 288*, 1987–1993.

Al-Sabwah, M. N., & Abdel-Khalek, A. M. (2005–2006). Four year cross-sectional comparison of death distress among nursing college students. *Omega, Journal of Death & Dying, 52*, 237–248.

Anderson, K. A., & Gaugler, J. E. (2006–2007). The grief experiences of certified nursing assistants: Personal growth and complicated grief. *Omega, Journal of Death & Dying, 54*, 301–318.

Anonymous (2005). Comment on "Job story." http://www.aboutmyjob.com/forums/showthread.php?t=40555.

Atkins, S., & Nygaard, J. (2004). Relationship between patient mortality and nurses' level of education. *Journal of the American Medical Association, 291*, 1320–1321.

Bromley, A. (2005). Mindfulness courses reduce stress among doctors, nurses—lead to more compassionate patient care. www.virginia.edu/insideuva/2005/mindfulness.html.

Chethik, N. (2001). *FatherLoss.* New York: Hyperion.

Corr, C. A., & Corr. D. M. (2003). Death education. In C. Bryant (Ed.), *Handbook of death and dying* (Vol. 1, pp. 292–301). Thousand Oaks, CA: Sage.

Feifel, H., & Strack, S. (2001). Thanatologists view death: A 15-year perspective. *Omega, Journal of Death and Dying, 43*, 97–112.

Figley, C. R. (Ed.). (1995). *Compassion fatigue: Coping with secondary traumatic stress disorder in those who treat the traumatized.* New York: Brunner/Mazel.

Freud, S. (1915). Thoughts for the times on war and death. In *Collected Works of Sigmund Freud*: Vol. 14. London: Hogarth Press.

Freud, S. (1917). Mourning and melancholia. In *Collected Works of Sigmund Freud*: Vol. 14. London: Hogarth Press.

Hedtke, L. (2002). Reconstructing the language of death and grief. *Illness, Crisis & Loss, 10*, 285–293.

Ifeagwazi, C. M. (2005–2006). The influence of marital status on self-report of symptoms of psychological burnout among nurses. *Omega, Journal of Death & Dying, 52*, 359–37.

Holloway, K. (2008). The passing of a repast. *The Forum, Association for Death Education and Counseling, 34,* 7.

Iserson, K. V. (1999). *Grave words. Notifying survivors about sudden, unexpected deaths.* Tucson: Galen.

Kalish, R. A. (1980/1981). Death educator as deacon. *Omega, Journal of Death and Dying, 11,* 75–85.

Kastenbaum, R. (1977). We covered death today. *Death Education, 1,* 85–92.

Kastenbaum, R. (1993). Ars Moriendi. In R. Kastenbaum & B. Kastenbaum (Eds.), *Encyclopedia of death* (pp. 17–19). New York: Avon.

Kastenbaum, R. (2002). Danse macabre. In R. Kastenbaum (Ed.), *Macmillan encyclopedia of death and dying* (Vol. 1, pp. 201–202). New York: Macmillan.

Kastenbaum, R. (2004). *On our way. The final passage through life and death.* Berkeley: University of California Press.

Kastenbaum, R., Barber, T. X., Wilson, S. G., Ryder, B. L., & Hathaway, L. B. (1981). *Old, sick and helpless: Where therapy begins.* Cambridge, MA: Ballinger.

Kastenbaum, R., & Schneider, S. (1991). Does ADEC have a prayer? A survey report. *The Forum Newsletter, 16* (5), 1, 12–13.

Kaufman, S. R. (2005). *And a time to die: How American hospitals shape the end of life.* New York: Scribner.

Kelly, B., & Varghese, F. T. N. (2006). The seduction of autonomy: Countertransference and assisted suicide. In R. S. Katz & T. A. Johnson (Eds.), *When professionals weep. Emotional and countertransference responses in end-of-life care* (pp. 39–54). New York: Routledge.

Kempson, D. A. (2000/2001). Effects of intentional touch on complicated grief of bereaved mothers. *Omega, Journal of Death and Dying, 42,* 341–354.

Lundberg, U. (2000). Workplace stress. In G. Fink (Ed.), *Encyclopedia of stress* (Vol. 3, pp. 684–692). New York: Academic Press.

Manion, K. (2005). The unspoken epidemic: Burnout in healthcare. www.worklifedesign.org/Resources/Burnout.pdf.

Maslach, C., & Leiter, M. P. (2000). Burnout. In G. Fink (Ed.), *Encyclopedia of stress* (Vol. 1, pp. 358–364). New York: Academic Press.

Maslow, A. H. (1954). *Motivation and personality.* New York: Harper & Row.

Maslow, A. H. (1968). *Toward a psychology of being.* New York: Van Nostrand Reinhold.

Mathers, P. (1974). (Trans.). *The book of the thousand and one nights:* Vol. 2. New York: St. Martin's.

Morrison, J. K., Vanderwyst, D., Cocozza, J., & Dowling, S. (1981/1982). Death concerns among mental health workers. *Omega, Journal of Death and Dying, 12,* 179–190.

Neimeyer, C. J. Behnke, M., & Reiss, J. (1983). Constructs and coping: Physicians' responses to patient death. *Death Education, 7,* 245–266.

Oliver, D. P., Porock, D., & Oliver, D. B. (2006). Managing the secrets of dying backstage: The voices of nursing home staff. *Omega, Journal of Death & Dying, 53,* 193–208.

Papadatou, D. (2006). Care providers' responses to the death of a child. In A. Goldman, R. Hain, & S. Lieber (Eds.), *Oxford textbook of pediatric palliative care.* Oxford: Oxford University Press.

Papadatou, D. (2009). *In the face of death.* New York: Springer.

Phillips L. R., & Reed, P. G. (2009). Into the abyss of someone else's dying. *Clinical Nursing Research, 18,* 80–97.

Powell, D. (2002, November 5). Presentation, Neuroscience Society Annual Meeting, Orlando, Florida.

Riordan R. J., & Saltzer S. K. (1992). Burnout prevention among health care providers working with the terminally ill: A literature review. *Omega, Journal of Death and Dying, 25,* 17–24.

Rogers, A. E., Hwang, W. T., Scott, L. D., Aiken, L. H., & Dinges, D. F. (2004). The working hours of hospital staff nurses and patient safety. *Health Affairs, 23,* 202–212.

Rosen, E. (1998). *Families facing death* (Rev. ed.). San Francisco: Jossey-Bass.

Rosenblatt, P. C. (2000). *Parent grief. Narratives of loss and relationship.* New York: Brunner/Mazel.

Salva, V. (2005). Job story: Burnout in my 5th year . . . another nursing statistic. http://www.aboutmyjob.com/forums/showthread.php?t=40555.

Schneider, S., & Kastenbaum, R. (1993). Patterns and meanings of prayer in hospice caregivers: An exploratory study. *Death Studies, 17,* 471–485.

Smith, L. R. (1996). Gillian's journey. *The Forum Newsletter* (American Association for Death Education and Counseling), 22(1), 14–16.

Sobel, H. (Ed.). (1981). *Behavior therapy in terminal care.* Cambridge, MA: Ballinger.

Speck, P. (2000). Working with dying people: On being good enough. In A. Obholzer & V. Z. Roberts (Eds.), *The unconscious at work: Individual and organizational stress at work* (2nd ed.) (pp. 94–100). London: Brunner-Routledge.

Taylor, J. (1977). *The rules and exercises of holy dying.* New York: Arno Press. (Original work published 1651.)

Tebrani, N. (2004). *Workplace trauma.* Florence, KY: Routledge.

Tolomiczenko, G. S., Kahan, M., Ricci, M., Strathern, L., Jeney, C., Patterson, K., & Wilson, L. (2005). Nursing and health care management and policy. SARS: Coping with the impact at a community hospital. *Journal of Advanced Nursing, 50,* 101–110.

Turnipseed, D., Jr. (1987). Burnout among hospice nurses: An empirical assessment. *Hospice Journal, 3,* 105–119.

Vachon, M. L. S. (1987). *Occupational stress in the care of the critically ill, the dying, and the bereaved.* Washington: Hemisphere.

Vahey, D. C., Aiken, L., & Sloane, D. M., & Vargas, D. (2004). Nurse burnout and patient satisfaction. *Medical Care 42* (2) (Suppl.), 57–66.

Walters, L. (2008). Sharing food at death across cultures. *The Forum, Association for Death Education and Counseling 34,* 7.

Wass. H. (2002). Death education. In R. Kastenbaum (Ed.), *Macmillan encyclopedia of death and dying* (Vol. 1, pp. 211–218). New York: Macmillan.

Winslade, J. (2001). Putting stories to work. *The Forum* (Association for Death Education and Counseling), *27*(2), 1, 3–4.

■ GLOSSARY

Ars moriendi The art of dying well. First presented in illustrated books of the fifteenth century.

Artificial hydration Providing fluids through an intravenous tube. ("Artificial nutrition" can also be provided in this way.)

Burnout An emotional exhaustion as a result of prolonged job stress.

Compassion fatigue A major factor in burnout for human service care providers.

Danse macabre A visual image of personified death leading people to their graves in a slow, dignified dance (first appearing in the thirteenth century).

Death threat index A self-report measure of some aspects of death anxiety.

Prosocial Thoughts, feelings, and actions that are motivated by the intention to help others.

■ ON FURTHER THOUGHT . . .

Useful online resources:

Association for Death Education and Counseling
www.adec.org

Bioethics.net
www.bioethics.net

Center for Death Education and Bioethics
http://www.uwlax.edu/sociology/CDEB/index.html
www.uwlax.edu/sociology/CDEB/index.html

Compassionate Friends, Inc.
www.compassionatefriends.org

Hastings Center
www.thehastingscenter.org

Medline Plus Health Information
www.nlm.nih.gov/medlineplus

National Institutes of Health Bioethics Resources on the Web
www.nih.gov/sigs/bioethics/

Help Wanted!

In recent years, more people have been helping more people cope with dying and grief. However, there are still large numbers of people whose distress is often neglected. These include people residing in nursing homes and geriatric facilities, and persons with mental retardation, especially if they are institutionalized. It is commonly thought that cognitive impairment or limitations will shield a person from anxiety and grief. This assumption is seldom tested and therefore becomes self-perpetuating. If you are or will become a human services professional, perhaps you would consider taking a leadership role in encouraging more awareness of the death-related thoughts and feelings of people with impairment and more attention to their needs. Some useful readings:

Casarett, D. J., Hirschman, K. B., & Henry, M. R. (2001). Does hospice have a role in nursing home care at the end of life? *Journal of the American Geriatric Society, 49,* 1493–1498.

Johnson, S. (2005). Living and dying in nursing homes. In K. J. Doka, B. Jennings, & C.A. Corr (Eds.), *Ethical dilemmas at the end of life* (pp. 237–250). Washington, DC: Hospice Foundation of America.

Kauffman, J. (2005). *Guidebook on helping persons with mental retardation mourn.* Amityville, N.Y.: Baywood.

Good Life, Good Death?

Trying to Make Sense of It All

Greek souls flew instantly out of the mouths of their possessors at the time of death, with no indication of fear or difficulty. Egyptian and Christian souls had a rather harder time of it.

—Rosalie Osmond (2009, p. 157)

I think we are doing a disservice to the family who's been told he's going to die, and they're waiting. And they think he's dead, or as good as dead. And he's just there, not dying.

—Nurse, quoted by Eleanor Stanton Chapple (2010, p. 173)

Civil War soldiers were better prepared to die than to kill, for they lived in a culture that offered many lessons in how life should end. But these lessons had to be adapted to the dramatically changed circumstances of the Civil War.

—Drew Gilpin Faust (2008, p. 6)

Esther Britt lay in an oversize casket the color of an overcast sky. She wasn't always so heavy, but relatives say a string of illnesses and unhealthy life choices pushed her weight past 350 pounds and led here Wednesday afternoon—lying at age 56 in Stevens Funeral Home. "Her body was just tired, worn out, her sister Mary Britt, 54, said. "This is better for her. Hard for us, but better for her."

—Therese Vargas (April 28, 2008)

What actually happens is that we leave it to others to make sense of our death.

—Herman H. van der Kloot Meijburg (2005, p. 53)

In those days people were born in places where people lived. Astonishing, but true. I came into this world, would you believe it, in this very room. It was my parents' bedroom and their bed was over there, against that wall. I was born in that bed.

—Alexander McCall Smith (2005, p. 6)

An analysis of e-mail, phone calls and voice mail messages from the World Trade Center shows that at least 353 of those who died in the towers were able to reach people outside, the New York Times reported Sunday.

—Associated Press (2002)

I am inclined to think that these muscles and bones of mine would have gone off long ago to Megara or Boeotia—by the dog they would, if they had been moved only by their own idea of what was best, and if I had not chosen the better and nobler part, instead of playing truant and running away, of endur-ing any punishment which the state inflicts.

—A prisoner awaiting execution in 399 B.C.

"My in-laws had started to treat us like outcasts and nobody would come near us or touch us," she said, adding that she can cope with the threat of death, but not with the stigma AIDS carries.

—Quoted in Hussain (2002)

As I walked into Dad's room I was struck by how small he looked. Above him an oscilloscope traced the electrical activity of his heart, and chrome IV poles framed the head of his bed. The IV in his left arm was attached to a bottle of saline, and a plastic bag of antibiotic solution was piggy-backed into the tubing at his wrist. Another IV, this one a large-bore catheter that entered the subclavian vein just below the midportion of his right collarbone, was attached to a three-way stopcock valve. Through it saline was flow-ing at a to-keep-open rate; also attached to the stopcock was a manometer that provided measurement of central venous pressure, a guide to his vol-ume status. The third channel led to a dopamine drip with its own infusion pump that was standing by, just in case that medication was needed to raise his blood pressure. Oxygen tubing ran from his nose. A call button was pinned to his pillow. A urine bottle hung at his bedrail. On his bedside table was a cafeteria tray with his untouched breakfast, a pitcher of water, and a menu of the next day's meals.
"Hi, Dad." I managed to say. "How are you doing?"

—Byock (1997, p. 15)

The party is still going on. I don't want to go.

—Billie S., a woman receiving hospice home care

Does a good life lead to a good death? Does a not-so-good death take something away from a good life? But first—what do we or should we mean by "good death?"

Almost always, we are really talking about end of life experiences, not the stubborn fact of death itself. In this chapter we explore phenomena and meanings associated with the "good death." [And now we will drop the quotation marks, but not forget that it is a concept susceptible to many interpretations.]

Greeks in ancient times are said to have believed that the soul-substance departs the body at death as a most natural event. It was just time to go. Egyptians and Christians struggled with the passage of their souls because death was a scary prospect—punishment and suffering almost beyond imagination. How the passage is experienced has much to do with how the destination is conceived.

Our perspective is radically altered by the second example. Here, the crux of the situation is not the passage of the soul to another realm, but the discomfort of nurse and family members because the patient was "as good as dead," yet not dying with sufficient diligence. What really matters, then? The individual's psychological and spiritual experience at the very end of life, or inconvenience for a particular family and staff member? Our perspective will continue to be challenged as we consider other situations.

In nineteenth-century United States, the good death was a powerful and pervasive concept. How a person died was crucial to determining how well he or she had lived and what the afterlife would hold. The American Civil War often violated the conditions for a good death, and it did so on an unprecedented scale. There was a profound effect on family survivors. According to historian Drew Gilpin Faust (2008, p. 2008):

> The nation was a survivor, too, transformed by its encounter with death, obligated by the sacrifices of its dead. The war's staggering human cost demanded a new sense of national destiny, one designed to ensure that lives had been sacrificed for appropriately lofty ends. So much suffering had to have transcendent purpose.

That Johnny Rebel and Jeremiah Union had given their young lives under horrific conditions required making good somehow. It must be that their sacrifice was itself good, noble, sacred.

Esther Britt's death was not considered good by either her friends or herself—other than the fact that it ended a life that had become increasingly burdensome. So many other women in southwest Virginia have been faltering toward early death from a difficult life that public health officials have become alarmed (Vargas, 2008). Life expectancy for women in communities such as Pulaski and Radford dropped nearly six years over a 16-year period: a radical decline, especially in a nation

This young woman is among the many victims of AIDS in India, one of several nations that have been slow to recognize and respond to this crisis.

with increasing longevity. Men in this region have also been declining in life expectancy, though not to such a degree. Poor diets and smoking are major contributors, but do not tell the whole story. The director of the local health district identifies the area's impoverished economy as a powerful influence: "If you are struggling to put food on the table, you don't have time to think about prevention." Few people can afford health insurance, and the price of gas discourages visits to the doctor's office. Women might be at particular risk because they put the welfare of others above their own, as seemed to be the case with Esther Britt, a former nurse. There are no active American Civil War battlefields in Virginia these days, but some people become "just tired, worn out" in a grinding life that terminates in what would be difficult to regard as a good death.

Dutch scholar Herman H. van der Kloot Meijburg (2005) confirms that often we do not have the opportunity to shape the end of our lives as we might choose. Statistics from the Netherlands (fairly comparable with those of the United States) indicate that only about one person in three can have much control over the way he or she dies. Most people either die suddenly and unexpectedly or slip away after an illness that was "diagnosed and treated over time, but never caused any reason for serious concern because it never culminated in a crisis whereby intervention was required" (p. 52). For about two out of three people, then, the "goodness" of a death is much dependent on the way it is interpreted by the survivors, and the stories they construct. There is growing awareness that end-of-life stories have much to do with the memories and well-being of family and caregivers (Gellfand, Raspa, Briller, & Schim, 2005).

Another hint about the good death is provided by a wise and worldly woman in Alexander McCall Smith's 2005 novel, *44 Scotland Street*. She offers guidance to a younger woman who has yet to discover who she is and where she is going. The older woman has a firm sense of place and identity: this gives her the security of feeling that death will complete her life within a coherent framework of experience. Why not die where she was born? That would somehow seem right.

Death sometimes makes itself known to us as a thought that curls around the edges of our minds for a moment before again disappearing. Sometimes it is the thrust of an invisible dagger we feel when we see the marks of mortal vulnerability in a person we love. Sometimes it is the bodies trapped in the crushed automobile or scattered at the scene of a mass murder. The varied contact points with aspects of death are hard to bring together within a coherent and comforting framework. It is in our nature, however, to try to make sense of our experiences.

Many people believe that a good life prepares the way for a good death. This has long been a component of religious beliefs as expressed, for example, by Jeremy Taylor (1665/1970) in his *Rules and Exercises of Holy Dying*. Some have drawn the lesson that we should live each day as though our last. Buddhist philosophy emphasizes a continuous flow in which life and death move together in everything we do (Gyatso, 1985). A good death is intrinsically related to a good life because what we call "life" and what we call "death" have always been companions.

Variations on this theme have continued to develop. For example, Avery D. Weisman (1972) introduced the influential concept of an *appropriate death,* that is, the death we would choose for ourselves if we really had a choice. The good death, then, might be very different from one person to another. Many writers focus on the importance of having lived a full and rewarding life. People who can accept their lives are thought to be more likely to experience a good death. This idea has been gaining favor in recent years, but firm evidence is difficult to come by.

THREE PATHS TO DEATH

The people who sent messages to their loved ones from the World Trade Center (WTC) towers on September 11, 2001, the condemned prisoner in Athens, and the AIDS victims in Gauhati, India, all raised difficult questions about a good death. The men and women who died in the WTC towers expected to return home for an evening with family or friends. They had no reason to expect that their lives would come to an abrupt end. It seemed in every aspect to be the opposite of good death:

- Individuality counted for nothing: The terrorist's goal was to compile a large body count.
- The sudden and unexpected catastrophe allowed no time for the victims to prepare

themselves spiritually for the end of their lives or to make practical arrangements for their families.

- Families were shattered, burdened with grief, deprived of companionship and support, and faced with the challenge of somehow going on with life despite this tremendous blow. The report of last-minute communications from victims to families does raise a question: Is it better to die swiftly or to become aware in advance? Most people say they would prefer to slip away from life, preferably from peaceful sleep. Awareness of imminent death is experienced as torment. Family members who received that last call from the WTC responded with shock and anxiety. Nevertheless, they cherished that last communication and used it as a transitional memory structure between the person they loved and the absence they now experience. The victims themselves were strongly motivated to make that final contact. Furthermore, the simple act of placing the call was something that one could still do—an expression of self against overwhelming catastrophe. So—perhaps there was that one last loving action that brought something positive to a catastrophic death.

- Socrates is generally considered to be the father of philosophical thought, although other insightful thinkers had preceded him. His death sentence was the unexpected outcome of bogus charges brought against him as payback for bruising some Athenian egos (Ahrensdorf, 1995; Kastenbaum, 2002). Socrates could have escaped execution by a few words of contrition or by boarding a ship provided by his friends while the authorities pretended not to notice. Within his prison walls, Socrates patiently reasoned with his friends about the meaning of life and death and sought to relieve their anxieties by his own serenity. When he accepted the cup of hemlock (if that's what it really was; see Ober, 1988) from the reluctant hands of a jailer, Socrates offered himself as a model for facing death with equanimity, along with his characteristic twist of humor. This was quite a bad death: miscarriage of justice, silencing one of humankind's greatest thinkers, depriving a great but troubled city-nation of an invaluable citizen. However, history also regards this episode as the very model of a very good death: bringing a clear and calm philosophical mind to the end of life and facing death in such a way as to affirm and fulfill all that has gone before. Despite the injustice of the situation, here was a good death that flowed from a good life.

- AIDS continues to be regarded throughout the world as a tainted pathway to death. Enlightened caregivers have had to contest with negative attitudes toward the disease and its victims. This pattern of avoidant behaviors exists both in developed nations and in countries that are struggling for stability and survival (including much of sub-Saharan Africa). Our example comes from India, where the actual number of people infected with HIV/AIDS has

Socrates, the gadfly of Athens, teaches his last lessons moments before he accepts the lethal cup of hemlock. The original 1787 painting by Jacques Louis David can be found in New York's Metropolitan Museum of Art.

been massively underestimated and where both the victims and their families are often ostracized by society, thereby impairing prevention and treatment efforts. It is estimated that there are now about 4 million HIV/AIDS cases in India, but this number could rise to 25 million by within the next few years. The human side is illustrated by the woman quoted at the start of the chapter. Her family was shunned while her husband suffered and then died from AIDS, and landlords would boot them out when they learned of his condition. The whole family was rejected by society not because the husband was dying but because he was dying of AIDS.

We take now a more extended example from our own society that raises the good death/bad death issue in a way that has become increasingly frequent.

A FATHER DIES: A MISSION BEGINS

Ira Byock, M.D., is founder of the American Academy of Hospice and Palliative Medicine and a leading advocate for improved care of terminally ill people. It was early in Byock's medical career that his father was struck with a fatal illness. Byock was stunned, moved, and instructed by this experience.

The hospital scene is described in the opening quotation. As a physician, Byock recognized the devices that were connected to the small-looking man in the bed. As a son, he felt disoriented by the barrier they established between his father and himself. How do you relate to a person who has become a component of a life support system? "Hi, Dad," I managed to say, "How are you doing?" One could hardly feel more awkward and unnatural.

But wait—the purpose of life support systems is to support life! Byock's father did recover with the assistance of these devices and devoted nursing care. This made it possible for the family to have more time together with him. Situations such as these caution us against simplistic conclusions about the relationship between life support systems and the "good death."

His father's death occurred later, peacefully, at home. Byock (1997) noted:

He appeared suddenly to be relaxed, as if the work, whatever it had been, was over. He was peaceful, no longer sweating, and his breathing

was easy and deep, though irregular. Mom stood touching his foot, and Anita and I sat on each side of the bed touching his arms, as he drew his last breath and left. For the next hour we continued our vigil: hugging one another, crying intermittently, grieving openly and together (p. 24).

Sy Byock seemed to experience the moment of death as a relief and release. There was no way of knowing how much awareness he had of the situation—but if he did, it would have been the loving presence of his family. A sense of unity and completion was experienced by the family itself, much different from the alienating hospital situation. All that Byock had learned about managing terminal illness as a physician now seemed inadequate. He realized that the health care system was at war with death and, therefore, with dying people as well:

If death on the wards was macabre, in the emergency room, it was ghastly. Passings that should have been peaceful turned gruesome. Nursing homes, for example, routinely sent patients only moments away from death to the hospital by ambulance, lights and sirens blazing. By transferring the almost-dead to the emergency room, nursing homes could claim a mortality rate of nearly zero, while providing evidence to families, and any interested attorneys, that "everything possible" had been done. This bizarre scenario extended not only to sudden deaths but also to people who were unconscious, in the final moments of dying, and expected to die (p. 27).

Futile medical procedures perpetuate the health care system's unwillingness to face the reality of dying and death and can even constitute a kind of assault on the patient in which respect and dignity lose out. Whatever else the good death might be, it is more likely to occur within a supportive interpersonal framework and without medical interventions that are both futile and alienating.

A SHIFT IN THE MEANING OF LIFE AND DEATH?

A person who regards death as destination and fulfillment may have a different set of expectations and priorities than one who regards death as end

TABLE 15-1 *Meanings That Have Been Given to Death*

- Death is an enfeebled form of life.
- Death is a continuation of life.
- Death is a perpetual development.
- Death is waiting.
- Death is cycling and recycling.

or outcome. Five alternative interpretations were considered in Chapter 3. These were structural or cognitive models. Each proposed its own version of the nature of death. We can refresh our memory with the help of Table 15-1.

Each of these interpretations has distinctive implications for how we might prepare ourselves for death. We have examined our feelings about death, especially in Chapter 3 when we focused on anxiety, denial, and acceptance. Shifts will continue to occur as we move deeper into the twenty-first century. Here we attend to the words of Billie S., the hospice patient who sighed, "The party is still going on. I don't want to go." She is not the only person who has felt this way. It seems to be a common sentiment among that most famous of generations, the baby boomers. A long life has become more attractive for many people. Throughout world history, people often feared growing old because of possible infirmity, suffering, and abandonment. The psalmist of the Old Testament records the lament: "Cast me not off in the time of old age; forsake me not when my strength faileth. . . . O God, forsake me not" (Psalm 71:9).

Death was often regarded as release from infirmity, suffering, and indignity. This attitude has not been restricted to elderly people because infirmity, suffering, and indignity can occur at any age. Suicide has been one way of acting on the feeling that life can be cured only by death. Another path has been systematic degradation of health and heightened risk taking, as by the abuse of alcohol and drugs. Less obvious is the silent withdrawal from life. Activities that once were attractive now seem either out of reach or only further sources of distress. Read history at ground level—the lives of everyday people—and we encounter repeatedly the scourges of poverty, famine, illness, bereavement, oppression, and war. Life was hard and dangerous. Many people had to ask themselves, "Why go on?" even as they struggled to go on.

Lulling to Sleep (or Death?)

Lullabies, those charming and comforting songs we sing to sleeping babies, have their origins in misery so deep and pervasive that the desire to live was strenuously challenged by the temptation to get it all over with. Kalle Achte (1989) tells us that:

> lullabies originated during the centuries that most people lived in agricultural communities, did hard work, and battled against the forces of nature. Famine was an ever-present threat, and epidemics killed many people, especially young children. . . . A woman's life was especially difficult at that time. Some mothers may have felt that death offered the only release from a joyless life and continuous labor. The mother's own depression and frustration may have been crucial factors in the origins of lullabies with death themes. Perhaps overworked and depressed mothers transferred their own death wishes to the child (pp. 177–178).

An example of a death-themed lullaby:

> Today Vanyushka will die the funeral will be held tomorrow we shall bury Vanya and toll the big bell (p. 177).

Death-ridden lullabies became less common as the conditions of life improved for many people—and that's the point here. Traditional attitudes toward death were forged when for most people life was hard, dangerous, and brief. As conditions of life have improved, aging has come to seem a less fearsome prospect, and death has not seemed to lurk so ominously around every corner.

Competing models of death emerged even when life was very difficult. The ancient "death as enfeebled life" model was challenged by the new Christian doctrine that life is only an interlude of waiting either for salvation or damnation. Today, this life on Earth attracts some of the attention formerly accorded to death. Many elderly men and women are active, vigorous, and strongly engaged with life. Attitude studies find that many elderly people are well satisfied with their lives. We would not want to exaggerate the differences between past and present attitudes. Many people treasured life and did all they could to survive in difficult circumstances. There were also people who "had it made" and were more interested in continuing a pleasant life than in entering a promised land after death. Nevertheless, death may be becoming less salient in everyday life (Hayslip & Peveto, 2004). We may still have our own individual mix of anxiety, denial, and acceptance and yet feel less intensely about death as either an overpowering catastrophe or a transcendent blessing.

Willa T., a woman in her mid-80s, nearly blind for the past several years, put it this way:

> *You can't change the past. All the bad stuff was part of all the good stuff. You can't really pick and choose. All in all, I've had more in life than I had any right to expect. But, listen, I want more. More life. I don't want to hear about "them pearly gates." I don't want to see them pearly gates any time soon. It's not that I have any problem with death. I don't. Do you understand? It's that I'm used to living and I haven't used up living. Poor Razzi was the same way. She died last night, you know, or early in the morning. I am not afraid of that happening to me, but, oh, it would be a shame, wouldn't it, to have to leave when there's so much more in front of you every day!*

Within this perspective, Death is not an awesome figure, terrifying or beatific. Instead, Death is more the spoilsport who turns out the lights and says "The party's over" before we are ready to go. Now it is time to once again challenge our perspective, this time with an ambitious international study.

FROM GOOD DEATH TO END-OF-LIFE CARE

Should everybody have one and the same kind of good death? Perhaps you would hesitate to say so, just as you would not care to have others tell you precisely what "good life" you should live. But what if we drew on the accumulated knowledge and experience of people from many nations who have been concerned with end-of-life (EOL) care? Perhaps there would be something to learn from the attempt to evaluate how and how well end-of-life care is managed throughout the world.

Such an attempt has now been made by the Lien Foundation's Economic Intelligence Unit (Murray, 2010.) Yes, this means that financial considerations are at the core, but the report also encompasses quality care, and cultural issues. Detailed information on the quality of care index and ratings of all nations surveyed can be found at www.qualityofdeath.org.

The palliative approach to a good death is still far from a universal practice:

> *Few nations, including rich ones with cutting-edge healthcare systems, incorporate palliative care strategies into their overall healthcare policy—despite the fact that in many of these countries, increasing longevity and ageing populations mean demand for end-of-life care is likely to rise sharply. Globally, training for palliative care is rarely included in healthcare education (p. 5).*

Forty nations are included in the survey. Of these, 27 are European, 7 are Asian, and 2 are African. Canada, Brazil, Mexico, and the United States represent the Americas. A total score for quality and availability of EOL care was computed, based on both quantitative and qualitative measures. Quality of care contributed the most to the overall ratings. The Quality of Death Index is one way of bringing "good death" into the universe of health care statistics.

Perhaps it is no surprise that the United Kingdom, the wellspring of the modern hospice movement, ranks at the top for quality care, followed closely by Australia, New Zealand, and Ireland. There is also something remarkable in these findings, though: England's overall health care system is afflicted with many problems, yet palliative care shines through. Other nations in the top 10 are Belgium, Austria, Netherlands, Germany, Canada, and the United States. At least two other nations have made outstanding progress. Hungary (ranked eleventh) has benefited from effective care advocates who have been well received by a responsive government. Taiwan (ranked fifteenth) was among the first Asian nations to recognize the need for EOL, providing high-quality service but not yet widely accessible. China, Mexico, Brazil, India, and Uganda have high-quality individual palliative care programs, but these reach only a small sector of the population.

Obstacles to the growth and utilization of palliative care programs were identified in the hospice chapter and continue to be encountered today, e.g., public taboos and misunderstandings about dying and death, physician reluctance to prescribe adequate pain medication, belief that providing comfort is giving up, even though aggressive treatment has become futile.

We can accept or reject the Quality of Death Index as a proxy for the good death. It provides useful information, however, and points to issues that require more attention. I am not 100 percent enthusiastic about replacing a rich, ambiguous, and value-laden concept with a statistical measure. Nevertheless, the report described was a competent and well-intentioned effort and, at the least, perhaps converting the good death into a statistic will encourage health care systems to give it a higher priority.

Are We Live or On Tape? The Life-and-Death Challenges of Virtual Reality

And still another challenge to our perspective are the ever more pervasive inducements of technologically mediated and transformed reality.

Face-to-face encounters almost completely dominated human interactions until technological innovations offered supplements, enhancements, and replacements. Photography not only altered our sense of identity but also transformed our relationship to the past, especially to loved ones, who now could still be with us just as they were. The tiny framed oval photograph of grandmother or the portrait showing the entire family as once it was became among the most cherished of possessions. Photographs provided a powerful new way for the dead to speak to the living. The emotional impact of the American Civil War has remained potent through the lens of photographers, the first to offer visual evidence of a major conflict. The dead also speak to the living in the movie *Dead Poets Society* as a teacher (Robin Williams) directs his students to study a photograph of an earlier generation of students. The intense aliveness of this vanished generation becomes a unique lesson to the present student generation. The dead were once young and full of life, just as the students of today. The lesson here: Seize the day! In this and in many other ways, the photograph has added an enduring visual context within which today's lives and deaths gain resonance.

The telephone had its own distinctive transformational effect. The human voice with all its subtle tones and inflections now could transcend distance. The pangs of separation and absence—so closely associated with bereavement—could be relieved by hearing the familiar reassuring voice. And so the process has continued, with every significant new form of communication having its effects on our symbolic relationship with both life and death. Sound recording not only revolutionized the place of music in society but rescued conversations and speeches from being carried away in the ever-flowing river of time. "Are we live or on tape?" became a question with philosophical as well as practical implications. (The rapid fading of "on tape" speaks to the continuing sea change wrought by technology. Does it really matter if the voice we hear is that of a person who is speaking to us in "real time" (another new concept)? The voice and message are the same if taped, even if the speaker is deceased. The ear processes the sound in the same way (given an accurate recording), whether the message comes live, on tape, or from the living or the dead.

Another important dimension has been the remarkable new ability to shift time. Those born into the age of electronics might take this ability for granted as they record a television show for later viewing. Nevertheless, shifting time is among the features that most distinguish present times from the human past. The role of time in human life was nailed by the Persian poet Omar Khayyam (1990) in the eleventh century:

> *The Moving Finger writes; and, having writ,*
> *Moves on: nor all your Piety nor Wit*
> *Shall lure it back to cancel half a Line, Nor*
> *all your Tears wash out a Word of it (p. 42).*

Time rules, then. Caught in the flow of time, life does not give us a second chance. Errors cannot be corrected, no failures repaired. No matter how clever or religious we might be, time will take its own course and, with that course, make off with all that we hold dear, including life itself.

How should we come to terms with death, given this view of time? People differed, then as now. Some, for example, attempted to prove Khayyam wrong by delving into alchemy or magic to prolong youth and life. The quest for perpetual youth was a desperate and occasionally inspired effort to bend time to human desire (Kastenbaum, 1995). Others decided to burn their candles brightly and live as intensely as they could within a shortened time frame. Still others sought to distract themselves from the disappearing sands of time by drink or other means. Time was not fragmented into stopwatch or nanosecond measures but regarded as the long, slow, implacable wave that swept away kingdoms as inexorably as it did the individual's youth and life.

Time's rule has now been challenged. We can convert immediate experience to the time-insensitive format of digital encoding. Essentially, time becomes number (or its electronic equivalent). Life remains perishable in the stream of time, but episodes within life can be stored "for later viewing at our convenience."

What are the implications for our views of life and death? In earlier chapters, we saw how difficult it is for children to develop and for adults to face the basic facts of death. The popularity of the idea that death is a kind of sleep also reveals our reluctance to recognize it on its own terms. We are often grateful for any opportunity to escape the recognition of mortality even (or especially) when in jeopardy. Technology's very good tricks of recording and shifting time can play right into our preference for keeping death out of awareness. Every time we take advantage of a time-eluding technology we might be making it that much easier to blur the difference between "virtual" and "real reality."

Consider a person who has had limited primary social interaction during infancy and childhood. Place a computer in front of that person and provide access to a vast universe of images and symbols. Give that person the opportunity to manipulate the images and symbols. Allow that person the power of trashing and deleting whatever does not please. Add the attraction of game playing. And to this game playing add a personal impulse that has been stimulated by mass media society since childhood: the pleasures to be found not only in victory but in destruction.

Some of the most popular computer-mediated games are variations on the shooting galleries that were long popular in carnivals and fairs. With the embellishments of vivid graphics, one can zap the alien invaders or blast away at other life form images. The most technologically updated aliens are the latest stand-ins for the Other: people who are not like us and therefore suitable as targets for our rage, pride, and entertainment. Competing to see who can run up the highest score of targets destroyed in a computer game is an activity that comes painfully close to representing our society's

aggressive edge. That the same group of people most attracted to zapping computer games also produces the most real-life killers is a connection that is as difficult to overlook as it is to interpret with any degree of confidence.

Many of us also enjoy a phantom-like interaction through chat rooms. The people with whom we interact may or may not be representing themselves honestly. This attenuated form of interaction competes with notoriously complex, shifting, and sometimes "messy" real-life relationships. Furthermore, the real people in our lives are not always available when we need them. Computer-mediated interactions, though, are just a mouse click away. Real-life relationships also have a way of making demands on us when we would rather not be bothered. One might often prefer the company of spirits generated or mediated in cyberspace to that of flesh-and-blood mortals. No heart stops beating when, with the touch of a finger, we trash or discard. Is it possible that our computer-bred, computer-linked person will fail to appreciate the crucial difference between the real death of real people and the pseudolethality that flourishes in virtual reality?

Perhaps it will become even easier with a few key strokes to endanger the lives of people we have never met. The 60 million peasants who starved to death during China's catastrophic farm reform movement were not family, friends, or neighbors of the leadership. The planners and leaders did not have to see the effects of decisions they made at a distance. When bombs were first dropped on a civilian population (Guernica, Spain), there was a widespread reaction of shock and outrage. Nevertheless, aerial assault on civilian populations persisted and intensified, because those who unleashed their bombs with the push of a button or the slide of a lever could not see the faces and mangled bodies below. The same action involved in pushing a button (or clicking a mouse) can have the effect of playing a game, sending a communication, or destroying lives.

We just don't know yet if coming generations will have a firm grasp of both virtual reality and the kind of reality that is experienced by mortal beings. There is another kind of virtual reality yet to explore, one whose long and influential history is seldom brought to mind: death and dying in imaginary places. We focus here on a blockbuster novel from the early sixteenth century.

Thomas More (1478–1535) described Utopia, an ideal commonwealth in which people could enjoy long lives that would end with respect and comfort. As friend, Henry VIII admired book and author; as monarch he had More's head chopped off.

UTOPIA: A BETTER DEATH IN A BETTER PLACE?

The endearingly clueless hero of Voltaire's *Candide* (1759) proclaims "This is the best of all possible worlds." A series of most unfortunate events promptly calls his judgment into question. This world actually could do with a bit of improvement, and this brings us to the Utopia tradition. Plato (370 B.C.) proposed a scientifically managed society to produce and enforce moral behavior. People would just have to be good whether they liked it or not. By contrast, sensualists and slackers throughout history have imagined idyllic places where they could loll about, enjoy delightful climate and abundant food, and treat themselves to such pleasures as they might desire. Not surprisingly, the carefree garden of delight was a popular alternative to Plato's rigorous Republic.

Centuries passed, and neither version of a better world came into being. In fact, the emergence of what historians call the "early modern period" did not help matters. Saint-to-be Thomas More (1516) was incensed by the violence, hypocrisy, and injustice of his times. He thought a more rational form of government might protect individuals and fulfill the legitimate needs of the commonwealth. The people would be physically fit, educated, and productive. With healthful activity, virtuous pleasures, and communal feeling within a just society, people would be more inclined to behave in accord with religious values. More called this new and improved society *Utopia* (1516) and placed it on a distant island unknown to mapmakers.

Utopia eventually became the inspiration for new communities that attempted to bring the system into palpable existence. It also became the progenitor of a robust literary tradition. Some versions have worked within More's concept of a well-managed commonwealth. Over the years, other versions have morphed into dystopias (scary and miserable realms) (George Orwell's *1984* is a towering example). These utopias-gone-bad often have outscored the amiable version in attracting public attention. Science fantasy versions of utopias and dystopias have escaped from the pages of pulp magazines to elaborate cinematic treatments. We will stick with the original here. Why is life better in More's Utopia? The positives can perhaps best be expressed through a list of negatives:

- *No money. No deprivation.* Nobody's rich. Nobody's poor. No mansions. No slums. All Utopians receive from the commonwealth what is needed for a decent and secure living. There goes the threat of crimes of desperation or ego-driven greed. There also goes the impulse for an individual to strut, flaunt, and boast, because everybody has pretty much the same economic standing and show-offs are scorned. The commonwealth is so well organized that agriculture and other essential activities assure prosperity.
- *No private property.* No land-grab schemes. No disenfranchising one group of people for the advantage of another. No setting one's self up as a power broker by accumulating properties. Nice!
- *No lawyers.* More was one of the great lawyers of his time, so he took particular delight in excluding this profession. Without lawyers, there

is no constant skirmish between one interest and another, no mind-numbing tactics, no societal preoccupation with contentious cases. Utopia gets along without lawyers because the laws are few, basic, and easily understood.

- *No unemployment.* Everybody participates in the work of society, therefore avoiding the dark clouds of alienation and anomie. Busy hands and duty-focused minds are also less likely to indulge in useless or uncitizen-like thoughts. The workload is not excessive, so there is plenty of time for people to improve themselves, for example, by reading good books (the only kind available), visiting museums, and the like.

- *No vice.* Utopians are schooled from early childhood in the virtues of responsibility, teamwork, and moderation. Temptation is neither stimulated nor countenanced. Visitors who might suppose Utopia to be a feast for sensual indulgence would be sorely disappointed. No frilled-up women, no stud-strutting men. No brothels, taverns, or other establishments of dubious propriety. Nothing but wall-to-wall virtue. Innocent citizenry 24/7!

- *No gambling.* Can you think of any other sinful temptations? Just add them to the list of indulgences that will not be found in Utopia. Premarital sex and adultery are, of course, no-no's. Sexual activity is normal and healthy as long as it is practiced within the bonds of matrimony. People are free to choose their own mates, but both partners must have reached a sufficient level of maturity. Both must also be satisfied with the physique of their prospective mates. (How? A betrothed couple is required to view each other in nature's own garment and express their approval of the one-and-only lifelong mate-to-be). A huge set of possible crimes and failings has thus been avoided. Within its proper limits, pleasure is obligatory. Utopia not only comes down hard on the few that stray from the marital path, but also does not prize ascetic wannabe martyrs who mortify their flesh.

- *No persecution.* In More's time, a realm that was free from brutal persecution would have been greatly cherished, even if none of the other features of Utopia existed. It was not unusual for property to be seized, or for people to be imprisoned, tortured, left to die, executed, or slaughtered in large groups. Strife within

Christianity was a major source of this brutality, primarily associated with the rift between the Catholic Church and the emerging Protestant Reformation. Thomas More himself would have his head separated from his shoulders at the command of his admiring friend, King Henry VIII, because he stayed true to his own religious beliefs in a conflict between church and state. The founders of Utopia knew the perils of religious intolerance. They allowed people to worship as they chose. It was expected that everybody would believe in a divinity that created and ruled the universe. People could choose their own comfortable way of worshiping this divinity, as long as they did not aggressively oppose other people's religions. Utopia was therefore mercifully free of acrimony and bloodshed between believers who called God by different names. The commonwealth's smooth-working machinery of governance also avoided armed hostilities based on opportunism, grudges, or rivals for royal succession. The blessings of peace were bestowed on Utopia. Naturally, though, from time to time the Utopians themselves found justifications for pouncing on somebody else's realm. They were wickedly effective diplomats and equally superior in military art and force.

Life in Utopia was purposeful and coherent. Luxury and self-indulgence were not part of the package, but it was far from a grim land. People were encouraged to participate in sports and keep themselves in excellent physical condition. There were satisfying communal meals with music and edifying conversation, pleasant places to stroll, and all of that. There were also limits on private initiative and activity. Perhaps Utopians did not think twice about the need to submit official requests in order to travel to another city—and to be observed and accompanied. Perhaps they also accepted without question a system of watchers: people who kept their eyes on other people. We might feel creepy and outraged in such circumstances, but this was the Utopian way of life and its citizens had known no other, and heard of no better.

Death in Utopia

What, then, about death in Utopia? I "visited" St. Thomas More's ideal commonwealth with that question in mind (Kastenbaum, 2005) and, again, with the related question of aging (Kastenbaum, 2008). Inflicted death is given more attention than natural passing away. We learn mostly about deaths associated with war and execution. Few people are put to death by the commonwealth. In this regard, Utopia differs appreciably from other nations at the time, reflecting More's anger at the infliction of capital punishment when the "crime" (if any) does not require so harsh a punishment. Nevertheless, the commonwealth does reserve the right to take the life of a citizen who violates a foundational principle of the society.

War was the far more common cause of inflicted death. The commonwealth was skillful in getting what it wanted without resorting to military action. Most potential enemies realized it would be folly to invade Utopia, with its well-disciplined forces and daunting defenses. Sometimes, though, the rational thing to do was to invade another realm that was not using its resources nearly as well as Utopia could. After the inevitable victory, Utopian forces took prisoners instead of slashing throats, which was the more common practice at the time.

People did die in battle, though, and here two discordant notes are sounded: (1) Spare the lives of one's own citizens by hiring fierce but dispensable mercenaries, many of whom would be killed anyhow and therefore not have to be paid; (2) affirm Utopian values by exposing whole families to battlefield death. The latter practice tells us a lot about the commonwealth's concept of the good life and the good death. When a man goes off to war:

> They place each wife alongside her husband in the line of battle . . . and all (his) children, kinsmen, and blood or marriage relations, so that those who have the most reason to help one another may be closest at hand for mutual aid. It is a matter of great reproach for either partner to come home without the other, or for a son to return after losing his father . . . hand to hand fighting is apt to be long and bitter, ending only when everyone is dead (More, 1975, p. 70).

Family values? Or commonwealth as monster? Shame avoidance is so powerful that an entire family is dispatched to its death. Utopia, the most enlightened and benign of realms, places the honor of the community above the lives of its citizens when the drums beat and the bugles blast. The state displays admirable restraint in executing so few offenders—but sacrificing entire families in battle is also considered admirable. The violent and painful death of "children, kinsmen, and blood or marriage relations" is good because it displays the values of the realm. Is it good from anybody else's perspective? *There is no other perspective.*

What of natural death in Utopia? In this compassionate realm, the sick and dying are tended by skillful physicians and comforted by priests and visitors in pleasant surroundings. People who are slipping away in final illness have consoling companions to the very end. Although More devotes only a few words to this process, it is worth observing that he does think it important to discuss the dying process.

Most later Utopian writers drew an implicit curtain around the death bed scene; they did not care to think about it. Sometimes, though, "the disease is not only incurable, but excruciatingly painful." Priests and public officials are up for this challenge. They remind the dying person that he or she is now unfit for any of life's duties, a burden to self and others. Life is good while one can serve the community and experience pleasure. Death is good when pleasure is gone and one can no longer be of use to others. Obey the priests! They are the interpreters of God's will. It will be "a holy and pious act" to accept a potion that leads to peaceful sleep and death. Compliance is expected. Assisted death (Chapter 9) is good because it is endorsed by the commonwealth. There is disappointment all around should a dying person decline this thoughtful suggestion, but it is not imposed, and care continues to be provided until the last breath. Priests shake their heads regretfully. This person had a wonderful opportunity to affirm his or her personal virtue by affirming the virtues of the commonwealth. Fortunately, though, most people in this circumstance accepted their responsibility to die on request.

Consider now another person who has suffered much and has but more suffering in prospect. This person might be in even more distress than the one who has been firmly "invited" to die. In despair, this person decides to take her or his life (perhaps even with the same recommended potion). This sufferer does not have to be advised by priests that he or she has become a liability, a noncontributing drag on the commonwealth. A good death this must be since it is well in line with the criteria for assisted death. It will probably not surprise you, however, to learn that the person "who takes his own life without the approval of priests and senate, they consider unworthy of earth or fire, and throw his body, unburied and disgraced, into the nearest bog" (p. 60). The smooshing splash of a suicide's body in a distant bog tells us something about the darker side of Utopian philosophy and practice.

A Better Death in a Better Place?

Utopia has many admirable features that were remarkable for their time. It has serious claim as a model design for a better place to live. How people die in Utopia is obviously connected with their way of life. Compassionate care for the sick and dying is consistent with obligations owed to citizens by the commonwealth. Assisted death also calls upon citizens to fulfill their obligations to the commonwealth. The harsh attitude toward people who take death into their own hands is paralleled by the unobtrusive but pervasive actions of the commonwealth to keep everybody "with the program." We note how this attitude reverses the situation in the United States today: Suicide is legal, not criminal, while assisted death is still caught up in controversy. For the guardians of Utopia, death is good when it conforms with the commonwealth's priorities. Both the person who has consented to assisted death and the person, equally suffering and failing, who chooses suicide have both escaped their pain and lifted the burden of support from society. In one instance, though, this is a virtuous death and, in the other, so despicable a death that the corpse is flagrantly dishonored. That a family should offer itself up for

Yvonne Quinn takes care of her prized pet, Amoeba, a sparrow she saved 3 years ago. She thinks the bird is attracted to her blue nail polish.

death in battle is an even more obvious example of commonwealth policy taking precedence over the lives and deaths of its citizens. In a very small nutshell, then: the good death in Utopia is the achievement of dying as a respectable citizen of the realm. Choose to live in Utopia and enjoy the many benefits and we have also chosen to die one of the approved deaths of the realm.

The United States is not Utopia, as most of us have noticed from time to time. Nevertheless, our personal feelings about the good death are also influenced by cultural expectations in many ways. It is time now to look more systematically at concepts of good and not-so-good deaths that compete for our favor.

"THE GOOD DEATH": FANTASY OR REALITY?

What can we say now about the relationship between a life and its death? Does having lived a good life contribute to ending with a good death? And what about the reverse: Can the way a person dies alter the meaning and quality of that person's entire life? There are many opinions to choose from, including views that dismiss the whole idea of a good death. Bring your own experience and judgment to the evaluation of the following propositions. You will notice that some of the propositions seem to be at odds with each other and that they draw upon different realms of observation, evidence, and belief. And so—to the challenge!

Proposition 1: We can agree that some forms of death are terrible even if we cannot always agree on what constitutes a good death. People should be spared such deaths. The terrible death is dominated by suffering. There is physical pain to the point of agony. There may also be extreme mental pain, as when a mother sees her child being killed while she herself is dying. Torture and humiliation, such as rape and murder in regions of subtropical Africa are still being used to destroy victimized people spiritually as well as physically.

It is reasonable to assume that people everywhere would fear a death marked by extreme physical, mental, and spiritual suffering. However, some people have believed that suffering is a valuable experience. We should suffer because this either helps to pay for our sins or promotes our spiritual growth. This belief can be held to a lesser or greater degree. In the not so distant past, the extreme position has been used to argue against providing pain relief to women in labor, a particularly cruel example of gender discrimination. There are also contemporary examples of withholding pain relief to terminally ill people for similar reasons. However, terminally ill people today rarely see any inherent value in suffering. It is an unfortunate situation when people in a position to provide care to the dying patient believe that people are meant to suffer.

Proposition 2: The good death should enact the highest values held by society. Both the individual and society benefit from such a death. Society is strengthened by having one of its members demonstrate allegiance to its values with the last breath. Utopia, as we have just seen, is one such example. Furthermore, each person's death is important as a possible test of both individual character and society's strength. This emphasis on how a person faces death contrasts sharply with the "failed machine" model that has often been implicit in medical management. The community and its health care professionals cannot turn away from a dying person if there is something important that all believe should be accomplished as life gives way to death. A good death is good for society.

But what precisely is to be accomplished at the end of life? The answer to this question varies. One of the most dramatic models is the heroic death. The person is to die bravely. The Kamikaze pilot and the Sioux warrior were among those who accepted combat missions in which their deaths were almost assured. In Norse mythology, the Vikings who died as battlefield heroes were rewarded with an afterlife in Valhalla. Both women and men are included among the martyrs—people who chose death rather than renounce their religious faith. The type of suicide that Durkheim described as altruistic (Chapter 7) may also belong here. The heroic death usually involves choice. Loyalty to one's people or God takes precedence over staying alive.

What the hero died *for* can be a troubling question. This was the case with American Civil War soldiers who mostly did not consider themselves heroes, although they often fought bravely, although not convinced that they were giving their lives for a just cause. Faust (2008, p. 270) quotes

Oliver Wendell Holmes as he attempted to make sense of the annihilation of so many youths:

> *The faith is true and adorable which leads a soldier to throw away his life in obedience to a blindly accepted duty, in a cause which he little understands, in a plan of campaign of which he has no notion, under tactics of which he does not see the use.*

Faust adds that "The very purposelessness of sacrifice created its purpose." Devastated by grief, the American public needed an explanation, a justification for the great slaughter. Keeping the United States united and abolishing slavery were significant justifications in historical perspective, but did not necessarily register profoundly on those in battle or visiting graveyards. Maybe, then, a death that could be called heroic because obedient to "a blindly accepted duty" was the way to wrest positive meaning from so much loss and destruction.

Heroic deaths seem to always have been exceptional and, therefore, especially admired and remembered. Not everybody has the opportunity or the ability to end his or her life in a way that dramatically affirms core social values. Many more people, however, have been able to demonstrate their social conscience by facing death with resolute allegiance to the values they cherish. Some people, for example, have acted in accordance with cultural expectations by going off to a particular place or even assuming a particular physical position when death is near. Some traditions also expect the dying person to offer memorable last words. A striking example is that of the *jisei* or farewell verse written by Japanese Zen Buddhists monks and haiku writers. It was often considered best to be sitting upright at the moment of death, using one's last words to offer a poem to those gathered around. In contrast to religious traditions in which last words are supposed to be pious, the *jisei* often is playful and surprising:

> *My last breath chases the first*
> *Two whispers at play*
> *In the garden of lost boys*

And:

> *Tell them whatever you like*
> *My jisei was perfect*
> *Or I coughed up a green toad*

If we embrace Proposition 2, then, we should expect to discover a great many variations—as many ideas about the good death as there are societal values. One of the most striking variations is *oppositional death*. People who have become bitter or disillusioned may use their last words and energies in attacking society's values. For example, a hospice chaplain spoke to me soon after having left the bedside of a dying woman who had rejected him and cursed God. He was shaken by this encounter but already starting to make sense of it:

> She couldn't have said anything that would have upset me more, and she knew it. Life had been a kind of poison to her for a long time, since her son, then her husband died. I think this was her getting the poison out and her using the strongest word she knew—that would be God. [A strange kind of prayer?] That's exactly what it was. A strange kind of prayer. I will go back to her—and she will take my hand.

It is likely that societal expectations influence the way we deal with the end of our lives, even if we are not attempting to achieve a particular kind of death. Experienced caregivers usually have learned to suspend their own expectations and attend instead to the cultural values that are most cherished by terminally ill people and their families. The situation can be more complex, however, in postindustrial societies where there are pluralistic beliefs and lifestyles instead of one dominating view. This has been found true, for example, in Japan (Long, 2003) and South Korea (Lee et al., 2008) as well as the United States.

Proposition 3: The good death is one in which our most significant personal relationships are affirmed. These relationships may also embody societal and religious values, but it is their personal meanings that are especially cherished. Our studies of deathbed scenes, actual (Kastenbaum, 1994, 2000, 2004b) and imagined (Kastenbaum & Normand, 1990) find that relationships are usually the uppermost concern. People most often desire the companionship of those who have shared their lives through the years. This does not mean that dying people want to have all the people in their lives with them all the time. Sometimes it is enough to be with a person a time or two in order to achieve a sense of closure in the relationship. A dying father in Kaliai, a region of Western New Britain, said to his daughter: "'Ah, now that you are here I can die easily.' He then closed his eyes and within two hours he was dead" (Counts & Counts, 1985).

There are also circumstances in which the dying person may feel more comfortable by having only indirect interactions with some people because of certain tensions or concerns. Even when interpersonal contact is minimal or indirect, however, the quality of the interaction may help to affirm the value of the relationship. That one smile or handclasp might be enough to let others know that they have been appreciated.

Effective palliative care has done much to provide opportunities for continuing and affirming relationships near life's end. Relief of pain without dulling consciousness has helped people to have many quality interactions that otherwise would not have occurred. Being able to spend more time at home has also enhanced the opportunity for natural interactions.

The good death as affirmation of our most meaningful personal relationships has many implications for the way in which we have shaped our lives. People whose interpersonal relationships have been prevailingly antagonistic, full of conflict, or distant are less likely to have loving companions at their sides near the end of life. Furthermore, nurses and other service providers may also find it difficult to establish caring relationships with people who have cultivated an abusive attitude toward others throughout their lives. Personal characteristics that earn the respect and affection of other people throughout the years often contribute to a warm and supportive interpersonal network at the end of life.

Proposition 4: The good death is one in which there is a transfiguring personal experience. As death approaches, one feels a profound sense of beauty, love, or understanding. The moment of death is also the peak experience of life. This construction of the good death has been with us in many forms throughout the centuries. The Moody-type near-death experience (Chapter 13) brought renewed attention to this mystical state of being. The final pages of Tolstoy's *The Death of Ivan Ilych* (Chapter 1) provide a dramatic literary example. There are also real-life people who seem to be having powerful and distinctive experiences near the end of their lives (Kastenbaum, 1994). The medieval fascination with deathbed conversions and miracles (Aries, 1981) has not entirely lost its hold on us.

There are several frames of mind that can be associated with the good death as a transfiguring experience:

- *A sense of adventure:* "Life has been a series of adventures—why not death as well?
- *A sense of mystical awareness:* "I just know there is more to life than the everyday, so the moment of death may open these mysteries to me."

- *A sense of escaping from a disappointing life:* "This transfiguring moment will make up for the hurts and sorrows I have experienced in life."
- *A need to avoid the stressful realities of dying and separation:* "I will get myself to think only of the beauty and wonder of dying, not the physical side of it, and not the interpersonal issues."

A special case here is the impulse to risk death for the thrill of escape or an exhilarating sense of being fully alive and keen-witted at the last moment. This is among the motives people have mentioned for running with the bulls at Pamplona and for picking fights with opponents who might kill them. Perhaps it is also an impulse for ardent rollercoaster riders (Chapter 1). The dying process is usually accompanied by declining energy and function. Some people, then, are tempted to adventure themselves to possible death while still primed for an exciting experience. At the end of their lives, some people seem to be having a distinctive and powerful experience that we cannot share. The first person I observed in this situation was an old man close to death who was sitting himself up in bed with a surprising display of renewed strength. He gestured eloquently while engaging in an animated conversation with a visitor who was visible or audible only to himself. This was a serious interaction in which, apparently, important matters were being discussed and resolved. For whatever it means, all of us felt that he was not out of his mind but had taken his mind someplace else. But we didn't know. And the next time I saw a dying person seeming to interact with a "spirit visitor," I still didn't know what was happening.

Other people near death slip away as into a deeper sleep, and we may choose to interpret this also as the outer manifestation of a transfiguring state of being. But do most people die with an exalted experience? That is a different question, and the answer is likely to depend on whether we rely primarily upon faith and hope or on what can be learned through direct observation.

Proposition 4 remains a significant model of the good death, but one that can distract us from the "ordinary" challenges that are faced by dying people and their families. "Healthy dying" (Kastenbaum, 1979) attempts to sugarcoat the actual stress and loss experienced by many terminally ill people. The model of the good death as transfigured life is sometimes used to avoid dealing with disturbing realities. The idea of the good

death as a peak experience is compelling enough on its own terms that it does not need an assist from denial.

Proposition 5: The good death is one in which people continue to be themselves as long as possible, preferably to the very end. This view is close to Weisman's (1972) concept of an appropriate death: the death a person would choose for himself or herself. It is not identical, though, because some people would prefer to take a different turning at the end of their lives (e.g., a heroic or transfiguring death).

Most of the terminally ill people in the National Hospice Demonstration Study (Chapter 6) who were asked about the last three days of their lives expressed a preference for a familiar routine: a day like any other, at home, with the people who meant the most to them. In a more recent study, elderly Israelis also emphasized the value they placed on continuity (Leichtentritt & Rettig, 2000). This value encompassed the funeral and memorial process as well. One respondent expressed his thoughts in this way:

> *My funeral should correspond with whom I am . . . [with] the way I lived my life. My family knows I do not want them to sit Shiva over me . . . I do not wish people to mourn after me in this way—it is not who I am.*

Another respondent had a different emphasis:

> *I am willing to suffer a lot. I am willing to tolerate pain, but I am NOT willing to tolerate a disrespectful process. . . . I have seen funerals in my life that were disrespectful—that is exactly what I do not wish for. . . . When I said that I wish for a respectful process . . . it does not end the moment I close my eyes (p. 237).*

Many people seem comfortable with the idea of ending their lives much as they have lived. This model of the good death is usually consistent with the model that emphasizes affirming one's closest interpersonal relationship. Again, the hospice movement has proved valuable in helping many people to continue being themselves through the final phase of life.

The Script and the Reality

Concepts of the good death can be likened to scripts: this is what should happen. The realities of end-of-life situations do not necessarily accord with anybody's script, however. Circumstances overmaster concepts. Bill Moyers (2000) presented real-life examples of people approaching the end of their lives in a four-part television documentary, *On Our Own Terms*. This was one of the most truly educational public explorations of dying as it is rather than supposed or desired. Anthropologist James Green (2008, p. 19) later commented on the discrepancy between the idea of a good death and the situational realities:

> Only a few of his subjects die as they planned. One man's victory is no more than dying sitting up because he insists he will not let death catch him lying down . . . in these four programs, of the image of the good death, let alone "a better death" is barely sustained. Each is different, each unpredictable and disrupted in some way, and only a few occur as hoped. Good deaths elude even the most meticulous planning.

And, of course, life often does not go as we would have supposed and desired either. Why should we expect otherwise of dying?

EXTINCTION: DEATH OF LIFE OR DEATH OF DEATH?

Trying to understand and come to terms with death is difficult enough. But—extinction? Perhaps we are ready to think about the total annihilation of life, perhaps not. Let's give it a try. We begin by consulting a man who was well accustomed to meditating on last things.

St. Paul's Cathedral, 1623

The physicians were doing what they could. As his life continued to slip away, they prepared draughts fortified with ingredients that are as well unmentioned. This failing, they next applied pigeons "to draw the vapours" from his head. Privately, he mused:

> But what have I done, either to breed or to breathe these vapours? They tell me it is my melancholy; did I infuse, did I drink in melancholy into myself? It is my thoughtfulness; was I not made to think? (p. 78)

He played with the idea of vapours even as the pigeons performed their ministrations. No, he decided, the most poisonous emanations come not from Nature's deadly creatures but from people who specialize in deceitful and mean-spirited actions. This meditation concluded with a simple message to the angel surrogates who were gathered around him: "Be a good pigeon to draw this vapour from the head and from doing any damage there."

What history remembers occurred a few days after the wine and pigeon treatments. He was edging ever closer to death but still could take pen in hand to record his thoughts. Lying abed so close to St. Paul's Cathedral (he was dean of this illustrious religious center), he could not help but hear the bells repeatedly tolling as one more soul departed this earth. Who was it this time? Will he be the next?

Anybody would be curious; it's in our nature.

> Who bends not his ear to any bell which upon any occasion rings? But who can remove it from that bell which is passing a piece of himself out of this world? No man is an island, entire of himself; every man is a piece of the continent, a part of the main. If a clod be washed away by the sea, Europe is the less. . . . Any man's death diminishes me, because I am involved in mankind, and therefore never send to know for whom the bell tolls; it tolls for thee (pp. 167–168).

This is an excerpt from the 17th of John Donne's Devotions (1623/1975), all of which are recommended to those who might be ready to consider the human condition without blinking too much. Donne knew life and death better than almost anybody. He reveled in the passion that binds lovers together, affirmed the bonds that unite all humans everywhere, and meditated on the mysterious relationship between a mortal soul and God.

All that lives should have compassion toward all that lives. In a sense, we are each other. Donne's message can help prepare us to consider extinction. Consider another implication from the same source. One of Donne's sonnets begins:

> Death, be not proud, though some have called thee
> Mighty and dreadful, for thou are not so;
> For those whom thou think'st thou dost overthrow

Die not, poor Death, nor yet canst thou kill me.

It concludes:

One short sleep past, we wake eternally,
And Death shall be no more: Death, thou shalt
die (p. 342).

This is an expression of the faith in the Christian promise that Donne labored to achieve through years of doubt. Whether or not one shares this faith, though, all can reflect on his confident dismissal: Death, thou shalt die. Hold on for a moment to the startling idea that death could die. Now introduce the idea of extinction. That death itself could perish becomes a less fantastic prospect. Death might die at its own hand. Every species extinguished perhaps reduces the power of death. Extinction of all life would be the supreme act of (let's call it) thanatocide. The Egyptians who honored the dung beetle by placing its likeness in the chest of dead pharaohs and queens had discerned that life needs death. But death also needs life.

Sigmund Freud (1920/1960) suggested that we have two basic instincts: one devoted to life (*Eros*), the other to death (*Thanatos*). This is the normal state of affairs. Eros and Thanatos scrimmage with each other throughout our lives, but the final outcome is never in doubt. The trick, thought Freud, was to keep the game going. Eros and only Eros would whirl us into a daze, and Thanatos, unrestrained, might suddenly destroy others as well as ourselves. Keep a little death in life, and enough life to counterbalance death. This facet of Freudian theory is itself nearly extinct now, but it is still another way of conveying the idea that impulses toward death are themselves inherently self-destructive or thanatocidal. Total extinction would be game, set, and match.

The Death of Species

Extinction usually refers to the destruction of an entire species or life form. Most famous perhaps is the termination of the dinosaur reign about 65 million years ago (although such estimates remain subject to revision). Mass extinctions have occurred at least five times in the distant past. It is also considered probable that there were a great many other episodes of mass extinction that did not leave enough evidence to analyze. Will there be a sixth mass extinction of life on Earth? "Look around," say the scientists: It's going on right now. The five most documented mass extinctions are summarized in Table 15-2.

Accidents in space traffic are suspected as the cause of most of the mass-extinction episodes. Collisions with asteroids can be devastating, and there can also be major casualties from exposure to meteor showers. Tumultuous changes in earth/sea formations and extreme climactic changes might also have been involved. At least one thing is clear: All these extinctions occurred without human contrivance or influence.

Many species have lost their struggle for life apart from the mass extinctions. This process was first brought to general attention by Charles Darwin (1869/1995) in his landmark book, *On the*

TABLE 15-2 *Mass Extinctions*

Geological Period	When?	Who Died?	Why?
Ordivician-Silurian	439 million years ago	85 percent of all species	Shifts in earth layers
Late Devonian	365 million years ago	75 percent of all species (marine life even more)	Asteroids, one or more
Permian-Triassic	251 million years ago	90 percent of marine and land vertebrates and many trees	Asteroid, volcano, falling sea levels
Late Triassic	200–214 million years ago	75 percent of all species; end of mammal-like reptiles	Asteroids, heavy rainfall
Cretaceous	65 million years ago	Dinosaurs, 18 percent of land invertebrates, 47 percent of marine life	Asteroid near Yucatan and Siberian eruptions

Origin of Species by Means of Natural Selection, or the Preservation of Favoured Races in the Struggle for Life. His observations led him to the conclusion that life forms are related to each other in a complex web of circumstances. (Echoes of Donne? No nematode is an island entire to itself.) The circumstances include everything that makes up the ecosphere (Broswimmer, 2002). Life forms have to contend both with each other and with the resources, limitations, and hazards of their environments or habitats. Over the course of years, some creatures are able to adapt themselves to their environments and continue to flourish; others are displaced or left helpless when circumstances change.

Species appeared and disappeared for millions of years by "natural selection" (or luck) long before humans came along to add our contributions to the process. Today it is our role in the continuing extinction of species that is arousing the most concern. Earlier in this book, a few examples were given, such as the frogs and vultures who are being decimated by pesticide and other agricultural or industrial residue. There are so many other examples, however, that one hardly knows where to start or stop. One example from the United States may serve to remind us of what the world has been losing in diversity of species and how our own kind has contributed:

> *Perhaps the most poignant of recent extinctions is the passenger pigeon, which was to be hunted into oblivion. At the beginning of the Civil War, this was one of the most successful bird species in North America, comprising an estimated 49 percent of the entire bird population. In 1870, a single flock one mile wide and 320 miles long flew over Cincinnati. In 1974 the last surviving pigeon died in that city's zoo. As of 2001, conservationists estimated that one in every six species of birds is in decline on the continent and could wane by half by the year 2030 (Kearl, 2002, p. 278).*

I have difficulty in trying to imagine that enormous flock of birds—and even greater difficulty in accepting the fact that our species contrived to eliminate theirs. What a sorry return for the good work of their feathered British kin who ministered to John Donne's vapours! Extinction occurs on such a scale and in so many ways that it does challenge our ability to take it all in. Planet Earth continues to change, change rapidly, and change in a great many ways—and, most often, in ways that

are leading to the death of species that might otherwise remain our companions.

Is death of species good or bad—or does it occupy a moral zone beyond our usual ways of thinking? For the limited purposes of this book, perhaps all we can suggest is to remember that we are not alone on this planet and our own lives and deaths may be as truly connected to all life forms as the dean of St. Paul suggested while the bells continued to toll.

FROM GOOD LIFE TO GOOD DEATH: A PERSONAL STATEMENT

Welcome back, now, to our own lives. Obviously, we cannot simply choose or create a model of the good death and take it home until needed. Circumstances not completely in our control are likely to affect the conditions of our death. Furthermore, we might hesitate to shape our lives around the end of our days. There is a case to be made for enjoying each day as it comes and not burying ourselves prematurely. Perhaps there is a way of integrating a realization of death into our ongoing lives that does justice to both. And perhaps no two of us would do this in quite the same way.

Here, then, is what I try to do, based in unequal parts on what I have learned, what I don't know, and what I feel. This statement is offered only as an example that might be useful in reviewing your own approach.

- I hope to achieve an ongoing balance between awareness of risk and danger and a free and open attitude toward life. I do not want to put myself or others in jeopardy by engaging overmuch in denial, resistance, compartmentalization, or other defensive strategies (Chapter 2). This awareness of possible threat to life encompasses physical, environmental, and man-made sources of danger. And yet I do not intend to crawl into a hole and pull the hole down with me. Like most other people who have been active in death-related studies, I enjoy life a lot and intend to keep doing so.
- I realize that I have a very limited ability to influence the large forces and events that influence how long people live and how they die. Nevertheless, I also notice how surprisingly many opportunities there are to do something

in a positive direction. Sometimes this is as simple as listening a little more intently or offering an alternative way to deal with a situation.

- I doubt that my death will be able to make up for the mistakes and shortcomings of my life. This means that I do not rely on a ninth inning rally, although that would be exciting. (While on the ICU, I managed to stay alive by fouling off enough pitches from The Closer to stay in the game a while longer.) Instead, I feel that I have to try for a good at bat in every opportunity that comes along. That may or may not influence the final score, but nevertheless seems the best way to play the game within the decided limits of my ability.

- The Buddhist and Hindu perception of what we call life and what we call death as a coexisting flow makes a lot of sense to me. No—not to the point that I dismiss the idea of death as the end of life as I have come to know it. But I do recognize at least some of the little births and little deaths that accompany us throughout life and from which we might be wise enough to learn.

- I know something of grief and loss, and so have some sensitivity to these feelings as they mark the faces, words, and lives of others. I try to be aware—at the right time, when it most counts—that this person with whom I am interacting may still be struggling with the pain of loss while trying to move on with life.

- I appreciate life the more. As a youth I went along pretty much assuming that life was both within and all about me and therefore could be taken for granted. Studies of dying and death, as well as personal experiences, have taught me to treasure life in all its forms. Yes, that does include the gigantic wolf spider that dropped down beside me one evening and decided I was okay while at the same time I was deciding he (she?) was okay; life in the trouble-making twinkle in an aged person's eyes; life in the open-eyed wonder of a young child; life in the here-right-now intensity of an athlete; and life in the who-cares-where-we-are engrossment of lovers. I can understand, I think, why encounters with death have soured some people on life. But it happens that death has given me—and I think many other thanatologists—an ever-fresh appreciation for life.

■ SUMMARY

This chapter has given us an opportunity to reflect on some of the issues we have encountered throughout the book. We were particularly interested in the meaning of the good death and how this might relate to the ways in which we live.

The American Civil War resulted not only in an astounding number of casualties but also in ways of dying that violated the nation's hopes and expectations for "the good death." Resonances from this experience remain with us today. The sharp reduction of life expectancy among women in some areas of West Virginia reveals a very different pattern in which difficult lives end in difficult deaths. Examples from World Trade Center victims, people shunned because they have HIV/AIDS, and the way a great philosopher accepted his death also introduced us to some of the dimensions and complexities of this issue.

A physician's response to the terminal illness of his father reminded us of how much both medical management and family support influence the outcome. Ira Byock, M.D., touched by his father's death and appalled by the mismanagement of dying people in the health care system, became an effective force for the improvement of terminal care. Eliminating futile medical procedures and providing opportunity for family and patient to have time together in natural surroundings could be seen as basic steps to prepare for "the good death." We were reminded that there are limits to our ability to control the conditions of our death and that "making sense" of the end phase of life often is a challenge that is in the hands of the surviving family and friends.

More people today are enjoying long, healthy, and materially enhanced lives. Death is therefore less tempting as release from the stresses and sorrows of life (as, for example, once a major factor in the lullabies sung to babies). We also noted that "not wanting to leave the party" is a trend that stands the regret theory of death anxiety on its head. According to regret theory, people who feel they have led satisfying lives are less anxious about death. However, more people may now regret (rather than fear) death just because life seems so pleasant that it should go on and on.

We acquainted ourselves with a major international study that attempted to evaluate the quality of end-of-life care in 40 nations. The study identifies achievements, but also continuing obstacles to providing quality care to terminally ill people throughout the world. We are also left to wonder about how well statistical measures can verify a "good death."

An influential new sociotechnological development also commanded our attention. Computer-generated and computer-mediated imagery are providing what amounts to an alternative universe of experience and interaction. We wondered about the possible impact of virtual reality on our conceptions of life and death, and, therefore, on the meaning of a "good death." Photography, sound recording, and time-shifting technology have also contributed to a sense of mastery over the transience of the moment and the inexorable flow of time. Will people who are born with two umbilical cords—one connected to their mother, the other to a computer—have full appreciation for real life and real death? Questions such as these were raised here in the hope of stimulating closer observation and thought.

An additional perspective was added with our exploration of death in an imagined society designed to provide a better life. Thomas More's Utopia raises provocative questions about the meaning and prospects for a "good death" in a thoroughly managed society. Five propositions about the good death were identified: (1) We can agree that some deaths are terrible, even if we cannot always agree on what constitutes a good death; the terrible death is dominated by suffering. (2) The good death should enact the highest values held by society; here the heroic and the oppositional death were given particular attention. (3) The good death is one in which our most significant personal relationships are affirmed. (4) The good death is one in which there is a transfiguring personal experience. (5) The good death is one in which people continue to be themselves as long as possible, preferably to the very end.

We were also encouraged to reflect on both the history and future of extinction, a process that continues to destroy entire species and which human values and actions continue to influence.

In conclusion, I offered a personal statement about the good life and the good death.

Good to begin well, better to end well.
—Advice from a fortune cookie

■ **REFERENCES**

Achte, K. (1989). Lullabies of death. In R. Kastenbaum & B. K. Kastenbaum (Eds.), *Encyclopedia of death* (pp. 176–178). Phoenix: Arno.

Ahrensdorf, P. J. (1995). *The death of Socrates and the life of philosophy*. Albany: State University of New York Press.

Aries, P. (1981*). At the hour of our death*. New York: Knopf.

Associated Press (2002, May 27). At least 357 killed in terror attacks made phone calls. www.ap.org.

Broswimmer, F. J. (2002). *Ecocide: A short history of mass extinction of species*. New York: Pluto Press.

Bulkeley, K., & Bulkley, P. (2005). *Dreaming beyond death*. Boston: Beacon Press.

Byock, I. (1997). *Dying well*. New York: Riverhead Books.

Chapple, H. S. (2010). *No place for dying. Hospitals and the ideology of rescue*. Walnut Creek, CA: Left Coast Press.

Counts, D., & Counts, D. (1985). *Aging and its transformations: Moving toward death in Pacific societies*. Lanham, MD: University Press of America.

Darwin, C. (1995). *On the origin of species by means of natural selection, or the preservation of favoured races in the struggle for life*. New York: Signet Classics. (Original work published 1869.)

Donne, J. (1967). "Death be not proud" in *The complete poems of John Donne* (p. 342). Garden City, New York: Anchor. (Original work published 1633.)

Donne, J. (1975). *Devotions*. Ann Arbor: University of Michigan Press. (Original work published 1623.)

Faust, D. G. (2008). *The republic of suffering. Death and the American Civil War*. New York: Alfred A. Knopf.

Freud, S. (1960) *Beyond the pleasure principle*. New York: Norton. (Original work published 1920.)

Gelfand, E. E., Raspa, R., Briller, S. H. & Schim, S. M. (Eds.). (2005). *End-of-life stories*. New York: Springer.

Green, J. S. (2008). *Beyond the good death. The anthropology of modern dying*. Philadelphia: University of Pennsylvania Press.

Gyatso, Tenzin, the 14th Dali Lama. (1985). *Kindness, clarity, and insight*. (J. Hopkins, Trans.). Ithaca: Snow Lions Publications.

Hallam, A., & Wignall, P. B. (1997). *Mass extinctions and their aftermath*. New York: Oxford University Press.

Hayslip, B., & Peveto, C. P. (2004). *Cultural changes in attitudes toward death, dying, and bereavement*. New York: Springer.

Hoffman, D. (2005, July 27). *60 Minutes*. [Television broadcast].

Hussain, W. (2002, December 1). Activist gives face to disease. Wants to make people aware others live in secrecy in India. Associated Press.

Kastenbaum, R. (1979). "Healthy dying": A paradoxical quest continues. *Journal of Social Issues, 35*, 185–206.

Kastenbaum, R. (1994). Is there an ideal deathbed scene? In I. B. Corless, B. B. Germino, & M. Pittman (Eds.), *Dying, death, and bereavement* (pp. 109–122). Boston: Jones & Bartlett.

Kastenbaum, R. (1995). *Dorian, graying: Is youth the only thing worth having?* New York: Baywood.

Kastenbaum, R. (2000). *The psychology of death* (3rd ed.). New York: Springer.

Kastenbaum, R. (2002). Socrates. In R. Kastenbaum (Ed.), *Macmillan encyclopedia of death and dying* (Vol. 2, pp. 769–772). New York: Macmillan.

Kastenbaum, R. (2004a). Death writ large. *Death Studies, 28,* 375–392.

Kastenbaum, R. (2004b). *On our way. The final passage through life and death.* Berkeley: University of California Press.

Kastenbaum, R. (2005). Is death better in Utopia? *Illness, Crisis & Loss, 13,* 31–48.

Kastenbaum, R. (2008). Growing old in Utopia. *Journal of Aging, Humanities, and the Arts, 2,* 4–22.

Kastenbaum, R., & Normand, C. (1990). Deathbed scenes as imagined by the young and experienced by the old. *Death Studies, 14,* 201–218.

Kearl, M. (2002). Extinction. In R. Kastenbaum (Ed.), *Macmillan encyclopedia of death and dying* (Vol. 2, pp. 275–283). New York: Macmillan.

Khayyam, O. (1990). The Rubaiyat of Omar Khayyam (E. Fitzgerald, Trans). (Original work published twelfth century.) New York: Dover.

Lee, H. J., Jo, K, H, Chee, H. C., & Lee, Y. J. (2008). The perception of good death among human service students in South Korea: A Q-Methodological approach. *Death Studies, 32,* 870–890.

Leichtentritt, R. D., & Rettig, K. D. (2000). The good death: Reaching an inductive understanding. *Omega, Journal of Death and Dying, 41,* 221–248.

Long, S. O. (2003). Cultural scripts for a good death in Japan and the United States: Similarities and differences. *Social Science & Medicine, 58,* 913–928.

Meijburg, H. H. (2005). The significance of dying well. *Illness, Crisis & Loss, 13,* 49–62.

More. T. (1516/1975). *Utopia.* (Original title: A truly golden handbook, no less beneficial than entertaining of the best state of the Commonwealth and new island of Utopia). New York: Norton. (Original work published 1527.)

Murray, S. (Ed.). (2010). *The quality of death. Ranking end-of-life care across the world.* Lien Foundation. www.qualityofdeath.org.

Ober, W. B. (1988). Did Socrates die of hemlock poisoning? In *Boswell's clap & other essays. Medical analyses of literary men's afflictions.* New York: Harper & Row.

Osmond, R. (2009). *Imagining the soul. A history.* Thrupp, UK: Sutton.

Orwell, G. (1949) *1984.* London: Secker & Warburg.

Plato. (1942a). Phaedo. In *Plato: Five great dialogues.* New York: Walter J. Black. (Original work published 370 B.C.)

Plato. (1942b). The republic. In *Plato: Five great dialogues.* New York: Walter J. Black. (Original work published 370 B.C.)

Smith, A. M. (2005). *44 Scotland Street.* New York: Anchor Books.

Taylor, J. (1970). *The rules and exercises of holy dying.* New York: Arno. (Original work published 1665.)

Tolstoy, L. (1960). *The death of Ivan Ilych.* New York: New American Library. (Original work published 1886).

Tomer, A., & Eliason, G. (1996). Toward a comprehensive model of death anxiety. *Death Studies, 20,* 343–366.

Vargas, T. (April 28, 2008). Southwest Va.'s mortality mystery. More than diet behind women's sharp life expectancy drop. *Washington Post,* p. A01.

Voltaire (1991) *Candide.* New York: Norton. (Original work published 1759.)

Weisman, A. D. (1972). *On dying and denying: A psychiatric study of terminality.* New York: Behavioral Publications.

■ GLOSSARY

Appropriate death The way a person would choose to have his or her life come to an end.

Genocide Killing people because of their nationality, religion, race, or any other group characteristic.

Horrendous death A premature and unexpected death caused by other people. Often violent and painful.

■ ON FURTHER THOUGHT . . .

- Characters die on television and in movies all the time. What comes to mind as the "most good" and "most not good" death you have seen in either format? And what made them so good or so not good? Perhaps this reflection will tell you a little more about your own hopes, fears, and priorities.

Photo Credits

Index